IISS

Strategic Survey
2007

published by

Routledge
Taylor & Francis Group

for

The International Institute for Strategic Studies
Arundel House I 13–15 Arundel Street I Temple Place I London I WC2R 3DX I UK

The International Institute for Strategic Studies

Arundel House | 13–15 Arundel Street | Temple Place | London | WC2R 3DX | UK

Strategic Survey 2007

First published September 2007 by **Routledge**
4 Park Square, Milton Park, Abingdon, Oxon, OX14 4RN

for **The International Institute for Strategic Studies**
Arundel House, 13–15 Arundel Street, Temple Place, London, WC2R 3DX, UK

Simultaneously published in the USA and Canada by **Routledge**
270 Madison Ave., New York, NY 10016

Routledge is an imprint of Taylor & Francis, an Informa business

This publication has been prepared by the Director-General of the Institute and his Staff, who accept full responsibility for its contents, which describe and analyse events up to 30 June 2007. These do not, and indeed cannot, represent a consensus of views among the worldwide membership of the Institute as a whole.

British Library Cataloguing in Publication Data
A catalogue record for this book is available from the British Library

Library of Congress Cataloguing in Publication Data

ISBN 978-1-85743-438-5
ISSN 0459-7230

Contents

Strategic Geography (after p. 184)

Index of Regional Maps

Index of Maps

Index of Figures

Events at a Glance
May 2006–June 2007

May 2006

25   **Timor Leste:** Australian and other foreign troops deployed to quell violence.

27   **Indonesia:** Earthquake in central Java kills 5,700 people.

28   **Colombia:** Alvaro Uribe easily wins second four-year term in presidential election.

29   **Afghanistan:** Accident involving US military truck sparks riots and looting in Kabul, leaving eight dead.

29   **Sri Lanka:** European Union places Tamil Tigers on list of banned organisations.

31   **Iran:** US says it is willing to take part in direct talks with Iran on nuclear issues provided that Tehran 'fully and verifiably suspends its enrichment and reprocessing activities'.

June 2006

1   **DR Congo:** German parliament approves deployment of 780 troops to lead EU mission to suppport Congo elections.

4   **Peru:** Alan Garcia wins presidential election, defeating Ollanta Humala who was supported by Venezuelan President Hugo Chávez.

5   **Somalia:** Union of Islamic Courts militia wins control of Mogadishu from warlords, and later extends control beyond capital.

6   **Iran:** Javier Solana, EU foreign policy chief, delivers package of proposals to Tehran agreed by P5 countries plus Germany. Iran says it includes 'positive steps'.

7   **Iraq:** US air strike kills Abu Musab al-Zarqawi, leader of al-Qaeda in Mesopotamia.

10 **United States:** Three prisoners commit suicide at US Guantanamo Bay detention facility in Cuba, the first deaths of inmates.

15 **Sri Lanka:** Attack on civilian bus, attributed to Tamil Tigers, kills 68 civilians.

20 **Iraq:** Japan announces plans to withdraw troops from Iraq.

22 **Somalia:** Union of Islamic Courts and Transitional Federal Government reach ceasefire agreement, but fighting continues.

25 **Israel:** Government threatens military action after Palestinian militants kill two Israeli soliders and abduct another in tunnel raid from Gaza into Israel at border post. Government demands return of kidnapped soldier.

26 **Sri Lanka:** Army deputy chief of staff killed by suicide bomber.

26 **Timor Leste:** Prime Minister Mari Alkatiri resigns, replaced by José Ramos Horta.

28 **Israel:** Air strikes launched against targets in Gaza, including power station. Israeli forces cross into Gaza. Israeli military's *Operation Summer Rains* to retrieve kidnapped soldier and attack targets in Gaza continues into August. *Qassam* rockets are fired from Gaza into Israel.

July 2006

2 **Mexico:** Presidential election results in Felipe Calderon winning 35.9% of votes and Andres Manuel Lopez Obrador 35.3%. After court challenge, Calderon, of the ruling National Action Party, is declared the winner on 5 September.

5 **North Korea:** Long-range missile and six shorter-range rockets launched in test. Long-range missile fails less than a minute after launch. UN Security Council on 15 July condemns tests, demands suspension of ballistic-missile programme and resumption of moratorium on tests.

10 **Russia:** Shamil Basayev, Chechen rebel leader, killed in explosion in Ingushetia.

10 **Afghanistan:** UK announces deployment of additional 900 troops to Helmand province, bringing total UK force in Afghanistan to 4,500.

11 **India:** Seven bombs on Mumbai commuter trains kill 207.

12 **Israel/Lebanon:** Conflict between Israel and Lebanon breaks out after Hizbullah fighters capture two Israeli soldiers and kill three more in cross-border raid into Israel, which immediately responds with air strikes and artillery fire. Israel later imposes naval blockade, sends forces into Lebanon and bombs Lebanese infastructure including Beirut airport, roads and power station. Israel bombs Hizbullah's headquarters and attacks its strongholods in Lebanon. Hizbullah fires hundreds of rockets into Israel, hitting as far south as Haifa. Many Lebanese flee their homes as hundreds of civilians are killed in Israeli attacks. Operations mounted to evacuate foreign citizens from Lebanon. US does not call for immediate ceasefire, saying it wants the root causes of the violence to be addressed. On 21 July, US Secretary of State Condoleezza Rice says: 'What we're seeing here, in a sense, is ... the birth pangs of a new Middle East'.

16 **Russia:** G8 leaders at St Petersburg Summit, in statement on Middle East, call on 'extremists' to halt attacks and on Israel to exercise 'utmost restraint'.

20 **Somalia:** Ethiopian troops enter Somalia to protect Baidoa, seat of Transitional Federal Government, from Union of Islamic Courts militia.

21 **Afghanistan:** UK Lieutenant-General David Richards, NATO commander in Afghanistan, says insurgency is 'extraordinarily dynamic' and is 'being waged across national borders'. Says lack of coordination between international organisations and agencies is 'close to anarchy'.

24 **Switzerland:** Pascal Lamy, director general of World Trade Organisation, announces indefinite suspension of Doha Round of trade negotiations following failure of US, European Union and others to make progress.

25 **Iraq:** President Bush, at meeting with Iraqi Prime Minister Nuri al-Maliki, announces additional troops to be assigned to Baghdad to curb rising violence.

26 **Venezuela:** President Hugo Chávez announces purchase of 24 Sukhoi-30 fighters from Russia.

26 **Sri Lanka:** Military launches air attacks on Tamil Tiger positions over access to canal. Fighting in following weeks in northeast Sri Lanka is heaviest since 2002 ceasefire.

26 **Israel/Lebanon:** Foreign ministers from the US, Europe and the Arab world, meeting in Rome, fail to agree on a call for an immediate ceasefire in Lebanon. Nine Israeli soldiers die in assault on Lebanese town of Bint Jubayl. The Israeli campaign has so far killed more than 400 Lebanese.

30 **DR Congo:** Presidential and parliamentary elections held. Though results remain unclear for three weeks, President Joseph Kabila wins 45% of presidential vote, and nearest challenger Jean-Pierre Bemba 20%, forcing a run-off. No party wins majority in parliament.

30 **Israel/Lebanon:** Israeli air raid on Qana, initially reported as causing about 60 deaths, causes outrage. Death toll later revised to 28, including 16 children.

31 **Germany:** Suitcase bombs are left on two trains leaving Cologne station. They fail to explode. A Lebanese student is arrested in Kiel on 19 August, and a second suspect is arrested in Lebanon on 24 August.

31 **Cuba:** Government announces President Fidel Castro handed power temporarily to brother Raul Castro, defence minister, and had surgery for intestinal bleeding.

31 **Iran:** UN Security Council passes resolution demanding Iran suspend uranium enrichment and reprocessing by 31 August.

31 **Afghanistan:** NATO takes over responsibility for security in southern provinces from US-led coalition.

August 2006

4 **Uganda:** Rebel movement Lord's Resistance Army declares unilateral ceasefire. Truce agreement takes effect 29 August.

4 **Ukraine:** Former Prime Minister Viktor Yanukovich, defeated by President Viktor Yushchenko in 2004 presidential election following the Orange Revolution, again becomes prime minister after his party's successes in parliamentary elections prompt a deal with Yushchenko.

10 **United Kingdom:** Police arrest 24 people as government says a plot to blow up transatlantic aircraft with liquid explosives had been thwarted. Arrests are also made in Pakistan.

11 **Israel/Lebanon:** UN Security Council calls for immediate ceasefire and agrees to expand UNIFIL peacekeeping force with up to 15,000 troops to enforce ceasefire and to police buffer zone in southern Lebanon. Calls on Lebanon to deploy forces into southern Lebanon and on Israel to withdraw. Ceasefire takes effect on 14 August.

22 **DR Congo:** UN-brokered ceasefire ends three days of fighting between supporters of Kabila and Bemba.

24 **Australia:** Government announces plan to increase size of Australian army in order to improve responses to regional instability.

25 **Israel/Lebanon:** European Union members agree to send 6,000–7,000 peacekeeping troops to Lebanon. On 31 August, donors' conference in Stockholm pledges $940m to Lebanon's reconstruction.

26 **Pakistan:** Pakistani military kills Baluch rebel leader Nawab Akbar Bugti in air raid on cave hideout, prompting rioting in Baluchistan.

September 2006

1 **United Kingdom:** Police arrest 14 people in London on suspicion of terrorist offences and search an Islamic school south of the capital.

2 **Afghanistan:** Fourteen British servicemen killed in crash of *Nimrod* reconnaissance aircraft in Kandahar province. Aircraft was supporting NATO's *Operation Medusa,* a two-week effort to target Taliban forces near city of Kandahar.

5 **Pakistan:** Pakistani government signs peace agreement with tribal chiefs in North Waziristan. Tribes agree to expel foreign militants and reduce cross-border attacks in Afghanistan. Pakistani military agrees to reduce presence and halt operations. Afghan officials say deal cedes control of area to pro-Taliban militants. US military reports sharp rise in Taliban attacks in south-east Afghanistan in following weeks.

5 **Denmark:** Seven people held under anti-terrorism laws in Danish city of Odense. Government says police prevented a terrorist attack.

6 **United States:** President Bush acknowledges existence of CIA prisons abroad and says 14 inmates have been transferred to Guantanamo Bay detention facility. He calls on Congress to pass legislation enabling detainees to be tried by military commissions. A previous plan for military tribunals was rejected by the Supreme Court. Congress later passes the Military Commissions Act.

8 **India:** Three bombs near a mosque kill 31 people in Muslim-dominated town of Malegaon, Maharashtra.

11 **Palestine:** Hamas and Fatah agree terms on forming a unity government, but formation remains stalled over refusal by Hamas to recognise Israel.

12 **Syria:** Syrian security forces foil car bomb attack on US Embassy in Damascus.

13 **Russia:** First Deputy Director of Russia's Central Bank, Andrei Kozlov, fatally shot by gunmen.

18 **Russia:** Natural resources ministry withdraws environmental approval for $20bn Sakhalin-2 offshore oil and gas project, led by Shell, Mitsui and Mitsubishi.

19 **Thailand:** Army takes power in bloodless coup from Prime Minister Thaksin Shinawatra while he attends United Nations General Assembly in New York. The army chief, General Sonthi Boonyaratglin, assumes control of government and promises elections in October 2007.

23 **United States:** Declassified National Intelligence Estimate, dated April 2006, says jihadists are growing in number and geographic dispersion. Says Iraq War has become cause célèbre for jihadists, breeding resentment of US involvement in the Muslim world and cultivating supporters for the global jihadist movement.

25 **Iraq:** An al-Qaeda leader, Omar al-Faruq, who escaped from Bagram air base in Afghanistan in July 2005, killed by British troops in a raid in Basra, Iraq.

26 **Japan:** Shinzo Abe, formerly chief cabinet secretary, elected prime minister by Diet (parliament) with 339 of 475 votes in lower house.

27 **Georgia:** Georgia's arrest of four Russian officers on espionage charges sparks row between Tbilisi and Moscow.

October 2006

3 **North Korea:** Pyongyang announces it will conduct a nuclear test. US says this would be provocative and would threaten peace and security.

5 **Afghanistan:** NATO's International Security Assistance Force (ISAF) expands its remit to the whole of Afghanistan, taking over from US command in 14 eastern provinces and increasing the number of troops under NATO command from 20,000 to 31,000.

7 **Russia:** Anna Politkovskaya, prominent investigative journalist, shot dead in her apartment block in apparent contract killing.

8 **Japan/China:** Japanese Prime Minister Shinzo Abe visits Beijing for first bilateral summit in five years. Both sides describe visit as a 'turning point' in relations. Joint statement says a nuclear test by North Korea would be 'unacceptable'.

9 **North Korea:** Pyongyang says it carried out a nuclear test, later estimated to have a yield of less than one kilotonne, suspected to have been significantly lower than intended. Test brings widespread condemnation, with China calling it 'brazen'. On 14 October, UN Security Council imposes sanctions, including ban on supply of nuclear-related and luxury goods, to be policed through cargo inspections.

13 **United Nations:** Ban Ki Moon, South Korean foreign minister, elected UN Secretary-General to succeed Kofi Annan.

16 **Sri Lanka:** Tamil Tiger rebels attack a convoy of buses, killing 92 naval personnel.

18 **Venezuela:** Spain cancels sale of military transport aircraft to Venezuela because of US pressure.

29 **Brazil:** President Lula da Silva re-elected in run-off poll with 60% of votes.

29 **Bangladesh:** President Iajuddin Ahmed takes over as head of caretaker government to oversee fairness of elections.

30 **DR Congo:** Run-off elections give Joseph Kabila victory in presidential poll with 58% of votes, announced on 19 November and confirmed by Supreme Court on 27 November following challenge by losing candidate, Jean-Pierre Bemba.

30 **United Kingdom:** Report for government by Nicholas Stern, former World Bank chief economist, warns of severe economic and other consequences from failing to tackle climate change.

November 2006

5 **Nicaragua:** Daniel Ortega, former Sandinista leader, elected president after 16 years out of power.

5 **Iraq:** Saddam Hussein, former president, and two others convicted of crimes against humanity and sentenced to death by hanging over the deaths of 148 people in the town of Dujail in 1982.

7 **United Kingdom:** Dhiren Barot sentenced to life imprisonment after plotting al-Qaeda attacks in Britain and United States.

7 **United States:** Democratic Party wins control of Senate by 51 seats to 49 and House of Representatives by 233 seats to 202. President Bush replaces Donald Rumsfeld as secretary of defense, nominating Robert Gates, former CIA chief, who is easily confirmed by Congress.

21 **Lebanon:** Pierre Gemayel, industry minister and prominent anti-Syrian, assassinated by gunmen in Beirut.

21 **Iraq:** Diplomatic relations between Syria and Iraq are restored after a 20-year break.

21 **Nepal:** Government signs peace agreement with Maoist rebels, under which the latter will lock up weapons and can take part in parliament and government. Following constitutional changes in January 2007, the rebels assume 83 of 330 parliamentary seats.

23 **Iraq:** Car bomb and mortar attacks on Shia-dominated Sadr City area of Baghdad kill 215 people.

23 **United Kingdom:** Alexander Litvinenko, a former KGB and FSB agent who became a dissident and sought asylum in the UK in 2000, dies in a London hospital, three weeks after being poisoned with polonium. People whom he had met and places where he had been were contaminated. He blamed President Putin for murdering him. Putin denied the accusation.

26 **Ecuador:** Rafael Correa, leftist economist and former finance minister, wins presidential run-off election with 57% of votes.

29 **Iraq:** *New York Times* reports that a memo by Stephen Hadley, US National Security Adviser, cast doubt on the ability of Nuri al-Maliki, Iraqi prime minister, to control sectarian violence. He suggested there was a government effort to consolidate Shia power in Baghdad and that more American troops may be needed in Baghdad. In response to the report, Maliki backs out of a dinner with President Bush in Jordan.

December 2006

3 **Venezuela:** Hugo Chávez re-elected president with 63% of vote.

4 **United Kingdom:** Following review, government announces plans to retain *Trident* nuclear deterrent with new generation of submarines but to reduce number of warheads 20% to less than 160.

5 **Fiji:** Commodore Frank Bainimarama, armed forces chief, takes power in military coup.

6 **Iraq:** Iraq Study Group, chaired by James Baker and Lee Hamilton, says the situation in Iraq is 'grave and deteriorating'. It recommends US diplomatic engagement with Iran and Syria. The US military should train and support the Iraqi army and should not engage in combat.

11 **Turkey:** EU foreign ministers partially suspend negotiations on Turkish membership because of Ankara's refusal to open its ports and airports to trade from Cyprus.

12 **United Kingdom:** UK and US sign memorandum of understanding on production of F-35 Joint Strike Fighter after US gives assurances on technology transfer.

14 **United Kingdom:** Government discontinues investigation by Serious Fraud Office into BAE Systems and the al-Yamamah arms deal with Saudi Arabia on grounds of national and international security. Tony Blair says relationship with Saudi Arabia is vitally important. The US is later reported to have filed a formal diplomatic protest against the British decision.

18 **North Korea:** Six-Party Talks resume in Beijing and recess after five days.

21 **Russia:** Royal Dutch Shell, Mitsui and Mitsubishi agree to cede control of Sakhalin-2 oil and gas project to Gazprom.

23 **Iran:** UN Security Council places sanctions on Iran for failing to halt uranium enrichment. It bans Iran's import and export of nuclear-related materials and provides for freezing the assets of people and companies supporting Iranian activities in nuclear weapons development and proliferation.

27 **Somalia:** Union of Islamic Courts withdraws from Mogadishu after a week of fierce fighting with troops of Transitional Federal Government and Ethiopia. Next day, government and Ethiopian troops pour into the capital. Anti-Ethiopian riots break out. On 1 January, Islamists abandon last stand in southern city of Kismayo.

30 **Iraq:** Saddam Hussein hanged. Film of him being taunted on the gallows draws international criticism.

January 2007

1 **Bulgaria/Romania:** European Union grows to 27 members with the admission of Bulgaria and Romania.

5 **United States:** Bush appoints John Negroponte, director of national intelligence, as deputy secretary of state, replacing him with Vice-Admiral Michael McConnell. Lieutenant-General David Petraeus appointed commander of US forces in Iraq, replacing General George Casey who is appointed Army chief. Zalmay Khalilzad, ambassador to Iraq, nominated as ambassador to UN, replacing John Bolton.

8 **Russia:** Russia, in dispute with Belarus over oil export duty, suspends oil supplies to Belarus through Druzhba pipeline, affecting supplies to Germany, Poland and other countries. Suspension ends after three days.

8 **Venezuela:** Chávez announces plans to nationalise the electricity and energy sectors.

8 **Japan:** Defence Agency upgraded to status of full ministry.

9 **Somalia:** US aircraft attacks suspected al-Qaeda targets in southern Somalia.

10 **Iraq:** Bush announces plans to send 21,500 more troops to Iraq, mostly to improve security in Baghdad. He says he has set benchmarks for progress by the Iraqi government, will not have talks with Iran and Syria but will seek more support from Arab countries.

11 **Bangladesh:** President Iajuddin Ahmed declares state of emergency, steps down as head of caretaker government and delays elections scheduled for 22 January. Decision follows mass demonstrations and violent clashes over allegations that the elections were being rigged. Fakhruddin Ahmed becomes interim leader of caretaker government and begins crackdown on corruption.

11 **China:** Kinetic kill vehicle launched by ground-based ballistic missile destroys Chinese weather satellite in test. Beijing, confirming the test on 23 January, denies it will take part in a space arms race.

15 **North Korea:** US official holds two days of 'substantive' talks in Berlin with North Korean vice foreign minister.

15 **Iraq:** Barzan al-Tikriti, Saddam Hussein's half brother, and Awad al-Bandar, former judge, executed by hanging.

16 **Iraq:** Bombs kill 70 people, mostly female students, at a Baghdad university. UN says at least 34,452 civilians were killed in 2006 and 470,000 forced to leave their homes since the bombing of the Golden Mosque at Samarra in February 2006.

17 **Israel:** Head of armed forces, Lieutenant-General Dan Halutz, resigns following criticism of handling of 2006 conflict with Lebanon.

19 **Turkey:** Murder of Hrant Dink, a Turkish-Armenian journalist who had been convicted in 2005 of 'insulting Turkishness', prompts widespread protests within Turkey, with Prime Minister Tayyip Erdogan saying 'a bullet has been fired at democracy and freedom of expression'.

23 **Afghanistan:** US pledges $10.6bn in additional economic and military aid to Afghanistan, with 3,200 troops also having their stay extended by four

months. Foreign ministers of other NATO countries signal general willingness to increase commitments. UK later announces it will send 800 more troops, bringing UK total to 5,800. On 4 February, US Army General Dan McNeill takes command of NATO's ISAF for one year.

25 **Lebanon:** Donor countries, meeting in Paris, pledge $7.6bn for reconstruction of Lebanon.

25 **Georgia:** Georgia discloses that it arrested in 2006 a Russian who had been carrying 100g of highly enriched uranium, but Russia had failed to cooperate in the case.

26 **Kosovo:** Martti Ahtisaari, UN-appointed mediator, presents plan for autonomous status for Kosovo, leading eventually to independence from Serbia. Serbian leaders later reject the plan.

28 **Iraq:** About 250 people, apparently members of a militant splinter Shi'ite cult, killed in fighting near Najaf with Iraqi and US forces on the eve of Ashura, a Shia holy day.

31 **United Kingdom:** Police arrest nine men in Birmingham in connection with alleged plot to kidnap, torture and behead a British Muslim soldier.

31 **Venezuela:** National Assembly grants President Chávez the right to rule by decree for 18 months.

February 2007

4 **Iraq:** Truck bomb kills 130 at market in Shia area of Baghdad.

9 **Palestine:** Hamas and Fatah agree to form unity government at talks in Mecca, Saudi Arabia. Ismail Haniya is given five weeks to form the government. The US and Europe react cautiously because the deal contains no explicit recognition of Israel.

10 **Russia:** President Putin, at Munich Security Conference, attacks US for promoting nuclear arms race and for unilateral over-use of military force.

12 **Guinea:** President Lansana Conte declares martial law, giving armed forces wide powers to deal with protests against his rule.

13 **North Korea:** North Korea agrees to shut down Yongbyon nuclear reactor within 60 days in return for 50,000 tonnes of fuel aid. Under the deal reached at Six-Party Talks in Beijing, it would receive a further 1m tonnes when it permanently disables its nuclear facilities. Inspectors are to verify the North Korean steps. The US, which calls the agremeent an 'important first step', agrees to begin removing North Korea from the list of states sponsoring terrorism and establishing diplomatic relations. Japan is also to discuss normalising relations.

14 **Iran:** Car bomb kills 11 Revolutionary Guards in southeastern city of Zahedan. Attack, claimed by Sunni group, prompts clashes between militants and security forces. On 19 February, a man is publicly hanged after being shown on television confessing to involvement in the bombing.

14 **France:** Police arrest nine people in Toulouse and two at Orly airport on suspicion of being involved with al-Qaeda and recruiting fighters for the Iraqi insurgency.

16 **United States:** House of Representatives, in 246–182 vote, condemns US troop 'surge' in Iraq. A 56–34 vote in the Senate to hold a similar debate falls short of the 60 votes needed.

19 **Poland/Czech Republic:** Leaders of Poland and Czech Republic agree they will look favourably on US request to site, respectively, missile interceptors and a radar station in their countries.

19 **India:** Bomb attack on train from Delhi to Lahore kills 68 people, many of them Pakistani.

21 **Iraq:** Britain announces it will reduce troops in Iraq by 1,600 to 5,500 in a few months, and Denmark announces it will withdraw its 460 troops.

26 **Serbia:** International Court of Justice in The Hague says Serbia was not directly responsible for genocide in Srebrenica massacre in 1995, though it failed to prevent the killings.

26 **Saudi Arabia:** Gunmen kill four French nationals in ambush near Madain Saleh.

26 **Afghanistan:** Britain announces it will send 1,400 more troops to Afghanistan in summer 2007, raising total to 7,700.

27 **Afghanistan:** Bomb attack on Bagram air base near Kabul kills nine people while US Vice President Dick Cheney is at the base.

28 **Bosnia:** European Union announces it will reduce its force in Bosnia from 6,500 to 2,500, with UK withdrawing all 600 troops. Germany is also to reduce its number from 850.

March 2007

1 **Somalia:** Ugandan troops begin deployment to Somalia as part of planned 8,000-strong African Union peacekeeping force. Sporadic fierce fighting in Mogadishu between the Ethiopian-backed government and insurgents kills more than a thousand people and displaces many more during March and April.

1 **Japan:** Prime Minister Shinzo Abe says Japanese military did not coerce 'comfort women' into sexual slavery in Second World War.

2 **Russia:** Ivan Safronov, defence writer for daily newspaper *Kommersant*, dies in fall from his apartment block.

3 **Iran:** President Ahmadinejad visits Saudi Arabia and agrees with King Abdullah on need to stop spread of sectarian strife.

4 **Côte d'Ivoire:** Government and rebels sign peace agreement providing for power-sharing government, joint army command, and removal of buffer zone patrolled by French and UN troops.

6 **United States:** Lewis Libby, former top aide to Vice President Dick Cheney, found guilty of perjury and obstruction of justice over his testimony to FBI and

a grand jury on leak of identity of a CIA agent. The case concerned doubts cast by the agent's husband, a former ambassador, on the Bush administration's case for going to war in Iraq.

9   **Pakistan:** President Musharraf suspends Chief Justice Iftikhar Muhammad Chaudhry for alleged misconduct. The decision prompts a nationwide wave of violent protests, as well as judges' resignations.

10 **United States:** Khaled Sheikh Mohammed, in statement to military tribunal at Guantanamo Bay, says he was responsible for 11 September 2001 attacks and was involved in 30 other plots.

10 **Iraq:** Meeting in Baghdad called by Iraqi government brings together US, Iranian and Syrian officials.

11 **Zimbabwe:** Opposition leader Morgan Tsvangirai is arrested at a rally and beaten up in custody, appearing in court two days later with head wounds. President Robert Mugabe tells Western critics to 'go hang'. African Union voices concern and calls for constructive dialogue. Opposition politicians are barred from going abroad.

23 **Iran/UK:** Iranian gunboats arrest 15 UK naval personnel carrying out routine patrols. Iran claims the British boats were in Iranian waters, but the UK says they were in Iraqi waters. On 4 April, President Ahmadinejad announces their 'pardon' and release.

24 **Iran:** UN Security Council passes Resolution 1747, tightening sanctions on Iranian arms exports and those involved in its nuclear programme, and giving Iran 60 days to suspend uranium enrichment.

26 **Australia:** David Hicks, an Australian held at Guantanamo Bay for five years, becomes first inmate to be convicted by a military commission under plea bargain that allows him to return home.

26 **Sri Lanka:** Tamil Tigers carry out aerial bombing raid on air base adjoining Colombo airport, killing three people.

28 **Saudi Arabia:** King Abdullah, at Arab League summit in Riyadh, says foreign occupation of Iraq was 'illegal' and calls for end to international boycott of Palestinian government.

April 2007

4   **Syria:** US House Speaker Nancy Pelosi, in move criticised by President Bush, holds talks with Syrian President Bashar al-Assad in Damascus.

11 **United States:** US military tours in Iraq and Afghanistan are extended from 12 to 15 months.

12 **Japan:** Chinese Prime Minister Wen Jiabao signals a thaw in relations with three-day visit including address to Japanese parliament.

12 **Algeria:** Two bombs kill 33 people in Algiers. Responsibility is claimed by an al-Qaeda-linked group.

16 **United States:** Student kills 32 people in gun rampage at Virginia Tech university.

16 **Sudan:** Government agrees to allow 3,000 peacekeepers into Darfur.

18 **Iraq:** Car bombs targeted mainly at Shia areas of Baghdad kill some 200 people.

21 **Nigeria:** Umaru Yar'Adua, ruling party candidate, wins presidential elections with 70% of votes but international observers say the results are not credible and opposition parties call for annulment.

24 **Ethiopia:** Separatist group attacks Chinese-run oilfield, killing 74 people including nine Chinese.

26 **Russia:** President Putin says Russia will suspend observance of the Conventional Forces in Europe Treaty in response to American plans to station a missile defence radar in the Czech Republic and missile interceptors in Poland.

27 **Saudi Arabia:** Saudi authorities say they arrested 172 men, broke up seven terrorist cells and seized weapons and cash.

30 **United Kingdom:** Five British men who were arrested in 2004 are sentenced to life imprisonment for conspiracy to carry out explosions. Links are revealed between them and the leader of the 7 July 2005 London bomb attacks.

May 2007

1 **United States:** President Bush vetoes war funding bill that called for timeline for Iraq withdrawal. A compromise bill, with no deadlines, is signed into law on 25 May.

2 **Estonia:** Government says websites under 'cyber attack' in row with Russia over Estonia's relocation of Russian war memorial away from centre of capital, Tallinn.

2 **Turkey:** Prime Minister Tayyip Erdogan calls early elections amid political crisis over nomination of Foreign Minister Abdullah Gul as president, which prompted opposition on the grounds that the country's secularism was being undermined.

6 **France:** Nicolas Sarkozy elected president with 53% of vote against 47% for Ségolène Royal.

8 **United Kingdom:** Power-sharing resumes in Northern Ireland after a five-year gap as loyalist leader Ian Paisley and Irish Republican Martin McGuinness are sworn in respectively as first minister and deputy first minister of a devolved government.

9 **United States:** Six men arrested over alleged plot to attack Fort Dix army base in New Jersey.

12 **Russia:** Russia, Kazakhstan and Turkmenistan agree to build gas pipeline linking the three countries via the coast of the Caspian Sea.

12 **Afghanistan:** Mullah Dadullah, Taliban's senior military commander, killed in southern Afghanistan.

17 **United States:** Paul Wolfowitz resigns as World Bank president after a Bank panel found he had breached its rules in awarding pay increase to his

companion Shaha Riza. Robert Zoellick, former US deputy secretary of state, nominated to replace him.

20 **Lebanon:** Heavy fighting breaks out between Lebanese forces and Islamic militants in refugee camp.

28 **US/Iran:** American and Iranian ambassadors to Iraq hold first bilateral talks between the two countries for almost 30 years.

28 **United Kingdom:** Government formally requests the extradition of Andrei Lugovoi, wanted for the London murder of dissident Alexander Litvinenko. Russia's prosecutor-general says extradition would be unconstitutional.

30 **Lebanon:** UN Security Council votes to establish special tribunal to try cases regarding the 2005 murder of former Lebanese Prime Minister Rafiq Hariri.

June 2007

4 **United States:** Four people charged with plotting to bomb fuel tanks and pipelines at New York's John F. Kennedy airport.

5 **Laos:** US prosecutors charge nine people, including a former Laotian general, with conspiring to mount a coup in Laos.

7 **Russia:** President Putin, in counterproposal to the US, suggests joint use of a radar system in Azerbaijan to detect incoming missiles.

8 **Germany:** G8 leaders, meeting at Heiligendamm summit, agree to seek substantial cuts in greenhouse gas emissions.

14 **Palestine:** Hamas takes control of Gaza after four days of fighting. Mahmoud Abbas, Palestinian Authority president, sacks Hamas-led unity government and asks former Finance Minister Salam Fayyad, an independent, to be prime minister of an emergency government. Western and Arab nations express support for Abbas and announce moves to unblock aid to the Palestinian Authority.

19 **France:** President Sarkozy is forced to reshuffle his just-appointed cabinet after his UMP party did less well than expected in parliamentary elections.

27 **United Kingdom:** Tony Blair steps down as prime minister and is replaced by Gordon Brown, previously finance minister.

1 Perspectives

The effects of the profound loss of authority suffered by the United States since its invasion of Iraq were felt throughout the world over the past year. The weak pillar in the world's security architecture was plain to see, and leaders across the globe sought to take advantage, or to protect themselves from the consequences.

This was despite the efforts of the administration of President George W. Bush to present, through new top officials, a more rational and conciliatory face, far removed from the naked assertion of American power that had been urged on the president by hardline neo-conservatives following the 11 September 2001 attacks on the United States. The failure to impose order on Iraq prompted nationwide reflection. After the Republican Party lost control of both houses of Congress in November 2006 elections, a weakened and discredited Bush was forced to become more accommodating. But the damage to American standing and credibility was likely to take years to repair – especially as problems such as Iraq's persistent violence and the Guantanamo Bay detention camp could not just be wished away.

It was therefore not surprising that some countries sensed an opportunity to flex their muscles in international affairs. Iran, for example, saw the political way clear to pressing ahead with its nuclear programme, even in the face of repeated United Nations Security Council resolutions that, ever so cautiously, imposed sanctions upon it. Tehran's calculation was perhaps that US military action, which could occur if Bush were to tire of diplomacy, would serve only to provoke international sympathy and to promote national unity. Meanwhile, Russia also sought to move into the vacuum left by the United States: President Vladimir Putin attempted to reassert his country's identity as a global power through verbal onslaughts directed at Washington – while at the same time using Russia's abundant gas and oil assets to the best diplomatic and financial advantage.

As Washington lost influence over the parties to disputes in the Middle East, there was constant conflict, with seemingly no strategies in place that could lead to solutions. In Iraq, a political settlement between Shia and Sunni factions seemed a distant prospect, with the United States apparently powerless to engineer it. The country remained trapped in a complex web of violence, from which Washington made flailing efforts to find an exit – it sought to lower the number of its troops deployed, then opted to send more, but considered plans to reduce them as the administration came under strong bipartisan domestic pressure. Meanwhile, after Israeli forces attacked Hizbullah fighters in Lebanon in mid 2006, the United States belatedly addressed itself to diplomatic efforts towards Middle East peace, with Secretary of State Condoleezza Rice making several visits. She gained little traction, and her efforts seemed to count for nothing when Hamas seized control of the Gaza Strip in June 2007. With two rival governments in Palestine, the West's rushed efforts to bolster the West Bank-based Palestinian Authority President Mahmoud Abbas seemed likely to be of questionable efficacy. There were few positive signs for the future.

Amid the continuing turmoil of the Middle East, the leaders of the al-Qaeda terrorist group were sitting pretty. From hide-outs probably in remote areas of Pakistan, they could continue to win adherents by claiming that there was an American-led crusade against Muslims, and they could argue that America's failure in Iraq showed that they were winning. They were at liberty to continue to build their organisation, and did so through new alliances and mergers. It became evident that, far from being smashed at the centre, al-Qaeda retained a core that still had the ability to instigate acts of terrorism around the world.

Gulf Arab states were left anxiously pondering their options for the future. Though maintaining close military ties to Washington, they had evident distaste for the American troop presence in Iraq, but equally were fearful of the potential consequences of American failure and withdrawal – including a poor fate for Sunnis in Iraq and an even more assertive, perhaps nuclear-armed Iran holding sway over Iraq and the region. The changing landscape caused by the Iraq imbroglio challenged old dividing lines. For example, while the issue of Palestinian suffering and future statehood independent of Israel remained a dominant issue for Muslims everywhere, Gulf states tacitly approved – at least for a while – of Israel's push against Iran-supported Hizbullah. Altogether, the risk of region-wide sectarian conflict appeared to have risen.

In East and Southeast Asia, where many states have long been dependent for regional security on bilateral alliances with the United States, leaders continued to emphasise the importance of these close relationships with Washington, and of America's pivotal role. Nevertheless, each of these allies was meanwhile proceeding to evolve a new set of security relationships and regional mechanisms, some of which did not involve the United States. However, a positive sign in this context was the engagement on many levels, including economic and military, of the United States and China. This continued in spite of America's expressed suspicions – rejected by Beijing – about the size and transparency of Chinese military spending, and also in spite of virulent protectionist anti-Chinese rhetoric in the US Congress. While this relationship will nevertheless continue to be awkward, it will be important for Beijing to ensure that no diplomatic problems can spoil the success of the Beijing Olympic Games in August 2008. With China acting as broker, there was a significant, if tentative, advance when North Korea agreed to steps that could, if carried out, put it on a path towards ending its nuclear-weapons programme. But this was only after Pyongyang chose in October 2006 to detonate a nuclear device in what was seen as a failed test.

Another positive trend could be found in relation to climate change. This was the year in which a consensus was forged among all leading countries that urgent action was needed to curb carbon emissions with the aim of capping the increase in global temperatures that has occurred since the industrial revolution. Publication of the latest reports from the Intergovernmental Panel on Climate Change, a body of experts established by the United Nations, gave new impetus to international efforts. Leaders of the Group of Eight industrialised countries, meeting in Germany in June, agreed to work through a UN framework for substantial cuts in carbon emissions. Years of diplomatic endeavour and further top-level agreements will, however, be required to introduce an effective regime, which will in turn take decades to have the desired effect on temperature. In the meantime global warming is expected to worsen poverty and to contribute to conflict, especially in Africa.

Overall, however, developments over the past year have been discouraging. In addition to those mentioned, there was renewed conflict in Somalia and Sri Lanka and a military coup in Thailand. Conflict in Afghanistan and the Darfur region of Sudan remained of wide international concern.

While the problems of international security are the regular meat of this annual volume, it would be myopic not to mention that much of the industrialised and developing world remains in the midst of a prolonged economic upswing that has hardly been dented by terrorism, proliferation or conflict. Even rises in oil prices have been absorbed, though when coupled with strong demand for other raw materials, the effect is being seen in global price inflation. To counter this, monetary authorities have been raising interest rates, which could curb demand. Large trade imbalances between Western and Asian countries, especially China, mean that there are lingering dangers of rupture in the economic field. If political and financial accidents are to be avoided, cooperative leadership will be needed – just as it is needed to in order more effectively to address the most serious common security threats. Cooperation has begun to be seen on climate change and – so far with limited success – in the confrontation with Iran. A new set of world leaders is emerging. Over the past year, German Chancellor Angela Merkel, who took office in 2005, has been joined by Shinzo Abe in Japan, Nicolas Sarkozy in France and Gordon Brown in the United Kingdom. A new Russian president is due to be elected in 2008. These leaders will have to wait until 2009 to deal with an American counterpart who has real authority. Concerted leadership will be needed to tackle the complex problems stretching from the Middle East to Pakistan, as well as the threats of terrorism and proliferation. Otherwise, the risk is that simmering international tensions will spill over and endanger global prosperity.

America's loss of authority

In November 2006, the change in the political tide in the United States that had occurred as a result of the Iraq War became obvious to George W. Bush. The 'capital' that he had claimed to have earned in his 2004 re-election had been lost. With the Republican Party having ceded control of both houses of Congress, Bush acknowledged a 'thumping' and sacked Donald Rumsfeld, who as secretary of defense was the principal planner and executor of the Iraq War. In the coming months, Bush was subjected to further indignities: a bipartisan commission co-chaired by James Baker, his father's secretary of state, recommended a reversal of policy on Iraq, including a phased withdrawal and dialogue with Iran and Syria; Speaker of the House Nancy Pelosi travelled to Syria and met its president; Bush was forced to veto a war-funding bill under which Congress set deadlines for withdrawal from Iraq. However, he appeared determined to stick to the course that he had set. His response to calls to withdraw from Iraq was to send more troops. He aimed, through a 'surge', to impose security on Baghdad in order to give Iraqi leaders what was intended to be a final chance to reach a political settlement.

In truth, Bush had already sought to change the international face of his administration away from the neo-conservative aggression of his first term. Condoleezza Rice, his closest aide, was in 2005 appointed secretary of state, re-establishing the White House's link to the day-to-day execution of foreign policy, in contrast to the tenure of Colin Powell, who had rarely had the president's ear. Her former deputy, Stephen Hadley, moved up to replace her as National Security Adviser. On Rumsfeld's departure in 2007, Robert Gates, who had headed the Central Intelligence Agency under the president's father, George H.W. Bush, was appointed secretary of defense and immediately set out on a path towards a rational, low-key defence policy in which he was at pains to adopt the reverse of Rumsfeld's approach. Meanwhile, the radical elements of the first administration in turn left the scene: Paul Wolfowitz, former deputy to Rumsfeld, went in 2005 to head the World Bank, though in 2007 he was forced to resign from that position as well; Douglas Feith, under secretary of defence for policy, left in 2005; Lewis 'Scooter' Libby, chief of staff to Vice President Dick Cheney, resigned when indicted in 2005 and was later found guilty of perjury and obstruction of justice; John Bolton went from the State Department to be ambassador to the United Nations through a procedure that temporarily bypassed Congress, but in December 2006 had to resign as Bush acknowledged that Congressional approval could not be obtained. The Iraq War had also taken its toll on the careers of senior US military officers, and in June 2007 Gates announced that he would not re-nominate General Peter Pace as chairman of the Joint Chiefs of Staff for a second two-year term on the grounds that the Congressional hearings would have focused 'on the past, rather than the future, and further, that there was the very real prospect the process would be quite contentious'.

These changes, however, left Cheney, the second most important author of Bush's Iraq strategy after the president himself, still in place. His role in guiding Bush's decisions, on issues such as treatment of prisoners and the president's own executive power, had been murky in the numerous books and memoirs written by former officials. However, a series of investigative articles in the *Washington Post* in June 2007 shed new light, revealing the secret manner of Cheney's exertion of influence, which had bypassed the usual mechanisms of policy-setting. It was unclear to what degree he was still able to hold sway over the president. His public utterances showed no signs of any moderation in his views.

The neo-conservatives had believed that, through the exercise of America's dominant, high-technology military power, they could decisively change the status quo in the Middle East, creating a new pattern in which democracy would override traditional ethnic, religious and sectarian rivalries. This, in turn, would reduce future threats to the United States. The first step in this agenda was the March 2003 invasion of Iraq. But no strategic success beyond removal of Saddam Hussein's regime has so far been achieved there. The reasons are well rehearsed: inadequate troop numbers, absence of planning, unwillingness to engage with Iraqi and regional political realities, inability to deal with a growing insurgency. American authority was lost not only because of the failure of an overambitious mission, but because America appeared to have departed from its core values: inhumane treatment of prisoners in Iraq and the absence of judicial process for detainees at Guantanamo Bay, as well as the killing of civilians in Iraq and Afghanistan, gave its critics ample ammunition. These failures have been universally recognised following the publication of numerous accounts. But over the past year, their consequences have become more apparent.

The effect has been twofold: firstly, the Bush administration itself has suffered from a much-reduced ability to hold sway both in its domestic agenda and in its international dealings. This was evident from Bush's failure in June 2007 to push through a new immigration bill, from the scant regard paid by the protagonists to Rice's efforts to take a hand in the Middle East, and from Bush's sudden acceptance of the need for international action on climate change just before the June 2007 G8 summit. To regain its former influence, it was not sufficient for the administration simply to show a more conciliatory, pragmatic face. However, this loss seemed temporary: a new president, of whatever political hue, would be unencumbered by the baggage of the Iraq War and could begin from 2009 to restore American authority at this tactical level.

The second and more fundamental loss of American clout was at the strategic level. It was evident that the exercise of military power – in which, on paper, America dominated the world – had not secured its goal. The United States clearly had the ability to overwhelm almost any country with its massively superior firepower and well-trained forces. But this had already been well known. Iraq showed that, as a nation, America had not been able to turn its muscular superiority to strategic advantage. In the period leading up to the Iraq invasion, it had almost gone out of its way to ensure that it did not marshal the international support and national instruments that would be required for ultimate success. The invasion plan was successful in slicing through weak military opposition, but allowed control of Iraq to be lost from the moment that Baghdad fell on 9 April 2003 and the looting began. Over the following four years, American military weaknesses were exposed: the effort to keep up an insufficiently large commitment of troops in Iraq over four years appeared to put almost unsustainable pressure on the armed services, and in particular the US Army – as well as incurring extremely high budgetary expense. The capabilities, both military and civil, that were needed to bring order and reconstruction to a large country were plainly lacking. Troops that had been vaunted as having extraordinary, technology-backed capabilities seemed highly vulnerable to attack, even if the casualty numbers were low by historical comparison. All these factors created a sense around the world of American power diminished and demystified. This seemed bound for the foreseeable future to limit the ability of the United States to have a determining effect in international crises, since the deterrent impact on opponents of the potential use of armed force would be reduced. All an adversary needed to do was to draw America into a prolonged engagement.

Many countries earnestly desire a strong America as an essential element of maintaining international peace and security. But the restoration of American strategic authority seemed bound to take much longer than the mere installation of a new president. Meanwhile, the fact that something pivotal to global order had been lost was a very large strategic reality to which other countries were bound, for better or worse, to respond.

Iran advances

This background provided a perfect setting for Iran to advance its regional and nuclear ambitions. Though by no means on strong political ground domestically, the government of President Mahmoud Ahmadinejad sought over the past year to gain the maximum advantage from America's perceived weakness. The US-led 2001 invasion of Afghanistan had relieved Iran of one regional adversary, the Taliban, and the US-led 2003 invasion of Iraq had removed another. American forces continued to be bogged down in both countries. America's inability to cajole a Shia-dominated Iraqi government into making political settlements played very much to the advantage of Tehran: the United States accused Iran and the Iran-supported Shia militia group Hizbullah of giving material help to Iraqi insurgents. The conflict in Lebanon in summer 2006 – to which Washington had refrained from seeking an end – left Hizbullah strengthened and Israel, Iran's mortal enemy and America's close friend, chastened and weakened. Iran, bizarrely, was able to cast itself as a champion of Arab nationalism – though this caused Sunni Arab states to view its rising power with heightened nervousness. Ahmadinejad was sufficiently emboldened to hold in December 2006 an international conference that assembled people who denied that the Holocaust, in which 6 million Jews were killed in the Second World War, had occurred. Meanwhile, Iran proceeded with its efforts to enrich uranium in defiance of successive United Nations Security Council resolutions.

If it succeeded in putting a planned 3,000-centrifuge enrichment plant into operation, Iran could in theory have enough material to make a nuclear weapon by 2009 or 2010 – though it denies that this is its intention. This extreme scenario remained subject to important caveats: Iran's technical progress towards its goal has been far from rapid; not only would the centrifuges need to be installed and successfully operated, but it would also need the ability to produce a weapon. Moreover, diplomatic options did not seem to be exhausted: there was scope for a continued tightening of sanctions on Iran through further UN resolutions, provided that Russia and China continued to acquiesce. The United States seemed willing to continue to travel along this route with its 'E3' European partners France, Germany and the United Kingdom, though negotiations with Tehran have so far been essentially fruitless. Under strong pressure, Bush went so far as to permit the first direct talks between Iranian and American officials for nearly 30 years, though the subject was Iraq rather than the nuclear programme. In considering progressively more punitive and painful sanctions, the international community would want to calculate their likely impact in Tehran. While it was possible that they could exacerbate divisions within Iran's political elite and lead to Ahmadinejad being weakened and Iran's nuclear stance relaxed, it was equally conceivable that the Iranian president could use more draconian UN sanctions to bolster his domestic political standing and to strengthen the country's resolve to continue with the enrichment programme.

Gulf Arab nations were thus confronted by the perceptible weakening of their principal ally and security guarantor, the United States, and the rise of nearby Iran, a Shia power that could in time be nuclear armed. Meanwhile, Iraq, which had been a regional balancing power, with a Sunni minority secular leadership but a Shia majority, was now rent asunder by sectarian, extremist and criminal violence from which the Shia majority seemed bound to emerge dominant. The spread of sectarian violence throughout the region would be catastrophic for all Gulf states. Therefore, it was not surprising to see them moving to hedge against the future, if in a somewhat uncertain fashion. Saudi Arabia sought to trace a path that was distinctively its own: though still maintaining a close relationship with the United States, it worked to build relationships with China and Russia. Riyadh revived its previous plan for Middle East peace, and brought the Palestinian factions to an agreement on a 'unity government' that proved short lived. It tried to limit Iranian influence, but had a series of contacts with Iran, including a visit to Riyadh by Ahmadinejad, who also visited Oman and the United Arab Emirates.

Persistent conflict: Iraq, the Middle East and Afghanistan

This was the year in which it became crystal clear to all that previous American strategy in Iraq was based on false assumptions and could not achieve a successful outcome. Robert Gates, in a Senate confirmation hearing, was asked whether the United States was winning the war in Iraq and replied: 'No, sir'. A US National Intelligence Estimate in January 2007 confirmed in careful language what many reports and commentaries had already indicated: it found 'an increase in communal and insurgent violence and political extremism', driven by weakness of Iraq's security forces and of the state, as well as all participants' 'ready recourse to violence'. There was, it said, 'a self-sustaining inter-sectarian struggle between Shia and Sunnis', and 'significant population displacement'. The previous month, the Iraq Study Group, made up of distinguished former American officials, had put it more baldly, reporting that 'the situation in Baghdad and several provinces is dire ... The level of violence is high and growing. There is great suffering, and the daily lives of many Iraqis show little or no improvement. Pessimism is pervasive.' The group advocated a comprehensive revision of policy: a sharp reduction in the American troop presence, with a shift in mission for those left to supporting the Iraqi army; engagement by Washington with Iraq's neighbours, including Iran and Syria; and stepped up pressure on the government of Iraqi Prime Minister Nuri al-Maliki to achieve national reconciliation, security and effective governance. President Bush, who treated the recommendations with disdain, produced the results of his own strategy review a month later. He was forced into a change of course, but not into retreat. There was, for him, no question of failure.

The new strategy dispensed with much of the wishful thinking of the administration's previous statements. It acknowledged rising sectarian violence, especially in Baghdad; al-Qaeda's growing role in Iraq; inadequate force levels; lack of popular support for the coalition because of poor security; the inability of Iraqi forces to impose security; and their infiltration by sectarian militias. To improve security in Baghdad and the surrounding region, Bush sent 31,500 more troops. General David Petraeus, who had acquired a high reputation for an enlightened approach in his previous commands in Iraq, was put in charge of coalition forces. Military tactics were changed, with troops deployed out of their bases to impose security in individual districts from mini-fortresses. The effect was to reduce violence in some districts, with signs that normal commerce and daily life were returning – though insurgents seemed to be displaced to other areas, or else to be biding their time. The key to the new strategy – as it was for the recommendations of the Iraq Study Group – was to place clear responsibility on the Iraqi government for the achievement of lasting political settlements between the country's warring communities, as well as for the exertion of governance over the whole country. Given the continuing complete absence of state capacity following the wholesale decapitation of the Ba'athist regime in 2003, this seemed a fatal flaw in the new American strategy – as it was indeed for the Iraq Study Group's proposals and other alternatives. The al-Maliki government appeared unlikely to be able to meet the 'benchmarks' that Washington was setting. Even as the surge strategy was being implemented, American commanders and officials, acutely aware of its doubtful prospects and of the pressure to bring troops home, were therefore busy devising the next strategy, likely to emerge during autumn 2007.

Prospects for resolution of the Israel–Palestine dispute worsened considerably, with Israel embarrassed by its performance in the 2006 military foray into Lebanon, and Palestinians dissolving into internecine warfare that left, by mid 2007, rival governments in the West Bank and Gaza respectively. The diminished leverage of the United States undermined its friends and emboldened its opponents. The Israeli military lost credibility, taking heavy criticism for its conduct of the Lebanon campaign, in which it relied too much on the effect of air power and at the same time found that its ground forces were ill prepared for an assault on territory controlled by Hizbullah. The year's events left the Israeli government of Prime Minister Ehud Olmert with little traction over events, though still able to limit the authority of the Palestinian Authority in the West Bank. Meanwhile, Palestine splintered. Following the June 2007 takeover of Gaza by the militant group Hamas, and the consequent demise of the Hamas-led 'unity government', Western powers and Israel sought to bolster Palestinian Authority President Mahmoud Abbas, leader of the rival Fatah faction in the West Bank. Palestinians lacked a credible, representative interlocutor. The creation of an eventual Palestinian state seemed even further distant – and this gave succour to the cause of jihadist extremism.

If the problems in Iraq and the Middle East seemed intractable, centuries of warlordism would suggest that the conflict in Afghanistan would be even more so. Here, history cautions against having too high expectations of what the involvement of international forces can achieve. Although NATO members and partner countries stepped up the commitment of troops to security and reconstruction operations, there was growing pessimism about the prospects for success, springing apparently from the realisation that the mission would have to continue for many years to come to make a lasting impact on the future of the Afghan people. Within NATO, which assumed responsibility for security throughout the country in 2006, there were persistent arguments about risk sharing. European countries with troops in the north of the country believed that the mission's success would lie in consultation, not combat, with local groups. They deplored the 'kinetic' approach of the United States, and found the deaths of innocent civilians strongly counterproductive. The United States, Britain, Canada and others with troops in the south – while seeking to win the favour of the local populace – found that a softer approach was not realistic, since they were in daily combat with hostile forces which were reinforced by flows of fighters from across the border with Pakistan. Afghan history suggests that the path towards conflict resolution would eventually involve the making of deals. Afghan President Mohammed Karzai showed signs of wanting to reach an accommodation with moderate Taliban elements, but it was unclear whether NATO and the international community in general were ready to support such an approach. Meanwhile, an expected spring 2007 offensive by the Taliban in the south appeared to have been blunted, but insurgency and extremism were spreading to previously peaceful areas, with a sharp rise in suicide bombings.

Islamic extremism: al-Qaeda's strengthened core

With the travails of Iraq, Palestine and Afghanistan still providing plentiful reasons for disillusion with the West, it was not surprising to find little diminution in the threat of terrorism from extremist groups. Indeed, evidence emerged from uncovered plots that the degree of direction from al-Qaeda's core leaders, believed to be based in ungoverned areas of Pakistan, had increased (see essay, pages 33–46)

While plots were foiled in many countries, Britain was a particular target. The trials of a number of British-based groups, as well as evidence about the 7 July 2005 London bombs, revealed that actual and would-be terrorists had made visits to Pakistan for training. Orders, instruction in techniques, operational planning and coordination, and other assistance appeared to have come from associates in Pakistan. The government of General Pervez Musharraf, Pakistan's president, therefore remained crucial to international efforts to curb Islamic extremism. However, it was at mid 2007 looking increasingly shaky. It had been forced into doing deals with tribal leaders in its ungoverned territories, and faced mounting popular discontent after Musharraf suspended the country's chief judge.

There were also signs of growing capability in the Iraq-based al-Qaeda in Mesopotamia, though that organisation lost its leader to an American air strike in 2006. However, there were two encouraging signs: firstly, local Sunni leaders in Anbar province, west of Baghdad, had begun to fight back against al-Qaeda's presence; and secondly, there was little evidence that al-Qaeda in Mesopotamia was instigating acts of terror outside the country. The US military, meanwhile, engaged in counter-terrorist strike operations in Somalia as that country's capital was taken over by the militant group Union of Islamic Courts, which was in turn expelled from Mogadishu by Ethiopian-backed government forces.

Old and new themes
The world at mid 2007 continued to be characterised by long-running conflicts and problems. But international dealings also featured some new themes.

Poverty, disease and conflict continued to bedevil Africa, though there were some positive signs. Implementation of the large international aid package agreed in 2005 was slow, but China's investment proceeded apace, albeit skewed strongly towards Beijing's own commercial and economic interests. In addition to renewed fighting in Somalia, conflict and humanitarian crisis persisted in the Darfur region of Sudan, spilling into neighbouring Chad. Elections were held successfully in the Democratic Republic of the Congo and less successfully in Nigeria, where guerrilla activity in the Niger Delta was a growing problem.

In Asia, the economic rise of China continued inexorably, and India again recorded strong growth. Sri Lanka's internal conflict worsened, and there was little advance in the Kashmir peace process between India and Pakistan. The military took a hand amid political turmoil in Bangladesh, and seized power in Thailand and Fiji. There was insecurity and violence in Timor Leste, the Solomon Islands and Tonga.

First steps were taken to ease the deadlock over North Korea's nuclear-weapons programme. However, this was only after Pyongyang itself had altered the regional balance, first by carrying out missile tests, and then by exploding a nuclear device. These moves were a major diplomatic setback for China, and prompted Beijing to switch its stance and vote for UN sanctions resolutions. Renewed diplomatic efforts by both Beijing and Washington then led to a February 2007 agreement under which, among various parts of a first phase, frozen funds would be returned to Pyongyang and the Yongbyon nuclear reactor would be shut down. It remained to be seen whether this agreement would have greater success than its predecessor, the 1994 Agreed Framework.

While these topics were familiar from previous years, there were also new elements at play in international affairs.

The first seemed a throwback to the confrontation of the Cold War. Russian President Vladimir Putin struck a more pugilistic stance towards the West and in particular the United States. His repeated accusations of old-style imperialism were fuelled by American plans to site missile-defence systems in Poland and the Czech Republic. The prospect of a highly capable American radar system being placed in the Czech Republic, even though intended to detect future Iranian missile launches, was not well received in Moscow. However, Western governments declined to respond in kind to Putin's aggressive rhetoric. Washington preferred to seek more opportunities to explain its missile-defence plans. Britain requested the extradition of a Russian suspect for the 2006 London murder – through ingestion of polonium – of Russian dissident Alexander Litvinenko. This set off a diplomatic row, but in general, Western governments expressed disappointment and resignation that a sticky period in relations with Moscow was inevitable as Putin approached the scheduled end of his tenure in 2008, and elections approached. US Defense Secretary Gates's response to Putin that 'one Cold War was enough' epitomised the Western attitude. Meanwhile, Putin skilfully outwitted European governments who were seeking to reduce their dependence on Russia for energy supplies, and continued to cement the nexus between Moscow's political and commercial interests.

The second new element was the sudden coalescence of international support for action to address climate change. This was triggered by 'An Inconvenient Truth', a documentary film featuring former US Vice President Al Gore – in essence, his slide show and lecture on rising global temperatures. German Chancellor Angela Merkel, who emerged during the past year as a formidable European leader, sought to make countering climate change the central theme of the June 2007 G8 summit, which she chaired. She succeeded in securing some softening of American opposition to coordinated action – though many difficult steps lay ahead, especially in persuading fast-growing nations such as China and India to limit carbon emissions. Meanwhile, there was a growing view that the consequences of climate change would have an effect on international security, especially in exacerbating factors that already contributed to conflict (see essay, pages 46–68).

Thirdly, Merkel had another notable success in beginning to move Europe out of the political malaise in which it had languished for two years following the collapse of efforts to introduce a 'constitution' for the European Union. Through intense diplomatic efforts she won support for a practical, less ambitious set of reforms with the aim of avoiding national referendums. A period of intense debate and jockeying over Europe's future beckoned with the election of

Nicolas Sarkozy as president of France and – by his party – of Gordon Brown as prime minister of the United Kingdom.

The emergence of Merkel, Sarkozy and Brown as Europe's leaders provided hope that fresh approaches could be brought to bear on the world's most unyielding issues. All three crossed normal party lines in forging their policies and governments (though Merkel, as the head of a 'grand coalition', did so of necessity). This raised the possibility of the development of 'new politics', combining pragmatism, flexibility and energy. All these, plus cooperation, will be required to address the pressing issues of the moment: Iraq, Iran, the Middle East, extremist terrorism and climate change. For the time being, however, such cooperation has to take place in the absence of an American administration lacking the degree of authority to which the world is normally accustomed. The damage to international security caused by the Iraq War and the ensuing loss of American standing will take some years to repair.

2 Strategic Policy Issues

Islamist Terrorism: al-Qaeda Resurgent

The threat from Islamist terrorism remains as high as ever, and looks set to get worse. This is evident from several developments that have become apparent over the past year. Firstly, there is increasing evidence that 'core' al-Qaeda is proving adaptable and resilient, and has retained an ability to plan and coordinate large-scale attacks in the Western world despite the attrition it has suffered. Secondly, a number of regional jihadist groups, notably al-Qaeda in Mesopotamia and al-Qaeda in the Maghreb, have not only sworn formal allegiance to al-Qaeda but, more importantly, have begun to demonstrate ambition beyond their parochial concerns in support of al-Qaeda's global objectives. Thirdly, the large number of terrorist plots that have come to light in Europe, Canada, the Arabian peninsula and the Maghreb point to a growing trend towards radicalisation within the Islamic world. Further factors pointing to a deteriorating situation include the continuing turmoil in Iraq, which has not only exposed the limits of US military power, but is also both a *casus belli* and a crucible for developing hardened jihadists with the potential to migrate elsewhere; the insurgency in southern Afghanistan which a NATO force is struggling to contain; and the associated problems of extremism in Pakistan. In sum, the United States and its allies have failed to deal a death-blow to al-Qaeda; the organisation's ideology appears to have taken root to such a degree that it will require decades to eradicate.

Europe: growing radicalisation
Plots disrupted by security authorities point to a continuing and worsening problem of radicalisation within Europe's Islamic diasporas – and the degree to

which terrorists were still being directed by al-Qaeda. In August 2006 the German authorities arrested a group of Lebanese who had attempted unsuccessfully to detonate bombs on passenger trains. In the latter part of 2006 Spanish services disrupted two major plots and French services three. Italian police arrested one Tunisian and two Algerian groups. Britain was a particular target. In July 2006 the British Security Service and police disrupted an alleged plot to detonate bombs on airliners over the Atlantic. In January 2007 they arrested another group whose alleged intention was to decapitate a British Muslim serving in the army. Two months later they arrested three people connected with those who carried out the July 2005 London bombings, and in April they arrested a further six people allegedly involved in inciting terrorist acts overseas and raising funds for terrorism. In April 2007 the year-long *Crevice* trial ended with five men jailed for life for planning attacks on a range of targets, using bombs made from ammonium nitrate fertiliser. In the same month six associates of self-confessed terrorist Dhiren Barot, who was sentenced in 2006 to life imprisonment for planning attacks on targets including Heathrow airport and the London Underground, pleaded guilty to terrorist offences. In June, two car bombs failed to explode in central London and there was a failed suicide car bomb attack on Glasgow airport. Several foreign-born doctors were arrested. By mid 2007, about 100 terrorist suspects were awaiting trial in the UK.

The scale of the problem in the United Kingdom was indicated in a rare public address in November 2006 by Eliza Manningham-Buller, then director-general of the Security Service, the domestic intelligence agency. She said the service was monitoring 30 terrorist plots involving some 200 groups and 1,600 individuals – the latter figure later rose above 2,000. A disturbingly high proportion of young British Muslims appeared to have been radicalised at least to the point where they took as a given the validity of the 'single narrative' – the idea that the complexities of the Islamic world could be reduced to the simple message that Muslims were suffering oppression at the hands of unbelievers. To counter the potential for violent acts arising from this phenomenon, the Security Service was expanded substantially, and began to establish a permanent presence in the British regions, working with regional police forces. Part of their aim was to develop a 'rich picture' of Muslim communities with a view to identifying anomalous behaviour at an early stage and acting on it. However, it remained unclear whether the Security Service had the resources needed to identify and deal fully with the problem.

The 2005 London bombings cast particular attention on the security issue arising from within its 800,000-strong Pakistani community. Three of the four 7 July bombers, who killed a total of 52 people on three Underground trains and a bus, were British citizens of Pakistani descent. This came as a shock to British intelligence and security services, which had previously been more focused on threats from the North African diaspora. By mid 2007, however, it was estimated that of the terrorist groups under investigation by the Security Service, two-thirds were made up of people of Pakistani origin, with people of Bangladeshi origin making up much of the remainder. A government report on the July 2005 bombings noted that 400,000 British nationals of Pakistani origin travelled each year to Pakistan, where they stayed for an average of 41 days, a volume of traffic well beyond the capacity of the British and Pakistani security authorities to monitor in detail. Al-Qaeda spotted the potential offered by this flow of people, and has proved adept at connecting with, developing and training already radicalised young men to undertake high-profile attacks. It became clear that the *Crevice* group of would-be fertiliser bombers, the 7 July 2005 London bombers, and the 21 July 2005 group whose bombs (also on three London Underground trains and a bus) did not explode, had all been directed from Pakistan, probably by Abd al Hadi al Iraqi; this was also almost certainly the case with the 2006 airline plot, for which suspects had not yet come to trial.

Awareness of the role of 'core' al-Qaeda (the remnants of the organisation under the direction of Osama bin Laden and Ayman al-Zawahiri in the Afghanistan–Pakistan border regions) in these plots forced intelligence and security services to reappraise a part of the movement that had been seen as being on the back foot and struggling to survive in the face of continued US and Pakistani pressure. Although relatively little was known about the composition and organisation of core al-Qaeda, it evidently retained both the will and the capability to plan and conduct ambitious terrorist operations and clearly constituted the main threat to the UK and, by extension, the United States, given the ease with which British nationals are able to travel there through a visa-waiver scheme. The predominantly Arab composition of the group has been supplemented by a significant influx of Pakistanis.

Recognition of the size of the problem led the British government to consider changes to its counter-terrorism strategy. This was encapsulated in its *Contest* or 'Four P' approach, which designated four pillars of counter-terrorist activity, each the responsibility of a separate committee of civil servants, intelligence and security officials, police and emergency services. The four pillars were to 'prepare' for terrorist attacks and put in place measures to deal with them; 'protect' potential targets through enhanced security measures; 'pursue' terrorists, disrupting their plans and bringing them to justice; and 'prevent' the creation of the next generation of terrorists by minimising the impact of jihadist ideology on young Britons. The strategy, though conceptually sound, had since its inception in 2003 suffered from uneven implementation. In particular, not enough had been done to push forward the 'prevent' strand, which was in effect the government's counter-radicalisation programme. A decision was reached in March 2007 to split the Home Office, the equivalent of an interior ministry, by separating out its responsibility for the criminal justice system and placing this in a new Ministry of Justice. National responsibility for counter-terrorism policy would be concentrated in the Home Office, with the creation of an Office of Security and Counter-Terrorism with responsibility for *Contest*, and a separate interdepartmental unit dedicated to taking forward the 'prevent' agenda. There would also be a ministerial committee chaired by the Home Secretary, designed to inject into the *Contest* process a degree of sustained top-level political engagement it had previously lacked. This increased focus has been generally welcomed, although there are some concerns within the UK's intelligence community that the structure risks giving an excessively domestic focus to an issue which is transnational in nature. It will however be some time before it becomes apparent how effective the new arrangements will be.

Elsewhere in Western Europe, the main terrorist threat continued to emanate from the Maghrebi communities which form the bulk of Muslim populations – although the increasing prevalence of Pakistani diasporas was giving rise to concern among European security officials, as was the potential threat posed by Kurdish and Somali diasporas, predominantly in northern Europe. In that context, an announcement by the Algerian Salafist Group for Combat (GSPC) in September 2006 that it had allied itself with al-Qaeda, rebranding itself as al-Qaeda in the Maghreb, was a potentially significant development. Initially it was unclear whether this was more than just a public-relations exercise by a group described by one Algerian minister as 'almost totally eradicated and no longer posing a serious threat'. But in April 2007, GSPC launched mass-casualty suicide attacks in Algiers, suggesting a renewed degree of ambition going beyond the stream of low-grade attacks that had taken place in the GSPC heartland of Kabylie in the preceding months. A further worrying factor was the degree to which aspirant jihadists had been directed away from Iraq and towards GSPC training camps in northern Mali in a manner seemingly co-ordinated with the Iraq-based al-Qaeda in Mesopotamia, giving rise to concern, articulated by French anti-terror judge Jean-Louis Bruguière, that such individuals could eventually migrate to Maghrebi communities in Western Europe. But so far this threat has remained hypothetical, and the main terrorist threat within Europe continues to emanate from indigenous Muslim communities.

Institutionally, Europe's response to the threat from Islamist terrorism has been mixed. The intelligence and security services of those European Union (EU) member states most affected by the threat have in the main evolved effective capabilities to counter it. Cooperation and intelligence sharing, both between European services and with key allies elsewhere, is better developed than is commonly supposed. But European services are still some way short of having a common 'toolbox' of professional capabilities and powers, which in part reflects distrust in some parts of Europe of reliance on an intelligence-based approach to counter-terrorism. Within the EU, terrorism is a national competence and the role of the European Council and the European Commission is limited to co-ordination. The EU's first counter-terrorism coordinator, Gijs de Vries, a former Dutch deputy interior minister, did much to raise awareness of the threat from Islamist terrorism among EU member states, but made little impact on EU insti-tutions. He departed in March 2007, and by mid year had not been replaced.

The United States: muscular approach

Radicalisation of elements of indigenous Muslim communities has not taken place in the United States to the extent that it has in Europe and elsewhere. Muslims in the United States appear to be better integrated than their European counterparts into the mainstream of society, and therefore less vulnerable to rad-icalisation. However, there have been some indications that this could begin to change. In May 2007 the Federal Bureau of Investigation (FBI) arrested a group of six US-based Islamists who had allegedly been planning to attack an army base at Fort Dix, New Jersey. So far as was known, the group had no external links. But this brought to 12 the number of home-grown plots investigated by the FBI since the 11 September attacks. The US Department of Homeland Security has uncovered a number of instances of radicalising activity by Islamic religious establishments in the United States, funded by individuals and groups from Saudi Arabia. In May 2007, a survey by the Pew Research Center found that the 2.4 million Muslim Americans were more assimilated than their counter-parts in Europe, and that very few were in the lowest income bracket. However, those aged below 30 were more likely to describe themselves as Muslim first and American second, and to attend a mosque. African-American Muslims, most of whom were converts, tended to have more radical views than others, with only 36% having a 'highly unfavourable' view of al-Qaeda.

An indication of what could be in store for the United States came from Canada, where in June 2006 the security authorities, following a two-year inves-tigation, detained 17 suspects, mostly Canadian citizens of various origins, who had allegedly been planning to carry out multiple terrorist attacks in the south-ern Ontario region and had procured ammonium nitrate fertiliser. Their targets allegedly included the Canadian Broadcasting Corporation, the Canadian Security Intelligence Service building in Toronto and the Canadian Parliament, which they had intended to storm, taking hostage and beheading the prime min-ister. Though the group were broadly supportive of the al-Qaeda ideology, no evidence emerged of external links or direction. Nevertheless, the arrests were a rude shock for a Canadian population which tended to believe that the coun-try's tradition of multiculturalism and its benign overseas image insulated them against such threats.

American counter-terrorism strategy, under the rubric of the 'global war on terror', has continued to emphasise the projection of hard power overseas and extensive and costly physical security within the US homeland. While there has been much debate about the term 'global war on terror' – seen by many as counter-productive because it is equated in many Muslim minds with a global war on Islam – President George W. Bush has made clear that its use will continue while he remains in office. The campaign has had some successes: the effort to detain or kill senior al-Qaeda operatives has been effective in reducing the capacity of core al-Qaeda to plan and execute major terrorist operations. Some 70% of Osama bin Laden's earlier commanders are now thought to be dead or captured: a significant recent example was Abd al Hadi al Iraqi, believed to be the controlling mind behind a series of terrorist plots in the United Kingdom. His capture in 2006 represented a major blow to al-Qaeda. However, US and European intelligence services believe al-Qaeda retains the resilience to survive a blow of this kind and to continue to generate attack planners with the same levels of ambition and capability as their predecessors.

Several aspects of US counter-terrorism policy have, however, appeared to be of questionable net value. These include the maintenance of a detention camp in Guantanamo Bay, Cuba; the practice of extraordinary rendition of suspects to third countries for interrogation; and 'enhanced' interrogation techniques that are often viewed as torture. On the one hand, the worth of these instruments in preventing and gaining information about terrorist activity, though often claimed by Washington as the justification for its actions, has yet to be publicly demonstrated. On the other, they have hindered the ability of judicial systems to bring terrorist suspects to justice; they have complicated the ability of the United States to act in concert with other governments against terrorists; and they have, through the sense of injustice that they have fostered, almost certainly stimulated recruitment into terrorist groups.

Guantanamo Bay in particular is perceived within the global Islamic community as a symbol of US oppression. International pressure on Washington has brought changes. Following a US Supreme Court ruling, the US Department of Defense accepted that prisoners were entitled to protection under the Geneva Conventions. Prisoners no longer deemed to pose a threat were released. Others were repatriated to their countries of origin to stand trial or be released on the grounds that the circumstances of their detention precluded judicial action. Some detainees have begun to appear before US military tribunals. But this left, as of mid 2007, nearly 250 detainees deemed by the US authorities to pose a continuing danger, whose own governments would not accept them and for whom no obvious solution existed. US Democratic Party politicians have made clear their desire to see the facility closed, but this is unlikely to be done during the remainder of Bush's tenure.

The past year saw an upsurge of international concern about extraordinary rendition, the process whereby the CIA has moved terrorist suspects to other jurisdictions for interrogation and detention without going through formal judicial processes. Some countries to which suspects are believed to have been transported are thought to practise torture. The Council of Europe and a Special Committee of the European Parliament conducted investigations into the extent of the CIA's use of extraordinary rendition in Europe, publishing reports in June 2006 and February 2007 respectively – though the latter was criticised as being short on hard evidence on the existence of 'black' detention facilities in Poland and Romania. The reports concluded there had been as many as 21 documented cases of extraordinary rendition, and a substantial number of CIA flights in and out of Europe between 2001 and 2005, some of which had been used to transport subjects of extraordinary rendition. Separately, an Italian prosecutor issued arrest warrants for 23 CIA officers thought to have been involved in the kidnapping of an Egyptian cleric, Abu Omar, in Milan in 2003. Prosecutors in Germany, Spain and Portugal opened investigations into other cases of extraordinary rendition.

Washington maintained its position, enunciated by Secretary of State Condoleezza Rice in 2005, that rendition was 'a vital tool in combating transnational terrorism'. It was unapologetic about the use of 'black' detention facilities, the existence of which was confirmed by Bush in September 2006. Reports of enhanced interrogation techniques led to an October 2005 ban, sponsored by Senator John McCain, on the use by the American military of 'cruel, inhuman or degrading interrogation techniques'. Those practised by the United States had been thought to include sleep deprivation, the use of stress positions and 'water-boarding', in which water is poured over a person's face to simulate drowning. The official US response was that it did not employ torture, and it was unclear whether techniques such as water-boarding were still being used.

Other aspects of US counter-terrorism policy were controversial on civil-liberties grounds rather than on their value as tools against terrorists: the use of subpoenas to access information on financial transactions in the SWIFT electronic banking system; the disclosure to the US authorities of details on airline passengers, which caused a transatlantic row; and the granting to US agencies of access to information indicating when, from where, by whom and to whom e-mails and other electronic communications passing through the United States had been sent.

Pakistan: the front line

Ever since Pakistani President Pervez Musharraf committed his country to cooperation with the United States in its war on al-Qaeda, Pakistan has been engaged in a delicate balancing act. While working with the CIA against al-Qaeda, Pakistan was also training and equipping militants infused with a strongly Islamist ideology to fight a proxy war against India in Kashmir. Simultaneously Musharraf, who was dependent on Islamic parties for a degree of political legitimacy, had to confront growing levels of sectarian violence, particularly in cities such as Karachi. Meanwhile, the Taliban, ousted from Afghanistan, had established itself in Quetta, capital of Pakistan's western province of Baluchistan, where its leadership is thought to be located; and in the Federally Administered Tribal Areas (FATA) of northwest Pakistan, a region over which the Pakistani government has never exercised effective control and where al-Qaeda's top leaders Osama bin Laden and Ayman al-Zawahiri are thought to be located.

In 2004 Musharraf recognised the need to counter domestic extremists, reduce the level of infiltration into Kashmir and reduce tension with India. He sent some 70,000 troops into the FATA to take on both the remnants of al-Qaeda and the resurgent Taliban. But by 2006, faced with mounting casualties and the need to counter a resurgence of separatism in Baluchistan, the Pakistani military struck an agreement with tribal leaders in the Wana region of South Waziristan, in the FATA. The army agreed to cease active operations and withdraw to barracks. In return the tribal leaders assumed responsibility for their own security, and agreed to drive out foreign fighters and to ensure that their territory was not used as a base for attacks on neighbouring states. This agreement was later replicated in two other areas of the FATA, most recently Bajaur in March 2007.

The agreements were received with scepticism by the United States, and subsequent events suggested this was well founded. The agreements provided the Taliban with a cross-border haven from which to send fighters into Afghanistan, and the numbers of these rose sharply. The CIA also feared that the agreements with the tribal leaders enabled al-Qaeda to re-establish safe areas, significantly enhancing its capability to plan and execute international terrorist operations. In February 2007 US Vice-President Dick Cheney, accompanied by CIA Deputy Director Stephen Kappes, reportedly handed over to the Pakistani authorities details of a number of locations in the FATA which the CIA believed to be al-Qaeda training facilities and operational bases. Both the US and Pakistani governments face the reality, however, that military force alone is unlikely ever to pacify the FATA, and that the only viable long-term solution is to try to integrate the region into the mainstream of Pakistani society – something that would take time, if it were achievable at all. Since Washington is therefore pressing for quick results that look undeliverable, it may feel compelled to consider unilateral action inside the FATA against al-Qaeda and Taliban groups. However, the wider negative consequences of such action in terms of Muslim public opinion worldwide would need to be weighed carefully against the potential short-term gains.

Pakistan's complexity and inherent instability will continue to make it a difficult ally for governments striving to tackle Islamist terrorism. However, there appears no alternative to continued engagement. Western governments face challenges in reconciling their desires to see progress towards democracy and improved human rights, to contain Pakistani nuclear proliferation, and to encourage Pakistani action against terrorism and extremism.

Iraq, Saudi Arabia and Iran

While much of the violence in Iraq has been sectarian, with Sunni and Shia groups pitted both against each other and against the US-led coalition, a significant proportion of recent attacks can be attributed to al-Qaeda in Mesopotamia, the organisation set up by Abu Musab al-Zarqawi in the wake of the US invasion. The death of al-Zarqawi in a US air strike in 2006 did not appear to dent the group's violence, which has been directed against the Shi'ites, coalition forces and Sunni tribes alike. Although al-Qaeda in Mesopotamia has sworn allegiance to bin Laden and has been led successively by a Jordanian and an Egyptian, it appears to be a predominantly indigenous organisation – though using foreign volunteers for suicide missions – whose aim is to establish sharia enclaves in Sunni areas.

Al-Qaeda in Mesopotamia has, however, suffered reverses in addition to the loss of al-Zarqawi. In Anbar province west of Baghdad, Sunni tribal sheikhs fought back against its uncompromising extremism, and by mid 2007, the group appeared largely to have been driven out of the province and to have switched its focus to Diyala, east of Baghdad. Unable to hold territory, it concentrated on car-bombings and other forms of mass-casualty attack. One feared consequence of al-Qaeda's involvement in Iraq has not materialised: 'blowback', the return of extremists to their own countries to cause trouble. Interest in foreign fighters among Iraq's contending factions has been mainly in those willing to volunteer for suicide missions. The number of foreign fighters crossing from Syria into Iraq each month is estimated in the low tens, and the border with Saudi Arabia is thought to be virtually sealed. Foreign aspirant jihadists are being redirected to training camps in North Africa. However, al-Qaeda in Mesopotamia is still being funded by private individuals and groups in Saudi Arabia, and there is also evidence that the Iranian Revolutionary Guard Corps is equipping the group, notwithstanding the latter's deep hostility to the Shi'ites, with the tactical aim of putting pressure on the United States.

In Saudi Arabia, the government's campaign against al-Qaeda has continued. By the end of 2004, the internal security organisation, Mabahith, had with US assistance largely dismantled the leadership of al-Qaeda in the Arabian Peninsula (AQAP), an insurgent movement mainly comprising Arabs returned from Afghanistan. Since then, there have been no large-scale successful attacks, though a foiled incursion into the Abqaiq oil refinery in February 2006 was a near miss. The Mabahith has regularly apprehended groups of AQAP activists, or has found itself in shootouts with militants who committed suicide rather than be taken. In April 2007 the Interior Ministry announced the arrest of 170 terrorist suspects of both Saudi and foreign origin who were alleged to have been involved in planning attacks. This included operatives taking flying lessons in neighbouring states, apparently with a view to conducting suicide operations against oil refineries and storage depots. Substantial quantities of weapons and cash were captured. These arrests, likely to have been the culmination of a long investigation, were a reminder of the resilience and regenerative capacity of Islamist terrorist organisations.

The Saudi government has developed counter-radicalisation measures, including guidance to parents on how to recognise signs of extremism, hotlines to enable them to seek help, and television soap operas depicting the suffering of surviving families of suicide bombers. The authorities have called for help on the religious authorities – the Ulema – which are an integral part of the state structure. However, official Saudi Wahhabist doctrines continue to contest with more liberal interpretations of Islam in the region and elsewhere, perhaps fuelling the very extremism that the government is committed to fighting at home. Although the Saudi authorities have clamped down on funding of extremist groups by official charities, groups and individuals in Saudi Arabia still provide significant financial support.

Iran's relationship with al-Qaeda has long been ambiguous. The official report on the 11 September 2001 attacks referred to the fact that much of the 'muscle' for the operation had been able to transit Iran with the host government's apparent complicity. There have also been suggestions that Iran offered bin Laden a collaborative relationship before 11 September, but was rebuffed. In 2003, following AQAP attacks in Riyadh which appeared at least in part to have been planned in Iran, Tehran admitted that it had detained a number of senior al-Qaeda figures who had fled Afghanistan, described metaphorically by one US official as 'al-Qaeda's management council'. The group, which includes bin Laden's son Saad, appeared in 2007 still to be under some form of detention, although there were unsubstantiated suggestions that Iran had allowed them some latitude to engage in terrorist planning. It was also alleged that Tehran was turning a blind eye to lower-level al-Qaeda operatives transiting Iran and even residing there. Iran undoubtedly saw the detainees as a potential negotiating card with the United States and the international community in the dispute over its nuclear programme.

Southeast Asia: continuing concern
No major terrorist episodes took place in Southeast Asia over the past year, but security authorities in all ASEAN states continued to be concerned about the risks of radicalisation and the continuing existence of elements within Jemaah

Islamiah (JI) committed to the use of violence. The relationship between JI and al-Qaeda is currently unclear. There is a shared ideology, although JI aspires only to creating a caliphate in Southeast Asia rather than in all Islamic lands, the al-Qaeda vision. Some prominent JI operatives such as Riduan Isamuddin, known by his *nom de guerre* of Hambali, fought in the Afghanistan jihad and developed personal relations with the al-Qaeda leadership. And JI played a role in facilitating the 11 September attacks. But intelligence officials have been puzzled by the recent absence of contact between the two organisations.

In April 2006 the Indonesian police raided several properties in central and west Java, killing one JI suspect and detaining several others. The principal target of the raid, JI leader Abu Dujana, escaped, but significant quantities of weapons, ammunition and bomb-making equipment were discovered. The Indonesian police also uncovered documents which showed that JI had reorganised the previous year into a new structure consisting of a central command council with five divisions: propaganda, education, economy, information and military. The military structure comprised seven groups (*ishobah*) each comprising ten people. The documents indicated that the focus of JI's military wing would be more local than previously, concentrating on activity within its Javanese heartland, and that there would be a shift away from hard to soft targets and a greater use of targeted assassinations. The apparently reduced ambitions of JI suggested that police pressure on the movement had had an impact. The reorganisation was also interpreted partly as an effort to isolate JI's chief bomb-maker, the Malaysian Noordin Top. On 10 June 2007 the Indonesian police arrested Abu Dujana in central Java and a week later arrested Zarkasih, the head of JI's military arm. It is expected that these arrests will generate further intelligence leading to a significant weakening of JI's capacity to conduct terrorist attacks.

There were two important qualifications to the successes of the Indonesian authorities. The first was that JI is a politico-religious movement, not all of whose members subscribe to violence as a tactic – there had always been a current within JI arguing for engagement in mainstream politics with the undeclared aim of bringing about the vision of a Southeast Asian caliphate ruled by sharia law. The second was that the government had shown an ambivalent stance towards JI, for example in its treatment of JI's spiritual leader, Abu Bakar Bashir, who was imprisoned in 2005 for his role in the 2002 Bali bombings but was released in 2006 and returned to teach in his Islamic boarding school in Java.

The southern Philippine island of Mindanao continued to serve as a training location and safe base for JI operatives, including some of the movement's most experienced bomb-makers. Philippine government pressure on Abu Sayyaf, an organisation which claims links to al-Qaeda, has continued with a number of senior Abu Sayyaf commanders having been killed in recent months. A three-year ceasefire between the Philippine government and the Moro Islamic

Liberation Front, which seeks to create a sharia state in Mindanao, came close to collapse following armed clashes. The lawless environment of Mindanao made it likely that JI and related groups would remain entrenched there, able to export violence to nearby locations including the Malaysian province of Sabah, where a substantial number of extremists linked to JI were arrested in 2006.

In Thailand, the conflict in the south between the Pattani United Liberation Organisation and the Thai army and police gave rise to widespread concern. A change from the hardline policy of former Prime Minister Thaksin Shinawatra to an ostensibly more emollient approach on the part of the military government headed by General Surayud Chulanont had no discernible impact on an insurgency which has been characterised by increasing levels of violence and brutality. There was little sign that the Thai government had a coherent strategy for dealing with the insurgency, which arose out of a perception among the ethnically Malay Islamic population in Thailand's four southern provinces that their interests and aspirations had been ignored by the Buddhist majority.

There is no evidence that the dispute has been exploited by JI, al-Qaeda or other extremist groups in support of a wider Islamist agenda, but Southeast Asian governments worry that if the conflict is allowed to continue unchecked, such external interference will in due course emerge. The conflict is of particular concern to the Malaysian government owing to its radicalising effect on Malaysians, especially in the four northernmost states, which are traditionally the most Islamic.

Africa: the Maghreb and Somalia
Following the end of an amnesty in August 2006, Algeria saw a significant upsurge in activity by the GSPC, renamed al-Qaeda in the Maghreb. The most significant event was a series of suicide bombings in Algiers, including an attack on the offices of the prime minister resulting in 33 deaths and over 200 injured. In Morocco, the authorities in September 2006 dismantled the Jema'at Ansar al-Mahdi group, which was allegedly involved in a plot to infiltrate the police and armed forces. Among 56 members arrested, many were middle class and some were women. A separate Moroccan network linked to GSPC was arrested for attempting to send volunteers to fight in Iraq. In Tunisia, the authorities in January 2007 killed 14 suspected GSPC members who had in their possession printouts from Google Earth detailing the US and UK embassies in Tunis.

Sub-Saharan Africa has long been seen by counter-terrorist analysts as propitious terrain for the growth of Islamist extremism, especially in the effectively ungoverned spaces of the Sahel region. To date this fear appears not to have been fully realised. However, there has recently been clear evidence of training camps in northern Mali, operated by the GSPC. The United States and European countries with historic links to the region have worked to establish close relations with the security and intelligence services of the Sahel states, focusing on developing their counter-terrorism and counter-insurgency capabilities. The United States, whose Trans-Saharan Counterterrorism Initiative has been funded by Congress to the tune of $500m, has adopted an integrated approach which brings together conventional counter-terrorism and counter-insurgency training with a focus on economic and social development. This approach has also been enshrined in the US military's new Africa Command (AFRICOM), now being formed. The extent to which the Sahel can be kept relatively free of Islamist extremism will be an important test of the effectiveness of such an approach.

In Somalia, the anarchy prevailing since the collapse of the Siad Barre regime in 1991 has created circumstances favourable to the growth of Islamist extremism. The indigenous Al-Ittihad al-Islamiya (AIAI) group, which is ideologically close to al-Qaeda, is believed to have provided support for the bombers who attacked the US embassies in Kenya and Tanzania in 1998, and had established training camps around Mogadishu attended by significant numbers of foreign fighters from both sub-Saharan Africa and Europe. In the absence of credible government the US and other Western intelligence agencies formed links with different warlords and with the governments of Somaliland and Puntland, both relatively stable and democratic enclaves, to contain AIAI. When the Union of Islamic Courts (UIC), a grouping of extreme Islamist warlords thought to be favourable to AIAI and al-Qaeda, occupied Mogadishu late in 2006 and established a national government, the United States backed the Ethiopian army, which invaded Somalia and installed the Transitional Federal Government (TFG), which had international recognition but until then had been impotent. AIAI activists and foreign fighters who attempted to leave Somalia via Kenya were detained by the Kenyan authorities and send to Ethiopia for interrogation. The UIC responded with an insurgency campaign which has led to heavy civilian casualties. The United States carried out air and missile attacks on groups of suspected al-Qaeda militants.

While South Africa has not fallen victim to Islamist terrorism, it has become apparent that within South Africa's substantial Muslim population there is a core of radicalised individuals engaged in facilitating the activities of extremists from other Islamic states, notably Pakistan. As a result, South Africa has become a popular transit destination for al-Qaeda activists seeking to disguise their travel patterns. In particular, al-Qaeda was quick to identify the potential offered by South Africa's unthreatening international image and passports which afford visa-free access to a wide range of destinations, a vulnerability publicly acknowledged by South African Intelligence Minister Ronnie Kasrils.

The war of ideas

Since the 11 September attacks, the threat posed by Islamist extremism has become more widely recognised. Nations and international bodies have begun to mobilise to confront it. Security and intelligence services have acquired knowledge and expertise in identifying networks and disrupting attacks. But these capabilities address the symptoms, not the root causes. Recent evidence suggests that al-Qaeda is proving a more resilient organisation than Western experts had thought, and has retained the capability to instigate and plan attacks around the world. The long-term challenge is to confront the extremist ideology which gives rise to terrorism, and which al-Qaeda has shown great skill and ingenuity in propagating. This requires governments to stimulate debates on interaction between Muslims and non-Muslims, and in particular on integration of Muslim minorities. In such debates, the 'single narrative' that sees Muslims as victims of non-Muslim aggression needs to be addressed. There is as yet no consensus on how best to do this. Islamic governments with de-radicalisation programmes tend not to contest the propositions of the single narrative but rather encourage individuals to contemplate non-violent responses to perceived injustices affecting their co-religionists. Western governments, to the extent that they have developed a response, incline more towards rebuttal. It may be that different responses are required for different cultural milieus. Whatever the approach, the need to develop effective, consistent, long-term policies which enjoy public support and political consensus will pose enormous challenges.

Climate Change: Security Implications and Regional Impacts

The year to June 2007 saw a coming together of several strands of thinking about climate change. Public recognition of the need for action has risen markedly. Perhaps the most significant development was publication of the latest findings of the UN Intergovernmental Panel on Climate Change (IPCC), whose reports are the most comprehensive and influential scientific studies on the subject. The Panel said in February 2007 that there was no doubt that there had been global warming over the past 100 years, that it had accelerated in the second half of the twentieth century, and that the majority of the rise was 'very likely' to be due to increased concentrations of man-made greenhouse gases.

Arguments that global warming demanded urgent action from politicians were given strong popular impetus by the 2006 Oscar-winning documentary film 'An Inconvenient Truth', featuring former US Vice President Al Gore, and his best-selling book of the same title. These significantly increased the level of popular debate and public awareness, at least in the Western world. In October 2006, the report of the Stern Review, commissioned by the UK Treasury, was published; the first comprehensive and rigorous analysis of the economic aspects of climate change, it made a convincing case that the costs of measures to reduce global warming were justified by the hugely greater damage to global growth that would otherwise occur, and that there was still time to address the issue. In January 2007 delegates to the annual meeting of the World Economic Forum in Davos, Switzerland identified climate change as the most important factor affecting the global 'shifting power equation' in the future, and the factor for which the world was least ready. In March 2007 European leaders agreed to set binding targets to reduce EU greenhouse gas emissions, and the UK government became the first to introduce legislation setting binding domestic targets. Climate change topped the agenda at the G8 Summit in Heiligendamm, Germany in June 2007, and the George W. Bush administration for the first time agreed that action was urgently needed.

The latest scientific evidence leaves no doubt that global and regional climates are changing significantly in response to global warming. Its effects seem bound to aggravate the difficulties of parts of the world that are already prone to conflict, famine and disease. But the impact will not be confined to such regions: global warming will have diverse implications for all regions, and while scientists can make careful projections based on known evidence, there seems also to be considerable scope for unpredictable – and catastrophic – changes. It is possible that, unless mitigated by remedial action to slow, stabilise and reduce greenhouse gas emissions, global warming may in time pose an existential threat even to states that are currently stable and secure. At the very least, it will accelerate migratory flows, increase competition in parts of the world for food, water, energy and other resources, and widen gaps between rich and poor – all classic factors that can help to give rise to conflict.

Arguments about taking responsibility for remedial action have by themselves the potential to cause considerable international tension. At the African Union summit in January 2007, Ugandan President Yoweri Museveni called global warming 'an act of aggression by the rich against the poor'. Because rapidly growing China and India are already huge producers of greenhouse gases, there will be tremendous pressure from the West on them to take expensive counter-measures – but they are likely to respond that the West created the problem, and that they have the right to the same economic benefits that Western countries obtained while doing so. Such views may complicate efforts to negotiate, implement and enforce a mitigation regime.

Even if the international community is successful in efforts that contribute to mitigating climate change – and in adapting to its consequences – the primary impacts on ecosystems, agriculture, human health and human security will profoundly affect the international security environment. Amidst growing recognition of the potential wide impact of global warming, United Nations Secretary-General Ban Ki Moon, who took office in January 2007, pledged to make climate change and resulting security threats one of his top priorities. However, governments are far from agreed that climate change is primarily a security issue. On 17 April 2007 the UN Security Council, whose remit is the maintenance of international peace and security, held a debate on climate change, chaired by then UK Foreign Secretary Margaret Beckett. China, Russia and Pakistan (representing the Group of 77 developing states), objected to the debate on the procedural grounds that climate change was an economic and social rather than a security issue, and was more appropriately dealt with by other UN organs. However, other developing countries, mostly in Africa, supported the debate. Two-thirds of the Security Council membership, and three-quarters of the speakers, agreed that climate change had a significant security dimension. Although the debate served its purpose of raising the issue higher up the international agenda, the reaction from many countries whose participation will be critical to any new mitigation regime to replace the 1997 Kyoto Protocol was a sign that negotiations would be long and difficult.

Documenting the emerging danger

The IPCC was established in 1988 by the UN Environment Programme and the World Meteorological Organisation to 'assess on a comprehensive, objective, open and transparent basis the best available scientific, technical and socio-economic information on climate change from around the world'. It publishes reports every five or six years, and the first half of 2007 saw publication of summaries of the latest reports of its three working groups. The full Assessment Report is due in November. The IPCC's reports are widely accepted as the most authoritative representation of global scientific opinion on a subject that attracts both unauthenticated doomsday predictions and denials that there is a man-made problem. Its First Assessment Report in 1990 was an important catalyst for the adoption of the 1994 UN Framework Convention on Climate Change (UNFCCC), first proposed at the Rio Earth Summit in 1992. The goal of this treaty was the 'stabilization of greenhouse gas concentrations in the atmosphere at a level that would prevent dangerous anthropogenic interference with the climate system ... within a time frame sufficient to allow ecosystems to adapt naturally to climate change, to ensure that food production is not threatened and to enable economic development to proceed in a sustainable manner'. The IPCC's second report in 1995 concluded that the balance of evidence suggested discernible human influence on global climate. This was influential in the adoption of the Kyoto Protocol to the UNFCCC, which committed signatories to individual targets for reductions in emissions or to emissions trading by 2012. The United States, which accounts for 20–30% of emissions, did not ratify the Protocol, which only entered into force in February 2005 when ratification by Russia put it over the threshold number of states and level of emissions.

The IPCC's Summary for Policymakers on the scientific basis for climate change, released in February 2007, concluded that global surface temperature increased by 0.57–0.96°C from the second half of the nineteenth century to the beginning of the twenty-first, with the rate accelerating to 0.10–0.16°C per decade over the last 50 years. Eleven of the last 12 years rank among the 12 warmest years since 1850. According to the IPCC report, warming will inevitably continue and raised temperatures will persist for centuries, even with the best possible efforts at mitigation, since there is a lag between emissions and warming and since important greenhouse gases stay in the atmosphere for decades to centuries.

A broad consensus is emerging amongst scientists, economists and policy analysts that to avoid the worst consequences of climate change, long-term warming needs to be limited to 2°C above the global average of the eighteenth century, before the industrial revolution, and that to achieve this, concentrations of greenhouse gases in the atmosphere must be stabilised below twice the level of the pre-industrial period. The Stern Review concluded that this was the best compromise between stabilisation targets and potential costs: targeting a lower overall temperature rise is already impractical, and permitting higher temperatures would increase the risk and costs of severe impacts of global warming without a corresponding decrease in the cost of the mitigation effort. The EU and the UK have in effect adopted this target, and a similar goal is likely to emerge from negotiations on the future shape of a global 'Kyoto II' regime.

At its meeting in Heiligendamm in June 2007, the G8, in consultation with Brazil, China, India, Mexico and South Africa (the G8+5), agreed to 'seriously consider' the EU target – also adopted by Canada and Japan – of cutting emissions by 50% by 2050. It acknowledged the UNFCCC process as the appropriate forum for future negotiations on a new global framework, to begin at the UNFCCC conference in Bali in December 2007 and to be concluded by 2009. The agreement was a step forward, but references to the 2°C target and other specific emissions targets were removed at the insistence of the United States. Similarly, the EU uses 1990 as a baseline for calculating the 50% reduction, while the United States proposes using 2007. Nevertheless, this represented a substantive change in stance on the part of the Bush administration.

The most recent international moves towards combating global warming represent a recognition, though this is still by no means universal, that if the emission of greenhouse gases, and hence climate change, is allowed to continue unchecked, the effects will be catastrophic – on the level of nuclear war – if not in this century, certainly in the next. As John Ashton, the UK Foreign Secretary's Special Representative for Climate Change, put it, 'policy failure on any scale ... is not an option'. Even if the international community succeeds in adopting comprehensive and effective measures to mitigate climate change, there will still be unavoidable impacts from global warming on the environment, economies and human security. These could contribute to geopolitical and strategic challenges and have important implications for the world's armed forces.

The science of climate projections

The science of global warming is not new. The underlying greenhouse concept – that heat is kept within the earth's atmosphere because carbon dioxide (CO_2), water vapour and some other gases are relatively transparent to sunlight but not to the infrared radiation given off by the warmed planet – was developed in the 1820s. The greenhouse effect is what keeps the planet at a temperature suitable to support life. Projections of global warming caused by increases in greenhouse gases generated by human activity were first made in the 1860s, and the effect was observed as early as the 1930s. But it was not until mean global temperatures began to rise significantly in the 1980s, and advances in computer technology allowed for better forecast models, that the phenomenon and its consequences began to be taken seriously outside the scientific community.

There are two main strands to the science of climate change. To know whether, and by how much, mean global temperature is changing requires knowing what the temperature was in the past. To know whether mean global temperature will change in the future, by how much, and why requires computational models incorporating complex interactions among factors such as atmospheric and ocean circulation, solar radiation, vegetation, snow and ice cover, volcanic and anthropogenic aerosols, and greenhouse gas concentrations. The models also involve assumptions about how these factors might vary in future, particularly in response to human activity.

Historical temperature records for most of the globe are only available for the last 100 years or so, and the longest continuous records cover no more than 350 years. These earlier records are of limited use in assessing global climate as they cover only a few locations or regions, but they are helpful in calibrating other 'proxy' indications of temperature that can be used to estimate earlier climates. Such proxies include patterns in tree-ring and coral growth, pollen deposition in lakebeds, fossil remains of plants and animals, ocean and lake sediments, and air bubbles trapped in core samples from glaciers or polar icecaps. Each of these proxies covers a different time range, and there are varying degrees of uncertainty associated with each. This is the issue underlying the notorious 'hockey stick' graph controversy. This graph of mean northern hemisphere temperatures over the past millennium shows temperatures as relatively constant from 1000 AD (the shaft) with a sharp rise in the twentieth century (the blade). Visually compelling, it featured prominently in the IPCC's Third Assessment Report and became a lightning rod for climate-change sceptics who argued it was based on bad data, was unreliable due to the uncertainties associated with proxy data, and was a statistical artefact. It was the focus of two reports commissioned by

Figure 1.1 **Overlap of uncertainty ranges of 12 Northern Hemisphere temperature reconstructions**

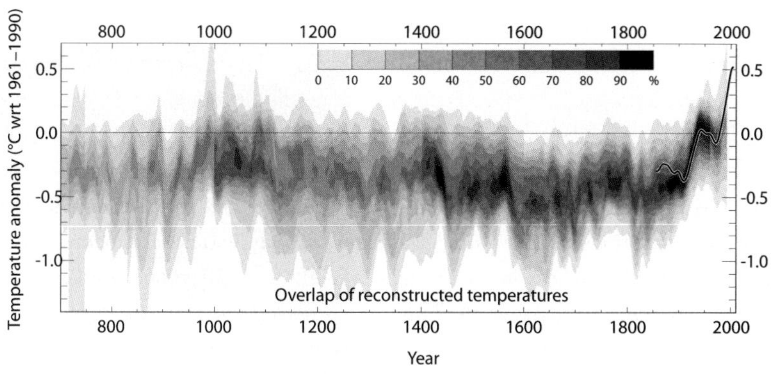

Source: IPCC Fourth Assessment Report, Figure 6.10c. Temperatures within one standard error of a given reconstruction score 10% and those within the 5–95% likelihood range score 5%. The black curve on the right shows the record of actual measurements since ca 1820.

the US Congress at the instigation of sceptics. However, it is now widely agreed that the 'hockey stick' graph is consistent with the overall scientific consensus on past climate trends, and it is one of 12 reconstructions compiled by the IPCC working group. Figure 1.1 shows the overlap of the uncertainty ranges from these 12 studies; the hockey-stick shape is clear in the trend of highest probability – where the various reconstructions are in closest agreement. Proxy data have allowed scientists to extend the climate record back at least 650,000 years with a high degree of confidence. At the beginning of the industrial era CO_2 concentrations were near the maximum for this entire span – typical for an interglacial period – but they are now significantly higher. Global mean temperature in the second half of the twentieth century was higher than at any time in the last 1,300 years, and continues to rise.

The link between CO_2 concentration and temperature over the past 650,000 years is well established both theoretically and empirically. It is reasonable to assume that the unprecedented levels of and continued rise in CO_2 and other greenhouse-gas concentrations generated by human activity will cause a similarly unprecedented warming. However, because this is uncharted territory, models or simulations of future climate have been developed. These can be run under various assumptions for the rate and level of greenhouse gas emissions. Most projections, including those in the IPCC reports and the Stern Report, use a set of standard scenarios published in the IPCC's Special Report on Emissions Scenarios (SRES). These scenarios incorporate different assumptions about future population trends and development of the global economy.

Figure 1.2 **Projected warming and climate change impacts to 2100, with and without mitigation**

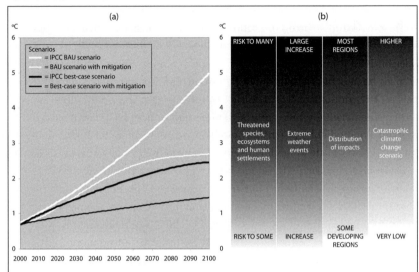

Business as usual (BAU) scenario = SRES A1F1 from IPCC Fourth Assessment Report; best-case scenario = SRES B1 from IPCC Fourth Assessment Report; BAU with mitigation is an overshoot scenario based on SRES A1F1 with a stabilisation target of 600 ppm CO_2e; best-case with mitigation is a slow-change scenario based on SRES B1 with a stabilisation target of 500 ppm CO_2e. *Source*: IPCC Third and Fourth Assessment Reports; B.C. O'Neill and M. Oppenheimer, *Proc. Natl Acad. Sci.*, vol. 101, no. 47, 23 November 2004, pp. 16411–16.

Figure 1.2a shows simplified trajectories for global mean temperature to 2100 for four scenarios. The first, a 'business as usual' scenario, assumes a world of rapid economic growth, a population peak at mid century followed by a decline, rapid introduction of new and more efficient technologies, convergence among regions, capacity building, increased cultural and social interactions, substantial reductions in regional differences in per capita income, and an emphasis on fossil fuels for meeting energy requirements. The second, 'best-case' scenario, uses the same population assumptions but assumes a world with rapid movement towards a service and information economy, new clean and resource-efficient technologies and reductions in material intensity, and global solutions to economic, social and environmental sustainability, including greater equity. These scenarios produce the highest and lowest global temperature increases of the six scenarios chosen by the SRES to illustrate the range of potential outcomes. The figure shows two additional scenarios, one based on each of the business as usual and best-case scenarios, but assuming an international regime to reduce emissions and stablise greenhouse gas levels. 'Business as usual with mitigation' assumes that greenhouse gas concentrations would overshoot the targets but then come down to stablise at the high end of the suggested range; 'best case with mitigation' assumes a slow and steady reduction in emissions to achieve concentrations at the low end of the target range. The margin of error in all four projections is such that temperatures could be one or even two degrees higher (or lower) than the mean projections shown.

Under 'business as usual with mitigation', temperatures would continue to rise slightly after 2100 but would soon level out and begin to fall, reaching an equilibrium level by the end of the twenty-second century. The peak average global warming would be at least one degree above the eventual stabilisation level. As Figure 1.2a shows, the temperature trajectory for this scenario is very close to that for the SRES best-case scenario, which does not include any climate change mitigation initiatives. This is because the best-case SRES scenario assumes that the technological and economic developments an effective mitigation and adaptation regime would incorporate would happen 'spontaneously' rather than as part of a formal mitigation regime.

The discussion that follows in this essay is based on the 'business as usual, with mitigation' emissions scenario. It assumes that society, especially in the developed world, will spontaneously adapt to climate change through enhanced coastal and flood defences, expanded irrigation infrastructure and fertiliser use, improved public health systems, and so on. The effectiveness of adaptation efforts is sensitive to the rate of climate change, so if global mean temperature increases faster than expected, even if it stabilises at the same level, the impact will be worse.

Consequences

Climate change will put stresses on nations in many ways. It is expected both to increase security challenges and to reduce the resources that would otherwise be available to nations for dealing with them. Figure 1.2b shows the types and degrees of impacts for different increases in mean global temperature. Impacts include rising sea levels and population displacement, disruption of water resources, increasing severity of typhoons and hurricanes, droughts, floods, extinctions and other ecological disruption, wildfires, severe disease outbreaks, and declining crop yields and food stocks. Many of these problems affect one another: flooding and water stress (where the demand for water temporarily or chronically exceeds available and useable supply) damage agriculture, malnutrition increases the susceptibility of a population to epidemics and chronic illness, etc.

Weather
It is never possible directly to attribute to global warming a particular weather event like Hurricane Katrina, which hit Louisiana and Mississippi in 2005, or the 2003 heatwave in Europe which cost more than 30,000 lives and over

$13bn. Weather is constantly subject – regardless of global warming – to variation, whether random or based on cycles lasting years or decades. Natural fluctuations in global circulation patterns such as El Niño produce cycles and extremes in regional weather and climate. However, as the mean global temperature rises, theory and models predict an increase in both the frequency and severity of extreme weather events – heatwaves, cold snaps, hurricanes, heavy rains, floods and droughts. Researchers at the UK government's Hadley Centre for Climate Change and Oxford University estimate that global warming has already doubled the chance of a heatwave in Europe like the one in 2003. By 2050, the 2003 European heatwave could be a normal summer, with more severe heatwaves also occurring with greater frequency.

Water
Global precipitation is increasing, and this trend is expected to continue over the next century. However, the worldwide trend will be less significant than changes in regional rainfall patterns. Even if overall global or regional precipitation levels were unaffected by global warming, the trend towards more extreme events would nevertheless increase water stress in many areas. Without massive investment in water-storage infrastructure, precipitation that comes at the wrong time, or all at once, could go to waste, or cause flood damage. Thus, even if there is increased precipitation in some water-stressed areas, they might not benefit. Measures to limit the consequences of extreme events could have their own effects: for example, improving local water storage could expand breeding sites for disease-carrying mosquitoes, and dams could affect water availability and ecosystems downstream.

Sea levels
Warming-induced rises in sea level will both have direct impacts and aggravate problems caused by extreme weather events. Sea levels have recently been rising by around 3cm per decade, and even with mitigation are projected to continue to rise at the same rate. These projections, however, disregard the possibility of rapid increases from accelerated melting of the Greenland and Antarctic ice caps. While there are still gaps in scientific understanding, there is a real risk that sea-level rise in this century could be twice as high as projected, even with effective mitigation. Rising seas will inundate low-lying islands and river deltas, displacing large numbers of people and affecting agriculture, and will damage coastal wetlands. By the 2020s, even with effective mitigation and enhanced sea and flood defences, hundreds of thousands more people will experience coastal flooding every year. Even without the rapid melting of icecaps, the impact of coastal flooding will increase if – as is not unlikely – temperatures rise more than 2°C above the late-twentieth-century mean. By

2080 the numbers affected could be in the millions. Without mitigation and improved defences, they would be several times higher. If coastal and flood defences fail as a result of rising sea levels and more intense storms, the consequences will be extremely severe.

Security implications and regional impacts

The effects of these and other phenomena resulting from global warming on people around the world are likely to be manifold. Different regions would be affected in different ways, but the overall impact is likely to be to increase the vulnerability of areas that are already prone to conflict, especially in Africa. Crop yields would be reduced not just by direct weather effects, but also by desertification, salination of coastal areas and increased frequency of pest and disease outbreaks due to climate-driven changes in species range. At sea, coral, which is highly sensitive to temperature increases, will be severely damaged by warming and acidification, potentially disappearing in the next few decades. This could lead to substantial reductions in fish stocks and further exacerbate the impact of severe weather events through the destruction of protective barrier reefs. Since coral reefs are made of calcium carbonate, their loss would also eliminate an important natural mechanism for removing CO_2 from the atmosphere.

Competition for resources and loss of livelihoods could cause large increases in numbers of migrants, refugees and internally displaced persons, creating humanitarian crises. In countries already at risk from conflict or from political, environmental and economic stress, there will be an increased danger of conflict and state failure.

Conflict and state failure caused in part by climate change will itself make adaptation to and mitigation of climate change more difficult, as state institutions are likely to be unable to implement measures, and international non-governmental organisations may not be able to operate in such conditions. State failures will also increase internal ethnic rivalries and create breeding grounds and safe havens for terrorist networks.

The developed world is better able than developing countries to adapt to the consequences of climate change. Poorer nations tend to be more closely dependent on climate-sensitive resources and less able to afford or implement adaptation measures. In developing countries, poor farmers will see their income drop on average, both in real terms and relative to wealthier sectors, in the next few decades – though some will see an improvement relative to urban populations as food prices increase.

Climate change has the potential to increase instability in some areas of the world, particularly Africa, which is already the continent most prone to conflict, poverty and disease. The demand for foreign interventions of all kinds – financial aid, civil support, humanitarian assistance and military intervention – seems likely to grow more than would be the case if there were no climate change. This will put increasing pressure on governments and international bodies, which might be hard pressed to find both resources and remedies.

Armed forces will face increased demands to deploy as part of crisis management efforts as a result of the increase in frequency and severity of extreme weather events, aggravated by sea-level rise. Operations like the US military missions to Honduras after Hurricane Mitch in 1998, Haiti after Hurricane Jeanne in 2004, and Mississippi and Louisiana after Hurricane Katrina in 2006, and international military relief operations such as those in response to the 2004 Indian Ocean tsunami and the 2005 Kashmir earthquake (which included the first uses of the fast-reaction NATO Response Force) are likely to be increasingly in demand as the climate becomes more volatile. There are, however, doubts as to whether existing military arrangements are adequate to deal with other possible climate-related contingencies. The European Union, for example, has as part of its crisis management approach established 1,500-strong battlegroups, of which two are on standby at any one time, ready for rapid deployment, particularly to Africa, but whether such arrangements are sufficient for handling large-scale instability and migrations to Europe is uncertain.

The impact of global warming will vary significantly among and within regions of the globe and its precise likely effect can only be properly considered through analysis of the different regional impacts. Projections of regional impacts are less robust than the global perspective due to limitations of the models, but important trends can be discerned. In the broadest terms, the carrying capacity – the population that can be supported by available resources and infrastructure – of tropical and sub-tropical regions will drop, while higher latitudes will see smaller declines in carrying capacity and, at least initially, even some potential benefits. The precise impacts are hard to predict. For example, higher levels of CO_2 can actually increase yields of wheat and rice (but not maize) if there are small temperature rises, other things being equal – a phenomenon called 'CO$_2$ fertilisation'. This effect, which is not fully understood, is an important variable in assessing climate change impacts. Recent findings indicate the effect may be lower in the field than in the laboratory, and any increase in yield may be offset by a decline in the food value of the crops, increases in pests and disease, declines in pollinating insects, and extreme weather events and pollution. Regardless of this effect, global rises in temperature will still produce a net decline in the world's cereal production, and will affect low-latitude, developing countries more than high-latitude, developed countries. Even taking CO_2 fertilisation into account, 65 countries are likely to lose over 15% of their agricultural output by 2100, and the gap between developed and developing countries will be greater. Efforts to adapt to changing

Map 1.1 **Aggregated climate change index**

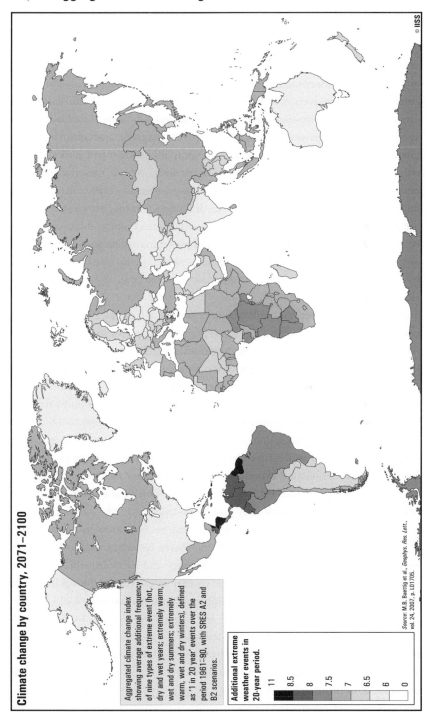

Climate change by country, 2071–2100

Aggregated climate change index showing average additional frequency of nine types of extreme event (hot, dry and wet years; extremely warm, wet and dry summers; extremely warm, wet and dry winters), defined as '1 in 20 year' events over the period 1961–90, with SRES A2 and B2 scenarios.

Additional extreme weather events in 20-year period.

11
8.5
8
7.5
7
6.5
6
0

Source: M.B. Baettig et al., *Geophys. Res. Lett.,* vol. 24, 2007, p. L01705.

© IISS

climate, such as shifting planting dates and changing crop varieties, are also more effective at higher latitudes.

This broad geographical pattern is likely to hold for extreme weather events as well (see Map 1.1). South and East Asia are expected to experience the worst coastal flooding impacts, as they do at present, and Africa's relative vulnerability will increase. Continental interiors are likely to see warming at twice the global average level. Coral reefs, which are under severe threat, are the basis of a vibrant ecosystem that feeds 30–40m people in tropical and sub-tropical regions.

Beyond these general trends, more specific impacts and security consequences can be identified. The region-by-region discussion that follows is based on a number of detailed studies (notably the IPCC reports, research commissioned by the Stern Review and surveys of the peer-reviewed literature) and the impacts are based on results from a range of models. The biggest variable among the models is the amount of precipitation, which affects agricultural and water resources. Localised trends are tentative and preliminary. The geographical divisions used are those specified by the Stern Review.

North America

Yields of the main food crops in the United States and Canada, maize and wheat, are likely to see small declines in the next two or three decades and moderate declines by mid century, with larger decreases if warming exceeds the mean projection. These falls will be smaller than the average decline worldwide. Although there should be no net change in water resources, precipitation patterns are likely to alter, with increased rainfall in the continental interior and east coast and decreases in the already arid southwest and on the west coast.

These changes in precipitation could cause problems with flood and river control in the Mississippi basin. Only costly efforts by the US Army Corps of Engineers have prevented a major change in the river's lower course in the last 50 years, which would have left New Orleans on a backwater and caused major disruption to industry and port infrastructure in the Gulf of Mexico. Even greater investment in flood control will be necessary in the next few decades to avoid disaster. In the west, the Sierra Nevada may see its annual snowpack decline by two-fifths by mid century and by nearly three-quarters by 2100, with peak melt runoff coming several weeks earlier. This will reduce water available for agriculture in California (which produces 13% of US crops by value, and more than half the fruit and vegetables), require further investment in water-storage infrastructure, and disrupt the delicate political system of water rights in this relatively arid region. Reduced runoff will lower the amount of hydroelectric power produced in the Pacific Northwest, much of it exported to California; loss of this low-carbon energy source will make mitigation efforts more expensive.

The frequency and severity of blizzards and cold snaps may increase. The severity, if not the frequency, of hurricanes along the Eastern Seaboard and Gulf coast may increase, and in the Pacific damage from storm surges could go up tenfold by the end of the century. With enhanced sea defences, however, there will be little increase in the number of people experiencing coastal flooding, unless warming exceeds the mean projection. Hurricanes are sufficiently rare that random variations in frequency unconnected to global warming are likely to be more important than increasing severity. Warmer temperatures in the Arctic may mean improvement in shipping and access to resources, but could also bring disagreements between the United States and Canada over sovereignty to the fore.

Central America

The key crops in the region are rice and maize, both of which are likely to be badly affected by climate change. There will probably be large and above-average falls in rice yields in the next few decades, and moderate, average declines in maize; both will continue to decline throughout the century. The region will probably experience moderate decreases in water resource availability in the next few decades, with large decreases by 2080 and very large decreases with higher temperatures. Increased impacts of coastal flooding will be minimal until later in the century, other than in the Caribbean island nations, and will only be severe if warming exceeds the mean projection. The Caribbean will be affected by early damage to coral reefs and associated fisheries, increased intensity of hurricanes, and sea-level rise. These factors will in turn damage tourism, a significant part of the economy.

Climate change is likely to exacerbate instability or slow progress towards stability and good governance in a region in which the United States has conducted a number of military interventions and proxy wars over the last 50 years. The United States will face increased immigration pressure from the region.

South America

Rice is the dominant crop in most areas, with wheat more important in Argentina and Chile and maize in Bolivia, Brazil and Venezuela. There is likely to be a large and above-average decrease in rice yield in the next few decades, and very large to extremely large falls if warming exceeds the mean projection. The fall in wheat yields will be moderate and above-average in the next few decades, large by mid century, and very large with higher temperatures. Maize will show moderate but average decreases in the next few decades, large decreases in the second half of the century, and very large decreases if warming exceeds the mean projection.

There will be small decreases in water resources in the region in the next few decades, and moderate decreases in the second half of the century. Peru, which relies on glacial runoff from the Andes, is likely to experience worse, and more immediate, problems. In Brazil, the Amazon basin may dry if temperature increases are greater than expected, with large parts of the rainforest becoming savannah, reducing biodiversity and a natural resource for removing CO_2 from the atmosphere. Increased impacts of coastal flooding will be minimal until later in the century, but will only be severe if warming exceeds the mean projection. Within the region, Argentina and Chile are likely to fare best and the Andean states worst.

Europe

The dominant food crop in Europe is wheat, which will see moderate and below-average decreases from now to the end of the century, with large decreases if warming exceeds the mean projection. In Mediterranean nations, maize is more important, and will see moderate but average decreases in yield throughout the century. There will be moderate decreases in water resources beginning in the next few decades, and large decreases with higher temperatures. Southern Europe will in general be hit the hardest.

The recent EU accession states (Romania and Bulgaria), EU candidates (Croatia, Macedonia and Turkey), and aspirants (Bosnia–Herzegovina, Serbia and Montenegro, and Albania) are all less able to cope with the consequences of climate change than the wealthier and more stable western, northern and central European states. The factors underlying Turkey's difficulties, in particular, are likely to be exacerbated by climate change. There could be increased migration and political stresses both within the EU and between the EU and its neighbours, in particular an increasingly arid North Africa.

Russia and Eurasia

This region will see significant impacts sooner than many other parts of the globe, with large and above-average falls in wheat yields in the next few decades and very large falls in the second half of the century. Due to increased precipitation, there will be moderate improvements in water resources in the next few decades and large increases in the second half of the century, but more extreme weather events mean that the frequency of bad harvests may triple, leading to increased intra-regional tensions and instability in the Russian Federation. Climate change will put stress on Uzbekistan and Kyrgyzstan in particular, and the rest of Central Asia is also vulnerable. Warmer temperatures in the Arctic may mean improvements in shipping and access to resources, but this could also create a new zone of potential conflict. Melting of Siberian permafrost could cause difficulties for infrastructure projects, notably proposed oil pipelines, with implications for Russia–China and Russia–Japan relations in particular.

The Middle East and the Gulf

States in the region will see large and above-average declines in food crops in the next few decades, with very large declines by the last quarter of the century, and extremely large declines if warming exceeds the mean projection. There will be moderate declines in water resources in this already water-stressed region in the next few decades and large declines in the second half of the century. Most states in the region already depend on outside sources for water and food, but efforts to solve existing conflicts and disputes will not be helped by these additional problems.

Africa

Africa as a whole is particularly vulnerable to climate change impacts, with some regional variations. Climate change will enhance the fragility of many African states. There will be moderate but average declines in most food crops in North Africa in the next few decades and larger declines by the end of the century. Maize, an important crop in Egypt, will see larger and above-average declines. These agricultural impacts are principally due to decreased rainfall in the region, one of the most robust regional climate change predictions. Declines in water resources are expected to be large in the next few decades, and extremely large by the second half of the century. Coastal flooding is likely to pose severe risks, particularly in Egypt's Nile delta, if warming exceeds the mean projection, but with enhanced sea and flood defences will be less of a problem at lower temperature increases. North Africa is likely to produce the first 'climate refugees' at relatively modest temperature increases, due to drought, and there is potential for conflict between Egypt and Ethiopia over water resources in the Nile basin.

The dominant crop in West Africa is maize, which will see moderate but above-average declines in the next few decades and large declines by the end of the century. There is a high degree of water interdependence between and among West African nations, and interstate conflicts over water resources could arise between Niger and Nigeria, Cameroon and Nigeria, Senegal and Mauritania, and Ghana and Burkina Faso. Besides being highly at risk of climate-influenced interstate conflict and humanitarian crises, this region is also strategically important as a significant source of strategic minerals and petroleum.

Eastern and southern Africa are likely to suffer the greatest impacts from climate change. Even under an effective international mitigation regime, mean temperatures here are likely to rise by up to 3°C more than the global average, with corresponding severity of desertification, water stress, disease and declining crop yields. Maize, the main food crop in most of the region, will see moderate and average declines in the next few decades, but large and above-average declines by mid century. Wheat, more important in Ethiopia, Eritrea and particularly Sudan, will see moderate but below-average declines in the next few decades but large and above-average declines in the second half of the century.

Wetlands ecosystems and fisheries in the Great Lakes region will be severely affected, removing a primary protein source for half of Malawi's population. There will be small declines in water resources regionally in the next few decades, with moderate declines by the end of the century. There is potential for conflict over water resources between Angola and Namibia, and Angola and Botswana. The number of people experiencing coastal flooding each year will increase faster than in other regions, nearly doubling by mid century, although the absolute numbers will be in the tens of thousands. Malaria will spread to higher altitudes, affecting Kenya in particular.

Climate change, in the form of a long-term drought in the Sahel in the 1970s and 1980s, has already been identified as an important factor contributing to the conflict in the Darfur region of Sudan. Global warming is likely to feed increased volatility in the region in the next few decades.

South and Southeast Asia

There will be moderate but below-average declines in rice yields in the region as a whole over the next few decades, with large but average declines by the last quarter of the century. Maize and wheat will see similar but above-average declines. Most countries in the region rely primarily on rice but in India, Iran, Afghanistan, Pakistan, Bhutan and Nepal these other crops are also significant. Temperature increases above the mean projection could lead to extremely large falls in rice and wheat yields.

One of the most important features of the regional climate is the monsoon, which provides most of the annual precipitation. The monsoon is likely to become, on average, warmer and wetter by the end of the century, meaning moderate increases in water resources in the next few decades and large increases in the second half of the century. This increase in precipitation will bring increased flood risk, particularly since more will fall as rain rather than snow, and since it will be more intense. There is also likely to be increased variability, with greater risk of particularly extreme years in either direction – failure of the monsoon in a single year can cause severe water shortages. To capture and store the additional water from heavier monsoons, more large-scale engineering projects like dams may become necessary, which could worsen disputes over water between South Asian nations. Stronger monsoons can also mean decreased precipitation in Indonesia, leading to increased risk of drought and forest fires there (with attendant release of further CO_2 to the atmosphere). Sea-level rise is of particular concern to states with both high population density and low-lying territory, like Bangladesh and Singapore. Enhanced flood defences could limit the percentage of the population at increased risk of coastal flooding, but the total will still be large. If warming exceeds the mean projection, the impact could be catastrophic, with millions at risk. Bangladesh is, furthermore, particularly at risk of river flooding from a combination of the progressive melting of the Himalayan glaciers and the expected increase in precipitation. This could increase pressure on India from migration flows.

East Asia

This region as defined by the Stern Review includes states such as Cambodia, Laos, Myanmar, Thailand and Vietnam, as well as China, Japan, Mongolia and the Korean peninsula. Rice, the dominant regional food crop, will only see small and below-average declines in yield in the next 20 or 30 years, with moderate but still below-average declines later in the century. Wheat and maize together contribute more than rice to China's agricultural output and will suffer similar impacts. There will be a small increase in available water resources in the next few decades, and moderate increases later in the century. Even with enhanced coastal defences the population at risk of coastal flooding is expected to increase significantly, but this is mostly due to population growth rather than the effects of climate change, which will be relatively small. Large-scale farmers are expected to benefit at the expense of smaller, and there will be disruption of fisheries in river delta regions, particularly the Mekong, where there is also likely to be increased tension over water resources.

The Chinese military expects to have to tackle more disaster-relief tasks in future, and to face refugee flows from Indonesia and the rest of Southeast Asia similar to those Europe may experience from North Africa. Meanwhile, geographical differences in impacts within China could affect internal stability.

Australasia, island nations and Antarctica

Australia is expected to see small, but below-average declines in wheat yields in the next few decades, with moderate but still below-average declines by the end of the century. Water resources are expected to increase marginally overall, though southern areas will be hardest hit where drought does occur. The country is particularly vulnerable to precipitation variation, as its current six-year drought illustrates. The situation reached crisis level in April 2007 when the government announced it would cut off all irrigation water to the main agricultural region if the drought persisted until June, to ensure adequate drinking water for the population. Sufficient rain fell in June and July to allow the government to postpone these measures. This demonstrates the problem with climate-change projections based on averaged impacts, and illustrates the scope for extreme variation from the norm.

Due to sea-level rise, the island nations of the Pacific and Indian oceans are particularly at risk from flooding and extreme weather events, but the threat of submergence, with its profound human and political consequences, will be marginal unless warming significantly exceeds the mean projection. Southern Ocean fisheries will be severely affected, but they contribute relatively little to global food production.

Addressing climate change

The Stern Review concluded that the total cost of climate change under business as usual, without mitigation, over the next two centuries would be equivalent to an average reduction of global annual per capita GDP of at least 5%, and possibly as much as 20%, beginning now. It would be most likely to be at the high end of this range. The low end of the estimate includes direct market costs from impacts on agriculture, energy use and forestry. The higher end incorporates impacts on the environment and human health; greater than projected warming due to 'feedback' effects like warming-induced releases from natural sources of additional greenhouse gases, which cause yet further warming; disproportionate regional impacts; and the risk of catastrophic climate change. In either case the estimates include the cost of 'autonomous' or individual-level adaptation measures such as changing crop-planting times, reducing energy use in response to market forces, etc. The bulk of both direct and indirect costs of climate change included in these averaged figures would be incurred in the twenty-second century, and is avoidable if mitigation efforts are made soon. The cost of climate change expected by 2050 is around 1.1% of per capita GDP per annum. Even if immediate mitigation efforts are made, though, only a small proportion of these shorter-term costs can realistically be avoided. According to Stern, mitigation efforts intended to achieve long-term stabilisation of greenhouse gas concentrations at twice the levels of the pre-industrial era would cost around 1% of GDP per annum by 2050 – though with a range of plus or minus three percentage points around this estimate. In other words, Stern estimates the cost of mitigation attempts could be as high as 4% of annual GDP, or as low as –2%, the latter figure representing a net gain to the world economy. Such gains might result because reductions in greenhouse-gas emissions would go hand-in-hand with reductions in other pollutants, reducing expected damages from these non-greenhouse emissions; or investments in new technologies needed to reduce emissions could have a stimulating economic effect; or modest temperature increases of 1 to 2°C could be beneficial for agriculture, particularly in high and mid latitudes. Given the 1.1% of GDP per annum averaged cost of unavoidable climate change over the next four to five decades, the combined cost of climate change and mitigation efforts in this period should be around 2% of the global economy. The IPCC Summary for Policymakers on mitigation options published in May 2007 is in broad agreement with Stern's conclusions.

Beyond Kyoto

The emissions targets set by the Kyoto Protocol applied only to a group of nations with industrialised or 'transition' economies (the latter being the post-communist states of Eastern Europe and the former Soviet Union, some of which were even permitted to increase emissions). These targets expire in 2012. Even if all nations meet their targets, through real reductions or emissions trading, any mitigation of expected climate change will be minimal. But the Protocol was only intended as an interim step that would establish a precedent and set up the sort of mechanisms that would be required for effective mitigation of global warming.

Formal negotiations over the next step – 'Kyoto II' – have yet to begin, and the exact form any such agreement will take is not clear. It is likely to aim for eventual stabilisation of atmospheric greenhouse-gas concentrations at twice pre-industrial levels, or around 25% above current levels. An effective mitigation regime will involve large transfers of resources and technology from developed to developing countries, whether directly or through market mechanisms. For the world's richer governments, this will in effect mean assuming the responsibility and the cost of reductions in emissions – in other countries as well as their own – that would in total be equivalent to reducing their own emissions to 20–40% of 1990 levels by 2050. Historical experience suggests that, except during economic recession, reductions in emissions of more than 1% per year are difficult to achieve, so any delay in reductions will have long-term consequences.

Emissions are closely correlated with GDP. Some nations, like Russia, have found it easy to meet their Kyoto emissions targets because their economies have been in recession. To reduce emissions without slowing or reversing growth in total or per capita GDP will require generating an increasing proportion of energy from low-carbon sources like solar, wind, hydro, geothermal and nuclear power and biofuels; increasing energy efficiency through technological improvements throughout the economy; and directly reducing emissions from fossil fuel use through carbon capture and sequestration (CCS). Fossil-fuel-fired power plants typically have lifetimes of at least 40 or 50 years, and large numbers will be constructed over the next two decades in both the industrialised world and countries such as China and India whose economies are expanding rapidly. Incorporation of improvements in generation efficiency and still-immature CCS technology into these plants would avoid locking in high levels of emissions for decades. Increased efficiency, especially in the expanding economies, is the main source of potential reductions in expected emissions until the middle of the century. Other reductions in emissions can be achieved through changes in land use, such as reforestation and soil carbon sequestration, worldwide.

An international mitigation regime could be structured, as some countries prefer, around technological targets – cooperative research and development, and international standards – rather than emissions targets, but this is not likely to be as effective. Technological cooperation and transfer, national and international standards, and national regulatory systems would still contribute to the success of any emissions-oriented mitigation regime. Such a regime is more likely to involve stringent long-term and more moderate interim emissions targets, with developing countries facing more lenient (or even no) targets in the short term. Implementation would use market-based instruments like national cap-and-trade systems and carbon taxes, and an international carbon market. The mechanisms and the targets must be perceived by all parties as fair.

The biggest portion of the projected increases of greenhouse gases in the next hundred years is expected to come from the rapidly developing economies of countries such as Brazil, Mexico, Indonesia and – especially – China and India. China is expected to overtake the United States as the largest emitter of greenhouse gases by the end of the decade, and possibly even by the end of 2007. To the extent these countries suffer disproportionately from the impacts of climate change, the easier it will be for the world as a whole to achieve mitigation targets, but the harder it will be to reach agreement on the mechanism.

The world's wealthier countries would benefit more than the developing countries from mitigation of climate change, since they will be better able to cope with the remaining impacts, but without mitigation the impacts on all actors would be catastrophic. Yet cooperation from the developing world, especially the rapidly developing Asian states, is vital to the success of any mitigation regime. The developed world thus needs to find politically palatable ways to compensate developing nations forced, in effect, to limit their own development through participation in a global mitigation mechanism.

Wider implications of mitigation and adaptation efforts
Efforts to remedy global warming have the potential to unsettle the world's established order in a number of ways. For example, reducing national and global reliance on fossil fuel sources as part of climate change mitigation, and reducing the relative proportion of such sources, will mean that many nations' security priorities could change. There could be reduced dependence on oil from the Persian Gulf and on gas from Russia. Countries whose economies are based on fossil-fuel production will lose out in a low-carbon economy.

Similarly, replacement of fossil fuels with biofuels, such as ethanol from wheat, maize or other crops, or biodiesel produced from vegetable oil, could provide new sources of income for developing countries in the tropics and subtropics, but these would compete with food production for limited water and land. Demand for biofuels in the developed world is already causing increased food prices in Mexico and declines in biodiversity in Malaysia and Indonesia as tropical forest is replaced by palm oil plantations. Within developing nations, a shift to biofuel production would benefit large-scale agricultural products at the expense of small farmers, potentially causing increased inequality and social unrest.

In some areas the untapped potential for low-carbon hydroelectric power may increase, but in others, expected to suffer from less reliable water supply, this power source may dry up. Efforts to cope with diminishing – or increasing but seasonally variable – water resources could involve new dams and other infra-structure projects. These, in turn, could cause tensions if they affect trans-border water supplies – though they could also lead to better regional arrangements and structures. Nuclear power, which already accounts for around a sixth of electrical generation, is likely to be an important alternative to fossil fuel, despite environmental concerns.

More broadly, a 'Kyoto II' agreement could affect the underlying structure of twenty-first century international relations as much as the Bretton Woods Agreements and their offshoots like the IMF and the World Bank did those of post-war era. New institutions – perhaps a World Environmental Organisation on the model of the World Trade Organisation – and new powers or roles for existing institutions will be needed to ensure the effectiveness of the mitigation regime.

Unforeseen consequences
Climate change could become a critical factor in international events, both by causing tensions in its own right, and by intensifying pre-existing frictions. It would become even more critical if temperatures were to exceed the best esti-mate. A degree of uncertainty is inherent in the science – the line representing projected temperatures for a worst-case emissions scenario in Figure 1.2a, for example, is the mid-point of a range of estimates that vary by up to 30% either way. It is unlikely that real events will follow the precise projections presented here – the impacts discussed will probably happen, but could occur later or earlier, faster or slower. There is an even chance that, an effective mitigation regime not-withstanding, warming will temporarily or permanently breach the target of 2°C above pre-industrial temperatures by as much as one degree. Higher tempera-tures mean worse impacts, and the severity of the impacts increases faster than the temperature.

Moreover, the IPCC scenarios each assume a particular trend for popula-tion increase and technological and economic development, but the models do not alter these assumptions in response to developments. In the event of rapid growth in emissions and rapid increase in global mean temperatures, there would be dramatic results sooner than expected – and those impacts would be strong enough to damp down the development trends which the models assume will continue unaffected. Economic slowdown, for example, could greatly affect global warming projections. In the decade after the collapse of the Soviet Union, its successor states saw fossil-fuel-related emissions fall by more than 5% per year. A similar collapse in large industrialised or rapidly developing economies could significantly reduce greenhouse gas emissions and help mitigate further global climate impacts.

The security challenges attributable to climate change will not simply be the foreseeable systemic stresses and changes in the global balance of power, but also increased volatility. While this has been an element in international relations since the end of the Cold War, climate change will make things even more unpredictable. It will in time need to be taken into account in all aspects of security planning. This is already beginning to happen within defence ministries in many countries, and a bipartisan bill introduced in the US Senate in March 2007 calls for a National Intelligence Estimate on the security threat of climate change. There have been calls for inclusion of climate-related threats and threat factors in the US National Security Strategy, National Defense Strategy and Quadrennial Defense Review. But since the real threat is to collective security, the response and the planning has to be international as well. The April 2007 Security Council debate and the G8 consensus in June 2007 were steps in this direction. National and international responses to climate change require a high level of organisation, mobilisation and cooperation.

Conclusion

The impact of climate change has to be taken into account in almost every field of policy, on both the national and international level. Discussion of the threat it poses has tended to be from an environmental and human-security perspective. But the security dimension will come increasingly to the forefront as countries begin to see falls in available resources and economic vitality, increased stress on their armed forces, greater instability in regions of strategic import, increases in ethnic rivalries, and a widening gap between rich and poor. Climate change is at the heart of both national and collective security.

In the next few decades, unavoidable warming due to past greenhouse-gas emissions and the necessary lead time for mitigation will lead to a world where current security concerns are multiplied and intensified under the influence of the changing climate. Fundamental environmental issues of food, water and energy security ultimately lie behind many present security concerns, and climate change will magnify all three. Action taken by individual nations and by the international community in the next few years will determine whether the second half of the century will see catastrophic climate change, increasing rivalry, instability, human tragedy and war; or an easing of and adjustment to climate change, with an international order increasingly rooted in cooperation and convergence.

The Military Use of Space

Space technology is an important factor shaping the modern world. The global space market will, at current growth rates, be 15 times its current size by 2025. Advances in new materials, nanotechnology, electronic components and information and communications technology will stimulate the space sector at an increasing pace. In addition, green-technology venture capital will flow increasingly into the space sector – such technologies, essentially running on sunshine, promise to replace carbon-intensive terrestrial infrastructure like television broadcasting or cellular telephone networks with environmentally preferable orbital platforms. Only a small fraction of the technological potential of satellites has yet been realised. Space could be transformed beyond recognition by a wave of investment. This could, in turn, quickly generate new options and implications for military use. However, there is a fundamental mismatch between the inherently global nature of the peaceful commercial opportunities afforded by outer space, and the lack of effective cooperation in organisation of the use of space for defence and security.

Satellites and space technology, beyond their historically central but operationally limited role in the days of the US–Soviet strategic nuclear confrontation, are still a rather recent addition to the inventory of armed forces. Their strategic significance, and their impact on the equations of power and vulnerability, are not yet fully established. However, some features of today's strategic priorities favour stronger attention to satellite technologies. These include the global scope of expeditionary operations; the ambition to prevent conflicts or halt them at an early stage; the networking concept that links commanders, units, sensors and weapons over large distances for well-directed effect; and, above all, the transformational impetus generated by the revolutionary ubiquity of digital information and communication technology, which is destined fundamentally to change the way operations are conceived and run.

Strategic significance of space

Satellites have a unique global reach for information gathering and communication. They provide a non-intrusive source of intelligence independent of the accessibility of an observed territory and the cooperation of its rulers. Availability of digital data from satellites, merged with information from other sources, has transformed the production of up-to-date maps from a matter of months or years to one of hours or days, with incomparably better, three-dimensional accuracy and at much lower cost. Superior weather information and forecasts can provide a decisive edge to armed forces.

The laws of physics permit a number of distinct classes of orbits that are of military value in different ways. Geostationary orbits (GEO) make a satellite

Map 1.2 **Successful launches to orbit, January 2001–June 2007**

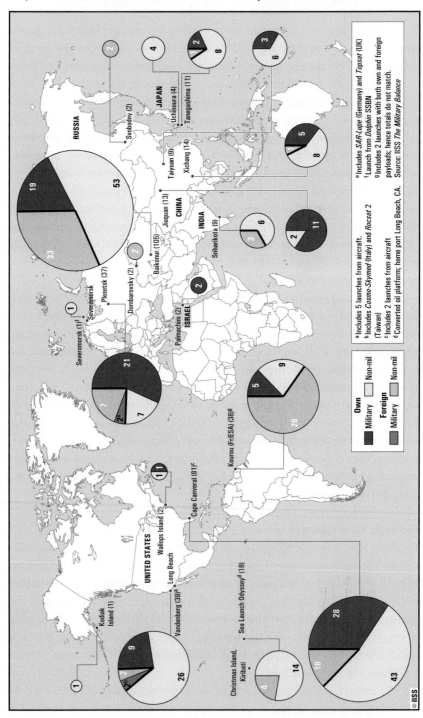

RUSSIA

Svobodny (2)

JAPAN
Uchinoura (4)
Tanegashima (11)

Taiyuan (9)
Xichang (14)

CHINA
Jiuquan (13)
Baikonur (105)

INDIA
Sriharikota (9)

Severomorsk
Plesetsk (37)
Dombarovsky (2)

Severomorsk (1)ᶠ

Palmachim (2)
ISRAEL

Kourou (Fr/ESA) (38)ᵍ

Cape Canaveral (81)ᶜ

UNITED STATES
Wallops Island (2)
Long Beach

Kodiak Island (11)
Vandenberg (39)ᵃ

Christmas Island, Kiribati
Sea Launch Odysseyᵈ (18)

Own
Military
Non-mil
Foreign
Military
Non-mil

ᵃ Includes 5 launches from aircraft.
ᵇ Includes *Cosmo-Skymed* (Italy) and *Rocsat 2* (Taiwan)
ᶜ Includes 2 launches from aircraft
ᵈ Converted oil platform; home port Long Beach, CA.
ᵉ Includes *SAR-Lupe* (Germany) and *Topsat* (UK)
ᶠ Launch from *Dolphin* SSBN
ᵍ Includes 2 launches with both own and foreign payloads; hence totals do not match.
Source: IISS *The Military Balance*

© IISS

appear stationary above a point on the equator, but at an altitude of 36,000km. Highly elliptical orbits (HEO) are chosen to maximise lingering time over specific non-equatorial regions. Circular or elliptic low Earth orbits (LEO) can bring satellites as low as 150km, but the lower they are, the more they are exposed to atmospheric drag, eventually leading to re-entry and decay. Satellites cover ground tracks between the northern and southern longitudes of their orbital inclination as determined by their place and direction of launch and later corrections. Only polar-orbiting satellites with approximately 90° inclination cover the globe as a whole. Launched with a westerly tilt, they become sun-synchronous: that is, they always cross any point on Earth at the same time of day. For other types of satellites such as navigation constellations, medium Earth orbits (MEO) a few thousand kilometres high are the preferred choice.

When the US Global Positioning System (GPS) all-weather navigation and timing satellites became available in the late 1980s, they initiated a new era for night and low-visibility operations and precision targeting. Through their secondary, openly available civil signal they also triggered spectacular new markets for geographical information. Automated asset tracking via satellite reduces the risk of failure in logistics support. In combination with satellite communications, navigation satellites also offer continuous tracking of a military's own forces and help avoid 'friendly fire'.

Effective use of satellites is an indicator of a country's ability to act, a measure of power and sovereignty in the age of global security. Without the global reach offered by secure satellite communications links, the ability to run effective operations worldwide and intervene in support of international peace and security wherever required rests on shaky ground.

Above all, advanced digital communications satellites play a key role for network-enabled operations, satisfying the exponential growth in bandwidth requirements as ubiquitous live video streaming, rich information browsing and instant access to worldwide communication even in remote regions become commonplace. This development is not restricted to the military sphere – the military has largely been trailing commercial developments in consumer electronics, taking advantage of off-the-shelf developments where possible. Communications also have a wide array of non-military security applications, often in conjunction with navigation and imaging capabilities that provide integrated services to users who may be unaware of the space component of the system. Examples include emergency services, safety at sea, search and rescue, container shipping security and pipeline operations.

The instant infrastructure offered by satellite communications has become indispensable for disaster relief operations. Hurricane Katrina, which hit the United States in 2005, and other disasters have shown that in areas of terrestrial devastation antennas on satellites provide the only means of communication when terrestrial wire, cable, radio and cellular links are broken or congested. Satellites are likely to become similarly indispensable for resilience and continuity of government capabilities as technology moves to digital mobile broadband satellites and the fusion of networks based on common protocols.

More broadly, the space sector is strategically important for technological and economic competitiveness. The harsh and demanding space environment, with its extreme weight and power-supply restrictions and the need for maintenance-free reliability, drives technological innovation and has catalytic effects in other sectors. Hardly any other field can match the positive effect of space activities in attracting students to mathematics, science and engineering in support of a society's skills base. Satellite broadcasting is of strategic importance as a vehicle of intercultural communication and education. Increasingly, services will include Internet access and interactive audiovisual links via satellites using miniaturised two-way ground antennas, circumventing gateways controlled and potentially censored by individual governments. Finally, in regions such as sub-Saharan Africa that lack established infrastructure, space technology offers the prospect of leapfrogging into the twenty-first century without the need for huge upfront infrastructure investment on the ground.

Costs and benefits of military space autonomy

The military space landscape is today marked by fundamental asymmetry. The United States, the only country with the full range of operational satellites for national security — optical and radar imaging, electronic intelligence, weather observation, communication, navigation and missile warning – is concerned about making even better practical use of its space assets. Russia, the only other country with a sizeable number of military satellites in orbit, still struggles with the burden of the ambitious space legacy of the Soviet Union. The *Glonass* navigation system, for example, is being rebuilt with the goal of restoring an operational constellation, but efforts appear to be plagued by technical problems that affect operational availability of satellites in orbit. Other countries are predominantly concerned with obtaining a modicum of space technology capability of their own for security and defence.

While there is a slow but steady spread of space capabilities, the group of countries that have decided to pursue military space to any significant degree is still remarkably small. Only the United States, Russia, China, India, Japan, France and Israel are space powers with their own launch facilities, launchers and operational satellites. The UK and Italy make up a second tier with operational military satellites in orbit, soon to be joined by Germany when its SAR-*Lupe* constellation of radar imaging satellites reaches initial operating capacity, planned for 2008. A third tier of countries, including Australia and Spain, does not maintain military satellites but relies on military co-use of civil or commercial satellites for communication, either through separate secure military transponders added to a civil platform or through guaranteed leased capacity. In addition, a number of countries have bought junior partner shares in the military space operations of major space powers, with a limited right of independent access. This includes, for example, the participation of Belgium and Greece in the French *Helios*-2 imaging satellite programme.

Routes to military space capability correspond to different levels of national ambition: building one's own satellites but using commercial launchers; operating foreign-built satellites; or contenting oneself with using imagery and communications services available from allies or in commercial markets. In addition, newcomers will normally seek to exploit dual-use civil–military synergies in remote sensing and telecommunication.

Wherever space operations are located organisationally — whether in the air force, in central defence services, with strategic forces or entirely separately — they develop lives of their own and generate growing demands. In both the US and Russian experience, given the considerable differences in technical and operational skill sets required in space and elsewhere across the forces, it was recognised as beneficial to cultivate a cadre of specialised officers who would spend their entire careers in space and missile operations. Furthermore, satellites need constant replacement. The expected lifetime of satellites in low orbit is usually not higher than five years. To make use of new satellites, new capacities and interfaces are also needed on the ground.

In effect, any country that embarks on the use of space for its defence will face the budgetary burden of an additional branch of the military. Justifying investments in space hardware is particularly difficult if other branches of the military see their own funds shrink. On top of that, space technology remains challenging and risky. Both Japan and Israel have experienced a high mission failure rate in their national high-resolution imaging intelligence satellite systems, leading to substantially higher costs than anticipated as gaps had to be filled to restore continuity of coverage.

While satellites are cost effective when compared to traditional, lengthy and intrusive ways of achieving similar results few countries could justify the high cost of constant, high-precision, global operation. High-altitude UAVs are increasingly able to fill some of the roles of satellites, including communications and remote sensing, though subject to geographical limits. Those who can afford both satellites and UAVs stress the synergies between the platforms for networked information flow, cross-cueing (using one platform to identify targets for another) and additional operational flexibility. Entry barriers are high, and strategic options for newcomers in military space are limited. Building an autonomous capability across the board will not usually be possible: Iran, for example, in spite of its clear ambitions, has so far had to content itself with portraying a suborbital sounding rocket as its entrée to the space club.

US defence space strategy

Given that the United States has by far the widest array of space assets and the largest budget, its policies are central to the future military use of space. Since the fall of the Soviet Union, the United States has accounted for an estimated 90% of worldwide R&D expenditure on military space. In terms of potential capability in military space, it will have no rival for a long time to come. In August 2006, the White House replaced the 1996 National Space Policy with an updated version that attracted considerable attention; it was interpreted, in line with general attitudes towards the Bush administration, as an example of unilateralism and confrontationalism. The headline message of the new policy was that the United States considered the protection of its own space capabilities and freedom of action in space as a matter of vital national interest, implying the will to use force in defence against aggression.

However, the 1996 policy had stated, equally clearly, that 'access to and use of space was central for preserving peace and protecting U.S. national security as well as civil and commercial interests'. The Clinton administration policy had also directed the Department of Defense (DoD) to 'maintain the capability to execute the mission areas of space support, force enhancement, space control and force application'. The 2006 policy does not go any further in respect of reserving the right to use force in space. There had been strong voices in the armed forces and the political debate who advocated a more forward-leaning 'space power' approach. Their views were not adopted, mainly due to the realisation that the United States stood to lose more than any other country if space became a battleground. The Bush policy put additional stress on the preservation and protection of the principle of freedom of navigation in space that underlies the existing multilateral legal regime of the 1966 Treaty on Principles Governing the Activities of States in the Exploration and Use of Outer Space, Including the Moon and Other Celestial Bodies (the Outer Space Treaty). The assertion that the new US policy mandates weaponisation of space cannot be supported from its wording or intent.

Since the 1980s, the United States has been largely on its own in conducting the debate on and coining new terminology for strategic thinking about military space. This was not the result of a deliberate effort to dominate, but the inevitable consequence of huge, continuing investments in space technology, microelectronics and related technologies and of possessing a highly capable science and engineering workforce in previous decades, unmatched in scale and competence by any other country. Today, the US government accounts for more than half of global civil and military space spending, and the DoD's space budget exceeds

$22 billion. Confidence in technological prowess is such that a statement from Donald Kerr, director of the US National Reconnaissance Office, that 'we need a capacity that will provide the United States with an integrated and automated world-wide trip-wire capability to detect anything of intelligence or operational interest' is taken as a serious and practical suggestion.

American enthusiasm for space's unique advantages must, however, be tempered by several caveats. Currently available space technology is not exploited well enough to make a crucial difference on the battlefield. The underlying problem appears to be more conceptual and organisational than technological or financial. The urban-centred stabilisation and counter-insurgency operations faced today were not on the minds of the designers of currently operational space systems. GPS service, for example, often fails in 'urban canyons', though the next generation GPS III is expected to overcome this limitation. Moreover, intelligence failures have occurred in spite of intense use of space: institutional secrecy and stovepiping make inter-agency intelligence fusion and timely cross-cueing an ever-elusive target. New, open commercial sources for geographical data are only half-heartedly adopted. Sensors and systems architectures remain tailor-made for problems of the past. The tradition of gold-plated, massive hardware blocks the transition to new technologies and more flexible architectures. As a result, the utility of costly space assets to warfighters and for homeland security remains limited.

The aim to have capacity for worldwide network-centric operations creates huge pressure to generate bandwidth. The data transfer rate of each of the new US military satellites scheduled to become operational in the near future is in the region of 2.5 gigabits per second or higher, roughly equivalent to 150 simultaneous high-definition video streams. This data rate for a single satellite exceeds the overall data rate required during *Operation Iraqi Freedom* in 2003, but is already considered by some to be at the low end of potential future requirements.

The planned Transformational Satellite Communications System (TSAT), with a first launch scheduled for 2013, will use laser communication links between satellites and from satellites to high-altitude long-endurance airborne platforms. Using standard Internet protocols, this system is designed to provide highly adaptable secure broadband connections to mobile users worldwide. Such a capability is bound to fundamentally change the way operations are conducted. It is unclear, however, if this will strengthen the autonomy, situational awareness, agility and protection of frontline troops or if it will simply lead to increased remote management of theatres of operation by commanders located in the United States.

A second caveat concerns procurement. Far from being 'transformational', for example, TSAT has turned into the heaviest and most complex geostationary satellite ever planned. Continued Congressional support remains uncertain.

Repeatedly, acquisition delays due to efforts to cram too many features on a platform have created a need for interim, gap-filling solutions that have themselves been delayed. At the same time, however, there have been innovative attempts within the defence space community to bypass the process, including buy-in of services from commercial spin-offs, demonstrators and prototypes that field initial capabilities, technology transfer to entrepreneurial start-ups to foster development of cheaper launchers, and funding from DARPA for generation-after-next technology.

A third caveat is recognised by US military leaders but seems to be lost on Congress and parts of the administration. By steaming ahead of allies and failing to bring them along through inclusive policies that respond to their interests, America is not just alienating other countries but also limiting business opportunities for space industries in the United States and abroad. Above all, a trend toward weakened interoperability between space-driven, fully digitised US forces and only partially transformed allies is likely to aggravate a defence technology chasm already visible today, hindering successful maintenance of a multilateral international security dependent on effective sharing of information.

European focus

Annual spending on military space in Western Europe is now above €1bn and expected to grow toward €2bn, with France accounting for the biggest slice. Even at the higher level, European spending will lag far behind that of the United States. Recent years have seen increasing, though not yet converging, military space cooperation among Europeans. There is also growing interest in the European Union in the use of space for security, though not expressly for defence. This is fuelled by realisation that the lack of cohesion among member states limits the overall power of the Union, and by a desire to narrow the gap with the United States in a high-technology field closely linked to the aerospace and defence electronics sectors, in which there is transatlantic competition.

This drive is still in its infancy. The future relationship between the EU and the European Space Agency (ESA), whose expertise is indispensable, remains institutionally undefined despite a framework agreement. Some member governments view Article 2 of the ESA Convention, which repeats the phrase 'exclusively for peaceful purposes' from the Outer Space Treaty, as preventing any ESA role in 'hard security'. It has until recently been interpreted as excluding all contacts with the world of defence.

The EU's *Galileo* navigation satellite initiative, aimed at building a large civilian European satellite constellation that complements the US-run GPS and puts new critical services such as satellite-driven airspace control on a commercially reliable basis, suffers from the same limitation. Only France has tentatively and unenthusiastically indicated that it might be willing to commit defence funds to *Galileo*. Meant to be pursued in a public–private partnership scheme, *Galileo* experienced an industry pull-out in 2007 exactly at the point at which industry had been expected to commit its own funds. At least €2.4bn in additional public funding needs to be authorised by the end of 2007 to rescue the programme.

So much money has already been sunk, and so much political capital invested, in *Galileo* that termination is not an option. One argument for *Galileo* had been that it would provide a global public service that would be an alternative to the American-controlled GPS system. However, this rationale was undermined when the United States ended the practice of deliberately reducing the accuracy of the public GPS signal in 2000. The United States also makes its precise military GPS technology available to allied forces to ensure interoperability. From a strategic viewpoint, the most remarkable aspect of *Galileo* so far has been the successful, though little publicised, US–EU negotiation process that led to a shared understanding of security aspects and a commitment to harmonise signals for improved performance and reliability.

Another big EU space project, Global Monitoring for Environment and Security (GMES), has been presented by the European Commission as an ambitious project to claim a major role in space. However, it is simply the contribution of EU countries to the Global Earth Observation System of Systems (GEOSS). It is essentially a repackaging of existing geoscience and Earth-observation satellite programmes, linking them conceptually and technically and embedding them in the EU's technology research funding programmes. This is intended to drive the transition from science to the provision of systematic, continuously available public-service applications, for example disaster prevention and management.

Gauging China's space ambitions

China's learning curve in space is still steep. The spectacular act of putting an astronaut into orbit in 2003, riding as a passenger on top of what was essentially an intelligence-gathering platform, obscured the fact that China's manned space programme had fallen considerably behind schedule and used ideas and equipment based on 1960s Soviet technology. In January 2007, China attracted considerable attention by destroying in low Earth orbit an ageing Chinese *Fengyun*-1C meteorological remote-sensing satellite with an anti-satellite (ASAT) missile fired from the ground. But this may have been the third attempt, after two previous failed tests were presented as test flights of a new truck-mobile satellite launcher.

It is therefore striking how little progress China's space efforts have made over the last decade. The set of Chinese military satellites in orbit is essentially unchanged. China still lacks a permanent very-high-resolution imaging and electronic intelligence collection capacity in space. China's navigation satellites only cover East Asia. The main characteristic of China's space programme has been its steady, dual-use nature, trying to satisfy military needs largely through the same platforms in communication, navigation and Earth observation as are used to meet civil government requirements.

Nevertheless, the ASAT demonstration seemed to resolve a decade-old debate among outside observers about the direction and motivation of China's space efforts. It suggested a systematic, determined and well-funded effort to counter US space dominance militarily, driven by defence modernisers who expect a high-tech regional war against the United States over Taiwan within their lifetimes – a view most likely not shared by the political leadership. Chinese publications about defence transformation and the role of space, some of them produced by military officers, support this interpretation, but there is room for doubt. Official figures paint only part of the picture of Chinese defence spending; the allocation and efficiency of use of military research and development resources are almost impossible to assess.

The People's Liberation Army (PLA) appears to be in control of the key operational aspects. The military space programme will likely benefit increasingly from China's rapid progress in the wider arena of technological development,which includes such space-relevant fields as electronics where huge numbers of well-trained, highly motivated graduates are produced each year and state-of-the-art manufacturing facilities are available. China is thus unlikely to remain two generations of technology behind the United States in space for much longer. On the other hand, the US military space effort is in the comfortable position of having decades of space-related and cross-sectoral advanced research and technology development still waiting to be translated into operational systems.

While China's future capabilities in the military use of space will be significant but limited, its intentions in this field are open to question. It seems more likely than not that these form part of Chinese military planning for a potential future war against the United States and its allies – and therefore that it would seek to gain asymmetrical advantage by striking US forces where they are most vulnerable, and potentially also to paralyse Western societies as a whole by shutting down critical orbital communications, navigation and timing infrastructure without which they would be unable to function. For the case of a future military confrontation with the United States, there is ample evidence in Chinese military writing that such action to exploit high-tech vulnerabilities would be considered.

However, China's own rapidly growing economy is just as dependent on this orbital infrastructure. Apparent disregard of defence planners for their own society's vulnerability to the consequences of action against an opponent's infrastructure in a globalised, networked economic environment runs the risk of creating a disconnect between military and political strategies. This tension may at some point offer an opportunity for developing a new shared understanding among China, the United States and other countries that would leave the sterile arms-control language of non-militarisation of space behind and instead focus on the common interest of keeping shared critical infrastructure in space in working order. This issue is not just of interest to the United States and China, and is not primarily an arms-control issue. There is no obvious forum in which it can be discussed, but a Group of Eight plus China format may be a good starting point for talks on the shared interest in space infrastructure security.

Space as a battleground?

In international law, space is recognised as one of the 'commons' that exist beyond the sovereignty of any state, along with the high seas and Antarctica. The Outer Space Treaty, a universally accepted, binding UN convention, outlaws deployment of weapons of mass destruction in space but otherwise places no restrictions on military use. The treaty's provision that space must be used exclusively for peaceful purposes is generally interpreted as permitting all non-aggressive use, including use of space for defence purposes. State practice at the time of the conclusion of the treaty, as well as subsequently, leaves little room for a more restrictive interpretation.

There is no legal basis for the common assertion that space was meant to be demilitarised. On the contrary, civilian space programmes were initiated in the 1950s with the deliberate intent to establish the right and practice of legitimate overflight in orbit for military purposes. There is also no current legal rule that bans ASAT weapons, even in orbit, so long as they are non-nuclear and are not used for aggression, as defined under the UN Charter.

Space is therefore not a sanctuary free of defence-related activities. Military satellites have played and continue to play a major role in strengthening international peace and security, above all as a means of transparency and confidence building. While there is much to be said in favour of preventing 'weaponisation' of outer space – the placing of actual weapons in orbit and the threat or use of force against space assets –the 'Prevention of an Arms Race in Outer Space (PAROS)' initiative frequently raised in international and bilaterial forums in support of this objective has essentially been an effort to impose legally binding obligations on the United States that would curtail its use of space in support of defence operations. The asymmetry of space capabilities between the United States and all others makes this approach a non-starter. It would make little sense for the United States to subscribe to restrictions that would apply in effect only to itself. There is also no evidence that their position on unrestricted use of space for defence creates the potential for an arms race. Even during the East–West arms race, space was treated as a separate matter, in recognition of the mutually beneficial stabilising role of military satellites as national technical means of verification and early warning.

There is little incentive to place a weapon in orbit to attack targets on the ground. With available and foreseen technologies, bombers or missiles could always achieve better results with much less effort. The movement to ban weapons in space has, therefore, always been closely linked with the debate on defence against strategic nuclear ballistic missiles, on the grounds that mid-course anti-missile missiles hit their targets in space. The original Strategic Defense Initiative concept included the futuristic technical option of perma-nently deployed missile-defence projectiles in orbit. Today that debate looks like a distraction from the real issues.

The concern is now more about potential destabilising effects of the increas-ing dependence on satellites and its exploitation by opponents through the use of force against satellite systems. As communications satellites have become the backbone of C4ISTAR (command, control, communications, computing, intelligence, surveillance, target acquisition and reconnaissance) networks for expeditionary operations, they have turned into high-value targets whose neu-tralisation before or during a conflict could theoretically have decisive effect by cutting the nerve between commander and forces. Similarly, other classes of mili-tary satellite have become very important for the conduct of operations, above all the GPS satellite constellation that guides troops on the ground as well as most modern weapons systems.

Most communications satellites are in high geostationary orbits, and naviga-tion satellites are in medium orbits, much less exposed to direct-ascent kinetic attacks from ground- or air-based missiles than satellites in low orbit. Attacking the hardware in orbit is unlikely to be the method of choice to disable, degrade or take over such satellites. Instead, ground-control stations may be cut off or attacked, uplink and downlink may be exposed to electromagnetic interference, or encrypted control channels may be broken into by means of cyber-warfare.

Protective countermeasures such as electromagnetic-pulse hardening, sophisticated frequency use and intelligent antennas that null jamming signals are routinely incorporated in military satellites. A number of Russian-built local GPS jamming devices were operated by Iraqi forces in 2003, but were quickly located and destroyed. For observation satellites, passive measures such as cam-ouflage during easily predictable overflights will often suffice to deny successful intelligence gathering. Temporary dazzling or permanent blinding by laser may also be pursued.

Though unlikely for the foreseeable future, on-orbit assaults and battles are a possibility. While it is very hard to hit a target at a distance of 36,000km from Earth, it may be relatively easy to affect a satellite in geosynchronous orbit through a small co-orbiting killer satellite or jammer. Such technology was developed during the Cold War, but deployed only in low Earth orbit. There have been reports that China has developed very small 'parasite satellites' with an ASAT mission, but these appear to be based on misinterpretation of a British–Chinese cooperative project that involved a UK nanosatellite demonstrator able to track and image other satellites in low Earth orbit. There is a risk that a very small ASAT payload, launched secretly with a legitimate commercial communications satellite, could pass undetected. The perpetrator of an attack would remain unknown. In response, valuable satellites may increasingly carry means of detection, evasion or defence.

Space control, or measures that assure situational awareness of the identity, position and velocity of all objects in orbit – similar to airspace and air traffic control – will soon become necessary. This poses a severe problem for the international system: only the United States has developed the use of space to a point where it needs to worry about space control to protect satellites it depends upon. With space a global commons, a purely national US space-control regime would inevitably be seen as an unacceptable claim to possession of space as a whole. Few in the United States have argued for a cooperative approach, and even fewer in other countries have indicated that they are willing to share the costs. There is nevertheless merit in working towards an agreed set of 'rules of the road' and a shared commitment to monitoring and mitigating threats to space security.

Moreover, there is increasing awareness that critical civil and commercial infrastructure in space is also at risk. This is not limited to threats to commercial communications satellites whose transponders are leased by the military, although this is an important factor given that even the United States routes more than half of its military communications traffic through such commercial platforms. At a time of increased worries about the vulnerabilities of modern industrialised and networked societies to various kinds of disruption, the space dimension requires attention because it has become embedded in the functioning of many non-space services which are taken for granted. If GPS service were lost, for example, not only would maritime navigation be significantly disrupted but terrestrial mobile networks and power grids would be affected worldwide, as would clearance systems in the financial markets, logistics chains and food supplies. There is reason to be concerned about threats to human security and social stability if protection against disruption of satellite systems that underpin public services is not pursued as an issue of wide international concern, requiring common action.

The January Chinese ASAT test – imitating a US test in 1985 before Congress banned the practice – highlighted not just the risk of direct attack but, much more importantly, the risks posed by deliberately created orbital debris as a means of warfare or terrorism, able to effectively deny the use of key orbits. The blast was by far the largest debris-producing event ever in space. It left more than 1,300 trackable pieces of debris and many more smaller particles, an estimated 35,000 of them larger than 1cm. By four months after the incident, less than 2%

of the trackable pieces had decayed from orbit and re-entered the atmosphere. Decay models show that the majority of trackable pieces will still be in orbit in 100 years' time. Collision with a particle of more than a few millimetres in size can disable a satellite since relative impact speed can reach 15km/s depending on the angle between orbital planes; hitting an object in the centimetre range causes destruction to satellites or space stations. Shielding against objects of that size is not possible. Aggravating the problem, objects of less than 5cm in diameter cannot be reliably tracked from the ground to allow evasive manoeuvres. The first satellite to be destroyed by debris collision is believed to have been the Soviet military navigation satellite *Cosmos* 1275 in 1981. The risk that operational spacecraft in low Earth orbit will be hit and disabled by debris has significantly increased since the Chinese ASAT test; additional shielding panels were deployed on the International Space Station in June 2007 in reaction to the increased risk. Politically the incident was worrying because the Chinese Foreign Ministry was apparently caught unprepared and needed two weeks to compose an explanation, an indication that decision-making is apparently more fragmented between the political and military leadership than often thought.

If done in anger or with intent to hurt orbital infrastructure, actions like the Chinese ASAT test could be classified as aggressive. The legal and conceptual parallel between naval and space matters — between protecting assets in Earth orbit and keeping the high seas lanes of communication open and secure for common use, for example — can provide some guidance, but the issue of orbital debris creation has no proper parallel. It is to some extent akin to sinking subsurface obstacles in international straits but, given the laws of orbital mechanics, its denial effect is potentially much more universal.

Sharing space benefits for international security

The deep secrecy that surrounded military space during the Cold War has given way to a more cooperative atmosphere. Few eyebrows were raised when the British small reconnaissance satellite *Topsat*, part funded by the Ministry of Defence, was launched from Russia in 2005 on the same launcher as an experimental Iranian satellite. Even in Europe, however, joint defence satellite procurement schemes of the 1990s such as the Franco-German *Helios/Horus* plan or the Franco-Anglo-German *Trimilsat* communications satellite programme fell through; specifications proved irreconcilable and shares of any commercial return were difficult to assign. Nations prefer to build hardware of their own choice at their own pace, and then enter into arrangements for shared use.

In the latest attempt at cooperation, a grouping of continental European defence ministries – those of France, Germany, Italy, Spain, Belgium and Greece – known as Besoins opérationnels communs (BOC) is trying to define joint requirements and specifications for common next-generation satellite systems.

In parallel, the European Defence Agency (EDA) is working towards better harmonisation of next-generation European military communications satellites, to be launched after 2020. There is still very little sharing of military space technology across the Atlantic, with the significant exception of British access to US national technical means on the basis of post-Second World War cooperation arrangements.

A major development over the last decade has been increasing reliance on commercial markets as an innovative form of international defence cooperation, after the United States decided in 1993 to allow some of its spy-satellite technology to be commercially exploited, prompted by Russian sales of high-resolution satellite photos for cash. The EU Satellite Centre near Madrid similarly provides EU institutions and member states that lack national capabilities with mapping and intelligence products derived from commercial imagery. Increasingly, such products are also made available for operations of the United Nations and the African Union. The new generation of British military communications satellites, *Skynet* 5, is operated by the private contractor Paradigm under a long-term, privately financed service contract for bandwidth with the UK government. Additional capacities are sold to NATO in a pooling arrangement together with the French *Syracuse* and Italian *Sicral* satellites, and to other countries, such as the Netherlands.

The defence ministries of countries with military imaging satellites of their own – especially the Pentagon – are today the most important purchasers of such commercial imagery. It provides wider geographical coverage, automated change detection and cueing of higher-resolution national reconnaissance tools. There is also the ability to exercise 'cheque-book shutter control' by buying up all commercial imaging capacity in crises to prevent other parties from access. However, only a certain portion of the feature set required for military use will be available. In recent US experience, even programmes like the Wideband Global System — previously known as Wideband Gapfiller — that are adapted from related commercial products have experienced serious delays and cost overruns.

The pace of innovation in the commercial space market poses a structural challenge to defence as procurement cycles for military satellites are still in the range of 10–15 years and specifications such as bandwidth needs will regularly be outpaced by rapid technological innovation by the time programmes become operational, burdening the military with either antiquated equipment or, in the case of space service provision by private contractors, excessive service bills. In the long run, increased commercialisation is likely to turn space into a less institutionalised market, less dominated by government demand.

Increasing attention to non-military aspects of security has some potential to change the dynamics of international space cooperation, as traditional cooperative civil space activities take on an operational security dimension. GEOSS, for example — supported by more than 50 countries and endorsed by the Gleneagles G8 summit in 2005 — is designed to provide warning of environmental risks and disasters and make Earth observation benefits available where they are needed. NASA, NOAA and ESA have already pooled their resources in a commitment to fly compatible instruments in space to ensure continuous measurement of key atmospheric and climate-change indicators. One current issue is the US decision to merge its national civil and defence polar-orbiting meteorological satellite programmes, raising concerns that existing international science commitments and the demands of operational continuity in a security-relevant field such as climate change may be pushed aside by the Pentagon in defining the next-generation US system.

There is currently little trust internationally in the willingness and ability of the United States to engage in sustainable and mutually rewarding cooperation. This affects perspectives on cooperation in space situational awareness, space traffic control, debris mitigation and protecting orbital infrastructure. These are, by their nature, multilateral tasks. It is neither reasonable nor financially feasible to duplicate ongoing national US efforts in these directions. There are no signs, however, that cooperative approaches can be found.

Conclusion

Space technology is both an enabler and equaliser of operational capabilities. Its impact can be understood as being similar in kind and dimension to the deep consequences of digital information and communication technology (ICT) across many military and non-military fields. In ICT, open standards and markets have enabled the wave of globalisation we have witnessed in the last 25 years, hugely improving the basis for the cooperative management of international security issues. In space technology, however, this openness and global market orientation is still blocked by the stranglehold of the US national security sector. It condemns some of the most promising bits of space technology to 'noforn' status – for US eyes only – and prevents their effective use. This policy denies key enabling capabilities to alliances and multilateral security efforts, prevents effective burden sharing in a networked world and could feed the emergence of new rivalries. A net assessment of vulnerabilities incurred by sharing and not sharing space technology for defence would be likely to produce strong arguments in favour of openness and cooperation. The strategic issue of making space technology work better for international security is worthy of being placed on the international political agenda at a significantly higher level.

3 The Americas

The United States: Facing Reality?

President George W. Bush has been many times accused of living in a state of denial, but his press conference on 8 November 2006 was a forthright display of lucid reckoning. In midterm elections the opposition Democrats had just won easy control of the House of Representatives, and in the Senate (though at press-conference time votes were still being counted), a one-seat advantage. 'It was a *thumping*', Bush declared, and he moved on to lay out a sober and conciliatory view of how – notwithstanding the bitterness of the campaign – he expected to find common ground with the newly empowered Democratic leadership.

The most difficult part of that search for common ground was clearly going to be Iraq. While there were significant domestic policy debates in deeper waters, the surface drama of American politics in 2006 and 2007 concerned foreign policy. This was a rare development – if Bush's 2004 re-election victory was one of the very few presidential campaigns decided by national-security issues, the 2006 election was something even rarer: a midterm foreign-policy contest. Going into the race, Republican candidates knew that their constituents were in a sour mood. Yet, because of the configuration of individual contests, they had been reasonably confident of holding onto the Senate and at least limiting losses in the House. In the event, the magnitude of their defeat was conveyed by another rarity: incumbent Democrats did not lose a single contested seat, a feat that neither party had accomplished since 1938. Exit polling was unambiguous: notwithstanding the considerable number of scandals that had tarnished Republican candidates, this was mainly a referendum on President Bush and the war that he was directing in Iraq, but which he seemed to have no prospect of

© IISS

CANADA

Ottawa

UNITED STATES

Washington DC

MEXICO

Havana

CUBA

HAITI

DOMINICAN
REPUBLIC

Santo Domingo

Atlantic
Ocean

Mexico City

BELIZE

JAMAICA

7

GUATEMALA

1

Kingston

2

3

HONDURAS

EL SALVADOR

NICARAGUA

4

5

COSTA RICA

TRINIDAD &
TOBAGO

Caracas

6

Panama City

Georgetown

Paramaribo

PANAMA

VENEZUELA

GUYANA

Cayenne

Bogotá

SURINAME

COLOMBIA

FRENCH GUYANA

Quito

ECUADOR

Pacific
Ocean

Lima

BRAZIL

PERU

Brasília

La Paz

BOLIVIA

PARAGUAY

Asuncion

CHILE

URUGUAY

Santiago

Buenos Aires

Montevideo

ARGENTINA

1 Belmopan   5 Managua
2 Guatemala City 6 San Jose
3 Tegucigalpa   7 Port-au-Prince
4 San Salvador   ■ Capital
─ Borders

Falkland Islands (UK)

South Georgia (UK)

1,000m

1,500km

finishing. This was bad for the Republicans, but it also posed a dilemma for the Democrats, who were coming to power under strong pressure from their partisan base and wider constituency to force an end to the war.

Bush said he recognised 'that many Americans voted last night to register their displeasure' about Iraq. His main concession to that displeasure was to fire Defense Secretary Donald Rumsfeld and replace him with former CIA Director Robert Gates. Gates, who after his government service had become president of Texas A&M University, was an exemplar of 'realist' Republicanism: a Cold War hawk, to be sure, but also associated with the foreign-policy traditionalists in the president's father's administration, including the senior Bush's secretary of state, James Baker, and his national security adviser, General Brent Scowcroft. Gates had been a member of the Iraq Study Group, an independent commission set up under the co-chairmanship of Baker and former Democratic Congressman Lee Hamilton to chart a way out of the Iraq quagmire. Bush that afternoon said that he was looking forward to the Baker–Hamilton Commission's recommendations, and to working with the Democratic Congress to 'achieve the objective'.

Yet here, precisely, were the limits to bipartisan comity, or even a common view of reality. Bush suggested that he was willing to compromise on everything but his commitment 'to victory' in Iraq, adding:

> Iraq is part of the war on terror ... I think back to Harry Truman and Dwight Eisenhower. Harry Truman began the Cold War, and Eisenhower, obviously, from a different party, continued it. And I would hope that would be the spirit that we're able to work together. We may not agree with every tactic, but we should agree that this country needs to secure ourselves against an enemy that would like to strike us again. This enemy is not going away after my presidency.

Democrats, however, increasingly rejected the idea that Iraq was part of the war on terror, or at least – since al-Qaeda's enthusiasm for fighting American troops there could not be doubted – they rejected the notion that this was a sensible place for the United States to carry on the fight. A few rejected the notion that 'war' was a logical construct for fighting terrorism in any event. As for 'victory' in Iraq, the new Senate majority leader, Harry Reid, voiced the sentiments of many if not most Americans when in April 2007 he blurted out his view that the war was already lost. A month after the elections, the Iraq Study Group had opened its report with the words: 'The situation in Iraq is grave and deteriorating'. Their recommendations were clearly aimed not at abstract victory but at minimising the scope of defeat. They called for US troops to be redeployed away from combat roles and drawn down, for significantly greater pressure on the Shia-dominated government to reach a compact with Sunni insurgents, for talks with Iran and Syria to explore the scope for common interests in stabilising Iraq, and for an Iraq Support Group – to include these and other neighbours along with Europeans and the UN – to hold the ring diplomatically against the country's meltdown.

The potential importance of the Iraq Study Group derived not so much from any special insight into how to turn the Iraq disaster around, as from a solid sense of what the American political traffic could bear. It was a case in which the much-abused label, 'bipartisan', was truly appropriate. Most of the nine elder statesmen, and one woman, had served or been close to the Reagan, elder Bush and Clinton administrations. Their report might have served as bipartisan cover for the gradual liquidation of a failing national enterprise: bitter for many Republicans to accept; much slower than many Democrats wanted; but less likely, by virtue of its provenance, to be the occasion for sustained partisan bloodletting.

Taking advantage of the report's political cover depended, however, on accepting the Iraq Study Group's grim assessment of real possibilities. President Bush quickly made it clear that he was not ready – at least not yet ready – to concede this much to Baker–Hamilton's version of reality. Instead, he chose a course that Baker–Hamilton had specifically recommended against – an escalation of troop levels. In January 2007 Bush announced a 'surge' of more than 20,000 additional troops for the purpose of providing security to Baghdad and, by extension, enough political calm for the Shia-dominated government to reach an national compact with enough disgruntled Sunnis to begin to quell the civil war.

By late June 2007, then, the question that Bush himself had imposed over his presidency was whether the surge could work – could work at all but also work within a short enough time-frame that Americans might give the war another chance. The signs were none too promising: in Iraq, where the level of suicide bombings and sectarian killings had returned, after an initial lull, to their pre-surge levels; and in Washington, where a growing number of Republican lawmakers were warning the president that they were unwilling to go into another election supporting a war that their voters had abandoned in droves.

The Iraq War tended to overshadow even the continued signs of a consolidated moderation in the Bush administration's foreign policies. Among the indications of a move to the centre were appointments of Gates-style traditionalists to high positions, the decision to engage in talks with Iran and reengage with North Korea, and President Bush's late conversion to at least the possibility of UN talks to curb global warming. In the domestic area, Bush pushed for an immigration-reform package that united him with such liberal Democrats as Massachusetts Senator Edward Kennedy but outraged the base of Republican conservatives by offering what they considered 'amnesty' to roughly 12 million illegal immigrants in the United States.

Bush's extreme unpopularity added immensely to the difficulties of gaining credit or traction for any of these more moderate policies. The last two years of a two-term presidency were bound to be problematic, as 'lame-duck' status deprived the president of political capital. Yet none of the other full two-term presidents of the post-Second World War era – Eisenhower, Reagan or Clinton – had finished their time in office with public approval ratings below 50%. Most surveys of Bush's public approval rating put him, throughout the first half of 2007, below 35%.

This created an odd dynamic in the 2008 presidential election campaign, which was already in full swing 18 months before the polling date. Republican candidates tried pretty consistently to escape association with the president who was the leader of their party. Yet rather than pitching for the political centre, they were trying to outbid one another on rightwing positions – such as 'enhanced interrogation' of prisoners in the war on terror, the possible use of nuclear weapons against Iran, and rejection of 'amnesty' for illegal immigrants. (The notable outlier adopting a different stance on at least some of these issues was Arizona Senator John McCain, but he joined his fellow candidates in remaining committed to 'victory' in Iraq without an entirely persuasive case for how to achieve it.) Meanwhile, the field of Democratic candidates seemed to be describing a different world. Although they might join Republicans in claiming that the threat from al-Qaeda was growing, they saw a world in which withdrawal from Iraq was a task of managing expectations; in which global warming loomed larger as a threat than Islamist jihad; in which America could expand its welfare state through near-universal health care and protection of gay rights.

Two worlds

This partisan dichotomy has been sharpened by the rhetoric and policies of the Bush administration. It is a dichotomy that can be expressed in two questions. Does the United States look at security problems primarily as a matter of confronting and defeating aggressors and despots? Or do Americans look at security problems as the consequences of systemic disorders that need to be fixed or at least ameliorated? Although President Bush may have expressed the former view more sharply than most, it is a familiar American strain of thought that derives especially from the popular historiography of the Second World War. Yet, the post-Second World War construction of the UN, the Bretton Woods financial institutions, and other organisations including NATO was largely based on the second vision of international security – one in which order and legality are global public goods that need to be cultivated and strengthened even without reference to any particular enemy or threat. The American founding fathers of these institutions were thinking not so much about confronting a Soviet threat – or not so much initially, anyway – as they were about ordering the world system to prevent the kind of rudderless chaos that they felt had characterised the inter-war years.

Both worlds can exist: it can be necessary to fight the forces of evil and to work on the underlying evils of the human condition at the same time. In Darfur, for example, there is a genocidal programme that might be opposed effectively with military force. As was the case in both Bosnia and Kosovo, an effective dem-onstration of escalation dominance by US or other Western forces could have a significant psychological impact. Just as obviously, however, there is a systemic disorder in Darfur – a series of droughts – and whether or not they are the direct result of anthropogenic climate change, the changing climate is likely to cause more such droughts. If the world community – meaning, in the first instance, its greater powers starting with the United States – cannot address this underly-ing systemic disorder, there will be many more Darfurs which no quantity of Churchillian resolve can prevent.

In 2006 and 2007, America in general, and the Bush administration in particu-lar, seemed to be vacillating between these two ways of conceiving its role in the world. The first conception was clear in the initial response of the administration and many of its most prominent supporters to the Lebanon war of summer 2006. The context included America's ongoing confrontation with an Iran that was enriched by rising oil prices and emboldened by US difficulties in Iraq. Iranian President Mahmoud Ahmadinejad was adding to the tensions with heated – and outrageous – rhetoric of religious apocalypse, Holocaust denial and wiping Israel off the map. In this already volatile summer, the Iranian-backed Hizbullah militia in Lebanon kidnapped two Israeli soldiers and killed others, provoking a ferocious Israeli air campaign against the militia's infrastructure that terrorised and killed many Lebanese civilians.

For Israel's principal ally, the United States, the crisis posed an immediate question: what is more important, to defeat Hizbullah or to stop the war? The immediate answer from President Bush and those who shared his world view was clear: America had a vital interest in defeating the terrorists and their Iranian backers. Some Bush administration officials – including, clearly, the president himself – saw this Israeli campaign as part of a proxy war against a terrorist group that was acting on behalf of Iran's hegemonic ambitions in the greater Middle East. White House officials lumped Shia and Sunni extremists together under the rubric of what the president called 'Islamo-fascism'. Former House speaker Newt Gingrich spoke of an emerging 'Third World War'.

Bush and Vice President Dick Cheney, with strong urging from Elliott Abrams, a National Security Council deputy, set the policy of the United States as, in effect, to let the Israeli operation take its course. This meant resisting early calls from Arab states, and from France and Russia, for a ceasefire resolution from the UN Security Council. Key players in the Bush administration saw the Israeli air-strikes as furthering US interests without the United States having to commit its own forces. This would happen, they reasoned, in four ways: by destroying as much of Hizbullah's weapons and forces as possible; by turning the Lebanese population against Hizbullah because of its role in fomenting the war; by allowing the Lebanese government to regain control of its country's south; and as a salutary demonstration to Iran of the refined power of Western air assets. There was a fifth, more general rationale in the lingering hope that disorder in the Middle East was preferable to the region's old, oppressive order, and would help to usher in a better, more democratic future for the region. Secretary of State Condoleezza Rice gave a rather unfortunate expression to this hope when she told a press conference that the war and suffering in Lebanon were part of the 'birth pangs of a new Middle East'.

The problem with this paradigm, however, was that it failed to account, or at least account adequately, for the narrative impact upon Muslims of the televised killings of Lebanese civilians. For Lebanon itself, the proposition that the Lebanese population would turn massively against Hizbullah reflected a familiar 'strategic bombing fallacy'. A bombarded population will rarely blame their misfortune on anyone but the people doing the bombing. The Israeli campaign arguably did considerable damage to Hizbullah's infrastructure, but Israel's inability to deliver a knockout blow, together with televised images of civilian death and suffering, inflated Hizbullah's prestige. Sunni Arab regimes, worried about Iran's power and rightly alarmed by Hizbullah's recklessness, were initially very critical almost to the point of siding with Israel. Yet the Sunni Arab street took the other side – blurring the Sunni–Shia divide.

Other members of the administration – including notably Secretary Rice – apparently came to understand that the extended war was damaging US interests. The four-week stalemate did not appear to be a success for Israel either, and in early August the United States and France finally came together to craft a successful UN Security Council resolution calling for a ceasefire.

The United States would continue to be caught up in the dilemmas of a 'hearts and minds' strategy that manifestly was losing Muslim hearts and minds: for example, in a policy that encouraged Palestinians to embrace democracy, then punished them with an embargo on the Hamas government that they had elected in January 2006. Still, the 2006 summer of crisis marked a dramatic stage in the halting, erratic and partial turnaround that had characterised the Bush administration's second term – towards a relatively greater attention to creating the conditions for peace rather than determination to achieve 'victory' in an ill-defined, global war.

Gates, the new defense secretary, was emblematic of this approach. In his 5 December confirmation hearing before the Senate Armed Services Committee, his candour caused press corps jaws to drop. Asked whether the war in Iraq had been a good idea, he ostentatiously declined to support the president's view: 'that's a judgment', Gates said, 'that historians are going to have to make'. Asked if the United States was winning in Iraq, he replied, 'no, sir'. When Senator Robert Byrd, the veteran West Virginia Democrat, asked about the prospect of an attack on Iran, Gates replied that the experience in Iraq should make Americans think more than twice. 'We have seen in Iraq that once war is unleashed, it becomes unpredictable.' The Iranians had many means of retaliation, he added. When the same question was applied to Syria, he answered, 'the Syrians' capacity to do harm to us is far more limited … [but attacking Syria] would give rise to a significantly greater anti-Americanism … [and] increasingly complicate our relationship with virtually every country in the region'. In June 2007, speaking to the International Institute for Strategic Studies Shangri La Dialogue in Singapore, Gates generated headlines that focused on his generally moderate approach to relations with China. Even more remarkable was the Cold War historiography that he employed to explain this moderation.

> My own view is that one of the ways in which conflict was prevented during the Cold War between the United States and the Soviet Union was a steadily growing range of interactions, first diplomatic and then in the military sphere. I have always believed that the years-long negotiations on strategic arms limitations may or may not have made much of a contribution in terms of limiting arms, but they played an extraordinarily valuable role in creating better understanding on both the Soviet and American sides about what the strategic intentions of each side were; what the strategic thinking was; what their motives were; where they were headed. That dialogue, which continued intensively for something like 20 years, built a cadre of people who were accustomed to working and talking with one another, people who were on opposite sides of a major conflict.

While such language might seem to express conventional reflections on the role of détente and negotiations in unwinding the Cold War, it was in fact entirely at odds with the version of Cold War history propagated by the neo-conservatives who had set the course of Bush's first-term foreign policy. In the neo-conservative version, détente and arms talks with the Soviets had been a snare and a delusion; only the belated toughness of the Reagan administration had persuaded the Soviets to seek an end to the confrontation. By these lights, détente with despots such as the clerics ruling Iran was also a delusion.

But Gates's way of thinking appeared, at least in certain policy areas, to be ascendant. The administration remained committed to the UN Security Council route of pressuring Iran on its nuclear programme – with diplomatic leadership by the European troika of Britain, France and Germany – even though few fruits of that diplomacy were forthcoming. The United States also engaged in its own direct, official talks with Iran for the first time since American diplomats were taken hostage in the 1979 Iranian revolution. The 28 May 2007 meeting in Baghdad between US Ambassador to Iraq Ryan Crocker and his Iranian counterpart was limited to the topic of stabilising Iraq, but there was talk of subsequent meetings and some speculation that such talking could become a habit that would spill over into other areas.

The possibility of military action to take out Iranian nuclear sites was not off the table. Bush had been quoted as telling associates that he would not leave the problem to his successor. The office of Vice President Cheney was using its formidable resources to stymie the diplomatic track. Moreover, the question of using military force was not a uniquely American choice. Israel was justifiably alarmed about the developing nuclear capability of a declared enemy whose president had announced the necessity of wiping the Jewish state off the map. (Though there was some dispute about the proper translation of his vitriol, there was no doubt about Iran's support of terrorism against Israel in addition to denying the legitimacy of the Jewish state's existence.) These were not circumstances under which Israel's public or politicians could be expected to find reassurance in theories about deterrence. Moreover, if Israel decided it had to take action, Washington would be unlikely to try to stop it, and might even decide that its own air-strikes would be preferable because they would be more effective.

Still, for the time being at least, the top levels of the State Department and, under Gates, the Pentagon were clearly unnerved by the prospect of action leading to a war with Iran. Diplomacy was to be given its chance.

Diplomacy also got its chance again in the ongoing confrontation with North Korea, where the Bush administration essentially completed a major policy shift in reaching a February 2007 agreement with Pyongyang, under which the North Koreans agreed to shut down the production of plutonium by sealing and disabling the Yongbyon complex. The deal was roughly similar to the 'Agreed Framework reached by the Clinton administration in 1994, with the important difference that, even if implemented in full, it was only freezing rather than forestalling the production of nuclear weapons. Dismantlement of the 5–10 nuclear weapons that North Korea had already produced was put off to a hypothetical future. The accord showed that the State Department was determined to deal with the nuclear situation as it presented itself, and now had the interagency clout to do so. The breakthrough also required abandonment of a long-standing administration taboo about direct bilateral talks with the North Koreans – the official deal in Beijing became possible after US envoy Christopher Hill met his counterparts in Berlin. In June he travelled to Pyongyang, pronouncing himself 'buoyed by the sense that we are going to be able to achieve our full objectives'. That this marked a major shift in Bush administration policies was certainly the judgement of one of the strongest proponents of the old policies, former

Undersecretary of State for Arms Control and UN Ambassador John Bolton, who wrote in the *Wall Street Journal*:

> This Pyongyang visit symbolizes the full return of Clinton-era, bilateral negotiations with North Korea … The Bush administration has effectively ended where North Korea policy is concerned, replaced for the next 18 months by a caretaker government of bureaucrats, technocrats and academics.

The administration also inched a little bit closer to the international consensus on the threat posed by global warming. One of President Bush's earliest challenges to transatlantic comity had been his March 2001 rejection of the Kyoto Protocol; at the time, Bush defiantly promised that he would never agree to a pact that would damage the US economy. This defiance was maintained right up to the brink of the June 2007 G8 meeting in Germany, despite the entreaties of two of his closest confidants among allied leaders, UK Prime Minister Tony Blair and German Chancellor Angela Merkel. Just a few days before the meeting, the United States reacted harshly to Merkel's bid for a new framework agreement to limit the twenty-first century's global temperature rise to 2°C above pre-industrial levels and decrease global greenhouse-gas emissions to 50% of 1990 levels by mid century; US officials sent a demarche claiming that the draft G8 statement 'runs counter to our overall position and crosses multiple "red lines" in terms of what we simply cannot agree to'.

Bush's concession at the G8 meeting, under intense pressure from allies, was to accept the principle of a UN framework for negotiating a post-Kyoto agreement, and although refusing to join the EU, Canadian and Japanese commitment to cut emission levels, he agreed that the United States would 'seriously consider' doing so in the future. On this basis Washington was not about to take up a leadership role on climate issues in the final 19 months of the Bush presidency. The administration continued to stress the role of technological innovation in reducing emissions, without recognising the argument that only government-imposed incentives such as energy taxes or cap and trade regimes could make such technology economically viable. Although Bush had moved gradually towards accepting the premise that global warming was a problem, most Republican members of Congress denied that it was even happening – or if it was happening, that human activity was the cause. This level of denial, together with enduring antipathy on the Republican right to the United Nations as an institution, suggested it would remain very difficult to launch the kind of major initiatives in global governance that would tackle the problem. On the other hand, both public-opinion surveys and the general buzz of popular culture – notably, the enthusiastic response to former Vice President Al Gore's Oscar-winning documentary film on the threat from global warming – indicated some readiness on the part of American voters for decisive, and perhaps even somewhat painful, government action. The new Democratic leadership of Congress, meanwhile, faced a dilemma. They could try to enact strong legislation, but it was unlikely to survive a presidential veto or even perhaps the Senate filibuster promised by Oklahoma Republican James Inhofe, who had repeatedly described the idea of man-made global warming as 'the greatest hoax ever perpetuated on the American people'. Under these circumstances, some environmentalists argued that it would be best to use the issue in the 2008 presidential campaign, and then pass more effective legislation for signature by a presumably more sympathetic president.

The limits of the Bush administration's move to the centre were most obvious in the president's continued assertions of broad powers to redefine the laws for holding and interrogating prisoners in the 'war on terror'. These assertions had provoked pushback from Congress and the courts, as well as the State Department and uniformed lawyers in the military services. Yet, with every setback the office of Vice President Cheney had worked to obfuscate the delineation of restraints on presidential power. In an interview on a talk radio programme, Cheney himself had called it a 'no-brainer' to subject terrorist suspects to a 'dunk in the water' to get information out of them. Though he later denied that he was referring to the practice of 'water-boarding' – a form of simulated drowning employed by the Spanish Inquisition and prosecuted by the United States after the Second World War as a war crime – it is hard to imagine what else he might have been talking about.

Many US military officers worried that the administration's relaxed attitudes about the abuse of prisoners had infected American culture to an extent that would compromise future training. In November 2006, US Army Brigadier General Patrick Finnegan, the dean of the US Military Academy at West Point, and three long-time Army and FBI interrogators met with producers and writers of the hit US television drama '24'. Finnegan and his team tried to convince the show's creators that the repeated portrayal of torture perpetrated upon terrorist suspects by the show's main character, federal agent Jack Bauer, propagated the myth that such 'ticking time bomb' scenarios were common and that violent interrogation tactics worked. The popularity of the show was such that it was damaging the Army's attempts to teach its troops that torture was immoral, illegal and ineffective, and that to cross the line was the opposite of heroism.

The torture debate of 2006 and 2007 was shaped in large measure by the US Supreme Court's 29 June 2006 decision in the case of *Hamdan vs Rumsfeld*. The Court declared unconstitutional the military tribunals that had been set up to hear the cases of detainees charged as 'unlawful enemy combatants' and insisted that the Geneva Conventions applied to this class of prisoner. In effect, the Court handed the issue to Congress, which replied after much struggle with the Military Commissions Act, signed into law on 17 October 2006. The act specifically prohibits torture, murder and rape, but does not resolve the problem of which interrogation techniques are to be designated as torture. Moreover, the Bush administration succeeded in limiting the legislation's applicability to Department of Defense personnel, exempting the CIA. So while the new law is stricter in paying heed to the Geneva Conventions, there is still a fundamental confusion, in some ways deliberate, as to what US personnel can and cannot do. A provision of the act gave the president the authority to issue an executive order to serve as a guideline for CIA interrogations, but that order is being fiercely debated and has yet to be issued. The Military Commissions Act also deprived 'unlawful' military combatants of the right to habeas corpus, which prominent senators such as Vermont Democrat Patrick Leahy and Pennsylvania Republican Arlen Specter said they would push to reinstate.

Republicans: facing the abyss?

One reason to assume that the torture debate remains open is that leading Republican candidates for the 2008 presidential election have declined to close it. Only Senator McCain, who was tortured as a prisoner of war in Vietnam, has taken the unequivocal position that the United States should stick to the laws of war and the standards for treating terrorist suspects that governed US military conduct before 11 September 2001. The other leading candidates, including former New York Mayor Rudolph Giuliani and former Massachusetts Governor Mitt Romney, maintained in their televised debates that 'enhanced interrogation' techniques were indispensable for winning the 'war on terror'. (They may have been unaware that 'enhanced interrogation' was a translation of an oft-employed euphemism in Gestapo documents.) Romney said that America should 'double Guantanamo'.

The early months of the campaign thus underlined the unsurprising reality that a sophisticated rethinking of American global strategy was unlikely to be generated by the Republican campaign. Giuliani, in particular, carrying the baggage of liberal positions on such issues as abortion and homosexual rights, staked out a position as early front-runner by casting himself as the '9/11 candidate' – on the basis of his role as New York's mayor on that day – promising to stay on the 'offence' against terrorism. In one extraordinary debate moment, the candidates endorsed the suggestion that tactical nuclear weapons might be employed against Iran's nuclear programme. Nor did the candidates evince anything in the way of second thoughts about the reasons for going to war in Iraq; Romney went so far as to state that the war had been necessary because Saddam Hussein would not admit weapons inspectors into the country – an historical confusion that did not seem to cause him much controversy.

None of them hesitated, however, to criticise the Bush administration's *conduct* of the war, and none showed much interest in associating himself more generally with the unpopular president. All sought to stake out the degree of separation that might give them a chance of not being caught in what *Time Magazine* columnist Joe Klein called the administration's 'epic collapse'.

The collapse continued in 2007 across three broad fronts. Firstly, the political toxicity of the Iraq War was only aggravated by the surge, a military escalation that the public rejected from the start. Two associated scandals brought further woe to the administration. An undercover investigation by the *Washington Post* revealed that severely wounded returning war veterans were being housed and treated in appalling conditions in housing annexes of the Army's Walter Reed Hospital in Washington. Then, in July 2006 President Bush decided to commute the three-year jail sentence of I. Lewis 'Scooter' Libby, a former aide to Vice President Cheney convicted in March of having committed perjury during a prosecutor's investigation of the administration's leaking to newspapers of the identity of an undercover CIA agent, Valerie Plame. Plame was married to former US Ambassador Joseph Wilson, and Libby's trial had documented the degree to which Cheney and others in the administration were obsessed with Wilson's public refutations of the claim that Iraq had sought uranium yellow-cake in Niger – one of the planks in the administration's case for war. Bush had a dilemma. Conservatives were furious that Libby could go to prison for perjury when no prosecution had been pursued for the supposed underlying crime (an argument eerily reminiscent of liberals' defence of President Bill Clinton almost a decade earlier on the charge of perjury about the underlying transgression of extramarital oral sex.) But a pardon or commutation was bound to invite the charge that there were further questions from the prosecutor or Congress that Bush and Cheney preferred Libby not to answer.

The administration was beleaguered on a second front when a series of revelations broke about the Justice Department's firing of nine federal prosecutors across the country. Prosecutors serve at the pleasure of the president, but evidence accumulated that many or most were dismissed after having investigated allegations of wrongdoing by Republican officials, failed to prosecute allegations against Democratic politicians, or failed to prosecute allegations of 'voter fraud'. The first two categories started to look particularly suspicious when it was revealed that from January 2001 until December 2006, of 375 federal investigations into political corruption nationwide, 298 of the targets were Democrats and only 67 were Republicans. The third category touched a raw political nerve in the United States. Since the civil-rights era there has been a stark disparity of interest in voter turnout between the two parties. Democrats have sought a high turnout to bring many first-time voters, often poor and black, to the polls, where they will presumably vote disproportionately for Democrats. Republicans have worried aloud that making the voting process too easy will infect it with fraudulent ballots. The potentially serious consequences of this argument were underlined in the 2000 dispute over Florida's ballot in the presidential election, decided by only a few hundred votes following an aggressive purging of the voter rolls under the state's Republican governor, Jeb Bush. Since then, the Justice Department under Republicans John Ashcroft and Alberto Gonzales has focused intensively on rooting out voter fraud, even though independent studies indicate that the problem is insignificant. Most cases turn out to be inadvertent – a black woman who wrongly thought she was eligible to vote while on probation for the offence of writing a bad cheque; a long-term resident from Pakistan who filled out a voter-registration form handed to him as he applied for a driver's licence. (The woman was jailed for her mistake and the Pakistani deported to Pakistan.)

The third front of administration woes was perhaps the one that was most revealing of the administration's sapped strength. Following failure in 2005 of his efforts to partially privatise the government pensions programme, known as Social Security, President Bush's domestic priority in 2006 and 2007 was for major reform legislation to address the reality of an estimated 12m illegal immigrants in the United States, roughly half of them Mexicans. As governor of Texas, Bush had made a point of emphasising policies that would be seen as welcoming to the state's large Hispanic minority. In the White House, his political adviser Karl Rove believed that reaching out to traditionally Democratic – but predominantly Catholic and presumably conservative – Hispanic voters was a critical element in his plan to engineer a long-term Republican electoral majority. The administration was able to assemble a broad coalition for reform, including traditionally Republican business interests that depended on cheap, often illegal immigrant labour, and West Coast and northeastern liberals who courted Hispanic voters out of both sympathy and political interest. The coalition had one gaping hole, however: Bush's own conservative base.

The immigration package included promises of tougher border control as well as provision for a new category of temporary visas for 'guest workers'. What angered conservatives was its provision for legalising the status of the 12 million. Proponents denied that the provision constituted amnesty – applicants for legalising their status would have to pay a hefty fine as well as back taxes, and go through a lengthy application process that involved a return to their home countries. What they would not have to do, however, was join the queue of applicants for the regular immigration process. The real dilemma was sharp. Proponents argued, convincingly, that it was not within the realm of possibility to deport 12m residents, many of whom had American-born children – to say nothing of the economic consequences of suddenly losing millions of low-wage workers. Opponents argued, just as convincingly, that periodic amnesties – by whatever name – just encouraged the next wave of illegal immigration. As evidence they cited the consequences of the last big immigration reform, during the Reagan administration, under which a reported 2.7m illegal immigrants were granted residency.

It was, perhaps, a bad time for a civil compromise. Heightened economic anxieties among the middle class overlaid a long-standing and more diffuse anxiety about demographic and cultural changes affecting the country. Spanish speakers were more visible in many more states across much more of the country than had been the case in 1986. The rage that could be heard on right-wing talk radio stations reflected, no doubt, an element of bigotry, but also a supreme lack of faith in the government's capacity to do what it said it would do to control America's long southern border. This collapse of faith derived, in part, from the failures of the Iraq War, the incompetence of the federal response to the Hurricane Katrina deluge of the Gulf Coast in 2005, and general disaffection with the Bush administration's performance. In the end, there was more passionate rage from opponents of the measure than there was genuine commitment from supporters. (Many liberals, for instance, were unhappy about creating a class of temporary guest workers.) Bush endured mass defections from his own party, and the bill failed twice – on 7 and 28 June 2007 – to win enough votes in the Senate to close off debate. It was considered, for the foreseeable future, to be dead.

This caused collateral damage to the Republican Party and the presidential ambitions of John McCain. The party was likely to suffer the disaffection of Hispanic voters, not a small problem if one anticipated that their share of the electorate would continue to grow. Bush and the Republicans had done unusually well among these voters in 2000 and 2004, but in 2006 amid the furore over immigration they returned to the Democratic fold. The damage to McCain came from the opposite direction. McCain had a fairly conservative record in the Senate, but also an independent streak: he sponsored campaign-finance reform, proposed government action to curb greenhouse gasses, vehemently opposed the torture or other mistreatment of prisoners, and generally disdained the moralising of the religious right. There had been extremely bad blood between McCain and Bush dating from what McCain considered a smear campaign against him directed by Bush operatives in the 2000 presidential primary in South Carolina.

In 2004 McCain had been courted by his friend, the Democrat John Kerry, as a possible unity-ticket vice presidential candidate, but he decided to stand by the president from his own party. This decision was helped by his strong conviction that, manifest mistakes notwithstanding, the United States had to persevere to victory in Iraq. But it was also the beginning of an expedient courting of the Republican right, including religious leaders such as Jerry Falwell. McCain became the presumed frontrunner for the 2008 Republican nomination by virtue of his high name recognition, his long-standing popularity among independents and some Democrats, and his generally acknowledged status as the new 'establishment' candidate of the kind that the Republican party, as a post-Second World War historical rule, almost always ended up nominating.

Yet it was starting to look, by mid 2007, as though the rule could be broken. The party's right-wing base by now knew him well, and apparently still didn't like him. His hard line on Iraq was negated to some extent by his strong opposition, unique among the leading Republican candidates, to torture. And he inspired intense anger among conservatives because of his support for the immigration bill.

In summer 2007 the McCain campaign reported that it had a meagre $2m in the bank, and would have to start laying off paid campaign staff. In public-opinion polls – admittedly of very limited value so early in the campaign – he consistently lagged well behind Giuliani, the new putative frontrunner. It was possible that Giuliani's position would erode precipitously, however, as voters in the primaries became aware of his liberal positions on social issues. Romney was having a bit more success packaging himself as the conservative candidate, but he faced two big pitfalls: firstly, that he was a Mormon running for the nomination of a party that depended heavily on evangelical Christians who considered Mormonism to be a cult; secondly, that he had his own very recent record of liberal positions on both abortion and gay rights, positions that had been more or less obligatory for his election as governor of liberal Massachusetts. There was a more authentic candidate of the religious right, Kansas Senator Sam Brownback. But Brownback seemed perhaps too religiously oriented to be a convincing national candidate.

Republican dissatisfaction with this field generated some considerable interest in a relative late-comer to the race, former Senator and Hollywood actor Fred Thompson. There was also talk, rather less convincing perhaps, of a political comeback by former House Speaker Newt Gingrich. In general, however, dispassionate Republican observers believed that their party was in trouble. The usual cycles of political alternation suggest that a two-term Republican presidency would be followed by a Democrat. Since the Second World War there have been five Democratic and six Republican presidents – in other words, it is not true that Republicans have naturally dominated the office. They have traditionally been dominant in political fundraising – yet by the second quarter of 2007 Democratic candidates as a whole had raised half again as much in campaign funds as the Republican candidates. Since candidates on both sides were regularly raising tens of millions – 2008 was expected to be the first billion-dollar campaign – the disparity was hardly conclusive, but it did indicate greater enthusiasm on the Democratic side. Democrats were still furious about the 2000 election and angry about Bush and his war. Republicans were weary about being saddled with an unpopular president and a toxic war.

Democrats: a different world?

Democratic Party leaders could look into the Republican Party's abyss and see opportunity. But they could also fall into it. The strategic hole that America found itself in did not have any obvious escape and so constituted a political trap for both political parties.

Both political calculation and the leaders' own national-security instincts meant that leading Democratic presidential candidates would not stray very far in their rhetoric from the Churchillian paradigm. Their views of global threats and the proper responses were more nuanced, to be sure, and included the frequent acknowledgement that international legal order and multilateral institutions were both valuable in themselves and assets for a more effective US foreign policy. They were far more likely than their Republican counterparts, for example, to present mandatory action against global warming as a global and US national-security imperative. At the same time, however, all of the leading Democratic presidential candidates joined their Republican counterparts in declaring that Iran's acquisition of a nuclear-weapons capability would be 'intolerable'. The Democrats were also ostentatiously pro-Israel – or, to be more precise, ostentatiously wary of directly criticising almost any policy that the Israeli government claimed was necessary for Israel's security. From abroad, this lockstep support is often cast in somewhat mystical and sinister – when not overtly anti-Semitic – terms, as the consequence of an all-powerful Israel lobby. The Israel lobby is indeed effective, but a large element of its success is that its arguments fall on the very fallow ground of an intrinsically pro-Israel American body politic. (The institutional lobby itself has moved progressively to the right in recent years, so that its agenda and affinities match more closely to the Republican Party, even though American Jews in general remain overwhelmingly Democratic in their voting habits.)

Such generalisations about an enduringly hawkish Democratic national-security establishment were borne out by the fact the leading candidates continued to lean against a heavy wind from the party's more dovish 'base', which was energised by deep anger over Iraq. Illinois Senator Barack Obama appeared well placed to exploit this anger, given that he was the only leading candidate to have eloquently, and presciently, opposed the Iraq War before it was launched. But even Obama made it his frequent refrain that he did not oppose war, 'just stupid wars'. His much vaunted April 2007 speech in Chicago to unveil a foreign-policy platform was notable in the first instance because of his insistence that US foreign policies under Bush had forfeited the confidence of the rest of the world, and in the second instance because he subordinated the fight against terrorism under a much larger vision of national security. But that vision was not particularly dovish. He called for America to 'lead the world in battling immediate evils and promoting the ultimate good', said that 'no president should ever hesitate to use force – unilaterally if necessary', and promised to raise 65,000 new army troops and 27,000 new marines for overstretched US military forces. The speech drew enthusiastic reviews from the likes of Robert

Kagan, one of the leading writers who defined the twenty-first century version of neo-conservatism.

In the same vein, New York Senator Hillary Clinton gave no hint of leading an American retreat to isolationism. Clinton was steadfast in her refusal to apologise for her 2002 vote authorising President Bush to use force in Iraq, despite the consternation this caused to likely Democratic primary voters. Many commentators assumed that this was a matter of political calculation, but this assumption was based on a misunderstanding of her 'liberal' persona. During her husband's administration, Clinton had often weighed in on the side of proponents of using military force in the Balkans, and she struck up a friendship and quasi-alliance on such matters with Bill Clinton's hawkish secretary of state, Madeleine Albright.

Those military interventions had been generally recognised, at least in retrospect, as Clinton administration successes. The early stages of the 2008 Democratic primary campaign also featured two 1990s flashbacks to controversies that had constituted President Clinton's earliest and most spectacular failures. The first, as it happened, was a failure in which Hillary Clinton had been intimately involved: the effort to fulfil a campaign promise to bring universal health insurance to the United States. In his first year in office, President Clinton had assigned his wife the role of leading a task force on how to end America's isolation as the only wealthy democracy that did not grant its citizens guaranteed access to health care. But lobbyists for private insurance companies mobilised quickly in opposition; Hillary Clinton's plan was pilloried as too complicated, and she was criticised for the secrecy of its formulation and the imperiousness with which she presented it. It went down to defeat in a Democratic-controlled Congress, a setback that helped the Republican takeover of 1994. The effort to institute universal health care, a Democratic priority since the Truman administration, looked moribund for at least another generation. By 2007, however, the inefficiencies and inequalities of the American system were again creating momentum for political action. All of the Democratic candidates were pushing proposals that would at least move the country closer to universal care.

Another Democratic cause that failed in the Bill Clinton administration had made a surprising comeback: for the rights of homosexuals to serve in the US armed forces. In 1993 Bill Clinton had been forced to retreat from his promise to allow homosexuals to serve, falling back to an awkward compromise dubbed 'don't ask, don't tell'. This meant that the military would no longer investigate and prosecute homosexuals on the basis of mere suspicion, but it would, according to its own policy guidelines, 'discharge members who engage in homosexual conduct, which is defined as a homosexual act, a statement that the member is homosexual or bisexual, or a marriage or attempted marriage to someone of the same gender'. That all of the 2008 Democratic candidates confidently promised to get rid of 'don't ask, don't tell' reflected astonishing progress in the acceptance of homosexuals across broad swathes of American society, and particularly among American youth.

There was another cultural taboo, though, that Democrats had learned not to touch. On 16 April 2007 at the Virginia Tech campus in Blacksburg, Virginia, a disturbed student named Seung-Hui Cho went on a shooting rampage that killed 32 people, making it the largest gun massacre in modern American history. Some observers' natural reaction would be to consider that this, like other mass killings from the guns of disturbed but heretofore non-criminal people, might indicate that guns in the United States were too easy to acquire. This indeed had been the position of many Democratic politicians in the not-so-distant past. There had evolved, however, a new political consensus that advocacy of even limited gun-control measures would merely reinforce the perception of Democratic 'liberals' as alien to the values of heartland America. (This emerging caution had gelled with the shock of Al Gore losing, in the 2000 presidential election, his home state of Tennessee.)

In 2006 the Democrats enjoyed an unusual winning streak in these southern or western 'Red States' – as in the victory in the Virginia Senate race of the anti-war populist James Webb, a Vietnam war veteran who had been Ronald Reagan's secretary of the navy. Their position for 2008 looked promising and, in contrast to the Republicans, there was considerable enthusiasm among prospective Democratic primary voters for their field of candidates: led by Obama, an eloquent and attractive young senator and the first black man to have a serious shot at the presidency; frontrunner Clinton, the first woman to have a serious shot, a senator of undoubted experience and shrewdness (though there were worries about the negative reactions she inspired from about half the electorate); and John Edwards, the 2004 vice-presidential candidate, a sunny, liberal populist who lagged in fundraising and national polling, but was maintaining a consistent lead in Iowa, which held the earliest contest and which he hoped might propel him to victory elsewhere. There was also, as of summer 2007, some speculation, albeit dwindling, that Gore might enter the race.

Public anger over Iraq fueled much of the Democrats' strength. It could also explode in their face. The dilemmas that it posed for the opposition party were demonstrated throughout the first half of 2007, as Senate Majority Leader Reid and the new House speaker, Congresswoman Nancy Pelosi from California, tried to make good on their promise to force an end to the war. In February, March and April they struggled for the votes in both chambers to set a deadline for withdrawal, or at least the beginning of withdrawal, of troops. They succeeded by very narrow margins to attach the deadline to the military spending bill, but this provoked President Bush on 1 May to use his veto for only the second time in his presidency. The House and Senate leaders had no stomach for engaging in a budget showdown that would leave them open to the accusation of de-funding troops in the field; in late May they engineered the appropriation of some $100bn for operations in Iraq and Afghanistan, without any timetable for withdrawal. Polls indicated that Congress was becoming as unpopular as the president.

Endgame

Though they held a thin majority in Congress, Democratic leaders did not believe they had the real power to force a change on the president. Supermajorities were required to overturn a presidential veto, or to close off debate in the Senate. Democrats could, if they had the stomach for it, basically close down the military appropriations process, but this route was generally considered political suicide – it had certainly backfired for the House Republicans under Newt Gingrich when they shut down the federal government in a confrontation with President Clinton.

This political mathematics meant that only the defection of large numbers of Republican lawmakers might have an impact. Many of these Republicans were worried about their chances in 2008, and a few started to argue that the troop surge was showing no convincing signs of working. Senator Richard Lugar of Indiana, a leading Republican voice on foreign-policy issues, in June 2007 joined a widening group of Republicans in publicly dissenting from the president's policy. 'Persisting indefinitely with the surge strategy', said Lugar in a Senate floor speech, 'will delay policy adjustments that have a better chance of protecting our vital interests over the long term'. Many analysts said the surge had a built-in expiration date in early 2008, when rotation schedules of overstretched forces made it almost impossible to continue at the same level of deployments. Bush himself had suggested in May, somewhat obliquely, that troops would move to a 'different configuration' after the surge was complete. Asked if there was a 'Plan B', the president replied, 'actually, I would call that a plan recommended by Baker–Hamilton, so that would be a Plan B–H'.

In limited ways, such as in narrowly proscribed discussions with Iran and Syria, the Baker–Hamilton recommendations had already been seeping into administration policy. There had not yet been, however, a decisive shift in strategy. Whatever changes might come in 2008, it appeared very likely that the president inaugurated in 2009 would have, as his or her first order of business, an unfinished war in Iraq.

Canada's Growing International Confidence

Canada's Conservative minority government, led by Prime Minister Stephen Harper, was elected in early 2006 largely on a domestic platform. The priorities on which the Conservative Party had campaigned against the previous Liberal government included the passing of a Federal Accountability Act; reduction in the federal goods and services tax; a crackdown on crime; increased aid for childcare; and waiting-time guarantees for hospital patients. Yet this domestic agenda has been overshadowed by the government's emphasis on expanding Canada's international presence, with new investments in 'hard power' assets and growing involvement in international issues, especially Afghanistan. Harper secured a parliamentary vote to extend until 2009 the mission of Canadian troops in Afghanistan, where 66 military personnel and one diplomat were killed from 2002 to mid 2007.

The renewed focus on international affairs had begun under the Liberal government, and the Conservative government followed its predecessor in acknowledging the urgent need to reinvest in Canada's international role. Harper said in 2006: 'We want Canada to be a player, at home and abroad, on the great challenges of the day.' Echoing the Bush administration, the government has emphasised the need for global promotion of democracy. It was quick to freeze ties with Belarus following that country's controversial March 2006 presidential elections. Its open criticisms of China's human rights record led to acrimony that nearly prevented a bilateral meeting between Harper and President Hu Jintao at the APEC forum in November 2006.

The government sees Canada's military as the primary asset in a more robust international security policy. Budget cuts in the 1990s, and indeed under-funding since the early 1970s, had resulted in the deterioration of key capabilities. Initial efforts to reverse this decline began in the aftermath of the 11 September 2001 attacks on the United States, and were accelerated by Paul Martin as Liberal prime minister. The 2005 Defence Policy Statement (DPS), the most recent strategic guidance document for the Canadian Forces (CF), was largely accepted by the Conservative government, partly due to the continuity provided by General Rick Hillier as chief of defence staff (CDS). Four new commands were assigned operational responsibilities in 2006: an Expeditionary Force Command for CF operations abroad; a Special Operations Command for special-forces operations at home and abroad; a Canada Command for domestic and North American operations; and a Support Command. The DPS also advocated creation of a Special Operations Task Force, including expanded first-tier and newly created second-tier special forces, and a Standing Contingency Group capable of rapid deployment for amphibious operations.

The Conservative Party, which had advocated a 'Canada First' approach to national security and defence, was keen to reform the CF into an expedition-oriented military force. Its approach involved expanded homeland defence, especially with regard to the country's northern Arctic region, as well as the capability to fulfil military obligations in NATO and elsewhere. The importance of expeditionary capabilities could clearly be seen in a C$20.3bn equipment acquisition package announced in June 2006, including a strategic and tactical airlift fleet; in-theatre transport capability to be provided by 14 medium-to-heavy lift helicopters; 2,000 medium transport trucks; and three multi-role Joint Supply Ships (JSS) for support and sealift. However, a leaked draft of a new Defence Capabilities Plan (DCP), which is expected to contain an additional policy statement of the 'Canada First Defence Strategy', raised questions about the long-term commitment to rearming the CF, with apparent plans to reduce platform numbers of the air force and navy. An election promise to acquire three armed heavy icebreakers appeared to have been replaced by plans to acquire a fleet of Arctic patrol vessels, while a proposed Standing Contingency Group with amphibious littoral capability seemed destined to remain a concept for study for the foreseeable future. The draft appeared to sanction further delays in recapitalisation projects: it was not clear that budget funding would be available for replacements for the navy's ageing destroyer and frigate fleet, the army's *Leopard* tanks, and the air force's CF-18 fighters.

Canada has taken a major combat role within NATO's International Security Assistance Force (ISAF) in Afghanistan, and its level of casualties reflects this. A 2,000-strong battle group sent to Kandahar in 2005 has undertaken robust counter-insurgency operations. Heavily armoured *Leopard* tanks have been deployed, and there are also plans to purchase tanks from the Netherlands and lease tanks from Germany. Canada's military strongly supports the mission, but the high costs and operational tempo could drain funds that would otherwise be spent on equipment modernisation, and divert spending from long-term projects to short-term equipment needs. Further escalation of the Afghan conflict could increase casualty rates at a time when popular support for the mission has gradually declined. The Liberal opposition under the new leadership of Stéphane Dion has moved to the left and seems set to keep up pressure on the government on Afghanistan. It is therefore not surprising that Canada has been among those countries urging fellow NATO members to eliminate caveats that set limits on their engagement in combat.

The government's emphasis on Canada's international role is not confined to the military. The Canadian International Development Agency (CIDA) is expected to double aid by 2010 from 2001 levels, including development assistance for Afghanistan totalling C$1bn from 2001 to 2011. The Department of Foreign Affairs and International Trade (DFAIT) had been declining in importance, but Harper overturned an earlier decision to break its component parts into separate departments. An expansion of foreign-intelligence capabilities is a distinct possibility in the near future, either through an expansion of the existing Canadian Security Intelligence Service (CSIS) or the creation of a new Foreign Intelligence Agency.

Canada's confident and less nuanced foreign policy can be clearly seen in a vocal tilt towards Israel. The government took the unusual step of abstaining on three UN resolutions that were critical of Israel in 2006, and it was also the first to suspend funding to the Palestinian Authority, in the amount of C$25m, after Hamas was elected to power. Canada's reaction to the 2006 Israel–Hizbullah conflict was also surprising. The prime minister defended Israel's response as an act of self-defence; even when this support became less strident in light of the escalating Israeli military operations, he still emphasised the plight of civilians in Israel as well as Lebanon. At the 2006 G8 summit in St Petersburg, a Canadian draft statement on the Israel–Hizbullah conflict was largely adopted, and Canada later succeeded in obtaining a less critical resolution on Israel at the Francophone Summit a few months later.

The 2006 Israel–Lebanon crisis highlighted the 'Canada First' requirement to protect Canadian citizens. There were an estimated 40–50,000 Canadians in Lebanon at the time of the conflict. With no military presence to provide lift and support, a sparsely manned embassy and a limited diplomatic presence in Cyprus and Turkey, Canada was ill-prepared to deal with a mass evacuation. However, it reassigned hundreds of government personnel and negotiated maritime and air transport charters. An estimated 15,000 citizens were brought out of Lebanon, the largest evacuation in Canadian history.

There was growing warmth in the Canada–US relationship. A softwood lumber dispute that had been a serious irritant was resolved, while an indefinite extension and a maritime-warning function for the North American Aerospace Defense Command (NORAD) were easily agreed. The government strongly supported efforts to deal with the nuclear ambitions of Iran and North Korea. Canada strongly condemned North Korea's nuclear test in October 2006 and sent its ambassador in South Korea to Pyongyang to press for dismantlement of the nuclear-weapon programme. While lacking the reflexive anti-Americanism of the previous government and keen to improve relations, the current government has, however, displayed strong willingness to defend against any perceived encroachment on Canadian sovereignty. The 'Canada First' emphasis on Arctic sovereignty, evident in plans for new Arctic vessels and surveillance capability, is intended to deter claimants from disputing Canadian territorial sovereignty. The United States remains one of the most important claimants, refusing to recognise the Northwest Passage as internal Canadian waters. Harper, though keen to maintain friendly stability in the Canada–US relationship, was characteristically blunt when the government's territorial claims and Arctic sovereignty plans were questioned by David Wilkins, American ambassador to Canada, in 2006: 'The United States defends its sovereignty and the Canadian government will defend our sovereignty', he said. 'It is the Canadian people we get our mandate from, not the ambassador of the United States.'

The higher priority on defence and a more outspoken stance on international issues indicate new confidence on the international stage. Yet the difficulties of the Afghanistan mission threaten to overshadow future elections and, perhaps eventually, to throw into question Canada's more robust approach. It remains to be seen whether the Conservative government's efforts to reinforce the hard-power foundations of Canada's international security policy will survive unscathed.

Latin America: The Limits of Populism

Latin America's recent wave of elections has been marked by widespread discontent with the Washington-backed liberal economic policies of the past two decades. The democratic leftist leaders brought to power have sought to soften these free-market policies with social welfare programmes that have fallen substantially short of wholesale economic revolution. However, this overall pragmatism has frequently been overshadowed by Venezuelan President Hugo Chávez's radical populist rhetoric and anti-American grandstanding.

The political currency of a more radical stance has been nowhere more evident than in the adoption of similar language by President George W. Bush. Embarking on a March 2007 trip to repair relations with the United States' neglected southern neighbours, Bush invoked the legacy of Bolívar, vowing to 'complete the revolution' for social justice. Washington has sought to counter Venezuela's quest for regional influence by engaging Latin America's moderate left while disengaging from combative discourse with Venezuela. Refusing to be ignored, Chávez launched a shadow tour of the American president, leading anti-Bush rallies in nearby countries.

Venezuela: Chávez and Latin American populism

Chávez's fiery anti-American rhetoric and talent for manufacturing media spectacles has made his radical populism the most prominent, though not the most popular, articulation of Latin American left-wing sympathies. Although Chávez is not the standard-bearer of Latin America's left-leaning governments, his polarising manoeuvres have earned him surprising regional power. Oil resources allot Venezuela disproportionate hemispheric influence, and Chavéz has been able to use radical populism to garner support. Persistent poverty and crime as well as the world's most pronounced inequality plague the region, fuelling angry rejection of the Washington-backed political and economic models dominant during the past 20 years. Chávez's regional ascendance and the appeal of his combative anti-capitalist rhetoric are symptomatic of these fundamental socioeconomic ailments.

The former army colonel's meteoric rise to power grew out of Venezuela's deeply rooted problems of socio-economic inequality and political exclusion. The rigid stability of Venezuela's two-party system, once hailed as the Latin American model, allowed these problems to fester as it masked oil-dependent clientelist structures that bred weak and unresponsive institutions. Sharply falling oil revenues in the 1980s left 80% of the country in poverty, showing the traditional political parties to have squandered over $250 billion in oil wealth since 1958. After entering the national arena with a failed 1992 coup attempt, Chávez took his fight to the ballot box in 1998 where he won a resounding victory with his relentless indictment of Venezuela's oligarchic elite and his revolutionary promises of social justice for the country's poor majority. His nationalist, populist Bolivarian Revolution eschewed the discredited institutions of representative democracy in favour of 'popular democracy' in which the president is directly accountable to the people. Chávez 'refounded' the nation in 1999 with a new constitution, which became the first in a long series of reforms that would concentrate power in the president and reduce institutional checks and balances.

Implementation of the Bolivarian Revolution's social agenda was hindered by the far from revolutionary nature of its sole economic policy: the politicised distribution of oil revenues. With oil prices at less than $10 a barrel, Chávez was forced to pursue the orthodox stabilisation policies he had so vehemently campaigned against. As the economic crisis deepened, so did the poverty of over one million Venezuelans, and the president's approval rating fell from 70% to 30% between 2000 and 2002. Exhibiting political resilience and acumen, Chávez weathered a coup attempt in April 2002, national strikes in 2002–03, and a recall referendum in August 2004. He turned the attempts to oust him into pretexts for purging institutions of disloyal elements and consolidating his power. Windfall oil revenues in 2004 reversed Chávez's political fortunes, allowing him to increase social spending, which in turn contributed to unprecedented growth.

The opposition was left in disarray after the failure of their recall referendum, and Chávez supporters secured control over 21 of Venezuela's 23 governorships as well as the position of mayor of Caracas in the October 2004 regional elections. By the December 2005 legislative elections, the president had extended his control over the Supreme Court, National Electoral Council, and the offices of the ombudsman, attorney general, and comptroller general. The opposition boycotted the elections, handing all 167 National Assembly seats to *chavistas*. All three branches of government were, and remain, in Chávez's hands. Three-quarters of the electorate turned out for the December 2006 elections, in which Chávez scored his largest margin of victory to date with 62% of the vote. Armed with this strong mandate, Chávez vowed to consolidate his self-proclaimed 'Bolivarian Revolution' by ushering in an era of 'twenty-first-century socialism'. Upon his electoral triumph the president announced, 'Long live the preordained popular victory. Long live the reign of socialism', and hailed his victory as 'another defeat for the North American empire' and 'another defeat for the devil'.

Diplomatic belligerence

Chávez has found a huge audience for his combative rhetoric by slating US imperialism as his new enemy. Bush's muted response to the 2002 coup attempt and continued support for Chávez's domestic opposition have fuelled Venezuelan accusations that regime change in Venezuela – including an American invasion – is part of a broader US agenda of Latin American domination. The Bush administration emphatically denies both involvement with the 2002 coup and Chávez's invasion warnings, dismissing them purely as inflammatory rhetoric. Polls show, however, that by the close of 2006 this rhetoric had convinced half of Venezuelans that the United States poses a significant military threat to their country.

Chávez has sought to counterbalance US influence in the region. This effort has centred primarily on Venezuela's extremely close alliance with the United States' hemispheric arch-enemy, Fidel Castro. Chávez similarly warns of US designs for an invasion of Cuba, declaring that in the event of such aggression, 'Venezuelan blood would run in defence of Cuba and its people'. Venezuela has alleviated Cuba's energy crisis with the delivery of 100,000 barrels of oil per day (b/d) and has been refurbishing a Soviet-era refinery, set to open in December 2007, which will transform Cuba into an oil exporter. Chávez has delivered approximately $5bn worth of oil since 2003, providing Cuba with a level of economic health not seen since the Cold War. In return, Cuba has helped Chávez implement his domestic social agenda. The approximately 22,000 doctors that the Castro regime has sent to Venezuela since 2003 have allowed the president to provide free health care to the country's poor. The popular programme has shored up support for Chávez, with November 2006 polls indicating a 74% approval rating among Venezuelans for his health-care policy. Castro's guidance has also allowed Chávez to replicate Cuba's literacy programme, under which approximately 1.5m Venezuelans have learned to read. Furthermore, Cuba sent a delegation in December 2006 to advise the government on the creation of an anti-corruption commission.

The Bolivarian Alternative for the Americas (ALBA), labelled an 'alternative trade agreement', has been the radical duo's counter to the US-backed Free Trade Agreement of the Americas (FTAA) and seeks to address social inequality along with its quest for regional integration. Under ALBA, Venezuela has helped finance the dramatic expansion of Cuba's eye-care programme *Operacion Milagro (Operation Miracle)*, providing service for nearly half a million people in 28 countries. Bolivian President Evo Morales joined ALBA in April 2006, and together the three countries have formed what they refer to as the 'axis of good'.

Venezuelan aid to Bolivia has come to rival that of the United States, as the latter has cut its anti-drug assistance by approximately 25% while Chávez has financed Bolivian production and export of coca, leading the United States to decertify Venezuela as a counter-narcotics ally in September 2006.

Venezuela has cultivated ties with Iran to further distance its foreign policy from American interests. Iranian President Mahmoud Ahmadinejad made his first Venezuelan visit in September 2006, adding 20 new agreements to the two countries' economic accords. Increases in Iranian investment as well as Chávez's defence of Iran's nuclear-power ambitions have made Iran Venezuela's most important ally outside Latin America. During the Iranian president's second visit in January 2007, he and Chávez agreed to fund projects to counter alleged US imperialist efforts in other countries in the region.

Chávez's alliances with Cuba and Iran and the White House's suspicion that the president was sending aid to Colombia's leftist insurgents provoked the Bush administration's May 2006 decertification of Venezuela as an anti-terrorist ally. The decision resulted in the United States banning its already meagre arms sales to Venezuela and ordering closure of the country's military acquisition offices located inside the United States. In April 2007, Venezuela and Cuba lobbed back Washington's accusations of terrorist complicity, requesting that the UN Counterterrorism Committee investigate the United States' release on bail of former CIA operative Luis Posada Carriles, a Venezuelan who has been charged with the 1976 bombing of a Cuban jet. Venezuela has been seeking Posada's extradition since the US government detained him in 2005 for immigration fraud. Both Venezuela and Cuba allege that the United States is in violation of UN Resolution 1373, an antiterrorism provision approved after the 11 September 2001 attacks.

More broadly, armed with Noam Chomsky's *Hegemony or Survival: America's Quest for Global Dominance*, Chávez warned that US imperialism poses a 'threat to the survival of the human race' and referred to Bush as 'the devil' before the UN General Assembly in September 2006. This divisive rhetoric, however, probably contributed to the failure of Venezuela to gain a temporary seat on the UN Security Council. Competition between Venezuela and Guatemala turned into a fierce voting battle in October. US-backed Guatemala was the front runner, but remained unable to secure the two-thirds support necessary to win the seat after 47 rounds of voting. Venezuela staunchly refused to concede, eventually prompting mutual withdrawal in favour of Panama as a compromise.

Mirroring his clientelist distribution of oil revenues domestically, Chávez is estimated to have spent a total of $16–$25bn pursuing support in over 30 countries. He claims to be promoting the Latin American integration envisioned by Bolívar and has attempted to achieve it in part through regional preferential oil agreements. Venezuela has supported allies in Bolivia, Ecuador and

Argentina with energy accords, debt relief and funding for Cuban-led medical care. Venezuela has allied with Argentine President Nestor Kirchner to spearhead creation of a new regional development bank, the Bank of the South, as an alternative to the Inter-American Development Bank (IDB) and the Andean Development Corporation. Bolivia, Ecuador and Paraguay have backed the new bank, and Brazil and Nicaragua may lend their support as well.

Chávez has sought to galvanise support by polarising Latin America into *chavista* and *imperialista* camps. However, his own 'you're either with us or against us' rhetoric, reminiscent of George W. Bush's in the 'war on terror', seems to have made Chávez as unpopular as the US president throughout the region. Opinion polls show that neither is held in high regard. Throughout the region there has been backlash against what many Latin Americans perceive as Chávez's meddling in their domestic affairs. Chávez's support for radical populist candidates in Peru and Mexico damaged these candidates at the polls. Successful candidates Daniel Ortega in Nicaragua and Rafael Correa in Ecuador wisely attempted to distance themselves from Chávez. Even among his allies Chávez's domineering attitude has been unpopular. Many Bolivians, for instance, see him as an unnecessary nuisance, and Brazilians tend to resent his attempts to usurp regional influence.

Venezuela's propensity to involve itself in its neighbours' affairs has added to concerns regarding the country's recent arms build-up. Arms spending rose by 12.5% in 2006, totalling over $4bn since 2005 and making Venezuela the top arms purchaser in Latin America. Among these purchases were 100,000 Kalashnikov assault rifles, 24 fighter jets and 35 helicopters from Russia. Chávez has also secured an agreement with Russia to build a Kalashnikov factory, saying, 'soon we will be selling them to countries in Latin America'. Chávez claims he is preparing for 'asymmetrical warfare' in the event of a US invasion. Having already formed 2m strong workers' councils called the Bolivarian Circles, in 'defence of the revolution', Chávez organised the Francisco de Miranda Front (FFM) in 2003 and the National Reserve and Territorial Guard in 2005 to defend against putative US aggression. These forces, however, are highly politicised and answer directly to the president, making them a potential tool of domestic repression. The FFM had 10,000 members as of mid 2006, and Chávez pledged to arm it with new Kalashnikovs. His military expenditures have caused concern that he will forcibly suppress internal dissent as well as spark a regional arms race.

Domestic dangers

Venezuela's soaring arms purchases have also helped fuel a broader domestic debate over Chávez's spending priorities. Many Venezuelans are frustrated with Chávez's highly publicised distribution of their oil wealth abroad and are less concerned with US imperialism than with domestic ills. Although Chávez has spent $20bn on social programmes since 2004, these funds have largely gone to 'quick fix' redistribution efforts, addressing the immediate needs of the poor without tackling Venezuela's problematic long-term socio-economic problems. UN estimates suggest that, while poverty has finally begun to decrease as a result of continuing economic growth (GDP increased by 9% in 2006), nearly 30% of Venezuelans still live on $2 or less per day. Furthermore, unemployment remains persistently high, at 10–20%, while half of the country's workforce is engaged in the informal sector.

Foremost among domestic concerns, however, is the epidemic of violent crime. Homicides have risen by 67% since Chávez took office in 1999 and have become the leading cause of death for 15- to 25-year-old males in Caracas. According to the UN, Venezuela now has the highest rate of firearm deaths in the world. Popular concern over violent crime increased when several high-profile kidnapping and murder cases led to street protests in April 2006. The government sought to quell public unrest with speedy arrests in these cases, but its aggressive action served merely to highlight the corrupt and inefficient practices of the Venezuelan police and judiciary. Chávez was generally quiet on the issue. Meanwhile, violent crime continued to spiral out of control, as homicides increased by 23% between January and August 2006, providing potent ammunition for Venezuela's fractured opposition ahead of the December presidential elections.

In mid 2006, the opposition managed to consolidate its forces behind a single presidential candidate, Provincial Governor Manuel Rosales. In addition to lambasting Chávez's anti-democratic consolidation of power, Rosales accused the president of fomenting the crime epidemic by politicising law enforcement and the courts. Rosales further contended that 'Chávez nourishes the anarchic forces that are tearing Venezuela apart with a discourse advocating aggression on all fronts'. Chávez's weakest issue in the presidential campaign was security, as even 75% of his supporters disapproved of his stance on crime. Rosales managed to garner 38% of the vote in the December election, a significant showing given Chávez's control over all the instruments of government and his populist pre-election spending sprees.

Following the December 2006 presidential elections, Chávez used his renewed mandate to further concentrate power. On 31 January 2007, the *chavista*-filled National Assembly passed a series of 'enabling laws' allowing the president to govern by decree for the next 18 months. Chávez thus had greater authority to circumvent the democratic institutions over which he had already consolidated power. The president announced his intention to amend Venezuela's constitution to allow for his indefinite re-election and embarked on a campaign – including recall referendums against Rosales as governor and Bareta Mayor Henrique Capriles – to weed out any potential contenders for power. But this strategy may backfire by uniting them instead. In response to Chávez's post-election power grab, leading opposition members joined Rosales's party, A New Time. With Rosales at the helm, the opposition has rallied together to oppose Chávez's attempt to shut down Radio Caracas Television (RCTV), which has long been critical of his government. Chávez declared he would not renew RCTV's licence in March 2007 despite the fact that the licence does not expire until 2020. Various international organisations, including the Organisation of American States (OAS), denounced the move as undemocratic.

Chávez has also attempted to tighten his grip on his supporters. At the start of his new term, he removed Vice President José Vincente Rangel and Minister of Justice and the Interior Jesse Chacón, both seasoned and respected politicians and the last relatively independent voices in the cabinet. Additionally, Chávez has sought increased control over Venezuela's fragmented party politics by transforming the loose coalition of parties supporting him into a single entity, the United Socialist Party of Venezuela. Several of these parties, however, are resisting the move. Ultimately, Chávez's seizure of political power may over-step his mandate. Venezuelans remain among the region's strongest supporters of democracy, and even many chavistas are wary of Chávez's attaining absolute or indefinite power. Rather than addressing rampant crime, unemployment or inequality, 'twenty-first-century socialism' appeared to entail little more than a series of nationalisations. Resistance to these autocratic measures will undoubt-edly increase if Chávez continues to fail to remedy the socio-economic problems of the Venezuelan people.

Along with solidifying plans to nationalise Venezuela's banking system and its electricity and telecommunications sectors, Chávez's government took over operations of foreign oil companies on 1 May 2007. Chávez couched his decree in the rhetoric of economic nationalism he has frequently employed to threaten US oil security and denounce Western oil companies. To this end, Chávez has courted Iranian investments and sought to expand oil exports to China. In the short term, however, Venezuela cannot afford to abandon the US market or evict oil companies, both of which provide the president with the oil revenues he depends upon to finance his Bolivarian Revolution.

Indeed, the state-owned PDVSA's oil production has declined from 3.5m to 2.5m b/d under the Chávez government, in part because Chávez has replaced its professional staff with cronies. In addition, his direct personal control over PDVSA has created an unstable investment climate which has discouraged foreign oil companies from funding research into processing Venezuelan super heavy crude or exploration of its oil fields. The president is looking to expand operations into the lucrative Orinoco Belt. That area, where foreign oil compa-nies are active, produces approximately 600,000 b/d and has the potential to make Venezuela the world's largest holder of proven oil reserves, ahead of Saudi

Arabia. Though most of the foreign oil companies are likely to stay in Venezuela and consent to contracts making them minority partners, they may be inclined to limit the extent to which they provide the country much-needed future investment and technical expertise. Additionally, PDVSA is already overstretched by joint energy ventures abroad, suffers from lack of re-investment as profits are distributed to social programmes, and is plagued by mishaps at its refineries. Taking over operations in the Orinoco Belt may prove a dangerous over-extension of the already ailing company.

On balance, Chávez's oil-rentism appears unsustainable. As a consequence, he may run short of the material resources required to shore up his political base in the absence of ameliorating the country's fundamental socio-economic problems. Lacking adequate channels of democratic representation, Venezuelans may be left with few viable alternatives for voicing their opinions and take their discontent to the streets. The potential for mass mobilisations to turn violent was evidenced in January 2007, when the police killing of a 17-year-old boy in a Caracas slum provoked a mob to burn down the police station in protest. Such events, in turn, may spark wider and more intense violence due to Chávez's militarisation of the political arena.

The Brazilian alternative

Brazilian President Luiz Inácio da Silva (generally known as 'Lula') staged a remarkable political recovery in 2006 after his administration was tarnished by the country's worst corruption scandal in a dozen years. Due to the scandal, Lula failed to secure the presidency in the first round of voting on 1 October 2006. However, he handily defeated his opponent, Geraldo Alckmin of the Brazilian Social Democratic Party, with 61% of the vote in the 29 October run-off, and by his inauguration on 1 January 2007, his popularity rating had risen to 71%.

Lula is Brazil's first working-class president, and the resilience of his popularity has been due, in large part, to the significant strides he has made against socio-economic inequality over the course of his first four-year term. He has kept Brazil's economy stable and inflation low, creating 7m jobs, while engaging in targeted poverty-reduction programmes such as *Bolsa Familia* (family fund), which has benefited 11m recipients. Lula is the most popular president in Brazilian history, and expectations for his second term are high, with 60% of the population believing it will be more successful than his first.

Serious problems remain, however, as sluggish growth, corruption, crime and poor education make some Brazilians frustrated with the slow pace of progress. Lula began his second term promising 5% growth in 2007, further poverty and inequality reduction, and a decrease in violent crime he labelled 'terrorism'. Violence directed by imprisoned gang leaders in São Paulo killed over 200 people in 2006. During the week preceding the presidential inauguration, violence in Rio de Janeiro killed at least 20 and the country was horrified by the news that eight people were burned alive in a bus. The political and economic reform needed, however, will be difficult to push through the country's fractious Congress.

The president's alliance with the Partido do Movimiento Democrático Brasileiro (PMDB) has helped him to secure a two-thirds majority in the lower house of Congress and a simple majority in the Senate. Several PMDB legislators, however, insist they will remain in the opposition, and in general there is little party discipline. Support from Lula's Partido dos Trabalhadores (PT) is also erratic, as the party is divided into several factions, and conflicts between the PMDB and the PT threaten to override the president's agenda both in Congress and in his own cabinet. Furthermore, many members of the PT felt betrayed by Lula's conservative economic policy and oppose the package of reforms his Acceleration Programme (PAC) has proposed. Lula has thus been forced to lobby for support among members of the opposition, which has caused even greater dissention among the ranks of his PT.

Lula's most spirited opposition has come from the landless movement (MST). In June 2006, for instance, they led an occupation of the congressional building in which they destroyed property in protest at the slow pace of land reform. Lula's general support for land reform, however, led the MST to call a 'truce' with his government ahead of the October elections. They have since resumed their battle with the government, and in April 2007 organised protests in 15 states and seized land in ten more. Past actions by the landless movement have sought to speed up reform, but recently the MST has begun questioning the commitment of Lula himself. They contend that his administration has inflated land reformation statistics, is protecting the interests of the rich by only redistributing land under state control rather than privately held properties, and is supporting agribusiness with its ethanol policy, which benefits sugar plantations.

Lula's ethanol policy, however, is unlikely to be changed by the landless movement because it is the key to Brazil's quest to increase its international standing. The country's ethanol production took on renewed importance in January 2007, when the United States shifted course in energy policy and President Bush launched a plan to use biofuels to reduce US oil consumption by 20% by 2017. US–Brazilian relations have flourished in recent months as the countries partner over ethanol production. The presidents discussed the future of such a partnership twice in March, when Bush visited Brazil and Lula became the first South American leader to visit Camp David in 15 years.

The Bush administration, furthermore, has placed ethanol production at the centre of its Latin American policy, and seeks to undermine Chávez's oil diplomacy with ethanol diplomacy, particularly in Central America and the Caribbean. Brazilians have been frustrated with the way in which Venezuela has managed to eclipse Brazil as the most prominent South American voice despite Brazil's status as South America's largest country and largest economy, and many have criticised Lula's conciliatory stance towards Chávez. Lula has endeavoured to influence Venezuela through engagement, supporting its bid for a rotating seat on the UN Security Council and spearheading the process that made it a full member of Mercosur in July 2006. Yet Chávez has caused several problems for Brazil, as he backed the nationalisation of the Bolivian hydrocarbon industry, in which Brazilian state-owned company Petrobras was an investor, and has politicised Mercosur.

Lula has attempted to minimise the impression of weakness vis-à-vis Chávez without antagonising him. In January 2007, he joined with President Néstor Kirchner of Argentina in warning Chávez that authoritarian measures in Venezuela could damage the international credibility of Mercosur as a whole, and in April Lula forced Chávez to back off from his indictment of ethanol production ahead of a regional energy summit that was held by Chávez in Venezuela. Additionally, Lula has failed to support Venezuela's plans for a Bank of the South and a South American gas integration scheme. On 26 April 2007, Lula took trips to Chile and Argentina in order to shore up alliances in an effort to prevent the radical populist agenda of Chávez and his counterparts from hurting Brazilian interests in the region. Bolstered by the prospects of ethanol diplomacy, Lula appears to be regaining Brazil's hemispheric leadership position, and thus strengthening the prospects for a leftist alternative to Chávez's radical populism and oil-brokered regional dominance.

Bolivia's grassroots indigenism

Bolivian President Evo Morales has emerged as Chávez's strongest South American ally. Venezuelan oil revenues distributed to La Paz have bolstered Morales's socio-economic policies as well as providing a measure of insulation from US influence. Morales's 'revolutionary' agenda has included nationalisation, land reform and a new constitution. Chávez has been a source of often-unsolicited advice on such matters. Yet the reforms underway in Bolivia emerged independently of Chávez. Furthermore, the indigenist framework Morales espouses has made advances where both Chávez's Bolivarian Revolution and Latin America's leftists more generally have failed: in the articulation of a coherent ideological alternative to the Washington-backed political and economic models of the past decades.

Much like Chávez, Morales rose to power in Bolivia primarily because of his promises to rectify the consistent failures of the country's highly imperfect democracy to improve fundamental social, economic and political problems. Despite possessing Latin America's second-largest gas reserves, Bolivia remains South America's poorest country, with over two-thirds of its population mired in poverty. The brunt of this poverty is borne by indigenous Bolivians, who make up 70% of the population.

An increasingly violent social protest movement has emerged in Bolivia in recent years, characterised by the mobilisation of radical indigenous groups, rejection of the traditional political elite, opposition to the neoliberal economic model, and resistance to US-backed drug-eradication policies. Appealing to each of these elements, Morales became a formidable opposition leader, particularly as he began to emphasise his Aymara lineage. In June 2005, social movements toppled their second president in 20 months, clearing the way for Morales's victory in the December 2005 elections. Morales's radical populist rhetoric won him 54% of the vote, making him Bolivia's first indigenous president and giving him the strongest mandate of any leader since Bolivia's return to democracy in the mid 1980s. His Movement Towards Socialism (MAS) won a majority in the legislature's lower house and fell just short of a majority in the senate.

Morales originally represented the interests of the coca-growing Chapare region, but he has increasingly claimed the mantle of a national indigenous leader and sought to lead a 'peaceful revolution' on behalf of Bolivia's impoverished and long-excluded indigenous majority. Morales's indigenist rhetoric has helped to reinvigorate struggles for native sovereignty throughout the region, particularly since increasing numbers of Latin Americans are beginning to identify themselves as indigenous. Rather than being imposed from above like Chávez's Bolivarian Revolution, Bolivian indigenism emerged from the masses and takes its cues not from the president's arbitrary agenda but from the guiding principles of the country's numerous indigenous communities and bitter memories of hundreds of years of foreign exploitation of natural resources. On Morales's hundredth day in office, 1 May 2006, he ordered troops to seize natural-gas fields as he decreed the nationalisation of Bolivia's gas sector and gave foreign companies 180 days to sign new contracts or leave the country. Contract renegotiations were already underway, but the president's grandstanding successfully boosted his declining domestic support from 68% to an unprecedented 81%. On 28 October 2006, just before the deadline set by Morales, the oil companies signed new contracts giving a state-owned company a majority share in all projects, restoring the president's approval ratings to over 60% after another slump.

According to the Bolivian government, the new terms will net Bolivia $4bn in annual gas revenues by 2010. But this victory did not come without significant conflict over and mismanagement of the nationalisation process. Technical problems and opposition foot-dragging delayed legislative ratification of the new contracts until 23 April 2007, and that occurred only after Morales threatened to go on hunger strike if the process was not expedited. Additionally, Morales's actions have soured Bolivia's relations with Brazil and have endangered the flow of gas to Argentina, threatening to curtail the benefits to Bolivia from its central location in the event of regional energy integration.

Other industries have become political battlegrounds as well. State-employed and independent miners clashed in the mining area of Haununi in early October 2006, leaving 16 dead and prompting Morales to nationalise Bolivia's mining sector. Later that month, after meeting with resistance from privately owned mining corporations, the president backed off his proclamation, citing lack of funds to carry out the project. Morales's supporters began to clamour about the slow pace of his natural resource nationalisation efforts, which encouraged him to accelerate the programmes in January 2007. He proclaimed the mining sector would be fully nationalised by the end of the year, and in February 2007 he deployed troops to seize a Swiss tin-smelting plant. Morales sought to further placate accusations that he was not moving quickly enough in April 2007 by decreeing the nationalisation of the telecommunications sector.

A mere two weeks after nationalising Bolivia's hydrocarbon sector, Morales began what his administration hailed as the most profound land reform in the country since the country's leftist revolution in 1952. In keeping with indigenous practices, lands are to be distributed communally rather than individually, which may facilitate the preservation of indigenous community structures rather than subverting them as other land reforms throughout Latin America have done. The government announced it would redistribute 12m state-owned acres before proceeding to privately held lands deemed unproductive by the state. Officials say that a total of 35m acres, approximately 13% of the country's area, could be reallocated to 2.5m people, or about 28% of the population, during the five years remaining in Morales's term.

While gas nationalisation enjoys wide support, land reform is a bitterly divisive issue. The government's May 2006 announcements promptly sparked hostile land takeovers by landless citizens as well as opposition protests among the country's wealthier people. The issue ignites the regional hostilities between the lighter-skinned residents of Bolivia's relatively opulent eastern lowlands and the impoverished indigenous communities of its Andean highlands. Most of the land under threat of redistribution is in the eastern states, where landowners not only seek to protect their private property but also to prevent an influx of residents from the highlands. Morales's primary opposition is from the eastern states of Santa Cruz, Tarija, Pando and Beni, which form a crescent-shaped region known as the 'Media Luna'. These states voted for greater regional autonomy in a July 2006 referendum, and they insist that land reform be implemented at the local level. Opposition senators sought to block the president's land-reform bill with a legislative boycott, but Morales called up two alternates from opposition parties to replace the striking senators, provide a quorum, and hold the vote with a MAS majority in the chamber. The opposition denounced the move as unconstitutional; nevertheless, the bill passed in November 2006 as thousands of indigenous protesters descended on La Paz.

Regional and racial divides have been similarly inflamed by Morales's promise to 'refound' the country with a new constitution enshrining indigenous mechanisms of governance. MAS fell short of a two-thirds majority in the Constituent Assembly elected in July 2006 to rewrite the constitution. The party then attempted to seize control of the assembly by declaring that a simple majority was sufficient to pass amendments rather than the two-thirds majority previously mandated. The power grab ignited fears that the president and his party sought to sideline middle-class and non-indigenous Bolivians altogether, and opposition deputies walked out on 1 September as they accused MAS of orchestrating an 'institutional coup'. A compromise was eventually reached in February 2007, but not before mass protests and violent clashes occurred over issues of regional autonomy.

Further, several regional governors denounced Morales as a threat to democracy in November 2006, whereupon he requested from Congress the power to sack uncooperative governors. An enormous protest effort ensued. Secessionist groups gained prominence despite their minority standing in the movement for autonomy, and the possibility of armed conflict loomed. Regional governor Manfred Reyes Villa announced in December that he would hold a referendum in Cochabamba to reconsider regional autonomy, which had been voted down by a small margin the previous July. Morales denounced the measure as unconstitutional and government supporters took to the streets in Cochabamba in an attempt to oust the governor. Protesters set fire to the seat of government and clashed with opposition forces, leaving two dead and over 60 wounded. Morales deployed troops to Cochabamba in January 2007. Facing criticism from both sides over the conflict, however, he adopted a more conciliatory tone toward opponents and sought to resolve the Constituent Assembly dispute.

When Venezuelan ambassador Julio Montes indicated that Venezuela might intervene militarily in the event of a secessionist crisis, Senator Oscar Ortiz denounced Morales's relationship with Chávez, saying that Bolivia had become a client state of Venezuela. Nevertheless, during the November 2006 senate boycott, Morales pushed through a military cooperation accord with Venezuela which could provide Bolivia with up to $47m in military assistance. Such aid has been used to increase the military presence in Bolivia's eastern lowlands, fuelling fears that Morales is building up his military in order to repress internal dissent. More generally, Venezuelan aid to Bolivia now rivals the $120m provided by the United States, which has long been the country's largest donor. Washington has decreased its anti-drug aid to Bolivia by 25% for 2007, and has threatened to let crucial trade preferences lapse while Chávez has poured assistance into the country and signed numerous economic accords. Venezuela provided $15m in

March 2007 for emergency flood assistance to Bolivia, dwarfing the $1.1m contributed by the United States. Bolivia has thus become more heavily dependent on alliance with Venezuela while reducing its susceptibility to Washington's disapproval of Morales's 'zero cocaine, but not zero coca' policy.

Chávez, furthermore, has helped his Bolivian counterpart 'industrialise' coca, much to the United States' vexation. In May 2006, the two South American presidents announced their intention to invest an initial $1m in research towards commercialising coca. Morales launched the construction of the first of two Venezuelan-financed coca-processing factories in December 2006, and Chávez has promised to purchase the goods produced. Venezuela also undoubtedly footed the bill for Cuba to send an investigative mission to Bolivia to explore the plant's medicinal benefits, which could lead to future pharmaceutical production and export of coca products. Such trade is prohibited by a 1961 UN resolution banning commerce in all forms of coca, but Morales hopes to challenge this prohibition. His argument is that coca is a traditional indigenous resource, cocaine a Western problem. The government has forgone the forced-eradication policies promoted by the US which led to numerous deadly conflicts and has replaced them with negotiated eradication efforts which seek to productively involve coca-growing communities. While Morales's coca policy has aggravated Washington, it has not placated all of Bolivia's coca growers, or *cocaleros*. The legal limit on coca crops is 12,000 hectares, but the UN estimates that this leaves an additional 13,000 hectares of illegal crops in the country. Efforts to eradicate unauthorised crops in the Yungas led 30 *cocaleros* in September 2006 to seize government offices in La Paz and hold officials hostage in protest.

The mobilisation of disaffected coca growers highlights the increasing pressure Morales faces from within his own constituency. The president has largely resisted redistributive spending of natural resource revenues, but this stance has left many Bolivians upset that nationalisation has led to little poverty relief. Radical protests on 2 February 2007 articulated this sentiment, calling for 'real nationalisation' of the hydrocarbons sector. Similarly, frustration with the slow pace of reform has created incentives for Morales to subvert the democratic process in order to push through legislation and produce results. Some of his more radical supporters are not overly concerned with the purity of a process which they believe has only benefited the elite over the years, but his machinations may produce backlash among his followers if they view him as using the instruments of government to further his own political interests.

Having raised impossibly high expectations in a country overdue for sweeping changes, Morales will have to focus on surviving the term at hand. His priorities are likely to be keeping a lid on secessionist tendencies in Media Luna and developing a functional working relationship with opposition politicians. The primary threat to the president's stability will come from discontent within the ranks of his supporters. While Morales has articulated an indigenist frame-work for Bolivian reform, it remains unclear whether he will be able to implement this vision on the federal level and within the constraints of the global economy. Unless he can forge effective avenues for channelling the discontent of both his enemies and allies, he will surely face the mass mobilisation of Bolivia's social-protest movement which he himself used to destabilise former governments.

Colombia's civil war

If the Bush administration may be accused of neglecting Latin America during its 'war on terror', Colombia surely has been the exception to the rule. Conservative President Alvaro Uribe, a staunch ally in US-led drug-eradication efforts, won re-election in May 2006 following a constitutional amendment allowing for consecutive presidential terms. His second term, however, has been beset by an unfolding scandal revealing connections between the president's supporters and Colombia's brutal paramilitary groups. The 'para-politics' scandal has damaged Uribe's personal credibility in the Democrat-controlled US Congress, where his close relationship with Bush has failed to protect him from threats to Colombian aid and trade agreements.

In many ways, the scandal is the result of Uribe's very success in demobilising the 30,000 fighters under the umbrella paramilitary organisation United Self-Defence Forces (AUC). Paramilitary chiefs have, in the past, bragged that they controlled a third of Congress and evidence of such connections was uncovered when the military seized the personal records of a top paramilitary commander last year. The diligence of the Supreme Court and attorney general's office in pursuing the investigation and prosecution of officials with paramilitary ties is a credit to Uribe's efforts to restore the rule of law in the notoriously lawless country. Over 25,000 Colombians have come forward as victims of paramilitary violence, and it is likely that deeper government–paramilitary collusion will be exposed as demobilised fighters make voluntary confessions in order to reduce their sentences. Salvatore Mancuso became the first top paramilitary leader to do so in January 2007.

The president's former chief of secret police, Jorge Noguera, was arrested in February 2007 on charges that he leaked information on union leaders to paramilitaries. The charge came at an inopportune time for Uribe, as criticism appeared to be escalating over the more than 800 deaths of labour organisers during his first administration. Disclosures about the trade-union killings have given ammunition to Democrats in the US Congress seeking to block the free-trade agreement President Bush signed with Colombia. The Colombian attorney general is pursuing the extradition of eight businessmen from the US-based coal company Drummond, as well as investigating Chiquita Brands, the fruit company.

In April 2007, US Senator Patrick Leahy suspended $55.2m in military aid in response to a leaked CIA document alleging that Colombian army chief General Mario Montoya collaborated with paramilitary organisations in operations against the Revolutionary Armed Forces of Colombia (FARC), Colombia's main leftist insurgency. Montoya is the highest-ranking official to be implicated in the scandal, is a close ally of Uribe, and has been a key partner of the US Department of Defense in carrying out the counter-insurgency and counter-narcotics programme known as Plan Colombia. Currently 80% of Plan Colombia aid, which has totalled $4.5bn since 2000, is directed toward the military. While the US Congress is unlikely to cut aid drastically, it may direct it more towards social and economic assistance in Plan Colombia follow-on programmes.

By mid 2007, 14 legislators and dozens of local and regional officials, most of them Uribe supporters, had been arrested on charges that they collaborated with paramilitaries, and Uribe's foreign minister was forced to resign after members of her family were implicated. None of these para-political scandals had been traced directly to Uribe, but in June 2007 video footage surfaced of the president shaking hands with a known paramilitary leader in 2001. Previously he had sworn he had never had contacts with the paramilitaries.

Allegations against Montoya, perhaps more importantly, threaten to further erode the military's domestic credibility. The Colombian Armed Forces have been embroiled in scandals since the revelation that the May 2006 killing of ten police anti-drug officers was not, as previously thought, a military mistake but rather the deliberate act of soldiers working with paramilitary drug traffickers, a widespread practice. Furthermore, the military has been accused of murdering civilians and disguising their corpses as FARC guerrillas in an attempt to claim they have exacted high guerrilla casualties.

The military's credibility is of the utmost importance, in terms of both waging war against FARC and keeping FARC from recruiting citizens angry over military abuses and paramilitary ties. Uribe's 'Plan Patriota' pushed the guerrillas out of the cities and has been responsible for enormous improvements in Colombian security, with marked declines in kidnappings, murders and terrorist attacks. FARC, however, has been engaged in a ruthless counter-offensive since 2005 and stepped up attacks during the 2006 elections and the start of Uribe's second term. It has become increasingly evident that a military defeat of FARC is unlikely, and support has been growing for negotiating a prisoner swap. Persistent FARC attacks, however, have made the Uribe administration unwilling to negotiate with the guerrillas, and consistent military advances will be necessary to bring FARC to the bargaining table.

Alleged paramilitary infiltration of government institutions has become particularly worrisome as evidence has emerged that, though disarming, the paramilitary organisations are using their networks to continue to profit from criminal activity. Promisingly, however, the left-wing Polo Democratico Independiente (PDI) has been growing in influence as PDI Senator Gustavo Petro has diligently led the attack on government–paramilitary connections. The rising prominence of the PDI is also indicative of the need for Colombian government to follow up its security successes with socio-economic development. The coercive arm of the state has extended its reach as the government has made territorial gains against FARC. The president's popularity remains high, with around 70% approval, and despite the paramilitary scandal Uribe appears compelled to focus on consolidating his victories by expanding the reach of political and economic government institutions over the course of his second term.

Argentina's continuing political evolution

The most important elections of the year for Latin America will take place in Argentina in October 2007. President Néstor Kirchner said in July that he would not stand, leaving the way clear for his wife, Senator Cristina de Fernández Kirchner, to run to succeed him. She was expected to be the front runner.

Kirchner was elected in 2003 with a mere 22% of the vote and without a genuine mandate after former president Carlos Menem withdrew from the run-off. However, his remarkable success in guiding Argentina out of financial ruin after its 2001 economic collapse has earned him enormous popularity. This support has eroded somewhat since January 2007, when the Kirchner administration tampered with inflation statistics, but the president remains popular. Former Finance Minister Roberto Lavagna, who declared his candidacy on 5 January 2007, has emerged as the primary contender for office. He is trying to build an anti-Kirchner coalition, courting the centre-right Propuesta Republicana, the Union Civica Radical and a new party (formed in November 2006) of dissident Peronists called Peronismo de Pie. Lavagna was fired by Kirchner in 2005 but claims credit for pulling the country out of economic crisis. He has an approval rating of only around 10%, yet if he could unite Argentina's dispersed opposition, he could pose a serious challenge.

Law and order has emerged as the president's primary weakness. While reported crimes purportedly declined by 3% in 2006, the year witnessed a wave of shocking high-profile incidents in Buenos Aires which fuelled massive anti-crime protests. In his effort to promote the rule of law through respect of human rights, Kirchner pledged he would not use force to quell the protests. His ardent adherence to this admirable vow has, however, created frustration among many Argentines, as the administration has stood by while social protest groups frequently erect roadblocks and engage in other tactics creating disorder. Additionally, the president has refused to intervene as protesters impede Uruguayan paper-mill construction on the border, damaging relationships with Argentina's neighbour and Mercosur partner.

Kirchner has, however, chosen to highlight the respect for the rule of law by diligently prosecuting the human-rights abuses of Argentina's 'Dirty War' (1976–83). In 2005 the Supreme Court annulled the amnesties granted by Menem, and over 200 former military officers are now charged with crimes against humanity. Kirchner's pursuit of justice has been extremely popular. In a manoeuvre calculated to capitalise on this popularity, Kirchner berated the judiciary in March 2006 for its slow progress and accused members of deliberately delaying justice. Yet, against his best intentions, the move merely provoked rebuke by the judiciary and highlighted a different sort of law-and-order problem: undemocratic concentration of executive power. In February 2006, Kirchner restructured the Magistrates' Council to increase his control over judicial nominations, and he has frequently bypassed Congress with executive decree-laws.

Kirchner also increased his populist profile by strengthening his ties with Venezuela and antagonising the Bush administration, moving himself farther from the political centre. In February 2007 he denounced US diplomatic overtures encouraging him to 'contain' Chávez and instead voiced his wholehearted support for Chávez and signed numerous accords with Venezuela. The following month he allowed Chávez to stage an anti-US rally in Buenos Aires when President Bush was visiting Uruguay. Venezuela has bought $3.5bn of Argentine bonds, and Kirchner's support for Chávez will certainly secure his assistance in the event of an Argentine energy crisis or shortfalls in gas supplies from Bolivia. Unlike other leaders in the region, Kirchner may benefit politically from his alliance with Chávez. An autumn 2006 Latinobarometro poll showed that Argentine support for Chávez is the highest in the region after Venezuela and the Dominican Republic, while Argentine support for Bush is the lowest in the region.

Peru: better governance at last?
Peruvian voters opted for the moderate populism of former president Alan García over the radical ethno-nationalism of Venezuelan-backed Ollanta Humala in a June 2006 presidential run-off. During García's first presidency (1985–90), his populist policies led to hyperinflation and economic collapse. The crisis paved the way for the rise of Alberto Fujimori's autocratic regime. Yet fears of another authoritarian presidency and resentment over Chávez's interference eroded Humala's support, helping to give García another shot at governance. García vows he has learned from the mistakes of his first term and now seeks to emulate Latin America's moderate left.

Populist resurgence in Peru reflects the failure of Alejandro Toledo's highly unpopular administration to translate the country's considerable macroeconomic gains into tangible benefits for the poor majority. Toledo's political ineptitude, furthermore, precluded reforms to democratically incorporate excluded sectors. Humala's radical populist agenda was most popular among these long-neglected populations. He won two-thirds of the vote in Peru's Andean highlands, home to deeply impoverished indigenous and *mestizo* communities. Meanwhile, García won majorities in the coastal regions and Lima where the benefits of economic growth have been concentrated. García's narrow five-point margin of victory in the country as a whole indicates the extent to which Peru is divided.

García has sought to safeguard the country's economic successes by continuing Toledo's free-market policies. He supports the free-trade agreement with the United States which Peru ratified in June 2006 under the previous administration, and he has strongly lobbied the US Congress to ratify it as well, though ratification appeared far from certain as of summer 2007. On the home front, he has attempted to foster an investment-friendly climate with the appointment of a finance minister known for his fiscal conservatism, backed off a campaign promise to raise mining taxes, and reduced bureaucratic business hurdles. Additionally, García has pledged to assist his middle-class supporters by making low-interest credit accessible to the country's small businesses.

García has also tried to distribute economic gains more widely. Upon taking office, he slashed his salary along with those of senior officials, and de-funded frivolous items such as presidential jet fuel, whiskey supplies and the inaugural ball. The new president said he would redistribute the $400m he hoped to save in the first six months to impoverished Andean communities and slums in the capital. He also announced that $1.6bn would be invested in roads, schools and health clinics for the rural poor during his first 17 months in office.

García has voiced interest in sweeping reforms in the judicial, health, security and tax sectors, though he is also undoubtedly seeking to defuse opposition demands, led by Humala, for a constituent assembly to reconstruct the entire state. Implementation of reforms will likely prove difficult, as García's APRA party holds only 39 of 120 congressional seats. APRA also fared poorly in local elections in November 2006, and the García administration faces increasing pressure from regional corporations. César Alavarez Aguilar, governor of the department of Ancash, has led the struggle for decentralisation, threatening strikes and protests if the central government does not acquiesce. Indeed, the first year of García's presidency has been plagued by demonstrations, often violent, from regions producing mineral wealth, oil and coca.

While García was initially conciliatory toward coca growers, escalating drug-related violence has moved him to toughen his stance. The violence characterising organised drug-related crime in Colombia and Mexico has become prevalent in Peru, and in July 2006 Federal Judge Hernán Saturno Vergara, who was presiding over a case against a Mexican drug cartel, was assassinated. Coca production rose by 38% last year. García once again faces destabilisation from the resurgent Maoist guerrilla organisation Shining Path (Sendero Luminoso), which instigated the Peru's internecine civil conflict in 1980; this time, though, the organisation has replaced its political aims with a profit-making agenda, threatening to import to Peru the narco-terrorism currently plaguing Colombia.

Ecuador's quest for stability

On 26 November 2006, Rafael Correa became Latin America's fifth leftist president elected in a little over a year. The US-educated economist and former finance minister rose to electoral prominence on a radical populist platform resembling that of Hugo Chávez. In the 15 October 2006 general election, Correa came in just behind banana magnate Alvaro Noboa, whose traditional variety of populism involved promises of grandiose social-welfare policies while maintaining a pro-American, pro-free-trade stance. After his first-round defeat, Correa toned down his radical populist rhetoric, distanced himself from Chávez, made conciliatory gestures toward the United States and international financial institutions and sought to reassure foreign investors. Focusing on his domestic political agenda, Correa won 56.67% of the vote in the November run-off.

While his presidency remains a boon to Venezuela's regional agenda, Correa has pragmatically sought to maintain his distance from Chávez and comparatively normal relations with Washington. Correa's most radical policies have been focused on the home front, where he is struggling to enact sweeping institutional reforms in South America's most politically volatile country. Correa is Ecuador's eighth president in ten years, and he aspires to be the first in this succession to survive a full term.

The failure of Ecuador's discredited and corrupt political elite to address socio-economic concerns had made the country ripe for the ascension of a populist leader, and the absence of democratic institutions to channel these concerns left mass mobilisation as one of the only viable policy tools available to the politically marginalised mass of the population. Lucio Gutierrez was elected on a populist platform, but in April 2005 he became the third president in nine years to be ousted by social protests after he pursued orthodox economic policies once in office. Interim president Alfredo Palacio sought to avoid his predecessor's fate through redistributive policies and frequent capitulation to protesters' demands. But the popular complaint is fundamentally political, not economic. Without democratic inclusion, no shifts in economic policy are likely to be sufficient to save Ecuador from popular uprising.

Correa initially attracted the Ecuadorian electorate by modelling himself on Chávez. Frequently invoking Bolívar, Correa praised Venezuela's regional agendas, and promoted a close alliance with the country. He publicly insulted President Bush, denounced Latin American trade agreements with Washington, and vowed to cancel the US military's air-base privileges in the coastal city of Manta. Correa attacked international financial institutions, proclaiming he would stop payment of Ecuador's 'illegal debt'. Most importantly, however, he issued a virulent indictment of Ecuador's political parties, claiming the country was governed by a 'party-docracy' rather than a democracy. Traditionally, government power has rested heavily in the legislature and the Congress has successfully unseated executives who have attempted to seize power. Correa's personal popularity, however, has enabled him to sideline Congress. Upon taking office on 15 January 2007, the president had an unprecedented approval rating of 73%, in stark contrast to the 68% of Ecuadorians who disapproved of Congress.

Lacking a party as well as any congressional representation, Correa advocated disbanding a Congress that he labelled a 'sewer' of corruption and calling a constituent assembly to 're-establish' the government. Correa forged a broad social alliance with Ecuador's highly organised indigenous movements at its centre and held widely attended rallies to campaign for a constituent assembly. These spurred legislators to approve a referendum on whether to hold a constituent assembly. By March 2007, however, the issue had provoked institutional crisis leading to the sacking by the Supreme Electoral Council (TSE) of 57 opposition deputies in Congress. Correa secured legislative control when two alternate deputies decided to replace their fired colleagues and to side with the president against their own parties. The move created a pro-government majority and restored the congressional number to just over the quorum needed to resume business. The following month, Correa refused to honour a ruling by the Constitutional Tribunal that the opposition deputies be restored. The president also had the state prosecutor issue arrest warrants for 14 sacked deputies who were holding parallel proceedings. The opposition has accused the president of a Chávez-like effort to concentrate power. Correa has insisted that his actions are legitimated by the 'will of the people'. A 15 April 2007 referendum reinforced the president's position, as 82% of the population voted in favour of a constituent assembly.

On the economic front, Correa declared that Ecuador's 'long dark night of neoliberalism' had come to a close. He has voiced his support for Palacio's decision to revoke the contract of US oil company Occidental Petroleum. Correa has further angered Washington and foreign investors by threatening to renew a lawsuit against US oil company Chevron–Texaco for environmental damage in the Amazon. The Occidental takeover prompted the United States to suspend negotiations of a bilateral free-trade agreement, but Correa had in any case strongly opposed the unpopular agreement. He does, however, seek to extend the preferential trade conditions the US government has granted Ecuador under the Andean Trade Preference and Drug Eradication Act (ATPDEA), and he backed off threats to suspend payments of Ecuador's foreign debt.

In the foreign-policy arena, despite Correa's attempts to distance himself from Chávez, Ecuador retains a close economic relationship with Venezuela. The two countries have signed energy-sector accords, and PDVSA is to invest in a $4bn oil refinery. The oil sector is crucial to the Correa government, as it bankrolls his distributionary social policies. Correa has not, however, become subservient to Venezuela. For example, Ecuador has signed ethanol cooperation agreements with Brazil despite Chávez's objections to biofuel production. The potential spillover of Colombia's domestic conflict, however, poses similar problems for Ecuador and Venezuela. Like Venezuela, Ecuador has been building up air and ground forces on its borders, and has criticised border crossings by Colombian troops which claim they are in 'hot pursuit' of FARC guerrillas. Colombia, for its part, has claimed that FARC has staged attacks from Ecuadorian territory. These security issues have increased diplomatic tensions between Colombia and Ecuador, particularly since the December 2006 resumption of aerial eradication along the border. Ecuador has opposed the spraying of glysophate as environmentally harmful, and has threatened to take its complaints to the International Court of Justice in The Hague. In April 2007, Correa launched 'Plan Ecuador' to promote border security, as a 'response of peace, justice, and development' as opposed to the 'militaristic and violent' US-backed Plan Colombia. Chávez allocated $135m to Plan Ecuador and called on the international community to match his government's contribution. It is unclear whether Correa will secure the investment he has solicited, though UN Secretary-General Ban Ki Moon praised Plan Ecuador as an 'important initiative'.

The main threat to Ecuadorian society remains the potential for violent conflict over the country's political reform process. On 13 March 2007 several of the deposed congressional deputies were injured in clashes with the police as they tried to re-enter the parliament building. After they returned to their parallel assembly, they were fired upon by citizens. On 12 April, an opposition deputy released teargas into Congress to protest the firings. Elections for the constituent assembly are to be held on 30 September 2007, and that body will be given 180 days to rewrite the constitution, which will then be presented to the people for approval in a referendum. But even a successful process to overhaul Ecuador's constitution may not quell popular discontent. The current constitution was adopted in 1998 and has not provided the country with stability. Correa may not be able to maintain control over the popular movements he now deploys against his opposition, particularly if his support begins to decay over the slow pace or unsatisfactory results of reform.

Central America, Mexico and the Caribbean

Central America and the Caribbean are becoming the newest fronts in the battle for regional influence between the Bush administration and Hugo Chávez. Both presidents wound up their March 2007 Latin American tours in the sub-region, with Bush in Guatemala and Chávez visiting Nicaragua, Haiti and Jamaica. Bush subsequently dispatched Health and Human Services Secretary Michael Leavitt to Central America with the message: 'We care about your plight'. Leavitt promised to open a regional healthcare training facility in Panama and emphasised that the United States had spent nearly $1bn on health initiatives in Central America since 2001. This 'health diplomacy' probably sought to counter the diplomatic influence Fidel Castro had garnered in the region through Venezuelan-financed eye care to several Central American countries, including Haiti, Nicaragua and Costa Rica. In February 2007, Honduras reopened diplomatic channels to Cuba after 46 years in return for the promise of three eye-care facilities.

Energy diplomacy, however, has been the major tool with which the United States and Venezuela have vied for regional influence. Chávez has launched Petrocaribe, which offers preferential terms for Venezuelan oil, in order to undermine the Bush administration's free-trade agreement, CAFTA-DR, with Costa Rica, Guatemala, Nicaragua, El Salvador, Honduras and the Dominican Republic. The United States scored a victory in the contest on 1 March 2007 when the Dominican Republic ratified CAFTA-DR, yet Dominicans remain the largest Chávez supporters outside of Venezuela. CAFTA-DR has been less successful in Costa Rica, where the political opposition has grown increasingly radical and the legislature has yet to approve the agreement despite the backing of President Oscar Arias. Chávez's oil diplomacy, however, has recently been countered by Mexican promises to build an oil refinery in Central America as well as US–Brazilian ethanol diplomacy.

Mexico – on track again?

After narrowly winning Mexico's highly polarised election on 2 July 2006, President Felipe Calderón has exhibited remarkable political skill and managed to govern the divided country. His predecessor Vicente Fox was Mexico's first democratically elected president from outside the Institutional Revolutionary Party (PRI). Fox failed to meet high expectations, presiding instead over stalled economic growth and unable to get necessary reforms through Congress. Frustration with the slow pace of change and widespread poverty helped fuel the rise of radical populist presidential candidate Andrés Manuel López Obrador. A former mayor of Mexico City, he mobilised a combative following among the country's poor, particularly those from Mexico's impoverished south. Calderón, a pro-business lawyer and former energy minister, managed to cast his opponent as a danger to both the Mexican economy and democracy, denouncing Obrador's connections to Hugo Chávez. Calderón emerged from the 2 July election with a lead of less than 1%, which Obrador contested as fraudulent. After nine weeks in which Obrador rallied supporters in a series of protests, on 5 September the Federal Electoral Tribunal unanimously declared Calderón the victor by a margin of 0.56%. Despite ongoing resistance from Obrador and his Democratic Revolutionary Party (PRD), Calderón was successfully inaugurated on 1 December in a midnight congressional session after which he and Fox quickly fled out the back door. Obrador, meanwhile, had been inaugurated as the 'legitimate' president of Mexico in a ceremony of his own.

Realising the weak position with which he took office, Calderón reached out to his opposition, calling for 'national reconciliation', promising to govern for all Mexicans and vowing to address the issues of the poor. He adopted several of Obrador's campaign promises, such as slashing the salary of the president and top officials, and launched an anti-poverty programme to assist the country's 100 poorest communities. Obrador's support waned as many legislators and local officials decided to work with the Calderón government, viewing Obrador's moves to create a parallel government as excessively disruptive. Calderón demonstrated his ability to decisively govern by launching an aggressive anti-drug campaign in which he deployed over 24,000 federal army and police troops to affected regions and extradited 15 kingpins to the United States. Drug-related crime took the lives of over 2,000 Mexicans in 2006, and while Calderón's offensive escalated the violence inflicted by narcotics-trafficking gangs, his efforts boosted his popularity ratings to 65%. In turn, his popularity and leadership have enabled him to create alliances with PRI legislators, and on 28 March 2007 the Mexican Congress passed an important pension-reform bill. If Calderón is able to maintain his working relationship with the PRI, Mexico may see the realisation of the many reforms Fox was unable to enact due to his lack of congressional support.

Significantly, Calderón has steered Mexican foreign policy away from its singular emphasis on immigration reform in the United States. While immigration policy remains important, Calderón has stressed to President Bush that the solution to the immigration issue lies not with a mere policy shift on the part of the United States, but rather in strengthening the Mexican economy to stem the tide of workers across the border. Furthermore, Calderón has placed increased emphasis on strengthening Mexico's relationships with its Latin American neighbours. The president has said he will seek to normalise relations with Cuba and Venezuela and take a greater role in hemispheric affairs. Calderón has broached the subject of entering Mercosur with Brazilian President da Silva and is working to revamp Plan Puebla-Panama to assist the poor regions of southern Mexico and its Central American neighbours. Rather than becoming a conservative antagonist to Hugo Chávez, Calderón's proven coalition-building abilities may enable him to provide a moderating influence to Latin America's radical populists.

In June 2006 violent conflict had erupted in Oaxaca when police raided a camp of teachers who had occupied the town's central square in protest. The police raid sparked clashes between protesters, now joined by other leftist groups angry over the government response, and the state government. The conflict turned violent as 12 died in the clashes and protesters burned government buildings. After the conflict raged unabated for months, President Fox ordered 4,000 federal police to restore order. While the crisis has since simmered down, protests have continued. Additionally, the crisis became a symbol for many in the Mexican left angry over government response to the people's demands for greater socio-economic justice.

Haiti – poverty and patronage

Haiti, which has the region's poorest population and weakest central government, has also recently become a theatre for US–Venezuelan diplomatic conflict. American troops have intervened in Haiti numerous times over the past century, most recently in 2004 after President Jean-Bertrand Aristide was overthrown and the country wracked by political violence. The Brazilian-led UN Stabilisation Mission (MINUSTAH) has since worked to stabilise the country, helping Haiti to elect a new government in 2006.

President from 1996 to 2001, René Preval was elected again in February 2006 in spite of the conservative interim government's efforts to hijack the election by fraud. In April 2006, Haiti held successful parliamentary elections. By June the legislature had confirmed a prime minister, and Preval was able to form a government. The UN mission, however, is far from being able to withdraw. The UN's over 8,000 troops are essential to keeping the country from drowning in violent crime. In February 2007, MINUSTAH launched an aggressive offensive against the pro-Aristide gangs that operated in the Cité Soleil slum. They frequently targeted UN workers and there were many kidnappings. While the offensive was largely effective, leading to the arrest of over 400 gang members and inhibiting the gangs' criminal activities, the underlying poverty and political instability that breed the criminality they displayed have yet to be addressed.

Better security led the Bush administration to release $20m in funds to stabilise areas plagued by gang- and drug-related violence, in addition to the $200m already slated for Haiti during 2007. The United States has spent over $800m in aid to Haiti since 2004, yet the Preval administration accuses Washington of fuelling the crime and drug problems it claims to be combating. In December 2006, the United States announced it would increase the number of criminal deportees to Haiti from 25 to 100 per month despite protests that the 2,000-plus criminal deportees returned over the past five years were exacerbating the already acute problem of violent crime. Additionally, in January 2007 Preval criticised the United States for failing to adequately help his country fight drug consumption, which stoked crime. The Bush administration defended its counter-drug efforts in Haiti, on which Washington has spent $40 million since 2004.

The Bush administration also attributed the increased flow of cocaine into Haiti to Venezuela, with one US official accusing Chávez of having established a 'narco-state'. Chávez denounced the US claims as an attempt to discredit him regionally and stepped up his oil diplomacy vis-à-vis Haiti with promises to double the flow of Venezuelan oil to the country and provide $20m in humanitarian aid. While the United States remains far and away the largest foreign-aid donor to Haiti, Chávez has managed to undermine its diplomatic monopoly on Haiti by inducing Preval to manoeuvre between Bush and Chávez to secure as much aid as possible. Haiti will likely continue to be a locus of US–Venezuelan political rivalry as the country's plans for ethanol production proceed.

Nicaragua: a newly pragmatic Ortega?

After a campaign in which both the United States and Venezuela became involved, former Nicaraguan revolutionary Daniel Ortega was elected with 38% of the vote, barely above the 35% needed to prevent a run-off, on 5 November 2006, 16 years after he was voted out of power. Ortega served as the front-man for the Sandinista Party's Marxist government from 1985 to 1990, which fought the US-backed counter-revolutionary Contras in a bloody civil war which cost the lives of around 30,000 people in a country of only 4m. Moderating his political stance, Ortega traded in his military fatigues for a white button-down shirt and campaigned as the candidate of 'peace and love', declaring he now followed God rather than Marx. Furthermore, Ortega made pro-business overtures, promising to respect private property as well as Nicaragua's free-trade agreement with the United States. US ambassador Paul Trivelli, however, warned that Ortega's newfound moderation was not to be trusted and would not last. Meanwhile, US officials threatened to cut off aid and to throw out trade agreements if Ortega was elected. Although the Organisation of American States chastised the Bush administration for its involvement in the election, former Reagan aide Oliver North travelled to Nicaragua during the campaign to spread anti-Ortega sentiments. Hugo Chávez, meanwhile, was rebuked by the Nicaraguan government for funnelling oil and aid to Sandinista mayors in an effort to boost Ortega's electoral prospects.

Chávez hailed Ortega's election as an anti-imperialist victory, promising to provide the struggling country with preferential oil prices, an oil refinery, $30m in forgiven debt, $20m in low-interest or interest-free loans, and $10m worth of aid for social programmes. Iranian President Mahmoud Ahmadinejad visited Nicaragua on 14 January 2007, pledging additional aid. Ortega joined Chávez's ALBA and welcomed the assistance from his leftist allies, having promised to solve the country's energy blackouts and eradicate the poverty which plagues 80% of Nicaraguans. At the same time, he sought to avoid jeopardising Nicaragua's ties with the United States, which provides $48m a year in aid, a market for 60% of the country's exports, and crucial investment. Ortega's position, in turn, has prompted a conciliatory shift in the Bush administration's Nicaragua policy. On 28 November 2006, US Assistant Secretary of State Thomas Shannon met with

President-elect Ortega, calling his visit 'an effort to bury an old hatchet' and indicating the United States' wish to maintain the close relations it has built with Nicaragua since 1990.

With the weakest mandate of any democratically elected Nicaraguan president and only 38 of 92 seats in the legislature, Ortega's government relies on a 1999 power-sharing pact between his Frente Sandinista de Liberación Nacional (FSLN) and former President Arnoldo Alemán's Partido Liberal Constitucionalista (PLC). Known as 'el pacto', this agreement lowered the threshold for a first-round electoral victory from 45% to 35% of the vote, a change essential to Ortega's 2006 victory. On 16 March 2007, Alemán was granted freedom of movement throughout the country while serving his 20-year prison sentence for corruption. In return, Ortega received the support of the PLC's 25 congressional deputies, allowing him to command a majority of the legislature. Ortega pushed through reforms which increased his control over the national police and armed forces as well as allowing him to create 'people's councils' which ominously resemble the Sandinista vigilante 'defence committees' of the 1980s as well as Chávez's 'Bolivarian circles'. Ortega has also effectively shelved reforms passed under his predecessor to diminish presidential authority and instead is seeking constitutional reforms which would allow him to run for re-election in 2010. While Ortega may have discarded much of his former socialist persona, his efforts to concentrate power indicate that he has not altogether shed his strong-man identity.

Cuba's pending regime change

Into the twenty-first century, Cuba has held its position as a stalwart opponent of the democratic tide washing over much of Latin America. The socialist agenda of Fidel Castro's regime, controversial as it may be, is generally regarded as the region's 'alternative' to the American model of republican government and free-market economics. Often considered the forerunner to populists like Chávez in Venezuela and Morales in Bolivia, Castro has rarely hesitated to remind the world of his nation's sovereignty, notwithstanding the powerful hemispheric influence wielded by the United States. In recent years, new dynamics have informed Cuba's domestic policy and, as a result, its international relations.

The Castro administration has tightened socialism's grip on Cuban society. It has developed new relationships with China and Venezuela. Moreover, the island nation's economy has stabilised since the 1990s and is now following a track of relentless expansion. In light of Cuba's 'globalisation', the Bush administration has made some adjustments to its Cuba policies. While maintaining the United States' long-standing trade embargo, the administration has sought alternatives for promoting change in Cuba. In particular, it has emphasised democratisation at the grassroots level, targeting subversives and dissident organisers for financial aid and leadership training. Yet it has also met with increased resistance from a bipartisan contingent in Congress, as well as the American business community, both of which consider restrictive trade policies outdated and inefficient.

On 31 July 2006, a wave of political uncertainty swept over Cuba, as Castro temporarily ceded executive responsibilities to his brother Raúl following intestinal surgery from which he was, as of summer 2007, still recovering. The first major interruption of Fidel Castro's administration since he took power in 1959, this was arguably the most significant political event in Cuba since the collapse of Soviet communism and the withdrawal of Soviet economic and military aid in 1991. Although there is a consensus in Havana that the elder Castro will return to power if his health improves, there was little indication of when this would happen, if ever. Given that Raúl Castro has made little effort to permit large-scale political and economic reforms on his watch, whether or not this disruption will mean the beginning of a new era for Cuba will depend largely on the ability of internal dissidents and pro-democracy organisations to secure a foothold in a society that has suppressed opposition for nearly half a century.

Leading up to Fidel Castro's illness, the Cuban government had pursued a comprehensive programme aimed at reviving the nation's sluggish economy and shoring up the socialist state. In 2002, anticipating his impending departure from the scene, the then-75-year-old leader secured a constitutional amendment that declared the socialist system 'irrevocable'. The legislation received exuberant support from a petition signed by more than 8m Cuban voters, though this must be taken with a grain of salt given the lack of political freedom in Cuba. The move was followed by an economic recentralisation initiative that began with the consolidation of the Central Bank and the reform of the Ministry of Finance. Then, in July 2003 the government removed the US dollar from the Cuban economy. It was to be replaced, the Central Bank announced, with the convertible peso system, which had no international exchange value. Castro hoped the move would punish the Bush administration for stiffening the trade embargo, as well as assert Cuba's economic independence. But the new system damaged many Cubans' confidence in national fiscal policy. It also resulted in an influx of euros, which were not only more stable than the convertible pesos, but also stronger than the US dollar had been.

Castro's government intended to further 'purify' the socialist state by clamping down on foreign investors. A series of stiff licensing fees was imposed on international businesses operating in Cuba, and Castro intensified his anti-imperialist rhetoric. When the government announced in November 2004 that foreign-owned enterprises operating in Cuban free-trade zones must form joint ventures with the Cuban government or leave, Cuba's policy of economic liberalisation – which had attracted substantial foreign investment throughout the 1990s – came to an abrupt halt. In 2005, Castro revoked self-employment licenses for several thousand small-business owners, forcing nearly 50% of Cuba's private entrepreneurs back into the public sector.

While Castro attempted to ensure the supremacy of the socialist system in Cuba with these recentralising policies, he also pursued a 'grand design' to restructure foreign exchange. Hoping to boost the nation's export earnings above dismal 1990s levels, the Cuban leader focused attention on biotechnology and medicine in the manufacturing sector and on high-value enterprise in the service sector. Medical care and education received heavy attention, and in 2004 Cuba hosted nearly 3,500 international medical students and began exporting its own physicians throughout Latin America. The nation also reached full production capacity of nickel in 2005, when nickel revenues increased to $1bn, up from $450m in 2001.

In perhaps his shrewdest decision of this period, Castro began to use his domestic socialist agenda to court Chávez and Chinese President Hu Jintao. In October 2000, Chávez and Castro signed the Integral Cooperation Accord, under which Cuba would receive subsidised petroleum in return for agricultural and manufacturing products, as well as subsidised (in fact, free) medical care. The two leftist leaders further strengthened their countries' ties in 2004, entering into the Application of the Bolivarian Alternative for the Americas agreement. The accords recognised the 'mutual interest' between the two countries, particularly countering American economic supremacy in the hemisphere. It deeply integrated the two economies, bilaterally eliminating duties and protective tariffs, providing tax exemptions for all benefits from investments in both countries, and laying a foundation for joint-venture enterprise between the two governments. Cuba's concessions permitted Venezuelan companies to own 100% of their investments in Cuba, whereas Western companies still can own only 49%; it also granted 2,000 scholarships to Venezuelan students in Cuba. In turn, Venezuela promised to finance infrastructure programmes and to give grants for technological research and development in Cuba. For Castro, these agreements secured much-needed markets for Cuban trade and emblematised his nation's independence from what he and Chávez considered the 'devil' of US economic imperialism.

Cuba's relations with China took off in 2001, when the leaders of both nations signed a series of agreements formalising cooperation in technological development, education and trade. Although the accords were neither as comprehensive nor as integrating as those between Cuba and Venezuela, they opened the door to Sino-Cuban exchange. China now primarily sends transportation equipment, tractors and heavy manufacturing equipment in return for Cuban nickel, sugar, medicine and biotechnology. This trade has been immensely profitable for Cuba. In 2006, Cuba's biotechnology sales to China rose 90%. China's markets also receive nearly 50% of Cuba's nickel, the price of which has leapt 160% in the past two years. All told, Sino-Cuban trade totalled $1.8bn in 2006, more than double the 2005 figure. These numbers parallel broader trends in Cuba's economy. In 2006, Cuba's goods and services exports approached $10.4bn, a 45% increase over 2005 figures, and imports reached $10.3bn, a 30% increase. The Ministry of the Economy and Planning in Havana reported an astounding 12.5% growth in GDP in 2006, though American and European estimates place it more conservatively between 7% and 9.3%. Still, the figures are impressive, surpassing those of Venezuela and Argentina, which are typically thought to have the fastest-growing economies in Latin America.

It is likely that Cuba's recent economic reforms were crafted with the end of Fidel Castro's rule in mind. Cuba's central planning committees seemed intent on preserving the nation's absolute sovereignty in the face of 'hegemonic' world powers. As of summer 2007, this appeared to entail a reassertion of social-ist dominance in Cuba. It remains to be seen whether the socialist programme will be able to sustain itself after Castro leaves office. Yet, in building up the socialist economy and partnering with foreign governments pursuing similar socio-political ends, the central planning committees have shown considerable fore-sight. When Fidel Castro makes his final exit from Cuban politics, the economic stability that Cuba has achieved in the twenty-first century may play a signifi-cant role in preventing a political meltdown.

Despite the dramatic upswing in the Cuban economy, the international com-munity – Washington in particular – has retained its fears about Cuba. Raúl Castro, whose confidence in the socialist machine remains strong, has made no effort to allay those fears. Raúl admitted recently in a meeting of the Council of State that the state-run transportation system was on the verge of collapse. High job turnover, poor infrastructure, a lack of discipline in the labour force, Cuba's unique transportation black market (conducted mainly in US dollars and euros) and a dearth of resources have pushed it to the edge of systemic failure.

Raúl's stance on human rights also remains a cause for concern. In 2003, the Cuban military arrested 75 pro-democracy activists and sentenced each to between six and 28 years for presenting a 'danger to the revolution'. The dis-sidents have suffered beatings, neglect and isolation, and several have been denied medical treatment. As of December 2006, at least 283 political prisoners and possibly as many as a thousand more people, held on charges of 'danger-ousness', remained incarcerated in Cuba. Exact figures are unavailable, as the Cuban government has denied visas to monitoring groups such as Human Rights Watch and Amnesty International. Moreover, Raúl Castro remains inflex-ible on freedom of speech, press and assembly, as well as prisoner release. During the 14th summit of the Non-Aligned Movement in September 2006, Raúl prohibited all gatherings that might harm the socialist regime's image. Political dissenters have remained subject to militant action by the paramilitary wing of the Department of State Security or by civilian justice organisations such as the Communist Youth League and the Committees for the Defence of the Revolution. In one striking case, on 10 December 2006, Raúl ordered 100 state paramilitary forces and at least 200 civilians from Communist vigilante groups to stop a silent march by 12 pro-democracy activists in Havana to commemorate Human Rights Day. They punched and kicked the activists to detain them, and then held them under arrest for several hours.

In spite of this incident, Cuba's internal opposition may be making some progress. Dissenters have recently found open outlets in the Cuban media and have urged Raúl to implement liberal political and economic reforms by promoting dialogue, revising property distribution and releasing political prisoners. Less than two weeks after the 10 December protest, Raúl delivered a speech before the Congress of the University Student Federation in which he advocated a more open political atmosphere. It appeared that the interim leader was waiting for a conclusion to his brother's political career before asserting a more definitive position on democratisation and human rights. Most signs, though, suggest that he, like his older brother, will only permit open discussion and free assembly if their objectives are in keeping with the narrow ideology of the Communist regime. Raúl may even tighten his grip on Cuban society when his power is assured. Cuba may thus see an increase in military control if Raúl decides to reward the allies he made while serving as minister of defence.

The Bush administration has indicated it will largely continue standing US policy, despite pressure from influential members of Congress, until Cuba allows significant democratic reforms. The administration appears to understand that the Castro regime's 'anti-imperialist' rhetoric has sunk deep into the Cuban social consciousness, and it is attempting to minimise its provocative presence as a hegemonic political and economic force. In the short term, the United States will probably refrain from forcing its own political model on the island nation. President Bush has waived all claims on US-held property nationalised during the early days of Cuba's Communist revolution, although the administration has remained unmoved in its intent to isolate the Castro regime. Influenced in part by the Cuban American National Foundation, the most influential Cuban-American group, Bush has upheld the comprehensive economic embargo instituted under the Cuban Liberty and Democratic Solidarity (*Libertad*) Act of 1996 (the Helms-Burton Act), denying all monetary and material assistance to the Castro regime. In 2005, he placed heavy restrictions on agricultural and medicinal exports to Cuba, which were permitted by President Bill Clinton just before he left office in 2001. Bush also renewed an inclusive prohibition on travel to Cuba for 2007.

Yet the administration's simple proposition that it will not recognise the 'tyrannical dictatorship' has been confounded by Cuba's recent economic development. US Senator Christopher J. Dodd (D-CT), one of the Senate's most ardent advocates of normalising relations with Havana, drafted a resolution in August 2006 declaring that the United States must not miss this 'tremendous opportunity' for hastening change in Cuba. On his side are several Democratic and farm-state Republican senators, as well as US business leaders and farmers who have argued that the unilateral embargo has been utterly ineffective, inflicting more damage on Cuba's suffering poor than on the persistent Communist regime. Furthermore, since Cuba recently partnered with Venezuela and China, it has found secure and protected markets to compensate for trade lost to the United States, rendering the economic restrictions effective only in principle. Advocates of lifting the embargo have also found support for their cause in the estimate that the market potential for US–Cuba trade exceeds $1bn annually. They reason that terminating the embargo now will enhance Cuba's economic boom and instil free-market principles in Cuban society at a time it is already ripe for broader liberal reform.

There has been speculation that the newly elected Democratic Congress will be able to pass legislation relaxing the embargo over the administration's veto. Indeed, throughout 2006, Democrats and some Republicans in Congress attempted to include anti-embargo and anti-travel prohibition language in the Agricultural Appropriations Bill and the Treasury–Transportation Appropriations Bill for the 2007 fiscal year. However, under threat of a presidential veto, the House and Senate conference committees excised the Cuba amendments. Concerned as the current Congress is with securing the withdrawal of American troops from Iraq, it likely will not devote serious attention to Cuba legislation in the near future. Furthermore, the Bush administration shows no sign of relenting in its resistance to legitimising Raúl Castro's regime unless there is meaningful reform. US efforts to promote reform have been active but ineffective. In 2003, the US government created the Commission for Assistance to a Free Cuba to identify efficient democracy-promoting initiatives and channel funds to grassroots Cuban pro-democracy organisations and families with relatives living in the United States. However, the White House's request for $40m to fund such efforts following the transfer of power to Raúl Castro met with congressional resistance, as a report by the Government Accountability Office revealed gross deficiencies in the programme's financial oversight and procedures for reviewing grant recipients. Critics of the administration's Cuba policy have cited this as evidence that such democracy-promotion schemes are at best inefficient, if not counterproductive.

As Cuba prepared for another series of parliamentary elections in spring 2008, there seemed to be little evidence that the country was moving toward a more open and democratic era. If Raúl remains in power until then, it is unlikely that he will attempt any dramatic reforms, while Fidel, who has announced that he plans to run again, remains alive. Any widespread political or economic change may need to come from the ground up, and grassroots political organisers will have to make considerable headway to secure open elections by 2008. Most likely, Cuba will undergo slow, evolutionary change, rather than a sweeping democratic revolution. If, however, Cuba's society begins to liberalise quickly, the island nation may witness a mass repatriation of Cuban-American exiles and refugees, which could upset its fledgling economy and portend a clash of ideologies that could cause tremendous political and civil unrest.

Stability with bluster

While consistently garnering headlines, Hugo Chávez has been largely unsuccessful in his populist crusade to isolate the United States. The United States has slowly regained regional influence as it has partnered with Mexico and Brazil to counter Venezuelan oil diplomacy. Chávez's regional influence, in turn, has waned as he has angered his neighbours by intruding into their domestic affairs. Accordingly, the time may be ripe for South America's more moderate leaders to forge an economically sustainable and socially responsible path for the hemisphere. Meanwhile, the United States and Venezuela are likely to continue their contest for influence primarily in Central America and the Caribbean.

4 Europe

Europe has over the past year begun to pull itself out of a period of internal discord and institutional atrophy. The divisions caused by the 2003 Iraq War had been followed by a setback in 2005 to the long-term project of European integration. The rejection by French and Dutch voters – British voters, if asked, would have done the same – of an EU 'constitution' had shown how disconnected from European electorates those who pushed forward the European project had become. National politics were, in a number of important countries, in the midst of change and introspection: only after this period had run its course could a substantive debate about the future of Europe be renewed.

In 2007, Nicolas Sarkozy was elected president of France and Gordon Brown became prime minister of the United Kingdom. German Chancellor Angela Merkel meanwhile consolidated her domestic position at the head of the 'grand coalition' formed in 2005, and established herself as a European leader to be reckoned with. All three appeared set to have polite, business-like but not overenthusiastic relationships with the Bush administration. Sarkozy moved to follow Merkel in improving links with Washington, while for Brown the relationship with President George W. Bush seemed bound to be less close than the personal bond enjoyed by Tony Blair, his predecessor. Taken together, the political changes in three main European powers seemed set to strengthen the transatlantic foundations of the West's approach to the world's immediately pressing challenges: Iran, the Middle East, international terrorism and climate change.

The new cast of leaders also addressed themselves to shifting the EU out of the limbo into which it had fallen in 2005. Holding the rotating EU presidency for the first half of 2007, Merkel sought through intensive consultation

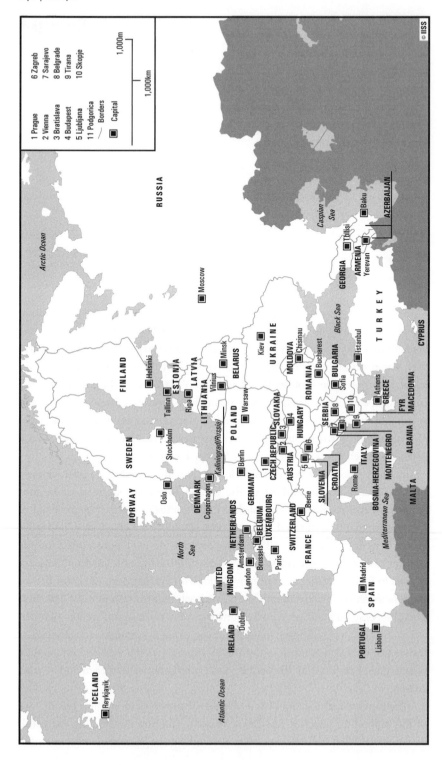

Legend:

1 Prague
2 Vienna
3 Bratislava
4 Budapest
5 Ljubljana
11 Podgorica
6 Zagreb
7 Sarajevo
8 Belgrade
9 Tirana
10 Skopje
■ Capital
— Borders

1,000km
1,000m

© IISS

with member governments to craft a slimmed-down set of institutional reforms – necessary because of the expansion of the EU to 27 members from 15 since 2004 – that could be enacted as a treaty rather than a constitution. Agreement at an EU Summit in June 2007 represented a considerable achievement: the EU's organisational structure will be simplified, and its voting system altered. The previous plan for an EU 'foreign minister' was watered down. The aim was to avoid a new round of referendums, yet the negotiating process led to fears of a reversion to the opaque backroom compromises, remote from ordinary people, which had contributed to disillusion among voters. Moreover, the summit discussions showed marked differences in philosophy, with Sarkozy insisting on the removal from the main text of a commitment to 'free and undistorted competition' in the EU internal market – it was retained via an attached protocol. This, for the EU, was a very traditional kind of argument. But Merkel had at least unfrozen the EU's institutional paralysis.

One reason why the future shape of Europe is hard to predict is that the politics of European countries are defining themselves along new lines that do not conform to traditional left–right stereotypes. Following the creation of the left/centre-right coalition in Germany, Sarkozy, who himself represents a modernist blend of conservatism and liberalism, invited socialists into his government in France. Brown made overtures outside the Labour Party in forming his government in the United Kingdom, his predecessor, Blair, having already embraced a market-led outlook that traditionally belonged to the Conservative Party. Such shifts and blends, reflecting the changing nature of European societies, will be a continuing theme that will set the direction of Europe for the coming decades.

While presiding over a peaceful and mostly prosperous Europe, leaders could not ignore persistent threats to security, which continued to absorb considerable resources. Terrorist plots were uncovered among extremist elements of Muslim communities. France, Germany and the United Kingdom continued to act in concert in confronting Iran's nuclear aspirations, though with little tangible result. European countries maintained their commitment to crisis-management efforts, with NATO taking over responsibility for security assistance in the whole of Afghanistan, and European troops sending forces to Lebanon following the 2006 conflict there as well as helping to oversee elections in the Democratic Republic of the Congo. The European troop presence in Iraq and Bosnia was reduced. Closer to home, there was tension over the future status of Kosovo, with Russia objecting to full independence, and European countries were concerned by the newly assertive tone of Moscow's foreign policy and by their dependence on Russia for energy supplies. Russia objected bitterly to American plans to site US missile-defence assets in Poland and the Czech Republic.

France: Towards a New Political Landscape?

France, in 2006, yearned for change. With the election of President Nicolas Sarkozy on 6 May 2007, a new era seemed set to begin, although it may well assume unanticipated forms. The desire for a different approach was primarily directed against one man, President Jacques Chirac, who for anybody aged under 60 had become a fixture in French politics. Appointed as Prime Minister Georges Pompidou's *chef de cabinet* in 1962, Chirac had subsequently held most major offices of state, including two terms as prime minister (1974–76 and 1986–88), almost 20 years as mayor of Paris (1977–95), and two successive terms as president of the republic (1995–2002; 2002–07). However, his presidency was marked by *immobilisme* ('stagnation'). During his first term this was a result of his misguided calling of early parliamentary elections in 1997, leading to five years of 'cohabitation' with the Socialist Party of Lionel Jospin. During his second term, it resulted from his miscalculation over the referendum on the European constitutional treaty which he resoundingly lost in May 2005. After the referendum, he effectively threw in the political towel.

But the desire for change went much deeper than Chirac's final bow. The Socialist Party (Parti Socialiste, PS) and the Gaullists (Rassemblement pour la République, RPR, then Union pour un Mouvement Populaire, UMP) had been alternating in power every few years since 1981, to little real effect. At one level, this was a political-institutional problem. The Fifth Republic Constitution of 1962 was devised to give strategic vision, oversight and durability to the president, who was elected by universal suffrage for a seven-year term, while the government, deriving from parliamentary elections every five years, was headed by a prime minister whose function was simply to govern. The president was considered above politics and could fire the prime minister, a convenient lightning rod if things went wrong. This worked well as long as the president and the prime minister came from the same political family, a situation which held (more or less) until 1986. But when in that year parliamentary elections produced a right-wing prime minister, Chirac, the socialist president François Mitterrand, who had been elected for a seven-year term in 1981, instead of resigning as strict constitutional purists argued he should have done, inaugurated the system of 'cohabitation'. This combination of a president from one side of the political spectrum and a parliament/prime minister from the other was to recur three times (1986–88; 1993–95; 1997–2002). It guaranteed political stagnation.

In October 2000, the constitution was altered. The presidential term was reduced to five years and the two sets of elections synchronised, with the parliamentary poll following only weeks after the presidential vote. In the 2002 and 2007 elections voters, having chosen their president, also opted to give him the parliamentary majority and the prime minister he needed to govern effectively.

However, Chirac, from 2002 to 2007, failed to capitalise on this opportunity. France's economic and social structures remained mired in outdated norms and procedures, the fruit of decades of compromise among a paternalistic and bloated state, a fractious and ill-led workforce, nervous employers and a political class reluctant to grasp the challenge of globalisation. Furthermore, mass immigration had, since the 1960s, transformed the urban landscape. Yet the inclusive ideology of the ('one and indivisible') Jacobin Republic refused to recognise the alienation staring it in the face. The suburban riots of November 2005 and the student protests of spring 2006 suggested the depth of the problems that were not being addressed and the extent of popular disillusionment with the political and social status quo.

The modernisation of French politics

By electing Sarkozy, the French people thus voted overwhelmingly for change. In some ways, it was unavoidable that they would do so. This was the first presidential election since the founding of the Fifth Republic in 1958 in which none of the leading candidates had been either a former president or a former prime minister. It was also the first presidential election in which all the serious candidates were born not only after Second World War, but in the 1950s. The leading contenders, Sarkozy (born 1955), Ségolène Royal (1953) and François Bayrou (1951), had all been high-school students in 1968. Royal triumphed in the Socialist Party primaries in part because she was not one of the old guard (familiarly known as the 'elephants'), men like Lionel Jospin (1937), Laurent Fabius (1946) or Dominique Strauss-Kahn (1949), who had held ministerial office for decades and were tarred with the brush of *immobilisme*. Moreover, all three main contenders for the first round in 2007 successfully passed themselves off as 'outsiders': Sarkozy as a social outsider, the son of immigrants; Royal as a political outsider who had taken on her own party and emerged triumphant; and Bayrou as the man who refused to be squeezed into either a Gaullist or a Socialist mould.

Yet, at another level, all the leading contenders had themselves been highly visible on the political scene for two decades. Royal had been an Elysée adviser to Mitterrand in the 1980s and held a succession of ministerial posts between 1992 and 2002, in addition to being the civil-partner of Socialist Party leader François Hollande and mother of their four children (after the 2007 elections their separation was announced). Bayrou had also been politically visible for decades as deputy (1986), minister of education (1993–97), MEP (since 1999) and party leader, having taken over the presidency of Giscard d'Estaing's Union pour la Démocratie Française (UDF) in 1998. As for Jean-Marie Le Pen, he first rose to national prominence in 1956 when he was elected – at 28 – as the youngest deputy in the National Assembly, a member of the right-wing populist Poujadist party. Since 1974, he has stood in every presidential election but one (1981, when he failed to receive the necessary 500 endorsements). Arlette Laguiller (born 1940), the Trotskyist candidate from Lutte Ouvrière, was the only candidate in 2007 to have stood in every presidential election since 1974. These were hardly 'fresh faces'.

Nor, at first sight, was Sarkozy, who had first made headlines in 1983 by becoming, at 28, the youngest-ever mayor of a major conurbation (the wealthy Parisian suburb of Neuilly-sur-Seine). A protégé of Chirac, he rose rapidly through the ranks of the RPR, becoming deputy secretary-general in 1992, secretary-general in 1997 and (briefly) grasping the leadership in 1999. The RPR was disbanded in 2002 when three other right-wing parties joined forces with it to create the UMP to support Chirac's presidential re-election bid. Sarkozy, who had broken with Chirac in 1995 when he backed Edouard Balladur's unsuccessful bid for the presidency, spent a period in the wilderness between 1999 and 2002. Chirac, who never forgave his protégé's 'betrayal', at first tried unsuccessfully to marginalise him and then, after re-election in 2002, to co-opt him by bringing him back into the government as minister of the interior and, in 2004, as finance minister. But Sarkozy refused to be either marginalised or co-opted. He intended to become president, and remarked in response to a television interviewer's 2003 enquiry as to whether he thought about the presidency each morning in front of his shaving mirror: 'Yes, and not just when I am shaving'. In 2004, two unforeseen events offered him a breakthrough: the resignation from the presidency of the UMP of former Prime Minister Alain Juppé, who had been convicted of abuse of public funds, and the collapse of support for the party itself in the regional elections owing to widespread disillusionment with Chirac and his prime minister, Jean-Pierre Raffarin. Sarkozy stood for the presidency of the UMP, won 85% of the votes, and then turned the party into a vehicle for his presidential ambitions. For the membership of the UMP in 2004, as for the French electorate in 2007, Sarkozy represented – above all – change. A poll published on the eve of the first round revealed that 50% of respondents thought that France should be reformed 'radically' (9%) or 'in depth' (41%), with a further 34% wanting some measure of reform and only 1% happy to leave things as they were. A poll published on the eve of the second round showed that 63% of respondents believed a Sarkozy presidency would represent genuine change whereas only 38% of voters felt the same about Royal.

The two rounds of presidential elections in 2007 differed significantly. Traditionally, in the first round, featuring multiple candidates representing the entire spread of politics from extreme right to extreme left, voters have tended to express their genuine political preference. In the second round, they have traditionally eliminated their perceived opponent. In the first round of the previous presidential poll in 2002, this form of political self-indulgence had led to the presence on the second ballot of Jean-Marie Le Pen. No fewer than ten 'frivolous' left-wing candidates, totalling 30% of the vote, had so bitten into Socialist Prime Minister Jospin's electorate as to give him (at 16.2%) a lower score than Le Pen's (16.9%). As a result, these practices were, in 2007, effectively reversed. In the first round, voters eliminated the frivolous candidates, and in the second round they chose their champion. However, this potentially important trend did not become clear until the first-round votes were counted. A record number of voters (almost 40%) remained undecided until the eve of the first round of polling. One explanation for this hesitation was the clear 'negative' factors in each of the main contenders. There were left-wing 'Ségophobes', feminist 'Ségophobes', centrist 'Sarkophobes', Chiraquien 'Sarkophobes', assorted 'Bayrousceptics' and millions of visceral 'Stop Le Penistes', many of whom also rejected the mainstream candidates but baulked at voting for a marginal candidate for fear of once again letting Le Pen through to the second round. Royal also suffered from being a woman, which in France is a double-edged sword: many women are attracted by a female candidate, but more are repelled. Royal achieved her lowest score (by far) of any category of voter among 'femmes au foyer' (housewives) at 11% on the first round (against 28% for Sarkozy and 25% for Le Pen) and 29% on the second round (against 71% for Sarkozy). She was also widely perceived as lacking expertise – and therefore competence – in many policy areas, including the presidential *domaine réservé* of foreign and security policy.

Sarkozy had a long-standing reputation as a political hothead, although in reality he talks tougher than he acts. Virulent opposition to his candidacy, from many different constituencies, fuelled the campaign and his electoral posters were regularly defaced with the addition of Hitler-style moustaches. Bayrou was widely perceived as a lightweight who had achieved only 6.8% of the vote on the first round in 2002 and who, even if he won, would have difficulty governing without the necessary party support in parliament. Nevertheless, despite – or perhaps because of – this uncertainty, since real change was very definitely in the air, voters turned out in unprecedented numbers (84%) to support their favoured candidate and the televised debate between the two second-round candidates was watched by more than half the population.

A superficial hallmark of change – but one revealing the degree to which old traditions are being breached – is what in French is called *le people-isation* of politics – meaning visual imagery and glitz (the word can exist in the singular – *un people* being used for a sexy gossip-column celebrity). Sarkozy's first public appearance after his victory on 6 May was when he dined with the crooner Johnny Hallyday and other media friends at the trendy Fouquet's restaurant on the Champs Elysées in Paris, wearing blue jeans. The president's private life is the subject of intense media attention. His wife Cécilia, the daughter of a Russian father and a Spanish mother, has boasted that she has 'not one drop of French blood' in her veins. She left her husband in mid 2005 for an affair and, although notionally reconciled with Sarkozy, conspicuously neglected to vote on polling day. Sarkozy's brief 2005 affair with a journalist was similarly blazoned across the newspapers. Since entering the Elysée palace, the 'first family' has appeared on the covers of glossy magazines, including Sarkozy's two sons from his first marriage and Cécilia's two daughters from an earlier marriage, as well as the couple's own son. Such a latter-day Camelot scenario – a clear sign of the Americanisation of French politics – would have been utter anathema to all Sarkozy's predecessors.

Change was also implicit in Prime Minister François Fillon's first government. Fillon himself is a reassuring moderate, with a solid ministerial career behind him, a Welsh wife, and sustained popularity in opinion polls. Whereas his predecessor Dominique de Villepin had governed with 32 ministers (only six of them women), the initial Fillon team was pared down to 15 ministers (including seven women) and four state secretaries. This was the greatest centralisation of authority and power under the Fifth Republic. Only five of the new ministers had been members of the previous government. More significantly, whereas prior to 2007, all French presidents had respected the constitutional formality whereby ministers are appointed by the president *after nomination* by the prime minister, Sarkozy dispensed with such niceties. Before even officially announcing the name of his prime minister, the president himself entered into intensive negotiations with most ministerial hopefuls and stamped his own indelible mark on the government. Fillon made it clear that the president was also the de facto head of the government. Sarkozy announced his intention of reporting on the implementation of his policies to the National Assembly once a year – a procedure which is technically unconstitutional since only the prime minister has this right. In another break from tradition, Sarkozy invited to the Elysée the main social partners, including leaders of the labour unions.

Sarkozy clearly reflected the France that elected him – a country which, in 2007, appeared to be unambiguously right wing. Royal had made regular incursions into what was generally considered right-wing territory by calling for young offenders to be sent to boot camp and demanding that every French family possess a national flag. Sarkozy tried to present himself as a defender of left-wing values by praising the great nineteenth-century socialist leader Jean Jaurès as a role-model. At one level, this was mere opportunism. But at a deeper level it revealed a significant shift in political parameters. The left has traditionally been culturally liberal, defending human rights, minorities, gender issues and abortion, whereas the right has been conservative, arguing for family and traditional (Catholic) morality. But in economics, the right embraces liberalism, individualism, profit and competition, whereas the left is increasingly conservative, clinging to state protection mechanisms and notions of social solidarity. Political science suggests that about 60% of the population can be situated on this uneasy diagonal axis running from cultural-liberal but economic-conservative to cultural-conservative but economic-liberal. Such people divide roughly 50:50 as between right and left. There are two other – more politically coherent – groups, one of which (15% of the population), the so called 'bo-bos' (bourgeois bohemians) is both culturally and economically liberal (and tends to vote left), the other (25% of the population), codenamed by pollsters 'the defiant', is conservative on both scores (and unambiguously on the right). This socio-political arithmetic, confirmed by the election result, produces a right-wing core of around 55%. Sarkozy epitomises the majority of the population which is culturally conservative and economically liberal. Old guide-posts based on class, role of the state and assertion of order no longer define the boundaries of political affiliation.

Another significant consequence of the 2007 elections was the potentially terminal crisis afflicting the Socialist Party. The French left, since the Revolution, had been driven by ideology, aiming at root-and-branch transformation of the capitalist system in France. Even Mitterrand in 1981 paid lip service to the notion of a 'rupture' with the capitalist system. Few believed this would happen, but it was necessary for the party's self-identity as the leader of the left to preserve the myth. In 1984 the party abandoned this ideology in a major turnaround on European macroeconomic policy, but never succeeded in devising a new legitimating discourse. In 2007 nobody knew how to translate the old ideological shibboleths into a winning electoral formula. Royal's campaign promises steered clear of identification with an unreformed Socialist Party and amounted to little more than updated Keynesianism – failing to impress more than a handful of the votes that needed to be won over from the right if the left was to have any chance of winning. The party is therefore in desperate need of renewal. It needs a new ideology, appropriate for the twenty-first rather than the nineteenth century, and new political allies, who can come only from the centre. There were calls during the 2007 election to form a tactical alliance with François Bayrou's centrist UDF party, but these were angrily brushed aside by Royal. After the first round, it might have been possible for her to forge a winning alliance with Bayrou, at the price of jettisoning some of her more antiquated socialist views, but she refused for fear of losing those traditional left-wing elements on which the PS has always relied. But those left-wing allies cannot bring victory. None of the party's current leaders has any chance of constructing a majority around a strategy of 'opening to the centre' – which alone could hope to forge an electoral victory – without splitting and destroying the hegemony on the left bequeathed by Mitterrand. A month after the election, the party seemed destined to engage in a bloody civil war.

Sarkozy's ambitious domestic agenda

The president initially appointed a cabinet that carefully included heavy political hitters from previous administrations – Alain Juppé, Michèle Alliot-Marie and Jean-Louis Borloo. However, he was quickly forced into a reshuffle when the UMP did less well than expected in parliamentary elections on 17 June. Though the UMP and its allies won 345 out of 577 seats in the National Assembly, this was well below the number for which it had hoped. Juppé lost his seat – though this had more to do with the peculiarities of Bordeaux politics than with the Sarkozy administration – and therefore had to resign. Borloo was blamed by some party colleagues for losing seats because he had revealed that the government was considering a rise in value-added tax. In what was seen as a demotion, Sarkozy switched Borloo from the finance ministry to oversee environment and energy, replacing Juppé. He appointed Christine Lagarde, former trade minister and labour lawyer, as finance minister.

The real ministries of 'reform' went to his closest associates: Brice Hortefeux, who heads a new Ministry of Immigration, Integration and National Identity; Rachida Dati, daughter of a Moroccan bricklayer and an Algerian housewife – the first ever appointee from such a background – who, as minister of justice, will oversee stiffer sentences for young offenders; and Xavier Bertrand (labour) who will steer major reforms in employment and pensions policy. Several other ministerial posts went to people of immigrant origins.

Perhaps the most significant move from an international perspective – and one that was welcomed in Washington – was the appointment of the charismatic Bernard Kouchner as foreign minister – a human-rights activist, co-founder of Médecins san Frontières (Doctors Without Borders), former socialist government minister, former UN special representative in Kosovo and supporter of the invasion of Iraq. Sarkozy also appointed two other former socialists: Jean-Pierre Jouyet as Europe minister and Eric Besson (forward planning), who resigned as Royal's economics adviser during the campaign. Other French presidents have demonstrated openness by appointing ministers from outside their own political party, but never before had anyone reached right across the political divide. Sarkozy's team also had many fewer *énarques* (graduates of the Ecole Nationale d'Administration, a traditional springboard for high officials), more businessmen and more representatives of civil society than previous governments.

Sarkozy vowed to carve out his long-term legacy within the first hundred days of his presidency. The main outlines were immediately perceptible. In economic, labour and social policy, the new president cut across political classifications, combining different aspects of the three traditional French right-wing families: Bonapartist/Gaullist (state instruments to minimise social disharmony); Orleanist/Liberal (freedom for market forces); nationalist/extreme right (core values, small businesses and immigration control). A first priority was to tackle France's excessive unemployment rate by introducing a 'single labour contract' to replace the existing distinctions between fixed-term and long-term contracts. The current system fails because it creates a labour market of 'insiders' with every manner of social protection and entitlements and 'outsiders' with neither guarantees nor benefits. Sarkozy's new scheme will go much further than de Villepin's well-intentioned but ill-fated *contrat première embauche* ('first employment contract') of spring 2006 and will seek to enlist the cooperation of the labour unions in the task of unblocking employment policy and regenerating growth – by embracing labour flexibility while preserving basic social rights. He will not repeal the Socialists' controversial 35-hour work week, but will simply short-circuit it by facilitating *heures supplémentaires* (overtime), which will be exempt from both quotas and taxation. This is intended to create both supply-side stimuli (there are hundreds of thousands of jobs available in the restaurant, construction and distribution sectors) and demand-side effects, since the increased earnings in the pockets of the additionally employed will boost growth.

The co-optation of the trade unions in delivering the president's policies could be seen in his approach to another campaign promise: to ensure a minimum service in public transport in the event of labour disputes. The state would respect the constitutional right to strike, but would not tolerate a total shutdown of the transport system, as happens often in France. In convening the labour leaders at the Elysée Palace, the president effectively told them to make proposals on how they would implement his objective.

On public expenditure, Sarkozy made an explicit commitment to a reduced public sector and healthy public finances. Only one out of every two retiring civil servants is to be replaced. However, Sarkozy dared not admit too openly his penchant for liberal economics. His early forays into positive comment on globalisation as an opportunity for France rapidly gave way to a traditional French discourse which offers the state as a guarantor against outsourcing and the chill wind of *mondialisation*. During the 2005 referendum on the EU Constitutional Treaty, Chirac had entrenched in French political culture a sense that only the French state could protect the population against unfair competition from abroad. The theme of 'protection' was prominent in the campaign literature of both leading presidential candidates. Sarkozy, in changing tack and repeating that his European policies would 'protect' French workers from externally driven job losses, appeared to have retreated into the same bunker as his predecessors. However, it was noticeable that he spoke of protecting French workers 'in' rather than 'against' globalisation.

The new immigration ministry is to embark on sweeping new reforms to break down the vicious circle of exclusion, marginalisation and anger which exploded in the suburbs in November 2005. Although Sarkozy at the time took an uncompromising stand on young urban rioters, his long-term practical proposals, while radical, are potentially constructive. Inflows of immigrants will be carefully managed by a series of restrictions on 'family regrouping' (only if an immigrant worker has a place to live and a steady job will family members be allowed to join him) and a requirement for proficiency in the French language. But for immigrants who are already in France, Sarkozy offered a range of policies designed to assist their integration into an indivisible Republic. A 'Marshall Plan' for the suburbs is in preparation, involving positive discrimination based on social and economic (rather than ethnic) criteria. No young person will be left idle: jobs and/or training schemes will be created, school class sizes halved in certain poor neighbourhoods, internships arranged on merit, French language classes made available to illiterate parents and the complete range of public services restored in the cities. Sarkozy's record both as minister of the interior and as minister of finance reveals a determination to create a new deal for excluded urban dwellers. Meanwhile, he adopted a tough approach towards young offenders, making it clear that recidivists would automatically go to jail and that being a minor (16–18) would no longer be considered mitigation.

Foreign policy: renewed ties with Europe and US

Foreign and security policy did not figure prominently in the election campaign. Foreign Minister Bernard Kouchner remarked in justifying his decision to accept the post: 'French foreign policy is neither right nor left. It defends France's interests in the world.' However, the outlines of a distinctive foreign and security policy immediately became apparent. Sarkozy's 'victory speech' on 6 May was a foretaste of change to come. On Europe, he promised to unblock the impasse over the Constitutional Treaty – rejected by French voters in May 2005 – by generating a slimmed-down text, focused primarily on institutions, which would not require popular ratification through a referendum. This was immediately acted on the very afternoon of his installation in the Elysée, when he flew to Berlin to meet German Chancellor Angela Merkel. He subsequently won round the leaders of Italy and Spain, which had already ratified the Constitutional Treaty. The results were clear at the European Council in June, when the outlines of a viable new institutional framework were agreed. In less than a month, he had helped unblock a situation which Chirac, during two years of inaction, had helped create and, during a further two years of hand-wringing, had failed to rectify.

Sarkozy insisted on his 'profound' attachment to the European Union, which he wishes to develop into a serious political force in the world. It is for this reason that he wants to adopt definitive borders by excluding Turkey and by launching his alternative grand scheme: the Mediterranean Union. This dramatic proposal – to create, between the countries on the two shores of the Mediterranean, a separate regional regime on the model of the EU – seems at first sight almost Utopian. Sarkozy presented this scheme in big-picture terms as both the ultimate solution to the clash of civilisations, allowing the world 'to overcome hatred and to make way for the dream of peace and civilisation', and as 'the pivot of a grand alliance between Europe and Africa which can become, within a globalised world, the counterweight to Asia and America'. However, persuading all the 15 countries involved – including Turkey and Israel – to fall behind such a plan is likely to be a tough challenge.

Sarkozy was careful in his early months as president to tread a fine line between his (unwarranted) early reputation as an Atlanticist and the knee-jerk anti-Americanism (unfairly) associated with Chirac. The tone and style of Franco-US relations is set to change: the new president will almost certainly forge close contacts with both Democratic and Republican hopefuls for the 2008 US elections. In his victory speech, he stressed France's lasting friendship with the United States, but noted that 'friendship means accepting that friends may think differently'. That difference is likely to surface rapidly over several key issues. While insisting that France is wholly committed to the Atlantic Alliance, Sarkozy has repeated that NATO must not become a global policeman or a rival to the UN. He will continue Chirac's policy of reviewing France's specific commitment to the struggle in Afghanistan, which is seen in Paris as too focused on the military dimension. He wishes the debate on the missile shield to be framed within a European (rather than a bilateral US–Polish or US–Czech) context. He has deplored Bush's positions on climate change and the Middle East peace process. There is plenty within this range of issues to continue to generate tensions between Washington and Paris. Sarkozy's biggest challenge in transatlantic relations will be to reverse Chirac's unfortunate tendency to divide the EU member states through his perceived anti-Americanism.

A fourth major element of Sarkozy's foreign policy is likely to be his almost Blairesque commitment to humanitarian intervention, an approach which he projects as central to France's values, identity and mission in the world. A robust leitmotif throughout the presidential election campaign was his rejection of realpolitik, which he dismissed as 'an effort to prevent change in the world'. He announced his firm intention of breaking France's 'silence' on oppression in Chechnya and Darfur as well as on human-rights abuses in China and Russia. He proclaimed solidarity with women throughout the world who were the victims of abuse, concern about child soldiers, and a crusading determination to promote the causes of 'tolerance, freedom, democracy and humanism'. The appointment of Kouchner seemed the logical extension of this emphasis on intervention. But while this interventionist platform aroused concern in Beijing and Moscow and was welcomed in London and Washington, in practice it seemed unlikely to turn French policy on its head.

On security and defence policy, the most outstanding feature – beyond the familiar incantation of France's nuclear independence – is a new and explicit commitment to Europeanisation at many levels: the defence industrial base, procurement policy, defence spending (all EU member states are being urged to raise their spending to the French level of 2.5% of GDP), pooling and specialisation. Sarkozy's aim is to support a political Europe capable of exerting serious influence on the world stage. His approach stresses complementarity between the EU's European Security and Defence Policy (ESDP) and NATO. Neither France nor the EU is, in his defence rhetoric, touted as a counterweight to the United States.

France's own defence planning is to be revamped in two main ways. First, a major defence review will take place under which every current project will be subjected to serious scrutiny. The Sarkozy review will be far more root-and-branch than the last defence *White Book* in 1994, and he made a campaign promise to cease France's longstanding habit of announcing procurement projects without matching funding. Secondly, the president has followed the US model and created a National Security Council within the Elysée Palace. This new body, headed by former French ambassador to the United States Jean-David Levitte, will become 'the central body for analysis, debate and reflection' in security and defence policy. It will give the president even greater direct control over defence policy.

The new emphases in foreign and defence policy, like those in domestic affairs, suggest a determination to reverse years of internal dissension and external friction both within Europe and with Washington – though Sarkozy is likely to prioritise Europe over the transatlantic relationship. There seems little doubt, as Sarkozy said during his victory speech, that 'France is back'.

Germany: International Demands Confront Domestic Restraints

Contrary to many predictions, the 'grand coalition' headed by Chancellor Angela Merkel after the September 2005 election showed staying power in 2006 and 2007. This was only the second time since the founding of the Federal Republic in 1949 that Germany had been governed by a combination of the centre-right Christian Democrats (Christian Demoractic Union/Christian Socialist Union, CDU/CSU) and the centre-left Social Democratic Party (SPD). Many had doubted that Merkel, a Christian Democrat – the first woman chancellor and the first from East Germany – could hold the government together: the CDU/CSU had just four more seats in the Bundestag than the SPD. There was concern that the coalition would tend towards the lowest common denominator on policy. However, well into the second year of Merkel's reign, such worries had largely abated. Merkel had emerged as a European leader. In fact, she was temporarily *the* de facto European leader, as changes of leadership loomed and then occurred in

France and the United Kingdom, and Germany simultaneously held the rotating presidencies of the European Union and the G8. At the same time, the coalition faced difficult challenges, as Germany was expected by its partners to assume a growing role in international security and defence.

Though Merkel's rapid rise among European leaders had to be seen in the context of the leadership vacuum elsewhere, opportunities for rapid improvements in Germany's foreign relations were also afforded by the legacy left by her predecessor, Gerhard Schröder, a Social Democrat. Schröder's opposition to the US-led invasion of Iraq in 2003 had proved popular domestically but left German–US relations in disarray. His attempts to build a united front with France and Russia on important international issues had backfired, leaving Germany uncharacteristically isolated in Europe and Schröder himself playing a secondary role to presidents Jacques Chirac of France and Vladimir Putin of Russia.

Merkel quickly moved to remedy this situation. At her first EU summit in December 2005, she brokered a deal on the EU's financial framework for 2007–13 by essentially ceding €100m earmarked for Germany to Poland. She assured the Bush administration that she was a committed Atlanticist and concerned about strengthening NATO. By doing so, she gained leeway to mildly criticise US policy on, for example, the Guantanamo Bay detention camp, which played well with the domestic audience in Germany.

These early successes made a potentially difficult domestic constellation easier to handle. During 2006 it looked as if failure to make significant inroads into domestic reform issues would undermine Merkel's international leadership role. Her approval ratings dropped as concerns about the stability of economic growth were fuelled by a value-added tax (VAT) rise from 16 to 19% which came into effect on 1 January 2007. However, by March 2007 unemployment had fallen over 12 months by 870,000 to 4.1m, tax revenues were stronger than expected and economic growth seemed by and large unaffected by the VAT increase. The domestic uncertainties had therefore eased.

There was also potential for conflict within the coalition on foreign and security policy. The Ministry of Foreign Affairs is headed by Schröder confidant Frank-Walter Steinmeier (SPD) and the Defence Ministry by Franz Josef Jung (CDU), a close ally of one of Merkel's chief party rivals, Roland Koch, minister president of the state of Hesse. However, pragmatism has been in evidence, for example, on the question of Turkey and the EU: while Merkel and the CDU–CSU prefer an as yet undefined special partnership with Turkey over EU membership, Steinmeier and the SPD would like to see it join. But the chancellor and her foreign minister have avoided public spats on the issue. On another issue, American plans to install parts of the US missile-defence system in the Czech Republic and Poland, Steinmeier, driven by a need to sharpen the SPD profile in light of falling poll numbers, was quick to point to Russian concerns over the plans, while Merkel, at least initially, preferred to keep a low profile on the subject, suggesting that it should be handled within NATO.

Debate on Germany's international role

In the UN, NATO and the EU, Germany has been urged to live up to its responsibilities as a major European power, especially through its participation and role in international crisis-management efforts. This pressure poses a real challenge for the coalition.

When it became clear during the Israel–Lebanon conflict of 2006 that reinforcements for the UN's UNIFIL mission in Lebanon would largely come from Europe, Germany experienced a domestic debate about the appropriateness of deploying its soldiers on the borders of Israel: the historic responsibility towards Israel was at odds with the potential nightmare of German soldiers confronting Israeli forces or citizens. In 2006, fighting in southern Afghanistan led to calls from NATO allies that Germany should move beyond the relative stability of the country's north, where the bulk of German forces were deployed, and come to the aid of allies who were taking casualties in combat. There was strong pressure from the United States, Britain and Canada for Germany to relax the caveats that limited its troops' operational roles. However, the German government and population proved unwilling. A request by then UN Secretary-General Kofi Annan for an EU military mission to support the UN during 2006 elections in the Democratic Republic of the Congo (DRC) pushed Germany into a lead-nation role that the government was reluctant to embrace – though it did so.

These episodes revealed a significant gap between international expectations of Germany and what was politically possible. Each successive government must balance growing external expectations of German involvement in managing crises with the persisting strategic culture of restraint. While cultural constraints have been reinterpreted since the mid 1990s, and German participation has expanded accordingly, they still remain powerful. The societal consensus that underpins participation in international missions is still fragile. Domestic debates about why German troops are being deployed and what exactly their mission is remain unfocused and confusing. Policymakers struggle to establish a direct link between the deployments and German national interests. Public opinion is more amenable to arguments stressing the humanitarian aspects of potential operations.

Merkel, like her post-Cold War predecessors, has had to perform this balancing act between managing external expectations and gradually changing the domestic debate. Schröder presided over the first post-war combat deployment of German armed forces during NATO's air war over Kosovo in 1999. He then staked his political survival on the deployment of German troops to Afghanistan to take part in both the US-led *Operation Enduring Freedom* and

NATO's International Security Assistance Force (ISAF). Merkel has maintained these commitments and obtained parliamentary approval for Germany to lead the DRC mission.

Publication in October 2006 of a long-awaited White Paper on German Security Policy and the future of the Bundeswehr, the first such document since 1994, served to fuel the debate on the country's international role. The paper focused on the threats of international terrorism, proliferation of weapons of mass destruction and their delivery systems, and the destabilising effects of regional conflicts, failing states and the privatisation of force. It favoured reinforcement of the transatlantic partnership, with the United States seen as the bedrock of German and European security. It argued that NATO remained the cornerstone of German security and defence policy, particularly in light of the political and military means it could bring to bear in peacekeeping and peace-restoration missions. Acknowledging the previous strained relationship with the United States, it called for the transatlantic link to be strengthened through continuous mutual consultation and coordinated action. At the same time, the EU would have to improve its capabilities and shoulder responsibilities for European security. The government saw NATO and the EU as complementary security institutions and pledged to work for better dialogue between them. NATO's comparative advantage was said to be in the field of robust and complex military missions, while the EU's strength was seen to be in the potential to combine a broad range of civilian and military means. Merkel told the annual Munich security policy conference in 2007: 'Strengthening Europe's security identity, separate from the Atlantic security partnership, is not a route I want to take. Both pillars are, so to speak, two sides of the same coin.' Jung said NATO 'continues to be the strongest anchor of German security and defence policy'.

The white paper, while acknowledging that international crisis-management missions were the most likely tasks and would therefore have overriding influence on the structure and capabilities of the German armed forces, still described national and collective defence as the central task of the Bundeswehr. It pointed to the growing overlap between internal and external security challenges such as terrorist attacks, and argued that the German constitutional framework, the Basic Law – which limits use of the armed forces within Germany strictly to assisting domestic authorities such as the police – needed amendment to address international terrorism. The paper called conscription 'an unqualified success', pointing out that some 20% of deployed German forces had begun as conscripts and extended their service, and arguing that conscription provided the services with a broad range of skills and a vast recruitment pool, as well as anchoring the armed forces in society.

Allies who expected a CDU-led government to increase defence spending were disappointed. The coalition did not perceive the need to respond in any significant way to pressure from the United States and NATO. The 2007 defence budget was set at €28.4bn, up from €27.9bn in 2006, including €4bn for pension payments which had in 2006 been included in the defence budget for the first time. However, the increase in the 2007 budget will partly be cancelled out by the rise in VAT and the costs of the Lebanon mission. According to press reports, there will be an annual gap of some €1bn between funding and planned procurement – a total of €8.4bn between 2007 and 2014. The draft budget for 2008 and planning assumptions up to 2011, which were presented in early July 2007, announced further limited increases to €29.3bn for 2008 and €30.0bn by 2010. The white paper argued that continuous transformation of the armed forces demanded a reorientation of the defence budget from running costs to acquisition, which is to take 27.6% of the budget in 2007, rising to 29% in 2009. However, there is likely to be continuing tension between the urgent operational requirements of the deployed forces and the long-term investment plans.

The white paper highlighted force protection, reconnaissance, command and control, missile defence, precision stand-off strike, and strategic deployability as central to the new capabilities profile. It confirmed previous plans to make up to 15,000 troops available for the NATO Response Force (NRF), of which up to 5,000 would be on stand-by. A pool of up to 18,000 troops are available to meet EU Headline Goal requirements. A further 1,000 troops are provided within the UN Standby Arrangement System, and 1,000 are available for unilateral rescue and evacuation tasks. The paper also confirmed differentiation of the Bundeswehr between three force categories with different roles: the response forces, 35,000 strong, are a joint rapid reaction force with network centric warfare (NCW) capability for high-intensity missions including combat. It is from this pool that Germany draws its NRF and EU battlegroup contingents, as well as troops for other demanding missions. Next come the 70,000 strong stabilisation forces, whose purpose is to serve in medium- and low-intensity peace-support operations. Up to 14,000 are to be deployable at any given time and sustainable for long-term missions. The stabilisation force will have partial NCW capability. Finally, the 147,500-strong support forces provide combat support for the response and stabilisation forces, such as logistics, transport, medical, and command and control. Only some elements of the support forces will have NCW capability. The rationale for this approach was to ensure an intervention capability within budget limits, since it was not feasible to modernise the whole force.

The white paper was expected to trigger a widespread and systematic domestic debate about German security policy. However, this did not occur: discussion continued to centre on deployment questions. The day the white paper was launched, the popular daily *Bild* published pictures of German soldiers posing with skulls and enacting execution scenes using human bones they discovered in Afghanistan. The resulting short-lived furore drowned out much of the white paper's impact.

Deployments mark growing participation

Germany's deployments, however, did mark steps forward in the country's international role. Its lead role in EUFOR RD Congo, to assist in elections in the DRC, was its first in Africa, which Germany had previously been happy to leave to other EU members with more recent colonial ties. The government was eager to make EUFOR as multinational as possible, and therefore did not wish to use EU battlegroups, which include troops from single nations or small groups. A leaked report revealed that the German general staff had advised the minister of defence that Germany had no direct interest in the DRC and hence a major commitment would be unwise. Nevertheless, Germany did lead the force and committed 780 troops, with 20 other countries also contributing. The German troops were restricted to Kinshasa, the capital, and a German infantry battalion was part of theatre reserve forces stationed in Libreville, Gabon. The operation passed off smoothly, apparently aided by the avoidance of heavy-handed responses to sporadic violence, especially following the first round of voting in the presidential election.

In Lebanon, Germany contributed a naval element, the strength of which has been limited to a maximum of 2,400. The actual deployment has so far fluctuated between some 750 and 950 sailors. On 16 October 2006, the German navy took command of the naval elements of UNIFIL with a mandate to intercept arms shipments along Lebanon's coast. Because of the risk that German soldiers could find themselves in confrontation with Israeli soldiers or citizens, the commitment of ground troops was explicitly avoided.

In Afghanistan, heavy fighting between NATO forces and insurgent groups in the south during 2006 threatened the solidarity of the alliance. Among the allies that had troops deployed in the south, the perception spread that Germany and some others were unwilling to join this demanding part of the mission and correspondingly were not willing to share the risks. Under intense pressure, the German government conceded that existing parliamentary mandates allowed for the temporary deployment of German troops throughout Afghanistan in order to come to the aid of allied contingents. NATO then asked Germany to fill a gap in reconnaissance capabilities by making *Tornado* jets available to ISAF. While based at Mazar-e-Sharif in the north of Afghanistan, the area of operations for the jets covers all of the country. They were declared fully operational as of 19 April 2007. While some in the grand coalition suggested that this would fall within the existing parliamentary mandate, a new vote of the Bundestag was deemed necessary. However, the government became concerned that a new mandate would open the door to even more demanding

NATO requests. Hence, the *Tornado* deployment was styled as an amendment to the existing mandate.

Germany has developed a consensus within society that permits participation in international missions defined in terms of international responsibility, humanitarianism and a comprehensive approach to crisis management – as long as casualties remain limited. However, the narrative that underpins this consensus is being undermined by the realities of recent deployments, especially in Afghanistan, which carry the risk of being asked to take part in active combat. German policymakers tend to downplay what the Bundeswehr is actually doing on operations. For example, media reports suggested that Defence Minister Jung refused to speak of a NATO spring offensive in early 2007 because it suggested an image deemed too aggressive. Similarly, he declared the deployment of *Tornado* reconnaissance jets to Afghanistan to be a purely defensive measure designed to reduce collateral damage from NATO actions. All this suggests that, in spite of the publication of the 2006 white paper, a serious debate about the purpose of the use of force is still to be had in Germany. German contingents take part in international missions with heavy limitations on the activities they are able to undertake. The gap between domestic constraint and international expectation seems likely to continue to grow, suggesting that the present state of affairs cannot be sustained in the long run.

Developments in European Defence

Both the European Union and NATO took steps to improve military capabilities over the past year, and the EU's involvement in a wide variety of operations continued to accelerate. The rapid deployment capacities of both institutions advanced significantly. However, the high tempo of military operations has been of concern to a number of individual European countries, with deployments in Lebanon added over the past year to the operations in Afghanistan and Iraq. Political debates in many countries centred on the purpose and sustainability of deployments, particularly in Afghanistan. Governments struggled to reconcile growing operational demands with long-term reform plans and flat or falling defence budgets. These problems did not sit easily with the NATO Comprehensive Political Guidance, endorsed at the Riga Summit in November 2006, which stated clearly that a greater number of limited but demanding operations could be expected, the precise nature of which would be both complex and unpredictable. Equally, a Long Term Vision document drawn up by the European Defence Agency (EDA), published in October 2006, expected some European Security and Defence Policy (ESDP) operations to be at the upper limit of intensity.

National debates on defence reform

While debates about international commitments and defence reform in the largest European states such as France, Germany and the United Kingdom receive most attention, similar challenges confront small countries as well.

Norway, for example, increased its commitments in Afghanistan during 2007 in response to a NATO request. It deployed more than a hundred special-operations forces to NATO's ISAF force in Afghanistan in April 2007, after having previously made similar deployments to the US-led *Operation Enduring Freedom*. The troops from the Forsvarets Spesialkommando (FSK) were tasked to prevent suicide and improvised explosive device attacks in Kabul. Norway also sent 400 soldiers to supply a quick-reaction capability for Mazar-e-Sharif in northern Afghanistan. Together with Provincial Reconstruction Team involvements and responsibility for Kabul international airport, the Norwegian effort in Afghanistan was substantial.

However, it raised both political and military issues. The left-wing socialist coalition partner in the Norwegian centre-left government had repeatedly ruled out deployment of the FSK, and forced a compromise that limited FSK activities to Kabul: a deployment of combat forces to the volatile south was in effect ruled out. Norwegian Defence Minister Anne-Grete Strom Erichsen nonetheless said Norwegian forces would 'come to the rescue of our allies if they are in a situation', including in the south. Meanwhile, the armed forces faced budget difficulties. The defence budget was increased slightly in real terms in 2007, with a little more money for procurement and international missions. However, it remained doubtful whether Norway's forces would have enough money to maintain their capabilities. The Armed Forces Command is expected to outline possible structural changes and savings, but Chief of Defence General Sverre Diesen indicated that structural underfunding of the armed forces was beginning to threaten their capabilities.

Another example was Slovenia. Its efforts to boost participation in international missions and to fulfil NATO force goals underlined the choices smaller European countries faced. Slovenia's ambition was to provide more in terms of both quantity and quality to international crisis-management missions, and at the same time to achieve greater operational autonomy. A battalion-sized deployment to NATO's Kosovo force in 2007 marks an important milestone. Under reforms adopted in November 2006, the Slovenian armed forces aimed to be able to provide a light battlegroup by 2010 and a medium battlegroup (some 1,400 troops) by 2012. Slovenian reform efforts were defined almost exclusively by international force goals drawn up in NATO and to a lesser extent the EU. This underlined the importance of closely aligning NATO, EU and national requirements, because smaller nations do not have the resources to pursue conflicting goals. For example, Slovenia viewed its patrol boats and trainer aircraft as priority assets, but NATO officials argued that they were not needed. Agreement on points such as this freed resources to invest in capabilities that are part of the planned reforms, such as 135 armoured vehicles contracted in 2006.

Some European countries have increased defence spending in order to pursue reform programmes and meet the costs of deployments. For example, Spain in 2007 announced the biggest rise in 20 years, increasing the defence budget by 8.6% to €8.05bn following a 6% rise in 2006 – though this had to be seen in the context of the comparatively low 1.2–1.3% of GDP that Spain spent on defence. The increased funding was to be spent on procurement, salaries, the national intelligence centre and the establishment of a military emergency force to assist civilian authorities in national emergencies.

Demand for EU missions

As of June 2007, the EU was running a total of ten crisis-management missions, of which eight were civilian in nature, one included both civil and military components (EU support to AMIS II in Darfur), and one was military (EUFOR-*Althea* in Bosnia). During the previous year, two missions under way had been completed, and one had been undertaken and completed: those that finished were a police advisory mission in Macedonia (EUPAT) and a monitoring mission in the Indonesian province of Aceh (AMM).

The EU's military mission to the Democratic Republic of the Congo, EUFOR RD Congo, was mandated by the UN Security Council to support the UN mission MONUC during presidential elections. The mission, lasting from the end of July to the end of November 2006, reached a peak strength of 2,466 soldiers from 21 contributor countries. The four biggest contingents came from France (1,090), Germany (730), Poland (130) and Spain (130), and the operational headquarters was provided by Germany. Some 1,100 troops were deployed to Kinshasa while the remaining 1,300 formed an over-the-horizon theatre reserve based in Libreville, Gabon. When fighting between supporters of the two main presidential contenders broke out in August 2006, some 400 additional troops were deployed to Kinshasa. Immediately before the population returned to the polls for a run-off vote in October 2006, EUFOR again reinforced its presence. Similarly, most of the over-the-horizon theatre reserve was deployed to Kinshasa in November to deter unrest in light of the final election results. The EU judged the mission to be a success and believed that its deterrent effect had limited the outbreak of serious incidents during the election period.

EUPOL Afghanistan was launched on 17 June, comprising some 160 police, law-enforcement and justice experts. Personnel are deployed in Kabul, five regional commands and on the provincial level. EUPOL will remain in place for at least three years.

Planning for further missions was under way. Following a joint action by the Council of the European Union in April 2006, an EU Planning Team deployed to

Kosovo to plan a future mission related to the rule of law, including judiciary, police, customs and correctional services. At an expected size of 1,300–1,500 civilian personnel, this would be the EU's biggest effort in civilian crisis management. Following approval in principle of an EU civilian mission to Afghanistan to cover rule of law and police issues, a detailed concept of operations was being developed.

The EUFOR *Althea* mission in Bosnia was being reduced and restructured following a decision by EU leaders in December 2006, taken in light of the improved security situation. Its size was being cut to some 2,500 troops from 6,000 during 2007, and it was to be centred on Sarajevo, with support from liaison and observation teams throughout the country. Most combat forces were withdrawing, and EUFOR was to rely on an over-the-horizon rapid-reaction capability shared with NATO's KFOR mission in Kosovo.

Capabilities development in the EU

As of January 2007, EU battlegroups, designed for rapid deployment in crises, had achieved full operational capability, meaning that there would always be two 1,500-strong battlegroups available for near-simultaneous use. In the first half of 2007, a German–Dutch–Finnish and a French–Belgian battlegroup were on standby, followed in the second half of the year by an Italian–Hungarian–Slovenian and a Greek–Cypriot–Romanian–Bulgarian battlegroup. The core of each group was an infantry battalion, with mission-tailored combat support and combat service support units. Norway and Turkey, though not EU members, will contribute to multinational battle groups in the first half of 2008 and the second half of 2010 respectively.

In parallel, discussions took place on maritime and air rapid-response initiatives. Under the EU Military Rapid Response Concept, land, air and sea elements could be used as stand-alone forces or in joint operations. An EU Maritime Task Group was activated in March 2007, consisting of vessels from Germany, Belgium, France and the Netherlands, operating under an interim Standard Operating Procedure drawn up by German Fleet Command. Meanwhile, an EU Operations Centre became operational in January 2007, providing the EU with a third option for the command of ESDP missions aside from using NATO assets and capabilities under the Berlin Plus agreement or relying on one of five national headquarters in France, Germany, Greece, Italy and the UK. The centre, with a permanent staff of eight, is able to generate an operational headquarters for a force of up to 2,000 troops, reaching full operating capability within 20 days with a staff of 89. It was activated for the first time during an EU military exercise in June 2007 to test the interaction between the centre as OHQ and a force headquarters provided by Sweden.

In the field of force planning, the EU was compiling a 'Progress Catalogue' that would list capability shortfalls. It used five illustrative scenarios to help identify the relevant military capabilities for its Headline Goal 2010: separation of parties by force; stabilisation, reconstruction and military advice to third countries; conflict prevention; evacuation operations; and assistance/humanitarian operations. Based on these scenarios a detailed list of required capabilities was defined, and this was translated into generic force packages, which in turn were the basis for the EU Requirement Catalogue of 2005. EU member states were asked to make pledges towards this catalogue, and contributions made were listed in the EU Force Catalogue of 2006. A comparison of these catalogues enabled the identification of shortfalls and their impact on potential EU operations, resulting in the Progress Catalogue to be completed by the end of 2007.

NATO Response Force enters full operation

The NATO Response Force (NRF), intended both to enhance rapid deployment capabilities and to be an instrument of transformation of European armed forces, gained momentum over the past year. After NATO members enhanced their pledges during a force-generation conference from 21 to 23 November 2006, the NRF was declared to have reached full operational capability on 29 November at NATO's Riga summit. General James Jones, then Supreme Allied Commander Europe (SACEUR), stated that additional pledges from Bulgaria, Canada, France, Germany, Italy, Norway, Romania, Spain, Turkey, the UK and the United States had helped to fill gaps. Additional troops, helicopters, transport aircraft, combat support and combat service support had been provided.

Following the entry into force of a Strategic Airlift Interim Solution (SALIS) in early 2006, NATO countries made further arrangements to improve capabilities in the field of strategic airlift. In September 2006, 13 allies signed a Letter of Intent to begin contract negotiations with Boeing for the purchase of up to four C-17 transport planes to be based at Ramstein Air Force Base in Germany. Delivery of the first C-17 had been expected for the second half of 2007 but was pushed back to mid 2008.

Despite the fact that the NRF was declared fully operational and conducted substantial live exercises, several problems persisted. Initial-entry operations, which are at the upper end of the operational spectrum, were problematic because capability shortfalls remained unresolved. Furthermore, the arrangements for funding of NATO operations were an obstacle to use of the NRF: the 'costs lie where they fall' principle meant that those countries who happened to be contributors to the NRF when a need for rapid deployment arose would have had to carry the financial burden almost exclusively. This, General Jones said, was a 'significant disincentive' to NRF deployment.

General John Craddock, who succeeded Jones as SACEUR, said the NRF 'was not conceived to be a static force that sits on the shelf after achieving full operational capability'. However, actual deployments of both the NRF and EU battlegroups were likely to be politically challenging. While on paper governments accepted that their forces were on call for the duration of six months, in reality no deployment would be possible against the will of a major contributing country. Existing commitments to operations, costs, political vulnerabilities and the character of the potential mission would all be factors influencing any decision to deploy forces.

United Kingdom: Brown Gets His Chance

On 27 June 2007, Gordon Brown's ten-year waiting period ended as he became prime minister. He immediately sought to distance himself from his predecessor, Tony Blair – using the word 'change' eight times in a short address before he entered 10 Downing Street, the prime minister's office and residence. Most of the previous year had in essence been a peculiar interregnum as Blair, facing a rebellion within the Labour Party over the timing of his planned departure from office, had announced on 7 September 2006 that he would leave within 12 months. This had the effect of finally ending the internal party battle that had been fought between the two men's respective camps for years. It left Blair to spend his remaining time on issues that, he hoped, would define a positive legacy. These included a political settlement in Northern Ireland, global action on climate change and reform of Britain's public services.

With Brown's accession, Britain had a 56-year-old prime minister who had been a member of parliament for 24 years, and chancellor of the exchequer (finance minister) for ten, but about whom it knew surprisingly little. A workaholic and a private man, he had long coveted the premiership with a degree of obsession. He had been successful in his stewardship of the economy, if with a tendency to meddle with tax mechanisms and to over-complicate them. But on matters away from his economics and finance brief, he seemed less comfortable. In the early months of 2007, he appeared awkward as he sought to address publicly the broader issues of government in order to appear a convincing and better-known leader.

Particular attention was therefore focused on how he would handle foreign-policy issues such as Iraq and Iran, but there were few clues to his likely attitudes. When combined with a domestic policy agenda including further reform of health services, and the need to counter better-organised opposition led by David Cameron, the Conservative Party leader, Brown had plenty of challenges to address before the next elections, which must be called by May 2010 but are likely to be in 2009 – unless Brown were to seek a mandate in a snap election.

Blair's tenure: the shadow of Iraq

Assessment of a ten-year tenure as prime minister is inevitably complex, and will in any case change in light of subsequent developments. The view of many in Britain was that Blair had done well in many respects, but that his premiership had been tarnished by his choice to tie the country so closely to the United States in the initiation and execution of the Iraq War. For many – especially on the left of his own party – this was a betrayal founded on false pretences, and one that fatally trumped his achievements in other areas.

Blair's personal style reflected the informality of thriving modern Britain – which, at least in its dominant capital city, has travelled a long way from its traditional image of staid, class-ridden stuffiness. With a private-school-educated accent sometimes infused with Cockney-like tones, and an unashamed liking for football and rock music, Blair epitomised the change. Only 54 on his departure, Blair had governed through a group of close advisers in what was caricatured as 'sofa government'. His ability to understand and give voice to the country's mood – for example, calling Princess Diana 'the people's princess' after her sudden death in 1997 – was in keeping with his achievement in leading the Labour Party in an unprecedented run of three successive election victories. To do this, he steered the party along a non-traditional path, combining economic orthodoxy and prudence (in which he was aided by Brown as finance minister) with a liberal approach on many isssues and a belief in strong, well-funded public services. Though the British people may have tired of Blair after ten years, there was no indication that they favoured any real revision of this approach: the dissatisfaction was with execution of the policies, and with Iraq.

Blair's tenure was full of contradictions. He was open and informal, willing to take on hostile audiences of voters on live television. It was therefore somewhat surprising that he lost the trust of many, accused of deceiving the country into war in Iraq. The 'sofa' style led to accusations of cronyism, fuelled by a long-running scandal in which his office was alleged to have made secret deals in return for party funding. His personal relaxed demeanour contrasted with Downing Street's manic attempts – especially during the first six years of his tenure – to manage media coverage. Blair's 'New Labour' approach, abandoning purist socialist tenets while still emphasising state-funded health care and education, was never fully accepted by many in his party, even though they probably owed their seats in Parliament to it. The phrase 'New Labour' was dropped from the party's website on the day he announced his departure date. Blair presided over a long period of healthy economic growth, as well as improvements in health services and education, for which, at least at the time of his departure, he was not fully appreciated. The one achievement for which he was universally praised was the apparent settlement through a power-sharing agreement of the bitter conflict in Northern Ireland: on 8 May 2007, loyalist leader Ian Paisley took office as first minister in a devolved assembly, with Irish Republican Martin McGuinness as his deputy.

Iraq was the main reason for popular disillusion with Blair. This was despite the fact that, in terms of domestic politics, the sting had to some extent been taken out of the issue by re-election in May 2005, by his announcement of his intention to stand down during his third term, and his September 2006 promise to do so within a year. Arguments over Iraq had consumed his second term from 2001 to 2005, a period which saw the prime minister's determination to stand close to the United States following the 11 September attacks lead him into evangelical enthusiasm for President George W. Bush's adventure. In the United Kingdom, the case for the invasion was made mainly on the basis of Saddam Hussein's programmes for weapons of mass destruction. But government dossiers and public statements about Iraqi weapons programmes were exposed after the invasion as exaggerations of the available intelligence, although inquiries absolved the government of deliberate falsification. Blair was seen as having followed Bush too easily and unquestioningly – more so as subsequent events in Iraq unfolded. If the UK government and military had raised in advance with American counterparts the issues which eventually doomed the mission to failure, they plainly had little or no effect on the American conduct of the post-combat phase. Not only were Britain's armed forces involved in a failure, but they appeared to have had limited success in their own area of operations, in and around the southern city of Basra. The Shia-dominated city descended into factionalism over which British forces had little control, their much-vaunted peacekeeping skills apparently unable to prevail in the face of a nationwide absence of security. Blair reduced the number of troops in Iraq from 7,100 to 5,500 by mid 2007, and Brown was expected to announce a further reduction. Since this step was likely to be taken over American objections, it would serve a useful political purpose for Brown in separating his approach from that of his predecessor.

Challenges for Brown: defence resources and counter-terrorism

A distinguishing feature of Blair's tenure – and that for which he was best known outside the United Kingdom – was his keenness for Britain to play an important role in the solution to the world's crises. In spite of Iraq, this enthusiasm had seemed undimmed, evidenced by Blair's high profile on the issues of African poverty and climate change. One question for Brown was whether he would maintain Britain's interventionist approach. Blair had sent British troops to Kosovo, East Timor, Sierra Leone, Macedonia, Afghanistan and Iraq, while maintaining commitments in Northern Ireland, Bosnia and the Falkland Islands. The United Kingdom has steadily increased its commitment of forces in Afghanistan, with the total due to reach 7,800 by September 2007. British troops in Helmand province were in mid 2007 involved daily in combat, and were regularly suffering casualties. Deployments of UK forces have remained at a constantly high level in spite of the withdrawal of 600 soldiers from Bosnia, and the reduction in forces in Northern Ireland to about 8,500 by March 2007.

The continuing high tempo of British troop deployments put pressure on Brown to consider the appropriate level of spending on defence. Over the past year, several senior serving officers publicly warned that the armed forces needed more resources if they were to maintain the level of operations. For personnel, persistently high commitments have resulted in insufficient gaps between deployments, and insufficient training. According to a 2006 report by the Defence Committee of the House of Commons, over 30% of units had serious or critical weaknesses compared with their planned ability to generate readiness for deployment. Welfare and accommodation were also inadequate. Just as pressing, the Ministry of Defence lacked the budgeted funds to pursue its programme for acquisition of equipment. Operations exposed serious shortfalls, for example in helicopters and air transport. At a deeper level, constant pressure on the Ministry of Defence (spurred by the Treasury when it was headed by Brown) to cut costs while keeping up a high tempo of operations had resulted by the time of Blair's departure in a loss of mutual trust between the government and the armed forces. Given all these concerns, one option open to Brown was to order a new defence review similar to that completed in 1998, which had set a course for modernisation through a consultative process viewed as a model by other governments. However, hopes within the armed forces for a new prime ministerial approach were not encouraged when the defence secretary, Des Browne, turned out to be the only cabinet minister kept in the same post by Brown – and was given the additional job of overseeing Scotland. For some – though judgements were obviously premature – this confirmed a long-standing impression that Brown was uninterested in defence and the armed forces.

A further pressing issue was the threat from Islamist terrorism. On 29 June, when Brown had spent just one full day in office, two unexploded car bombs were found in the centre of London, and on the next day an attempt was made to explode a car bomb at Glasgow airport. Those arrested immediately after the incidents were mainly foreign-born doctors working in British hospitals. Brown said it was 'clear that we are dealing, in general terms, with people who are associated with al-Qaeda'.

The dimensions of the problem afflicting the United Kingdom had become clearer during the year to mid 2007. In August 2006, police said they had uncovered a plot to blow up transatlantic airliners with liquid explosives, prompting additional security measures to be taken at airports. Seventeen people with addresses in London and surrounding towns were charged variously with terrorist and other criminal offences. The 7 July 2005 bombings which killed 52 people in London had caused particular shock because they appeared to be domestically generated, with three of the bombers born in northern England and the fourth brought up there from infancy. More evidence subsequently emerged. Although the bombers had been radicalised in Britain, the role of al-Qaeda leaders based in Pakistan seemed to have been greater than was previously thought. Two of the group had undergone terrorist training in Pakistan with members of another British group, who were arrested in 2004 and whose trial ended in April 2007. The trial of the latter group, who were planning fertiliser-bomb attacks, shed light on the part played by outsiders in British-based terrorist groups. Of the seven on trial, of whom five were convicted, all but one were second-generation British nationals of Pakistani origin in their twenties, from towns around London. Of Britain's 2.3m Muslims, some 800,000 are of Pakistani origin, and many of these visit Pakistan regularly. The possibility that even a small number of these might attend terrorist training camps creates a serious vulnerability for the UK.

A rare speech in November 2006 by Eliza Manningham-Buller, then head of the domestic intelligence service (MI5), shed light on the scale of the problem. She said that five major conspiracies had been foiled since July 2005, that some 1,600 individuals in some 200 groups, still at large, had been identified as 'actively engaged in plotting, or facilitating, terrorist acts here and overseas'. She said: 'More and more people are moving from passive sympathy towards active terrorism through being radicalised or indoctrinated by friends, families, in organised training events here and overseas, by images on television, through chat rooms and websites on the internet.' The service, she said, was aware of nearly 30 plots then under way. 'These plots often have links back to al-Qaeda in Pakistan and through those links, al-Qaeda gives guidance and training to its largely British foot soldiers here on an extensive and growing scale.' In response, the UK government has expanded its intelligence services and has refined its counter-terrorism strategy through organisational changes that allow the Home Office (interior ministry) to focus more clearly on countering terrorism and crime.

Brown's first steps

In shaping his government, Brown took a leaf from the book of Nicolas Sarkozy, newly elected president of France. The changes that were required, he said, could not be met by 'old politics'. In spite of Labour's strong majority in parliament, he went outside party-political lines to tap the experience of former officials – though the cabinet was still made up of well-known and rising Labour figures, minus some 'Blairite' stalwarts. A former Conservative MP who had switched to Labour was made Northern Ireland Secretary – reportedly after Paddy Ashdown, the former Liberal Democrat party leader and High Representative in Bosnia, was barred by his party leadership from accepting the job. Mark Malloch-Brown, former deputy secretary-general of the United Nations, was made a Foreign

Office minister responsible for Africa, Asia and the UN. A former navy chief, Admiral Alan West, was made a security minister in the Home Office, and a former police chief, John Stevens, was made the prime minister's international security adviser.

Brown's intended agenda for the period until the next election seemed likely to be primarily domestic. He proposed constitutional reforms to increase the accountability of government to the electorate, in an effort to rebuild voters' trust which he saw as having been damaged. Under his proposals, parliamentary approval would be required to declare war and for international treaties. He would set up a national security council and regularly publish a national security strategy. Health was also likely to be a key theme: while Blair's tenure had seen substantial improvements in the delivery of health care by the state's National Health Service, there remained a widespread belief that reforms and a huge increase in financial resources had not yet produced an adequate result. Education and housing would also be priorities. In addition, Brown repeatedly expressed a desire to promote British values – a response to the phenomenon of extremism among immigrant communities and to the perceived failure of the 'multicultural' approach to community integration. More generally, Brown signalled an end to 'sofa government', stopping the practice of ministerially appointed 'special advisers' giving orders to civil servants, and promising a more formal approach to cabinet decision-making. After one retired top civil servant had accused Brown of a 'Stalinist' approach and of having 'a very cynical view of mankind and his colleagues', he was clearly making an attempt to reassure the administrative branch. But there remained questions about how Brown's tendency in the Treasury to make decisions with little consultation – and brooking no dissent – would translate to the demands of leading the government.

It was even less easy to divine the likely tenor of Brown's foreign policy. He had a great deal of international experience in the financial and economic sphere, and had said nothing to indicate any radical departure from Blair's overall approach. There was no reason to believe that he would have anything other than cordial relations with the United States, and within Europe – where Brown had prevented Blair from joining the euro – the stage seemed set for jousting over the continent's future direction among Brown, Sarkozy and German Chancellor Angela Merkel. As well as the continuing issues of Iran, Iraq, the Middle East and Afghanistan, Britain found itself in a diplomatic confrontation with Russia as it sought to extradite a Russian suspect in the murder in London of Alexander Litvinenko, a former Russian dissident killed in 2006 with polonium-210, a highly radioactive isotope. Another looming diplomatic issue was disquiet – in the United States and elsewhere – over Blair's decision in 2006 to end a corruption inquiry into arms manufacturer BAE Systems, because of the risk to intelligence cooperation with Saudi Arabia.

If Britain was entering a new era under Gordon Brown, it was therefore difficult to define its likely nature in the first few days of his premiership. He gave all the signs of someone who had long planned the steps he would take when the day came – but as soon as it did, events took a hand.

The Balkans: Year of Frustration

The past year was one of disappointment and delay for the people of Serbia, Bosnia-Hercegovina and Kosovo. Serbia spent much of it in political paralysis; progress towards political reform in Bosnia stalled; Kosovo's status remained unresolved as Russia put up stiff opposition to its independence.

Montenegro, Macedonia, Albania and Croatia progressed to a greater or lesser extent on paths towards membership of the EU and NATO. Macedonia was bogged down with political problems after its July 2006 election as the winning ethnic Macedonian party chose the smaller of the two main ethnic Albanian parties as a coalition partner. However, there was no return to the tensions seen during the brief period of armed conflict there in 2001. Montenegro proclaimed independence from Serbia on 3 June 2006 after a close-fought referendum. It proceeded to address domestic issues which had been neglected over the previous decade when politics was dominated by the issue of independence.

Status of Kosovo: the Ahtisaari plan

Kosovo was the central issue in Balkan affairs over the last year thanks to the mission of former Finnish President Martti Ahtisaari, who had in 2005 been appointed by Kofi Annan, then UN Secretary-General, as special envoy to lead a political process to determine the territory's future status. Talks between Serbia and the Kosovo Albanians took place throughout 2006 but proved desultory and inconclusive, with the two sides unable to agree on the final status. In the end Ahtisaari drew up a plan which he presented to the Security Council on 26 March 2007. He proposed independence, under international supervision for an initial period.

Kosovo has been problematic because, unlike the six former Yugoslav republics, its legal status is that it is a province of Serbia. Some 90% of its two million people are ethnic Albanians who want independence. About 130,000 are thought to be ethnic Serbs, although the number fluctuates. Less than half of these live in an area of northern Kosovo abutting Serbia, while the remainder live in enclaves scattered throughout the rest of the territory.

Resolution 1244 of the UN Security Council, which ended NATO's 78-day bombing campaign of Yugoslavia in 1999, contained a central contradiction which has bedevilled policymakers seeking a solution of Kosovo's status. While on the one hand it recognised the territorial integrity of the then Federal Republic of Yugoslavia, to which Serbia is the legal successor state, it also demanded that full account be taken of the 1999 Rambouillet accords, which spoke of a final settlement 'on the basis of the will of the people'. Since the 1999 war, Kosovo has been run by the UN administration in Kosovo, UNMIK, with much power devolved to Kosovo's elected institutions. Serbs are allotted reserved seats in parliament giving them greater representation than their numbers warrant, but have boycotted Kosovo's institutions on the orders of Belgrade. Ultimate authority rests with the UN's Special Representative of the Secretary General (SRSG), since September 2006 Joachim Rücker, a German diplomat. Security is provided by 17,000 NATO-led troops, plus a UN police mission supporting the Kosovo Police Service.

While the Ahtisaari plan represented a blueprint for an independent state, it offered concessions to Kosovo's Serbs. Reflecting the fact that Kosovo's Serbian enclaves, and especially the north, are run, or at least strongly influenced, by Belgrade, the plan allowed for 'decentralisation', under which Serbs would be able to run their own districts with special links, including financial, with Serbia. Areas with important Serbian Orthodox churches and monasteries would also have special status. However, Ahtisaari reported that Serbs and Albanians have 'diametrically opposed positions' and that 'no amount of additional talks, whatever the format, will overcome this impasse'. His conclusion was that 'the only viable option for Kosovo is independence, to be supervised for an initial period by the international community'.

NATO troops would stay in Kosovo but direct UN supervision would end 120 days after the passing of a Security Council resolution endorsing the plan. Although Kosovars would be running their new state, two new outside organisations would have significant powers. The larger of the two, with more than 1,500 international staff, including police, and almost 900 local staff, would be an EU body deployed as a European Security and Defence Policy (ESDP) mission. Its job would be to 'monitor, mentor and advise on all areas related to the rule of law in Kosovo. It shall have the right to investigate and prosecute independently sensitive crimes, such as organized crime, inter-ethnic crime, financial crime, and war crimes.' The second body would be an International Civilian Office (ICO) headed by an International Civilian Representative (ICR). According to the Ahtisaari report on what is termed the 'Settlement', the ICR, who as in Bosnia would be double-hatted as the EU Special Representative, 'shall be the ultimate supervisory authority over the implementation of the Settlement. The [ICR] shall have no direct role in the administration of Kosovo, but shall have strong corrective powers to ensure successful implementation of the Settlement. Among his/her powers is the ability to annul decisions or laws adopted by Kosovo authorities and sanction and remove public officials whose actions he/she deter-mines to be inconsistent with the Settlement.' This body would be dominated by the EU, but would not technically belong to it, so as to allow for the participation of Americans and other non-EU citizens. In every respect it would resemble the Office of the High Representative (OHR) in Bosnia. Kosovo would thus become, in effect, an EU protectorate.

Among the assumptions of Western diplomats was that Russia, though uncomfortable with independence for Kosovo because of what it saw as a prec-edent for post-Soviet frozen conflicts, would agree to it and thus not block a new Security Council resolution. However, Russia strongly opposed the Ahtisaari plan, saying that only an agreement between Kosovo Albanians and Serbs was acceptable and that there should be more talks. Russian diplomats implied they would veto a Security Council resolution. While Washington's initial reaction was that Kosovo should declare independence unilaterally, and that the United States would recognise it, the United States later seemed to be backing away from such a commitment. In mid 2007 discussions were under way among US, Russian and EU leaders. The EU view was that if independence was declared in the absence of a UN resolution, there could be no new EU mission and ICO to replace UNMIK. Chaos might ensue as the UN mission, its clout by now extremely weak, would probably have to wind down drastically or even withdraw, leaving the Kosovar authorities to cope on their own. This could encourage more clearly defined par-tition in the north of Kosovo and the possible flight or expulsion of the Serbs from the enclaves.

One suggestion was for a compromise under which the Ahtisaari plan would be adopted but with provisions relating to statehood and international recogni-tion postponed for later review, perhaps after a year. It was pointed out that Moscow was not against a new resolution and an EU and ICO mission in Kosovo, but simply opposed formal independence. However, EU officials disliked this idea, believing that the biggest-yet EU mission might be doomed to failure from the start. It seemed that Kosovo's fate could be caught up in Moscow's broader tensions with the West on issues such as missile defence, Iran and possible NATO membership for Ukraine and Georgia.

Serbia: political wrangles mar international progress

The fate of Kosovo was a key factor in the domestic political paralysis that gripped Serbia for much of the past year. Serbian politics also contributed to delaying the Ahtisaari plan. Serbian leaders oppose the loss of Kosovo and propose that it should be an autonomous part of the country. In a sudden, surprise push, they reached agreement on a badly needed new constitution, rushed it through parliament and called a referendum to endorse it. They then asked Ahtisaari to delay handing over his plan to the UN on the grounds that after the referendum they needed to hold a general election. If he delivered a plan proposing Kosovo's independence before the elections, they argued, the only beneficiaries would be the extreme nationalist Serbian Radical Party, whose leader Vojislav Seselj is currently on trial at the UN's International Criminal Tribunal for the former Yugoslavia (ICTY) in The Hague. Ahtisaari agreed to a delay.

Serbia's constitutional referendum was held on 28–29 October 2006 and, despite an aggressive campaign, only 54% of the electorate voted, with 95% of those who did approving the constitution. The low turnout was in spite of the fact that much was made of the constitution's preamble describing Kosovo as an 'integral part' of Serbia. Serbian leaders had also argued that people should vote because a new constitution would help Serbia to join the EU.

When the general election was held on 21 January 2007, all the parties were disappointed by the results. The conservative nationalists of Prime Minister Vojislav Kostunica's party took 16% of the vote, while the more liberal, more pro-Western Democratic Party of President Boris Tadic won 23% and the far-right Serbian Radical Party 28.5%. Until May, Serbia had no effective government as the parties wrangled. As a 15 May deadline for the formation of a government approached, there were moments of high drama. On 8 May Kostunica's party voted in favour of electing Tomislav Nikolic, acting leader of the Radicals, to the post of parliamentary speaker – a shock both domestically and abroad. Nikolic declared that he was against Serbia joining the EU because of EU support for the Ahtisaari plan, that deputies from other parties were traitors, and that because of Kosovo a state of emergency could be declared. It was unclear whether Kostunica had hoped to frighten Tadic into closing a deal by supporting Nikolic. However the drama came to a head when agreement was finally struck on the composition of the new cabinet. Kostunica remained prime minister of a coalition comprising his and Tadic's party and two others. Nikolic resigned. The deal was confirmed 28 minutes before the deadline after which new elections would have had to be called.

Amid relief abroad at this outcome, Olli Rehn, the EU Enlargement Commissioner, immediately went to Belgrade to say that talks on a Stabilisation and Association Agreement (SAA), the first step towards EU membership, would be resumed. These had been broken off in May 2006 because of Serbia's failure to deliver General Ratko Mladic, the former Bosnian Serb wartime commander wanted by the ICTY on charges of genocide, and believed to be in Serbia. The Mladic condition seemed to have been dropped. NATO had also appeared to take this important step in November 2006 when Serbia, along with Bosnia and Montenegro, was invited to join the alliance's Partnership for Peace.

In what then seemed to be a remarkable coincidence, an apparent joint operation of the Serbian police with that of their counterparts in the Serbian part of Bosnia led to the arrest on 31 May of Bosnian Serb General Zdravko Tolimir, who was taken next day to face trial in The Hague. With Tolimir's arrest, out of 161 people indicted by the ICTY only five Serbs remained on the run, of whom the most important, apart from Mladic, was Radovan Karadzic, wartime leader of the Bosnian Serbs. The arrest occurred a few days before the planned visit of Carla Del Ponte, the ICTY's chief prosecutor, who is required to certify whether Serbia is cooperating with the ICTY.

Bosnia: struggles over political reform

Political reform in Bosnia, of which much had been hoped in 2007, met obstacles and delays. The legacy of the Bosnian war of 1992–95 and the Dayton accords which ended it was a complex and inefficient system of government. The country's 3.8m people emerged from the conflict divided into two main entities, the Serbian Republika Srpska (RS) and the Federation of Bosnia-Hercegovina, which encompasses the overwhelmingly Bosniak (Bosnian Muslim) and Croat regions of the country. While the RS has a unitary system of government, the Federation is subdivided into ten cantons. Apart from these entities, the city and region of Brcko is a separate autonomous district. Some functions are pooled in a weak central government. These levels of governance and administration overlap, making for inefficiencies, for example in the area of policing: inter-entity police cooperation is weak, but criminal activity occurs across the entities.

There is widespread recognition of the need to rationalise and modernise the political system. To this end, the EU set 16 conditions which were fulfilled as a condition for opening talks on an SAA in November 2005. Much of the cajoling of Bosnia's leaders had been done by the international community's high representative in the country, who until 31 January 2006 was Britain's Paddy Ashdown. He was replaced by Christian Schwarz-Schilling, a German former minister and businessman with considerable Bosnian experience, who came to the post with a strong belief that it was time for Bosnians to stand on their own feet and for his job to be terminated. He announced that he would only use his considerable legal powers in exceptional circumstances. He said he would remain in Sarajevo after the Office of the High Representative (OHR) had been phased out, but would use only his influence as the EU's special representative.

In this mood of optimism two key decisions were taken. The first was that OHR would close down on 30 June 2007. The second was that the EU's 6,000-strong military force in the country (EUFOR) would be drastically pruned to some 2,500 personnel. As the armies of the three wartime rivals to all intents and purposes no longer existed, and a unified Bosnian army with a single Ministry of Defence had been created, and there was no military threat foreseen, it was seen as unnecessary to keep so many EU-led soldiers in the country, in their barracks and with little to do.

The first sign that things were not going to plan came in April 2006 when relatively modest constitutional reforms, which had received US backing, failed to gain the two-thirds of votes necessary to pass through parliament. The main opposition came not from Bosnian Serbs, who are often blamed for obstructionism, but from the Bosniak party of Haris Silajdzic, the wartime premier. He argued that the reforms did not go far enough because they did not tackle what he saw as the main impediment to Bosnia's future, the power of the entities over the state as a whole. Silajdzic favours abolishing the entities, a solution seen by Bosnian Serbs as a recipe for Bosniak domination of the whole country.

The next sign of stalled progress came when Milorad Dodik, premier of the RS, stated in the wake of the Montenegrin referendum on independence that he could not see why Bosnian Serbs should not have the same right. To those who responded that the RS as a part of Bosnia did not possess the same rights as the former Yugoslav republics, he asked why, if Kosovo as a province of Serbia might be recognised as an independent state and could break away on ethnic grounds, this right should be denied to the Bosnian Serbs.

These manoeuvres set the stage for general elections on 1 October 2006, in which Silajdzic won the Bosniak vote and Dodik swept the board in the RS, each benefiting from the rhetoric of the other. Silajdzic was elected as the Bosniak representative on the country's tripartite presidency while Dodik remained premier of the RS. The success of his party gave him the right to nominate Nikola Spiric as premier of the central government. Following months of horse-trading, a cabinet of seven parties was finally sworn in on 9 February, but divisions between Bosnian Croats meant that the Federation was left without a new government until 30 March.

Given these mounting difficulties Schwarz-Schilling and foreign diplomats began to lose faith that the country was ready to be run without the OHR. Schwarz-Schilling also clashed with Dodik. In February 2007 it was decided to delay the OHR's closure until 30 June 2008, and to replace Schwarz-Schilling with Miroslav Lajcak, a former Slovak ambassador to Belgrade who had presided over the Montenegrin referendum on behalf of the EU. Pending his arrival, much of the management of the OHR fell to Raffi Gregorian, an American who was Schwarz-Schilling's deputy. In spite of the delay to the OHR's closure, the EU proceeded to cut the size of EUFOR to 2,500 troops.

Domestic politics was further complicated when the International Court of Justice (ICJ) in The Hague ruled on 26 February 2007 on Bosnia's case against Serbia (as successor state to Yugoslavia) accusing it of genocide. The court's judgement was that genocide had taken place at Srebrenica in 1995 when Bosnian Serb forces killed up to 8,000 Bosniak men and boys as the town succumbed after a siege of more than three years. However, it ruled there was no proof that Serbia was responsible, as opposed to the RS military and police, even though Belgrade financed them during the war. It also concluded that Serbia was guilty of failing to prevent genocide at Srebrenica but that it was not appropriate for Bosnia to demand reparations.

After the judgement it emerged that transcripts of the then Yugoslav Supreme Defence Council had been given to the ICTY by Serbia, but only on condition that these would not be given to the ICJ, precisely because they might contain incriminating evidence. Silajdzic argued that the judgment was proof that the RS was founded on genocide and should be abolished, and Bosniak returnees in Srebrenica demanded that the town should be taken out of RS jurisdiction. Dodik, meanwhile, argued that Bosnia should be reconstituted as a federation of three entities, splitting the Federation into two separate Bosniak and Croat parts.

This bad blood and political wrangling meant that reform ground to a halt. However, international efforts to reinvigorate the process continued. Following negotiations throughout 2006 on an SAA, the EU said it was ready to sign the agreement when Bosnia had completed a number of political tasks including police reform; improved cooperation, especially from the RS, with the ICTY; public administration reforms and the adoption of a public broadcasting law in the Federation. On 16 March 2007, Rehn made a speech to parliament in Sarajevo in which he urged Bosnian leaders to put their quarrels aside and compromise. He said: 'Do you really want to miss the European train by quarrelling endlessly at the station? That is what is now happening. Do not ask for any sympathy from me for that.' Immediately afterwards Bosnian leaders came close, but not close enough, to striking a deal on police reform. They agreed that a State Ministry of Interior should be created and the RS police would be part of this structure. However, Dodik said that in order to sell this deal to his public the name of the RS must be retained for police forces within the entity. Silajdzic rejected this as unacceptable, especially in the light of the ICJ judgment. In May 2007 Dodik and Silajdzic had three days of talks at the State Department in Washington, where US officials attempted to persuade them to agree not just on police reform but also on restarting stalled talks on constitutional reform. The meeting ended in failure after Dodik claimed that Douglas McElhaney, the US ambassador to Bosnia, had threatened to have him removed from office. A State Department statement said that unless the men could reach agreement it would be 'impossible for Bosnia and Hercegovina to proceed on its path to full integration into Euro-Atlantic structures'.

Stalled progress in Bosnia, Serbia and over the fate of Kosovo left the prospects for the Balkans gloomy at mid 2007. Serbia remained hostage to the Kosovo issue, which unless resolved will hugely complicate Serbia's hoped for accession to NATO and the EU. Serbia's ability to become a normal country remains hobbled by the Kosovo issue. Equally, Kosovo will continue to linger in the background of Bosnian politics, where it is a powerful card to be played. In Kosovo itself the situation on the ground remained calm, but whether this was the calm before the storm remained to be seen. In the short term, those who might be tempted to return to arms appeared to have understood that to do so would only be to fall into a trap laid by the Serbs and the Russians, because such actions would discredit the Kosovo Albanian cause. At the level of the EU there were debates about whether it might be possible to have an ESDP mission without independence or even with unilateral recognition, but the issue seemed destined to be postponed until at least September.

Turkey: New Uncertainties

After years of political and economic stability, and troublesome but manageable foreign relations, Turkey suddenly faces a more uncertain future. The political crisis that began in spring 2007 seemed most unlikely to be resolved by early elections that were called for July. Social tensions, not least the simmering struggle between religious and secular forces, deepened. Questions of civil–military relations that many had thought resolved came back to the centre of political debates, with the potential for a military coup openly discussed. Nationalism emerged as a vibrant force, and is now a common denominator of the right and the left. PKK (Kurdistan Workers' Party) violence increased, alongside a rise in terrorist incidents in urban areas. By June 2007, Turkey was poised for a possible military incursion into northern Iraq to address the PKK challenge, and perhaps to forestall the emergence of a Kurdish state. Taken together, these developments had significant implications for Turkey's longer-term stability. They could seriously affect Turkey's already strained relations with the European Union and the United States. The regional consequences could be far reaching at a time of growing insecurity in Iraq, a looming confrontation between Iran and the West, and new tensions with Russia.

Domestic crisis with deep roots
The proximate flashpoint for the current crisis was the nomination of a candidate to succeed President Ahmet Necdet Sezer, whose term was set to expire on 16 May 2007. The Justice and Development Party (AKP) government, led by Prime Minister Recep Tayyip Erdogan, with a strong majority in the Grand National Assembly, saw the opportunity to shape the election of Turkey's next president and the future of a key Turkish institution by nominating a figure with political leanings closer to those of the governing party. For a period it appeared that Erdogan would put himself forward as a candidate. The prospect of Erdogan,

whose wife wears a Muslim headscarf, occupying the presidential palace sparked demonstrations in Ankara, Istanbul and Izmir. The headscarf carries enormous symbolic meaning for Turkey's secularists, as well as for the AKP's more religious supporters. In the event, the party decided to nominate Foreign Minister Abdullah Gul. Though his wife also wore a headscarf, he was a more moderate choice apparently designed to assuage criticism and perhaps to mollify the military, which is the traditional guardian of Turkish secularism. Erdogan rejected the option of selecting a more secular or technocratic figure, apparently under pressure from conservative elements within the AKP.

It was not enough. Parliamentary opponents boycotted the vote, triggering a constitutional debate over its validity. The Turkish General Staff issued a cryptic late-night warning in a memo posted on the Internet. Large rallies followed, with perhaps one million people marching in Izmir. In this highly charged atmosphere, Turkey's constitutional court on 1 May annulled the results of the first rounds of presidential balloting. Erdogan called parliamentary elections for 22 July, earlier than expected – they had been due by November 2007. Parliament approved an AKP-led constitutional amendment providing for the direct election of the president, but this was promptly vetoed by the now caretaker President Sezer and thrown back to the constitutional court.

The AKP was well placed to fight the elections, with its commanding majority in the Assembly and high standing in public opinion polls. Under the Turkish election system, a party must win 10% of the national vote to be represented in parliament, and in 2002 only one other party, the leftist Republican People's Party (CHP), crossed this threshold. In the run-up to the July 2007 elections, the National Action Party (MHP) also looked set to meet the 10% hurdle. While the AKP would perhaps be able to form a new majority government, it was also possible that an unstable coalition might be necessary.

These events were presaged by a period of growing turmoil and debate within Turkish society, dating back a year or more. In this period, the underlying social and political cleavages in Turkish society came increasingly to the fore.

One divide was between liberal reformers and nationalist champions of a security-conscious state. This friction was pushed to prominence by the January 2007 murder of Turkish-Armenian journalist Hrant Dink, editor of a bilingual weekly. His murder exposed long-simmering tensions over the constitution's controversial Article 301, which criminalises insults to 'Turkishness'. Dink had been prosecuted under this law, which had also spurred cases against a number of writers and intellectuals, including the Nobel laureate novelist Orhan Pamuk. A 17-year-old with ties to an extreme nationalist network was charged with the murder of Dink, whose funeral was attended by some 100,000 people. The government strongly condemned the murder and invited Armenian representatives to attend the funeral. There were allegations of police complicity in this and other instances of nationalist violence, and many Turks remained suspicious of state institutions in cases of political extremism.

Turkish nationalism has also been fuelled by a resurgence of PKK violence, with perhaps 1,500 deaths since the ending in 2004 of a five-year-old ceasefire. In 2006, the PKK claimed to have killed some 900 Turks in 500 separate attacks. In the first few months of 2007, roughly 100 Turks were killed in PKK attacks, the majority against army and gendarmerie patrols. In a number of cases, remote-controlled mines were employed, on the pattern of insurgent attacks against coalition forces in Iraq and Afghanistan. In 2006–07, there was also a rise in bomb attacks in urban areas, although not all of these were claimed by the PKK, and fringe Kurdish or other groups may have been responsible. Funerals for soldiers killed in PKK attacks became flashpoints for well-publicised opposition protests, especially by MHP supporters.

A second key divide is between secularism and Islamism. Many in Turkey's highly secular elite have been wary of AKP's religious roots, and suspect that the AKP leadership harbours a hidden Islamist and possibly anti-democratic agenda. There has been little in AKP's behaviour since coming to power to support this view, and most Turks remained supportive of the party's populist agenda. Indeed, AKP's list for the July 2007 parliamentary elections showed a marked emphasis on less overtly pious and centrist candidates. But suspicions persisted, and the country's political struggle was increasingly seen by Turks and international observers as a test of Turkey's secular future.

These conflicting approaches reflect increasingly visible social divides, against a backdrop of considerable economic dynamism. Turkey's secular, Kemalist establishment, as embodied in the military leadership, the large business community based in Istanbul, and much of the intellectual and social elite, is increasingly embattled and hard pressed. While the political success of the AKP at the expense of this establishment may be due partly to its religious background, it probably owes more to the rise of an alternative elite, more conservative and religious, less cosmopolitan and less overtly Western, and with roots in Anatolia. Populism and nationalism have been part of this mix, reinforced by Erdogan's charismatic persona and the AKP's efficient approach to local and national politics. These are likely to prove durable forces, supported by an expanding and diversified economy with multiple centres of activity outside Istanbul and western Turkey. According to recent surveys, Turkey now counts over 20 dollar billionaires (slightly less than the 25 or so in Japan). Some of these are associated with the leading Turkish holding companies, but others have emerged from the far less secular AKP milieu.

A third source of friction is the position of the state in Turkish society. Liberal reformers and groups such as Alevis — a traditionally secular and left-leaning sect, viewed with some suspicion by both mainstream Turkish Muslims and elements of the secular establishment – and Kurds harbour deep grievances and are suspicious toward and often strongly opposed to Turkey's 'strong state'. When Turkey's EU candidacy was progressing well, and the AKP-supported programme of reforms was in full swing, many such tensions seemed headed toward resolution – or might at least be tamed through steady convergence with European norms. As Turkey's candidacy encountered mounting ambivalence – in Europe as well as among Turks – and some very real political obstacles, confidence that the strong state would wither away waned. A sustained struggle over the future of state and society could therefore ensue, and Turkey's international partners may increasingly find themselves dealing with multiple interlocutors – secular and religious, national and internationally minded, reformist and conservative. The future looks increasingly complex and potentially chaotic.

The changing role of the AKP is a factor in this debate. It too has become part of the state, building on its strong position in local and national politics to place its people in the pervasive state bureaucracy, including the interior and education ministries. AKP-oriented figures have begun to appear in some of the bastions of Turkish secularism, including the foreign ministry. In the increasingly divided debate over the future of the country, this trend has variously been seen as the normal course of a successful political movement or the harbinger of an Islamist takeover of society, depending on the ideology of the observer.

As these divisions have persisted or widened within Turkish society, the role of the armed forces has changed. Under pressure of reforms oriented towards EU accession, the military has steadily withdrawn from its traditionally active role in national policymaking in the political as well as the security realm. The powerful National Security Council is now chaired by a civilian, and military budgets have become more transparent. But personalities and political culture still matter. The appointment in 2006 of a harder-line figure, General Yaşar Buyukanit, as head of the Turkish General Staff, and a continued attachment to the role of the military as a trusted institution by many Turks, has offered an opportunity for the military to shape Turkish politics, at the margins if not directly. The possibility of a 'soft coup' – or even a coup of the more direct and traditional kind, however unlikely – is now openly debated. Even short of this, terrorist incidents on the pattern of the 22 May 2007 suicide bombing in Ankara, which killed six and for which no group has claimed responsibility, and bolder PKK attacks on civilian and military targets, including a 4 June attack on a gendarmerie station in Tunceli province, in which seven people died, put national security questions at the forefront and increased the scope for military influence in policy if not politics per se.

In contrast to Turkey's last political crisis, which led to the financial collapse of 2000–01, Turkish markets held up reasonably well. Over the last five years, Turkey's economy has grown at 6–7% per year, the highest sustained rate of growth in the OECD. The volume of foreign direct investment has equalled the total inflow since the founding of the Turkish republic. Much new investment from Europe, Russia, the United States and the Gulf is in the form of tangible holdings such as real estate, giving investors a structural stake in the Turkish economy. With a restructured banking sector, Turkey is less vulnerable to the sort of capital flight and financial collapse that was provoked by a relatively minor cabinet dispute in 2000. However, international investors will find much to worry about if Turkey's political and security crises are prolonged.

The security dimension

Internal security now dominates the Turkish policy agenda. After a period of tentative relaxation on Kurdish cultural rights, and a more open debate on ethnic and identity issues in Turkey in general, the public mood has grown more tense and intolerant, and this has been reflected in the approach of political parties, including the AKP, once a champion of a more open policy. Meanwhile, the political crisis itself, and the rise of more confrontational politics, may increase the risk of terrorism and political violence carried out by elements on the margins, whether extreme nationalists or Turkey's small but dangerous network of Islamic extremists, many hailing from the Kurdish southeast, or new groups with a mixed religio-nationalist agenda. There was some evidence that a network of this kind was responsible for the Dink murder and other recent attacks on individuals. Many Turks also worry about the scope for action by rogue elements within the police and security establishment. Against these troubling possibilities must be set the encouraging reality that Turkey has seen very large scale and entirely peaceful public demonstrations over the past months. Violence has not been a feature of these, despite the emotional and highly charged character of the political discourse.

The resurgence of PKK violence also raised the spectre of more general friction between Kurds and Turks beyond the troubled southeast. This may be avoided: the insurgency and counter-insurgency during the 1990s claimed the lives of some 30,000 people without provoking a wider ethnic conflict. But the new factor in the present conflict is the chaos in Iraq, with at least the possibility of a separate Kurdish state emerging there. A year ago, even Turkey's security establishment was beginning to consider whether Turkey might be able to tolerate an independent Kurdish entity on its borders – since this 'Kurdistan' would be highly dependent on Turkey in economic and probably security terms. But the combination of Ankara's political crisis and renewed PKK violence hardened attitudes and left Turks searching for more vigorous means of dealing with the PKK and its alleged supporters within the Kurdish administration of northern Iraq.

It is widely understood that Turkey has maintained a discreet special-forces presence across the Iraqi border since its multiple large-scale ground and air operations in the 1990s. It remains unclear, however, whether it will opt for a more aggressive cross-border strategy to address the PKK problem. The bulk of PKK fighters are probably inside Turkey, where the threat also comes from PKK offshoots such as the Kurdistan Liberation Hawks, operating in Turkish cities. It is unlikely that trained PKK fighters operating from bases in northern Iraq number more than 2,000–2,500, while PKK strength in Turkey may be several times that number. Brief strikes against PKK strongholds across the border might have political and symbolic value in the current circumstances, but their operational effect would probably be limited. A build up of Turkish forces along the border, combined with an explicit threat of a military intervention, almost certainly encouraged the PKK to move out of exposed positions around Kandil mountain and elsewhere. A more extensive and sustained cross-border operation, on the pattern of the division-level interventions of the mid 1990s, would be aimed at pressuring the autonomous Kurdish administration in northern Iraq, headed by Masoud Barzani, to change its permissive attitude toward the PKK presence. It might also aim at establishing a cordon sanitaire inside Iraq to inhibit PKK infiltration. But an intervention of this kind would also incur costs, both regionally and in Ankara's relations with Europe and the United States.

The PKK issue and the future of northern Iraq has become the centre of gravity for Turkish foreign and security policy, as well as for Turkish–Western relations. Turkish frustration with American policy in Iraq and on the PKK issue has reached a high level. A bilateral working group on the PKK issue, led by retired high-ranking officers on the Turkish and American sides, operated over the past year with little visible effect (it was more active in countering PKK networks in Europe than in addressing the problem in northern Iraq). The Bush administration has been reluctant to divert American military assets and attention to deal with what has been seen in Washington as a marginal aspect of the Iraq mission – especially at a time of deteriorating security in Iraq and intense debate in Washington over Iraq strategy. This reluctance has arguably been reinforced by continuing disenchantment with Turkey's failure to allow the opening of a northern front in the invasion of Iraq in 2003. For many Turks, the perceived absence of American support on the PKK issue has become an argument for reassessing the strategic relationship with the United States and a cause of negative public attitudes towards Washington. By contrast, Turkish views toward Tehran have warmed as Iran has launched its own attacks on PKK-affiliated bases near the Iranian border.

Strategic implications

Turkey's political and security travails could have a range of strategic consequences for Turkey, its region, and the West. A sustained political crisis and widening social divisions could make the country more inward looking and nationalistic. Progress on EU-oriented reforms, already stalled, could shift into reverse. This could make negotiations on Turkish EU membership far more difficult, and would strengthen the hand of European political leaders who prefer to hold Turkey at arms' length. Debate about Turkey's foreign-policy orientation under AKP rule could be overtaken by more basic questions about Ankara's ability to pursue an effective external strategy.

The security dimension of US–Turkish relations, long at the core of the bilateral relationship, would in turn face even more severe strains. At a time when Iraq is a central strategic concern for both Ankara and Washington, a concerted approach will be even more difficult to achieve. Turkish security depends critically on the evolution of American policy in Iraq. Many of the possible options for American redeployment or disengagement would depend on Turkish support, both political and logistic. A politically divided and insecure Turkey is less likely to be a positive contributor to regional security, in Iraq or elsewhere. Turkey's international partners will have a keen stake in the resolution of the country's travails.

Strategic Geography 2007

GLOBAL ISSUES

EUROPE

MIDDLE EAST/GULF

ASIA-PACIFIC

AFRICA

AMERICAS

Legend

——————— subject country international boundaries

– – – – – – other international boundaries

·············· province or state boundaries

ANBAR province or state

▣ capital cities

● state or province capital cities

● cities/ towns/ villages

GLOBAL ISSUES: Projected carbon-emissions trends

Although there are many differences of opinion within the scientific community about the most precise way of measuring the impact of human activity on global warming, there is one point on which the majority agrees: increased levels of anthropogenic greenhouse gases in the atmosphere have accelerated the process of global warming. Even though the figures cited here reveal differences of methodology between individual studies, the trends they demonstrate are clear: carbon emissions will continue to rise over the coming century with the largest growth occurring in newly industrialised nations such as China, India and Brazil.

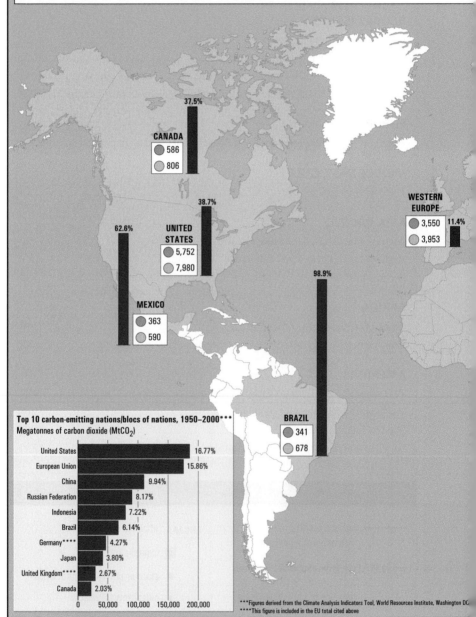

CANADA 37.5%
586
806

UNITED STATES 38.7%
5,752
7,980

62.6%

MEXICO
363
590

WESTERN EUROPE 11.4%
3,550
3,953

BRAZIL 98.9%
341
678

Top 10 carbon-emitting nations/blocs of nations, 1950–2000***
Megatonnes of carbon dioxide (MtCO$_2$)

Nation		Value
United States		16.77%
European Union		15.86%
China	9.94%	
Russian Federation	8.17%	
Indonesia	7.22%	
Brazil	6.14%	
Germany****	4.27%	
Japan	3.80%	
United Kingdom****	2.67%	
Canada	2.03%	

0   50,000   100,000 150,000 200,000

***Figures derived from the Climate Analysis Indicators Tool, World Resources Institute, Washington DC
****This figure is included in the EU total cited above

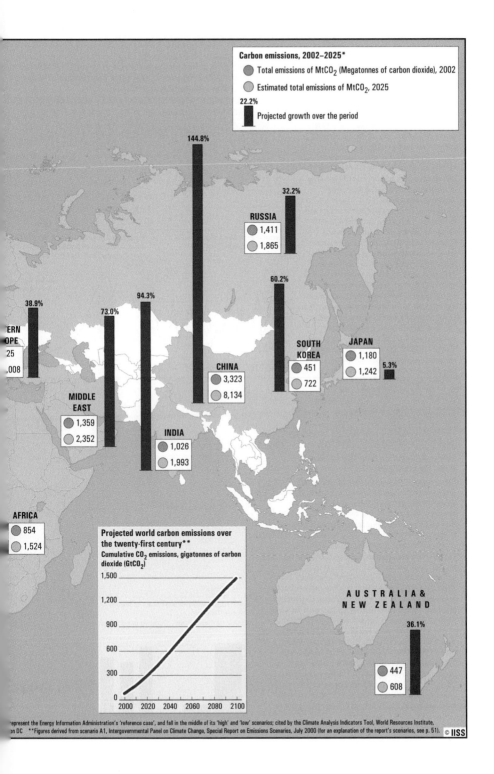

Carbon emissions, 2002–2025*

⬤ Total emissions of MtCO$_2$ (Megatonnes of carbon dioxide), 2002

◯ Estimated total emissions of MtCO$_2$, 2025

22.2%

▮ Projected growth over the period

144.8%

32.2%

RUSSIA
⬤ 1,411
◯ 1,865

60.2%

38.9%

94.3%

73.0%

SOUTH KOREA
⬤ 451
◯ 722

JAPAN
⬤ 1,180
◯ 1,242

5.3%

'ERN OPE
25
,008

MIDDLE EAST
⬤ 1,359
◯ 2,352

CHINA
⬤ 3,323
◯ 8,134

INDIA
⬤ 1,026
◯ 1,993

AFRICA
⬤ 854
◯ 1,524

AUSTRALIA & NEW ZEALAND

36.1%

⬤ 447
◯ 608

Projected world carbon emissions over the twenty-first century

Cumulative CO$_2$ emissions, gigatonnes of carbon dioxide (GtCO$_2$)

1,500
1,200
900
600
300
0

2000 2020 2040 2060 2080 2100

epresent the Energy Information Administration's 'reference case', and fall in the middle of its 'high' and 'low' scenarios; cited by the Climate Analysis Indicators Tool, World Resources Institute,
on DC   **Figures derived from scenario A1, Intergovernmental Panel on Climate Change, Special Report on Emissions Scenarios, July 2000 (for an explanation of the report's scenarios, see p. 51).   © IISS

GLOBAL ISSUES: Selected migration patterns

The International Organization for Migration estimates that in 2005 there were 191 million migrants worldwide, representing 3% of global population. They include refugees, returnees, asylum-seekers, internally displaced or stateless persons, as well as economic migrants. The factors causing people to migrate are manifold. These case studies provide a snapshot of five global migration patterns, and examine their causes.

US–Mexico border

Plans to construct a 1,100km-long security fence across the 3,145km-long US–Mexico border in order to stem the flow of illegal migrants and to aid anti-terror efforts are currently the subject of much scrutiny across the Americas and have come to be considered by some as a symbol of deteriorating relations between the US and its southerly neighbours. Illegal migrants play a key role in the US economy, taking unskilled jobs in sectors such as agriculture, healthcare, construction and the hospitality industry. The Council on Foreign Relations has highlighted the lack of evidence that increased security measures actually serve to reduce illegal immigration levels, saying that in 1986 there were 2.5m illegal immigrants in the US, while in 2005, after funds directed at border control measures had 'skyrocketed', there were approximately 10.3m undocumented workers in the US, of whom 53% were thought to be Mexican. The 'push' factor of weak Latin American economies and the 'pull' factor of strong demand for cheap labour in the US must be addressed for a real change in levels of illegal immigration, regardless of additional security measures, it said.

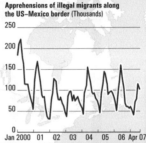

Apprehensions of illegal migrants along the US–Mexico border (Thousands)

World Bank figures indicate that, like many other economic migrants across the world, those Mexicans most likely to migrate are 16–30 years of age

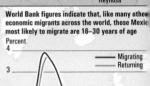

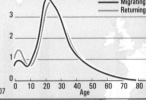

US–MEXICO BORDER

WEST AFRICA TO CANARY IS.

Economic migration from West Africa to the Canary Islands

Paying around €1,000–2,000 each for their passage, West African economic migrants depart from Senegal, Mauritania, Western Sahara and southern Morocco for the Spanish territory of the Canary Islands. The journey of up to 8–10 days over approximately 800km is perilous: the most common vessel is a pirogue or cayuco, a large fishing canoe equipped with two or three 40-horsepower outboard motors, in which up to 100 migrants are packed together. While many lose their lives along the way, those who do make it and are not repatriated upon arrival are often sent to mainland Spain where many are released pending expulsion hearings – the number of illegal immigrants turning up for their court hearings is inevitably low. In the latter half of 2006, Madrid launched a joint monitoring mission with Frontex, an independent EU agency which assists member states with border patrols, deploying ships, helicopters and planes in order to curb the flow of migrants. Frontex reported that of the 14,572 arrivals in the Canary Islands between early August and mid December 2006, it had intercepted 3,887. Madrid also established a joint scheme with Dakar, in which 4,000 Spanish work permits would be issued to Senegalese nationals – although the scheme was widely welcomed, it was thought unlikely to have much impact on current levels of illegal immigration.

Flow of illegal immigrants into and out of Spanish territories (Thousands)

Arrivals in the Canary Islands

Expulsions by the Spanish authorities*

*arrivals on the Spanish mainland, as well as the Canary Islands

Sources: Council on Foreign Relations, World Bank, Pew Hispanic Center, International Organization for Migration, BBC, Frontex, Spanish Interior Ministry, International Medical Corps, United States Institute of Peace

q's internally displaced population

International Medical Corps (IMC) estimates that in February 2007 546,078 Iraqis been internally displaced over the course of the previous 12 months. Significantly, of those accounted for had fled from Baghdad, and the IMC predicted that a er million Baghdad residents could be displaced in the following months. Of the nally displaced population, the IMC reported that 350,550 were Shia, 156,510 e Sunni and 16,218 were Turkmen, Christian and Kurds. Sectarian-motivated cks in the city are the main catalyst for these population movements, with a wave adly car bombings and mortar attacks on 23 November 2006 in Baghdad's Sadr having triggered further sectarian violence.

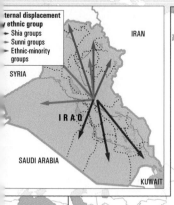

ternal displacement
ethnic group
→ Shia groups
→ Sunni groups
→ Ethnic-minority groups

Afghanistan–Pakistan

The 2,400km-long Afghanistan–Pakistan frontier stretches across Baluchistan, the Federally Administered Tribal Areas and North West Frontier Province, and is divided by the disputed Durand Line. The harsh, mountainous terrain is notoriously difficult to patrol: Islamist militias are thought to enjoy relative freedom to launch insurgent operations in both countries, while al-Qaeda leader Osama bin Laden has long been thought to be using the area as a hideout. Because of the treacherous nature of the terrain, there exist very little data as to migration flows across it. Approximately 90,000 Pakistani soldiers patrol the frontier, and according to the United States Institute of Peace, they had killed 194 foreign militants and 552 'local supporters' between mid 2002 and late 2006. These foreign fighters were thought to be of Uzbek, Chechen and Arab origins. There are thought to be 2–3m Afghan refugees in Pakistan.

Sudan's Darfur region

For 21 years a civil war raged between Sudan's mainly Muslim north, and Christian and Animist south, which is estimated to have claimed the lives of two million people, uprooted a further 4m and forced 600,000 to flee the country as refugees. Two years of negotiations finally culminated in a comprehensive peace agreement between the government and the Sudan People's Liberation Movement/Army in January 2005, in which the southern rebel forces were granted relative autonomy and the prospect of a referendum on independence after six years. In early 2003, as a peaceful solution to the civil war was being discussed, instability began to spread in the country's western Darfur region, as Janjaweed Arab militias began a programme of ethnic cleansing against the black African population. Even though the African Union's (AU) peacekeeping force struggled to stem the violence, the Sudanese government had resisted calls for the expansion of the UN's mission in Sudan (UNMIS), which had been monitoring the implementation of the 2005 comprehensive peace agreement. Although in August 2006 its mandate was amended to include the Darfur region, UN figures show that the current IDP population has reached an all-time high, while the instability has spread into neighbouring Chad and the Central African Republic, and there are fears that the current conflict could lead to a wider regional insurrection.

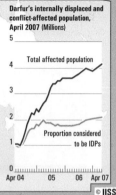

Darfur's internally displaced and conflict-affected population, April 2007 (Millions)

Total affected population

Proportion considered to be IDPs

© IISS

GLOBAL ISSUES: The dynamics of the US–China relationship

In spite of China's rapid economic growth, the size of the US economy far outstrips that of China. However, the two countries are closely linked by trade, with China's large surplus fuelling its foreign-exchange reserves, some which are in turn invested in US securities.

Demographic indicators

	US	China
Total population	301,139,947	1,321,851,888
Labour force	ε151,400,000 (including unemployed)	ε798,000,000
Labour force by occupation	Farming, forestry, and fishing: 0.7%	Agriculture: 45%
	Manufacturing, extraction, transportation, and crafts: 22.9%	
	Managerial, professional and technical: 34.9%	
	Sales and office: 25%	Industry: 24%
	Other services: 16.5%	Services: 31%
Total area	9,826,630km²	9,596,960km²

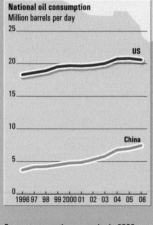

■ Washington DC

Energy indicators

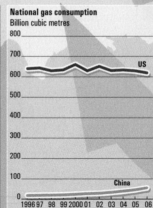

National oil consumption
Million barrels per day
US
China

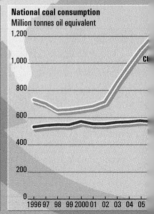

National gas consumption
Billion cubic metres
US
China

National coal consumption
Million tonnes oil equivalent
Cl

Energy consumption per capita in 2006

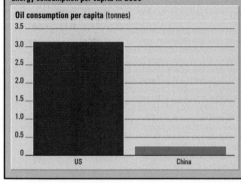

Oil consumption per capita (tonnes)

US   China

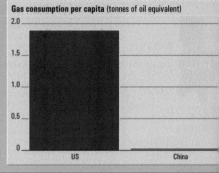

Gas consumption per capita (tonnes of oil equivalent)

US   China

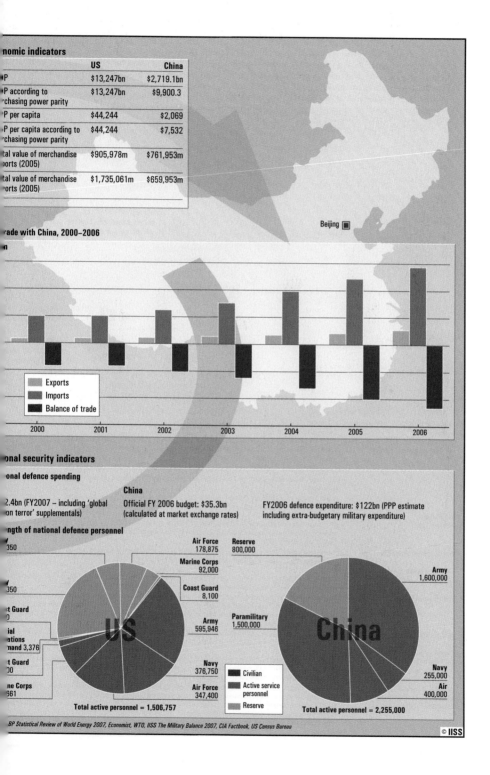

nomic indicators

	US	China
P	$13,247bn	$2,719.1bn
P according to chasing power parity	$13,247bn	$9,900.3
P per capita	$44,244	$2,069
P per capita according to chasing power parity	$44,244	$7,532
tal value of merchandise orts (2005)	$905,978m	$761,953m
tal value of merchandise orts (2005)	$1,735,061m	$659,953m

Beijing ■

ade with China, 2000–2006

- ▨ Exports
- ▨ Imports
- ■ Balance of trade

2000　2001　2002　2003　2004　2005　2006

onal security indicators

onal defence spending

China

2.4bn (FY2007 – including 'global on terror' supplementals)

Official FY 2006 budget: $35.3bn (calculated at market exchange rates)

FY2006 defence expenditure: $122bn (PPP estimate including extra-budgetary military expenditure)

ngth of national defence personnel

350

350

t Guard
0

ial
ations
mand 3,376

t Guard
00

ne Corps
561

Air Force 178,875
Marine Corps 92,000
Coast Guard 8,100
Army 595,946
Navy 376,750
Air Force 347,400

US

Total active personnel = 1,506,757

Reserve 800,000
Paramilitary 1,500,000

China

Army 1,600,000
Navy 255,000
Air 400,000

- ■ Civilian
- ▨ Active service personnel
- ▨ Reserve

Total active personnel = 2,255,000

BP Statistical Review of World Energy 2007, Economist, WTO, IISS The Military Balance 2007, CIA Factbook, US Census Bureau

© IISS

GLOBAL ISSUES: The US ballistic missile defence system: expanding into Eastern Europe

Described as an 'integrated layered defense' by the US Missile Defense Agency (MDA), the Ballistic Missile Defense System (BMDS) is a network of sensors and missiles designed to protect the US mainland from attack b ballistic missiles launched from 'rogue states' such as Iran and North Korea. Based in large part on the National Missile Defense Program launched during the Clinton administration, and incorporating a number of separate missile defence programmes, the BMDS is controlled centrally by the Missile Defense Agency.

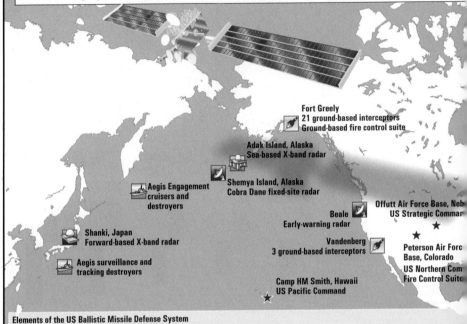

Fort Greely
21 ground-based interceptors
Ground-based fire control suite

Adak Island, Alaska
Sea-based X-band radar

Shemya Island, Alaska
Cobra Dane fixed-site radar

Aegis Engagement
cruisers and
destroyers

Beale
Early-warning radar

Offutt Air Force Base, Neb
US Strategic Comman

Shanki, Japan
Forward-based X-band radar

Vandenberg
3 ground-based interceptors

Peterson Air Forc
Base, Colorado

Aegis surveillance and
tracking destroyers

US Northern Com
Fire Control Suite

Camp HM Smith, Hawaii
US Pacific Command

Elements of the US Ballistic Missile Defense System

Element	Description
Command, Control, Battle Management and Communications (C2BMC)	Key to the cohesion of the entire BMDS and described by the MDA as 'the nervous system of the BMDS', its infrastructure is based on the operations of the six strategic command centres and relies on a system of sensors to gather and pass on informa and directives to each component of the system, including:
	Forward-based radars – air and sea transportable radars capable of detecting missiles early in their flight
	Sea-based X-band radars – advanced X-band radars with semi-submersible platforms, which can be positioned anywhere in the world
	Space Tracking and Surveillance System – currently consists of two satellites in low-earth orbit; each is equipped with infrared and visible sensors for detecting and tracking ballistic missiles
Boost phase **Airborne Laser**	This chemical oxygen iodine laser, fitted on a Boeing 747-400, is designed to detect, track and destroy missiles within a range several hundred kilometres during the boost phase. Currently in development, a test of its ability to shoot down a ballistic miss flight is scheduled for 2008.
Kinetic Energy Interceptor	Also in development, this is a programme of next-generation fixed-site and mobile interceptors designed to destroy medium- an intermediate-range, as well as intercontinental, ballistic missiles.
Midcourse phase **Aegis Ballistic Missile Defense**	Capable of intercepting short- to medium-range missiles, Aegis cruisers and destroyers are equipped with Standard Missile-3 interceptors; designed to operate alongside the Aegis Combat System already installed on US Navy ships.
Ground-based Midcourse Defense	The network of radars and satellites used to track and transmit information via the C2BMC system about enemy missile launc supplies that information to a ground-based fire control suite, which then launches a ground-based interceptor (made up of a booster vehicle and accompanying exoatmospheric kill vehicle) on a collision course with an intermediate- or long-range missile during the midcourse phase of flight.
Multiple Kill Vehicles	Designed to combat medium-range and intercontinental ballistic missiles equipped with multiple warheads, with individual 'kill vehicles' being launched from a single carrier vehicle. The first test flight is scheduled for 2010.
Terminal phase **Terminal High Altitude Area Defense**	Due to come into service in 2009, this uses 'hit-to-kill' technology to shoot down short- to medium-range missiles in the termi phase of flight, whether within or beyond the earth's atmosphere. It consists of truck-mounted launchers, interceptors, radars fire control/communications, and can be transported around the world by air within a matter of hours
PATRIOT Advanced Capability-3 (PAC-3)/ Medium Extended Air Defense System (MEADS)	Already deployed by the US Army during *Operation Iraqi Freedom*, the PAC-3 is a surface-to-air missile used to shoot down short-range ballistic missiles. In partnership with Germany and Italy, the US Army is developing the MEADS, which will replac PAC-3 and widen the range of threats it can tackle, with the intention of bridging the gap 'between short-range maneuver air missile defense systems and the long-range BMDS elements'. The MDA is working closely with the US Army on this project i order to ensure its cohesion with the BMDS as a whole.

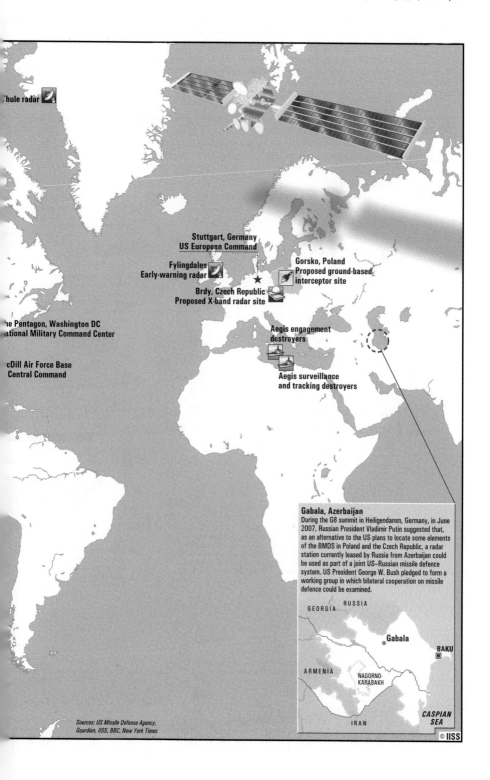

Thule radar

Stuttgart, Germany
US European Command

Fylingdales
Early-warning radar

Gorsko, Poland
Proposed ground-based
interceptor site

Brdy, Czech Republic
Proposed X-band radar site

The Pentagon, Washington DC
National Military Command Center

McDill Air Force Base
Central Command

Aegis engagement
destroyers

Aegis surveillance
and tracking destroyers

Gabala, Azerbaijan
During the G8 summit in Heiligendamm, Germany, in June
2007, Russian President Vladimir Putin suggested that,
as an alternative to the US plans to locate some elements
of the BMDS in Poland and the Czech Republic, a radar
station currently leased by Russia from Azerbaijan could
be used as part of a joint US–Russian missile defence
system. US President George W. Bush pledged to form a
working group in which bilateral cooperation on missile
defence could be examined.

RUSSIA

GEORGIA

Gabala

BAKU

ARMENIA

NAGORNO-
KARABAKH

IRAN

CASPIAN
SEA

Sources: US Missile Defense Agency,
Guardian, IISS, BBC, New York Times

© IISS

EUROPE: The EU at 50 and its members' troop deployments

May 2007 marked the European Union's fiftieth birthday. European countries have troops deployed in crisis-management missions around the world. This chart demonstrates where EU members and candidate countries have troops deployed.

Date	Event
1950	Schuman declaration on the establishment of a European Coal and Steel Community founded by six countries: Belgium, Germany, France, Italy, Luxembourg and The Netherlands
1957	Treaty of Rome expanded common market values and established the European Economic Community (EEC)
1973	Denmark, Ireland and the UK join the EEC
1981	Greece becomes a member
1986	Spain and Portugal join
1990	With the unification of Germany, the East German Länder are now included in the EEC
1993	Maastricht Treaty on the creation of the European Union comes into force
1995	Austria, Finland and Sweden join
2002	Euro notes and coins introduced
2004	Ten countries accede to the EU, representing the largest enlargement to date and consisting to a large extent of former Soviet bloc countries: Czech Republic, Estonia, Cyprus, Latvia, Lithuania, Hungary, Malta, Poland, Slovenia and Slovakia
2005	French and Dutch referendums on the European Constitutional Treaty result in 'no' votes. The treaty was an attempt to simplify decision-making processes and to deepen member states' ties to the EU.
2007	Bulgaria and Romania join
	Three countries now being considered for EU membership: Croatia, Macedonia and Turkey

NETHERLA

16.3m € 3.60% $35,077.76
Afghanistan - 1,889; Bosnia-Herzegovina - 26
DRC - 3; Germany - 2,600; Iraq - 15;
Lebanon - 150; Middle East - 13;
Netherlands Antilles - 20; Serbia - 4; Sudan

60.4m 5.40% $35,051.39
Afghanistan - 7,800**; Ascension Island - 23;
Belgium - 183; Belize - 30; Bosnia-Herzegovina - 590;
Brunei - 1,120; Canada - 557; Cyprus - 3,275;
DRC - 6; Germany - 22,000; Gibraltar - 340; Iraq - 5,500*
Kenya - 20; Liberia - 3; Nepal - 63; Netherlands - 120;
Northern Ireland - 3,000-5,000; Oman - 133; Serbia - 20
Sudan - 3; United States - 692

UK

10.4m € 7.80% $34,477.59
Afghanistan - 265; Bosnia-Herzegovina - 51;
DRC - 11; Lebanon - 365; Middle East - 1;
Serbia - 420; Sudan - 5

IRELAND

BE

4.2m € 4.30% $44,087.20
Afghanistan - 7; Albania - 1; Bosnia-Herzegovina -58;
Cote d'Ivoire - 2; DRC - 3; Former Yugoslavia/Albania - 5;
Georgia -1; Lebanon - 41; Liberia - 322; Middle East - 12;
Montenegro - 1; Serbia - 215; Sudan - 3;
Western Sahara - 3

5.0m € 4.90% $80,471.40
Afghanistan - 10; Bosnia-Herzegovin
Lebanon - 2; Serbia - 26

FRANCE

63m € 9.00% $30,693.10
Afghanistan - 220; Bosnia-Herzegovina - 450; Chad - 1,050; Cote d'Ivoire - 3,987;
DRC - 17; Djibouti - 2,850; Egypt - 15; Ethiopia/Eritrea - 1; French Guyana - 1,470;
French Polynesia - 800; French West Indies - 800; Gabon - 700; Georgia - 3;
Germany - 2,800; Haiti - 2; Indian Ocean - 1,000; Lebanon - 208; Liberia - 1;
Macedonia and Bosnia-Herzegovina - 60; Middle East - 3; New Caledonia - 1,540;
Senegal - 610; Serbia - 2,455; Tajikistan - 150; Western Sahara - 17

8.3m € 4.50% $36,031.44
Afghanistan - 5; Bosnia-Herzegovina - 287
Cyprus - 4; Ethiopia/Eritrea - 2;
Former Yugoslavia/Albania - 6; Georgia -
Middle East - 7; Serbia - 554;
Syria/Israel - 367; Western Sahara - 2

PORTUGAL

SPAIN

10.6m € 8.00% $22,677.46
Afghanistan - 166; Angola - 11; Bosnia-Herzegovina - 193; Burundi - 1;
Cape Verde - 2; DRC - 39; Timor Leste - 4; Guinea Bissau - 1; Iraq - 8;
Lebanon - 18; Mozambique - 7; Sao Tome e Principe - 6; Serbia - 310

45.1m € 8.30% $27,522.08
Afghanistan - 625; Bosnia-Herzegovina - 495; DRC
Ethiopia/Eritrea - 4; Lebanon - 1,393; Serbia - 751

Sources: Troop deployments extracted from IISS The Military Balance 2007, unless otherwise indicated (some deployment totals may have changed since January 2007 publication o
Deployments listed as being part of Operation Enduring Freedom now listed as Combined Joint Taskforce-82. Other sources: www.eu.int; Economist *2005 figure **Figure updated

© IISS

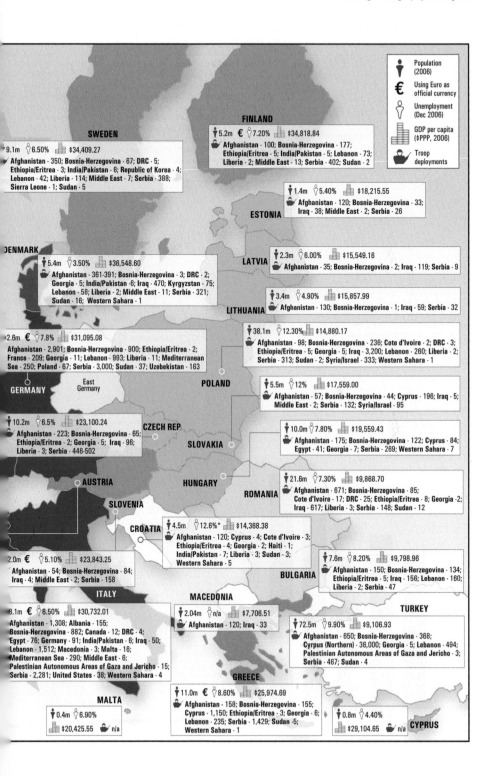

Legend:
- Population (2006)
- € Using Euro as official currency
- Unemployment (Dec 2006)
- GDP per capita ($PPP, 2006)
- Troop deployments

SWEDEN
9.1m · 6.50% · $34,409.27
Afghanistan · 350; Bosnia-Herzegovina · 67; DRC · 5; Ethiopia/Eritrea · 3; India/Pakistan · 6; Republic of Korea · 4; Lebanon · 42; Liberia · 114; Middle East · 7; Serbia · 388; Sierra Leone · 1; Sudan · 5

FINLAND
5.2m € 7.20% · $34,818.84
Afghanistan · 100; Bosnia-Herzegovina · 177; Ethiopia/Eritrea · 5; India/Pakistan · 5; Lebanon · 73; Liberia · 2; Middle East · 13; Serbia · 402; Sudan · 2

ESTONIA
1.4m · 5.40% · $18,215.55
Afghanistan · 120; Bosnia-Herzegovina · 33; Iraq · 38; Middle East · 2; Serbia · 26

DENMARK
5.4m · 3.50% · $36,548.60
Afghanistan · 361-391; Bosnia-Herzegovina · 3; DRC · 2; Georgia · 5; India/Pakistan ·6; Iraq · 470; Kyrgyzstan · 75; Lebanon · 58; Liberia · 2; Middle East · 11; Serbia · 321; Sudan · 16; Western Sahara · 1

LATVIA
2.3m · 6.00% · $15,549.16
Afghanistan · 35; Bosnia-Herzegovina · 2; Iraq · 119; Serbia · 9

LITHUANIA
3.4m · 4.90% · $15,857.99
Afghanistan · 130; Bosnia-Herzegovina · 1; Iraq · 59; Serbia · 32

GERMANY
82.6m € 7.8% · $31,095.08
Afghanistan · 2,901; Bosnia-Herzegovina · 900; Ethiopia/Eritrea · 2; France · 209; Georgia · 11; Lebanon · 993; Liberia · 11; Mediterranean Sea · 250; Poland · 67; Serbia · 3,000; Sudan · 37; Uzebekistan · 163
East Germany

POLAND
38.1m · 12.30% · $14,880.17
Afghanistan · 98; Bosnia-Herzegovina · 236; Cote d'Ivoire · 2; DRC · 3; Ethiopia/Eritrea · 5; Georgia · 5; Iraq · 3,200; Lebanon · 260; Liberia · 2; Serbia · 313; Sudan · 2; Syria/Israel · 333; Western Sahara · 1

CZECH REP
10.2m · 6.5% · $23,100.24
Afghanistan · 223; Bosnia-Herzegovina · 65; Ethiopia/Eritrea · 2; Georgia · 5; Iraq · 96; Liberia · 3; Serbia · 446-502

SLOVAKIA
5.5m · 12% · $17,559.00
Afghanistan · 57; Bosnia-Herzegovina · 44; Cyprus · 196; Iraq · 5; Middle East · 2; Serbia · 132; Syria/Israel · 95

HUNGARY
10.0m · 7.80% · $19,559.43
Afghanistan · 175; Bosnia-Herzegovina · 122; Cyprus · 84; Egypt · 41; Georgia · 7; Serbia · 269; Western Sahara · 7

AUSTRIA
SLOVENIA
2.0m € 5.10% · $23,843.25
Afghanistan · 54; Bosnia-Herzegovina · 84; Iraq · 4; Middle East · 2; Serbia · 158

ROMANIA
21.6m · 7.30% · $9,868.70
Afghanistan · 671; Bosnia-Herzegovina · 85; Cote d'Ivoire · 17; DRC · 25; Ethiopia/Eritrea · 8; Georgia ·2; Iraq · 617; Liberia · 3; Serbia · 148; Sudan · 12

CROATIA
4.5m · 12.6%* · $14,368.38
Afghanistan · 120; Cyprus · 4; Cote d'Ivoire · 3; Ethiopia/Eritrea · 4; Georgia · 2; Haiti · 1; India/Pakistan · 7; Liberia · 3; Sudan · 3; Western Sahara · 5

BULGARIA
7.6m · 8.20% · $9,798.96
Afghanistan · 150; Bosnia-Herzegovina · 134; Ethiopia/Eritrea · 5; Iraq · 156; Lebanon · 160; Liberia · 2; Serbia · 47

ITALY
58.1m € 6.50% · $30,732.01
Afghanistan · 1,308; Albania · 155; Bosnia-Herzegovina · 882; Canada · 12; DRC · 4; Egypt · 76; Germany · 91; India/Pakistan · 6; Iraq · 50; Lebanon · 1,512; Macedonia · 3; Malta · 16; Mediterranean Sea · 290; Middle East · 6; Palestinian Autonomous Areas of Gaza and Jericho · 15; Serbia · 2,281; United States · 38; Western Sahara · 4

MACEDONIA
2.04m · n/a · $7,706.51
Afghanistan · 120; Iraq · 33

TURKEY
72.5m · 9.90% · $9,106.93
Afghanistan · 650; Bosnia-Herzegovina · 368; Cyrpus (Northern) · 36,000; Georgia · 5; Lebanon · 494; Palestinian Autonomous Areas of Gaza and Jericho · 3; Serbia · 467; Sudan · 4

MALTA
0.4m · 6.90% · $20,425.55 · n/a

GREECE
11.0m · 8.60% · $25,974.69
Afghanistan · 158; Bosnia-Herzegovina · 155; Cyprus · 1,150; Ethiopia/Eritrea · 3; Georgia · 6; Lebanon · 235; Serbia · 1,429; Sudan ·5; Western Sahara · 1

CYPRUS
0.8m · 4.40% · $29,104.65 · n/a

MIDDLE EAST/GULF: The Baghdad security plan

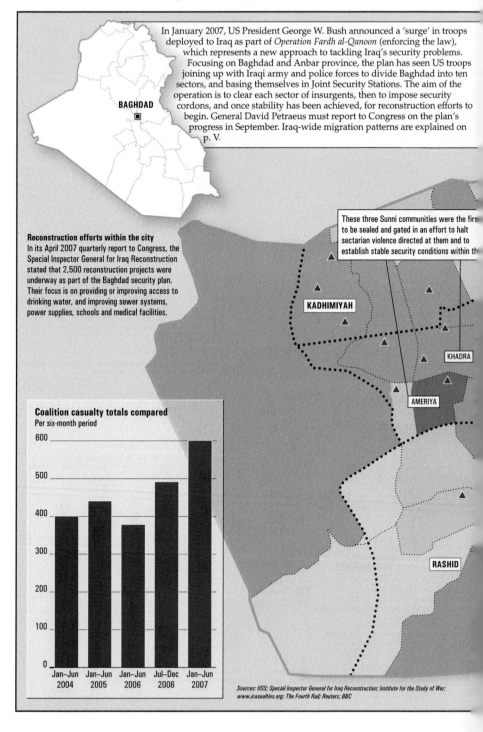

In January 2007, US President George W. Bush announced a 'surge' in troops deployed to Iraq as part of *Operation Fardh al-Qanoon* (enforcing the law), which represents a new approach to tackling Iraq's security problems. Focusing on Baghdad and Anbar province, the plan has seen US troops joining up with Iraqi army and police forces to divide Baghdad into ten sectors, and basing themselves in Joint Security Stations. The aim of the operation is to clear each sector of insurgents, then to impose security cordons, and once stability has been achieved, for reconstruction efforts to begin. General David Petraeus must report to Congress on the plan's progress in September. Iraq-wide migration patterns are explained on p. V.

BAGHDAD

Reconstruction efforts within the city
In its April 2007 quarterly report to Congress, the Special Inspector General for Iraq Reconstruction stated that 2,500 reconstruction projects were underway as part of the Baghdad security plan. Their focus is on providing or improving access to drinking water, and improving sewer systems, power supplies, schools and medical facilities.

These three Sunni communities were the firs to be sealed and gated in an effort to halt sectarian violence directed at them and to establish stable security conditions within th

KADHIMIYAH

KHADRA

AMERIYA

RASHID

Coalition casualty totals compared
Per six-month period

Period	Total
Jan–Jun 2004	400
Jan–Jun 2005	440
Jan–Jun 2006	375
Jul–Dec 2006	485
Jan–Jun 2007	600

Sources: IISS; Special Inspector General for Iraq Reconstruction; Institute for the Study of War; www.icasualties.org; The Fourth Rail; Reuters; BBC

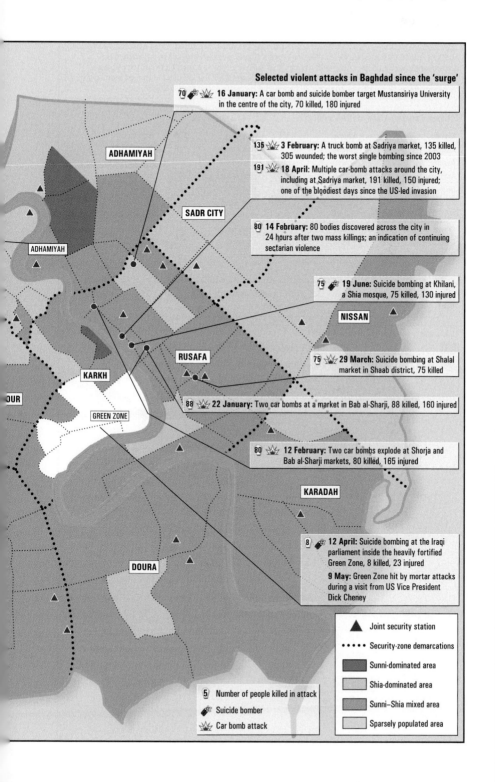

Selected violent attacks in Baghdad since the 'surge'

70 **16 January:** A car bomb and suicide bomber target Mustansiriya University in the centre of the city, 70 killed, 180 injured

135 **3 February:** A truck bomb at Sadriya market, 135 killed, 305 wounded; the worst single bombing since 2003

191 **18 April:** Multiple car-bomb attacks around the city, including at Sadriya market, 191 killed, 150 injured; one of the bloodiest days since the US-led invasion

80 **14 February:** 80 bodies discovered across the city in 24 hours after two mass killings; an indication of continuing sectarian violence

75 **19 June:** Suicide bombing at Khilani, a Shia mosque, 75 killed, 130 injured

75 **29 March:** Suicide bombing at Shalal market in Shaab district, 75 killed

88 **22 January:** Two car bombs at a market in Bab al-Sharji, 88 killed, 160 injured

80 **12 February:** Two car bombs explode at Shorja and Bab al-Sharji markets, 80 killed, 165 injured

8 **12 April:** Suicide bombing at the Iraqi parliament inside the heavily fortified Green Zone, 8 killed, 23 injured
9 May: Green Zone hit by mortar attacks during a visit from US Vice President Dick Cheney

ADHAMIYAH
SADR CITY
ADHAMIYAH
NISSAN
RUSAFA
KARKH
DUR
GREEN ZONE
KARADAH
DOURA

▲ Joint security station
• • • • • Security-zone demarcations
Sunni-dominated area
Shia-dominated area
Sunni–Shia mixed area
Sparsely populated area

5 Number of people killed in attack
Suicide bomber
Car bomb attack

ASIA-PACIFIC: Afghanistan: ISAF's deployments

NATO's International Security Assistance Force's (ISAF) mission is to assist Afghanistan's government, while cooperating with its national security forces, to establish security in the country and to aid reconstruction efforts. Since February 2007 the US has led the mission, assisted by troops from 37 countries, running 25 provincial reconstruction teams (PRTs).

*Estimated contributions of ISAF nations

Albania	30	Estonia	130	Lithuania	130	Slovenia	50
Australia	500	Finland	70	Luxembourg	10	Spain (Sp)	650
Austria	2	France	1,000	Macedonia	120	Sweden (Sw)	260
Azerbaijan	20	Germany (Ge)	3,000	Netherlands (Nl)	2,200	Switzerland	2
Belgium	300	Greece	170	New Zealand (NZ)	7	Turkey (Tu)	1,200
Bulgaria	100	Hungary (Hu)	180	Norway (No)	500	United Kingdom (UK)	6,700
Canada (Ca)	2,500	Iceland	9	Poland	1,100	United States (US)	17,000
Croatia	180	Ireland	5	Portugal	150	NATO-ISAF	35,500
Czech Republic	150	Italy (It)	1,950	Romania	750	Non-ISAF troops*	5,500
Denmark	400	Latvia	35	Slovakia	60		

PRT lead countries

*National support elements

ISAF Provincial Reconstruction Team (PRT)

ISAF Forward Supporting Base (FSB)

NATO HQ

ISAF expansion stages and completion dates

Stage 1 (North) 2004
Stage 2 (West) 2005
Stage 3 (South) July 2006
Stage 4 (East) October 2006

Regional Command North 3,700

KUNDUZ TAKHAR Faizabad (Ge)
JAWZJAN
BADAKSHAN
Mezar-e Sharif (Sw) Kunduz (Ge)
FARYAB BALKH Pul-e Kumri (Hu) NURISTAN
SAMANGAN PANJSHER Nuristan (US)
Meymaneh (No) BAGHLAN Panjsher (US) KUNAR
SARI PUL Bagram (US) KAPISA LAGHMAN Asadabad (US)
BADGHIS PARWAN KABUL Mehtar Lam (US)
Wardak (Tu) KABUL Jalalabad (US)
Qal'eh-Now (Sp) Bamiyan (NZ) NANGARHAR
Chaghcharan BAMIYAN WARDAK LOGAR
Gardez (US) Regional Command Capital – Kabul 5,000
Herat (It) Khost (US)
GHOR DAIKONDI PAKTIA
HERAT Ghazni (US) KHOST
GHAZNI
Regional Command West 2,000 URUZGAN Sharan (US)
FARAH ZABUL PAKTIKA
Tarin Kowt (Nl)
Farah (US)
Qalat (US)
Lashkar Gah (UK) Kandahar (Ca)
Regional Command East 16,500
NIMRUZ HELMAND KANDAHAR
Regional Command South 9,000

Sources: ISAF, IISS

© IISS

ASIA-PACIFIC: Afghanistan: opium poppy cultivation

Despite efforts to provide farmers with incentives to choose alternative crops, to prosecute perpetrators and to eradicate plants, in its 2007 Opium Winter Rapid Assessment Survey, the UN Office on Drugs and Crime (UNODC) reported that the 2007 opium poppy harvest would top the record harvest of 2006. It also warned of a year-on-year increase in cannabis cultivation, estimating that in 2005 30,000 hectares had been planted with cannabis, rising to 50,000 hectares in 2006 and predicting that this would again rise in 2007. Tackling these issues is central to establishing Afghanistan's long-term security: the UNODC describes it as 'the most obvious case in the world of how drug cultivation, refining and trafficking fund political violence, and vice versa'.

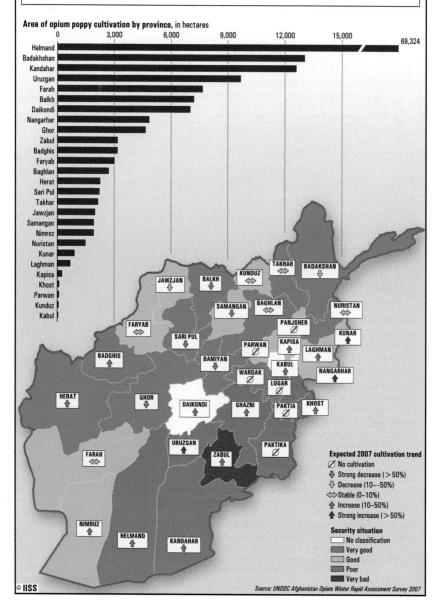

Area of opium poppy cultivation by province, in hectares

© IISS

Source: UNODC Afghanistan Opium Winter Rapid Assessment Survey 2007

ASIA-PACIFIC: Pacific island strife

Faced with creaking infrastructures, high levels of deprivation, populations who speak well over 1,000 languages between them and a multitude of ethnic divisions, as well as the lingering threat of natural hazards, governments of the Pacific islands must surmount significant challenges in establishing stable security conditions.

But as internal conflicts have flared up across the region, Australia and New Zealand have assumed primary responsibility for regional security and committed significant military resources towards achieving it.

The alternative prospect of being surrounded by a group of failed states would have serious implications for these two regional powers.

PAPUA NEW GUINEA

Head of government: Prime Minister Sir Michael Somare
Population: 5,795,887   **GDP per capita (PPP):** $2,700

October 2006	Diplomatic relations with Australia hit a low amid accusations that the government transported Julian Moti, the Australian-born Attorney General of the Solomon Islands who is wanted in Australia to face child sex abuse charges, to the Solomons
30 June– 10 July 2007	General elections to be held in which under-resourced security forces must tackle lawless and increasingly well-armed gangs; with high levels of crime, a weak government mandate and lying only 100km north of the Australian mainland, Canberra will be watching developments closely

Military personnel

Police personnel

Military/police personnel

PAPUA NEW GUINEA

Port Moresby

Dili
TIMOR LESTE

TIMOR LESTE

Head of state:
President Jose Ramos Horta
Population: 1,084,971
GDP per capita (PPP): $800

LIQUICA · DILI · MANATUTO · BAUKAU · LAUTEM
ERMERA · AILEU · VIQUEQUE
BOBONARO
AINARO · MANUFAHI
KOVA LIMA

AUSTRALIA

UN Integration Mission in Timor Leste (UNMIT)
1,674 total uniformed personnel, including 1,641 police; 33 military observers; supported by 234 international civilians, 846 local civilian and 289 UN volunteers.

Australia 925; **New Zealand** 142

May 2002	The nation of Timor Leste is born after 25-year Indonesian occupation and bloody struggle for independence – high poverty and unemployment rates mean that the new nation must rely on external assistance if long-term stability is to be secured
May 2006	Splits between East Timor's new army and police, as well as frustrations at high levels of deprivation, cause street-fighting and looting to erupt, requiring an Australian-led intervention and renewed UN police operation
May 2007	Ramos Horta elected president with 70% of the popular vote
June 2007	Volatile situation in Dili in the run-up to legislative elections at the end of the month, with two people killed during election campaigning on 3 June. However, Ramos Horta attributes this instability to gang rather than political violence

VANUATU

Head of state:
President Kalkot Matas Kelekele
Population: 211,971
GDP per capita (PPP): $2,900

Iles Banks
Espiritu Santo
Maéwo
Pentecote
Malakula
Forari Etaté
Port-Vila
Erromango
Tabba
Anatom

March 2007	State of emergency imposed after ethnic violence erupts in a squatter camp outside Port-Vila, killing three people. The camp is home to thousands of settlers who have migrated from outlying islands

Sources: IISS, Sydney Morning Herald, CIA Factbook, BBC, VOA, Jane's   *Denotes that totals for individual forces are not available

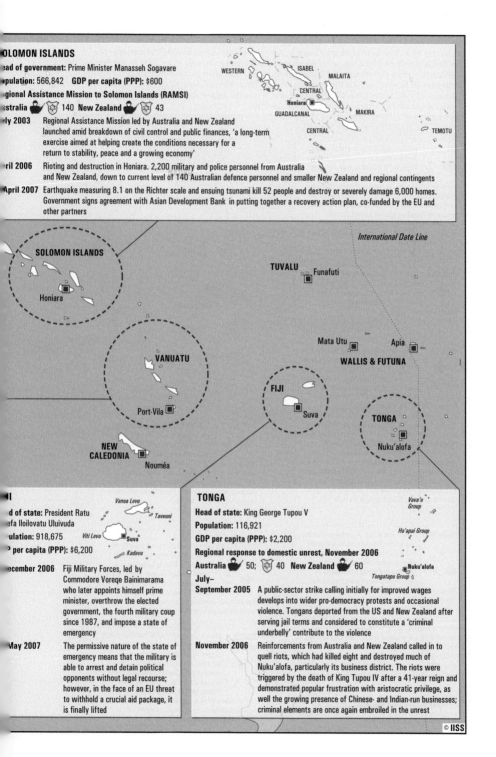

SOLOMON ISLANDS

Head of government: Prime Minister Manasseh Sogavare
Population: 566,842   **GDP per capita (PPP):** $600
Regional Assistance Mission to Solomon Islands (RAMSI)
Australia 140 **New Zealand** 43

July 2003 Regional Assistance Mission led by Australia and New Zealand launched amid breakdown of civil control and public finances, 'a long-term exercise aimed at helping create the conditions necessary for a return to stability, peace and a growing economy'

April 2006 Rioting and destruction in Honiara. 2,200 military and police personnel from Australia and New Zealand, down to current level of 140 Australian defence personnel and smaller New Zealand and regional contingents

April 2007 Earthquake measuring 8.1 on the Richter scale and ensuing tsunami kill 52 people and destroy or severely damage 6,000 homes. Government signs agreement with Asian Development Bank in putting together a recovery action plan, co-funded by the EU and other partners

FIJI

Head of state: President Ratu Josefa Iloilovatu Uluivuda
Population: 918,675
GDP per capita (PPP): $6,200

December 2006 Fiji Military Forces, led by Commodore Voreqe Bainimarama who later appoints himself prime minister, overthrow the elected government, the fourth military coup since 1987, and impose a state of emergency

May 2007 The permissive nature of the state of emergency means that the military is able to arrest and detain political opponents without legal recourse; however, in the face of an EU threat to withhold a crucial aid package, it is finally lifted

TONGA

Head of state: King George Tupou V
Population: 116,921
GDP per capita (PPP): $2,200
Regional response to domestic unrest, November 2006
Australia 50; 40 **New Zealand** 60

July–September 2005 A public-sector strike calling initially for improved wages develops into wider pro-democracy protests and occasional violence. Tongans deported from the US and New Zealand after serving jail terms and considered to constitute a 'criminal underbelly' contribute to the violence

November 2006 Reinforcements from Australia and New Zealand called in to quell riots, which had killed eight and destroyed much of Nuku'alofa, particularly its business district. The riots were triggered by the death of King Tupou IV after a 41-year reign and demonstrated popular frustration with aristocratic privilege, as well as the growing presence of Chinese- and Indian-run businesses; criminal elements are once again embroiled in the unrest

© IISS

AFRICA: China's investments in Africa

China is now close to overtaking France as Africa's second-largest trading partner after the US; bilateral trade, which is dominated by Chinese oil purchases, has increased fivefold since 2000, to $55.5bn last year. China essentially offers infrastructure-building services and consumer goods in exchange for energy and raw material supplies. In November 2006 the third Forum on China–Africa Cooperation (FOCAC) summit was held in Beijing attended by delegates from 48 African nations, it was the largest summit to date. This chart shows Chinese investment activity in ten selected African countries.

ALGERIA Algeria is one of China's most important African partners in terms of bilateral trade totals. In 1993 China National Petroleum Corporation (CNPC) bought several oil refineries for US$350m. As well as continuing interests in established refineries, in March 2007 CNPC reported that an appraisal well that it had started drilling in early 2006 had started to produce crude oil and gas. Chinese companies are also involved in infrastructure projects, such as contracts worth more than $6bn to build two sections of an east–west highway.

SENEGAL In June 2007 Senegal received a $48.7m loan from China to build an electricity distribution network in Dakar, consisting of five new power plants. Other deals are thought to include a telecoms project.

NIGERIA China's presence in Nigeria is significant. As well as oil interests, such as China National Offshore Oil Corporation's 2006 purchase of a $2.7bn stake in an offshore oil field, China has a contract to generate 2,000 MW of hydroelectric power from the Mambila Plateau worth $1.5bn. Infrastructure-related projects include a contract worth $8.3bn for the modernisation of the Lagos–Kano railway line, and during the FOCAC 2006 summit China signed a deal worth $300m to upgrade one of Nigeria's highways. In May 2007 China launched a communications satellite for Nigeria as part of a $311m contract, enabling broadcasting, telecoms and broadband internet services to Africa (Nigerians were trained to run its accompanying tracking station). In 2006 Nigeria received F-7 multirole fighters with missiles, and could well turn to China for equipment to fight rebels in the Niger Delta.

ANGOLA In 2006 Angola temporarily became China's largest supplier of crude oil, ahead of Saudi Arabia. As well as China National Petroleum Corporation's oil exploitation deals with Luanda, since 2004, China has given Angola loans worth a total of $5bn, thus enabling Luanda to turn its back on the IMF. Other projects include China's contract to rebuild the Benguela railway to connect coastal regions with mining regions in Zambia and the DRC.

ZIMBABWE China is Zimbabwe's second-largest trading partner after South Africa. Its relationship with Robert Mugabe's regime has attracted international condemnation, but there are signs that Beijing might be trying to distance itself from Harare, such as Hu Jintao's failure to stop in Zimbabwe during his tour of the region in early 2007. Mugabe launched his 'Look East' policy in 2003 and has welcomed Chinese loans which served to bolster the failing economy, as well as Beijing's refusal to condemn his regime. Harare has bought two batches of six K-8 jet trainer aircraft from China over the past two years, and in May 2006 it received 424 Chinese tractors and 50 trucks. In 2003 Zimbabwe was designated as an 'official approved travel destination' by China, which resulted in a 40% surge in tourists from Asia in that year.

BOTSWANA As well as providing soft loans for the construction of roads and municipal facilities, in 2006 an agreement was signed for China to send trained medical staff to Botswana. The country is listed as an 'official approved travel destination' and China has an interest in Botswana's coal reserves which are thought to amount to 300bn tonnes.

SOUTH AFRICA China's mineral-exploration interests in South Africa are focused on platinum, manganese, copper, cobalt, bauxite and iron ore (copper, in particular, is a key component in electronics manufacturing). Considered by Beijing to be a valuable market for its consumer goods, Pretoria has had to handle protests over the rise of Chinese clothing imports which threaten native industries. South Africa is included on Beijing's list of 'official approved travel destinations'.

Sources: Africa Research Bulletin, China Statistical Yearbook 2005, Financial Times, BBC, Bloomberg, IISS, Time, China Industry Daily News, Middle East Newsline, gov.cn, allafrica.com

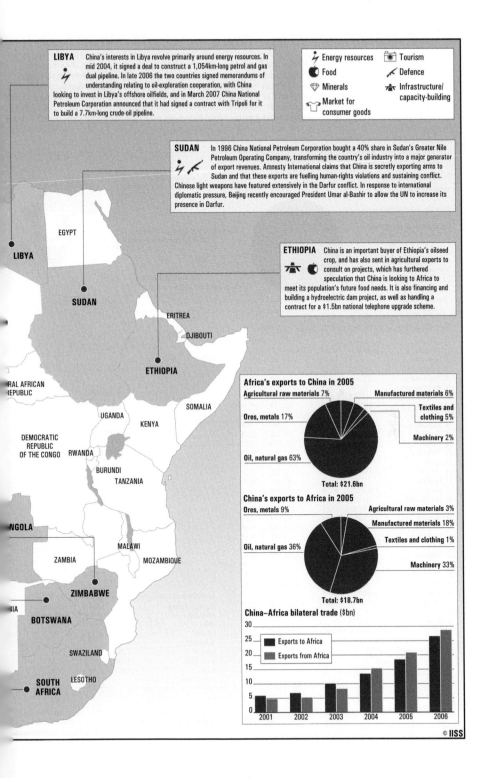

LIBYA China's interests in Libya revolve primarily around energy resources. In mid 2004, it signed a deal to construct a 1,054km-long petrol and gas dual pipeline. In late 2006 the two countries signed memorandums of understanding relating to oil-exploration cooperation, with China looking to invest in Libya's offshore oilfields, and in March 2007 China National Petroleum Corporation announced that it had signed a contract with Tripoli for it to build a 7.7km-long crude-oil pipeline.

⚡ Energy resources   📷 Tourism
🌐 Food   ⚔ Defence
💎 Minerals   🚜 Infrastructure/capacity-building
👕 Market for consumer goods

SUDAN In 1996 China National Petroleum Corporation bought a 40% share in Sudan's Greater Nile Petroleum Operating Company, transforming the country's oil industry into a major generator of export revenues. Amnesty International claims that China is secretly exporting arms to Sudan and that these exports are fuelling human-rights violations and sustaining conflict. Chinese light weapons have featured extensively in the Darfur conflict. In response to international diplomatic pressure, Beijing recently encouraged President Umar al-Bashir to allow the UN to increase its presence in Darfur.

ETHIOPIA China is an important buyer of Ethiopia's oilseed crop, and has also sent in agricultural experts to consult on projects, which has furthered speculation that China is looking to Africa to meet its population's future food needs. It is also financing and building a hydroelectric dam project, as well as handling a contract for a $1.5bn national telephone upgrade scheme.

EGYPT
LIBYA
SUDAN
ERITREA
DJIBOUTI
ETHIOPIA
CENTRAL AFRICAN REPUBLIC
SOMALIA
UGANDA
KENYA
DEMOCRATIC REPUBLIC OF THE CONGO
RWANDA
BURUNDI
TANZANIA
ANGOLA
MALAWI
ZAMBIA
MOZAMBIQUE
ZIMBABWE
BOTSWANA
SWAZILAND
LESOTHO
SOUTH AFRICA

Africa's exports to China in 2005
Agricultural raw materials 7%
Manufactured materials 6%
Ores, metals 17%
Textiles and clothing 5%
Machinery 2%
Oil, natural gas 63%
Total: $21.6bn

China's exports to Africa in 2005
Ores, metals 9%
Agricultural raw materials 3%
Manufactured materials 18%
Textiles and clothing 1%
Oil, natural gas 36%
Machinery 33%
Total: $18.7bn

China–Africa bilateral trade ($bn)
■ Exports to Africa
■ Exports from Africa
2001 2002 2003 2004 2005 2006

© IISS

AFRICA: The Democratic Republic of the Congo: fragile after elections

Despite the relatively smooth implementation of the first democratic elections in the Democratic Republic of the Congo in 40 years, in which Joseph Kabila was elected president with 58% of the run-off vote, the country's stability remains fragile and the humanitarian needs of the population extreme. The possibility of civil unrest threatens western areas where the vast majority supported opposition candidate Jean-Pierre Bemba. Militia activity has continued in the east. At the end of the civil war, militia groups were to disband and integrate with th' national army; some now wear the army uniform but remain loyal to their erstwhile commanders, continuing the cycle of violence. Meanwhile, the weak judicial system is unable to keep pace with developments. In this climate, the mandate of MONUC, the largest and most expensive UN operation anywhere, is crucial if long-term stability and prosperity are to be secured.

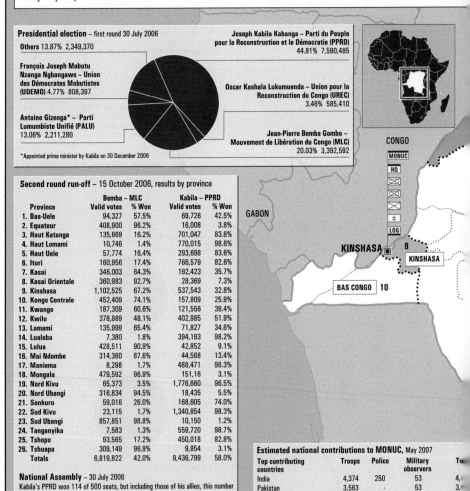

Presidential election – first round 30 July 2006

Others 13.87% 2,349,370

François Joseph Mobutu Nzanga Ngbangawe – Union des Démocrates Mobutistes (UDEMO) 4.77% 808,397

Antoine Gizenga* – Parti Lumumbiste Unifié (PALU) 13.06% 2,211,280

*Appointed prime minister by Kabila on 30 December 2006

Joseph Kabila Kabanga – Parti du Peuple pour la Reconstruction et le Démocratie (PPRD) 44.81% 7,590,485

Oscar Kashala Lukumuenda – Union pour la Reconstruction du Congo (UREC) 3.46% 585,410

Jean-Pierre Bemba Gombo – Mouvement de Libération du Congo (MLC) 20.03% 3,392,592

Second round run-off – 15 October 2006, results by province

Province	Bemba – MLC Valid votes	% Won	Kabila – PPRD Valid votes	% Won
1. Bas-Uele	94,327	57.5%	69,726	42.5%
2. Equateur	408,900	96.2%	16,008	3.8%
3. Haut Katanga	135,669	16.2%	701,047	83.8%
4. Haut Lomami	10,746	1.4%	770,015	98.6%
5. Haut Uele	57,774	16.4%	293,698	83.6%
6. Ituri	160,956	17.4%	766,579	82.6%
7. Kasai	346,003	64.3%	192,423	35.7%
8. Kasai Orientale	360,983	92.7%	28,369	7.3%
9. Kinshasa	1,102,525	67.2%	537,543	32.8%
10. Kongo Centrale	452,409	74.1%	157,809	25.9%
11. Kwango	187,309	60.6%	121,556	39.4%
12. Kwilu	378,889	48.1%	402,985	51.9%
13. Lomami	135,999	65.4%	71,827	34.6%
14. Lualaba	7,380	1.8%	394,193	98.2%
15. Lulua	428,511	90.9%	42,852	9.1%
16. Mai Ndombe	314,360	87.6%	44,568	13.4%
17. Maniema	8,298	1.7%	488,471	98.3%
18. Mongala	479,592	96.9%	151,16	3.1%
19. Nord Kivu	65,373	3.5%	1,776,660	96.5%
20. Nord Ubangi	316,834	94.5%	18,435	5.5%
21. Sankuru	59,016	26.0%	168,605	74.0%
22. Sud Kivu	23,115	1.7%	1,340,854	98.3%
23. Sud Ubangi	857,851	98.8%	10,150	1.2%
24. Tanganyika	7,583	1.3%	559,720	98.7%
25. Tshopo	93,565	17.2%	450,018	82.8%
26. Tshuapa	309,149	96.9%	9,854	3.1%
Totals	6,819,822	42.0%	9,436,799	58.0%

National Assembly – 30 July 2006

Kabila's PPRD won 114 of 500 seats, but including those of his allies, this number was closer to 200. The remaining seats were divided up among 67 different parties and another 63 independent candidates.

Senate – 19 January 2007

The PPRD won 22 of 108 seats, while Bemba's MLC won 14.

CONGO

MONUC

HQ

GABON

KINSHASA 9

KINSHASA

BAS CONGO 10

Estimated national contributions to MONUC, May 2007

Top contributing countries	Troops	Police	Military observers	To
India	4,374	250	53	4,
Pakistan	3,563	.	53	3,
Bangladesh	1,326	250	29	1,
Uruguay	1,323	.	46	1,
South Africa	1,157	.	15	1,
Nepal	1,031	.	20	1,
MONUC Total	.	.	.	18,

Miles	200
Km	320

CENTRAL AFRICAN REPUBLIC

SUDAN

Ⓐ Fataki
Ⓑ Mongwalu

20

23 Gemena

1

5

HQ

⚓

∞

ORIENTALE

Aru Mahagi

HQ
CSS
SF

18

EQUATEUR

Ⓐ Ⓑ Kwandroma

Bunia Nizi L. Albert

6 Marabo Tchomia

LOG

Kisangani

2

andaka

26

DEMOCRATIC REPUBLIC
OF THE CONGO

Beni

Butembo

19 Lubero

NORD KIVU

Rutshuru

Walikale Masisi Goma

UGANDA

HQ

HQ
⚓

CSS

Kindu 17

21

∞ Adikivu L. Kivu RWANDA
Bukavu

Walungu Panzi

22 Uvira

KASAI ORIENTALE

BANDUNDU

SUD KIVU BURUNDI

MANIEMA

7

KASAI OCCIDENTALE

TANZANIA

Kananga

8 13

15 Mbuji-mayi

Nyunzu Kalémie

24

L. Tanganyika

ANGOLA

∞ Manono

4

Pweto

Kamina Mitwabe

14

KATANGA

3

Lubumbashi

MONUC Mission headquarters

HQ Sector, brigade or division
headquarters

⊠ Infantry

⊠ Mechanised infantry

∞ Support helicopters

⊠ Army aviation

⚓ Navy

LOG Logistics base

⊞ Medical unit

Ⅲ Engineers

SF Special forces

CSS Combat service support

IDP population
of September 2006

■ more than 400,000

■ 200,000 to 400,000

■ 100,000 to 200,000

□ 40,000 to 100,000

□ less than 40,000

ZAMBIA

© IISS

AMERICAS: Two years after Hurricane Katrina: reconstruction efforts in New Orleans

Hurricane Katrina has cost $125 billion so far, the most expensive storm in US history. From 23–31 August 2005 Florida, Louisiana, Mississippi, Alabama and Tennessee all felt its force, with winds of over 140 miles per hour hitting the Louisiana coast. Levees designed to protect New Orleans were breached and many areas of the city became flooded in up to six metres of water, rendering large areas of the city uninhabitable. Approximately 20,000 people, many of them the city's poorest and most vulnerable residents, converged on the Louisiana Superdome – images of the chaotic conditions that greeted them shocked the world. While the international community pledged many offers of assistance, according to the State Department by January 2006 only a minority of the offers had been accepted. Amid accusations that the US domestic infrastructure was ill-equipped to handle an emergency on home soil, it emerged that of the $475 million committed in aid, only $126m had been claimed and just $40m had reached Katrina's victims.

Immediate impact of Hurricane Katrina on New Orleans:

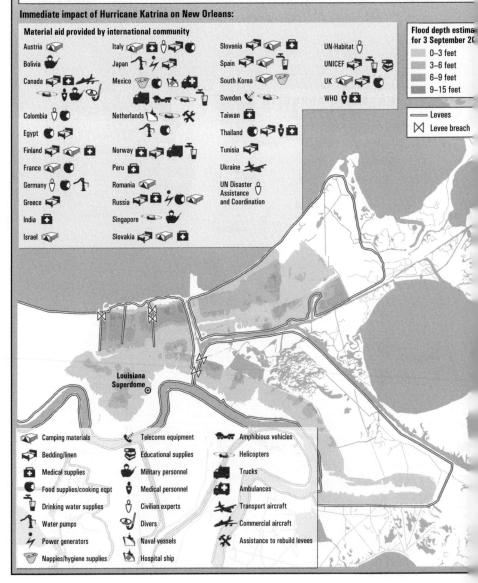

Flood depth estimate for 3 September 2005

- 0–3 feet
- 3–6 feet
- 6–9 feet
- 9–15 feet

Levees
Levee breach

Material aid provided by international community

Austria, Bolivia, Canada, Colombia, Egypt, Finland, France, Germany, Greece, India, Israel, Italy, Japan, Mexico, Netherlands, Norway, Peru, Romania, Russia, Singapore, Slovakia, Slovenia, Spain, South Korea, Sweden, Taiwan, Thailand, Tunisia, Ukraine, UN Disaster Assistance and Coordination, UN-Habitat, UNICEF, UK, WHO

Louisiana Superdome

Camping materials · Bedding/linen · Medical supplies · Food supplies/cooking eqpt · Drinking water supplies · Water pumps · Power generators · Nappies/hygiene supplies · Telecoms equipment · Educational supplies · Military personnel · Medical personnel · Civilian experts · Divers · Naval vessels · Hospital ship · Amphibious vehicles · Helicopters · Trucks · Ambulances · Transport aircraft · Commercial aircraft · Assistance to rebuild levees

ew Orleans in 2007

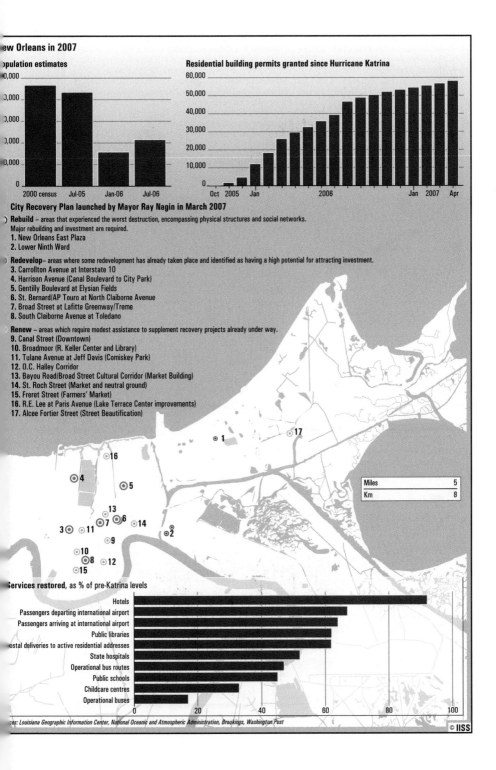

opulation estimates

Residential building permits granted since Hurricane Katrina

City Recovery Plan launched by Mayor Ray Nagin in March 2007

Rebuild – areas that experienced the worst destruction, encompassing physical structures and social networks.
Major rebuilding and investment are required.
1. New Orleans East Plaza
2. Lower Ninth Ward

Redevelop– areas where some redevelopment has already taken place and identified as having a high potential for attracting investment.
3. Carrollton Avenue at Interstate 10
4. Harrison Avenue (Canal Boulevard to City Park)
5. Gentilly Boulevard at Elysian Fields
6. St. Bernard/AP Touro at North Claiborne Avenue
7. Broad Street at Lafitte Greenway/Treme
8. South Claiborne Avenue at Toledano

Renew – areas which require modest assistance to supplement recovery projects already under way.
9. Canal Street (Downtown)
10. Broadmoor (R. Keller Center and Library)
11. Tulane Avenue at Jeff Davis (Comiskey Park)
12. O.C. Halley Corridor
13. Bayou Road/Broad Street Cultural Corridor (Market Building)
14. St. Roch Street (Market and neutral ground)
15. Freret Street (Farmers' Market)
16. R.E. Lee at Paris Avenue (Lake Terrace Center improvements)
17. Alcee Fortier Street (Street Beautification)

Miles 5
Km 8

Services restored, as % of pre-Katrina levels

Hotels
Passengers departing international airport
Passengers arriving at international airport
Public libraries
ostal deliveries to active residential addresses
State hospitals
Operational bus routes
Public schools
Childcare centres
Operational buses

ces: Louisiana Geographic Information Center, National Oceanic and Atmospheric Administration, Brookings, Washington Post

© IISS

AMERICAS: The Guantanamo Bay detention facility

About 780 people have been held at the Guantanamo Bay detention facility since it was established in 2002 to house people captured in the US 'war on terror'. Of these about 415 have been repatriated to Albania, Afghanistan, Australia, Bangladesh, Bahrain, Belgium, Denmark, Egypt, France, Germany, Iran, Iraq, Jordan, Kuwait, Libya, Maldives, Morocco, Pakistan, Russia, Saudi Arabia, Spain, Sweden, Sudan, Tajikistan, Turkey, Uganda, United Kingdom and Yemen, according to the US Department of Defense. In July 2007 some 360 people remained, of whom 80 had been determined eligible for transfer or release. In 2006, three detainees committed suicide. One person, David Hicks of Australia, has been convicted by a military tribunal of providing material support to terrorism after pleading guilty under a plea bargain arrangement. Guantanamo Bay was leased by the US from Cuba in 1903 and is the site of a US naval base.

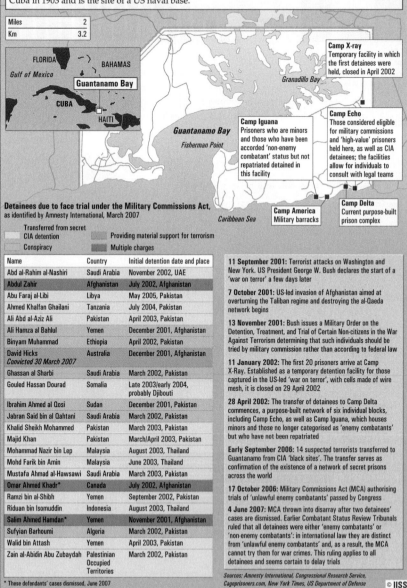

| Miles | 2 |
| Km | 3.2 |

FLORIDA
BAHAMAS
Gulf of Mexico
Guantanamo Bay
CUBA
HAITI

Granadillo Bay

Guantanamo Bay
Fisherman Point

Camp X-ray
Temporary facility in which the first detainees were held, closed in April 2002

Camp Iguana
Prisoners who are minors and those who have been accorded 'non-enemy combatant' status but not repatriated detained in this facility

Camp Echo
Those considered eligible for military commissions and 'high-value' prisoners held here, as well as CIA detainees; the facilities allow for individuals to consult with legal teams

Camp America
Military barracks

Camp Delta
Current purpose-built prison complex

Caribbean Sea

Detainees due to face trial under the Military Commissions Act, as identified by Amnesty International, March 2007

- Transferred from secret CIA detention
- Conspiracy
- Providing material support for terrorism
- Multiple charges

Name	Country	Initial detention date and place
Abd al-Rahim al-Nashiri	Saudi Arabia	November 2002, UAE
Abdul Zahir	Afghanistan	July 2002, Afghanistan
Abu Faraj al-Libi	Libya	May 2005, Pakistan
Ahmed Khalfan Ghailani	Tanzania	July 2004, Pakistan
Ali Abd al-Aziz Ali	Pakistan	April 2003, Pakistan
Ali Hamza al Bahlul	Yemen	December 2001, Afghanistan
Binyam Muhammad	Ethiopia	April 2002, Pakistan
David Hicks Convicted 30 March 2007	Australia	December 2001, Afghanistan
Ghassan al Sharbi	Saudi Arabia	March 2002, Pakistan
Gouled Hassan Dourad	Somalia	Late 2003/early 2004, probably Djibouti
Ibrahim Ahmed al Qosi	Sudan	December 2001, Pakistan
Jabran Said bin al Qahtani	Saudi Arabia	March 2002, Pakistan
Khalid Sheikh Mohammed	Pakistan	March 2003, Pakistan
Majid Khan	Pakistan	March/April 2003, Pakistan
Mohammad Nazir bin Lep	Malaysia	August 2003, Thailand
Mohd Farik bin Amin	Malaysia	June 2003, Thailand
Mustafa Ahmad al-Hawsawi	Saudi Arabia	March 2003, Pakistan
Omar Ahmed Khadr*	Canada	July 2002, Afghanistan
Ramzi bin al-Shibh	Yemen	September 2002, Pakistan
Riduan bin Isomuddin	Indonesia	August 2003, Thailand
Salim Ahmed Hamdan*	Yemen	November 2001, Afghanistan
Sufyian Barhoumi	Algeria	March 2002, Pakistan
Walid bin Attash	Yemen	April 2003, Pakistan
Zain al-Abidin Abu Zubaydah	Palestinian Occupied Territories	March 2002, Pakistan

* These defendants' cases dismissed, June 2007

11 September 2001: Terrorist attacks on Washington and New York. US President George W. Bush declares the start of a 'war on terror' a few days later

7 October 2001: US-led invasion of Afghanistan aimed at overturning the Taliban regime and destroying the al-Qaeda network begins

13 November 2001: Bush issues a Military Order on the Detention, Treatment, and Trial of Certain Non-citizens in the War Against Terrorism determining that such individuals should be tried by military commission rather than according to federal law

11 January 2002: The first 20 prisoners arrive at Camp X-Ray. Established as a temporary detention facility for those captured in the US-led 'war on terror', with cells made of wire mesh, it is closed on 29 April 2002

28 April 2002: The transfer of detainees to Camp Delta commences, a purpose-built network of six individual blocks, including Camp Echo, as well as Camp Iguana, which houses minors and those no longer categorised as 'enemy combatants' but who have not been repatriated

Early September 2006: 14 suspected terrorists transferred to Guantanamo from CIA 'black sites'. The transfer serves as confirmation of the existence of a network of secret prisons across the world

17 October 2006: Military Commissions Act (MCA) authorising trials of 'unlawful enemy combatants' passed by Congress

4 June 2007: MCA thrown into disarray after two detainees' cases are dismissed. Earlier Combatant Status Review Tribunals ruled that all detainees were either 'enemy combatants' or 'non-enemy combatants': in international law they are distinct from 'unlawful enemy combatants' and, as a result, the MCA cannot try them for war crimes. This ruling applies to all detainees and seems certain to delay trials

Sources: Amnesty International, Congressional Research Service, Cageprisoners.com, New York Times, US Department of Defense

© IISS

AMERICAS: The UN mission in Haiti

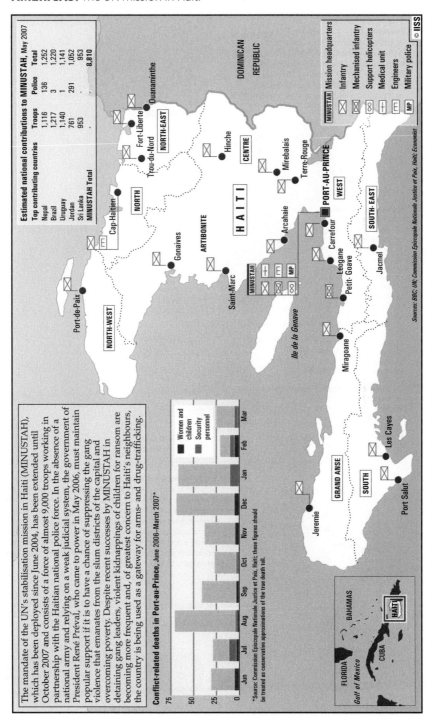

The mandate of the UN's stabilisation mission in Haiti (MINUSTAH), which has been deployed since June 2004, has been extended until October 2007 and consists of a force of almost 9,000 troops working in partnership with the Haitian national police force. In the absence of a national army and relying on a weak judicial system, the government of President René Préval, who came to power in May 2006, must maintain popular support if it is to have a chance of suppressing the gang violence that emanates from the slum districts of the capital and overcoming poverty. Despite recent successes by MINUSTAH in detaining gang leaders, violent kidnappings of children for ransom are becoming more frequent and, of greatest concern to Haiti's neighbours, the country is being used as a gateway for arms- and drug-trafficking.

Estimated national contributions to MINUSTAH, May 2007

Top contributing countries	Troops	Police	Total
Nepal	1,116	136	1,252
Brazil	1,217	3	1,220
Uruguay	1,140	1	1,141
Jordan	761	291	1,052
Sri Lanka	953		953
MINUSTAH Total			**8,810**

Conflict-related deaths in Port-au-Prince, June 2006–March 2007*

- Women and children
- Security personnel

*Source: Commission Épiscopale Nationale Justice et Paix, Haiti; these figures should be treated as conservative approximations of the true death toll.

Sources: BBC; UN; Commission Épiscopale Nationale Justice et Paix; Haiti; Economist

© IISS

MINUSTAH Mission headquarters
Infantry
Mechanised infantry
Support helicopters
Medical unit
Engineers
MP Military police

AMERICAS: Another year of elections in Latin America

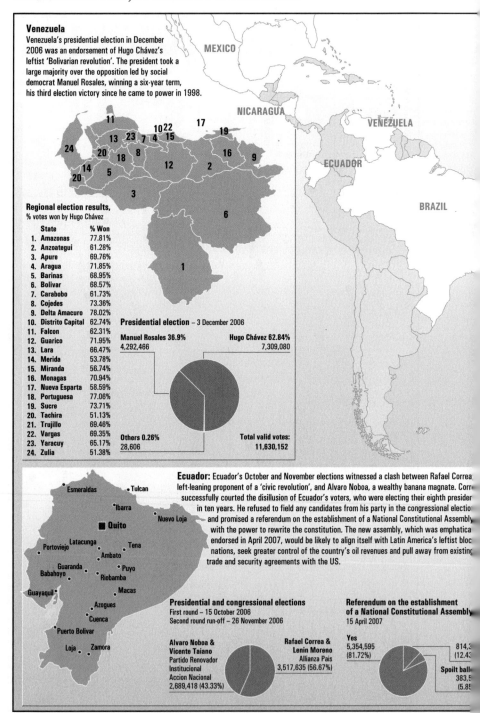

Venezuela

Venezuela's presidential election in December 2006 was an endorsement of Hugo Chávez's leftist 'Bolivarian revolution'. The president took a large majority over the opposition led by social democrat Manuel Rosales, winning a six-year term, his third election victory since he came to power in 1998.

Regional election results,
% votes won by Hugo Chávez

	State	% Won
1.	Amazonas	77.81%
2.	Anzoategui	61.28%
3.	Apure	69.76%
4.	Aragua	71.85%
5.	Barinas	68.95%
6.	Bolivar	68.57%
7.	Carabobo	61.73%
8.	Cojedes	73.36%
9.	Delta Amacuro	78.02%
10.	Distrito Capital	62.74%
11.	Falcon	62.31%
12.	Guarico	71.95%
13.	Lara	66.47%
14.	Merida	53.78%
15.	Miranda	56.74%
16.	Monagas	70.94%
17.	Nueva Esparta	58.59%
18.	Portuguesa	77.06%
19.	Sucre	73.71%
20.	Tachira	51.13%
21.	Trujillo	69.46%
22.	Vargas	69.35%
23.	Yaracuy	65.17%
24.	Zulia	51.38%

Presidential election – 3 December 2006

Manuel Rosales 36.9%
4,292,466

Hugo Chávez 62.84%
7,309,080

Others 0.26%
28,606

Total valid votes:
11,630,152

Ecuador: Ecuador's October and November elections witnessed a clash between Rafael Correa, left-leaning proponent of a 'civic revolution', and Alvaro Noboa, a wealthy banana magnate. Correa successfully courted the disillusion of Ecuador's voters, who were electing their eighth president in ten years. He refused to field any candidates from his party in the congressional election, and promised a referendum on the establishment of a National Constitutional Assembly with the power to rewrite the constitution. The new assembly, which was emphatically endorsed in April 2007, would be likely to align itself with Latin America's leftist bloc nations, seek greater control of the country's oil revenues and pull away from existing trade and security agreements with the US.

Presidential and congressional elections
First round – 15 October 2006
Second round run-off – 26 November 2006

Alvaro Noboa &
Vicente Taiano
Partido Renovador
Institucional
Accion Nacional
2,689,418 (43.33%)

Rafael Correa &
Lenin Moreno
Allianza Pais
3,517,635 (56.67%)

Referendum on the establishment of a National Constitutional Assembly
15 April 2007

Yes
5,354,595
(81.72%)

814,3
(12.43

Spoilt ball
383,5
(5.85

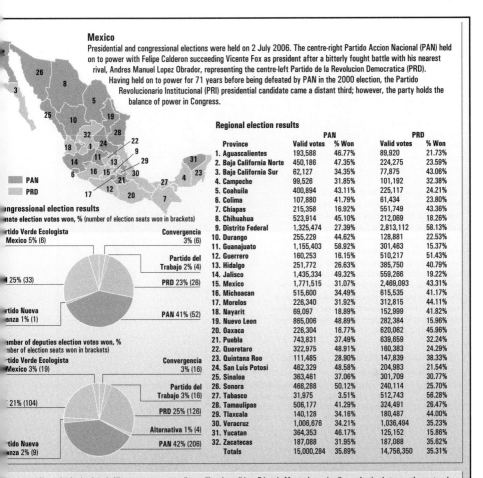

Mexico

Presidential and congressional elections were held on 2 July 2006. The centre-right Partido Accion Nacional (PAN) held on to power with Felipe Calderon succeeding Vicente Fox as president after a bitterly fought battle with his nearest rival, Andres Manuel Lopez Obrador, representing the centre-left Partido de la Revolucion Democratica (PRD). Having held on to power for 71 years before being defeated by PAN in the 2000 election, the Partido Revolucionario Institucional (PRI) presidential candidate came a distant third; however, the party holds the balance of power in Congress.

PAN
PRD

Regional election results

		PAN		PRD	
Province	Valid votes	% Won		Valid votes	% Won
1. Aguascalientes	193,588	46.77%		89,920	21.73%
2. Baja California Norte	450,186	47.35%		224,275	23.59%
3. Baja California Sur	62,127	34.35%		77,875	43.06%
4. Campeche	99,526	31.85%		101,192	32.38%
5. Coahuila	400,894	43.11%		225,117	24.21%
6. Colima	107,880	41.79%		61,434	23.80%
7. Chiapas	215,358	16.92%		551,749	43.36%
8. Chihuahua	523,914	45.10%		212,069	18.26%
9. Distrito Federal	1,325,474	27.39%		2,813,112	58.13%
10. Durango	255,229	44.62%		128,881	22.53%
11. Guanajuato	1,155,403	58.92%		301,463	15.37%
12. Guerrero	160,253	16.15%		510,217	51.43%
13. Hidalgo	251,772	26.63%		385,750	40.79%
14. Jalisco	1,435,334	49.32%		559,266	19.22%
15. Mexico	1,771,515	31.07%		2,469,093	43.31%
16. Michoacan	515,600	34.49%		615,535	41.17%
17. Morelos	226,340	31.92%		312,815	44.11%
18. Nayarit	69,097	18.89%		152,999	41.82%
19. Nuevo Leon	865,006	48.89%		282,384	15.96%
20. Oaxaca	226,304	16.77%		620,062	45.96%
21. Puebla	743,831	37.49%		639,659	32.24%
22. Queretaro	322,975	48.91%		160,383	24.29%
23. Quintana Roo	111,485	28.90%		147,839	38.33%
24. San Luis Potosi	462,329	48.58%		204,983	21.54%
25. Sinaloa	363,461	37.06%		301,709	30.77%
26. Sonora	468,288	50.12%		240,114	25.70%
27. Tabasco	31,975	3.51%		512,743	56.28%
28. Tamaulipas	506,177	41.29%		324,491	26.47%
29. Tlaxcala	140,128	34.16%		180,487	44.00%
30. Veracruz	1,006,676	34.21%		1,036,494	35.23%
31. Yucatan	364,353	46.17%		125,152	15.86%
32. Zacatecas	187,088	31.95%		187,088	35.62%
Totals	15,000,284	35.89%		14,756,350	35.31%

Congressional election results

Senate election votes won, % (number of election seats won in brackets)

Partido Verde Ecologista Mexico 5% (6)
Convergencia 3% (6)
Partido del Trabajo 2% (4)
PRI 25% (33)
PRD 23% (26)
Partido Nueva Alianza 1% (1)
PAN 41% (52)

Number of deputies election votes won, % (number of election seats won in brackets)

Partido Verde Ecologista Mexico 3% (19)
Convergencia 3% (16)
Partido del Trabajo 3% (16)
PRI 21% (104)
PRD 25% (126)
Alternativa 1% (4)
Partido Nueva Alianza 2% (9)
PAN 42% (206)

Nicaragua: November's elections in Nicaragua were, according to liberal candidate Eduardo Montealegre, 'really an election between the past and the future'. In electing President Daniel Ortega, Nicaragua's voters chose to revisit their past. Despite cautions from the US that victory for Ortega might jeopardise bilateral relations and its commitment to giving aid to Nicaragua, the leader of the Frente Sandinista de Liberacion Nacional, who led the country from 1979–90 and was widely expected to align himself with the wider leftist movement in Latin America, won 38.07% of the popular

Presidential election results, by state*

	PLC Jose Rizo		FSLN Daniel Ortega		ALN Eduardo Montealegre	
State	Valid votes	% Won	Valid votes	% Won	Valid votes	% Won
Boaco	26,279	46.03%	14,978	26.24%	14,773	25.88%
Carazo	10,878	14.31%	28,749	37.81%	27,291	35.89%
Chinandega	18,765	10.77%	82,985	47.62%	63,975	36.71%
Chontales	28,051	37.71%	19,616	26.37%	25,530	34.32%
Esteli	26,575	25.91%	48,012	46.81%	24,211	23.60%
Granada	13,379	16.34%	27,464	33.55%	33,714	41.19%
Jinotega	61,773	46.20%	47,089	35.22%	22,851	17.09%
Leon	26,290	15.93%	75,948	46.02%	51,512	31.22%
Madriz	25,831	37.99%	31,773	46.72%	9,503	13.97%
Managua	115,865	19.15%	217,060	35.88%	189,759	31.36%
Masaya	23,553	17.34%	49,158	36.19%	50,594	37.25%
Matagalpa	74,375	39.85%	76,162	40.81%	32,723	17.53%
Nueva Segovia	28,023	32.79%	37,143	43.46%	18,950	22.17%
Rio San Juan	20,548	51.63%	13,527	33.99%	5,391	13.55%
Rivas	10,288	13.21%	30,431	39.07%	34,177	43.88%
Totals	588,304	26.21%	854,316	38.07%	650,879	29.00%

Legislative election results, by party (number of seats won)

Partido Liberal Constitucionalista 25
Frente Sandinista de Liberacion Nacional 38
Movimiento de Renovacion Sandinista 5
Alianza por la Republica 1
Alianza Liberal Nicaraguense Nacional 23

*The autonomous regions of Atlantico Norte and Atlantico Sur are excluded from these results.

© IISS

AMERICAS: Another year of elections in Latin America

Brazil

Presidential and legislative elections were held in Brazil in October 2006. Amid fresh allegations of corruption within his party following on from the 2005 congressional cash-for-votes scandal, President Luiz Inacio 'Lula' da Silva of the Partido dos Trabalhadores (PT) failed to win the required 50% of votes in order for him to claim an outright victory in the first round and faced a run-off vote against the Partido da Social-Democracia Brasileira (PSDB) candidate and former governor of São Paulo state, Geraldo Alckmin. Lula won the run-off with 60.83% of the vote. Despite his leftist credentials, since his election in 2002 he has pursued a centrist agenda by lowering inflation, securing a moderate level of growth and using a surplus in international reserves to pay off the country's debt to the IMF, while winning the support of the poor by expanding welfare programmes. Legislative elections saw 27 of 81 seats in the Federal Senate and all 513 seats in the Chamber of Deputies contested, with Lula's PT failing to win a majority in either house.

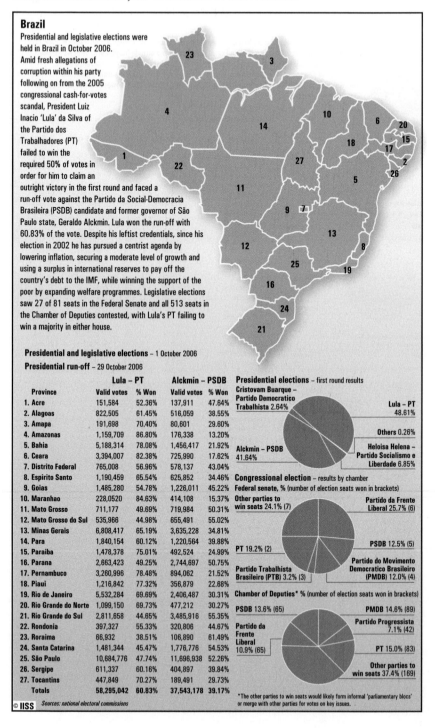

Presidential and legislative elections – 1 October 2006

Presidential run-off – 29 October 2006

	Lula – PT		Alckmin – PSDB	
Province	Valid votes	% Won	Valid votes	% Won
1. Acre	151,584	52.36%	137,911	47.64%
2. Alagoas	822,505	61.45%	516,059	38.55%
3. Amapa	191,698	70.40%	80,601	29.60%
4. Amazonas	1,159,709	86.80%	176,338	13.20%
5. Bahia	5,188,314	78.08%	1,456,417	21.92%
6. Ceara	3,394,007	82.38%	725,990	17.62%
7. Distrito Federal	765,008	56.96%	578,137	43.04%
8. Espirito Santo	1,190,459	65.54%	625,852	34.46%
9. Goias	1,485,280	54.78%	1,226,011	45.22%
10. Maranhao	228,0520	84.63%	414,108	15.37%
11. Mato Grosso	711,177	49.69%	719,984	50.31%
12. Mato Grosso do Sul	535,966	44.98%	655,491	55.02%
13. Minas Gerais	6,808,417	65.19%	3,635,228	34.81%
14. Para	1,840,154	60.12%	1,220,564	39.88%
15. Paraiba	1,478,378	75.01%	492,524	24.99%
16. Parana	2,663,423	49.25%	2,744,697	50.75%
17. Pernambuco	3,260,996	78.48%	894,062	21.52%
18. Piaui	1,216,842	77.32%	356,879	22.68%
19. Rio de Janeiro	5,532,284	69.69%	2,406,487	30.31%
20. Rio Grande do Norte	1,099,150	69.73%	477,212	30.27%
21. Rio Grande do Sul	2,811,658	44.65%	3,485,916	55.35%
22. Rondonia	397,327	55.33%	320,806	44.67%
23. Roraima	66,932	38.51%	106,890	61.49%
24. Santa Catarina	1,481,344	45.47%	1,776,776	54.53%
25. São Paulo	10,684,776	47.74%	11,696,938	52.26%
26. Sergipe	611,337	60.16%	404,897	39.84%
27. Tocantins	447,849	70.27%	189,491	29.73%
Totals	58,295,042	60.83%	37,543,178	39.17%

Presidential elections – first round results

Cristovam Buarque – Partido Democratico Trabalhista 2.64%

Lula – PT 48.61%

Others 0.26%

Alckmin – PSDB 41.64%

Heloisa Helena – Partido Socialismo e Liberdade 6.85%

Congressional election – results by chamber

Federal senate, % (number of election seats won in brackets)

Other parties to win seats 24.1% (7)

Partido da Frente Liberal 25.7% (6)

PT 19.2% (2)

PSDB 12.5% (5)

Partido Trabalhista Brasileiro (PTB) 3.2% (3)

Partido do Movimento Democratico Brasileiro (PMDB) 12.0% (4)

Chamber of Deputies* % (number of election seats won in brackets)

PSDB 13.6% (65)

PMDB 14.6% (89)

Partido da Frente Liberal 10.9% (65)

Partido Progressista 7.1% (42)

PT 15.0% (83)

Other parties to win seats 37.4% (169)

*The other parties to win seats would likely form informal 'parliamentary blocs' or merge with other parties for votes on key issues.

Sources: national electoral commissions

5 Russia / Eurasia

Russia's relations with the United States and some European countries deteriorated throughout 2006 and the first half of 2007, in the midst of increasingly assertive, even hostile, rhetoric from the Russian leadership, including President Vladimir Putin. Traditional sources of tension, including Russia's retreat from democracy and Russian–US rivalry in the countries of the former Soviet bloc, were reinforced by US plans to deploy elements of missile defence in central Europe, NATO's plans to consider membership for Georgia and Ukraine, disagreements over the future status of Kosovo, deadlock in EU–Russian talks, and Russian–UK tensions over the murder in London, with radioactive polonium, of Russian dissident Alexander Litvinenko. The year also saw diplomatic confrontations, backed by economic sanctions, between Russia and two small neighbouring states, Georgia and Estonia – the latter a member of the EU and NATO. And in a race to outmanoeuvre the West, which is seeking ways to diversify its energy imports away from reliance on Russian oil and gas, Russia moved to secure greater control over transport to Europe of Central Asian natural gas through an agreement with Kazakhstan and Turkmenistan.

Increasing Russian resentment towards US and European policy, and its new international ambitions, were summed up in an uncharacteristically strongly worded statement by Putin at a security conference in Munich. He accused the United States of attempting to dominate other nations, to ignore international law and to interfere in the domestic affairs of other states under the slogan of democracy promotion. The confrontational tone of Russian diplomacy was a direct result of Russia's new wealth from high oil and natural gas prices. As the opportunity for external influence over Russian policy declined, Moscow adopted a more assertive foreign policy centred on its ambition to be a major

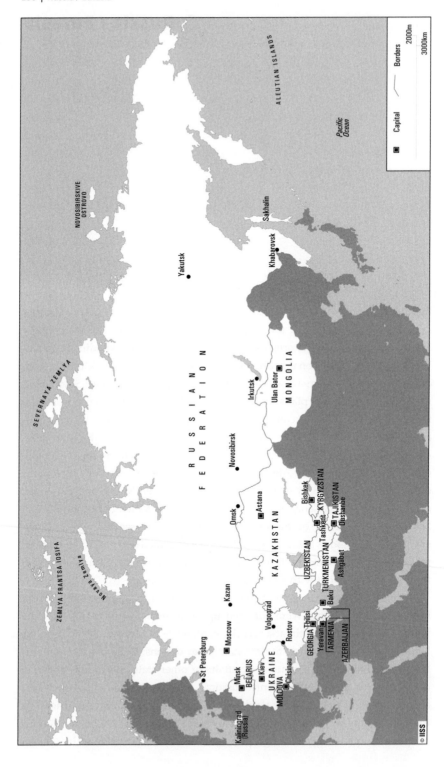

global power. Russia's first G8 chairmanship in 2006, viewed by Moscow as a major diplomatic success, helped to consolidate this image domestically and, to some extent, internationally.

Tensions with the West were partly a by-product of domestic Russian politics. The last year was marked by growing tensions over presidential elections scheduled for March 2008, which are due to mark the end of Putin's second term. Under the constitution, he must step down at that point and a new leader elected in a direct nationwide vote. Despite this clear constitutional position and Putin's repeated assertions that he intends to step down, there is no certainty about whether, and how, the change will take place. However, one thing is clear: the presidential elections will not be free and fair, given that the Kremlin has consolidated control over the media, imposed constraints on the activities of opposition parties, changed the electoral laws to benefit the party in power, and shown willingness to use administrative resources to pressure the opposition. The succession could still be competitive (between two candidates from the ruling elite) or merely symbolic (if Putin nominates a single candidate as his successor). In parliamentary elections due to take place in December 2007, Kremlin-controlled parties will likely prevail. However, marginalised opposition groups have a better chance to present a united front under a new proportional voting system. The forthcoming elections have provoked new tensions both within the Russian ruling elite and in relations with Western democracies, seen by the elite as trying to influence Russia's murky political process.

Leadership succession

The succession issue looms over Russia's political, economic and security agendas. If Putin, while still popular, young, healthy and with more influence than anyone else in the Russian Federation, voluntarily gives up power in accordance with the constitution, it will be a first. Russian leaders never relinquished power voluntarily during the Soviet and post-Soviet periods, or under the tsars. The last Soviet leader, Mikhail Gorbachev, was forced out when Boris Yeltsin made his job redundant by dissolving the Soviet Union. Yeltsin himself had to resign the presidency when his health deteriorated, his popularity plummeted and he lost his grip on power. In earlier times, Soviet Premier Nikita Khrushchev was removed from power by a Politburo-orchestrated conspiracy after he had launched unpopular reforms and lost the respect of and power over Communist Party apparatchiks. Several tsars were removed from power by force – Paul I and Peter III were murdered, Alexander II was killed and Nicholas II was ousted by the 1918 revolution.

There has been much open support for a third Putin term, or extension of his current one. In the first part of 2007 signatures began to be collected in several regions to support amending the constitution to allow him to stay. The speaker of the Federation Council wrote to many regional legislatures to explore attitudes in their regions towards such a development. The mechanics are simple: post-Soviet leaders in Belarus, Kazakhstan, Uzbekistan and Tajikistan have already held referendums to extend their constitutional terms. If Putin were to take this path, he would likely win a referendum with an overwhelming majority. According to opinion polls, 35% of Russians would like to see Putin given the presidency for life.

The Russian political elite and bureaucracy, who have greatly benefited from oil and gas revenues over the past few years, are not keen to see Putin depart. They have a lot to lose. Most top Russian officials are on the boards of powerful and rich state-controlled companies, making them direct stakeholders in the 'petroleum state' economy. In the regions, officials and members of parliaments fear that a change of leadership could put their jobs on the line. Another powerful group of stakeholders – former security officials whom Putin promoted to the top of the political and business community – have the most to lose if the succession goes wrong. According to recent studies, over 70% of top Russian civil servants had links to the KGB or FSB at some point in their careers and over 35% served on the agencies' books. They may be stirring up perceptions of growing threats from the West, including a Western conspiracy to exert influence over the elections. Putin has made strong statements about foreign-funded non-governmental organisations and about US State Department reports, branding them as attempts to meddle in Russian internal affairs. He also claimed that some foreign leaders had encouraged him to stay.

In spite of all this pressure, it appeared in mid 2007 that Putin was determined to follow the constitution and leave office in March 2008, at the age of 55. It would be ironic if the leader who encouraged what the West sees as a Russian retreat from democracy were to set such a precedent.

State-managed pluralism

If Putin does step down, it is unclear whether he will propose a candidate for confirmation by the electorate, or seek a competitive vote. There were signs that he could take the latter course – albeit with candidates that the Kremlin would endorse. The parliamentary polls scheduled for December 2007 will feature competition between two Kremlin-created parties, both loyal to Putin: the centre-right United Russia, which dominates the Kremlin-controlled and largely powerless parliament (Duma), and the centre-left Just Russia (or Russia of Justice). Their creation in 2006 represented a kind of political engineering project based on Putin's desire that Russia have a two-party system.

This new alignment introduced an arguably healthy tension within the Russian political elite. For the first time, Kremlin loyalists, who used to be guaranteed seats in parliament, were forced to make choices in support of – albeit marginally – different political agendas. This choice did not mean that affiliation was driven by belief rather than opportunism. However, these two parties provide an embryonic system of checks and balances. Other parties are inherently weak, and were further marginalised by a recent significant decline in support for the traditional left – the communists – and continuing single-digit support for democratic and liberal parties. It appeared that support for nationalist parties – such as the Motherland Party, which unexpectedly won 9% of the vote in the 2003 elections – was captured by the mainstream pro-Kremlin parties which support Putin's tougher line on the West and neighbours like Estonia and Georgia, as well as revival of patriotic symbols like the old Soviet anthem and Soviet-era parades.

The presidential poll could therefore be between candidates hand-picked by Putin and backed by different parts of the Kremlin administration. Two potential candidates were promoted to deputy prime minister in 2005 and were given time on state-controlled media as well as tasks to test their skills and introduce them to the electorate. They were endorsed by some officials, but Putin was careful never to publicly declare them as candidates for the succession.

The first was Dmitry Medvedev, a 41-year-old lawyer from Putin's native St Petersburg. Before joining the Putin administration in 2000 first as deputy head and then head of administration, he taught at St Petersburg State University. Medvedev is very close to Putin and has been a trusted ally not only in the administration but also as chairman of Gazprom, the state-run natural gas company – a post he held since 2002. In 2005 Medvedev was made deputy prime minister and was given responsibility over so-called 'national projects'. These programmes in housing, health care, education, agriculture and other areas are funded from extra oil and gas revenues to answer public criticism that windfalls from high energy prices fail to benefit ordinary Russians. Putin saw these projects as a good opportunity for Medvedev, who was not well known around the country, to get public exposure. However, ineffective government, corruption and regional bureaucracy made it impossible to achieve quick results and the role may prove to be an obstacle rather than a platform for Medvedev's presidential ambitions. Medvedev, who lacks charisma, is believed to share Putin's views about the strong state, but also supports more liberal economic reforms and might support more cooperative relations with the West and a less aggressive policy in Eurasia. With strong support from the Kremlin, praise for his work on national projects, and large amounts of time on state television, his approval rating in early May was 25–29%, a significant improvement on his single-digit rating last year.

The second potential successor was Sergei Ivanov. Like Putin, he came from a security-service background, having served in the KGB and its successor the FSB from 1981 to 1998, including many years in the Foreign Intelligence Service. He had experience of dealing with foreigners, and excellent English.

From 1998 Ivanov was secretary of the Security Council, and from 2001–2007 he was defence minister. A much more public person who is comfortable making speeches, Ivanov had a stronger track record in foreign policy, where he was a strong supporter of Russian national interests as defined by the current Kremlin elite. He used strong rhetoric against Georgia, at one point threatening to mount a preventive attack against Russia's South Caucasus neighbour for allegedly aiding Chechen separatist forces. He was part of Russia's campaign to reassert its influence in the CIS and to oppose the United States on a number of issues, from Kosovo to arms control to US deployments in Central Asia after 11 September. He was the first to advocate that Russia should suspend implementation of Russia's obligations under the 1999 Adapted Conventional Forces in Europe (CFE) Treaty – which was ratified by the Russian Parliament but still has not entered into force since most of the other CFE signatories have failed to ratified it. However, his track record in the ministry of defence was mixed at best, marked by an inability to form a strong reform-minded team. Like Medvedev, Ivanov was given the opportunity to prove himself and to gain popularity – his portfolio includes innovation projects designed to save the Russian science sector. Yet his ability to understand and speak on anything from nanotechnology to space projects is unlikely to win him as many votes as his continuing hardline stance on foreign-policy issues, including the clash with Estonia over removal of a war memorial and graves of Russian war dead from the centre of Tallinn. Although Ivanov is seen as a hardliner, he is also a pragmatist: given his experience in working with the United States and Europe, he would seem unlikely to revive the Cold War.

In early May 2007 a Levada Center poll indicated that if a second-round presidential run-off were held then between Ivanov and Medvedev, the former would get 55% and the latter 45% – an exact reversal of the December 2006 position. The same poll showed that if Putin himself were to take part Ivanov and Medvedev would each get less than 5%. And 41% of respondents said they would vote for whatever candidate Putin proposed. Putin therefore still had room for manoeuvre and he may still be considering other candidates. An announcement was unlikely before the parliamentary elections.

In the meantime, uncertainty over which of the two pro-presidential parties will prevail in various regions in the parliamentary elections, and who will be Putin's successor, paralysed the bureaucracy, which was not accustomed even to Potemkin-style pluralism. Senior bureaucrats preferred to keep their options open, given how much is at stake for them: almost all key officials in the presidential administration, and even some ministers, are board members of state-controlled companies. A similar overlap between the state and big business is also common in the regions.

Another important question is what Putin will do when and if he steps down in 2008. He has made no secret of his intention to retain influence over decision-making, but it is unclear how he can do this. Given the overall weakness of political institutions, undermined by Putin's drive for centralisation, there is no institutional post that would allow Putin to remain a powerful player. He has dismissed speculation that he would join Gazprom, and it seems unlikely that Putin could assume a more international role like that of former US Presidents Jimmy Carter and Bill Clinton, given his reputation in the West as the man who turned Russia away from democracy. Opinion polls in March 2007 showed that 57% of Russians believed that after 2008 power would remain in the hands of Putin's inner circle, wielding influence through informal levers. But if his successor were to implement real reforms, moving the country closer to the rule of law, such informal power could not be sustained.

Growing tensions with the West

The new assertiveness of Russian foreign policy was linked to Moscow's perception that it has secured its rightful place among the world's great powers. Backed by energy-derived wealth and determined to safeguard its independence and sovereignty, Russia was keen to stress that the West should not take its cooperation for granted. On the contrary, Russian and Western interests have diverged, with the list of disagreements growing longer in 2006–07. The tone of Russian diplomacy changed to be not merely assertive, but increasingly inclined to reject and resent Western messages. Moscow decided that being critical of US policy could win it more friends in the world and more support at home than could any attempt to soften differences and to save whatever was left of US–Russian and EU–Russian strategic partnerships. By early 2007 Russian relations with the West had hit their lowest point since the collapse of the Soviet Union.

In February 2007 Putin strongly criticised American policy at the Munich security conference, saying the United States had 'overstepped its national borders in every way', and accusing it of imposing its policies on other nations and of making excessive use of military force. Putin warned this was extremely dangerous: no one felt safe because no one felt that international law could protect them. Those who lectured Russia about democracy 'do not want to learn themselves'. The model of a US-dominated unipolar world was 'unacceptable' and could not be a moral foundation for modern civilisation. Putin claimed that NATO had broken its promise, given as part of the security guarantees at the time of German unification, not to expand the alliance to the east. Europe was trying to 'impose new dividing lines and walls' on Russia.

Many of the claims were not new, but this was the first time the president had delivered them so bluntly, sparking speculation about the dawn of a new Cold War. Putin continued the attack in April in his annual address to the Duma, when he announced that Russia would suspend its obligations under the 1999 adapted CFE Treaty until the United States and European states ratified it. They refused to do so until Russia pulls its forces out of Georgia and Moldova as part of commitments made by Yeltsin. Russia claimed these commitments were not binding, while the West insisted that they were part of the compromise reached among all the parties to permit agreement on the terms of the adapted CFE. In May 2007 Putin went even further; addressing the Victory Day parade in Red Square, he appeared to compare America with the Third Reich: 'in our time, these threats are not diminishing … In these new threats, as during the time of the Third Reich, are the same contempt for human life and the claims of exceptionality and diktat in the world.' The Kremlin later denied that Putin was referring to the United States.

Areas of disagreement

Putin's anti-Western rhetoric was backed by an even stronger campaign of criticism to which ordinary Russians were regularly exposed through the state-controlled media. At the centre of Russian concerns were a number of key issues.

First, there was growing resentment of foreign criticism of domestic developments, particularly the lack of democracy. Many Russians saw such criticism as an attempt to interfere in their domestic affairs or to belittle Russia's role in the world. Kremlin ideologues have branded Russia's domestic system a 'sovereign democracy', underlining their determination to keep external influence over domestic development to a minimum. The Kremlin appeared concerned that the West could try to influence the outcome of the presidential elections and to embolden the opposition to challenge the authorities. Putin accused the West of using non-governmental organisations as vehicles of foreign influence. Democratic opposition parties, on the contrary, blamed the West for offering too little public criticism of Putin's regime and failing to raise the issue at the July 2006 G8 summit in St Petersburg. As the elections approach, domestic political events, including bans on demonstrations and potential election irregularities, are bound to get more attention in the West, threatening to deepen mutual suspicion even further. In an attempt to silence criticism, the government pressed the Organisation for Security and Cooperation in Europe (OSCE) to shift its focus away from election monitoring and human rights, threatening that Russia would withdraw from the OSCE if this did not occur.

A second point of resentment was the growing perception in Russia that the United States and NATO were implementing a new containment strategy. In Moscow's eyes, the evidence for this was discussion of NATO membership for Ukraine and Georgia, the US decision to deploy elements of ballistic-missile defence to Poland and the Czech Republic, and the failure of the United States and Western Europe to ratify the Adapted CFE Treaty. This perception was rooted in Cold War thinking and in a lack of trust.

US plans for deployment of around a dozen missile interceptors in Poland and a radar in the Czech Republic were particularly badly received. Despite US attempts to reassure Moscow that these systems would be defensive – aimed only at neutralising Iranian missile launches – and could not negate the Russian nuclear deterrent, Moscow continued to question US motives and long-term intentions. Russia believed that the American plans would lead to a new arms race in which Russia would have to invest in modernising and maintaining its own nuclear and missile forces. On 30 May Russia tested a new missile, the RS-24 ICBM, capable of carrying multiple, independently guided re-entry vehicles (MIRVs). This test was advertised by the Kremlin as a response to US missile defence. Washington termed 'ludicrous' Moscow's assertion that its proposed system could threaten Russian nuclear deterrence, which was still backed by over 500 ICBMs (some MIRVed) and many SLBMs. In a clearly escalatory move, Putin suggested that Moscow would target its missiles on Europe, or base them in the Kaliningrad enclave in eastern Europe, should the US system be deployed. This return to Cold War rhetoric raised new concerns in the West. However, Putin acted to cool down tensions during the G8 summit in Heiligendamm by proposing that, instead of deploying its systems in Central Europe, the United States should use the Gaballa radar station, located in Azerbaijan and leased by Russia, to monitor Iranian missile tests. Washington's reaction was to express cautious interest, though the proposal seemed unlikely to be accepted.

Moscow views any decision to establish a permanent military base in Central Europe as a violation of assurances given to Russia under the 1997 NATO–Russia Founding Act, and at the time of NATO enlargement in 1999, that no military bases would be placed in new member states. The missile defence deployment was seen, therefore, as a first step towards more extensive deployments in future. Moscow also questioned why the United States wanted to deploy the systems via bilateral agreements instead of under the NATO umbrella. The NATO–Russia Council has for years been working on cooperation on theatre missile defence and has advanced to discussions on information and technology sharing. At the same time, Russia was sceptical of US proposals for US–Russian cooperation on missile defence in Europe, dismissing them as symbolic and not mitigating Russian concerns. Chief of General Staff General Yuri Baluyevsky said Russia would not cooperate in developing a system that was directed against itself. Even those in Moscow who agreed that US missile-defence plans did not challenge the Russian nuclear deterrent still opposed them on the grounds that if the United States felt less vulnerable against attack, it would be even more prone to use force in resolving differences with states like Iran. Russians were worried by Congressional testimony from US Secretary of Defense Robert Gates in which he included Russia in the list of potential threats to the United States.

US support for Ukraine and Georgia joining NATO was the third bone of contention. This was linked to a number of Russian insecurities. For example, there was growing speculation in Moscow that elements of US national missile defence could also be deployed in the South Caucasus, even closer to Russia's borders. Moreover, as NATO approached Russia's borders to the south as well as to the west, there was a feeling of encirclement. Russia believed NATO membership for Georgia, with which Moscow has particularly difficult relations, could further complicate NATO–Russia cooperation, which was already stagnating under the burden of growing mistrust. It was also worried about escalation of frozen separatist conflicts in Georgia. NATO has never admitted a country with two internal unresolved conflicts, and even some NATO members feared that Georgian membership could one day lead the Alliance into direct confrontation with Moscow. Georgia in turn accused Russia of supporting separatist regimes, and claimed that making conflict resolution a precondition of membership could give Russia a permanent veto over Georgian integration into the Alliance. Concerns over Ukrainian membership included the future of the Russian Black Sea fleet and the unresolved border dispute in the Kerch Strait. Despite Russia's vocal opposition, however, it appeared that Georgia was moving nearer to membership and might be granted a Membership Action Plan (MAP) at the 2008 NATO summit. Although some Western European states remained sceptical, the Georgian bid was strongly supported by newer NATO members and the US Senate, which on 22 March 2007 approved a special bill authorising funding and expressing support for Georgian and Ukrainian membership.

Further complicating relations was geopolitical rivalry between Russia and the United States (and increasingly Europe) in post-Soviet Eurasia. This was particularly apparent in the energy sector, where Europe and the United States sought ways to bypass Russia in the transport of Caspian and Central Asian oil and gas to Europe. Following the 2006 interruption in gas supplies to Europe as a result of Russia's dispute with Ukraine, officially over pricing but believed to be politically motivated, Europe was concerned about energy security and dependence on Russia for its growing demand for hydrocarbons. In 2007 new concerns emerged when Russia interrupted supplies via Belarus in another price dispute and also stopped supplies of oil to a Lithuanian refinery, allegedly due to an accident with a pipeline. Many European governments, especially in Central European states overwhelmingly dependent on imports from Russia, have been exploring projects which could transport oil from Kazakhstan via the South Caucasus and the Black Sea to Ukraine and onwards to Poland and Western Europe. Another project, a trans-Caspian gas pipeline from Turkmenistan, was actively promoted by the US administration following the sudden death of Turkmen leader Saparmurat Niyazov in December 2006. This would connect with the proposed Nabucco pipeline, planned to transport natural gas from Turkey to Austria via Bulgaria, Romania and Hungary.

However, Russia moved to counter these efforts. Moscow proposed an alternative to Nabucco: extending the Russian Blue Stream pipeline from Turkey and making Hungary a hub for Russian gas distribution. In March 2007 Putin attended the signing in Greece by Russian, Bulgarian and Greek partners of an agreement for the construction of the long-awaited oil pipeline connecting the Bulgarian Black Sea port of Burgas with the Greek port of Alexandroupolis in the northeastern Aegean. It was expected to transport 35m tonnes of crude oil per year with the possibility of increasing output to 50m tonnes. In May Putin, Kazakh President Nursultan Nazarbayev and the new Turkmen leader Gurbanguly Berdymukhammedov signed an agreement committing most Kazakh oil and Turkmen gas to be sent to European markets via Russia. The three leaders said they had instructed their respective governments to proceed with the construction of a new export pipeline to Russia along the Caspian Sea coast. The declaration said a final agreement on the Caspian shore gas pipeline would be signed by 1 September and that its implementation would begin in the second half of 2008. The summit was held at the same time as a meeting in Krakow, Poland, attended by the leaders of Ukraine, Azerbaijan and Georgia, at which the Kazakh leader had been expected to agree to bypass Russia. These events left US and EU policy on Caspian energy in ruins.

The past year saw aggressive moves by Russian state-controlled companies to limit Western control over the oil and gas sector. The main targets were two production-sharing agreements from the early 1990s, Sakhalin-1 and Sakhalin-2, under which consortia comprising only foreign companies were granted rights to extract oil and gas in Sakhalin. Gazprom had its eye on Sakhalin development, particularly liquefied natural gas infrastructure, and in 2006 moved to take a controlling stake in the Sakhalin-2 consortium. Under pressure from government inquiries over environmental violations and cost overruns, stakeholders in Sakhalin-2 were compelled to surrender control. On 18 April Gazprom completed the purchase of a controlling share in Sakhalin-2, buying half the stakes owned by Royal Dutch Shell, Mitsui and Mitsubishi for $7.45 billion. The status of Sakhalin-1 remained unchanged. Gazprom's next target could be the lucrative Kovykta gas field, where BP-TNK, a joint venture half-owned by BP of the United Kingdom, holds the licence but has so far been prevented from developing infrastructure for shipping gas to China.

At the same time, Russia continued to pursue its so-called 'reciprocity policy', under which it granted Western European companies access to some Russian oil and gas production assets if Gazprom was given shares in gas distribution in the companies' home countries. An agreement signed in November 2006 between ENI and Gazprom promised the Italian company access to Russian gas exploration and production in exchange for investment opportunities in the consumer side of the natural gas business in Europe. Russia was keen to establish similar arrangements with other European companies – Gazprom already has interests in 16 out of 27 EU states – but some EU states remained uneasy about letting it acquire a stake in distribution. These issues will remain central to EU–Russian relations in the years to come as Europe's dependence on Russia for oil and gas grows.

Although Europe and Russia are becoming more interdependent in trade and investment in the energy sector and elsewhere, EU–Russian relations reached a low point in 2006–07. Following a Russian ban on the import of Polish meat on the grounds that some meat re-exported by Poland from third countries into Russia did not meet Russian sanitary norms, Poland vetoed the opening of EU–Russian negotiations on a new Strategic Treaty to replace the Partnership and Cooperation Agreement due to expire in December 2007. Attempts by the Finnish presidency in December and the German presidency in May failed to resolve the Polish–Russian dispute, and negotiations remained blocked. The EU–Russia Energy Dialogue also made no progress as Russia refused to ratify the EU Energy Charter.

In May 2007 the Estonian government's decision to move the Russian war memorial and Second World War graves from the centre of Tallinn to a military cemetery sparked riots among Estonia's Russian population and provoked a major reaction from Russia, which called for the resignation of the Estonian government. Moscow initiated limited economic sanctions, allowed demonstrators to blockade the Estonian Embassy in Moscow for several days, and allegedly orchestrated cyber-attacks against the computer systems of key Estonian government agencies, banks and media. This pressure met a slow but firm response from the EU, which backed Estonia and, in a show of solidarity which infuriated Moscow, said the Estonian problem was an EU problem. Russia accused Estonia of attempting to rewrite history and of disrespect for its war dead. With tension mounting between Russia and Central European states, the EU is unlikely to develop a constructive and productive dialogue with Russia in the near future. Even if negotiations on the new treaty are allowed to begin, it is hard to see how these could be completed or a treaty ratified by all 27 parliaments. EU–Russian relations will therefore be confined to low-key dialogue and small ad hoc cooperation programmes, hardly amounting to the ambitious strategic partnership that was previously hoped for. New leaders in France and the UK – Nicolas Sarkozy and Gordon Brown – are likely to take a more critical stance towards Russia and to embrace EU solidarity, taking into account the concerns of Russia's neighbours in Central and Eastern Europe.

Another point of disagreement between Russia and the West was the future of Kosovo. Washington and Brussels wanted Kosovo to transition towards *de jure* independence from Serbia within the framework of the plan developed by UN Special Envoy and former President of Finland Martti Ahtisaari. Russia opposed the Ahtisaari plan, which was rejected by Serbia, advocating instead continuation of negotiations between Belgrade and Pristina until the two sides reached a mutually acceptable compromise. Neither Washington nor Brussels believed that such a compromise was possible. They wished to grant Kosovo independent status before, as they feared, the region plunged into another round of violence. Russia made it clear that it was prepared to veto any resolution in the UN Security Council which followed the logic of the Ahtisaari plan. Furthermore, Russia initiated a special Security Council fact-finding mission to Kosovo in order to assess the implementation of UNSC Resolution 1244 of June 1999. This obligated the Kosovar authorities to respect the Serbian minority and to create conditions for the return of Serbian refugees. The mission discovered that many of these obligations had not been implemented and that Serbs had been leaving Kosovo over the past six years. Russia argued that any solution imposed on Serbia would not be sustainable. It believed that separation of part of a sovereign state's territory against its will would create a dangerous precedent and would violate the principle – a Kremlin obsession – of strictly upholding norms of international law where sovereignty was at stake. Russia's unwavering opposition to granting Kosovo 'supervised independence' remained intact even after pressure for a compromise at the G8 summit in Heiligendamm. Russia rejected a proposal by Sarkozy to delay the decision on status for six months to leave room for Serbia and Kosovo to negotiate further. Although Moscow favoured further negotiation, it wanted no deadlines to be imposed on Serbia.

The Balkans remained an emotional issue for Russia. Many Russians criticised Moscow's cooperation with NATO towards the end of the 1999 bombing campaign, and the presence of Russian peacekeepers during the mass exodus of Serbs from Kosovo and destruction of Orthodox churches. Although Putin withdrew Russian peacekeepers from Kosovo, there remained a perception of Russian complicity in anti-Serbian and anti-Orthodox policies. Moscow hinted that it considered Kosovo's potential independence as a precedent for unrecognised separatist states in Eurasia – Abkhazia, South Ossetia (both part of Georgia) and Transdniester (part of Moldova) – which it backed. Although the United States and Europe rejected the parallel, arguing that each conflict should be considered on its own merits, Kosovo's independence would be likely to be viewed as a precedent in the Caucasus and elsewhere. If Moscow felt compelled to recognise these separatist entities in response to unilateral recognition of Kosovo by the West, neither Georgia nor Moldova, nor the international community, would accept such recognition. This would further complicate the process of conflict resolution and worsen relations between Russia and the West, as well as between Russia and some of its neighbours.

Despite the long list of disagreements and increasingly strong rhetoric in US–Russian relations, both sides dismissed speculation about a crisis in bilateral relations, emphasising that they continued to cooperate on a number of important issues, particularly Iran's proliferation challenge. Indeed, US–Russian cooperation on Iran, which over the years had been clouded by disagreement and mistrust, developed more smoothly in 2006–07. Following initial disagreement over referring the Iranian dossier to the Security Council, imposing sanctions on Iran and adopting a resolution under Article 7 of the UN Charter – all originally opposed by Moscow – Russia finally supported all three resolutions on Iran adopted since July 2006. While UNSCR 1696 of 31 July 2006 was the most difficult to negotiate, UNSCR 1747, adopted on 24 March 2007, took just weeks to finalise and created almost no tension between the United States and Russia, despite coming in the immediate aftermath of Putin's Munich speech. Moscow was increasingly irritated that Iran was taking its support for granted and did not reciprocate it. At the end of 2006 Iran criticised Russia for failing to meet its obligations in the construction of the nuclear reactor at Bushehr, and even briefly suspended payment to the Russian company undertaking the work. The Russian manoeuvre at the Security Council was in part intended to compel Tehran to pay. Two days after UNSCR 1747 was passed, Iran made a payment towards the Bushehr costs. However, by June 2007 Iran again owed Moscow over $105m for work in the preceding five months. Nonetheless Moscow expected to complete construction of the power plant, which has been marred by long delays. Moscow also used its backing for UNSCR 1747 to secure US support for its plans for developing an international centre for reprocessing nuclear fuel. The aim of such a centre would be to supply fuel to countries which could be seen as a proliferation threat, but wanted to develop nuclear power for peaceful purposes. Given high oil and gas prices and growing concerns over energy security, demand for civilian nuclear energy has been growing in many parts of the world and Moscow could earn billions of dollars from such a facility. However, Russia has to first complete negotiations with other powers on the terms under which such a scheme could work. Moscow thus refused to supply fuel for the Iranian reactor, hoping instead to negotiate a comprehensive agreement for Iran to acquire fuel from the international reprocessing centre.

Russian support for UNSCR 1747 may have been purely tactical. It remained unclear whether Moscow was committed to implementing its provisions in both letter and spirit. In April 2007, just over a week after the resolution was passed, an Iranian general on the list of officials whose international travel should have been restricted appeared in Moscow, apparently by official invitation from a government ministry. Tehran argued that the visit showed that UN sanctions could not be enforced. Another concern involved continuing Russian weapons sales to Iran. In January 2007 Defence Minister Ivanov acknowledged that Russia had sold Iran *Tor* 1 air-defence systems. Later in May it was reported that Russia had also sold *Pantsir* S1 anti-aircraft systems to Iran indirectly via Syria. Ivanov denied that Russia knew Syria intended to re-export any of the *Pantsir* systems to Iran. Russian journalist Ivan Safonov, who was investigating the sale, fell to his death from the top floor of his apartment building in Moscow in suspicious circumstances in March 2007. There was further speculation, also denied by Ivanov, that Russia might sell S-300 anti-aircraft missiles to Iran via Belarus. Russia and Iran were also discussing other sensitive issues, such as the creation of an OPEC-style gas cartel, which Putin and Iranian President Mahmoud Ahmadinejad discussed at the fifth anniversary summit of the Shanghai Co-operation Organisation in June 2006. Russian and US positions on Iran might again diverge if, as appeared likely, Tehran fails to suspend uranium enrichment. Unlike the United States, Russia was in principle open to the idea of allowing Iran some enrichment capacity, which could be a face-saving measure for the regime. Russian leaders viewed a nuclear-armed Iran as a lesser threat to its security than any US military action against Iran, which could destabilise not just Iran but its entire neighbourhood – to which Russia itself belongs.

No area of disagreement was more sensitive and divisive than Washington's democracy-promotion agenda, also supported by some European states. Although 2006–07 did not see any of the so-called 'colour revolutions' which Russia viewed as externally orchestrated and aimed at weakening Russian influence in Eurasia, Russia's own record on democracy came under increasing scrutiny, particularly by the US Congress. The murder of prominent journalist and Putin critic Anna Politkovskaya in the elevator of her apartment building on 7 October 2006, which Putin dismissed as insignificant, caused uproar among human-rights activists around the world. A study by the International News Safety Institute, an NGO set up by journalists, conducted over a ten-year period (1996–2006) ranked Russia second only to Iraq in terms of the number of journalists killed on the job. The Politkovskaya murder was followed by the murder in London of ex-KGB and FSB officer Alexander Litvinenko, who had accused the Kremlin of orchestrating the explosions in apartment buildings across Russia which killed 300 people in August 1999 and using them as a pretext for the second war in Chechnya, boosting the unknown Putin in his presidential ambitions. Litvinenko, who held a UK passport and lived in exile in London, died on 23 November 2006 from acute radiation poisoning caused by polonium-210, a highly radioactive, short-lived and for the most part commercially unavailable substance manufactured by only a few countries, but mostly in Russia. In his final message Litvinenko accused Putin of authorising his murder. Scotland Yard discovered traces of polonium-210 in various locations across London and in several British Airways aircraft. On 22 May 2007 the UK director of public prosecutions asked Russia to extradite Andrei Lugovoi, who had also worked with the FSB in the past and ran a private security firm, to London to be charged with the murder. Litvinenko met with Lugovoi and two other Russians at the Millennium Hotel in London on 1 November, and fell ill immediately afterwards. Lugovoi denied the charges and the Russian government made it clear that the Russian constitution rules out extradition of Russian citizens for trial abroad. According to Putin, there was still a possibility that Lugovoi might be tried in Russia, if Moscow received compellilng evidence of his guilt. However, such a trial would not been seen as objective by the UK. British authorities stopped short of accusing any Russian government agency of involvement in the murder, although there was a widespread perception that without some official involvement Lugovoi and his putative accomplices could not have obtained polonium-210. The Litvinenko affair cast a long shadow over the already tense UK–Russian relationship. Moscow accused London of granting refuge to two people – oligarch and former political manipulator Boris Berezovsky and Chechen separatist leader Akhmed Zakayev. Russia's repeated demands for their extradition were refused. Berezovsky acknowledged that he continued to fund organisations in Russia which intended to overthrow the current regime.

While the murders of Politkovskaya and Litvinenko affected Western perceptions of the Putin regime, the Russian authorities grew increasingly suspicious that the West was plotting to interfere in the Russian elections in 2007 and 2008. In April 2007 a US State Department report entitled 'Supporting Human Rights and Democracy: The US Record' sparked an uproar in Russia. The report did not call Russia a democracy, but rather a country with a 'weak multiparty political system with a strong presidency', and described US aid programmes to strengthen democratic institutions and promote free elections. The report claimed that 'continuing centralization of power in the executive branch, a compliant State Duma, political pressure on the judiciary, corruption and selectivity in enforcement of the law, continuing media restrictions and self-censorship, and government pressure on opposition political parties eroded the public accountability of government leaders'. In response the Russian government and parliament accused the United States of interfering in Russian internal affairs. In his state of the nation address on 26 April, Putin accused the West of 'making skilful use of pseudo-democratic rhetoric … to return us to the recent past, some in order to once again plunder the nation's resources with impunity and rob the people and the state, and others in order to deprive our country of its economic and political independence'. In his traditional attack on foreign-funded non-governmental organisations he claimed that 'there has been an increasing influx of money from abroad being used to intervene directly in our internal affairs'. In 2006–07 Washington funnelled most of its money for democratisation in Russia through the US Agency for International Development, which spent $84m in 2006 and earmarked $60m for 2007. In 2006 $38m went to programmes to strengthen democracy, with $28m budgeted for 2007. The Kremlin feared that some of this money might be used to encourage grassroots mobilisation of the kind that helped topple corrupt regimes in Georgia and Ukraine.

Beyond 2008

Although most attention was on the succession to Putin, important trends emerged which are likely to be sustained beyond 2008 regardless of who is in power in the Kremlin.

The first was that Russia was unlikely to become more democratic in the foreseeable future, and was more likely to move in an authoritarian than a pluralist direction – in spite of recent moves towards a form of managed pluralism. According to recent opinion polls, only 20% of the population favoured democracy and a market economy, the lowest in any transition economy. State institutions were too weak and not ready for democratic processes and the bureaucracy, with widespread corruption, was even less so. With growing corruption and centralisation, Russia moved further away from a culture of the rule of law. Groups who support democracy do not enjoy broad domestic support, and it is likely to take many years for a new pro-democracy elite to emerge. A poll on Russian attitudes and aspirations published in April 2007 by the European Bank for Reconstruction and Development showed that the majority of Russians were better off then than five years earlier, happy with their economic situation and optimistic about the future. Optimism was strong among the new middle class, which accounted for up to 25% of the population. However, it has so far been excluded from the political process. The political awakening of the middle class could eventually be an impetus for future change.

Russia will remain assertive in its foreign policy and aggressive in its neighbourhood, where it will compete for influence with the United States and Europe. Oil- and gas-driven wealth has translated into more self-confidence and a desire to act independently in both domestic and foreign policy. The political elite is united in seeing Russia as a new pole of power in the world and the key player in post-Soviet Eurasia. Moscow is acting on this premise, challenging Western policies on many fronts, regaining influence in Central Asia and reasserting its role as a permanent member of the UN Security Council. Firmly rooted in geopolitics and a perception of zero-sum competition with the United States in its neighbourhood, Russian foreign and security policy is set to follow its own course.

This means that relations with the United States and Europe are likely to get worse before they can start to improve. Russian energy exports have become not a vehicle for greater closeness between Russia and Europe, but a source of growing disagreement. Putin's successor will take office at a time when Russian relations with the EU and the United States are at their worst since the end of the Cold War, and when its relations with other major powers – such as India,

China or Japan – are yet to develop beyond a modest trade and business agenda. Russia's unilateralist and nationalist foreign policy has hindered development of a strategic vision for relations with other powers. Whether or not speculation about a new Cold War is exaggerated depends on whether Russia feels it can afford to escalate tensions with the West at a time when it has been unable to win other powerful strategic partners.

Economic arguments support greater interdependency between Russia and the West. While it will be increasingly difficult to draw a clear line between private economic interests and the Russian national interest, Russia is likely to remain a growing economy and an attractive investment opportunity, continuing to integrate into the global economy. Despite a failure to diversify the economy and regardless of pervasive corruption, there is a growing consumer sector across Russia: household consumption increased by 11% in 2006 and is set to rise further. The trade surplus, which exceeded $140bn in 2006, will remain high due to oil and gas exports. Investment also continues to increase – in 2006 fixed investment increased by over 13% against 10% in 2005. According to the Central Bank's estimates, net private capital inflow into Russia in 2006 reached an all-time high of $41.6bn (against $1.1bn the year before), largely as a result of liberalisation of the currency regime on 1 July 2006 and many initial public offerings (IPOs) by Russian companies. This made operations in Russian financial markets more attractive for foreigners and investment companies. IPOs of Russian companies (some state controlled), mostly in London, have raised over $17bn, and about 150 companies intend to make IPOs in the next two years, which could bring in $30–50bn.

However, Russia will be increasingly preoccupied with domestic problems, particularly modernisation of social services and infrastructure. Putin failed to achieve this in spite of a favourable economic environment. Major projects remained unimplemented, such as modernisation of the electricity grid and reform of the social security system, pensions and health care. Immigration policy remained undeveloped at a time when continuing economic growth depended on a steady inflow of workers. Putin's successor is also likely to face growing instability in the North Caucasus.

Putin's presidency was viewed in Russia as largely positive: reversal of economic decline; improved quality of life and levels of security, stability, predictability and prosperity which Russia has not seen for at least a century. But for many ordinary Russians, and for a large part of the bureaucracy and political elite, this stability was associated with one man. It lacked the necessary foundation of strong institutions, rule of law and civil society, all three of which have been weakened under Putin. As the 2008 elections approached, the myth of Russian stability was starting to unravel and systemic vulnerabilities were coming to the surface. The country that Putin will leave to his successor was no longer in crisis, as it was at the end of Yeltsin's second term, but it was less prepared for the comprehensive economic and political reform that was urgently needed if Russia was to maintain domestic stability, diversify its economy and preserve the role it aspired to play in the world.

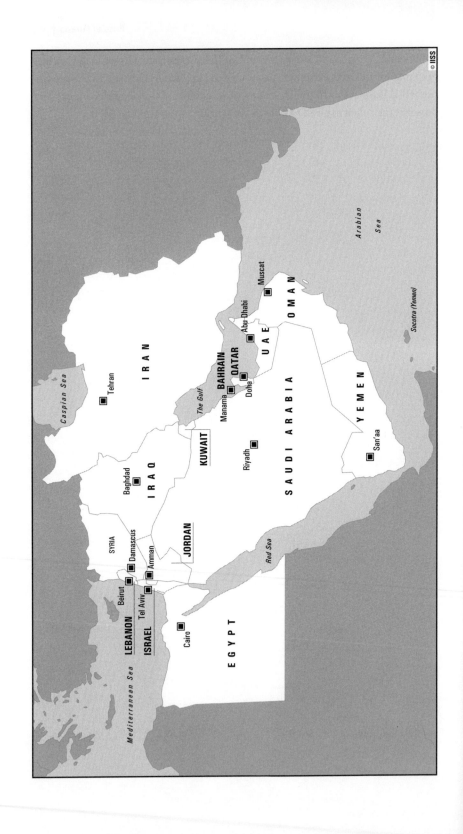

6 Middle East / Gulf

It was a year of unmitigated gloom in the Middle East and Persian Gulf region. The conflict in Iraq continued unabated, with a high death toll. The Bush administration, under growing pressure to bring American troops home, wrestled with options for the future. Iran's confrontation with the West over its nuclear programme brought a series of condemnatory United Nations Security Council resolutions and no progress in negotiations, although the first direct contacts between Iranian and American officials since 1979 were seen. President Mahmoud Ahmadinejad kept up his anti-West and anti-Israel rhetoric but was under domestic political pressure to deliver on economic promises. The Middle East saw an incursion by Israel into Lebanon that achieved little and left its government and military embarrassed, while strengthening the Hizbullah militia. However, the cause of the Palestinians was not advanced as they split into factional fighting that broke up their 'unity government' and left rival governments in the West Bank and Gaza. Gulf Arab states viewed all these developments with alarm, fearing the spread of sectarian violence and a rise in Islamic extremism. Saudi Arabia sought to develop its international relationships so that it was less dependent on its close relationship with the United States.

Iraq: Persistent Conflict

Iraq over the past year continued to be dominated by profound instability with roots in the almost complete collapse of state capacity in the aftermath of the US-led invasion in March and April 2003. Over the four years since then, the security vacuum created by state failure and then compounded by the disbanding of the Iraqi army drove a steady increase in violence. Initially, insecurity was primarily caused by criminality and looting. However, from summer 2003 onwards a disparate but coalescing group of insurgents began to launch hit-and-run attacks on US forces, attempting to drive them from the country. Attacks also focused on infrastructure and nascent Iraqi Security Forces to incite chaos and undermine the Iraqi transitional governments. In 2004 insurgent groups allied with al-Qaeda in Mesopotamia began to incite sectarian violence mainly through mass murder attacks. By 2005 this struggle took on an increasingly inter-communal dynamic, enabling militias deploying sectarian ideology to dominate Iraqi society. This potent mix of criminality, insurgency and sectarian violence killed, according to United Nations estimates, 34,452 Iraqi civilians in 2006.

During 2006–07 the United States diplomatic and military presence in Iraq struggled unsuccessfully to contain this multifaceted conflict. For much of 2006 the US military, under the leadership of General George Casey, pursued a policy of transition, handing over military as well as political responsibility to the Iraqi government and armed forces as quickly as was possible. However, by the beginning of 2007, as violence continued to increase, President George W. Bush had announced a dramatic change in policy, increasing the number of US troops deployed in an attempt to halt Iraq's descent into civil war. Bush appointed General David Petraeus to implement this ambitious new policy.

Since the Iraqi elections of 2005, America's political strategy focused on strengthening the government of Prime Minister Nuri al-Maliki. After tortuous negotiations, al-Maliki took office in May 2006 and afterwards spent a great deal of his time desperately trying to impose his authority on a fractious cabinet. There were still profound doubts in Washington that al-Maliki was able, or even willing, to build a government of national unity that could act as a vehicle for both state building and reconciliation. Al-Maliki had to fend off American doubts while trying to overcome his constitutionally weak position.

Increasing violence and the fractured nature of the government left Iraqi society both traumatised and brutalised. The result was a mass movement of the population, with 1.7 million people internally displaced: 700,000 Iraqis living in Jordan, and 1 million in Syria. Against a background of increasing domestic volatility, the potential for Iraq to act as a cockpit for a wider regional conflagration increased, with neighbouring states fuelling the violence by funding proxies. If indigenous violence continues to increase then Iraq will remain a major source of regional instability.

Political violence: overlapping disputes
The violence that dominated Iraq was far from a straightforward civil war. The primary motor driving the conflict was state collapse and the resultant security

vacuum. Profound lawlessness gave rise to several overlapping disputes that unfolded across the country. Outside Baghdad, violence was both inter- and intra-communal. In Iraq's second city, Basra, Shia militias fought amongst themselves for control of revenue from oil smuggling. In Anbar province, to the northwest of Baghdad, Iraqis increasingly turned against al-Qaeda, sparking a violent intra-Sunni conflict. Amongst these conflicts the epicentre of violence remained Baghdad itself, where a quarter of the country's 26.5m population live.

The conflict within Baghdad had three aspects. The first was criminal, with armed gangs motivated by profit preying on what was left of Iraq's middle and upper classes. Secondly, Baghdad was a major area of operations for insurgents fighting to drive US forces from the country. Thirdly, during 2006 Baghdad's dominant conflict became sectarian, pitching militias and insurgents against each other, using the defence of their specific communities as justification for a sharp increase in levels of violence. The sectarian aspect of this conflict was certainly present in 2004, and increasingly in 2005. However it was the destruction of the al-Askariyya Mosque in the city of Samarra at the end of February 2006 that brought it to ascendancy. The mosque is one of Shia Islam's holiest shrines and its destruction by al-Qaeda in Mesopotamia (AQM) was an act calculated to drive Iraq into civil war. The bombing triggered a 90% rise in violence across Baghdad and set a pattern for the rest of 2006. From February onwards a cycle of sectarian killings dominated the capital. Al-Qaeda in Mesopotamia launched repeated mass-casualty attacks using car bombs or suicide bombers. These attacks were primarily aimed at Shia neighbourhoods and mosques. In the wake of such attacks Shia militias retaliated, abducting and murdering Sunni men. The cycle of atrocity and counter-atrocity resulted in the central mortuary in Baghdad logging between 1,500 and 1,800 dead bodies a month through spring and summer 2006. Some were victims of car bombs, but the majority of the dead had been bound, frequently tortured and then shot in the back of the head, the work of Shia death squads.

As well as al-Qaeda in Mesopotamia, the main perpetrators of sectarian violence in Baghdad are the Shia militias: the Badr Brigade and the Jaish al-Mahdi (JAM). The 15,000-strong Badr Brigade is the military arm of the Supreme Council for the Islamic Revolution in Iraq (renamed the Supreme Iraqi Islamic Council in 2007). They infiltrated the Ministry of Interior's Special Commandos and before February 2006 were one of the main groups involved in the sectarian cleansing of Baghdad. However in the aftermath of the Samarra attack, the 50,000-strong JAM became chiefly responsible for murdering Sunnis in Baghdad. Jaish al-Mahdi was organised around the offices of the Martyr al-Sadr, the religious charity of the radical young Shia cleric and politician Moqtada al-Sadr. Each office was run by a cleric appointed by al-Sadr's headquarters in the southern town of Kufa, with full-time fighters paid as much as $300 a week.

Throughout 2006 JAM used its base in Sadr City, a slum containing 2m people in eastern Baghdad and its presence in other neighbourhoods, such as Kadhimiyah and Shuala, as a platform from which to purge the Sunni-dominated areas of western Baghdad. Under the cover of darkness convoys of armed men would leave Sadr City, moving into mixed or predominately Sunni neighbourhoods. As many as 60 men at a time would be seized. Their bodies, bearing the signs of torture, would be dumped the next morning on the peripheries of Sadr City.

Although the trigger for this cycle of violence was Sunni jihadist attacks on the Shia population, the extent of the coordination and planning behind the cleansing of Baghdad suggests that the Shia militias had a much larger strategic goal. From mid 2006 onwards JAM death squads swept from their base in Sadr City across the north and west of Baghdad in a pincer movement. Their ultimate aim appears to have been to drastically reduce the number of Sunnis resident in the capital. Previously affluent suburbs like Mansour and Yarmouk were targeted for violent population transfer. Militia campaigns of murder and intimidation were combined with the withdrawal of banking services and health care by government ministries controlled by Badr and al-Sadr supporters. The Sunni population was increasingly corralled into a shrinking enclave in western Baghdad and gradually pushed out into Anbar province to the northwest. By early 2007 the western suburbs of Mansour, Yarmouk, Ameriya and Ghazaliya had become increasingly deserted, their markets and shops closed, their populations trapped inside their houses or forced to flee.

Moqtada al-Sadr, along with other prominent Shia religious leaders and politicians, repeatedly called for calm in the aftermath of the al-Askariyya attack. Since the 2003 invasion, al-Sadr has deployed a militant Iraqi nationalism, demanding the withdrawal of US forces and stressing the unity of the Iraqi nation under Islam. The protracted involvement of his militia in the systematic cleansing of Baghdad suggested that his public commitment to Iraqi nationalist rhetoric was at least temporarily suspended in the wave of outrage that greeted the bombing in Samarra. In addition, the speed with which his militia was built after regime change, its two military conflicts with the US army in 2004 and al-Sadr's prolonged absence in Iran for the first five months of 2007 took a toll on its organisational coherence. JAM commanders became financially independent of Kufa through widespread hostage-taking, ransom and the smuggling of antiquities and petroleum. Al-Sadr repeatedly tried to instil discipline by removing disloyal brigade commanders, but the movement remained disparate and ill-disciplined. On balance, however, it was highly probable that al-Sadr sanctioned JAM's campaign of violence in Baghdad during 2006. Against this background his calls for Iraqi unity are unlikely to be treated seriously by those who have suffered from his militia's violence.

The cycle of sectarian violence that unfolded in 2006 left Baghdad a deeply divided city. The people that remained retreated into their respective neighbourhoods and erected makeshift barriers in an attempt to hinder the death squads and suicide bombers. Those neighbourhoods not already dominated by established militias either organised or had imposed on them ad hoc military groupings extracting money from the communities to whom they were claiming to offer protection. By the end of 2006 Baghdad had been transformed into a series of fortified ghettoes, geographically reorganised along sectarian lines.

Outside Baghdad the security vacuum led to instability taking several different forms. An intra-Shia struggle erupted in Basra in April–May 2006 and then again in Amara in October. In Basra, which has a very small Sunni population, the fighting in April, responsible for the deaths of 174 Iraqis, was not caused by religious or ideological differences, but by money. Basra was the centre of Iraq's oil export trade and the conflict was primarily concerned with the division of the spoils. The conflict was a four-way struggle between the Badr Brigade, JAM, the militia of a local political party, Fadillah, and criminal gangs. In the conflict's aftermath, a brittle stand-off kept a rough and ready peace, as each group managed to engage in enough corruption to stop them fighting. The violence in Amara in October was between JAM and Badr, struggling to dominate the town once British forces left. In both cities, none of the groups involved was strong enough to win an outright victory, so the conflict continued to simmer, with sporadic outbreaks triggered by rival machinations and Iranian interference. The continued reduction of British troops stationed at Basra airport during 2007 may trigger renewed fighting.

Anbar province, at the centre of the so-called 'Sunni triangle' northwest of Baghdad, was the epicentre of the insurgency from 2003 to 2006. However, the conflict in this predominately Sunni governorate was transformed during 2006. Al-Qaeda in Mesopotamia dominated territory, especially around the city of Ramadi. As its grip on the area increased, it violently enforced adherence to a very strict Islamic code and sought to replace the influence of Iraqi rural leaders with its own jihadi emirs, controlling self-styled Islamic emirates. Al-Qaeda's brutality, combined with its attempt to enforce its own rule over the population, produced an Iraqi backlash. Harith al-Dahri, one of the most important Sunni religious figures in Iraq, complained in May that al-Qaeda had 'gone too far' in trying to impose an Islamic state on Anbar. 'Iraqis will not accept such a system', he predicted. The struggle between Iraqi Sunnis and AQM ignited when rural leaders in Anbar gathered together to form a 'Salvation Council' and raised militias to fight the jihadis. This indigenous backlash against al-Qaeda was quickly seized upon by both the US military and the Iraqi government, which offered funding and weapons. This dynamic was further encouraged by negotiations aimed at solidifying an alliance of convenience between former insurgents now fighting al-Qaeda and the US and Iraqi governments. The results of this policy were mixed. Violence directed at US troops in Anbar decreased, and al-Qaeda was thrown on the defensive. However, AQM struck back using car bombs to kill several notable members of the Anbar Council in Falluja, Ramadi and Baghdad itself.

Switch in military policy

US military planning in Iraq has had to balance a constant steam of American casualties and the increasing unpopularity of the war at home with the incapacity of Iraq's ruling elite and the continuing instability and lawlessness in Iraq. The US response to the rising tide of violence though 2006–07 can be divided into two broad phases, corresponding to the commands of Generals Casey (until January 2007) and Petraeus. Throughout 2006, Casey doggedly focused on plans to reduce the number of US troops in the country. In June, he drew up a three-stage schedule for a complete handover of military responsibility to the Iraqi government. The first stage would have seen US troop numbers drop by 30,000 to 100,000 by the end of the 2006. Under the second, the Iraqi government's authority would be restored by summer 2008. The final stage would end in 2009 with the Iraqi armed forces becoming self-reliant. The drawdown was to be accompanied by a reduction of US bases across the country from 69 to 11 by the end of 2007.

Under Casey's plan, an increased security vacuum was to be avoided by speedy training of the Iraqi army. The Multi-National Security Transition Command had trained 100,000 Iraqi soldiers by March 2006. In May the Iraqi army was said by the US military to be in command of 50% of the battle-space across the country with plans for this figure to rise to 100% by year end. However, as the security situation deteriorated through the summer, Casey's optimism began to wane. In August he revised his timetable, stating that it would now take another 18 months for the Iraqi army to become self-sufficient. Even this new-found caution did not stop formal command of Iraq's military being handed over to the Iraqi government in September as regional responsibility for security was handed back to individual provincial governors. In October Casey claimed the coalition was three-quarters through its mission to train the army.

Such optimism could not disguise the fact that the security situation in Baghdad was steadily deteriorating. Al-Maliki had announced a new security plan when he took office in May, but by June Bush had acknowledged that the situation in Baghdad remained 'terrible'. The remedy was *Operation Together Forward* and *Together Forward II*, meant to increase Iraqi and US troop numbers in Baghdad through the summer and autumn. However, the attempt to control the situation by deploying 7,000 extra US troops and 4,000 Iraqis proved unsuccessful. After an initial drop in the Baghdad death toll in August, the plan was undermined by the Iraqi government's inability to deliver more than 1,000 troops. Several Iraqi battalions refused orders to deploy to Baghdad. US commanders also had to counter sustained political interference in their operations from the highest levels of the Iraqi government. The finance minister, the former Badr commander Bayan Jabr, was repeatedly accused of obstructing reconstruction initiatives designed to rebuild support for the government in the Sunni neighbourhoods of Baghdad. Moreover, many Iraqi Security Forces tacitly approved of or were complicit in the sectarian cleansing of Baghdad and other mixed areas.

Militarily, 2006 saw a series of hasty and unsustainable plans designed to reduce US troop numbers and hand over responsibility for security to Iraqis as quickly as possible. This policy exacerbated an already deteriorating security situation in Baghdad, Diyala province, Maysan province, and other areas. General Ray Odierno, Petraeus's deputy commander in Iraq, said: 'We've rushed the transition and soon lost many areas that we had before'.

The failure of *Operation Together Forward* triggered a major policy rethink in Washington. This process was given added urgency by the Republican Party's loss of both houses of Congress, and the Iraq Study Group of prominent former officials recommending a dramatic change in policy – which was not adopted. Under Bush's new military approach, announced in January 2007, the number of US troops was increased. The 'surge', Baghdad Security Plan or *Fardh al-Qanoon* (imposing the law) as it is called in Arabic, began in mid February. A departure from Casey's approach, it involved raising American force levels by over 15%, with 30,000 extra troops to be added to the 132,000 already in the country, with particular emphasis on Baghdad where the number of US soldiers would rise to 32,500.

The new US policy sought to deliver order to Baghdad by giving American troops a much higher public profile. They were moved out of the large heavily fortified military bases on the edge of the city to be stationed amongst the population. This was achieved by occupying 28 Joint Security Stations (JSS) or mini-forts, and 28 combat outposts scattered across the city. US forces shared these bases with members of both the Iraqi army and police force, in an attempt to oversee but also to train indigenous security forces. Joint Security Stations, the most visible sign of government capacity in each area, were meant to deliver security and then reconstruction.

The Baghdad Security Plan was divided into two specific phases, each with separate aims. The first stage started in Baghdad on 14 February and was timetabled to reach its peak in terms of troop deployments by mid June, with the number of US soldiers in Iraq topping 160,000. The immediate aim was to secure the central areas of Baghdad on both sides of the Tigris, with the broader goal to reduce the alienation felt by the country's Sunni population and hence facilitate their full participation in government. To do this the widespread religious cleansing of Sunnis from Baghdad needed to be stopped.

The security plan set about replacing makeshift blockades erected by the local population in west Baghdad with concrete barriers, designed to impede death squads and car bombers. Gated communities were set up behind the perimeter walls. The US army cleared armed groups from the areas they designated as a priority, conducting local censuses and then putting an identity-card system in place. Once specific areas were secured, the barriers built and the security stations staffed, American battalion commanders used Commander's Emergency Response Programme funds to begin rebuilding governmental services in the areas they now controlled. Local councils were empowered to hire street cleaners, sewage systems were renovated, schools were redecorated and reopened, and electricity sub-stations were repaired. This approach brought tentative improvements in security, infrastructure and economic activity, though these were highly local and dependent on US military funds. The rate of sectarian murders fell, a limited number of formerly displaced Sunnis returned to their homes and economic life was rejuvenated in the shopping and market areas west of the Tigris. Government and US military statistics backed up early anecdotal evidence.

By late April, however, the militias and insurgent groups had started to reorganise, and there was a marked increase in sectarian-motivated violence. Although a US-led military campaign in January had driven al-Qaeda in Mesopotamia out of its stronghold along Haifa Street in the Karkh area on the western bank of the Tigris, this did not reduce its ability to deploy mass violence. AQM was still able to launch suicide car bombs into predominantly Shia areas, reigniting the vicious sectarian cycle of atrocity and counter-atrocity.

On the other side of the civil war there was strong evidence to indicate that the initial decline in sectarian-motivated violence was largely due to a tactical decision taken by Moqtada al-Sadr's militia. Al-Sadr himself fled to Iran for the first five months of the surge. JAM took its forces off the streets, reducing its operations to avoid confrontations with the US military. The tactical decision to withdraw forces from US-dominated areas meant there was no mass disarmament of those responsible for the previous upsurge in killings. Instead, JAM chose not to fight the United States and merged back into its host community, retaining the majority of its weapons and its coercive capacity.

The second stage of the surge started with the arrival of the final wave of US troops in June. These were sent to Baghdad's outer suburbs, the so-called city 'belts', the major source of post-surge violence. Their task was to seek out and defeat both AQM and JAM. At mid year it was clear that to be successful, US forces would, over the summer, have to enter Sadr City. If the US military managed to gain control of it, to impose security and to begin rebuilding its crumbling infrastructure, it would have made a major inroad into the geographic, military and political basis of al-Sadr's strength and Baghdad's insecurity. If however the United States did not have the troop numbers or political will to control Sadr City, then JAM would continue to have a platform from which to cleanse Baghdad of its Sunni population and drive Iraq further into civil war.

Secondly, the American military would have to impose control on the turbulent areas surrounding Baghdad, to where AQM has relocated. These were situated to the east of Baghdad in Diyala province, and to the south. Diyala, an area with a mixed Sunni and Shia population, has seen a steep increase in violence since the Baghdad Security Plan began. Al-Qaeda, restricted in its ability to operate in Baghdad, fomented religious tension in Diyala instead. This violent instability needed to be curbed over the summer to prevent the area being turned into another platform to launch attacks against Baghdad.

The focus to the south of the capital was the area including the towns of Mahmudiyah, Latifiyah and Yusufiyah. This area sits on a sectarian fault line: it was where Saddam Hussein, in the final years of his rule, deliberately encouraged the growth of Sunni Islamic radicalism. The aim was to create a barrier separating Baghdad from the Shia holy cities of Najaf and Karbala. Since 2005 the area's high levels of violence earned it the moniker the 'triangle of death'. It was in this largely rural area, divided by a myriad of agricultural canals, that the US military would need to open up a second front against al-Qaeda in Mesopotamia.

Until February 2007 US military strategy was primarily shaped by US domestic opinion and electoral timetables. As Iraq descended further into chaos and civil war, Casey, under pressure from then Secretary of Defence Donald Rumsfeld, continued to plan for American troop cuts. In spite of compelling evidence to the contrary, Casey insisted that the Iraqi military were ready and able to take over responsible for security. In January 2007 Bush recognised the unsustainability of this approach. The surge was a profound reversal of US policy – the president's final attempt to impose sustainable security on Iraq before he left office. However, Petraeus repeatedly stated that the ultimate success of this final American attempt to create stability in Iraq would be delivered in the political arena. The momentum delivered by the surge was meant to trigger and ultimately be sustained by the transformation of the Iraqi state. The unanswered question was whether the Iraqi ruling elite were able to meet this challenge.

Politics: the al-Maliki dilemma

The nationwide elections of 15 December 2005 brought to power Iraq's first full-term post-regime-change government. US policy thereafter focused on trying to support Prime Minister al-Maliki, looking to him as the chief vehicle for reforming the government and rebuilding the state. However, al-Maliki faced a series of major problems that constrained his freedom of action. First, he was the head of a government with very little administrative capacity. The Iraqi state had not been rebuilt since its collapse in 2003; al-Maliki has few governmental institutions with which to influence Iraqi society. Secondly, within the government itself the position of prime minister is constitutionally weak. In the aftermath of the 2005 elections the successful political parties divided up the ministerial positions and the resources they brought with them. Against this background al-Maliki did not dominate or even direct his cabinet. Instead he was, at best, a facilitator, attempting to create a degree of consensus amongst his ministers and between them, their powerful party bosses and the US Embassy and military. To make matters worse, al-Maliki was not the first or even second choice for prime minister. He was appointed after a protracted series of negotiations and gained the job only after al-Sadr gave him his support. This meant that for much of 2006 al-Maliki was a very weak prime minister, dependent on both the United States and the radically anti-American al-Sadr for his job.

In trying to influence al-Maliki, US diplomats became increasingly worried about the weakness of his position. By late 2006 this concern turned into scepticism that al-Maliki was committed to national reconciliation. Doubts reached a peak at the end of October 2006 when Bush decided to impose a series of benchmarks on him to judge his commitment and ability. Deadlines were to be set for al-Maliki to disarm the militias, improve electricity supplies and provide equipment and reliable wages for the Iraqi army. Mindful of not only his dependence upon Sadrist support but also his reputation across Iraq, al-Maliki hit back publicly, stating he 'was not America's man' and would pursue an independent policy of his choosing. To demonstrate his resolve he criticised a US military raid on Sadr City and demanded that the American military lift its road blocks surrounding the area. Given that the blockade was imposed in an attempt to release a kidnapped American soldier, this assertion of the prime minister's independence was especially problematic.

Bush dispatched National Security Adviser Stephen Hadley to Iraq in the first week of November. The memo Hadley wrote upon his return was indicative of the United States' ambiguous relations with al-Maliki. Hadley's priority was 'to determine if Prime Minister Maliki is both willing and able to rise above the sectarian agendas being promoted by others'. He listed a series of reasons for US concern about al-Maliki, including the government's 'non-delivery of services to Sunni areas, intervention by the Prime Minister's office to stop military action against Shia targets and to encourage them against Sunni ones, removal of Iraq's most effective commanders on a sectarian basis and efforts to ensure Shia majorities in all ministries'. Combined with JAM's murderous campaign to drive Sunnis from Baghdad, this made Hadley gravely concerned about the prime minister's motives. However, ambiguity began to dominate Hadley's analysis when policy prescriptions were sought. It was less than clear, he argued, whether 'Maliki is a willing participant' in the sectarian actions of the government and JAM. Instead, the national security adviser advocated a package of incentives to strengthen al-Maliki's position and build a platform of moderate political opinion from which the prime minister could gather enough strength to tackle sectarian actors within his own cabinet, party and private office.

Hadley's November 2006 memo, leaked in its entirety to the *New York Times*, summed up the tensions in the US government's relationship with al-Maliki. Washington was aware that a number of the prime minister's close advisers and supporters were actively pursuing a covert and violent sectarian agenda against Iraqi Sunnis. However, there was profound doubt amongst US diplomats about the wisdom or even the ability of the United States to remove him from office. In 2007, with limited choices, US diplomacy continued to give al-Maliki the benefit of the doubt, attempting to strengthen his position while creating incentives for non-sectarian behaviour at the pinnacle of the Iraqi government. Meanwhile his cabinet was ineffective. Part of the problem was widespread corruption present throughout the Iraqi administration, from cabinet level downwards, thought to cost Iraq $4 billion a year. The government was also undermined by its lack of institutional capacity – indicated by the fact that the government spent only 20% of its capital budget in 2006. Government ministries were able to spend $8bn on wages and $6bn on food and fuel subsidies but did not have the capacity to spend more than a small percentage of the $6bn set aside to rebuild the Iraqi state.

After the surge

The Baghdad Security Plan was the final major attempt by the United States to change realities on the ground. At mid 2007, the odds against its success were high. Firstly, US forces, even with the increase in troop numbers, had not yet succeeded in reducing the death toll from sectarian violence. There was increasing evidence that they had not been deployed in sufficiently large enough numbers to bring a fundamental change in the situation in Baghdad. At the height of the surge one US government survey suggested that American forces controlled only 146 out of 457 neighbourhoods in Baghdad. In May, 736 murder victims were found in Baghdad, 50% lower than in January but triple the number killed in February, the first month of the surge.

If the new US policy fails on the security front, the chances of it succeeding with the larger political task are remote. For the surge to deliver sustainable stability the Iraqi government needs to rebuild the state, drastically increasing its administrative capacity and establishing the rule of law. There are grave doubts about the ability, let alone the willingness, of the Iraqi government to do this. If this proves to be the case Bush will face a series of stark choices during his final year in office. The heightened level of US troops in Iraq will probably last until February 2008. If the surge has not delivered sustainable security and political compromise by that date, it will be very difficult to deny that it has failed. Bush will then face two stark choices: to pursue a broadly similar policy in Iraq in the face of continuing troop losses and very high disapproval ratings at home or to embark on a final dramatic change of policy. However, if the latter course is taken, it is much more likely that the policy change would involve a new prime minister as opposed to a dramatic reduction in the American troop presence.

Iran: Ahmadinejad's Brittle Presidency

Iran experienced another turbulent year as international pressures mounted over its nuclear programme and its hardline president, Mahmoud Ahmadinejad, came under increasing criticism at home for the mismanagement of the economy. Ahmadinejad's honeymoon period, prolonged by a heady mix of populism at home and crisis abroad, encountered its first serious setback in the midterm municipal elections held in December 2006. In spite of extensive government restrictions on campaigning, a reinvigorated coalition of reformists and moderate conservatives swept the board and deprived Ahmadinejad's political allies of control of any of the country's municipal councils. Ahmadinejad was characteristically undeterred by the results and answered his critics by pursuing his own policies with increased vigour. The immediate consequence was a further polarisation of politics and, with the arrest of the former senior nuclear negotiator, Hossein Mousavian, the clearest indication of a serious rupture within the political elite of the Islamic Republic.

Ahmadinejad defined his presidency against that of his predecessor, the reformist Mohammad Khatami. Khatami's policies were anathema to Ahmadinejad and his supporters, who regarded the idea of 'reform' as little less than heresy, and the notion that Iran could negotiate with the West as little short of treason. Through 2006, Ahmadinejad moved quickly to take credit for the nuclear programme. While Secretary of the Supreme National Security Council Ari Larijani, Iran's chief negotiator, sought talks with the European Union, Ahmadinejad sought maximum exposure and association with Iran's apparent technological breakthroughs in the nuclear field. This cagey management of the international crisis – pressing ahead with uranium enrichment despite Western protests, and presenting Iran's achievements as a technological and economic milestone – enhanced his domestic political leverage, and allowed him to play a more disruptive role in Larijani's efforts than the latter had imagined. These efforts, which had already been limited by Larijani's condemnation of his predecessor's 'flexibility', were now further hindered by Ahmadinejad's constant interference. At times, it appeared as though Iran's nuclear negotiations were dictated as much by this personal rivalry as they were by Iran's interests.

Regional provocations

Iran came under considerable pressure from major powers on the basis not only of its nuclear programme but also its activities in Iraq and Lebanon. US President George W. Bush, in outlining his new 'surge' plan for Iraq on 10 January 2007, vowed to stop Iran providing material support for attacks on US troops, and the next day US forces seized five Iranian officials at an Iranian government office in the Kurdish regional capital of Irbil. US forces in Iraq provided evidence to back claims that Iran was orchestrating increasingly deadly attacks on Americans in Iraq – in particular, by providing Shia militias with lethal shaped charges known as explosively formed penetrators, or EFPs – although US Secretary of Defense Robert Gates backed away from allegations that this was on the orders of the senior leadership in Tehran. In February, the United States deployed a second carrier strike group, led by the USS *John C. Stennis*, in the Persian Gulf. The *Stennis* and the USS *Dwight D. Eisenhower* participated in military exercises in the Gulf on 27 March. Naval officers were also appointed as head of US Central Command and chairman of the Joint Chiefs of Staff, reinforcing perceptions that the United States, despite the Iraq quagmire, still saw armed conflict with Iran as a real possibility.

In March 2007, media reports surfaced over the embarrassing disappearance of former Iranian Islamic Revolutionary Guard Corps (IRGC) commander Ali Reza Askari, who apparently had defected while visiting Turkey in December. In what may have been a response, on 23 March the IRGC seized 15 British sailors and marines on charges of having entered Iranian territorial waters in the Persian Gulf. The Iranians undoubtedly saw the British as a soft target that would not respond militarily. After several days of fruitless calls to Tehran, Britain publicised evidence that the naval personnel had in fact been in Iraqi territorial waters and sought UN and EU support. Iran initially reacted negatively to the public pressure and paraded the British personnel, who 'confessed' to violating Iranian territory, on television. On 4 April, however, Ahmadinejad announced Iran was returning the personnel as 'a gift' to Britain, gaining a propaganda victory in much of the world by appearing conciliatory.

In Lebanon, unlike Iraq, Iran has been less provocative than advertised. Speculation that Iran had an immediate and direct hand in the initiation of hostilities between the Lebanese Shia militia group Hizbullah and Israel in summer 2006 appeared misplaced. While Hizbullah's abduction of two Israeli soldiers on 12 July 2006 coincided with the decision of the EU to refer Iran back to the Security Council, there is little evidence that Iran was seeking to divert attention away from the nuclear crisis. While there was little doubt, contrary to Iranian denials, that Iran had been supplying Hizbullah with weapons, including missiles used against Israel, this activity formed part of an overall Iranian strategy of deterrence. Iranian military strategists had long concluded that the best way to deter a US attack was to threaten retaliation against Israel. As with any deterrence strategy, the key element was to maintain the threat, and not to risk its elimination through the reckless abduction of Israeli soldiers. At the same time, once the conflict began, Iran was disinclined to abandon its protégé, and as Israeli miscalculations became increasingly apparent, Iran was only too anxious to take the lion's share of the credit. By the end of the conflict, Ahmadinejad seemed to be riding the crest of a regional wave. Hizbullah had survived the Israeli onslaught, intensified perceptions of a 'rising Shia crescent' in the region, and burnished its credentials as a leader of Arab nationalism. The Arab street, in stark contrast to the criticisms that had emerged from the leadership of countries like Saudi Arabia, seemed increasingly enthralled by Hizbullah. A triumphant Ahmadinejad pointed out to Washington that the lesson of the Lebanese conflict was that no amount of high-tech hardware could crush a resistance founded on deep faith and conviction.

To an extent, Ahmadinejad's bluster backfired. Sunni Arab leaders saw Hizbullah's political success in the summer war as evidence of the unacceptable growth of Shia and Iranian power in the region. With the rising Shia crescent as a pretext, both Western and Arab capitals began to consider the resurrection of a post-Oslo regional order in which moderate Arab states would re-align themselves with Israel and the United States against Iran. This fear reached a particularly dramatic peak in the aftermath of the December 2006 execution of Saddam Hussein, which was regarded by many Arabs as not only an act of Shia vengeance, but a peculiarly 'Persian' misdeed. Lebanese Druze leader Walid Jumblatt, for example, characterised the Iranians (and Shi'ites) as fire-worshipping *magi*. Thus, Ahmadinejad's overplaying of Hizbullah's success hastened the formation of a broad anti-Iranian commonality of interests. But the issue that subjected Iran to the greatest outside scrutiny and opprobrium was its determination to develop nuclear weapons.

Nuclear tensions

Tension over Iran's nuclear programme steadily escalated from mid 2006 as the UN Security Council repeatedly set deadlines for Iran to suspend uranium enrichment which Iran repeatedly defied. When Iran defied the 28 April 2006 first deadline for suspension set by the Security Council, the five permanent members (P5) were split on how to respond. While the United States, Britain and France sought prompt enforcement action, Russia and China argued that sanctions would only fan Iran's belligerence. To win their support for sanctions at a later stage, the United States agreed to join the other P5 members plus Germany in offering Iran an upgraded package of incentives. Presented in Tehran on 6 June by EU foreign policy chief Javier Solana, the inducements included direct US engagement in the negotiations and state-of-the-art nuclear technology as well as other economic and political incentives that the E3 had unsuccessfully offered in August 2005. Washington baulked at including a security guarantee in the package, but did agree on a review mechanism under which enrichment would be possible after Iran had restored international confidence. Iran was asked to forgo enrichment for a period, not give it up forever. Unlike the August 2005 offer asking Iran to make a 'binding commitment' not to pursue fuel-cycle activities, the June 2006 proposal asked Iran to suspend its fuel-cycle activities during the negotiations and said the moratorium would be reviewed when 'international confidence in the exclusively peaceful nature of Iran's civil nuclear programme has been restored'.

While the P5 may have seen the offer as generous, Iranian leaders did not believe that Washington would ever agree that Iran had restored confidence, and they did not find the offer of US engagement as enticing as the Europeans had expected. Washington's willingness to join negotiations was a major change in policy, however, which set the stage for punitive measures when Iran refused to suspend enrichment activity as a precondition to negotiations. In mid July, the foreign ministers of the P5 plus Germany announced they would return to the Security Council to discuss sanctions against Iran. On 31 July 2006, the Security Council adopted its first sanctions resolution against Iran by a 14–1 vote (Qatar opposing). UNSCR 1696 made Iranian suspension of all enrichment-related and reprocessing activities mandatory under Chapter VII of the UN Charter. The resolution also required that Iran fully cooperate with the International Atomic Energy Agency (IAEA). If Iran failed to meet these measures by 31 August, the resolution expressed the council's intention 'to adopt appropriate measures', but said these would be under Article 41 of the UN Charter – i.e., economic sanctions and not military measures.

A week before the deadline, Iran responded to the June incentives package by saying that it was ready to discuss suspension during the course of negotiations but not beforehand. In a 21-page counter-proposal, Iran set its own conditions for negotiation, including termination of Security Council discussion of the issue and a commitment that the talks would aim not at limiting Iran's nuclear activities but only at ways to provide assurances of their peaceful nature. An IAEA report of 31 August confirmed that Iran had not met any of the conditions of Resolution 1696, and that, in addition to rejecting IAEA requests for additional information to resolve outstanding questions, Iran was resisting the increased inspection tempo the IAEA sought at the Natanz pilot enrichment facility. Iran had, however, delayed plans to move from the single 164-centrifuge cascade it was operating at Natanz to the six cascades originally forecast to be finished by the end of the summer. Because Russia and China still baulked at sanctions, the transatlantic allies agreed to allow further exploration of Iran's position before initiating Security Council discussion of a follow-on resolution. The P5 plus Germany set early October as a new deadline for Iran to suspend nuclear activity, and US Secretary of State Condoleezza Rice signalled that a temporary suspension by Iran might be enough to allow direct negotiations.

To explore whether negotiations could begin on the June proposal, Solana met Larijani in early September. Larijani signalled that once talks began, Iran could suspend enrichment for two to three months. A tentative plan emerged under which the United States would join negotiations immediately after the suspension was in place. However, Larijani found his room for manoeuvre restricted by an uncompromising mood in Tehran, where Supreme Leader Khamenei sided with hardliners who argued that Iran did not need to make any concessions. With its protégé Hizbullah having fought Israel to a standstill, America hopelessly bogged down in Iraq, and Iran reaping the benefit of record oil prices, Tehran believed it was in a strong position. Ahmadinejad announced on 28 September that Iran would not suspend enrichment for even one day, and Larijani had to break off the pre-talks with Solana. When the transatlantic allies then resumed Security Council consultations on a sanctions resolution in October, Iran responded by beginning operation of a second centrifuge cascade at Natanz to signal that it would not bow to pressure.

After the 31 August deadline set by Resolution 1696, it took the P5 nearly four months to agree on a second resolution imposing sanctions. On 23 December, the Security Council adopted Resolution 1737, this time unanimously, which banned technical and financial assistance to Iran's enrichment, reprocessing, heavy-water and ballistic-missile programmes and froze the foreign-held assets of 12 Iranian individuals and ten organisations involved in those programmes. The resolution also put some restrictions on IAEA technical cooperation. This provision became effective in early February through follow-on action by the IAEA Board of Governors to cut about one-third of the agency's projects in Iran. Earlier the board had blocked Iran's request for technical assistance for a heavy-water moderated research reactor at Arak because such a reactor would be ideal for producing weapons-grade plutonium. Iran is nevertheless proceeding with construction of the 40-megawatt reactor, which is targeted for completion in 2009.

The technology ban in Resolution 1737 was significantly weaker than what the E3 authors originally proposed. The drafters also had to cut back on their original demand for a mandatory travel and training ban on individuals involved in Iran's nuclear and missile programmes. Instead, the resolution called on states to 'exercise vigilance' in allowing travel by Iranians involved in these activities or training to Iranians in disciplines that would contribute to these programmes. In deference to Moscow, the E3 drafters also exempted all work relating to the Bushehr reactor Russia was completing in Iran, including delivery of reactor fuel. The council set a new deadline of 60 days for Iran to suspend enrichment, after which further measures would be adopted under Article 41.

More significant than the actual measures imposed by Resolution 1737, from a political standpoint, was the unanimity of its adoption and the universal application of its provisions. Iranians appeared to be taken aback by the united front lined up against them and by the fact that China and Russia had not blocked sanctions. Ahmadinejad came under fierce criticism over his handling of the nuclear issue. Former nuclear negotiator Mousavian warned that Iran could not ignore the Security Council, only to be arrested a few months later. A group of Majlis (parliament) members signed a letter blaming Ahmadinejad's rhetoric for the sanctions, and the parliament held a public debate on whether the defiant attitude of the government was providing the basis for additional sanctions. A major reformist party, the Islamic Participation Front, called for public discussion to inform the people of the depth and scope of the costs and benefits of the nuclear programme. A newspaper reputed to reflect the views of Khamenei editorialised that the resolution 'is certainly harmful to our country' and that it was excessive for Ahmadinejad to call it 'a piece of torn paper'. The newspaper also accused Ahmadinejad of endangering public support for the nuclear programme by hijacking it as a personal cause. Yet Iran did not stop its drive towards a nuclear-weapons capability.

Throughout 2006, hardline newspapers and Majlis members had demanded that Iran respond to any sanctions by pulling out of the NPT. That, however, would destroy the legitimacy of Iran's nuclear programme and play into the hands of American hardliners. Instead, in line with a new law obliging the government to revise cooperation with the IAEA, Tehran banned 38 IAEA inspectors from Canada, France, Germany, the UK and the United States, demanded that the IAEA remove its section head for Iran, and refused to install remote monitoring cameras in the underground facility at Natanz. The IAEA had a sufficient number of other inspectors but warned that further restrictions could impede the agency's ability to meet its verification task.

The day after Resolution 1737 passed, Iran also announced it would begin to install centrifuges in the underground enrichment facility at Natanz, in furtherance of its goal of standing up a module of 3,000 centrifuges there. By June, approximately 2,000 centrifuges were installed in the underground facility, spinning at sub-optimal speeds and with small amounts of uranium hexafluoride feed material for testing purposes. They were not yet operational. Installing 3,000 centrifuges in the plant, connecting them together and getting them to run smoothly and continuously will take until 2008 or 2009 at the earliest. Once a 3,000-centrifuge enrichment plant is operational, Iran could produce a weapon's worth of highly enriched uranium (HEU), enriched to over 90% concentration of fissionable isotope uranium-235, in nine to eleven months, if Iran chose to break out of the NPT.. Thus, 2009 or 2010 is the earliest possible date Iran could produce a nuclear weapon, assuming that in the same time it could also develop and fabricate the weaponisation package. The estimates also assume that Iran's domestically produced uranium hexafluoride is of sufficient purity, which most analysts now believe is the case despite early indications that it was contaminated with other heavy metals. Iran's stock of uranium hexafluoride feed material – 270 metric tonnes according to an Iranian announcement in March – is enough, when enriched, for at least 30 implosion-type weapons.

A second UN sanctions resolution, 1747, followed with surprising speed and again with unanimity on 24 March, this time just one month after Iran defied the 21 February deadline imposed by Resolution 1737. Although new council members South Africa and Indonesia sought to drop new punitive measures, they reluctantly agreed to support the text largely as agreed to by China and Russia. Resolution 1747 doubled the list of Iranian entities subject to an asset freeze because of their involvement in Iran's nuclear and missile work, including seven more IRGC officers. Also included on the list was Bank Sepah, Iran's fifth-largest bank. The only new mandatory sanction barred Iranian arms exports. UN member states were only asked to 'exercise vigilance and restraint' in transferring arms to Iran, and were called upon, but not required, to cut off financial assistance and concessionary loans. In addition, the resolution required member states to report whether any individuals sanctioned by the council had entered through their territory, but these persons were not subject to a travel ban.

The US determined that unity and speed in adopting a second resolution was of more importance than holding out for tougher measures, and was satisfied with this incremental increase in pressure. In targeting more elements of the IRGC, the new resolution was a form of smart sanctions, focused on the leadership rather than the people as a whole. The scope was not insignificant, given the IRGC's control of large financial assets and economic resources. The day after the resolution was passed, Iran announced it would further restrict its cooperation with the IAEA. Instead of giving the IAEA the customary advance notification of new nuclear facilities and renovation, as it had promised to do in February 2003, Iran said it would revert to providing such information only 180 days before the introduction of nuclear material into such facilities. Iran's refusal to allow remote monitoring cameras, to accept new inspector designations, and to allow the frequency of inspection access the IAEA requested all threatened to provide another basis for the IAEA to find Iran in non-compliance with its safeguards obligations. The IAEA Secretariat sought to avoid confrontation, however, and Iran was able to successfully exploit legal grey areas in its safeguards agreement. But Iran's defiance produced a tougher Russian attitude toward Tehran. In March 2007, Moscow postponed the scheduled delivery of low-enriched uranium fuel for Bushehr. Though the delay was ostensibly over a financial dispute, Moscow used the opportunity both to send Iran a signal and to honour Russian President Vladimir Putin's 2003 pledge to President Bush that Iran would not obtain nuclear weapons on his watch. Postponing the fuel for Bushehr had the unintended consequence, however, of strengthening Iran's insistence that it must produce its own enriched fuel because of the unreliability of outside sources.

Economic pressure has undoubtedly hurt Iran. Washington has urged all nations to interpret the Security Council resolutions aggressively by cutting ties with any businesses involved with the sensitive nuclear and missile programmes and the IRGC. In September 2006, Oil Minister Kazem Vaziri-Hamaneh suggested that, with no new investment, output from Iran's fields would fall by about 13% a year. Based on internal risk assessments, several European and Japanese financial institutions ceased operations in Iran or stopped new investments and dollar transactions. In mid September 2006, the US Treasury barred one of Iran's major banks, Bank Saderat, from any business with US financial institutions, because it was Iran's channel for funnelling money to Hizbullah. The action prevents Bank Saderat from conducting operations in US dollars. Several other countries joined the action against the bank. In January 2007, the US Treasury took similar action against Bank Sepah on grounds of its transactions with Iranian entities named in Resolution 1737. In February, the members of the European Union agreed to go beyond the requirements of 1737 by barring Iran from importing all items on international missile and nuclear control lists, and banning visas to all individuals named in the resolution. Credit guarantees for exports to Iran have declined in volume because of market nervousness over doing any business with Iran.

Domestic perils

Even more threatening to Ahmadinejad were looming domestic challenges. The December 2006 elections for the municipal councils and the Assembly of Experts constituted the first electoral tests of Ahmadinejad's presidency. The composition of the Assembly of Experts, elected every eight years, could determine, through its role in selecting the next Supreme Leader, the direction that would be taken by the Islamic Republic. The municipal elections were a broad gauge of Ahmadinejad's popularity. In order to ensure a high turnout, it was decided to schedule the two elections on the same day.

One of the many paradoxes of the political system in the Islamic Republic of Iran is that, for all the disdain shown to the electorate by the hardliners within the regime, they remain wedded to the idea of popular legitimation. This legitimation does not need to be democratic, but it should be popular: a regular show of public acclamation. Ahmadinejad's role following his assumption of the presidency in 2005 was to secure that acclamation, and to erase the 'heresy' of reform once and for all from the public imagination. His populism rested on this message, and his popularity had appeared more durable than his critics had predicted. But this popularity had been predicated on economic performance and his flamboyant public persona. The political and intellectual elites remained resolutely sceptical of his ability to deliver. In the event, his economic populism – which involved abruptly cutting interest rates and doling out cash handouts to the poor – simply fuelled inflation. Nevertheless, Ahmadinejad, increasingly confident of his own charisma, was sure that he would benefit from a high turnout.

Others in the hardline alliance (in particular, religious fundamentalists) were less convinced. They decided to run separate lists of candidates in the elections. Ahmadinejad too ran his own list, poetically labelled 'The Sweet Scent of Service'. His reformist and moderate conservative opponents, however, led by former president Khatami and Hashemi Rafsanjani, respectively, settled their differences and combined campaigns. Organising cells and coordinating through mobile-phone text messaging, Ahmadinejad's opponents achieved a degree of social cohesion they had not enjoyed since 2001. As a result, Rafsanjani topped the Assembly of Experts poll, winning more than double the votes of his chief rival, ultra-hardliner Ayatollah Misbah Yazdi. Crucially, this ensured that the assembly would remain under the control of the moderate conservatives, and that Rafsanjani would chair any transition council for the leadership. If the assembly elections were politically more important, the municipal elections were more dramatic. Ahmadinejad and his allies, running on different lists, lost control of every municipality in the country. In the important Tehran city election, the reformists captured as many seats as their hardline opponents, while overall control fell to the moderate conservatives under the leadership of Mohammad Baqer Qalibaf. Qalibaf is a bitter opponent of Ahmadinejad and has barely disguised his ambition to run again for the presidency in 2009.

The election reinvigorated Ahmadinejad's opponents, and the press suddenly came alive with broad criticism of his policies, especially with respect to the economy and international affairs. In particular, critics were quick to point out that Ahmadinejad had dismissed the possibility that the UN would impose sanctions over the nuclear issue. With substantial US forces in the Persian Gulf, questions arose as to the president's judgement, and in one revealing television interview he responded to criticisms of his style with the answer that he had always preferred to rely on instinct, and that logic was an over-rated concept. This naturally drew even more fire from both left and right. Especially telling was the domestic response to the Holocaust Conference, which following Ahmadinejad's direction was hosted by the Foreign Ministry in Tehran in December 2006 with the purpose of questioning whether the Holocaust had taken place. Reformists openly condemned the revisionism of the conference, and even conservative clerics queried whether the support of European neo-Nazis was something the Islamic Republic should be seeking.

While Ahmadinejad appeared stubbornly impervious to the mounting criticism of his political style and substance, his greatest vulnerability lay in the economy. Having campaigned on a programme of economic egalitarianism and the redistribution of wealth, Ahmadinejad was under attack for actually increasing the disparities. In a concerted effort to consolidate his popularity, he had spent liberally from the oil reserve fund that had been built in the Khatami administration, injecting an estimated $5 billion into the economy, much of it in cash handouts to the poor. In addition, he had instructed the banks to cut interest rates to allow smaller businesses to borrow. Both these measures resulted in a steady rise in inflation. With wealthier Iranians moving their money abroad, the rial weakened and stood to improve exports, but the cash injection to the poor ensured that many basic goods witnessed a dramatic increase in price. In one celebrated incident, while presenting the annual budget to the Majlis, Ahmadinejad confronted a deputy who had heckled him about the price of tomatoes, retorting that he was clearly shopping in the wrong part of town. Such flippancy won him few friends.

More uncertainty on the horizon

The incoherence of Ahmadinejad's economic policies brought an economy dependent on trade to the brink of stagnation. With the recent introduction of petrol rationing, popular discontent is likely to match that of the business elite. Ahmadinejad's response to this mounting criticism was to repress it. His populism translated into a kind of imperial presidency, to the point where he was unfavourably compared with the Shah. But in suppressing dissent at home, he appeared to enjoy the support of the Supreme Leader, Ayatollah Khamenei, whose tendency is to balance political factions. The fact that Tehran had serious worries about the anti-government and even irredentist impulses of indigenous Kurd and Azeri Sunni minorities, who feel oppressed by Iran's intolerant Persian-oriented culture, and the sectarian opposition of Iranian Sunnis, also tended to underwrite Ahmadinejad's repressive disposition. At the same time, the arrest of the British sailors and their subsequent very public pardon, along with the arrests in spring 2007 of various Iranian-American academics (characterised as part of a global conspiracy to foment regime change), and that of Mousavian (who has not disguised his contempt for Ahmadinejad), reflected an administration acutely aware of its vulnerabilities, determined to make a very public show of strength, and disinclined to undertake genuine substantive engagement with external actors. Ahmadinejad seemed to find political sustenance in closely managing international crises, especially the ongoing one over Iran's nuclear ambitions. But Ahmadinejad's political adversaries saw vulnerabilities in this tendency. Accordingly, the parliamentary elections in February 2008 are likely to be bitterly fought.

In late autumn 2006, hopes emerged in various capitals that American engagement with Iran could be the key to resolving the impasse. Support within the US for talks with Iran grew when the bipartisan Iraq Study Group, led by former Secretary of State James Baker and former Congressman Lee Hamilton, advised opening talks with Iran and Syria about ways to end the violence in Iraq. Advocates of engagement hoped that talks with Iran about security in Iraq could expand to include other issues between the two countries. Iran, for its part, has signalled its interest in comprehensive talks with the US, but President Bush ruled out talks unless Iran first suspended enrichment. Although Secretary of State Rice and Iranian Foreign Minister Manuchehr Mottaki joined a 3 May conference to stabilise Iraq in Sharm al-Sheikh, that occasion failed to produce any substantive discussion. The first real bilateral engagement occurred on 28 May, when the US and Iranian ambassadors to Iraq met face-to-face in Baghdad, for what each described as positive, albeit inconclusive, talks that may continue. While the potential for a negotiated accommodation may have increased slightly, however, it appears a long way from being realised.

The Middle East's Deepening Dysfunction

Even against the backdrop of post-Camp David II violence and political frustration, the past year in the Middle East was exceptionally bloody and futile. The 2006 Palestinian elections that brought Hamas into government triggered violence in Gaza, punctuated by Israeli air strikes, targeted killings and armoured incursions. In mid 2007, a Hamas-led 'unity government' dissolved after Hamas seized control of Gaza, leaving rival Palestinian governments in the West Bank and Gaza. In summer 2006, a successful Hizbullah kidnapping of two Israeli soldiers had unleashed a fierce Israeli response that left parts of Lebanon in rubble, while hundreds of thousands of Israeli civilians were relocated in the face of Hizbullah rocket launches. That war weakened both the Fouad Siniora government in Beirut and the Israeli government in ways that left them unable to respond effectively to the growing crisis. The crowning irony was that these events left only the Bashar al-Assad regime in Syria stronger. There was no outside power to arrest the slide. The United States government was, for the most part, preoccupied with a deteriorating situation in Iraq and an assertive opposition at home. When it did intervene in the Levant, its actions had the unintended effect of reducing its leverage on the contending parties.

The summer war

The chain of misfortune began with the decision of Hamas officials to kidnap an Israeli soldier from within Israeli territory on 28 June 2006 and hold him for the ransom of hundreds of Palestinian prisoners in Israel. Whether the Hamas Gaza leadership under Palestinian Authority (PA) Prime Minister Ismail Haniya was a witting accomplice in the hostage taking is unclear. It is possible that responsibility lay with the so-called external leadership of Hamas in Damascus, commanded by Khaled Meshal. Meshal, previously the target of a bizarre Israeli assassination attempt, represents a harder line on the legitimacy of agreements with Israel, and it was arguably in his interest to disrupt any tacit accommodation that might have been in the making among the Fatah leader and PA President Mahmoud Abbas, Haniya and Israel. Moreover, Israeli reprisals would not have put Meshal at serious risk.

In the event, both Fatah and Hamas officials in Gaza argued that they were unaware of the precise location of the Israeli soldier, but did admit that he remained in Gaza. This gave the new Israeli government under the then-caretaker Prime Minister Ehud Olmert little choice, from the standpoint of domestic politics, but to authorise a significant Israel Defense Force (IDF) armour and infantry incursion into Gaza through Rafah, its southern gateway. The Israeli Air Force (IAF) attacked Gazan infrastructure, destroying a key power station.

The IDF force met resistance from a mix of Palestinian security forces and Hamas militants. The goal of putting sufficient pressure on the PA so that it would force Hamas to surrender the soldier necessitated attacks against economic targets, and the dense urban geography of northern Gaza meant an extremely high civilian casualty rate. The use of heavy weapons, particularly artillery, took a heavy toll; for example, an entire family on a beach holiday was wiped out by an errant shell. The collapse of the de facto truce that had moderated Hamas–Israeli relations for the year preceding the kidnapping led to a resumption of Israel's so-called targeted killing operations. These seemed to have been conducted on the basis of good human and technical intelligence, given the number of militant commanders that, according to Arab reporting, were killed during this period. The apparently high degree of Israeli intelligence penetration was a harbinger of intra-Palestinian tensions that were to get much worse during the course of the year.

The Palestinian response was to continue firing *Qassem* rockets from Beit Lahiya and Beit Hanoun, towns in northern Gaza, towards the nearest Israeli city, Sderot. During the Palestinian intifada, which had seemed to be petering out in the preceding months, up to 800 of these weapons were fired at Israel. Although the rockets were primitive and imprecise, and lethal casualties were few over the ensuing months, the fact that the main target of the missiles was the home town of then-Labour leader and Defence Minister Amir Peretz created additional political pressures to suppress the missile launches. As Israeli ground forces withdrew, air strikes became the preferred way to balance military effectiveness against the public-relations need to avoid IDF and, to a degree, Palestinian casualties. The redeployment of Israeli forces, first to cantonments within Gaza, then back across the ceasefire line, was followed by desultory and ultimately fruitless negotiations with the PA over the release of the soldier whose kidnapping began the confrontation.

The combination of rocket launches and the kidnapping of the soldier decisively undercut the programme of Olmert's Kadima party. The party had been founded the year before by then-Prime Minister Ariel Sharon on a platform of unilateral withdrawal from Gaza and eventually from large parts of the West Bank. Sharon's term had been 'severance' from Gaza and the Palestinian majority areas of the West Bank. Olmert's more marketing-savvy term was 'coming together' of Jewish Israelis in Jewish majority areas. The animating concept was the belief that there was no Palestinian leadership capable of negotiating and then delivering on a bilateral agreement, which called for bold, unilateral action by Israel. Moreover, Israelis asserted that only in the absence of Israeli occupation forces would Palestinians be able to develop the institutions essential to a negotiated peace with Israel. Opponents of unilateral withdrawal had argued that removal of Israeli forces from Gaza would be construed by Palestinian militants as a victory akin to Hizbullah's in Lebanon, which they would then seek to exploit. Other sceptics contended that Palestinians would not respect an Israeli initiative of this kind if it did not account for Palestinian concerns.

The emergence in early 2006 of an elected Hamas government that would not recognise Israel, renounce violence or unambiguously agree to abide by pacts reached by Israel and prior Palestinian administrations had already raised questions in Israel about the viability of Kadima's platform. Subsequent provocations seriously undermined the party, its programme and its leadership. Events in Lebanon in July 2006 appeared to hammer nails into Kadima's casket. On 12 July, Hizbullah's fifth attempt to kidnap Israeli soldiers, to lend support to Hamas, succeeded with the capture of two enlisted men following an assault on their patrol in which three other soldiers were killed. The immediately preceding events in Gaza combined with the prime minister's and defence minister's weak military credentials added to the pressure on the Israeli government to act strongly. It started with extensive air strikes and naval bombardments so as to destroy launchers for longer-range missiles in Hizbullah's arsenal and kill as many fighters as possible at main Hizbullah installations, and to coerce the Lebanese government into removing Hizbullah forces from the southern part of the country by inflicting severe damage on the national infrastructure. Power generation plants as well as the newly completed Beirut airport were hit.

Because Hizbullah was part of the Lebanese government, however, the government was institutionally incapable of taking the decisive action – namely, a deployment southward of the Lebanese Army – that would have met Israeli requirements. While many Lebanese considered Hizbullah's kidnapping of the Israeli soldiers a reckless provocation, the severity of the Israeli response made it politically impossible for a nationalist government to so act without appearing to capitulate to Israeli demands. Hizbullah, which, according to its secretary general, Hassan Nasrallah, had not expected such a strong Israeli reaction, was nevertheless prepared to react. On 13 July, a sweeping missile barrage of northern Israel erupted from prepared *Katyusha* launch sites across southern Lebanon.

Throughout the 33-day war, Hizbullah displayed unprecedented sophistication and precision in its rocket fire. Some 3,970 rockets were fired Although the targets were concentrated around northern Israeli population centres such as Metula, Carmiel, Tiberias, Kiryat Shmona and other towns, there were a significant number of impacts as far south as the port city of Haifa and Hadera, 80km from the border and one of the largest road junctions in Israel. In the first ten days, an average of 150–180 rockets per day were fired. Hizbullah later increased its missile barrage, unleashing 250 rockets on 13 August, the final day of the war. Haifa had been hit 93 times and more than a thousand rockets had struck Kiryat Shmona. Most of the rockets fired were short-range *Katyushas*, the IAF having knocked out many of Hizbullah's medium-range *Zelzal* and *Fajar* missiles early on. More than two million Israelis (one-third of the country's population) were exposed to Hizbullah's missiles; 6,000 homes were hit and 300,000 people were displaced.

On 14 July, Hizbullah launched a Chinese-made, Iranian-upgraded C-802 radar-guided missile at the *Hanit*, an Israeli missile boat patrolling off the Lebanese coast. The crew, unaware that Hizbullah was armed with these missiles, had not activated the ship's defences. Four sailors were killed and the ship limped back to Ashdod, her home port. While this sort of strike was not attempted again, the episode revealed both the sophistication of the weapons transferred by Iran to Hizbullah and significant gaps in Israeli intelligence about Hizbullah's capabilities. It became apparent to Israeli policymakers that airpower would not suffice to subdue Hizbullah, or motivate the Lebanese government to intervene. IDF Special Forces had been conducting ground operations in southern Lebanon since 17 July, and a ground invasion began in earnest on 22 July, when Israel sent 2,000 soldiers and a tank brigade into the Hizbullah stronghold of Maroun al-Ras.

The IDF encountered stronger than expected resistance in villages throughout the area, with the heaviest fighting occurring at Maroun al-Ras and nearby Bint Jubayl. Armed with AK-47s, M-16s and M-4s, Hizbullah fighters engaged in house-to-house combat with Israeli soldiers in villages throughout southern Lebanon, managing to ambush and then pin down members of the elite Golani brigade. Those fighters, many of them villagers who joined the full-time force of about 1,000, operated in squad-sized units of 7–10 men. They were granted enormous freedom by the group's leadership to make battlefield decisions, while simultaneously remaining in contact with the leadership in southern Beirut through a complex system of radio and cell-phone communications and reportedly cracking Israel's radio communications codes. Skilled Hizbullah anti-tank teams delayed Israel's advance with their use of AT-3 *Sagger* and AT-14 *Kornet* E anti-tank missiles, striking up to 46 Israeli tanks, destroying five, and killing 30 Israeli crewmen during the war. Markings on captured *Kornets* showed that the Russian-manufactured missiles were supplied by Syria from Syrian Army stocks. These missiles had a disproportionate effect on the ground campaign because they forced armoured and other vehicles off the roads onto cross-country routes that made progress slow and severely complicated resupply of forward units.

The IDF ground forces were relatively unprepared for the war of manoeuvre and assault they were called on to fight in Lebanon. Reservists had done most of their duty time in the West Bank and, until the withdrawal, in Gaza. Their operational responsibilities consisted mainly of military police work: maintaining civil order through regular patrolling, guarding checkpoints, inspecting traffic and cargo as well as individual credentials, and conducting raids into Arab neighbourhoods ringed by Israeli forces in search of militants. Proper training for major military operations had not been provided, apparently in the belief that the Lebanon front would remain quiescent. Unlike isolated terrorist cells in the West Bank and Gaza, the adversary in Lebanon was well armed and organised and enjoyed some territorial and vertical depth. Southern Lebanon was honeycombed with tunnel systems that resembled those used by the North Vietnamese Army and Viet Cong. Hizbullah carefully prepared and used these, as well as private and public civilian structures, as sheltered launch areas for surface-to-surface missiles.

The poor performance of the IDF was also attributable to the failure of Israeli political leaders to establish a workable, coherent set of war aims at the outset of the conflict. Israeli officials initially vowed to destroy Hizbullah. Six days into the war, in an address to the Knesset, Prime Minister Olmert said the war would continue until the two kidnapped soldiers had been freed, rocket attacks on Israel had been halted, and the group's terrorist infrastructure destroyed. Halfway through the war, on 27 July, Lieutenant-General Dan Halutz, the IDF chief, articulated the more realistic aims of freeing the kidnapped soldiers, re-establishing border security against Hizbullah, weakening Hizbullah and consolidating the sovereign territorial authority of the Lebanese government. In contrast, Hizbullah throughout the conflict had the clear and achievable intention, in the words of one former UN official, 'to bleed the IDF, not to defeat it'.

The international response
The Hizbullah misjudgement that sparked the war, Israel's confused and inept response and the rapid escalation of violence to civilian areas were compounded by tardy and stumbling international diplomacy. The United States was inclined

to let the fighting play out in the hope that Hizbullah could be destroyed now that Israel had taken the gloves off. Halutz, the first IAF officer to become chief of staff, appeared to have convinced the militarily naive political leadership, on the basis of NATO's successful campaign against Serbia in the 1990s, that airpower alone could bring Hizbullah to its knees by compelling the Lebanese government to act.

The same skewed expectations seemed to have influenced Washington's thinking. The US leadership might also have drawn a geopolitical analogy between the summer war of 2006 and the 1973 Yom Kippur War. Whereas in 1973, Washington viewed the conflict through the lens of the Cold War with the Soviet Union, in 2006, the Bush administration saw the Lebanon war as a manifestation of a larger confrontation with Iran, Hizbullah's key sponsor. A decisive victory would be essential to demonstrate to others that Iran's regional pretensions could be punctured, and to deter Iran from further challenging American interests.

This understanding of the conflict was informed by Iran's supplying highly effective explosive devices to Shia militias in Iraq, Tehran's insistence on proceeding with uranium enrichment, Iranian support for Hamas, and Iranian President Mahmoud Ahmadinejad's denial of the Holocaust and Israel's right to exist. Against this background, Iran looked increasingly revisionist. If appeased, Iran's leaders would only be emboldened. On this argument, it was therefore essential that Iran be stopped somewhere, just as Hitler should have been challenged in 1938. Lebanon would be the high-water mark of Iranian aggrandisement. Insofar as Hizbullah's military capabilities were largely due to Iranian training, money and equipment, and Hizbullah's support from Syria bolstered by Iran's diplomatic support of and investment in that country, the Bush administration's understanding of Iran's role was not far wrong. Washington's net assessment of Israeli and Hizbullah respective levels of operational effectiveness and vulnerabilities, however, was not quite so well judged.

The American miscalculation turned a strategic sidelining of diplomacy into a diplomatic setback. Within a week of the war's start, Saudi Arabia, Jordan and Egypt had publicly deplored Hizbullah's provocation and implicitly endorsed the Israeli response. European capitals were lining up reluctantly on Israel's side. Criticism of Hizbullah was also voiced within Lebanon. The temper of the moment was reflected in Nasrallah's public concession that, in retrospect, the kidnapping had been a mistake. Believing that strategic gains lay in a more thorough bruising of Hizbullah, the US administration fended off UN Security Council action and shielded Israel from pressure for a ceasefire. But the exigencies of combat changed the setting in which the parties were acting. On 30 July, Israeli aircraft seeking to destroy a Hizbullah firing position at Qana, near Tyre, mistakenly hit a nearby building housing civilian refugees. The death toll was initially reported as 60, including children, though it was later revised down to 28.

Although Hizbullah had deliberately co-located a military target with civilian facilities to either deter an attack or yield a propaganda victory, regional Arab states were politically unable to sustain their critical stance towards Hizbullah. European publics became intensely agitated. While the United States continued to oppose a ceasefire, Washington and Jerusalem were increasingly isolated. Media-distributed images of destruction caused by Israeli air strikes created the understandable, if inaccurate, public impression that Israel had laid waste to the entire country. The precipitating event was now largely forgotten by constituencies anxious to see their governments end the fighting as rapidly as possible. Even the Pope registered his concern.

By the time the Qana attack occurred, the pummelling delivered by Israel had only strengthened Hizbullah and weakened the players that Washington and Jerusalem had been counting on to show some steel. The failure of Siniora's government to act raised the prospect of Lebanon's turning into a failed state, essentially run by a consortium of Hizbullah terrorists and Syrian gangsters. On the weekend before the attack, the Saudi foreign minister, national security adviser and ambassador to Washington descended on the White House to deliver a confidential letter from King Abdullah to President Bush indicating, according to Bush administration sources, that the United States would lose Riyadh's diplomatic support if Washington failed to force a ceasefire on Israel. This démarche carried special force in the context of the US administration's evolving policy toward Iran. From the US perspective, rolling back and containing Iranian assertiveness in Iraq, Lebanon, Palestine or the Gulf, or in the nuclear arena, required Saudi cooperation on account of the kingdom's prestige, money and contacts. In Lebanon, Washington was already beginning to work through intelligence channels with the Saudis to strengthen the Lebanese government and undermine Hizbullah's influence.

US interest in a ceasefire was the signal European capitals needed to begin thinking systematically about how to respond to the crisis. Negotiation of UN Security Council Resolution 1701, passed on 11 August, proceeded relatively quickly. Among its central provisions were the withdrawal of Hizbullah and Israeli forces above the Litani River and on the Israeli side of the blue line, respectively, an exception for Israeli defensive operations and the deployment of a much larger UN Interim Force in Lebanon (UNIFIL) as well as Lebanese army detachments to southern Lebanon. Contributions to UNIFIL II, as it was called, included French, Italian and Spanish forces. The German navy undertook the maritime component of the overall operation. Significantly, the UNIFIL II rules of engagement were more liberal than were those regulating the operations of the predecessor troops. UNIFIL II was also more heavily equipped with armour

Map 6.1 **UNIFIL deployments in southern Lebanon**

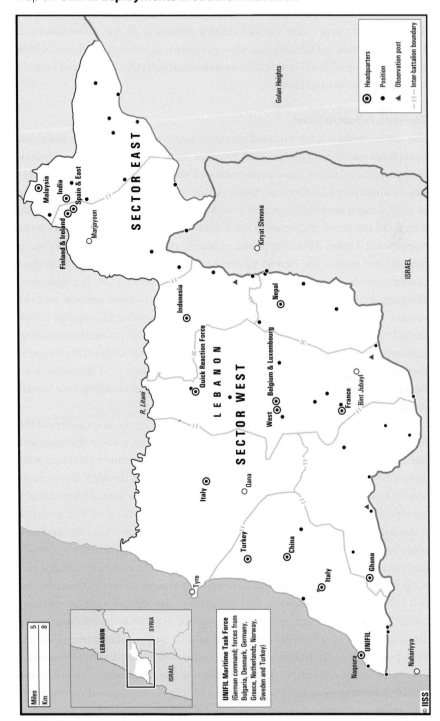

and artillery. If the war could be said to have any positive outcome, it was the unexpectedly robust military involvement of western European states and the deployment, 17 years after the Taif Accord providing for the disarmament of Lebanese militias, of Lebanese government forces to Hizbullah's backyard. Other things being equal, UNIFIL II will be an important deterrent to renewed fighting between Hizbullah and Israel.

The war's fallout in Israel

The war nevertheless left both Lebanon and Israel worse off. In both countries, hostilities unsettled fragile political balances. In Israel, the public was disconcerted by the relatively poor performance of the IDF, which was indisputably caught unprepared by the tenacity and skill of the Hizbullah fighters. The failure to get the major part of the ground assault underway until late in the game also perplexed the Israeli public and raised questions about the government's basic competence. Under mounting public pressure, after a shambolic process spanning several weeks, the cabinet approved the establishment of the Winograd Governmental Investigative Committee by a vote of 20–2 on 17 September, charging it 'to look into the preparation and conduct of the political and the security levels concerning all the dimensions of the Northern Campaign which started on July 12, 2006'. The government committee was granted the ability to subpoena witnesses and grant immunity to witnesses, but critics still charged it was insufficient. Demonstrations outside Olmert's residence in Jerusalem continued into October, with reservists among the most vocal in calling for a formal state commission to replace the Winograd Committee.

The committee released a preliminary report covering the first six days of the war on 30 April. The report singled out the prime minister, defence minister, and IDF chief of staff for criticism and concluded that 'the decision to respond with an immediate, intensive military strike was not based on a detailed, comprehensive and authorised military plan'. The committee said the government did not consider the whole range of options in making the decision to go to war, showing a 'weakness in strategic thinking'. The interim report noted that the declared goals were unclear and too ambitious. The report also commented that Olmert had made up his mind hastily and failed to ask for a detailed military plan when none was submitted, and did not have enough experience in external political and military affairs. The committee's criticism of the defence minister was also harsh. Noting that Peretz lacked knowledge or experience in military, political or government affairs, the committee said he had impaired Israel's ability to respond well to challenges. Halutz, who had resigned in January, was taken to task for failing to alert the political echelon to the complexity of the situation and to shortcomings in the preparedness and fitness of the armed forces. More broadly, the committee noted that these and other failings, including those relating to operational doctrine and organisational culture, stemmed from the failure to update and fully articulate Israel's security strategy doctrine. To wit, the leadership was operating under the flawed assumption that the country's ground forces would only be needed for low-intensity asymmetrical conflicts, not 'real' wars. For this form of complacency, the committee declared, there would be no quick solution.

Somewhat improbably, as of summer 2007, Olmert had kept his premiership. His smaller coalition partners were unwilling to risk their Knesset seats in early elections. As a consequence, there were no critical defections from Olmert's coalition. The Labour Party did see a shake-up as the party committee dethroned Amir Peretz and reinstated former Prime Minister and former IDF Chief of Staff Ehud Barak, who had lost to Ariel Sharon in 2001, as leader. Barak's accession to the defence portfolio will probably inject some small measure of credibility into a tattered government.

The Israeli–Palestinian conflict
As Israel became distracted by the war in Lebanon and its political aftermath, the situation in Gaza became increasingly tense. The election of Hamas to the leadership of the Palestinian Authority in January 2006 created an unsustainable political balance. Fatah, the loser, retained the presidency, a monopoly on international legitimacy and the channel to Israel. Hamas had a large, although scarcely exclusive, claim on legitimacy in the street, as well as control of the barely functioning ministries of state. Neither side had been willing to concede either turf or authority. Both sides sought outside support. Fatah leader and PA President Mahmoud Abbas looked to Israel for the release of withheld tax revenues he could pay to his thousands of retainers and to the United States for weapons and training for his multiple militias. Hamas turned to Tehran for aid and Syria for protection of its external militant leadership, including Khaled Meshal, who lives in Damascus.

In late 2006 and early 2007, the positions of both sides hardened, even as they agreed to a tactical alliance in the form of a unity government arranged under Saudi auspices in Mecca in February 2007. Disappointed and possibly angered by Washington's ineffectual approach to the growing crisis in Palestine, especially against the background of chaos in Iraq and Iranian encroachment, the Saudis were determined to introduce some stability into an increasingly untenable situation. In doing so, they were prepared to run roughshod over the Bush administration's preferred approach, which was to isolate, delegitimise and ultimately marginalise Hamas. Indeed, the unity government agreement brokered by the kingdom and accepted by Fatah did not require Hamas to do any of the things – such as renouncing its opposition to the state of Israel – that the United States had been insisting upon as a condition for recognition.

At the same time, Fatah was unprepared to accept Hamas as an equal partner, or to defer to Hamas's prerogatives under the Palestinian constitution. Strong US support and tacit backing from Israel and Egypt no doubt stiffened Abbas's spine. Thus, he formed an army to counter Hamas's forces and placed it under the command of his interior minister, Mohammad Dahlan, who had earned a villainous reputation among Hamas members for his brutal and humiliating treatment of them during previous crackdowns. The United States offered to train, equip and fund this private army, initially for nearly $90m in reprogrammed foreign-aid funds. Congress baulked at this dispensation, wondering whether the guns would wind up in the wrong hands, and permitted the administration to expend a little over $50m for training and 'non-lethal' equipment.

The appointment of Dahlan set in motion a series of tit-for-tat attacks, punctuated by upsurges in violence. This escalating dynamic peaked in June 2007, with Hamas fighters routing Fatah forces in Gaza. It appeared that fighting had been propelled by the two factions throwing each other's senior officers to their deaths from the roofs of Gaza office towers. While Fatah's Executive Protection Force was competent enough, the majority of Fatah fighters were untrained, poorly organised and seemingly uncommitted to the fight. Hamas personnel, in contrast, were highly disciplined, skilled and fought effectively under a unified command. In mid June, Hamas essentially carried out a successful military coup. Fatah, physically ejected from Gaza, retained control of the West Bank, where it immediately rounded up the Hamas activists known to be in the area, dissolved the existing government – of which Ismail Haniya of Hamas had been prime minister – and appointed a new emergency cabinet on 17 June.

The mini-civil war and its peculiar outcome took both the United States and Israel completely by surprise. Plausible policy responses were hard to identify, especially given the paltry thought and diplomatic energy given to the festering situation in Gaza even though US Secretary of State Condoleezza Rice had made five trips to the region during the previous year. In summer 2007, instincts in both Washington and Jerusalem were to focus development efforts and political concessions on the West Bank to consolidate Abbas's position and show Gazans how agreeable, relatively speaking, life could have been if they had voted differently in January 2006. On 18 June, the United States released to the PA tens of millions of dollars of aid that had been embargoed since Hamas rose to power, with the European Union announcing that it would follow suit, and a day later President Bush publicly threw his weight behind Abbas and his emergency government when Bush met Olmert in Washington. In a show of support for Abbas, Egypt then organised a summit meeting involving Abbas and Israeli, Egyptian and Jordanian leaders in Sharm al-Sheikh, while Riyadh encouraged Hamas and Fatah to renew the unity government. On 24 June, Israel announced it would release to Abbas's emergency government $350m in Palestinian tax revenues withheld since Hamas's electoral victory.

Given the political weakness of the Olmert government, the threat of an election contest against an invigorated Likud, and an unpopular lame-duck administration in Washington consumed by its engagement in Iraq, it is difficult to see how a 'West Bank first' strategy could succeed. With minimal effort, Hamas could disrupt any improved West Bank situation with a few well-timed and placed explosions and thus restore the unpleasant status quo ante there. Indeed, Hamas Gaza leader Mahmoud Zahar threatened as much after Fatah began to assert control more aggressively in the West Bank following its ouster from Gaza.

In light of developments in Palestine and Lebanon, it seems likely that Israelis will go to the polls in spring 2008, at which point former Likud Prime Minister Benjamin Netanyahu will challenge either Olmert or Barak. Netanyahu has taken a hard line on both Iran and the emergence of Islamists – Hizbullah and Hamas – as major players on Israel's borders. Thanks to the summer war of 2006 and the Palestinians' burgeoning internal political strife, he will be a formidable candidate.

Lebanon's relentless difficulties

The summer war also played havoc with Lebanese politics. Hizbullah's prestige as defender of Lebanon against Israeli aggression, albeit precipitated by Hizbullah's own adventurism, was high, while the Siniora government appeared feckless. Hizbullah was not inclined to leave its new status unexploited. In the aftermath of the war, the organisation demanded that cabinet decisions be taken on the basis of consensus voting rather than majority rule. This would in effect give the two Hizbullah ministers in the cabinet a veto over all decisions before the government. On some issues, including compliance with UN requirements, or cooperation with the investigation of the 2005 murder of former Prime Minister Rafik Hariri, Hizbullah had a large interest. Attempting to apply the lessons of the Orange Revolution in Ukraine, Hizbullah organised a massive sit-in in Beirut aimed at a soft coup, bringing the government to a halt. As of summer 2007, however, Hizbullah's strategy had not worked, and the organisation, aware of its limitations and burdened by growing popular resentment for having put party interests above national ones, had opted for a more pragmatic stance. Whether this posture will hold is uncertain.

The modus vivendi struck between Hizbullah and its political rivals proved to be timely, given the outbreak of a separate crisis in the north of the already jittery country. On 20 May 2007, Lebanese police pursued a gang of bank robbers into the Nahr el-Barad camp, housing thousands of Palestinian refugees, near Jounieh. The chase ended in a gunfight that sparked a continuing, intense battle between members of Fatah al-Islam, an al-Qaeda-affiliated group that had staged the robbery, and the Lebanese Army. More than 120 people, including at least 60 Fatah al-Islam militants, 46 soldiers and 20 civilians, were reported killed in the fighting. There was widespread physical destruction owing to the use of heavy weapons by Lebanese forces in the close confines of the refugee camp. Fatah al-Islam had not been suppressed after a month of close combat. Apparently, its multinational membership – it includes few Palestinians – had sufficient control over its sector of the camp and enough firepower to secure an indefinite stalemate. The eruption of violence in Jounieh was another indication of the appeal of religiously oriented revolutionary movements in the region, and the increasingly difficult challenge that secular governments faced in containing them.

Bleak horizon

The Israeli–Palestinian conflict remains the most significant problem in the region owing to the fuel it supplies to jihadism and the political traction it affords Iran, Syria and Hizbullah, all of which are spoilers. The summer war of 2006 reduced Israel's control over events in the Middle East, and caused Lebanon's to dwindle from little to nothing, while the Iraq War has caused the United States' position in the region to deteriorate and diminished its leverage. Iran's and Syria's positions have been proportionately strengthened. While Saudi Arabia and Egypt have tried to lend some diplomatic support to a conflict-resolution effort that was in tatters, they have sent divergent signals to the Palestinians.

The 'West Bank first' strategy adopted by the United States and Israel is more a convenient acquiescence to new realities on the ground than an authoritative and well-considered sequencing of steps towards ameliorating the conflict. Serious progress appears virtually impossible without fuller and more enterprising American and Israeli engagement. With the Bush administration bogged down in Iraq and the Olmert government seemingly facing a slow but ineluctable demise, such engagement is unlikely to materialise over the course of 2007–08. In the near term, perhaps that best that can be hoped for is that Hizbullah remains politically pragmatic and that the Israeli electorate's roundly negative assessment of the 2006 summer war translates into a broader and more positive political consensus. Substantial help from the US will probably have to wait until 2009, when Bush's successor takes office.

Saudi Arabia and the Gulf States: Cautious Hedging

The emergence of a new dynamism in Saudi Arabia's foreign policy was the most important development in the politics of the monarchical states of the Gulf over the past year. Alarmed at the deterioration of the situation in Iraq and at Iran's aggressive efforts in the region to take advantage of its power, Riyadh set about containing and, where possible, rolling back Iranian influence. The Saudi approach was clear, but subtle. While aimed at arresting the trend toward growing Iranian power in the broader Middle East, it did not seek direct confrontation with Tehran, and was open to Iranian offers of cooperation. At the same time, Saudi Arabia put symbolic distance between itself and the United States, which was seen by Riyadh as increasingly unable to achieve its goals – in Iraq most notably but in the wider region as well. Again, the Saudi signals were subtle. There was no intent to burn any bridges with Washington: the overarching relationship with the United States remained the cornerstone of Riyadh's long-term security policy. But after a number of years of diplomatic passivity following the American invasion of Iraq, it clearly wanted to set its own regional course, one that was not completely in accord with Washington.

Despite the decline in world oil prices from mid 2006 highs of around $75 per barrel to around $50 per barrel in early 2007, the economies of the Gulf states remained buoyant. The recovery of oil prices back up over $70 per barrel at mid 2007 promised another year of abundant revenues. While there were underlying economic concerns, and stock markets continued their declines from the dizzying heights of previous years, economic issues did not create political problems for Gulf rulers. The year saw continued evidence of modest but real moves toward greater political openness in the smaller Gulf states (less so in Saudi Arabia), though the spill-over of Iraqi events increased domestic sectarian tensions in the area.

Saudi Arabia: diplomatic activism, domestic continuity

Saudi diplomatic activism during the past year was spurred by the escalation of conflict in both Iraq and Lebanon, conflict which the United States seemed either unable (in Iraq) or unwilling (in Lebanon) to manage. The Saudi leadership feared that both conflicts would strengthen Iranian regional power. This fear led to new Saudi diplomatic initiatives on a number of fronts – Lebanon, Palestine and the Arab–Israeli conflict. While Riyadh achieved a number of successes, the limits of its regional influence were clear in its uncertain handling of the deteriorating situation in Iraq.

Lebanon and Iran

The outbreak of violence between Hizbullah and Israel in July 2006 placed the Saudi leadership in a difficult position. Riyadh did not want to see Hizbullah's position, and that of its patron, Iran, strengthened in Lebanese politics. It also did not want an Arab–Israeli conflict to polarise regional politics, allowing Tehran, with its uncompromising anti-Israeli position, to assert regional leadership.

Therefore, at the outset of the conflict, the official Saudi Press Agency quoted an unnamed Saudi official characterising Hizbullah's kidnapping of Israeli soldiers – the spark for the crisis – as 'irresponsible behaviour' and drawing a distinction between 'legitimate resistance [to Israel] and uncalculated adventures'. As the fighting escalated, Arab public opinion strongly backed Hizbullah. The Saudi government changed its tune. On 25 July the Royal Court issued 'an appeal and a warning to the international community … in particular the US' threatening that 'if the peace option is rejected due to the [sic] Israeli arrogance then only the war option remains'. The Saudis wanted to dampen down the crisis, but were expecting American assistance with the Israelis. When that was not immediately forthcoming, they chose not to stand against the wave of Arab opinion despite their worries about how the crisis increased Hizbullah's, and thus Iran's, regional popularity.

The crisis emboldened Hizbullah to challenge the government of Prime Minister Fouad Siniora, demanding a de facto veto over government policies. As the Lebanese crisis shifted from an Arab–Israeli fight to an intra-Lebanese quarrel, Arab public opinion (guided by Arab governments like Riyadh) began to take a more critical view of Hizbullah. With the contemporaneous increase in Sunni–Shia conflict in Iraq, the Lebanese crisis was increasingly depicted as part of a region-wide sectarian struggle between Iran and its Shia allies in the Arab world on one side and Sunni Arab governments on the other. The Saudi government did not discourage that view, and Saudi-owned Arab media outlets propagated it.

As the focus of public opinion shifted from Arab–Israeli confrontation, which benefited Iran and Hizbullah, to a potential sectarian confrontation, in which Arab Sunnis would far outnumber Arab Shi'ites, Saudi Arabia began to play an active part in constraining Iranian influence. Riyadh provided strong support to the Siniora government in its confrontation with Hizbullah. The *Washington Post* reported in December 2006 that Saudi National Security Adviser Prince Bandar bin Sultan, the former Saudi ambassador in Washington, had been paying regular secret visits to Washington to urge a common front against increasing Iranian regional influence, particularly in Lebanon.

Saudi worries about Iran are often portrayed as sectarian, but they have more to do with classic balance of power politics than with Sunni–Shia identity politics. The fall of Saddam Hussein's regime in Iraq, though viewed as welcome by the Saudi leadership, removed a useful buffer to Iranian influence in the Arab world. Fulfilling the warnings that Riyadh had given to Washington before the Iraq War, Iran quickly increased its influence in Iraq, not only with Iraqi Shia organisations with which it had long had strong relations, but also among Kurdish and even some Arab Sunni groups. The election of Iranian President Mahmoud Ahmadinejad in 2005 accelerated Iran's nuclear programme, which is widely believed in Saudi Arabia to be aimed at producing nuclear weapons. Iranian connections with Hizbullah and the Palestinian Islamist group Hamas extended Tehran's influence into the Levant. From Riyadh's perspective, taken together, these Iranian moves indicated a play for regional dominance. Saudi diplomacy set out to balance and, where possible, limit Iranian influence.

Riyadh's strategy toward Iran sought, at the same time, to avoid a direct confrontation with Tehran. On the contrary, when Iran was willing to talk, Saudi Arabia was more than willing to listen. In January 2007, as regional sectarian tensions were rising (spurred on by the Iraqi government's botched execution of Saddam Hussein at the end of December 2006) and Hizbullah's confrontation with the Lebanese government continued, Iranian National Security Adviser Ali Larijani visited Riyadh to seek common ground. Prince Bandar paid a visit to Tehran a few weeks later, with Larijani returning to Riyadh in February amid news reports about Saudi–Iranian efforts to defuse the Lebanese crisis. In March 2007 Ahmadinejad met King Abdullah in Riyadh, after which Saudi Foreign Minister Saud al-Faisal told reporters that the two countries 'have agreed to stop any attempt aimed at spreading sectarian strife in the region'. King Abdullah also met with Hizbullah representatives in January 2007, as part of this diplomatic initiative. While the Lebanese crisis remained unresolved as of May 2007, the Saudi–Iranian contacts had contributed to some mitigation of regional sectarian tensions.

Saudi Arabia clearly was not going to accept an Iranian leadership role in the region. It even gave very public indications that it would develop its own nuclear capabilities if Iran continued on its nuclear course. However, Riyadh was also very wary of direct American–Iranian confrontation, fearing that it would be the target of Iranian retaliation for any American strike against Tehran's nuclear programme. It was seeking to constrain Iran without direct conflict, blocking Iran's efforts to increase its influence in the Arab world, but willing to work with Tehran on joint approaches, such as in Lebanon.

Palestine and the Arab–Israeli conflict

Saudi activism in Palestinian and Arab–Israeli issues over the past year has also been driven largely by Riyadh's desire to reduce Iranian influence and reassert Saudi leadership in the Arab sphere. With the West largely boycotting the Hamas-led government formed after the Palestinian elections of January 2006, Iran emerged as its most public and generous supporter. Saudi Arabia and other pro-American Arab governments, wary of being seen in Washington as supporting a group officially branded as terrorist by the United States and supportive of the stalled Palestinian–Israeli peace process, kept at least some public distance from Hamas. This offered Iran a new opportunity to increase its influence in the Arab world, building upon its long-standing support for Hamas and their shared rejection of the Arab–Israeli peace process.

When tensions between Hamas and Palestinian Authority President Mahmoud Abbas, leader of the nationalist party Fatah, erupted into open conflict in late 2006, the clashes offered Saudi Arabia an opportunity to play the role of broker in Palestinian politics. Unlike Iran, it had ties to both sides of the intra-Palestinian conflict. In February 2007 King Abdullah brought Abbas and Hamas leaders Ismail Haniya (the Palestinian prime minister) and Khaled Meshal (the head of Hamas's Syrian-based leadership) together in Mecca. The king brokered a deal under which a new Palestinian unity government was formed, still headed by Haniya but including a number of Fatah and independent ministers. Saudi Arabia then called on the international community to end its boycott of the Palestinian Authority. Though the unity government proved short lived, the Mecca agreement was a forceful reassertion of Saudi leadership in Palestinian politics and a direct effort to counter Iran's increasingly close relationship with Hamas. The Saudi priority – limiting Iranian influence in the Palestinian arena – was clear. The effort to unite Hamas and Fatah ran counter to the American preference to isolate and sideline Hamas in the hope that a new Fatah-led government would move quickly toward negotiations with Israel. Riyadh was willing to go against the United States on this issue in order to challenge Iran for influence with Palestinian Islamists.

King Abdullah took another high-profile position on the Arab–Israeli issue at the Arab League summit meeting Saudi Arabia hosted in March 2007. At Riyadh's behest, the summit reaffirmed Abdullah's 2002 plan, adopted at the Arab League summit that year, promising Arab recognition of Israel in exchange for the establishment of a Palestinian state in the West Bank, Gaza and Jerusalem. This public diplomacy followed reports that Prince Bandar had secretly met with a high-ranking Israeli official in late 2006, indicating a new sense of urgency in Riyadh about the Arab–Israeli situation. Saudi Arabia, joined by Egypt and Jordan, sees continued Arab–Israeli tensions and crises as an avenue through which Iran and its regional allies, like Hizbullah, can mobilise Arab public opinion and create problems for pro-American Arab governments. Thus King Abdullah is willing to engage diplomatically on Arab–Israeli issues. However, he has given no indication that he is willing to make a dramatic public gesture toward Israel, like a visit to Jerusalem or Saudi diplomatic recognition of Israel, to promote a diplomatic breakthrough. Such moves would probably place him, and Saudi Arabia, too far out in front of domestic public opinion, and Arab opinion more generally, for comfort.

Iraq and relations with the United States

The deterioration of the security situation in Iraq highlighted the dilemma which has largely paralysed Saudi policy towards that country since the American invasion in 2003. On the one hand, Riyadh has worried about the growth of Iranian influence in Iraq, represented by Tehran's close ties to the parties in the Iraqi government and to their militias. On the other hand, it fears the regional effects of the chaos arising out of Iraq's civil strife, much of it driven by the Sunni Arab insurgency. To the extent that al-Qaeda and its ideological allies are playing an important role in the insurgency, it presents a direct threat to Saudi regime security. The *New York Times* reported that at least some of the Saudis arrested in late April 2007 for plotting attacks against targets in the kingdom had trained in Iraq. Moreover, the Sunni Arab insurgency is killing American troops in Iraq, and thus support for it would greatly damage Saudi–American relations. Riyadh is thus reluctant to support the Iraqi government but unwilling to back the armed opposition against it.

This Saudi paralysis on Iraq is reflected in the somewhat conflicting positions Riyadh has taken toward American policy in Iraq. There was a real fear in Riyadh in autumn 2006 that the Bush administration might be reconsidering its Iraq policy. The Democratic victory in the 2006 Congressional elections and the rumours surrounding the work of the Iraq Study Group (the Baker–Hamilton Commission) led to a belief that American troops might be leaving Iraq sooner rather than later. Saudis further feared that an American decision to withdraw would lead to a new American diplomatic initiative toward Iran, acknowledging Iranian primacy in Iraq in exchange for an orderly withdrawal. An American withdrawal from Iraq would remove the one barrier to the consolidation of Iranian influence in Iraq. Saudis, most prominently the outgoing Saudi ambassador in Washington, Prince Turki al-Faisal, very publicly urged the United States not to withdraw precipitously from Iraq. Saudi officials and those close to them raised the prospect of direct and indirect Saudi intervention in Iraq if the United States were to leave and warned Washington against a policy of engaging Iran. The threats of Saudi military intervention were undoubtedly a bluff, but the intimations that Riyadh might adopt a policy of supporting elements of the Sunni Arab insurgency were more believable.

Riyadh was thus relieved when the Bush administration reaffirmed its commitment to keeping American forces in Iraq. In reaction, Saudi Arabia in April 2007 agreed to a long-standing American request that it write off most of Iraq's debt to it. However, the American inability to achieve its goal of stabilising Iraq led the Saudis to put distance between themselves and Washington on this issue. In his opening statement to the Arab League summit held in Riyadh in March 2007, King Abdullah termed the foreign occupation of Iraq 'illegitimate'. It remained to be seen whether his use of the term was a bow to general Arab opinion with little policy relevance, or the beginning of a new turn in Saudi policy towards Iraq. The king also refused to receive Iraqi Prime Minister Nuri al-Maliki, who had hoped to visit Saudi Arabia before the May 2007 regional summit on Iraq in Sharm al-Sheikh, Egypt. Into the fifth year of the Iraq crisis,

Saudi Arabia's inability or unwillingness to adopt a clear and active role on this issue continued.

The tensions between Saudi Arabia and the United States on Iraqi and Palestinian issues led to questions being raised in Washington about the direction of Saudi policy and whether the two countries were following different paths in the region. Those questions were not without foundation. King Abdullah quietly turned down an offer to come to Washington on a state visit in 2007, indicating that all was not well on the bilateral level. However, it seemed unlikely that the American questioning, which resembled similar episodes in the past, would lead to a fundamental change in the Saudi–American relationship. Overall, the bilateral relationship between Washington and Riyadh remained strong, with Saudi and American officials consulting regularly on regional issues. When there were reported threats of terrorist attacks against Saudi oil facilities in October 2006, US Navy ships were reported to be patrolling the waters off those facilities. A number of arms sales were concluded in 2006, and other arms sales were in the works, though Congressional approval was somewhat in doubt given Israeli objections. In December 2006 Ambassador al-Faisal announced his resignation amid reports that Prince Bandar bin Sultan, the former ambassador and current chairman of the Saudi National Security Council, was pursuing back-channel contacts with the Bush administration. He was replaced by Adel Jubeir, Prince Bandar's former deputy in Washington and a close foreign-policy adviser to King Abdullah. Jubeir's appointment promised to end the incoherence that had begun to characterise the Saudi position in Washington.

Saudi Arabia continued to cultivate good relations with other world powers. After the high-profile exchange of visits by King Abdullah and Chinese President Hu Jintao in early 2006, the king received Russian President Vladimir Putin in Saudi Arabia in February 2007. China is Saudi Arabia's fastest-growing energy customer; Russia and Saudi Arabia are the world's two largest oil producers. While economic issues are the most important element of bilateral Saudi relations with both these countries, Riyadh anticipates a more multipolar world power distribution in the future. Its relations with Russia and China can therefore be expected to become more strategically important over the years. In the immediate future, however, the decades-long strategic relationship with the United States is set to remain the centrepiece of Saudi Arabia's security policy.

Oil

The past year witnessed gyrations in the world oil market. Prices approached $80 per barrel in summer 2006, fell close to $50 per barrel at the beginning of 2007 and then rallied back to $70 per barrel at mid year. There was much speculation about how Saudi Arabia, as the world's leading oil exporter and OPEC's key member, would react to the price roller-coaster. Some suggested that the Saudis were encouraging the fall in prices in late 2006, as part of their overall effort to contain Iranian regional influence. However, Saudi decisions on oil production demonstrated, to the contrary, that Riyadh was interested in maintaining oil prices well above $50 per barrel. With oil prices at historic highs in the first half of 2006, Saudi production fell from a high of 9.5 million barrels per day (b/d) in February 2006 to 9.1m b/d in June 2006. As prices began to fall in September 2006, the Saudis continued to cut production, averaging 8.75m b/d in December 2006 and January 2007. As prices strengthened in the early months of 2007, the Saudis maintained roughly that same production level. These were not the actions of a government seeking to drive prices down. While Riyadh may have been anxious with oil at $80 per barrel, fearing moves to reduce world consumption through conservation and switching to alternative fuels, it did seem comfortable with oil prices in the $60–70 range, even if that meant that the Iranian government had extra money as well.

Meanwhile, Saudi Arabia did announce an important step to reassure markets about long-term oil availability. In September 2006 Oil Minister Ali Naimi said the kingdom planned to increase its total production capacity to 12.5m b/d by 2009, up from an official capacity of 10.5–11m b/d. However, Saudi Arabia and the United Arab Emirates were the only major Gulf oil producers that were implementing plans to boost production capacity. According to international estimates, these increases will not bring the region anywhere close to the level of production necessary to meet growing demand over the coming two decades.

The Saudi economy

For the Saudi government, domestic political and economic concerns are more important than external factors in determining the oil price level with which it is comfortable. The high prices of the last three years have sustained an economic boom, buoying the local economy and filling the government's coffers, so that King Abdullah was able to announce in December 2006 that he was cancelling a planned increase in petrol prices. Saudi GDP grew by 4.2% in 2006 and the non-oil element of the Saudi private sector was estimated to have grown by 6.3%. Per capita income grew by more than $1,000 between 2005 and 2006, according to figures compiled by Saudi–American Bank.

Good economic times helped to smooth over political tensions, providing the Saudi regime with a relatively placid domestic political environment. Sustaining the economic boom is the single most important domestic political goal for Riyadh.

Not all the economic news was good. The Saudi stock market lost nearly 45% of its overall value (measured by the leading market indicator) in the year to the beginning of May 2007, continuing its fall from historic highs in February 2006. Many Saudis had invested in the market, and grumbled at the government over its decline. Unemployment, particularly among young males, remained a structural weakness of the economy. The Saudi government reported in April 2007 that male unemployment was 9.1% of the total male workforce. Female unemployment was much higher, but women make up only a small percentage of the total workforce. Perhaps most troubling, the oil boom began to stimulate inflation, which rose to 2.3% in 2006, the first time since 1995 that it had exceeded 1%. Nevertheless, the country's economic performance was a point of strength for the regime.

Domestic Saudi politics: terrorism, political reform and sectarianism
The Saudi government continued a crackdown on violent domestic opposition, represented by al-Qaeda in the Arabian Peninsula. In late April 2007 Saudi security forces announced the arrest of 172 suspects, mostly Saudis, who were accused of plotting attacks within the country, including on oil facilities. This continued the pattern of the past few years, with the security forces seeking to take the initiative against the underground opposition and to break up cells before they could conduct attacks. However, the arrests were a reminder that al-Qaeda and its sympathisers continued to present a threat to public security. For example, in February 2007, four French expatriates working in the kingdom were killed by gunmen on the road between Medina and Tabuk after a tourist outing. While the emphasis of the anti-terrorist campaign was on ensuring security, there was also an active effort to rehabilitate people arrested on suspicion of involvement with al-Qaeda and like-minded organisations. In August 2006 the authorities announced that they had released 700 suspected militants over the previous three years after regime clerics had 'corrected' their thinking.

It was clear that the government was taking the fight to al-Qaeda and its affiliates in the kingdom, and with measurable success. However, it was debatable whether the Saudi government was using all the resources within the country's vast religious establishment to combat extreme interpretations of Islam that could lead to political radicalism. While steps were taken to confront al-Qaeda's ideological appeal, the regime was careful to distinguish between official Wahhabism and what it termed 'deviant' interpretations of Islam. It was unwilling to alienate important constituencies, both in the official religious establishment and among Islamist activists, by encouraging an open reassessment of the religious and ideological bases of the political order.

On the issue of political reform, activism has subsided after emerging from the more open political environment encouraged by then Crown Prince Abdullah in response to 11 September and the violent attacks in the kingdom in 2003. More recently, the government has sought to discourage and suppress such activism. The municipal elections of 2005 re-energised the political arena, but only briefly: the councils took months to get organised, and little of note emerged from them. In February 2007 the Saudi authorities announced the arrest of ten people accused of raising funds for 'suspicious bodies'. It subsequently turned out that a number of those arrested were involved in efforts to pressure the government for political reform. Three were among the organisers of a new petition to the king published that month, similar to those around which reform activism centred in 2004 and 2005, calling for constitutional reform, an elected parliament and government guarantees of individual rights. As of May 2007, there was no indication that the king had agreed to receive the petition, as he did a similar, if more mildly worded, effort in 2004. The political reform movement has thus made very little headway over the past year. High oil prices and public focus on the sectarian violence in Iraq, and its possible spill-over effect, allowed the government to ignore pressures for greater political freedom. In what was widely interpreted in Saudi Arabia as a signal of the government's stand-pat attitude, not a single minister was replaced when the new cabinet was announced in March 2007.

The rise in regional sectarian tensions had its reflection domestically in Saudi Arabia. Saudi authorities arrested a number of Saudi Shi'ites for demonstrating in favour of Hizbullah during the 2006 conflict between Hizbullah and Israel. Expressions of support for Hizbullah in the Saudi Shia community ran against government policy, but were not contrary to Sunni opinion in the country. In December 2006, 38 Saudi religious scholars posted an online call for the Sunni world to rally to the support of the embattled Sunni minority in Iraq. The declaration referred to Shi'ites as *al-rafida*, a defamatory label identifying them as rejecting the true Islam. Some well-known Saudi Salafist activists further stirred the pot by issuing fatwas condemning the Shi'ites as non-Muslims. While this kind of clerical opinion was not new in the Wahhabi tradition, the timing of the fatwas pushed the sectarian issue to the forefront at a time of heightened regional tensions. The circumstances surrounding the execution of Saddam Hussein in late December 2006 exacerbated the sectarian issue for many Saudis who were not normally sympathetic with either the more extreme elements of the country's religious establishment or with the former Ba'athist regime in Baghdad.

The Saudi government did not encourage this rise in local sectarian tensions. Saudi Shi'ites were permitted in January 2007 to perform publicly the rites of *ashura*, the commemoration of the martyrdom of Imam Hussein, for the third consecutive year after decades of official bans on such observances. In that same month King Abdullah told an interviewer that he thought Sunni–Shia tensions were 'a matter of concern, not a matter of danger', and that if handled correctly those tensions would not become dangerous. In his speech opening the new session of the Consultative Council in April 2007, the king said sectarian disputes were against Islam and a threat to 'national unity and the security of the state'. However, the government did not crack down in any public way on those Wahhabi clerics and activists who were raising the sectarian temperature. These mixed signals disquieted Saudi Shia leaders, who had been encouraged by the government's more open attitude toward their community in the past few years. As long as Iraq continues to be roiled by sectarian fighting, sectarian divisions in Saudi Arabia will be exacerbated. However, there have been no indications so far that the government wants to use those divisions to suppress the Shia community.

Succession and the ruling family

In October 2006 plans were announced to create a new body to manage succession issues within the ruling Al Saud family. The 'Allegiance Institution' is to consist of the surviving sons of the late founder of the modern kingdom, King Abd al-Aziz (Ibn Saud), one son of each of the deceased sons of Abd al-Aziz, one son of the king and one son of the crown prince. This was the first time that members of the third generation had formally been brought into the succession process. Under the plans, the next king would propose between one and three candidates for crown prince to the institution, which would then vote on its preference (or to approve or reject, if a single candidate is nominated). The institution may reject all nominees and propose its own. In the event of a difference between the king and the institution, a majority vote of the Institution's members would select the crown prince. This procedure changes the Saudi Basic Law promulgated in 1992, which declared that the appointment of the crown prince was the sole prerogative of the king.

The Allegiance Institution will also have the power to seek a medical judgement on the competence of the king to continue to rule, in the event that he falls ill. The institution is empowered to consider the medical judgement and then to decide whether the crown prince should temporarily assume the powers of the king or even replace him – or whether no action should be taken. This was clearly a response to the long illness suffered by King Fahd, which left executive authority in Saudi Arabia in question for years in the late 1990s and early 2000s, until his death in 2005. The new body will only take effect when Crown Prince Sultan becomes king. If Sultan should predecease King Abdullah, it is not clear whether Abdullah would be bound by the new procedure in selecting a new crown prince. In practical terms, however, it seems unlikely that the new institution will play a central role in succession until it comes time for the generation of the grandsons of Abd al-Aziz to produce the king. As long as sons of the founding king remain able to rule, succession seems likely to continue to pass from brother to brother. The naming of a crown prince among the surviving brothers will more likely be settled through consultation among them than by votes in the new committee.

The Gulf States: political openings and foreign-policy continuity

The smaller Arab monarchies of the Persian Gulf were almost the mirror image of Saudi Arabia during the past year: domestic political developments pointed towards more open and participatory political systems, while foreign policies were virtually static. All seemed happy to continue their role as close allies of the United States and home to important American military facilities. Like Saudi Arabia, they worried about the direction of events in Iraq and about the prospects of a confrontation between Washington and Tehran. But unlike Saudi Arabia, they took no diplomatic steps to distance themselves from the United States.

On the domestic front, there were hotly contested parliamentary elections in Kuwait (June 2006) and Bahrain (November–December 2006). The United Arab Emirates held its first, though limited, election for members of the (largely powerless) Federal National Council in December 2006. There were municipal elections in Qatar in April 2007, with parliamentary elections likely before the end of 2007. Oman will hold consultative council elections in October 2007.

Developments in Kuwait strengthened the power of parliament relative to the government and the ruling family. The ruler, Sheikh Sabah al-Ahmad Al Sabah, was compelled to dissolve the parliament in May 2006 and to call for new elections in the face of public and parliamentary pressure for a redrawing of the electoral districts. The June 2006 parliamentary elections returned a solid majority of representatives supporting the reformist call for an electoral system of five districts, rather than the existing system of 25. The reformists crossed ideological lines, with liberals and Islamists, Sunnis and Shi'ites, supporting the new electoral system. The new parliament shortly thereafter passed legislation establishing a new, five-district system, and the government accepted that change. Parliament asserted itself again in March 2007, forcing the resignation of the cabinet as it was poised to remove the health minister, a member of the ruling family, from office. The new cabinet did not include the unpopular minister.

Bahrain's parliamentary election, held in two rounds in late November and early December 2006, was a controversial affair. Political groups representing the island state's Shia majority actively campaigned for seats, after boycotting the 2002 elections to protest constitutional changes that reduced parliament's powers. They accused the government, headed by the Sunni ruling family, of favouring candidates from the minority Sunni community and produced evidence of a government plan to tilt the elections toward its favoured candidates. In an interesting electoral alliance, the major Shia group coordinated with a bloc of liberal and nationalist candidates against Sunni Islamists, who were seen as supporting the government. Opponents of the government were able to win 18 of the 40 seats, with the Shia Islamist group al-Wifaq taking 17. One woman, a pro-government independent, was elected unopposed in her district, making her the first elected female parliamentarian in the Gulf states. The elections, with voting largely on sectarian lines, combined with regional events to raise sectarian tensions, never far from the surface in Bahrain.

These electoral experiments in the Gulf states did not signify the spread of genuine democracy. In each state – even in Kuwait, where the parliament has demonstrated real power – ultimate decision-making power continued to rest in the hands of the ruling families who appoint and control the governments. Nevertheless, the trend throughout the Gulf states was towards greater public participation in politics, through elections to legislative and consultative assemblies. Some indicated interesting trends. For example, while Islamists did well in Kuwait and Bahrain, mirroring the trend throughout the Arab world, in each case political alliances did not fall along a neat Islamist–secularist line. In Kuwait Islamists and liberals joined together in a tactical alliance to push for electoral reform. In Bahrain Shia Islamists and liberals cooperated against pro-government Sunni Islamists. The significance of Islamist successes thus depended very much on local political factors.

7 Africa

While a more buoyant mood prevailed in much of Africa, the past year was uneven for political developments on the continent. The most dramatic turn of events came with Ethiopia's US-supported intervention in Somalia in December 2006. After six months during which the Union of Islamic Courts had given Somalia its closest approximation to effective rule for more than 15 years, the intervention achieved an unexpectedly swift victory for Somalia's previously impotent transitional government. However, a subsequent sharp escalation in fighting with insurgents and clan militias delayed Ethiopian plans for withdrawing and handing over to African Union forces.

The fighting in Somalia rekindled tension between Ethiopia and Eritrea, while the four-year-old crisis in Sudan's Darfur region spread westwards to unsettle the country's precarious neighbours. A new pattern of conflict began to emerge in a swathe between Africa's northern and equatorial regions, from the Horn of Africa to Chad. Elsewhere, instability was more isolated. Smouldering conflicts in West Africa were mostly being contained, and Nigeria agreed to a UN-brokered deal for its troops to leave the Bakassi peninsula after a two-decade dispute with Cameroon. But fresh uncertainties arose, notably over militia activity in the Niger Delta and the consequences of unsatisfactory Nigerian elections – one of a series of political milestones in 2007 in key regional countries – as well as continued risks to security in the post-transition Democratic Republic of the Congo (DRC).

The announcement in February 2007 of a new unified US combatant command for the continent (AFRICOM) signalled growing US attention to African security. American concerns focus both on access to oil and gas, for which China is also competing, and on fears about collapsed or weak African states becoming

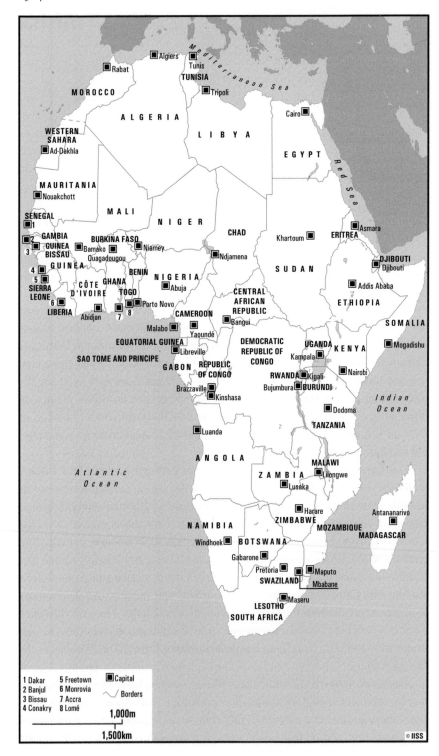

1 Dakar   5 Freetown   ■ Capital
2 Banjul   6 Monrovia
3 Bissau   7 Accra   ⟋ Borders
4 Conakry 8 Lomé

1,000m
1,500km

© IISS

magnets for Islamic extremists – fears that are already starting to be realised in Somalia. Air strikes in January against suspected al-Qaeda terrorists in southern Somalia marked the first direct action in the country by the United States since the fiasco of 1993. In April, the terrorist threat echoed across North Africa with two al-Qaeda-linked attacks in Algeria and a string of suicide bombings in Morocco.

Worries about African security failed to prevent a strengthening of economic confidence in many countries, with the main exception of Zimbabwe, which continued its slide. The International Monetary Fund raised its 2007 growth forecast for Africa to more than 6%, after 5.5% in 2006, but the outlook depends heavily on commodity prices. In spite of debt relief, extra donor support is so far falling well short of ambitions set at the Gleneagles G8 summit in 2005.

Somalia and Sudan: a Web of Conflicts

Chaos in Somalia

Between June 2006 and January 2007, the nominal government of Somalia – which has not been truly governable or governed for 16 years – changed twice by force of arms. In June, the Union of Islamic Courts, a political coalition of 11 Islamist militias, wrested de facto control of Mogadishu, Somalia's capital, from local secular militias aligned with the secular Transitional Federal Government (TFG). Only Sudan formally regarded the Islamic Courts as Somalia's official government. About six months later, the TFG, which was recognised by the United Nations, ran the Islamic Courts out of Mogadishu and assumed national leadership with the help of several thousand Ethiopian troops. In February, however, heavy fighting erupted in Mogadishu between the TFG and the Islamists. By early spring, low-intensity warfare had forced an estimated 320,000 of Mogadishu's two million residents to flee and take refuge outside the city in camps that, because of insecurity, could not easily be supplied by aid organisations. Fatalities from mid March to mid April were conservatively estimated at 1,000. Most of the victims were civilians caught in heavy-arms crossfire between insurgents and TFG forces.

Persistent political instability in Somalia poses moderate but not insignificant threats to Western interests as a source of and inspiration for transnational jihadist terrorism and as a potential site of regional war. A narrow counter-terrorism approach, consisting of military containment plus covert support to pro-Western factions, has not appreciably mitigated these threats. There remains every possibility that, sometime in the near future, the Islamists will again hold sway in Somalia. In that case, al-Qaeda or groups affiliated with it would enjoy greater

Map 7.1 **Somalia**

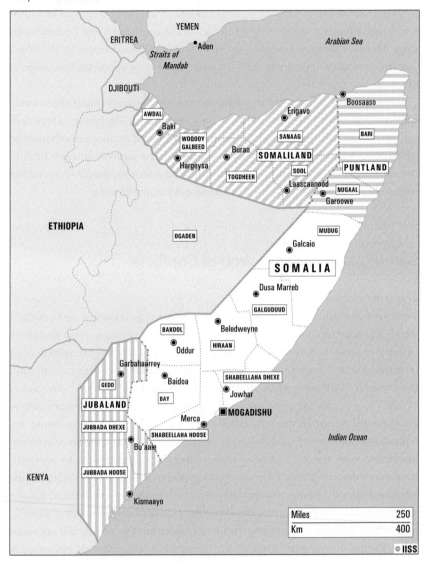

political traction there, and could seek to resume infiltration of Somalia and East Africa.

Unending disarray

The southern two-thirds of Somalia has been in a state of chaos for the past 16 years, as the clans that form the basis of Somali society have battled for territorial control, and two sub-sovereign republics – Puntland and Jubaland – have been declared. By contrast, the northwest third of the country consists of the break-away self-declared republic of Somaliland, which is relatively peaceful and well governed.

The current problems started in 1991, when strongman President Mohammed Siad Barre was overthrown in a civil war. Competing clans were able to commandeer weapons supplied alternately by the Soviets and the Americans during the Cold War to the now-toppled government, and the country devolved into a patchwork of clan fiefdoms without central authority. Then came drought and famine that an ineffectual United Nations mission was unable to ameliorate, prompting the United States to intervene in December 1992 with the relatively narrow intention of facilitating humanitarian relief in the service of a 'new world order'. In bootstrapping a humanitarian mission into a coercive peace enforcement effort, however, the United States antagonised Somali clan militias. Their fury culminated in the infamous October 1993 'Black Hawk Down' attack in which 18 US Army Rangers and hundreds of Somalis died. This disaster precipitated a hurried American withdrawal, stoked anti-Americanism and strengthened al-Qaeda's hand in East Africa. Osama bin Laden and second-in-command Ayman al-Zawahiri are fond of calling the United States a 'paper tiger' with no staying power, and their favourite examples are the American pullouts from Lebanon after Hizbullah's barracks bombing in 1983, and from Somalia after 'Black Hawk Down'.

Since then, over a dozen governments formed in exile have tried and failed to govern. The latest is the TFG. It was established in October 2004, with UN support, by clan delegates who had been meeting in Kenya over the preceding two years. But the TFG has a clan-based cabinet, while most of the conflict in Somalia occurs on the sub-clan level. The TFG, as presently constituted, therefore does not reflect the realities of Somali power politics, and consequently finds it difficult to exert control. In 2005 and most of 2006, Mogadishu was not safe for the TFG, which set up a temporary headquarters in Baidoa, 150 miles northwest of the capital. Several TFG ministers, while refusing to resign from the cabinet, joined a rival quasi-governmental grouping, the so-called Somali Rehabilitation and Redemption Council (SRRC), which in 2005 consolidated under the banner of the 'Alliance for the Restoration of Peace and Counterterrorism'. To increase its political viability and attract US support, the TFG stressed its 'anti-terrorist' credentials and TFG President Abdullahi Yusuf Ahmed's strongly secular mindset.

A number of suspected al-Qaeda operatives surfaced in Somalia in late 2005. They included Fazul Abdullah Mohammed of the Comoros Islands, probably the most important al-Qaeda figure in sub-Saharan Africa, believed to have helped organise the 1998 US Embassy bombings in Kenya and Tanzania. The Central Intelligence Agency (CIA), through its Nairobi station, then chose to actively support the SRRC, but its approach backfired. When the SRRC warlords tried to forcibly dominate Mogadishu, the Islamic Courts gathered clan support, and took control of the city. Al-Ittihad al-Islamiya, the small Somali radical Islamist movement led by Hassan Dawer Aweys, then sided with the Union of Islamic Courts. Al-Ittihad advocates the unification of Somalia with the ethnically Somali Ogaden region of Ethiopia, which Somalia unsuccessfully tried to annex in the 1977 Ogaden War, and Aweys wants to make Somalia a unified Islamic republic. He was appointed leader of the 'Somali Supreme Islamic Courts Council', replacing the more moderate Sharif Sheikh Ahmed, who had shown some interest in working with Western powers.

In early December, the UN Security Council unanimously adopted US-sponsored Resolution 1725, authorising the deployment of an African force in Somalia to protect the TFG. But the United States and Europe were (and remain) too overstretched in Iraq and Afghanistan to provide serious armed help. The resolution barred the participation of neighbouring countries under the UN's aegis, and only Uganda firmly offered troops. The Islamic Courts harboured and backed Ethiopian separatist groups and supported Ethiopian Islamists. Christian-dominated Ethiopia, for its part, had strongly supported Abdullahi Yusuf Ahmed's appointment as president of the TFG. It stepped in to fill the security vacuum, sending several thousand troops to reinforce the TFG's increasingly besieged position in Baidoa. The Islamic Courts, emboldened by the expansion of their control to much of southern Somalia, then overplayed their hand. In late December, backed by Eritrean troops and probably a few hundred foreign jihadists, they launched an attack outside Baidoa, were pushed back towards Mogadishu by TFG and Ethiopian forces, and then were forced to abandon Mogadishu when local clans withdrew their support. With a wink and nod from Washington as well as some intelligence assistance, the Ethiopian troops – many of them American trained – pressed their advantage. Within a few days the Islamists had dispersed and gone underground, and the TFG and Ethiopians – joined by a few small US special-operations teams – held sway.

On 7 January 2007, the TFG gave its consent for US special-operations forces to launch a strike from an AC-130 gunship on terrorist suspects in Somali territory. The initial strike was followed by several more. The operations killed about ten suspected militants, but missed the three al-Qaeda figures who were the key targets. Somalis' anger towards the United States – latent since the mid 1990s – was revived. On 19 January, the African Union authorised an 8,000-strong African peacekeeping force for Somalia. Uganda again offered the lion's share of the nine battalions deemed necessary by a fact-finding mission, and Malawi and Nigeria also tendered forces. As of April 2007, however, only about 1,500 Ugandan soldiers had arrived, and most of them were hunkered down at Mogadishu's airport rather than patrolling its streets. One had been killed by artillery fire.

At first blush, a victory for secular interests seemed to bode well for the containment of Islamism in the Horn of Africa, as well as for newfound peace and stability for the Somali people. Somalis, though 98% Sunni Muslim, generally prefer a relatively relaxed, traditional and moderate brand of Islam to the militant strain of Wahhabi-influenced Salafism that bin Laden has spread. The Islamic Courts movement, however, had brought order to several key areas in Somalia, and increasing numbers of Somalis had been willing to submit to sharia law for the sake of greater security. To thwart poverty and insecurity, most had pragmatically come to support the Islamists. When the TFG assumed control of Mogadishu, the lives of Somalis did not materially improve. Indeed, they became considerably worse: in spring 2007, there were no hospital beds left in Mogadishu, commerce had shut down, and food convoys were being attacked. The two sides could not reach a sustainable ceasefire. It was not lost on Somalis – who are nationalistic as well as clan oriented – that Abdullahi Yusuf Ahmed was close to the Ethiopian leadership, and rising Ethiopian brutality increasingly tainted him. Unsurprisingly, Somali public opinion was turning against the TFG. If the Islamists, in the manner of Hizbullah and Hamas, again offer solutions to social problems that secular entities cannot or will not supply, Islamism could still take firmer root in Somalia. Somalia, then, still presents palpable threats to African, European and American interests in countering transnational terrorism and preserving regional stability. The overarching challenge facing outside powers is one of serving those interests without neglecting the humanitarian needs of Somalia.

Regional and global threats

Since the US Embassy bombings in East Africa in 1998, and perhaps even since bin Laden's residence in Sudan from 1991 to 1996, the US has viewed East Africa as a potential exporter of Islamist terrorism to the West. Since the 11 September 2001 attacks, and especially after the defeat of the Taliban in late 2001, Western threat perceptions have stayed at a relatively high level. The fear has been that al-Qaeda holdouts fleeing Afghanistan would seek and find refuge in failed or failing states in sub-Saharan Africa and reconstitute their operational base, including training camps and indoctrination centres. The leading candidate for such jihadist colonisation has remained Somalia, in light of its homogeneously Sunni Muslim population, the absence of state enforcement mechanisms, and proximity to the Persian Gulf. Yet Somalia has not thus far ripened into a full-fledged global terrorist threat. Even bin Laden, when contemplating his next stop after Sudan in 1996, felt that clan militias were too untrustworthy to provide reliable security in an otherwise ungoverned country.

Accordingly, the United States and its partners have been content to maintain a posture of vigilance and containment via train-and-equip programmes with African states, financial assistance to their security sectors, and deployments such as the 1,800-strong Combined Joint Task Force–Horn of Africa in Djibouti to collect intelligence and take direct action if necessary. However, the temporary ascendancy of the Islamic Courts from June 2006 demonstrated that Somalis would, under certain conditions, accept indigenous quasi-state institutions sympathetic to the jihad. Although relatively few Islamic Courts members are militant jihadists in the mould of bin Laden, the fear is that, if they hold sway again in Somalia, they could play host to foreign jihadists and perhaps to al-Qaeda leaders, just as the Taliban hosted bin Laden and Arab jihadists from 1996 to 2001. The hardcore jihadists, in turn, could also dispatch terrorists – perhaps directly to the United States, but more likely to infiltrate Europe, the Middle East or elsewhere in Africa.

Some Islamist elements in Somalia, such as al-Ittihad, have already helped propagate terrorism. The explosives used in the December 2002 attack on Israeli tourists in Mombasa, Kenya probably came from Somalia. The perpetrators of that attack and the nearly simultaneous attempted shoot-down of an Israeli airliner leaving Mombasa used Somalia as a bolt-hole. Two Somalis, an Eritrean and an Ethiopian were among those convicted for the attempted London bombings on 21 July 2005, and at least one Somali was among 17 people arrested in Canada in June 2006 on suspicion of terrorist activity. According to an unverified and widely questioned UN report, some 700 Somalis went to Lebanon to help Hizbullah battle Israeli forces in 2006 in exchange for military training.

Furthermore, the Somali diaspora is large and widespread, and holds potential for the build-up of 'self-starter cells' and terrorist support networks. Expatriate Somalis would tend to be more inclined to radicalise locally if they perceived their host nations and allies as harming their country and countrymen, and that grievance would find reinforcement in the aggressive Salafist ideology that has come to permeate the global community of Muslim believers (the umma). The Somali diaspora reportedly repatriates up to $700m a year, and the Islamic Courts organised a moderately successful fundraising campaign in the UK in late 2006. Al-Barakat, the large Dubai-based Somali *hawala* organisation that handled about $140m annually, was shut down by US authorities after 11 September, but smaller outfits have arisen to take its place. More generally, the reciprocal encouragement of indigenous Somali Islamists and the Somali diaspora to radicalise could increase jihadist recruitment in the region, and more widely. A continuation of the Islamist-fuelled insurgency in Somalia that began to gather momentum in early 2007 could also force increasingly unmanageable numbers of Somali refugees to flee over Kenya's border – potentially destabilising a country that has been, at least by default, the anchor of stability in East Africa.

Finally, Eritrea remains a potential geopolitical spoiler. Although about half Muslim and half Christian, Eritrea's support for the Islamic Courts rests on its strategic enmity towards Ethiopia. The Ethiopian government and the country's Eritrean population fought a brutal civil war that culminated in Eritrea's secession in 1993. A bloody border war erupted in 1998 and continued until 2000. The peace since then has been fragile, and reciprocal military mobilisations on the border occurred in late 2005. A direct military confrontation has been discouraged by a 2,300-strong UN ceasefire monitoring force on the border. Ethiopia's presence in Somalia on the TFG's behalf, however, provides Eritrea with an opportunity to use the Islamic Courts as a proxy with which to bleed Ethiopia with less fear of direct repercussions on Eritrean soil.

Impediments to progress

Ethiopia's expeditious suppression of the Islamic Courts has damped down both the terrorist and the insurgent threat in the short term by installing a pro-Western secular government in the form of the TFG. However, the TFG's regime security is entirely dependent on Ethiopian troops, and they cannot stay for long. Addis Ababa stated only days after ousting the Islamic Courts from Mogadishu that it could not afford a protracted deployment, and its troops started to withdraw in late January. Guerrilla activity rose sharply as the troops started to leave. Ethiopian military persistence, then, cannot be counted on. Without more diplomatic work on the Somali polity, the TFG's tactical success probably will not translate into strategic victory.

Somalia remains a 'failed state' on most objective criteria. The TFG does not collect taxes or provide effective social services, and has not established a civilian law-enforcement organisation. It clearly enjoys nothing like a monopoly on the use of force, and cannot make collective decisions for the populace. Thus, even though the TFG is a UN-sanctioned government and remains in nominal control by virtue of Ethiopian-assisted military coercion, it is highly vulnerable to the Islamist insurgency. In turn, the rise of indigenous Somali Islamisation at the grassroots level has stoked both insurgency and transnational terrorism. Since that rise is driven largely by poverty and insecurity, there is little reason to believe that the TFG's secularism will check the trend. Only if the TFG enhanced Somalis' well-being could it consolidate its competitive popular political advantage vis-à-vis the Islamic Courts and begin to mould Somalia into a viable state.

There is no evidence that it will be able to do so. Al-Qaeda's core leadership has portrayed Ethiopia's intervention as the act of the infidel, and would inevitably cast a more extended commitment as the non-Muslim occupation of a Muslim land – especially if it were to receive more overt or abundant US support. As in Iraq, this characterisation has both drawn foreign jihadists into the conflict and stands to accelerate the Islamisation of Somalis themselves, respectively fuelling jihadist terrorism worldwide and strengthening the Islamic Courts, which declared jihad when the prospect of a peacekeeping force arose. Within days of

Mogadishu's liberation from the Islamic Courts, anti-Ethiopian protests began, and armed attacks on Ethiopian troops ensued.

A key counter-insurgency task is to identify those who firmly support the government and ensure their continued support by protecting them from those who oppose it. Amidst Somalia's perplexing maze of clans and sub-clans, and their perpetual angling for momentary advantage, this challenge has thus far proven impossible for the TFG, Ethiopia and other external actors to meet. Both the Islamic Courts' victory in June and the TFG's counterstrike the following December turned on the support of the same local clan elders in Mogadishu: during that six-month period, they simply changed their minds about what group they should back. Likewise, many of the SRRC militiamen recruited by the United States to counter the Islamic Courts undoubtedly fought against American forces for Somali warlord Mohamed Farah Aideed in 1992–94; the SRRC's co-chairman is Aideed's son Hussein, a former US Marine.

In light of past experience and present problems, there is likely to be very little enthusiasm among Western powers for a substantial military deployment to Somalia in the foreseeable future. Without substantial diplomatic efforts, even a fully deployed force of 8,000 troops, as prescribed by the AU, would have no realistic chance of controlling a factionalised, and widely and heavily armed, Somali population. Even if an externally supported counter-insurgency campaign were possible and effective, its very success could stoke a regional war in which Ethiopia and Eritrea exploited the TFG and the Islamic Courts as proxies for prosecuting longstanding border conflicts, or render Somalia a more fertile field of jihad. A UN monitoring group has already reported that Egypt, Djibouti, Iran, Saudi Arabia, Yemen, Libya and Sudan, as well as Eritrea, have contributed funds, arms and technical support to the Islamic Courts' cause.

Better options?

The establishment of the TFG rendered overt US military action on Somali soil politically easier, and American AC-130 strikes targeting al-Qaeda players made sense from a strictly counter-terrorism standpoint. But they also inflamed Somali anti-Americanism (some civilian casualties were reported) that had been latent since the mid 1990s, on top of anti-Ethiopian sentiments that had already surfaced. The European Union's acquiescence to the Ethiopian occupation – even as it has evolved as a brutal one – has turned Somali opinion against Europe as well as the United States. So, the net result of Ethiopia's intervention and the closeness of the TFG's relationship with the United States and Ethiopia may well fuel the Islamists' continued popular appeal. It appears that there is no satisfactory coercive solution to the quandary of Somalia, and more enterprising and assertive outside diplomatic engagement is needed to ameliorate Somalia's parlous situation.

Diplomacy by outside powers, though perennially frustrating when it comes to Somalia, appears obligatory. But time may be short. No effective UN peace-keeping force is likely to materialise in the short term. Accordingly, once most of the Ethiopian troops have left, the Islamic Courts may well be emboldened to ramp up guerrilla operations further and threaten the TFG's dominant but embattled position. On the other hand, the Islamic Courts have suffered a serious military defeat, and have less leverage than they had in the latter part of 2006. Sharif Sheikh Ahmed, who remains head of the Islamic Courts' executive com-mittee, surrendered himself in Kenya on 21 January and has appeared interested in political reconciliation.

It would make sense for the Islamic Courts to be part of any political talks. Carrots and sticks could further increase the Islamic Courts' incentives to com-promise. For instance, the TFG might concede that Ethiopian troops should stay out of Somalia, and clan elders might forswear future tactical alliances with the Islamic Courts. Outside powers should also manifest greater awareness of the complex alignments within and among clans that determine who wields power in Somalia. The TFG tends to be regarded as a mouthpiece for Darod clan inter-ests, the Islamic Courts as one for Hawiye interests (ten of the Islamic Courts' 11 militias are composed of members of the Hawiye clan). And there are indica-tions that the Islamist insurgents leading the resistance against the TFG have been joined by secular Hawiye militias, Somali nationalists, and businessmen. In April, Hussein Aideed, though a deputy prime minister in the TFG, went to Eritrea and joined an alliance of former Islamist leaders, proclaiming the Ethiopian counter-insurgency campaign a 'genocide'. A negotiating framework would also need to offer some incentives for all of these parties to stand down in favour of dialogue. With a palpable stake in the political status quo, even if the Islamic Courts continued to have jihadist designs, the Courts would be less likely to return to violence, just as Hizbullah and Hamas have shown greater restraint as they have gained political traction.

Who should broker any talks is an open question. After the United States' counterproductive intervention in the early 1990s and its partisan backing of the SRRC and Ethiopia, Washington may have little credibility among Somalis as an honest broker. The European Union is probably more trusted by the Somalis, but its toleration of perceived TFG misrule through Ethiopian muscle has lowered its stock. Nevertheless, newly inclusive diplomacy is more likely than continued partisan coercion to win over the Somali populace. Furthermore, if the United States and the EU positioned themselves alongside a regional power – say, Kenya – they could obtain the political cover needed to regain the Somalis' respect. The EU, in fact, showed some appreciation of the gravity of the crisis when, on 8 December 2006, EU Development Commissioner Louis Michel held separate talks in Baidoa and Mogadishu with the TFG and the Islamic Courts in hopes of lowering tensions. The United States and the EU have some additional leverage as, respectively, Somalia's largest bilateral and largest multilateral donors. They could extend the TFG residual military guarantees and perhaps set the table for the deployment – by consent – of a small UN force to monitor the implementation of a new agreement.

Kenya has been the most active and effective broker in the region on Sudanese as well as Somali issues, usually under the auspices of the Intergovernmental Authority on Development (IGAD), and has sponsored the TFG. But in the latest confrontations between the TFG and the Islamic Courts, Nairobi has appeared constrained by the rising cross-border threat from the Islamic Courts and political pressures from its own substantial ethnic Somali population. Although IGAD tried in 2007 to address the Horn of Africa's acute regional security problems, including Somalia's instability and tense relations between Ethiopia and Eritrea, its efforts have seemed tentative and half-hearted, and politically damaged by Eritrea's withdrawal in mid April 2007 on grounds of 'a number of repeated and irresponsible resolutions', mainly with respect to the Ethiopia–Eritrea border controversy.

The prospect that renewed armed conflict could send hundreds of thousands of refugees over Kenya's border, however, may induce Nairobi to abandon its timidity and push for more focused negotiations. Religious leaders in Kenya have urged as much. The day after Eritrea withdrew from IGAD in April 2007, Kenya took the lead in imploring it to return. With the EU's diplomatic and bureaucratic sponsorship and residual US support, an IGAD-based diplomatic push might at least enforce a pause and bring the principals to the table. If effective diplomacy does not materialise, only further escalation would be able to bring decisive attention from major powers – possibly in the form of the military 'coalition of the willing' mooted by UN Secretary-General Ban Ki Moon in April. Such an escalation may well be in the cards.

Sudan's regional knock-on effect

Three peace agreements in the space of two years with rebel movements in different parts of Sudan are by no means an insignificant achievement for a country that has been at war with itself for most of its post-colonial history. But they fall short of an overall solution for the relationship between Khartoum and the peripheral regions of the largest national territory in Africa or the Arab world. The concentration of development and wealth around Khartoum, an imbalance since the pre-1956 period of British–Egyptian condominium, has been at the centre of a complex set of grievances over regional inequality, identity, power, access to land and natural resources and, in Southern Sudan's case, religion.

The Darfur crisis, continuing to fester despite a partial deal in May 2006, has taken on wider importance as its impact has spilled over into fragile neighbours,

Chad and the Central African Republic. Whereas Sudan's hostilities were previously contained largely within its borders, there were increasing signs of the conflict becoming enmeshed with rebellions in those countries, whose regimes blamed the Khartoum government for fuelling wider destabilisation.

All Sudan's main recent conflicts are connected and have points in common, and the three peace documents bear strong similarities. But the accords do not make a coherent whole, and their efficacy can be categorised in a range between uncertain and minimal. Deals in 2006 for Darfur and Eastern Sudan were both modelled on the January 2005 Comprehensive Peace Agreement (CPA) for Southern Sudan and its provisions for sharing power through the allocation of posts and parliamentary seats at national and state level. But their scope was also limited by having to fit in with the CPA arrangements, which were built into a subsequent interim constitution. The agreements have provided no convincing answers to vexed issues relating to land rights, which have been exacerbated by population movements and climate change. Politically they appear to have had the effect of reinforcing rather than diluting the dominance of President Umar al-Bashir's National Congress Party (NCP). As a combination, it is to be doubted whether they are capable of bringing stability.

World attention has continued to concentrate on the clearest example of failure in this respect, the emergency in Darfur, four years after the eruption of rebellion in the region. It was widely accepted that deaths resulting from the fighting had reached 200,000 with more than 2m uprooted from their homes, exposing the impotence of the UN and the AU in attempts to halt attacks against civilians by government-backed forces. International opprobrium prevented Khartoum from assuming the AU presidency in 2007, as it was originally expected to do in 2006, while the International Criminal Court's prosecutor applied to start the first proceedings for war crimes and crimes against humanity (against a junior Sudanese minister and an alleged militia commander).

With the 7,000-strong AU monitoring and protection force clearly out of its depth and under-equipped, Sudan's government stalled in the early months of 2007 on allowing a joint UN–AU operation in the region. The UN Security Council had in August 2006 expanded the mandate of the 10,000-strong UNMIS mission deployed in Southern Sudan and called for up to 22,000 army and police personnel in Darfur. The climate worsened in October when Sudan declared the UN envoy Jan Pronk persona non grata for remarks in his personal weblog about the morale of government forces following defeats in Darfur.

In November the government agreed in principle to a 'hybrid' UN–AU force but rejected a UN command and later sought to limit the UN role to advisory, technical, logistic and financial support. Subsequent talks revolved around a three-phase approach, with Sudan eventually dropping objections in mid April to an intermediate 'heavy support' plan involving about 3,000 UN troops with attack helicopters. The European Union, meanwhile, earmarked further stopgap funding for the overstretched AU mission.

President George W. Bush issued a strongly worded warning in April, giving the Sudanese government a 'last chance' to end the violence and promising economic sanctions if it failed within 'a short period of time' to agree to a full UN deployment, stop support for Janjaweed militias in Darfur and enable delivery of aid. Envisaged sanctions would involve banning Sudanese state companies from doing business in the United States and blocking dollar transactions by the Sudanese government within the US financial system. Pressure also intensified on China, Sudan's main oil partner, over its support for the regime, including calls for a boycott of the 2008 Beijing Olympic Games. As a token of greater involvement in promoting a resolution, China named a special envoy to the region in May 2007. But frustration continued to mount in the United States and other Western nations about the lack of conclusive progress.

All this was a far cry from the optimism in the build-up to the CPA, signed more than 21 years after the resumption of war between north and south. That deal was ambitious and far reaching but, despite its name, in no way comprehensive as an approach to a new federal structure. Although steps were taken to accommodate other parties, it was essentially a pact between two forces, the Arab-dominated NCP regime and the Sudan People's Liberation Movement (SPLM). In the interim period before a secession referendum in Southern Sudan in 2011, it brought the SPLM into a national unity government and gave it leadership of an autonomous regional administration. In addition to splitting revenues, it allowed for two armies with mixed units, and specified separate arrangements for three areas outside the border of Southern Sudan but with affinities to it – Abyei, Southern Kordofan (Nuba Mountains) and Blue Nile.

Implementation fell behind on numerous fronts in the first two years, in part reflecting a critical shortage of capacity and infrastructure. Aid agencies complained that promised funds, either from Khartoum or from the $4.5 billion pledged by donors in 2005, were slow to surface. With Southern Sudan almost wholly dependent on its oil fields as an internal source of government funding, the deal provided for 2% of net oil revenues to go to oil-producing states and the remainder from Southern Sudan's output to be split 50:50 between the Southern Sudan and national governments. The national finance ministry said it transferred an over-estimated total of $1.2bn in 2006, based on an excessively optimistic prediction of oil output of 500,000 barrels per day, compared with an actual average of 365,000. Concerns were raised, however, about the transparency of the calculations, determined by NCP-controlled government departments. Southern officials also expressed suspicion that boundary rulings might exclude some oil reserves from the sharing arrangement.

Tension is likely to mount ahead of elections due across Sudan in 2008, and the 2011 referendum deadline. The charismatic former SPLM leader and Sudanese First Vice-President John Garang had faced a hard task bringing opinion in Southern Sudan around to maintaining links with Khartoum. Following Garang's death in a helicopter crash in July 2005 and his replacement by his deputy Salva Kiir, previously considered to favour independence, the prospect appeared harder still. There seemed to be as little chance of the south voting for unity as of the north acceding easily to secession.

Anxiety on the part of the United States and other sponsors of the north–south peace talks to ensure their successful completion led to insufficient attention being paid to the crisis in Darfur in its early stages. By its timing, the Darfur rebellion could clearly be seen as a bid for a share in the carve-up of power and wealth. As the government resorted to the tactic of proxy militias that it had long used in the south, a conflict rooted in old frictions rapidly defined itself along the lines of Arab and non-Arab ethnic identities.

This time, international pressure for a deal led to an accord being signed in the Nigerian capital Abuja by only one faction of the rebel Sudan Liberation Movement, leaving out another faction and the Justice and Equality Movement, which was fighting on a broader national agenda. Continuing to hold out, these then regrouped as the National Redemption Front. Negotiations had been marked by mistrust. The deal provided for wealth sharing through transfers from Khartoum, a reconstruction fund and a compensation commission. It offered the rebels a new position of senior assistant to the president and leadership of a transitional Darfur authority. Four thousand combatants were to be integrated into the security forces. But rebels would not have to disarm until the government disarmed and controlled Janjaweed irregular forces, as it had previously committed itself (and failed) to do. A subsequent deterioration in security, deployment of government reinforcements, continuing air and land attacks and factional infighting brought the agreement's workability into question.

The third piece in this ill-fitting jigsaw was added in October 2006 with the signing in Asmara, the Eritrean capital, of the Eastern Sudan Peace Agreement, following a decade of low-level conflict. Covering the states of Kassala, Gedarif and Red Sea, a marginalised and largely arid region that nonetheless holds strategic importance for its sea access and oil pipeline terminal, negotiations were concluded in about four months. The deal between the government and the Eastern Front, grouping the long-established Beja Congress with the Free Lions from the semi-nomadic Rashaida tribe, was facilitated by Eritrea, which had links with the rebels, without other international participation. Like the other deals it involved a figurehead post (an assistant to the president), assembly seats, a reconstruction plan and absorption of militia members into the armed forces.

Prospects for peace dividends will be limited, however, as long as the Darfur situation remains unresolved. Counting on the reluctance of China, Russia and Arab nations to support tough punitive measures, Sudan's government has continued to brazen it out against international pressure, apparently reluctant to abandon its pursuit of a military response in Darfur. Already, that conflict has begun to merge with others across Sudan's western borders, in what threatens to develop into a wider crisis.

Chad and the Central African Republic

Armed activity in eastern Chad and northern parts of the Central African Republic (CAR) intensified in 2006 and early 2007, fuelled by Sudanese support for rebel movements. While the two governments laid the primary blame on Sudan, rejecting ritual denials from Khartoum, it was also clear that their insurgencies were based on internal causes and not just outside interference. What has emerged is a complex web of conflicts, each with their own dynamics but interlinked. Rebel attacks, incursions and counter-insurgency retaliation in the past two years have combined to cause extensive destruction in frontier areas of both Chad and the CAR. The number of displaced people from or in these areas had risen to about 600,000 by mid 2007, including Darfurian and Central African refugees in Chad and Chadian and Central African refugees in Darfur. France, with troops stationed in both countries and fearful of a political vacuum, has provided military support to their governments in the form of logistics and intelligence and, recently in the CAR, more direct participation backed by Chad-based *Mirage* F1 fighters and helicopters.

After initially cooperating with Sudan over the Darfur conflict, Chad's President Idriss Déby came to be seen by the Sudanese government as playing a double game, allowing Darfur rebels to operate from Chadian territory. His own Zaghawa ethnic group forms the military backbone of Darfur's rebel forces. In return, his government reiterated charges that Sudan was pursuing a 'sinister Chad destabilisation project' by arming and supporting Chadian defectors using bases in Darfur. At the same time, eastern Chad suffered raids by Janjaweed Arab militias and violence by various Chadian militias. Rebel forces seized eastern towns for short periods and in October 2006 a column attempted to repeat a thrust that reached the outskirts of the capital N'Djamena in April.

In December, the government made a deal with a rebel general, Mahamat Nour Abdelkérim, and appointed him defence minister. But rebel forces regrouped, with three main formations active, principally the Union of Forces for Democracy and Development (UFDD). The war of proxy rebellions came close to direct confrontation in April 2007 when Chadian troops skirmished with Sudanese forces after crossing into Darfur. Libya repeated earlier attempts to reconcile the Chadian and Sudanese leaderships and defuse tension. UN

Secretary-General Ban Ki Moon proposed sending 11,000 peacekeepers to the Chad and CAR borders. But Chad rejected a full-scale UN peace mission, echoing opposition from Libya, which said it was sending its own observers instead. Other countries joined the mediation efforts, including Saudi Arabia, which hosted the signing of an agreement between al-Bashir and Déby in early May for each country to stop supporting rebellions in the other.

Even further removed from world attention, fighting in the CAR escalated in late 2006 when rebels occupied key northeastern towns for several weeks before being ousted. Birao, near the Chad and Sudanese borders, was devastated. Chad, participating in a small regional peacekeeping force, sent more troops and France reinforced its small contingent. Peace deals were reached in February with one rebel organisation active in the northwest, and in April with another in the northeast. But the region remained prey to other armed groups and vulnerable to precarious security in Chad.

Progress in Northern Uganda

In the nexus of conflicts connected with Sudan, one that clearly benefited from recent developments was the obscure 20-year bush war in northern Uganda. The cultish Lord's Resistance Army (LRA), waging a low intensity but particularly brutal campaign of killing, child abduction and mutilation, had long operated from bases in Sudan, receiving support from the Sudanese government or military along with other armed groups enlisted as allies during the north–south civil war. The LRA's relationship with the Khartoum government was uneven, however, and in 2002 Sudan agreed to let Ugandan forces cross the border.

Sudan's north–south peace agreement in 2005 changed the circumstances of the conflict. What had previously been seen as a remote and bizarre guerrilla campaign became part of the regional security puzzle. The new autonomous government of Southern Sudan wanted to be rid of a conflict on its territory that hindered development. With the relocation of Sudanese forces from the region making it harder to receive supplies and the deployment of UN peacekeepers hampering its ability to roam freely, the LRA set up camp instead in the DRC's Garamba national park.

Southern Sudan's Vice-President Riek Machar took on the role of chief mediator, meeting the reclusive LRA figurehead Joseph Kony in May 2006. Talks were launched in Juba, the Southern Sudan capital, in July, and the next month brought a formal cessation of hostilities. The LRA, which had been adept at using small, fast-moving units and had spread its campaign beyond its original field of combat in the Acholi ethnic region, was by then reduced to a few hundred armed fighters, according to Ugandan officials, but other estimates put total membership at several thousand.

Despite subsequent violations by both sides, northern Uganda has since enjoyed effective peace, albeit with more than 1m still living in 'protected' camps. Previous peace efforts involving church groups had stumbled on without success, and prospects were complicated by outstanding International Criminal Court arrest warrants – the first issued by the court, in 2005 – against Kony and other top figures. Pressure mounted, however, on Uganda's President Yoweri Museveni to seek a settlement and address the development lag in the north, a stronghold of opposition in his controversial re-election in February 2006 for an additional term. Talks faltered and the LRA broke them off in a climate of distrust in January 2007. But after a strengthened mediation effort, with former Mozambique President Joaquim Chissano acting as UN envoy and support from Kenya and South Africa, a deal was signed in April on the Southern Sudan–DRC border, renewing the expired ceasefire and giving the LRA six weeks to assemble its forces. While still dilatory, the process is now moving inexorably towards a solution.

Hurdles for African Democracy

After a wave of democratisation in the 1990s, with wider acceptance of multi-party politics, progress in Africa in recent years has been slow and irregular. High points since mid 2006 were elections in the DRC after more than 40 years of dictatorship, war and transition; and Mauritania, which successfully staged its first fully democratic presidential contest in March 2007. But Nigeria's April elections, the third since the end of military rule, set a dismal example. Other key events in leading regional countries were looming in late 2007, with elections in Kenya and a crunch point for the ruling African National Congress party in South Africa.

Nigeria's failed test
Even by Nigerian standards, the elections of April 2007 in Africa's most populous country were a mess. While they produced the expected victory for Umaru Yar'Adua, the chosen successor to President Olusegun Obasanjo, the extent of the ruling People's Democratic Party's win at both national and state levels defied credibility. Evidence of widespread rigging and arguments over the exclusion of candidates left the results open to legal challenges, the reputation of important institutions damaged and the new president's legitimacy and authority under question.

The elections took on wider importance because of Nigeria's role as West Africa's dominant economic, diplomatic and military power and Africa's largest exporter of oil, mainly to the United States. Worries about post-election stability became a prominent factor in oil markets already nervous about insecurity in Nigeria's Niger Delta region. The contest should have been a democratic milestone in a nation of 140m, eight years after it emerged from military rule, an unprecedented third election in a row. Never before has an elected Nigerian administration handed over successfully to another. On two previous occasions when this might have happened, in 1964–65 and 1983, election malpractice and violence led to military takeovers.

The temperature rose a year in advance with an aborted bid to change the constitution to allow Obasanjo to run for a further term. The run-up to the ballot became more chaotic when the Economic and Financial Crimes Commission (EFCC), which had been bold in pursuing corruption in high places, produced an advisory list of 135 candidates for office who were liable to be charged and therefore disqualified. Alongside state governors and former ministers, it included Obasanjo's estranged vice-president Atiku Abubakar, already indicted by a panel of inquiry in 2006 over alleged misuse of funds. A panel of government appointees was set up to review 77 cases, and after two days indicted 37, effectively barring them from standing. As a result of this manoeuvre, both the EFCC and the Independent National Electoral Commission (INEC) were exposed to accusations of partisanship. After a supreme court decision, Abubakar's name was finally allowed onto the presidential ballot papers just five days before the poll.

Violence surrounding the votes for state governors and legislatures on 14 April and for the presidency, Senate and House of Representatives on 21 April caused dozens of deaths. All three main contenders were from the predominantly Muslim north, in line with an understanding that the presidency should alternate between north and south to ease tensions. Results gave Yar'Adua almost 26.8m votes, about 70%. Muhammadu Buhari, a former military dictator running for the second time for the All Nigeria People's Party, was given 6.6m and Abubakar just 2.6m, although his Action Congress party dominated in the key state of Lagos. Yar'Adua might have won anyway, but the margin was implausible. On the positive side, the campaign showed the court system to be robust, and international observers acknowledged that there was freedom of expression and assembly. But they also reported numerous irregularities including removal of ballot boxes, shortage of election materials and falsification of results sheets. European Union and non-governmental US monitors said the vote fell short of international standards and Commonwealth observers pointed to 'significant shortcomings'. Although voting was well conducted in many areas, the elections overall were deemed to have been worse than the already flawed 2003 contest, further sapping public trust in the workings of the political system. INEC announced re-runs for some state contests, but opposition parties and local observer groups called for the entire exercise to be held afresh.

As well as tarnishing Obasanjo's prestige as an African statesman and peace-maker, the contested elections raised questions about his successor's ability to govern and push forward with reforms begun in the last four years. Yar'Adua, a one-time chemistry teacher whose brother was vice-president in an earlier army regime headed by Obasanjo, is Nigeria's first non-military head of state since the early 1980s. Previously governor of the northern state of Katsina, he is little known in the south, and there has been speculation about his health. He and his vice-president Goodluck Jonathan, who comes from the Niger Delta, will need to establish authority in the oil-producing region following an escalation of militia activity there in 2006 and early 2007. More than 100 foreigners were taken hostage during this period. Groups operating under the banner of the Movement for the Emancipation of the Niger Delta have shown growing sophistication in equipment and tactics, attacking government forces and oil installations. A fifth of Nigeria's potential oil output has been shut down, while tens of thousands of barrels are illegally siphoned off daily. The threat of further action, anger over the elections and a questionable mandate make a combustible mix. It will be a feat if the low-key Yar'Adua can prevent it exploding.

West Africa: pulling back from the brink

There were some encouraging signs in the past year of West Africa beginning to get over its convulsions. Both Sierra Leone and Liberia, seats of regional turmoil through and beyond the 1990s, made progress towards consolidating peace. Sierra Leone managed without UN peacekeepers, following the end of a suc-cessful mission. In neighbouring Liberia, where Ellen Johnson-Sirleaf completed the first year of her post-transition presidency, a cautious drawdown of the UN's 15,000-strong force was expected. In June 2006 Liberia's former President Charles Taylor, who had been caught trying to flee Nigeria and then been whisked through his own country to respond to charges by Sierra Leone's special court for war crimes and crimes against humanity, was flown to The Hague to stand trial using the facilities of the International Criminal Court.

Possibly the most hopeful development came in Côte d'Ivoire after four years of unresolved confrontation that bisected the country, long considered one of the continent's most advanced and still West Africa's biggest economy after Nigeria. In November 2006 the UN Security Council agreed for President Laurent Gbagbo to extend his stay in office for a further 12 months, but called on him to hand effective power to Prime Minister Charles Konan Banny. A demurring Gbagbo decided to pursue his own plan instead, and in March signed an agreement in Ouagadougou, capital of Burkina Faso, with Guillaume Soro, leader of the rebel Forces Nouvelles movement, paving the way for a transitional power-sharing government with Soro as the new prime minister. The sensitive post of defence minister, one of the bitterest points of contention over the Linas–Marcoussis accords brokered by France back in 2003, was assigned to a member of Gbagbo's own party. The deal provided for a general amnesty, disarmament, a timetable for restructuring the army under joint command and an identification process for elections, already postponed twice and now set to be held by the beginning of 2008. In a symbolic step towards reunification, work began in April on dismantling checkpoints along the 'confidence zone', a 20km-wide buffer strip separating the rebel-held north from the government-controlled south, where 11,000 UN and French troops were to hand over progressively to mixed patrols by government and rebel soldiers. Although the agreement marked a breakthrough in Côte d'Ivoire's neither-war-nor-peace stalemate, optimism was tempered by the failure of a series of earlier accords and mediation efforts, difficulties with demobilisation and doubts about whether the planned elections would be conducted fairly.

Conflicts in the region have a tendency to re-ignite or, after being damped down in one place, to flare up in another. A long awaited crisis in Guinea erupted in early 2007 when a month and a half of protests left scores of dead and offices and homes ransacked. Guinea had up to then been largely spared from the violence affecting its neighbours, although it received large numbers of refugees from fighting across its border and various armed factions used it as a rear base. Its ailing strongman President Lansana Conté, in power for 23 years behind a façade of sham elections, had survived an army mutiny in 1996 and an alleged assassination attempt in 2005, but had never been challenged in such large numbers. After 18 days of a general strike, called in January to protest against collapsing living standards, mismanagement and corruption, he agreed to delegate powers to a prime minister. But his appointment of a close associate, Eugène Camara, sparked renewed protests, to which he responded by decreeing a state of siege, a curfew and martial law. Under a deal negotiated by West African regional leaders, alarmed by the risk of spreading insecurity, Conté agreed to name a consensus prime minister, Lansana Kouyaté, a diplomat who was on a list submitted by the unions. France was quick to offer financial and political support. Under pressure to bring rapid change, the new government sought to address economic grievances by intervening to moderate staple food prices and launching a review of mining contracts, including bauxite, of which Guinea is the leading world exporter. But further violent disturbances took place when soldiers rioted over pay, forcing the dismissal of the defence minister and the armed forces chief of staff. It was unclear whether the appointment of new faces would be the start of a genuine transition or, more likely, just the dying phase of Conté's regime.

Congo's tricky new phase
Elections in the DRC in July and October 2006 ended the transition set in train in 2003, when an interim government was formed after almost five years of war.

But they did not complete the peace process. Intermittent outbreaks of serious violence followed in several parts of the country. In March 2007, suppression of armed opposition in central Kinshasa left several hundred dead in two days of heavy fighting, marking a setback to hopes for Congolese democracy.

Held more than a year behind schedule, the presidential and parliamentary contests promised to be the country's first successful open elections. Since independence there had been only one multi-party legislative election, in 1965, which paved the way for Mobutu Sese Seko's 32 years of predatory dictatorship. The importance of a smooth outcome for the region was obvious, considering the DRC's pivotal position, with nine international borders, and following a war in which seven African nations sent troops.

The risk in pressing ahead with elections, and thereby exacerbating factional confrontation, had to be weighed against the unsustainable and unwieldy nature of the transitional government, which had four vice-presidents. The European Union committed 2,000 troops as a temporary back-up for the 17,000-strong UN mission, MONUC. The largest exercise of its kind under UN auspices, costing donors $500m, the voting itself was less marred by violence or blatant irregularities than many expected. Joseph Kabila, president since succeeding his assassinated father in 2001, took a strong lead in a field of 33 candidates that included former warlords. But, relying on support mainly in the volatile east, he fell short of an outright majority with just under 45%. The run-off three months later gave him 58% over his rival Jean-Pierre Bemba, a wealthy former rebel leader and vice-president. Results of both rounds provoked battles in Kinshasa, a stronghold of Bemba's support. After initially challenging the count, Bemba accepted taking the role of opposition leader, with a Senate seat. But growing tension over his insistence on maintaining a separate armed guard culminated in March 2007 in a bloody defeat at the hands of regular forces loyal to Kabila. Under threat of treason charges, Bemba took refuge in the South African Embassy, then flew to Portugal for medical treatment.

The period immediately following Kabila's inauguration as elected president saw a worrying trend towards concentration of power, creating a quandary for international donors constrained to support the new government. The indirect election of governors by provincial assemblies in January and February 2007 placed Kabila allies, either members of his Alliance of the Presidential Majority coalition or pro-government independents, in 10 of 11 provinces, provoking allegations of vote buying. Bemba's Union for the Nation coalition secured only his northwestern home province of Equateur. Kabila's faction was thus able to establish dominance over key institutions even in opposition areas. However, the uncertainty of his control was exposed when his party's nominee for the presidency of the senate surprisingly lost to Léon Kengo wa Dondo, a former Mobutu prime minister who had given his support to the Bemba camp.

The other worrying flaw in the DRC's new dispensation was security, as a result of delays in the process of demobilisation, armed forces reorganisation and justice reform. The national army, at the heart of abuses in the Mobutu period, has been regarded more as a security threat than a protector, subject to poor discipline, wages and living conditions, while army integration has meant incorporating members of militias with a record of human-rights violations. Many local conflicts are unresolved, and armed groups, including Rwandan Hutu fighters, remain at large. The activity of dissident general Laurent Nkunda's forces within the new framework of mixed army brigades has caused particular concern. With security reform probably needing many years to complete, the role of MONUC, the largest and costliest of current UN peacekeeping operations, will therefore remain vital. Much will depend on how fast Kabila's government can deliver economic benefits. Congo's minerals, forestry and water resources should make it Central Africa's economic engine. But the International Monetary Fund has complained about failure to meet economic objectives, and the pace of recovery slowed to 5% in 2006 from 6.5% the year before. Beset by corruption, the lack of a strong political class, and the readiness of warlords to return to arms, the country remains at risk of a relapse into violence.

Kenya's slow reforms

Presidential and parliamentary elections due in Kenya in December will be the first since the country's democratic turning point in 2002. Mwai Kibaki's sweeping victory then, ending 39 years of rule by the Kenya African National Union (KANU), was hailed as a model for ousting entrenched regimes peacefully. But the promise of 'comprehensive political and economic changes' has gone unfulfilled in important respects. As a consequence, Kenya's reputation in the initial post-election euphoria as a beacon for democracy in East Africa and the rest of the continent has been greatly tarnished.

After pledges to eradicate corruption and rewrite Kenya's patched-up 1963 constitution, the momentum of reform soon ran out. The victorious National Rainbow Coalition (NARC) proved a wobbly alliance and succumbed to infighting, the septuagenarian president became a closeted figure, and Kenya failed to shake off a mode of politics governed by ethnic and regional power bases and vested interests. After anti-corruption measures, bribery showed signs of declining for the first two years and then, according to Transparency International, appeared to increase. To the dismay of donors, the authorities were seen as being more interested in unearthing past corruption than current abuses. There were damaging disclosures about security-related procurement contracts ostensibly being used for party financing. But two ministers who resigned in February 2006 over corruption scandals were reinstated in November.

The need for a new constitution remains unresolved, following a protracted review process, the dropping of proposals to clip the president's powers, and a watered-down final draft that voters rejected in a November 2005 referendum. Despite this snub, Kibaki was expected to stand for a second term amid indications that he was still the most popular candidate, with the advantage of incumbency. The opposition Orange Democratic Movement-Kenya, an awkward and fractious alliance formed around the referendum 'No' campaign, suffered from a surfeit of heavyweight contenders. Among these were the last election's defeated KANU candidate Uhuru Kenyatta and two high-profile defectors who joined the NARC bandwagon in 2002, ex-ministers Raila Odinga and Stephen Kalonzo Musyoka. But the reasons for Kibaki's apparent strong standing were also linked to vivid memories of the dismal Daniel arap Moi regime that he replaced, characterised by economic stagnation, rising poverty and self-enrichment on a grand scale by government cronies.

Since 2004 economic growth has been stronger and the 6% recorded in 2006 was the highest for two decades. Kenya's report from the African Peer Review Mechanism in mid 2006 highlighted unequal wealth distribution and a poor record in implementing programmes, but many Kenyans, especially in Nairobi, feel their lot has improved. Most importantly, Kenyans enjoy much greater freedom, the media have become bolder and, despite the failings of the political elite, there are signs of an increasingly confident grassroots democracy. While the government has squandered opportunities to make politics more inclusive and tackle corruption decisively, the electorate does not yet appear to be in the mood to experiment with another change.

Choice in South Africa, blockage in Zimbabwe

Tensions that have built up inside the African National Congress (ANC) since the first post-apartheid elections in 1994 are coming to a head as South Africa's governing party prepares for its five-yearly national conference in the northern city of Polokwane in December 2007. The event, setting the stage for the succession to President Thabo Mbeki when his second term ends in 2009, is shaping up to be its most difficult hurdle since it came to power.

Such is the ANC's dominance, with 70% of National Assembly seats and control of all nine provinces, that its internal battle has greater importance than any near-term election in determining the country's future path. By tradition it has anointed its leaders without a fight, and the last transition from Nelson Mandela to Mbeki went smoothly. But its divisions have been out in the open, along with allegations of irregularities at party branches. The core divergence is over economic policy, between the government's broadly orthodox, market-oriented approach and greater interventionism to tackle poverty, unemployment and inequality. But the rift has also formed around personalities. The temperature rose in 2006 amid further legal controversy surrounding Jacob Zuma, the ANC's number two. A popular figure contrasting with Mbeki's aloof style, he has been a figurehead for grievances among many left-wing and youth members frustrated with the pace of change. Sacked as deputy president in 2005 when his financial adviser was convicted for fraud and corruption linked to a defence deal, Zuma survived two controversial trials in 2006 – an acquittal in May in a bizarre rape case involving a woman he knew to be infected with HIV, followed by the collapse of the corruption case against him in September. The affairs rallied support behind Zuma especially in the Zulu community, South Africa's largest ethnic group. But the threat of renewed legal troubles and cavalier comments on gender relations, HIV/AIDS and homosexuality probably reduced his comeback chances as a leadership front-runner. Efforts within the hierarchy were concentrating on forging unity behind a new policy platform.

The limit on Mbeki's mandate as South African president does not stop him standing for a further stint as party leader. This would mean finding a mechanism for selecting another candidate for national president, to be chosen by the parliament elected in April 2009. If the battle between the Mbeki and Zuma camps proves too divisive, the party may settle on a compromise candidate. The names of high-profile activists turned businessmen Cyril Ramaphosa and Tokyo Sexwale have been frequently mentioned but might be too contested. Other options include ANC Secretary-General Kgalema Motlanthe, party strategist Joel Netshitenzhe and the foreign affairs minister, Zuma's ex-wife Nkosazana Dlamini-Zuma. But the most likely would be to let Mbeki hold the ANC fort and manage the succession.

Widely criticised for his failed 'quiet diplomacy' policy towards Zimbabwe, Mbeki was again invited to mediate between President Robert Mugabe's Zimbabwe African National Union-Patriotic Front (ZANU-PF) government and the Movement for Democratic Change (MDC) opposition. Following an international outcry over the detention and beating of Morgan Tsvangirai, leader of the divided MDC's main faction, an emergency summit of the Southern African Development Community (SADC) in March 2007 in Dar es Salaam, Tanzania, appointed Mbeki to facilitate dialogue, in spite of deep distrust towards him within the MDC. Any harsh words were kept behind closed doors at the meeting, which expressed solidarity with Zimbabwe, reaffirmed SADC's view that Mugabe was fairly re-elected in 2002 and called for the dropping of travel and other sanctions imposed by the United States, European Union, Australia and New Zealand.

Zimbabwe's worsening political and economic crisis has, however, become increasingly uncomfortable for its neighbours, South Africa included, not least because of the stream of Zimbabweans leaving the country. A security cooperation agreement between Zimbabwe and Angola in March provoked concern, although Angola denied plans to send paramilitary forces to back Mugabe's regime. Immediately after the SADC summit, ZANU-PF's central committee endorsed Mugabe to stand again in March 2008, when he will be 84. An earlier proposal to extend his term by two years to coincide with parliamentary elections was dropped and plans for bringing forward parliamentary elections adopted instead. Pre-election intimidation tactics were already in evidence. Changes were being rushed through to enlarge both houses of parliament with more rural seats, which would favour ZANU-PF, and ensure that parliament could replace Mugabe on his death without triggering an automatic election. The MDC wants a new constitution and repeal of repressive laws on the media and public meetings before going into an election. But time was short for a thorough constitutional review.

An uncertain factor was the impact of Zimbabwe's economic collapse, which worsened with annual inflation surpassing 2,000% by March, a tumbling exchange rate and a lack of foreign reserves to meet a gaping shortfall in supplies of maize, the staple food. As go-between, Mbeki appeared to place hope on Mugabe being persuaded to step down ahead of the election. But Zimbabwe's leader has been cunning in playing off different factions in his party. Prospects for an early handover have been aired before without materialising.

Africans voting with their feet

The waters between Africa and the islands and mainland of the European Union have become a front line for international migration. Shortage of opportunities for young adults in African countries has prompted unprecedented numbers to attempt the journey by increasingly hazardous means. It is by now apparent that European efforts to plug the flow have had the effect of displacing this movement more than reducing it, giving rise to a shifting pattern of migration routes and trafficking networks and creating new dilemmas for African transit countries.

According to the UN Population Division, migration from Africa to developed countries now runs at 400,000 a year, a third more than in the 1990s, and is expected to stay near this level to 2050. Other experts estimate the annual number of 'irregular' migrants crossing the Mediterranean at 100,000-plus. The overall flow from Africa is smaller than from Asia or the Latin America–Caribbean region, but causes growing alarm in southern Europe because of the relatively sudden concentration of migration pressure in countries such as Spain and Italy and the appalling spectacle of corpses washed ashore.

In the 1990s clandestine crossings took place mainly in the Strait of Gibraltar, 14km across at its narrowest point. As vigilance tightened, the emphasis shifted eastwards to routes from Libya and Tunisia to Italy's southern islands and Malta, and southwest to Spain's Canary Islands, which lie at the nearest 100km from

Africa. At the same time, while migrants were at first predominantly North Africans, the majority of those intercepted are now from sub-Saharan Africa, fleeing zones of chronic unemployment and recurrent conflict. On the Canaries route alone at least 3,000 were reckoned to have died in 2006, and local officials put the probable figure at 6,000, five times the previous year's estimate.

Cooperation between the EU and Maghreb countries, coupled with more effective surveillance, led to a shift away from previous embarkation areas and the Spanish North African enclave territories of Melilla and Ceuta, the scene of border-fence shootings in autumn 2005, to departure points further south, first in Mauritania, and then principally in Senegal. Thus, despite apparent success in containing the small-boat traffic from Morocco to southern Andalusia, the number of seaborne migrants apprehended by Spanish authorities in 2006 multiplied more than threefold to 39,000, mainly in the Canaries. About 7,000 others were stopped attempting the crossing. Most travel in wooden fishing canoes, sometimes specially constructed to carry 100 or more passengers, but cargo vessels have also been used. The organisers may be criminal gangs or local opportunists. The route has also attracted migrants from Asia, usually arriving in West African capitals by air. This transcontinental traffic was highlighted by a diplomatic standoff in February 2007 when a trawler carrying 370 passengers, mostly South Asians, broke down in Mauritanian waters after apparently setting out from Conakry in Guinea.

Joint patrols off the African coast involving the Spanish Guardia Civil were backed up between August and December by the deployment of vessels and aircraft from several EU countries by Frontex, the EU's border-control agency. There were some signs of a drop in arrivals in the Canaries in early 2007, when Frontex mounted a follow-on mission. Spain meanwhile extended a range of bilateral agreements with African governments, tying financial and other support to the repatriation of unauthorised migrants. It sent back 21,000 in 2006, mainly Moroccans and Senegalese. Italy began large-scale returns to Libya under a similar arrangement in 2004.

Repatriation policies get more complicated, however, when migrants start out from third countries. Overland journeys to departure points often last weeks and require stage-by-stage payment. Established trans-Sahara routes used by West Africans run via Gao in Mali or Agadez in Niger, from where one fork goes through Algeria towards either Morocco or Libya and another directly into Libya. Other routes connect the Horn of Africa to Libya or the eastern Mediterranean. Towns along these routes have seen their populations swollen by stranded travellers. Countries such as Morocco and Senegal are simultaneously sources of emigration, destination countries and transit countries. South Africa, which has become a magnet for African asylum seekers, is also seen by many as a first stop on the way to Europe, North America or Australia. This complex pattern of cross-border movements has produced backlashes against foreign residents, such as violence between police and Sudanese migrants in Egypt.

Ways of securing greater African cooperation in stemming the exodus were discussed at a European–African conference in Rabat in July 2006 and a further meeting of EU and African Union ministers in Tripoli in November. Up to now, the EU's approach has been mainly security driven, geared more to controlling borders and pushing back migration than addressing its causes or the conditions to which migrants are subjected. But it is beginning to look at targeted development assistance schemes and increased facilities for legal migration. Reluctance by African governments to collaborate by clamping down on emigrants may in part reflect their reliance on remittances from abroad, but also the deep unpopularity of such measures. Since the disparity in average income compared to Europe has widened in the past 30 years, social pressure for emigration is strong. Sending migrants back has limited deterrent effect, since many are prepared to repeat the attempt. Increasing controls may encourage people to try to leave while they still can. The expectation is that numbers will rise before they decline.

Assisting Africa: the G8 and China

Africa has seen very little of the large increase in aid promised two years ago at the G8 summit in Gleneagles, Scotland. Under the grandiloquent plans adopted at that meeting, overall assistance to developing countries was to rise by $50bn a year by 2010. Half the extra money was earmarked for Africa, enough to double the volume of aid to the continent. Emphasis was given to funding the infrastructure needed to boost economic growth and help Africa's poorer countries become more self-reliant. But the momentum that Gleneagles was supposed to impart is at best only beginning to materialise. In the first two years, aid going into development programmes in Africa has been flat. Efforts to improve aid effectiveness have also made slow progress, while changeable flows and a proliferation of donor agencies strain the capacities of recipient countries to implement projects.

Official aid figures during this period have been swollen by emergency humanitarian operations and most of all by debt cancellation, which figured prominently among the G8's pledges. The biggest beneficiary of this in Africa has been Nigeria, which has managed to wipe off most of the $35bn it owed abroad. Other African countries began to benefit in 2006 from the elimination of remaining debts to the World Bank and other multilateral institutions, a facility limited to poor countries that had already fulfilled the conditions to qualify for debt relief. The number of African countries in this category has since risen from 14 to 18, out of a global total of 22. The measure has eased burdens on national budgets, but the money released from debt service payments falls a long way short of meeting priority financing needs. Although the US administration's budget request for the 2008 fiscal year included a sharp increase in aid for Africa, especially for HIV/AIDS, it would still leave Western donors with a big lag to make up in order to meet expectations. Leaving debt relief aside, provisional figures from the Organisation for Economic Co-operation and Development (OECD) for 2006 indicated that aid to Africa was virtually static. Globally, it calculated that core development funding would need to start increasing by 12% a year, three times the average of recent years, to attain the 2010 target.

A central idea in the Gleneagles plan was that it should be a two-sided bargain, and that development and stability depended first of all on Africa taking steps to overcome its general record of bad governance. Invited African leaders committed themselves to promote poverty reduction and growth programmes, strengthen democratic institutions, increase transparency, fight corruption and remove obstacles to cross-border trade within the continent. The principle that foreign support should be linked to better African governance was not new, having been established from the launch in 2001 of the New Partnership for Africa's Development (NEPAD), an ambitious but diffuse economic plan subsequently absorbed by the African Union. The record on Africa's side has been mixed. Improved economic management has helped bring more consistent performance, although recent growth rates averaging 5–6% have been mainly the result of high prices for export commodities. Bureaucratic barriers have started to be lowered, especially in countries such as Ghana and Tanzania, but still do more to obstruct business than in other developing regions. Measures against corruption have been mostly superficial, with some exceptions such as Rwanda. Half the countries of Africa have signed up for the showpiece African Peer Review Mechanism for political and economic scrutiny, but the process has been painfully slow. The African Union has reinforced its commitment to democracy and the rule of law, but the 2007 assessment by Freedom House, the Washington-based advocacy organisation, found more setbacks than gains for political rights and civil liberties across Africa. At the same time, while donors have sought to coordinate their efforts to ensure aid is better allocated and used, Africa's traditional partners have faced increasing competition for influence in the continent.

China's evolving role
One part of the African development equation largely overlooked at the time of Gleneagles was increasing involvement by China (and, to a lesser but sig-

nificant extent, India). After figuring prominently in the ideological rivalries played out in Africa in the 1960s and 1970s, China then showed waning interest. But a spectacular commercial and political thrust in Africa over the past few years has extended its power beyond its own region, providing an alternative ally for African governments and posing a challenge to Western policies. China has obtained diplomatic dividends, and by 2007 only five of Africa's 53 countries were still holding out by maintaining relations with Taiwan instead. The prime force behind China's return to prominence in Africa is economic, fuelled by Beijing's massive accumulation of foreign-exchange reserves and dominated by its need for energy sources and raw materials to keep powering its industrial growth. Africa has become a key oil supplier, providing almost a third of China's crude imports, and a source of other natural resources from base metals to timber and cotton. Two-way trade climbed by 40% in 2006 to $55.5bn, a threefold rise in nominal terms in three years, putting China close to France in the front rank of Africa's trading partners, behind the United States. Chinese companies have invested extensively in energy, construction and telecommunications, often in countries where Western business has been timid. An illustration of this was a Chinese oil exploration facility in eastern Ethiopia where more than 70 people, including nine Chinese, were killed in a rebel attack in April 2007. For African governments, China offers long-term export contracts and long-term finance, as well as the capacity to build key infrastructure such as power plants, roads and bridges relatively cheaply and quickly. Reported Chinese loans for infrastructure in Africa in 2006 far outstripped those of the World Bank and African Development Bank (AfDB). The importance of the Chinese connection was underlined by the presence of 43 heads of state at a China–Africa summit in Beijing in November 2006 and the decision of the AfDB, which is preparing to assume a lead financing role in the continent, to hold its 2007 annual meeting in Shanghai.

Chinese support mirrors benefits provided by Western partners such as duty-free access for many African products, grant aid, soft loans, debt relief, training and scholarships, as well as hospitals and public buildings. But there are clear differences with China's state-centred approach to cooperation, relying heavily on investment by state companies and often de facto barter arrangements. One example was an unsuccessful proposal that Nigeria should channel revenues from oil exported to China into an escrow account for payment of Chinese goods and services. Much of China's lending is directly linked to supply commitments, and not subject to the same rules and agreements – on untying aid, for instance – as that of other creditors. Serious concern was raised by the US Treasury and the World Bank in 2006 that African countries might be incurring excessive debts as a result of unconditional Chinese loans, undermining debt-relief arrangements agreed with Western donors.

The aspect of China's policy that most appeared to set it on a collision course with the United States, however, was its support for authoritarian regimes in countries such as Sudan, which sends most of its oil exports to China and Zimbabwe. An Africa policy paper in early 2006 re-iterated China's stance of non-interference in internal affairs. In Angola, which in 2006 temporarily overtook Saudi Arabia as China's biggest oil supplier, multi-billion-dollar Chinese credit facilities have provided an effective financial shield, enabling the government to turn its back on the International Monetary Fund and fend off pressure for greater accountability. In recent months, however, Chinese policy has shown signs of evolving in response to Western criticism. In Sudan, while it continued to resist UN Security Council sanctions over the conflict in Darfur, it backed efforts in early 2007 to negotiate the deployment of UN forces as part of a beefed-up peace operation. China had already sent troops for UN peacekeeping in Southern Sudan, as well as Liberia and the DRC. After controversy over links with Zimbabwe, including the supply of military aircraft, Chinese President Hu Jintao pointedly avoided visiting the country in a tour of the region in January–February 2007, his second African trip in ten months.

While African countries can relate to China's recent experience as a rapidly developing economy, the Chinese presence is far from being universally popular. Controversies have erupted over Chinese competition in the clothing industry, the use of Chinese labour, and in Zambia over mineworkers' conditions under Chinese ownership. Angola, buoyed by rising oil revenues, has shown increased assertiveness towards both Western and Chinese partners, a tendency signalled by its accession in early 2007 to the Organisation of the Petroleum Exporting Countries (OPEC).

South Africa's President Thabo Mbeki cautioned in December 2006 against replicating 'the historic colonial economic relationship' in which Africa was used as a source of raw materials and an outlet for manufactured goods. There is no disguising the fact that the China–Africa relationship is driven more by China's interests than by Africa's. But that at least could be deemed to display a clarity of purpose that is lacking in the discourse of the traditional donor community. The presence of another leading player in the field may help to concentrate minds about what aid policy is supposed to achieve.

Competition for influence and resources is nothing new on a continent that was a platform for the rivalries of both colonialism and the Cold War. The pledges of extra Western backing and the sharply increased involvement of China have coincided to bring Africa more into international focus. Debt relief, sounder finances, flourishing trade with Asia and the premium on oil and metals have all been factors in an improved economic outlook, which is now the strongest for many years. But rising growth has not been matched by a corresponding increase in employment, nor is it yet sufficient to put more than a handful of

African countries on course to achieve UN poverty-reduction targets. Additional external support and financial resources for governments have done nothing to widen the distribution of power or wealth. The tendency has, if anything, been to reinforce the propensity of ruling elites to entrench their positions. Thus, while political unheavals have become rarer than in the past, potential causes of further instability continue to be present in many African countries.

The economic rise of China and India dominated developments in Asia over the past year. While trade and investment ties between China and the United States became ever closer, the relationship between the two capitals was characterised simultaneously by closer engagement and verbal fencing. India developed its relations with China and the United States, but the slow steps towards the hoped-for India–US civil nuclear agreement suggested that long-standing mutual suspicions had not completely dissipated. The complex jigsaw of inter-Asian relationships was altered by a thawing of relations between Tokyo and Beijing, and by North Korea's nuclear test and subsequent agreement to make moves that might eventually lead to denuclearisation.

Events in a number of countries across the region gave cause for concern. The conflict in Afghanistan showed signs of spreading into previously peaceful areas, and Pakistan faced multiple problems including growing disaffection with the government of President Pervez Musharraf. Sri Lanka's long-running conflict worsened, while in Bangladesh the prospects for democracy were uncertain after the military acted to stem electoral chaos. Nepal, however, edged towards resolving its Maoist insurgency. The outlook for restoration of democracy in Thailand was unclear following a military coup. Australia and New Zealand were concerned by violence and institutional weaknesses in a number of small states in the Pacific, and a military coup also occurred in Fiji.

China: Growth and Engagement

The scope and nuance of Chinese diplomacy continue to widen and deepen. Beijing's well-known and well-established objectives are first and foremost eco-

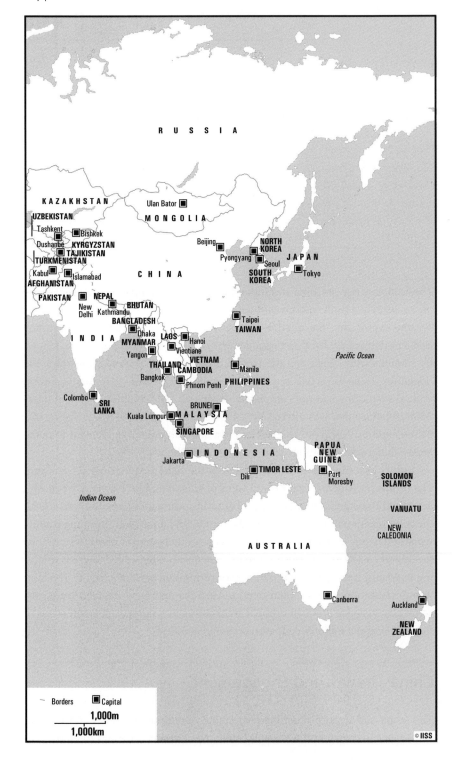

RUSSIA

KAZAKHSTAN

UZBEKISTAN

Tashkent

Dushanbe ■Bishkek

KYRGYZSTAN

TAJIKISTAN

TURKMENISTAN

Kabul ■ ■Islamabad

AFGHANISTAN

PAKISTAN ■ NEPAL

New ■

Delhi Kathmandu

BHUTAN

BANGLADESH

Dhaka

INDIA

MYANMAR

Yangon

Ulan Bator ■

MONGOLIA

Beijing ■

Pyongyang ■

NORTH
KOREA

Seoul

SOUTH
KOREA

JAPAN

■Tokyo

CHINA

■Taipei

TAIWAN

LAOS ■

Hanoi

Vientiane

THAILAND VIETNAM

CAMBODIA

Bangkok ■

Phnom Penh

Manila

PHILIPPINES

Colombo ■

SRI
LANKA

BRUNEI ■

Kuala Lumpur■ MALAYSIA

SINGAPORE

■ INDONESIA

Jakarta

PAPUA
NEW
GUINEA

Dili

■ TIMOR LESTE

■Port
Moresby

SOLOMON
ISLANDS

VANUATU

NEW
CALEDONIA

Pacific Ocean

Indian Ocean

AUSTRALIA

■Canberra

Auckland ■

NEW
ZEALAND

Borders   ■Capital

1,000m

1,000km

© IISS

nomic development and political stability at home, to be achieved by ensuring and enlarging China's access to markets and resources overseas, and by avoiding, where possible, the distractions of foreign conflicts and tensions. This means that great powers, intrigued and unsettled by China's breathtaking rise, must be engaged and, not infrequently, assuaged. Smaller neighbours, tempted to widen their strategic options by enlisting larger powers in precautionary alignments against Beijing, have to be persuaded that they will be lifted up rather than dashed against the rocks by a rising Chinese tide.

Beijing employs attentive amiability against sceptics who note less kindly inflexions in Chinese diplomacy: for example, its bristling rejection of any foreign pressure that Beijing sees as intended to influence the shape of its political and social arrangements, or at setting limits on and standards for relationships with governments whose policies invite controversy; and the shrillness with which Beijing pronounces on foreign-policy matters that are connected to the credibility or legitimacy of the ruling Chinese Communist Party. Others note China's evident desire for stature and sway in the international system – an impulse expressed not only in efforts to play, within the confines of national self-interest, a 'responsible' role in world affairs, but also in moves to acquire the military paraphernalia of a great power.

Most importantly, China must achieve workable relations with the United States – a country which in equal measure inspires fascination and suspicion in Chinese minds. In the United States, there is similarly no political consensus as to whether China's rise is a predominantly good thing with some unpleasant side-effects, or an overwhelmingly bad thing with some fringe benefits. No other country is as sensitive as the United States to the possibility of eventual strategic displacement by Beijing, and none is more suspected by Beijing of attempting to contain China or to change it politically. No other country is as economically important to China and yet so intimately entangled and interested in all of the most sensitive questions and disputes – from the status of Taiwan and North Korea's nuclear aspirations to Japan's gradual strategic resurgence – that Beijing regards as vital determinants of its future security.

Among China's neighbours, dealings with Russia are outwardly the most comfortable, couched in an implicit but definite common resistance to aspects of Western policy and a shared realist-statist mindset. Yet each side doubts the dependability of the other. Relations with India and Japan have historically been antagonistic. These increasingly extrovert powers are closely aligned not only with the United States but with each other on many security questions, including their aversion to a China that is strategically preponderant in Asia. But from China's perspective this antagonism has begun to look counterproductive.

There is a contest among the larger Asian powers for influence and opportunity regarding the ten members of the Association of Southeast Asian Nations

(ASEAN), which are conversant enough with their self-interest to welcome all suitors simultaneously. This requires China to pay constant attention to ASEAN's concerns and interests. In Northeast Asia, China faces security challenges in North Korea's nuclear appetite and Taiwan's efforts to detach itself more formally from the mainland. Both of these flashpoints continue to draw the United States militarily into the region and provide some of the rationale – or, as seen from China, a plausible excuse – for the continuing American defence relationships with South Korea, Japan and others.

In the case of North Korea, Chinese interests lie foremost in avoiding a regional conflict and then in dampening North Korea's tendency to stimulate Japan's normalisation as a military power. Adoption of the role of constructive mediator in the dispute has provided China with an important element of control over regional diplomacy. It serves the long-term Chinese goal of influencing the terms of an eventual reunification of a Korean Peninsula that might be drawn more closely into China's ambit. But the ease with which China might become a hate-object of Korean nationalism requires Beijing to tread lightly. Another reunification, that of China and Taiwan, remains a paramount if long-term objective for Beijing. Here it faces dilemmas, not least on how best to calibrate military deterrence of a Taiwanese declaration of independence: too overt a posture might drive the island away, justify US military deployments in the region and swell the number of those who doubt that China's wider strategic intentions are benevolent; too little emphasis on military deterrence might embolden pro-independence sentiment and set in train events that could lead to a conflict China wishes to avoid if at all possible.

Further afield, the European Union's economic heft, comparative detachment from the tangles of Asian security and empathetic view of China's convoluted socio-economic transition make it an attractive and valuable interlocutor – although probably less so than imagined by Beijing. In the resource-rich areas of the Middle East, Africa and Latin America that are becoming important for China's economy, Beijing must ingratiate itself with targeted countries, acquaint itself with unfamiliar and complicated regional politics, and remain alive to the attitudes of other outside powers with stakes and interests to defend.

On the whole China worked reasonably well in the last 12 months to square all of these accounts with skill, patience, flexibility and pragmatism. But amid steady progress and the occasional, notable diplomatic breakthrough, there were also significant reversals. And in addition to the challenges confronting China abroad, increasing and immediate demands were made of Beijing on other fronts, such as the economy, that have their own consequences for foreign policy.

The domestic scene
China has continued its strong growth in output, accompanied by expanding trade surpluses and accumulation of the world's largest foreign-exchange

reserves of well over $1 trillion. Some of these reserves have been deployed into a new state investment fund which is making its presence felt in international markets. However, these developments have not smothered the impression – at home or in global financial capitals – that the government lacks the means to impose order and balance on an economy prone to bouts of fever caused by structural ailments.

Recent spectacular growth in trading on China's equity markets, occasionally eclipsing the combined daily turnover on all of Asia's other exchanges, did not reflect the sudden appearance of an abundance of sound corporate stock on the bourses. Rather, it resulted from the inability of China's banking sector to provide attractive returns to savers. The consequent infectious volatility of China's markets became a matter of significance to global financial governance. Meanwhile, China's monetary and exchange-rate polices were a controversial topic of economic discourse and diplomacy. It seemed unlikely that China would soon develop adequate regulatory mechanisms, or that trade flows would very quickly be restructured in a way that would defuse politically charged observations that Beijing was practising a species of mercantilism. In some respects, the pace at which the government has responded to economic realities has been curiously slow. It was only at the annual session of the parliamentary National People's Congress in March 2007 that political resistance was overcome to a long-tabled law enshrining and giving standing to private property – an initiative that had caused offence to some nostalgic members of a Chinese Communist Party that is now presiding over a rough-and-tumble 'turbo-capitalism'.

Mastery of this central anomaly has been the political aim of a leadership that was preparing for the 17th five-yearly Communist Party Congress scheduled for autumn 2007. Significant leadership personnel matters will be predetermined and then announced at the Congress. President Hu Jintao – who is also Secretary-General of the party and the head of the Central Military Commission – and Premier Wen Jiabao were both expected to be confirmed for second terms. Elsewhere, however, the party's now well-established restrictions on the maximum age (70) at which high office may be occupied will require a sweeping turnover: four of the nine members of China's highest decision-making body, the Politburo Standing Committee, will be replaced; half of the wider Politburo will be changed; and only about 40% of the membership of the Central Committee, from which the members of the other two bodies are drawn, will remain in place. The secrecy with which such personnel matters are decided, and uncertainty among outside observers about the wider criteria on which decisions are made, make it difficult to anticipate with any great certainty the full implications of these changes. But they are at the very least likely to carry some significance for factional balances within the party's power centres. This is not least because all those expected to leave the Politburo Standing Committee were closely associated with the 'Shanghai faction' of the former president, Jiang Zemin, who perhaps somewhat reluctantly made way for Hu Jintao in 2002 – but not before ensuring that his own supporters were abundantly and strategically placed to exert influence. That influence, the extent and flow of which was never easy to pin down, will now be diminished. Many observers read into Hu Jintao's unceremonious dismissal on corruption charges of Shanghai Party Secretary Chen Liangyu in September 2006 a growing confidence in dealing with Jiang Zemin's previously panoplied protégés. The future of a principal figure of the Shanghai faction, Vice President Zeng Qinhong, once thought a credible and serious rival to Hu Jintao, seemed uncertain too: at 68, his age appeared to preclude his serving out a full second term, and it was speculated that he might retire at the Congress or be given a sinecure. Another strand of speculation held that Zeng had seen the writing on the wall and so worked to develop an accommodation with Hu. The death of Vice Premier Huang Ju in June removed another prominent member of the Shanghai faction. Hu Jintao thus had room for manoeuvre and the occasion to shape his own Politburo Standing Committee. A wider question was whether the construction of new power centres would provide clues to the identity of the fulcrum of a 'Fifth Generation' of leaders, perhaps drawn from party secretaries of significant provinces, in the same way that Hu Jintao's appointment to the Standing Committee in 1992 signalled his designation by then paramount leader Deng Xiaoping as the 'core' of the 'Fourth Generation'.

Despite their intensity, these intrigues are not particularly animated by clashing policy perspectives: where there are differences, they tend to focus on emphasis and presentation. Broad continuity can therefore be expected in the domestic policies Hu has gradually set out in his first term. These have often been advanced under the rubric of aspiring to the creation of a 'harmonious society' that is 'moderately well-off in an all-round way'. The objectives are a rapid, job-generating but more efficient manner of growth; greater regard for inequalities and social fissures thrown up by China's transformation; dealing with the effects of staggering environmental dislocation insofar as economic imperatives allow; improving the responsiveness of government; punishing official corruption where it reaches egregious levels; and strengthening China's idiosyncratic and rudimentary legal processes – and through these and other devices, staving off challenges to the party's authority and its monopoly of political power.

China and America

The extension of 'harmony' to international society is a goal often expressed by China's leadership and diplomats, albeit rarely in a precise or programmatic way. In Beijing's view this 'harmony' would generally be advanced by levelling out international power along broadly multipolar lines (some poles will be more equal than others). The principle of 'non-interference' in the internal affairs of one state by another would be more closely observed, while relationships would be founded on the basis of 'mutual benefit' and 'peaceful coexistence'. Military alliances, especially those that might take an interest in China, would be disestablished. Lest it be thought that a strengthening China would seek in some way to impose this harmony, however, reassurances are offered. The 'peaceful rise' theory, propounded for a time by advisers close to Hu Jintao, in essence claims that China will be the exception to the rule that rising powers tend to wilfully disrupt and disorganise the international system, inviting the resistance of other powers and so ultimately sowing the seeds of their own gradual exhaustion over time. There is a large and receptive international audience for these protestations which, however, sit uneasily with historical precedent and the increasing nationalist confidence of a country manifestly on its way up.

All these matters go to the heart of China's relationship with the United States. There are too many points of difference – contrasting political systems, complicated economic exchanges, American sympathy for Taiwan, China's ties to 'rogue' regimes, and others – to bear much 'harmony'. Yet, over the last 12 months at least, no dispute has proved unmanageable. Moreover, on the nuclear aspirations of North Korea and Iran, China and the United States found themselves working more closely together in the UN Security Council to censure both states. This collaboration was forced mainly by the flagrancy of the provocations and recalcitrance demonstrated by North Korea and Iran, pushing China into a tougher public line contrary to its private preferences. It owed rather less to any sudden emergence of a tight Sino-American consensus on the nature of these problems and how best to remedy them. Indeed, the expectation that China, with Russia, would shelter both Pyongyang and Tehran from American and European wrath was presumably a key consideration for the two proliferators in deciding to act in the way they did. Neither appeared decisively intimidated by the adjustments in China's public stances.

Bilateral dialogues on the broadest issues continued to flourish as fixtures on the diplomatic calendar. Indeed, the relationship seems to have become substantially more process-oriented in the last two years, in recognition of the fact that entrenched differences will not quickly be overcome, and that the importance of each country to the other has grown such that episodic or ceremonial contacts can no longer serve. Thus the now regular Senior Dialogue brings prominent officials from Washington and Beijing together to discuss international security issues, just as the Global Issues dialogue allows the two sides to assess and coordinate responses to transnational challenges ranging from crime and human trafficking to the environment and health. Perhaps the most impressive expression of this new yearning for contact has been the Strategic Economic Dialogue inaugurated in December 2006, led on the US side by Treasury Secretary Henry Paulson and on the Chinese side by Vice Premier Wu Yi. At the inaugural meeting in

Beijing, the US cabinet secretaries for energy, commerce, health and labour were present as well as Paulson, as were the US trade representative and the chairman of the Federal Reserve. A similarly imposing Chinese delegation made its way to Washington for the second round of the Strategic Economic Dialogue in May 2007. Against a backdrop of considerable Congressional exasperation and threatened legislation to punish China, American calls for a further revaluation of the renminbi were pressed, with the aim of achieving more even trade balances between the two countries. The Bush administration has often appeared to be a mediator between Beijing and Capitol Hill in such encounters.

It seems to be recognised that these and other high-level exchanges have value even if they do not produce immediate policy results. This is a remarkable adjustment for a Bush administration that in its earliest days had almost blithely designated China a 'strategic competitor' of the United States and seemed dismissive of the close engagement of Beijing which the Clinton administration had, after some prevarication of its own, eventually sought. It is occasioned at least in part by the tendency of Washington's preoccupation with the wars in Iraq and Afghanistan, and with international terrorism, to crowd out other seemingly less immediate challenges. But there has also been a genuine rethink, perhaps more in the State Department and National Security Council than the Pentagon. Washington continues to make strong demands for changes in China's policies and practices, but it now does so in the guise, at least, of a tutor in the art of 'responsible stakeholding' in the international system. Some US policy advisers have taken this approach even further. An April 2007 report by the Council on Foreign Relations, produced by a 'task force' of China-watching luminaries, urged the United States to do a better job of communicating its own strategic intentions to China. It suggested that problems in the bilateral economic relationship were not simply a function of cynical mercantilism by China, but at least as much a symptom of deficient US policies at home and structural imbalances in the US economy. It recommended active efforts by the United States to achieve China's closer integration with the G8 and other global institutions. While stressing the need, in light of Chinese military modernisation efforts, for continuing investment in defence capabilities that will secure American predominance in Asia, the report counselled greater efforts to draw China into inclusive security dialogues with US defence allies and other partners in the region. This was presented as a way of seeking Beijing's 'understanding and appreciation for a continued US leadership role', in return for which Washington should be 'prepared to welcome a growing role for China in regional and global security affairs'. Similar sentiments infused policy recommendations regarding efforts to stem proliferation, promote sustainable development and encourage political reform, the rule of law and respect for human rights in China.

But these are hardly dominant views. The 2006 Report to Congress of the US–China Economic and Security Review Commission, published in November, was, true to past form, far less sanguine. Many of its views resonated inside the Bush administration and beyond. It voiced strong criticism of Chinese proliferation practices; protested on national-security grounds the relocation to China of US production activities in the technology sector; expressed concerns about the impact of Chinese policies on the stability of world energy markets; charged that front-companies of the People's Liberation Army (PLA) were tapping US capital markets; worried about the growth in new Chinese relationships around the world that might prejudice various American regional interests; anticipated that China's internal instabilities would spill over into the region; criticised Chinese trade and industrial policies that stood in violation of World Trade Organisation norms; and found much more worthy of complaint. In tone, many of the dense passages of the report read like an extended objection to the existence of the People's Republic, and its policy prescriptions were invariably of a heavily muscular sort.

Beijing seems fully aware of how finely balanced American debates on China can be, and how the substance and atmospherics of the relationship can suddenly alter for better or worse. It senses that now may be a moment of particular fragility. The distractions and controversy of the Middle East which initially caused Washington to put its relations with China on a less antagonistic footing have lately also made the United States sensitive to the suggestion that Beijing has exploited these encumbrances to make diplomatic advances at America's expense – be it in Asia, Europe, the Middle East, Latin America or Africa. At the same time, it seems likely that the gathering 2008 US presidential election campaign will in various ways cast an unwelcome spotlight on China. Although Sino-American relations will have far less prominence as a foreign-policy issue than Iraq, they are certain to receive more attention than in the 2004 race, when they were largely absent as an issue. Few of the candidates for the nomination of either party have had positive things to say about China, with criticisms ranging from labour, trade, environmental and human-rights practices to China's relations with countries such as Sudan, Zimbabwe, Iran, North Korea and Venezuela. For these reasons, Beijing has, while publicly disapproving of American military intervention in Iraq and other elements of US foreign policy in guarded terms, tended to go out of its way to signal that it does not intend to exploit Washington's considerable strategic predicament. Such considerations predisposed China to an extremely intensive programme of engagement, and it has worked to create political room for them.

Indeed, the attention being paid by Washington and Beijing to the full breadth of their relationship provides some assurance of forethought and restraint in handling differences. But it is hard to understate the degree to which the competitive military relationship between the two powers, which at various points has begun to resemble a classic 'security dilemma', now shapes strategic perceptions and calculations. In the last year, the two powers made particular efforts to improve and enlarge military-to-military contacts. Nevertheless, official assessments and public pronouncements tended to reflect the rather dim views still taken by each side of the other's posture and programmes. Moreover, mutual suspicion tended to ensure that even the recently stepped-up military exchanges and joint exercises retained a primarily ceremonial quality and in particular failed to achieve the standards of transparency for which the United States was pressing.

Notable exchanges over the course of the last year included a July 2006 visit to the US Third Fleet in San Diego by General Guo Boxiong, Vice Chairman of the Central Committee, followed by an onward visit to Washington for calls on Secretary of State Condoleezza Rice, then-Defense Secretary Donald Rumsfeld, Chairman of the Joint Chiefs of Staff General Peter Pace and National Security Adviser Stephen Hadley, and a short 'drop by' meeting with President George W. Bush. In September 2006 the People's Liberation Army Navy (PLAN) guided-missile destroyer *Qingdao* made a port call in San Diego and took part in a joint Sino-American search-and-rescue exercise off Hawaii. A further such exercise was held around the time of the November visit to China of Admiral Gary Roughead, commander of the US Pacific Fleet, who met among others PLAN Commander Admiral Wu Shengli and the commander of PLAN's South Seas Fleet, Vice-Admiral Gu Wengen. During Roughead's visit the press reported, via a leak, that a PLAN *Song*-class diesel-electric submarine had in October shadowed and then surfaced within five miles of the US aircraft carrier *Kitty Hawk* in waters near Japan. Roughead used his meetings to express concern about the vigour with which China was pursuing submarine capabilities and highlighted the need for closer communication when significant military assets were in close proximity. Exchanges continued into January 2007 with the visit to Pacific Command in Honolulu, the West Point military academy and Washington of General Ge Zhengfeng, deputy chief of the General Staff of the PLA.

By this time, however, the tone of the military-to-military relationship had reverted to its traditional, problematic form. In December, Beijing published a white paper on China's National Defence in 2006 – a biannual document intended to answer the charge that transparency in Chinese military affairs is lacking, and an opportunity to make pointed comments about the defence policies of other powers. While noting that 'China's overall security environment remains sound', it complained that the United States is 'accelerating its realignment of military deployment to enhance its military capability in the Asia-Pacific region'. America and Japan, it continued, 'are strengthening their military alliance in pursuit of operational integration', while Japan now sought to 'revise its constitution and exercise collective self-defence'. Its military posture was becoming 'more external-oriented'. While the more vigorous military threats issued against Taiwan's independence leanings were absent from this iteration of the white paper, Washington was cautioned to cease arms transfers or other forms of military assistance to Taiwan, and to uphold the 'one China' policy. The white paper observed that 'a number of countries have stirred up a racket about a "China threat", and intensified their preventive strategy against China and strove to hold its progress in check'. Observers generally gave credit to China for including in this report more detail and data than in previous white papers, where it had been almost entirely absent. Particularly noted, although not with much sense of reassurance, were some of the more forward-leaning aspirations set out for the various service arms of the PLA: the navy should possess reach outside of China's nearest coastal waters; nuclear and conventional rocket forces needed to expand their range and sophistication; the air force should effect a shift from a defence role to combining offensive and defensive elements in its posture. Shortly after publication of the report, Hu Jintao, in his capacity as chairman of the Central Committee, donned his military tunic to argue in a speech that China 'should make sound military preparations for military struggles and ensure that the forces can effectively carry out missions at any time'.

More significant than these developments to US–China military relations, however, was the successful testing by China on 11 January of a direct-ascent anti-satellite (ASAT) missile, which was not notified in advance or subsequently made public by China until Washington issued a statement of complaint on 18 January. The US military has designated the weapon system the SC-19, and has assessed it as an interceptor mounted on a solid-fuelled medium-range missile fired from a mobile launcher. The target of the test was an obsolete Chinese weather satellite in a 760km low Earth orbit, estimated to have disintegrated into 1,600 debris fragments upon impact with the kinetic kill vehicle. American criticism focused on the lack of Chinese disclosure. Attention was drawn to the threat China might now pose to space-based communication assets on which America's high-technology armed forces increasingly depend. The scattering of a new circle of debris was, moreover, attacked as putting at risk 'the assets of all space faring nations' and as posing dangers to human space flight.

In view of the sharp and surprised international response to the test, which seemed to undo much of the efforts of Chinese diplomats in recent years to project a non-threatening image, debate soon began to focus on how Beijing's usually more surefooted leadership could have allowed this set of circumstances to develop. No conclusive answer has been found. One line of thought holds that there may have been an alarming lack of coordination and consultation between China's civil and military hierarchies, holding out the possibility of future 'freelancing' by the PLA, and suggesting inadequate capacity in China for crisis-management in any future military-related contingencies over Taiwan.

According to another strand of interpretation, the civilian leadership was fully informed and approved of efforts to develop and test this new capability, but had merely underestimated the international reaction. It has also been suggested that the test was part of a strategy to force American receptivity to Chinese efforts to engage Washington on a treaty or protocol that would prevent the militarisation of space, about which China has in the past voiced concern. China's Foreign Ministry in fact took up this theme in February. But some US military analysts noted that the most recent Chinese defence white paper had, perhaps with some premeditation, omitted customary protestations on this point, suggesting China is now perhaps set on another course.

In the months that followed, fiftul bilateral defence diplomacy continued. During the March 2007 session of the annual National People's Congress, Beijing announced that defence spending would rise by 17.8% this year to $44.94 billion. This drew customary American accusations of understatement and prompted calls for greater explanation of the purposes to which funds were being put. The equally customary Chinese reply was that this defence budget was miniscule in comparison to US outlays, that most of the increase was allocated to salary increases for service personnel and other general overhead costs – and that, in any case, the United States rather than China was embroiled in foreign wars. Issues of transparency were rehearsed later in March, when General Pace made his first visit to China for discussions with his counterpart General Liang, as well as Defence Minister Cao Gangchuan and General Guo. These meetings did not appear to result in any notable policy initiatives. Then, in May, Admiral Timothy Keating, the newly appointed commander of the US Pacific Command, led a US military delegation to Beijing for meetings with members of the Central Military Commission before travelling to view various military facilities and institutions in Nanjing, Chongqing and Nanchang.

May 2007 also saw the publication of the Pentagon's congressionally mandated Annual Report to Congress on the Military Power of the People's Republic of China. The ASAT test and increases in Chinese defence spending received prominent and critical attention, but many other issues disconcerted the Department of Defense. In briefings, these developments were couched in terms of 'surprise' – indicating puzzlement at Chinese intentions and hinting at the increasing success and deliberation with which China appeared to be concealing its energetic military programmes. Missile forces were to the fore. It noted that China had deployed 'roughly 900' short-range ballistic missiles opposite Taiwan. Among China's longer-range forces, the report said a road-mobile, solid-fuelled DF-31 intercontinental ballistic missile would soon achieve operational status, if it had not done so already, while a variant with longer range, the DF-31a, would 'reach initial operational capability in 2007'. The efforts exerted on these fronts triggered speculation about the extent to which China may be contemplating adjustments to nuclear doctrine, currently fixed to a 'no first use' policy, in order to strengthen deterrence through doctrinal ambiguity and flexibility as well as more survivable capabilities that provide greater second-strike credibility. In this regard, the reported development of five new Type 094 *Jin*-class nuclear-powered submarines, to be fitted with a new JL-2 submarine-launched nuclear-capable ballistic missile, was also regarded as important. Also in the naval realm, the report noted deliveries to China by Russia of two *Sovremennyy* II-class guided-missile destroyers at the end of 2006, as well as two *Kilo*-class submarines, bringing China's holding to eight. Amongst surface vessels, China was reported to have begun production of its first guided-missile frigate, the *Jiangkai* II. These and other procurement activities and alterations in deployments were seen as part of an emphasis on anti-access and denial strategies directed at US and Japanese forces in respect of China's maritime periphery.

Sino-American defence diplomacy was practised at senior levels in a more public setting during the sixth annual IISS Asia Security Summit, The Shangri-La Dialogue, held on 1–3 June in Singapore. Both delegations appeared in conciliatory mood. US Secretary of Defense Robert Gates, while rehearsing some of the findings of the Pentagon's study, also conveyed grounds for optimism about the bilateral relationship, and was prepared to say that military-to-military talks had inherent value even if they produced little of concrete substance in the short term. They would contribute to greater confidence and understanding. Similarly, Lieutenant-General Zhang Qinsheng, Deputy Chief of the General Staff of the PLA, and the most senior Chinese officer to have participated in The Shangri-La Dialogue to date, did not refrain from a sharp rebuke of US commentary on Chinese defence policy, but he also used the occasion to indicate that he hoped to reach agreement on the establishment of a military hotline when he travelled to Washington in September 2007 for the Ninth US–China Defense Consultative Talks. While this was widely welcomed as of strong symbolic worth, it is not yet clear whether such a hotline would actually facilitate greater connectivity between the two countries' decision-making structures.

Watching Taiwan

In view of the arduous complexities of the Sino-American relationship, both sides will have been somewhat relieved by the absence of any particularly acute crises over developments in Taiwan in the last 12 months. Moreover, to the extent that China has recently been somewhat unsettled by gathering political uncertainties surrounding the island's electoral cycle, featuring legislative elections in December 2007 and presidential polls in March 2008, it implicitly looks to Washington to act on Taipei as a calming and restraining force. For its own part, meanwhile, it seems unlikely that Washington will lament the passing of the two-term administration of Taiwanese President Chen Shui-bian of the Democratic

Progressive Party (DPP), whose strong pro-independence instincts and penchant for slippery brinkmanship it found as irritating as Beijing found them alarming.

Beijing will have taken satisfaction in the financial scandals which have enveloped Chen and his wife since spring 2006, chronically disorganising the business of the government and triggering large protests calling for Chen's resignation. These developments seemed certain to confirm the revival in the fortunes of the opposition Kuomintang (KMT), and smooth the way to the presidency for its widely popular leader, former Taipei mayor Ma Ying-jeou. But the path has been unexpectedly bumpy. Although stripped of credibility and political capital, Chen survived three efforts, beginning in June 2006 in the Legislative Yuan, to unseat him through a recall motion. Moreover, with his back against the wall, and looking to establish a political legacy, he began to advance the more radical components of his campaign to secure a distinct international identity for Taiwan. Having at the start of his tenure formulated a 'Four Noes' policy intended to reassure both China and the United States – under which, provided China had no intention of using force against Taiwan, he would not declare independence, change the island's formal designation, alter the constitution in regard of sovereignty questions or prepare referendums on questions of independence or reunification – Chen now began to propound a 'Four Wants' policy. He argued that the island wanted independence, 'rectification' of its official name, a new constitution and more 'development'. Chen also ruminated on the merits of a 'Second Republic' constitution, including a redefinition of national territorial boundaries. In May 2007, he announced that the island would in September, for the first time, apply to join the UN as a full member under the designation 'Taiwan' rather than the Republic of China. All of these initiatives teetered on the brink of Beijing's red lines.

A parallel development which gave Chen some breathing room was the partial fall from political grace of Ma Ying-jeou, whose reputation for probity was seriously challenged by embezzlement charges, which led to his resignation as chairman of the KMT in February 2007. His trial began in April and a verdict was expected by the end of the year. Yet Ma, rejecting the allegations, retained his political prominence among opposition forces and secured the KMT's nomination for the presidency in May. The selection process for the DPP presidential candidate, meanwhile, eventually produced a strong challenger to Ma. Former Prime Minister Frank Hsieh, who had recommended himself not least by making deep inroads into the KMT stronghold of Taipei as a candidate in the December 2006 mayoral election there, made a strong showing in the first round of DPP primaries, so that the other three candidates – the pro-independence firebrand Vice President Annette Lu, then-Prime Minister Su Tseng-chang and DPP Chairman Yu Shyi-kun – all effectively conceded defeat. For Beijing there might have been worse outcomes: Hsieh has repeatedly urged better, but not supplicant, relations with Beijing. Both he and Ma would be inclined to develop more stable and predictable interactions with the mainland. The December 2007 legislative elections will be a key barometer of the candidates' prospective fortunes, with the added possibility that a verdict against Ma by the end of the year might throw the KMT campaign into considerable disarray. Under these uncertain circumstances, Beijing is likely to continue to exercise its new-found caution and avoid the temptation to intervene directly in Taiwanese politics for fear of provoking a backlash. The same will not be true in the wider diplomatic context. Here, the contest for recognition between China and Taiwan has continued in its familiar, bad-tempered way, by what might be thought of as an auction in which substantial largesse is on offer. In the latest round, Chad in August 2006 decided to recognise China in preference to Taiwan, which then succeeded in inducing the Caribbean island of St Lucia to recognise it in May 2007. The following month, however, Costa Rica switched its diplomatic recognition to China. This 'dollar diplomacy' is now a fixture among the smaller states of Latin America, Africa and the South Pacific.

Setback and breakthrough in Northeast Asia

If the ultimate likely implications of recent developments in Taiwan are still ambiguous, they are clearer in regard to North Korea's nuclear activities. Events of the past year were a major setback for Beijing in a theatre of diplomatic action where it had become used to acclaim for its interlocutory skill with both Pyongyang and Washington. In retrospect, the high-water mark of China's diplomatic role was the Joint Statement of 19 September 2005, reached at its urging by members of the Six-Party Talks process (North Korea, the United States, China, South Korea, Japan and Russia). It was only then that, after three years of talks, the general objective – the denuclearisation of the Korean Peninsula – were formally established and some specific commitments were made. Through the principle of reciprocal (albeit poorly defined) steps, North Korea pledged to return to the Nuclear Non-Proliferation Treaty and abandon all nuclear weapons and programmes. The United States declared that it had no intention to attack North Korea. The provision to Pyongyang of a light-water reactor for power generation would be an eventual matter for discussion. Washington and Pyongyang would work towards normalising their relationship, and a peace regime for the peninsula would be investigated. But the Joint Statement which Beijing had pressed so hard for left many issues – such as the status of North Korea's clandestine uranium-enrichment programme – unaddressed. Questions about an implementation mechanism and a sequence of further steps were unanswered. Critics cited this statement as evidence of Beijing's preference for smoothing over difficult issues that it did not wish to see forced at the cost of greater friction; its main objective was to preserve a vague regional stability that was to be achieved by not confronting North Korea, and it hoped that even episodic engagement among the six parties would help to contain such proliferation risks as existed. These critics were unsurprised when the diplomatic process began to unravel almost immediately upon publication of the statement, as the various parties to it, and especially the United States and North Korea, described their opposing interpretations of the general text. From this point onwards, Beijing lost the diplomatic initiative and became more reactive. There was also a definite, if reluctant, estrangement from Pyongyang.

The imposition of punitive financial measures on Pyongyang by US Treasury authorities in autumn 2005 in response to North Korean money laundering, a prime result of which was the freezing of some $25 million in North Korean accounts held at Banco Delta Asia in Macao, confirmed this trend. Beijing, along with Seoul, opposed the measures on grounds of their predictably prejudicial impact on the Six-Party Talks, which stalled as North Korea demanded the repeal of the measures as a precondition for the resumption of dialogue. With Washington as yet unable to disentangle the requirement under US law to act against financial improprieties where they are identified, and North Korea feeling the effects of international financial isolation, tensions mounted. The series of tests of short-, medium- and long-range missiles carried out by North Korea on 5 July 2006 were intended to place direct pressure on the United States in this regard, as well as to mobilise indirect pressure from Chinese and South Korean quarters presumed to be sympathetic. In fact China, having urged North Korea against the impending tests, demonstrated irritation and exasperation. Although it worked with Russia in the UN Security Council to dilute a draft censure resolution introduced by Japan, it ultimately voted in support of UNSCR 1965. This went against the grain of China's traditional stated preference for avoiding referral of North Korea to the Security Council, and it introduced a marked chill into relations between Beijing and Pyongyang. Perceiving itself strategically more hemmed in and needing to visibly strengthen a posture of deterrence, Pyongyang conducted a nuclear test on 9 October. Beijing received a cursory 20-minute notification of the test, leaving it to scramble to inform the United States and others of what was about to take place. These circumstances made it both necessary and possible for Beijing to support a second resolution, UNSCR 1718, on 14 October to sanction North Korea. But Beijing was palpably relieved when adjustments in the US position allowed for bilateral exchanges between Washington and Pyongyang, leading to encounters later in October and again in January 2007 that paved the way and set an agenda for a resumption of the Six-Party Talks in February.

On 13 February the parties reached a multi-phased agreement that in its initial stages would principally involve the verified shutting down of North Korea's nuclear reactor at Yongbyon and the provision to Pyongyang of 50,000 tonnes of heavy fuel oil, and in the latter stages result in the 'disabling' of nuclear facilities and a full declaration on activities, including weapons programmes, by North Korea in exchange for 950,000 tonnes of heavy fuel oil. The United States, in another significant adjustment to policy, also took steps to ensure that North Korea would have access to funds deposited with Banco Delta Asia. North Korean concerns about whether these arrangements would end its de facto exclusion from the wider international financial system held up implementation of the agreement, although by June it appeared that a satisfactory formula had been developed. From Beijing's perspective, the primary benefit of the 13 February agreement – in effect the previously lacking implementation mechanism for the September 2005 Joint Statement – is that it has, at least for the time being, prevented a major escalation of tensions, provided an agreed basis for discussion, and structured incentives that in theory give Pyongyang good reason to follow through on its commitments. Still, Beijing is all too aware of the complications which lie ahead. Moving beyond the first phase is likely to involve tortuous negotiation that will be subject to the constant risk of breakdown. And there remains the central question of whether Pyongyang really wishes to deprive itself of its primary strategic asset. The most convincing answer is that it does not. If this is more definitely established at some future point, parties to the 13 February agreement will be forced to decide whether to adjust their aims and set their sights on the limitation of Pyongyang's nuclear programme, or to adhere to present objectives and pursue them even at the cost of increasing tension. Beijing is unlikely to opt for the latter course.

A breakthrough in China's regional diplomacy over the last year partially compensated for the reversal suffered with North Korea. Relations with Beijing's largest neighbour, Japan, were put onto a reasonably civil footing after years in which bilateral high-level summitry and strategic dialogue had, for all intents and purposes, dried up. Even as economic relations widened and deepened, the two countries had settled into sullen and bitter attitudes. Then-Japanese Prime Minister Junichiro Koizumi's determination, despite pointed Chinese (and South Korean) protests, to persist in visiting the Yasukuni shrine, which holds the remains of Japanese Class-A war criminals among others, was the most immediate focus of a quarrel rooted in historical antagonism, dishonesty and contemporary suspicion. On occasion, Beijing has found it politically expedient to burnish its nationalist credentials at home by playing upon anti-Japanese sentiment. The ugly form which this has taken in recent years, from time to time getting out of hand and resulting in riots and harassment of Japanese in China, is not in keeping with the calming and reassuring messages at the centre of Chinese diplomacy. However, officials of both powers now speak publicly of efforts to 'melt the ice'. Such steps were made possible by Shinzo Abe's succession to the Japanese premiership on 25 September 2006. Caught on the one hand between China's long-standing demand that prime-ministerial visits to the Yasukuni shrine must be permanently ruled out before talks could resume, and on the other by domestic conservative opinion cautioning against 'submission' to China on this point, Abe had developed a position of studied ambiguity. This provided Beijing with just enough assurance that there would be nothing in Abe's actions that would cause China immediate embarrassment. It therefore proved possible for Abe to travel to Beijing reasonably soon after his appointment as prime minister for his first foreign visit. On 8–9 October, he held meetings with Hu Jintao and Wen Jiabao. North Korea's nuclear test injected a good deal of substance into what had been intended as a mainly ceremonial, carefully orchestrated re-acquaintance. The joint press statement at the conclusion of the summit committed the two powers to work together towards a resolution of the nuclear issue, but also to engage each other on wider bilateral security questions, such as seemingly intractable territorial disputes over resource-rich portions of the East China Sea and over the Diaoyu/Senkaku islands. The document referred to a 'solemn responsibility' to manage a relationship that was fundamental to their interests and so to contribute to regional stability. Wen travelled to Tokyo for meetings on 11–13 April, and the two sides indicated that they wished to build a 'mutually beneficial relationship based on common strategic interests'.

Much indeed remained to be discussed. In the security field alone there was a distinct uneasiness on each side about the defence posture of the other. China worried about a possible operational integration of US and Japanese forces, and saw the elevation of the Japan Self Defense Agency to a full cabinet-level Defence Ministry as signalling a more forward-leaning defence identity for Japan. It was unsettled by Abe's recent engagement of NATO and his advocacy of constitutional reforms that would remove the bar on practising collective self-defence. And China continued to offer resistance to Japan's bid for permanent membership of the UN Security Council. Tokyo, meanwhile, in its most recent defence white paper again raised concerns about Chinese military modernisation efforts and Chinese air and maritime reconnaissance activities intruding into or in the vicinity of its airspace and waters. It was encouraging, therefore, that it proved possible in late November 2006 to reactivate defence exchanges at vice-minister level for the first time in 20 months, with the aim of establishing dialogue at cabinet level; and that historic joint naval exercises and port calls were planned for later in 2007. These marked tentative but important steps in establishing a broader framework for communication, without which the security architecture of Asia would be structurally flawed and certainly more inclined toward attrition and conflict.

Other big powers

While mending fences with Japan, China in the last year also worked with Russia to add momentum and content to their vaunted 'strategic partnership'.

Indeed, 2006 was declared the 'Year of Russia' in China, albeit without evident public enthusiasm. Both countries at least had cause to take satisfaction from the endurance of a totemic strategic accomplishment. The Shanghai Co-operation Organisation (SCO) celebrated its fifth anniversary in June 2006 with a summit in its eponymous city. The organisation has overcome doubts about its relevance. These were voiced particularly after 11 September 2001, when the Sino-Russian construct appeared set to be overwhelmed and sidelined by the rapid development of American defence and security relationships in Central Asia. The SCO now addresses itself to a wide field of security and economic issues and, including countries such as India and Iran who have been admitted as observers, is the principal multilateral mechanism linking Central Asia to East, South and Southwest Asia. Lacking in institutional strength, much of its direction must be provided by Moscow and Beijing. It has become clear, however, that Russia and China are increasingly tugging the SCO in different directions. For both, the SCO is a forum in which they compete in a reasonably civil way for regional influence: China seeks to establish a stronger economic identity for the grouping, which would give it increased diplomatic clout; while Russia would stand to gain status and initiative from an emphasis on security policy. Neither side wishes to force the issue, however, so the SCO will likely continue to evolve in fits and starts.

More concerted steps were taken over the last year to outline a bilateral foreign-policy agenda. Having met in Shanghai in June 2006 and then again at the St Petersburg meeting of the G8 in July, Hu Jintao and Russian President Vladimir Putin met for a third time in Moscow on 26–28 March 2007 during a state visit by Hu. A joint statement committed the two powers to strengthening cooperation in the UN, where both are permanent members of the Security Council. Common, basic positions were set out on the questions of Iraq, the Arab–Israeli dispute, Afghanistan, Asian regional security, the SCO, North Korea and Iran. Yet while the two sides maintained in their practical diplomacy a good degree of coordination on many of these points, Beijing seemed to have become uneasy about the direction of Russia's relations with the United States and the European Union – where Moscow appeared to be set on diplomatic confrontation over such matters as the prospective deployment of missile-defence radars and interceptors in eastern Europe and the question of independence for Kosovo. Beijing may sympathise with many of Moscow's grievances, but is alarmed by the revanchist rhetoric in which they are now commonly draped. China fears that, as the disagreements deepen, it may be boxed into narrower policy positions of which it does not inherently approve – but would be expected to observe in public for the sake of lending meaning to the Sino-Russian strategic partnership.

China's relations with India continued to evolve in a more sedate manner. The high-point was the four-day visit to India by Hu Jintao in late November

2006, the first by a Chinese head of state in ten years. It was a measure of the greater regard now being paid by Beijing to India as that country's economic and political-military emergence gathers pace. Chinese strategic objectives with regard to India are fairly transparent. Beijing wishes to detach India from any putative constellation of democracies in Asia, involving the United States, Japan, South Korea and Australia, who might try to project a hedge against China or contain it. This concern is probably overdone: India seems unlikely, in view of the independence it has tended to demonstrate in foreign and security policy, to allow itself to be imprisoned by a construct of this kind. From Beijing's perspective, however, a more intimate engagement was also warranted by the importance of the nuclear and conventional military dynamic between China and India. The nuclear posture of each is directly informed by that of the other (India cited China's strategic modernisation as a spur to the nuclear test carried out in 1998), just as each country looms large in the planning that underpins respective conventional military modernisation efforts. Meetings in Beijing between Chinese Defence Minister Cao Gangchuan and then Indian Defence Minister Pranab Mukherjee in May 2006 laid the basis for greater military-to-military contact, and the two capitals in May 2007 advanced discussions on the aim of holding joint land exercises to build upon naval exercises already carried out.

The extent to which India's new foreign-policy extroversion has caused it to become an emerging diplomatic player in Southeast Asia and the Persian Gulf, both regions China considers vital to its interests, gives Beijing further incentive to talk to Delhi. One of the requirements of this engagement has been the effective 'de-hyphenation' of Beijing's diplomacy towards India and Pakistan: support for Islamabad is now less centrally motivated by the desire to provide a preoccupation for India, but instead is more informed by Pakistan's importance to the strategic theatres of Central and Southwest Asia, and by its ability to provide China, through port facilities, access to the Indian Ocean and Persian Gulf. For India, this de-hyphenation is to be encouraged, since it provides relief from strategic claustrophobia. Better relations with Beijing are also a prerequisite to the management and eventual resolution of the substantial territorial disputes that remain between them: China's claim to the state of Arunachal Pradesh; and India's claim to 38,000km² of Kashmir held by China. These matters are now the subject of regular meetings of special representatives, the most recent round of which was held in April 2007 between Indian National Security Adviser M.K. Narayanan and Chinese Executive Vice Foreign Minister Dai Bingguo. There are limits to how far along the road these and other interactions will travel: the entrenched mutual suspicion that pervades respective national-security establishments, Chinese resistance to India's aspirations to join the UN Security Council as a permanent member, and Beijing's sense that India's improving ties to the United States and Japan are intended to give it greater strategic depth against China are among the larger potholes to be negotiated.

Engaging ASEAN

In a largely process-driven engagement intended to offer reassurance about the meaning of China's rise, Beijing publicly subscribes to ASEAN's principle of non-interference in internal affairs. It has worked to resolve or put into abeyance maritime territorial disputes, demonstrated its increasing comfort with various ASEAN-driven multilateral processes and worked to institute new ones. It has reinforced such exchanges with intensive bilateral contacts and mobilised its economic appeal as the basis for stronger political relations and, increasingly, security ties. The last year provided further evidence of the intensity of China–ASEAN interactions.

The ASEAN Regional Forum meeting in Kuala Lumpur in July 2006 brought Wen Jiabao into extensive dialogues with regional counterparts. In late October, Wen hosted a summit in the Chinese city of Nanning to mark the 15th anniversary of ASEAN–China dialogue, using the occasion to urge not only further progress towards a China–ASEAN Free Trade Area, but also the enhancement of a security dialogue touching on issues ranging from counter-terrorism and transnational crime to non-traditional security challenges such as infectious disease. The Asia Pacific Economic Cooperation summit in November 2006, followed by the January 2007 ASEAN+3 meeting and East Asian Summit in Cebu, Philippines, were also part of an exhausting regional diplomatic calendar. In between there were a series of high-level bilateral exchanges, exemplified by Hu Jintao's state visits to Vietnam and Laos in November.

Aspects of China's Southeast Asian diplomacy also continued to attract controversy from within and outside the region. The acquiescent response of much of the international community to the Thai military coup of September 2006 meant that China's description of it as a purely internal affair did not provoke particular criticism or comment. Sino-Thai relations have matured significantly in both economic and security terms: Thailand is a key economic outlet for China's southwestern provinces, while its status as a major non-NATO ally of the United States has not prevented it from exploring better defence ties with China, from whom it has purchased weapons systems in the past. Thaksin Shinawatra's removal as prime minister might have been privately regretted by Beijing: it was under his stewardship that recent progress was made, and Beijing was aware that his toppling might yet produce more instability. But China will now be keen to engage the military-led government on a pragmatic basis.

Pragmatism of a more controversial sort continued to be in evidence in Beijing's dealings with Myanmar. Many in ASEAN looked on with disappointment as Beijing failed to respond to urgings that it use its influence to encourage

economic and political reforms. Disappointment in ASEAN was matched by irritation in other quarters, especially the United States and Europe. In September
2006, China successfully led efforts to frustrate a US-sponsored UN resolution
to censure and mandate action against the Myanmar junta in light of its repres-
siveness. China objected on the grounds that internal developments in Myanmar
could not be construed as of relevance to international security and thus ought
not to come before the Security Council. China–Myanmar relations are unsen-
timental and transactional. Beijing sensed that failure to provide Yangon with
diplomatic protection might prejudice the aim of gaining access through
Myanmar to the Indian Ocean (bypassing the possible choke-point of the Strait
of Malacca) and might push Yangon into the open arms of Delhi, which has been
cultivating the junta for some time.

Regional entanglements

Over the last year China found itself drawn more closely into the affairs of a
number of other regions – partly by active choice, and partly by the force of
events which overwhelmed its traditional reticence. The most glaring example
of the latter was China's increasing involvement in international diplomatic
efforts to address concerns about Iran's nuclear activities, which despite Tehran's
protestations are widely presumed to be directed towards the development of a
weapons capability. Beijing's initial policy line was informed by scepticism about
the immediacy of the problem and the desirability of confronting Iran through
the UN Security Council. Beijing believed that Security Council action might
simply antagonise Tehran, raise the stakes of the confrontation and prejudice any
other, more flexible diplomatic approaches that might be undertaken outside the
glare of the UN spotlight. It also remembered how the Security Council process
towards Iraq before 2003 had appeared in its later stages to acquire a mechanis-
tic momentum of its own, and was then taken in pro-war circles as conferring
a legal basis for the military action the United States and Britain were to take.
Narrower interests, too, were in play for Beijing, which has sought to enhance its
access to Iranian supplies of energy that might be jeopardised by any sanctions
regime intended to pressure Tehran. Over the last year, China National Offshore
Oil Company and China National Petroleum Corporation have engaged Tehran
on the question of further investments in the South Pars and North Pars gas
fields.

In a significant adjustment in Chinese policy, Beijing lent its weight to Security
Council efforts to arrive at a suspension in Iranian uranium enrichment to pave
the way for a wider negotiated solution. Beijing provided support to UNSCR
1696 of 31 July 2006, having first agreed with Russia that no reference would
be made to the possibility of action under Article 42 of Chapter VII of the UN
Charter, relating to military force. The passage of half a year and the failure of

various diplomatic overtures to Tehran caused Beijing to back UNSCR 1737 on 29 December 2006, which set a deadline of 60 days for Tehran to comply with the call for a suspension; and, this having produced no notable effect, to back UNSCR 1747 of 24 March 2007.

China's hand was clearly forced by Iranian intransigence, which also removed some of the ambiguity about Tehran's ultimate intentions regarding a nuclear-weapons capability. Beijing saw the risk of proliferation in the Middle East, and the possibility of further instability, in starker terms. In particular it had to take account of the sensibilities of various regional powers it has attempted to engage on mainly economic and energy-related but also political fronts. Beijing sensed that there would be risks in the pursuit of a policy of detachment from – or resistance to – the line being adopted by the United States and the E3 of Britain, France and Germany, with variable contributions from Russia. Such an approach might be construed as accommodative to Iranian nuclear aspirations; and the more progress Tehran made, the more blame would attach to Beijing. The consequences of an Iranian nuclear-weapons capability would not be parochial. It would increase the strategic pain that Tehran might feel capable of inflicting on the United States in Iraq without fear of ultimate retaliation. It would lend Tehran greater confidence in seeking to establish its strategic pre-eminence in the Middle East in a way that would antagonise and draw a reply from Saudi Arabia, with which Beijing is seeking to develop a strategic energy relationship. The other members of the Gulf Co-operation Council, many of which are also important to Chinese energy requirements or have begun to make large investments in the Chinese economy, will also continue to urge Beijing to play a strong role in halting an Iranian nuclear programme that is acting as spur to closer Gulf defence links to the United States. Nuclear capability would also embolden Iran in respect of any intentions it has to further harass Israel through its support of Hizbullah in Lebanon. This possibility, and the apocalyptic terms in which Iranian President Mahmoud Ahmadinejad has voiced his antagonism towards Israel, would have been rehearsed at length during Israeli Prime Minister Ehud Olmert's 11 January 2007 meeting in Beijing with his counterpart Wen Jiabao. Related to this was Beijing's long-standing desire to obtain Israeli defence technology to reduce its dependence on Russian transfers that often stop short of the most sophisticated items. Other regional powers such as Egypt and Turkey that China would like to have closer ties with will also be monitoring China's Iran policy with care.

All of these considerations will continue to press upon China in holding the current collective Security Council line, but this will not be perpetually sustainable in the absence of Iranian compliance. The longer Iran holds out, the greater will be the pressure on the P5 and others to formulate alternative, more coercive approaches. In the first instance this would include a hardening of economic and political sanctions, but if Iran showed signs of being willing to absorb the resulting pain the question of military action to destroy or significantly retard its nuclear programme would loom more insistently. Beijing would be willing to contemplate further sanctions, but would offer resistance to military action for fear that its wider consequences – in particular the probability that a cycle of retaliation and counter-retaliation would lead to a general war – could not be contained. Since the United States and its allies seem to recognise these dangers too, the more likely question for China will be whether it would be willing to participate actively in containment of Iran. This is not inconceivable, though it would not subscribe to such a policy by name.

Somewhat less arduous dilemmas confront China in other regions. Chinese diplomacy towards Africa, powered by growing energy and natural-resource requirements and smoothed by offers of trade, aid and infrastructural support that come without the conditionalities advanced by the West, has attained a particular intensity. A January 2006 white paper on China's African policy laid down principles for Chinese–African exchanges, which, it said, are to be grounded in 'sincerity, friendship and equality'; 'mutual benefit, reciprocity and common prosperity'; 'mutual support and close coordination'; and 'learning from each other and seeking common development'. It set out, too, the mechanism through which these objectives were to be furthered: high-level visits, exchanges between legislatures, political parties and local government; the establishment of consultation mechanisms; and 'cooperation in international affairs'. The document mainly described forms of economic interaction to be encouraged, but also stated a strong interest in building up security ties. Military exchanges would be encouraged and China would assist in training defence forces. China would support the African Union and others in conflict resolution and peacekeeping operations. It would provide help to judicial and law-enforcement agencies, and assist in tackling transnational crime.

Many of these various aspirations were rehearsed at the November 2006 meeting in Beijing of the Forum on China–Africa Cooperation (FOCAC), to which 48 of 53 African countries sent senior delegations. In May 2007 Shanghai was the venue for the first meeting outside the African continent of the African Development Bank. China used the occasion to present itself as Africa's champion on the world stage, calling for Europe and America to provide better market access to it, and contrasting this with China's willingness to provide increasing quantities of aid and debt relief. During the meeting, plans were finalised for the creation of a $5bn China–Africa Development Fund, supplementing the increasing presence on the continent of China ExIm, the trade finance bank that is estimated to have advanced over $7bn in loans to Africa in the last three years alone – thereby reportedly raising concerns among the World Bank and International Monetary Fund about a fresh accumulation of foreign debt in

Africa. In addition to working within these multilateral settings, China's bilateral diplomacy has proved highly energetic. Examples in the last year included Hu Jintao's third visit to Africa in three years, taking in South Africa, Sudan, Cameroon, Liberia, Zambia, Namibia, Mozambique and the Seychelles in a single swoop in January 2007.

Yet the last year also demonstrated that closer contacts require more careful stewardship of relations and balancing of objectives, and that there is a risk of a backlash to China's expanding presence in Africa. In particular, it became apparent to China that its close ties to Sudan, with which it has developed strong oil interests and which it has shielded from international sanctions intended to force Khartoum to bring an end to killings in the Darfur region, is not only objectionable to America and Europe but to large swathes of Africa as well. The habit of offering diplomatic protection to a government complicit in the killing of black Africans by Arab-Sudanese militias, and a track record of selling arms to that government, are clearly not aligned with the objective of strengthening ties to West African and sub-Saharan states. A combination of highly public Western pressure and private African irritation seem to have forced a change in approach. In May 2007, China appointed Liu Guijin its special envoy to Africa, with a particular remit to focus on the crisis in Darfur. That same month, Beijing announced that it would deploy around 300 military engineers to support the beleaguered African Union peacekeeping mission in Darfur, and it began efforts to encourage Khartoum to accept a UN-mandated peacekeeping force of 20,000 troops.

External criticism also appeared to prompt China to begin to rethink the value of the relationship it has assiduously built up with Zimbabwe, despite the political repression practiced by President Robert Mugabe. Observers noted Hu's failure to visit Zimbabwe on his most recent tour of the continent, perhaps embarrassed by Mugabe's tendency to advertise his contacts with China as a success of his 'Look East' policy of turning his back on Western critics. Equally, Beijing might have concluded that it had little to gain from investing political capital in a government which, while brutally resilient, seemed to have a shortening life expectancy. Other problems presented themselves to China in Zambia, where the September 2006 presidential election campaign was notable for the extent to which Michael Sata, leader of the opposition Patriotic Front, incorporated anti-China sentiments in his challenge to President Levy Mwanawasa. Sata alleged that Mwanawasa was allowing Chinese companies in Zambia to behave in exploitative ways, paying low wages and having little regard to health and safety issues. The risk of entanglement in African conflicts was highlighted by the April 2007 killing of nine Chinese energy workers by the separatist Ogaden Liberation Front in the Ogaden region of Ethiopia that borders Somalia. Such incidents and reactions can be expected to become more common as Chinese companies fan out across the continent, requiring China to familiarise itself better with local conditions and develop astute political as well as economic strategies.

The same principle is likely to apply to China's contacts with Latin America, which, while busy, are of a lower order of magnitude. Indeed, while China has a strong and continuing incentive to diversify its sources of supply of energy and minerals, and to fashion political relationships to permit and facilitate this, many observers argue that Latin America is unlikely to approach the importance of the Middle East and Africa in this regard – and that political relations will be limited and circumscribed to a commensurate degree. An awareness of American sensitivity to China's closer involvement in the affairs of the region will also play a part. Nevertheless, the last year was marked by tentative efforts to develop greater political-military links, as Chinese Defence Minister Cao Gangchuan travelled to the region in May 2007 to hold meetings in Argentina, Chile and Cuba, having in April received the commander in chief of the Bolivian Army, Wilfredo Vargas, in Beijing. China's ties to Venezuela remained both its strongest and weakest suit in the region. The strength derived from the progress made in boosting energy cooperation: in August 2006, Beijing and Caracas announced the creation of a $6bn energy fund to finance exploration and production in the Orinoco basin and help construct three heavy-oil refineries in China, with the aim of lifting Venezuelan oil exports from 150,000 to 800,000 barrels a day. The weakness, however, derived from the diplomatic costs of association with the idiosyncratic and extravagantly anti-American Venezuelan president, Hugo Chávez, who seems to harbour wider international ambitions than to cause mere irritation to the United States. It remains to be seen whether the kind of policy adjustment China has practiced with regard to Sudan and Zimbabwe might in time also be replicated in this context.

Efforts to conceive frameworks and principles for China's dealings with developing regions were matched in the last year by significant initiatives to do the same in Europe. At the 9th EU–China Summit in Helsinki in September 2006, the two sides announced plans to begin negotiation of a Partnership and Cooperation Agreement that would update a much narrower document produced in 1985. It would reflect the EU's own evolution and expansion since then, more fully capturing the wide extent of present Sino-European relations and setting out an agenda for future action. As part of this process, a Communication from the [European] Commission to the Council and European Parliament was issued in October 2006. Subtitled 'EU–China: closer partners, growing responsibilities', it was notable for the expectations and demands the EU now seems keen to place on China, and for its willingness to put the principle of reciprocity at the centre of the relationship. The document's focus on security as well as trade issues, meanwhile, bore witness to the gradual evolution in European thinking on China. It stressed that the EU has a strong interest in developing good relations with all of Asia's major powers and urged an improvement in Sino-Japanese ties. The EU would take 'an active interest' in the cross-Strait dispute and would maintain strong trade links with Taiwan. It noted 'increasing concern' about Chinese military expenditure and called for improvement in EU analytical capacity towards China's armed forces. It offered China no real hope in the short term of a repeal of the EU arms embargo against the PLA. All of this demonstrated that the hopes voiced by some in China and Europe in the wake of the bitter transatlantic divisions over Iraq for a true strategic alignment between Brussels and Beijing were over-optimistic. European policy has instead become a variant of the 'responsible stakeholder' concept originating from the United States, and the alignment thus runs in a direction more to the opposite of the one previously imagined.

Olympian diplomacy

Many in Beijing are now looking forward to the 2008 Olympic Games, which will be an occasion to showcase the image China wishes to project. The efficient and hospitable organisation of a sporting occasion might well boost China's standing and confidence, especially if unaccompanied by unattractive national-ist clamour. More decisive, however, will be the attitudes Beijing strikes and how it performs in a kind of pentathlon of diplomacy – towards great powers, other rising regional powers, its neighbours, the developing world and international institutions. The task is only likely to become more difficult over time.

Korean Security: Roller-Coaster Ride

A nuclear test on 9 October 2006 altered the balance of power in Northeast Asia. It demonstrated that the Democratic People's Republic of Korea (DPRK) pos-sessed the ultimate deterrent, although whether it could deliver such a weapon with its *No-dong* missiles remained unknown. Coming three months after a series of North Korean ballistic-missile launches, the nuclear test severely tried China's patience and drew together North Korea's neighbours in support of a tough UN sanctions resolution against that country. But ultimately the test had another impact: Washington was persuaded to change course, to talk to North Korea bilaterally and to lift money-laundering sanctions on $25 million in North Korean bank accounts in Macao that North Korea had posited as a reason to boycott the Six-Party Talks.

Washington's policy shift and new willingness to engage bilaterally set the stage for a February 2007 agreement on steps to halt North Korea's nuclear pro-gramme. The agreement did not address the existing weapons stockpile; it was aimed only at stopping the production of more weapons. Whether it will achieve that goal, however, remains in doubt. Difficulties associated with releasing the Macao bank accounts delayed implementation of what were supposed to be the easy first steps, boding ill for the more difficult issues to follow. These include how North Korea will account for the uranium-enrichment equipment it procured in the late 1990s, and the sequencing of reciprocal steps called for in the February agreement.

The missile and nuclear tests further exposed a gap in threat perceptions between the United States and the Republic of Korea (ROK) and further weakened leftist South Korean President Roh Moo Hyun's public support, due to the obvious failure of his unconditioned engagement policy toward the North. Based on early opinion polls, the conservative party is likely to win the December election and move the United States and South Korea into greater harmony. Ratification of a seminal free-trade agreement between the two countries, agreed subject to legislative approval at the end of intense negotiations on 2 April 2007, would also mend relations and boost both economies.

Missile test

On 5 July 2006, North Korea carried out seven tests of unarmed ballistic missiles: two or three presumed to be short-range *Scuds*, three or four intermediate-range *No-dongs*, and one longer-range *Taepo-dong* 2. The latter launch failed after 42 seconds, but the others were successful. The tests broke a moratorium in place since the 1998 first test of the *Taepo-dong* sparked intense diplomatic efforts by the Clinton administration to put constraints on North Korea's missile programme. Although world attention focused on the failure of the longer-range missile, North Korea's success in multiple launches of the other missiles in quick succession, three of them at night, and with evident precision, demonstrated a significant operational capability.

North Korea conducted the missile tests both to demonstrate and enhance its deterrent capability and because it judged that it had nothing to lose diplomatically. Pyongyang had declared in March 2005 that the earlier moratorium was no longer valid because normalisation talks with the United States and Japan on which it was based had long since ended. Washington was tightening its pressure policy, epitomised by the freeze the US Treasury caused to be placed on North Korean bank accounts in Macao in October 2005 on charges of money laundering. In demonstrating its military strength and resolve, North Korea sought to persuade the United States to remove this pressure. North Korea may also have wanted to demonstrate its missile wares to Iran, which, according to unconfirmed media reporting, sent observers to the tests.

The missile tests provoked all of North Korea's neighbours. Japanese Chief Cabinet Secretary and soon-to-be Prime Minister Shinzo Abe led other nationalist politicians in condemning North Korea and reasserting Japan's right to initiate military action if it were under threat. Japan led deliberations on a harsh Security Council resolution. The tests embarrassed China and South Korea, which had explicitly pleaded with Pyongyang not to go ahead with the launch preparations that had been apparent for two months. However, Seoul responded more strongly to Japan's harsh reaction than it did to the missile launch itself. China watered down some of the provisions in Japan's resolution, but for the first time accepted UN sanctions on North Korea. UN Security Council Resolution 1695, which passed unanimously on 15 July, condemned the tests, demanded that North Korea suspend its ballistic-missile programme, and required all UN members to prevent transfers of missile-related technologies and financial resources for missile programmes to North Korea. Separately, Japan put a six-month ban on ferry service and charter flights to North Korea and tightened restrictions on export controls and bank remissions. Several other countries froze North Korean bank accounts.

Nuclear test

If China's support for the Security Council resolution shocked the North Korean leadership, as many observers at the time believed, Pyongyang's ensuing actions were anything but conciliatory. It began making visible preparations to conduct an underground nuclear test near Punggye in the remote northeast corner of the country. The United States hinted that it could increase pressure by re-imposing economic sanctions that President Clinton had lifted in 2000. Concurrently, to try to entice North Korea along a peaceful path, the US signaled procedural flexibility, saying that Assistant Secretary for East Asia Christopher Hill, US chief negotiator in the Six-Party Talks, could visit North Korea even before the next round began, if Pyongyang indicated it would rejoin the talks. This willingness to meet bilaterally – 'in the context of Six Party Talks', according to Washington parlance – acceded to a longstanding North Korean demand. Nevertheless, on 3 October, Pyongyang announced that it was set to conduct a nuclear test 'in the future' as a deterrent and in response to what it called the 'US extreme threat of a nuclear war and sanctions and pressure'.

North Korea carried out that test on 9 October. Twenty minutes beforehand, Pyongyang gave Beijing advance notification, saying the yield would be 4 kilotonnes. Seismic readings, however, measured a yield of 0.5–0.9kt. Even the projected yield was small in comparison to the first nuclear tests of other countries (which ranged from about 9kt for Pakistan's 1998 test to 60kt in the case of the French 1960 test). This may mean North Korea tested a small weapon designed to fit the *No-dong*, although most experts believe North Korea would have started off with a simpler device. North Korea may also have purposely sought to conserve its small plutonium stockpile and to minimise radioactive emissions. The sub-kilotonne actual yield, which could have been due to any of several technical problems, led some commentators to question whether it was a nuclear test at all. US Director of National Intelligence John Negroponte put this question to rest by stating that air samples detected radioactive debris confirming an underground nuclear test explosion. Unnamed US intelligence sources confirmed that the air samples showed the test device to have been made from plutonium, not highly enriched uranium.

Producing as little as one-eighth the planned yield, the nuclear test was a fizzle in the technical sense. In achieving nuclear criticality, however, the 9 October test was a success in other ways, giving North Korea a basis to declare itself a nuclear-weapon state. Whether the nuclear device is usable and reliable as a deliverable nuclear weapon is another question.

In deciding to conduct the October test, Kim Jong Il must have believed that confirming the nuclear deterrent was a military and diplomatic necessity. He perhaps feared the US policy of pre-emption, and wanted to respond to some US suggestions that only regime change could resolve the North Korean nuclear issue. In carrying his 'military first' (*songun*) policy to the logical extreme, Kim was convinced that establishing North Korea as a nuclear power was the best and perhaps only way to guarantee regime viability. With nuclear weapons, the North Koreans reinforced their demand that they be treated as an equal by the United States.

Coinciding with the ninth anniversary of Kim Jong Il's elevation to the chairmanship of the Korean Workers Party, the nuclear test enhanced his status and strengthened his internal position, while reaffirming his close ties to the military. An atomic bomb is a powerful symbol of defying the enemy, as well as a means to boost national pride. North Korean billboards after the test lauded it as a signal achievement in the 5,000-year history of the Korean people. After years of South Korean dominance in conventional forces, economy, culture, science, technology and diplomacy (the test came on the day the Security Council approved South Korean Foreign Minister Ban Ki Moon as the next UN Secretary-General), the North Koreans could finally best their southern kin in one key area.

Kim also judged he had little to lose from the test and little to fear from external powers. The North Koreans, making the assessment that India and Pakistan 'got away with it', were asking to be treated the same as India, with US cooperation in nuclear energy. Having already endured over 50 years of US sanctions, they insist they can endure more. They also could count on China and South Korea to continue their engagement policies, since they compete for influence in the North and fear conflict escalation – and most of all, North Korean disintegration. In this regard, North Korea's biggest trump card is its own potential demise.

The immediate impact of the test was to reinforce North Korea's isolation, but Kim proved correct in guessing that this would be manageable. Japan banned imports from North Korea and stopped North Korean ships and citizens going to Japan. Drawing a red line, President George W. Bush said the United States would regard a North Korean 'transfer of nuclear weapons or material' to other states or terrorist groups as a 'grave threat', implying it would bring a US military response. South Korea suspended food and fertiliser aid, and subsidies of visits by students and veterans to the Mt Kumgang tourist attraction, but did not otherwise use the tourism project or the Kaesong Industrial Zone joint venture as a means of retaliation or leverage against the North. China called the test a 'brazen' act, a term usually used for adversaries.

China went along with another UN Security Council sanctions resolution, adopted swiftly and unanimously on 14 October. Under Chapter VII of the UN Charter, Resolution 1718 banned the export of heavy weapons and luxury goods to North Korea and the export of any heavy weapons from North Korea, required the freezing of funds connected with the nuclear and missile programmes, and called on all member states to take cooperative action to inspect cargo to and from North Korea to prevent trafficking in nuclear, chemical and biological weapons or ballistic missiles. The economic impact of such sanctions depends largely on North Korea's two closest neighbours and largest trading partners, China and South Korea. Although there were reports that China had stopped the supply of military spare parts to North Korea, China made clear that it disapproved of the cargo-inspection provision of the resolution. South Korea also indicated it would not be participating in any maritime interdictions of North Korean vessels. Even the United States let pass what some media reports alleged to be an Ethiopian violation of the arms embargo in January 2007 because Addis Ababa needed spare parts for Soviet-origin equipment in its military offensive against Islamic militias inside Somalia.

Back to diplomacy: the 13 February agreement

International coordination of steps to implement cargo inspections never took place, as diplomacy brought a resumption of the Six-Party Talks later in the year. This resumption started when China arranged a three-way meeting on 31 October with Hill and North Korean Vice Foreign Minister Kim Kye Gwan. In a follow-up three-way meeting in November, Hill suggested a package proposal that called for North Korea to close down its nuclear facilities and declare its nuclear programmes in exchange for Washington lifting financial sanctions and making other concessions. When the six parties convened in mid December, however, they made no progress, as Kim refused to engage on the nuclear-weapons programme until the United States abandoned its 'hostile' policy by lifting all sanctions. Hill then privately signalled his willingness to meet elsewhere bilaterally, and a meeting was set up for 16–18 January in Berlin. There, the two negotiators reached an unannounced understanding that would form the basis of a formal agreement the next month.

Based on the discussions in Berlin, the Six-Party Talks on 13 February produced an agreement on 'initial actions for implementation of the [19 September 2005] Joint Statement'. North Korea agreed to shut down and seal the nuclear facility at Yongbyon and to invite the International Atomic Energy Agency (IAEA) to conduct the necessary verification, all within 60 days. Shutting down Yongbyon is not a painful sacrifice for the DPRK. Having extracted, in 2003, the plutonium from the 8,000 spent fuel rods that had been under seal under the terms of the 1994 Agreed Framework and having carried out an additional reprocessing campaign in 2005, the DPRK already has enough for a minimum nuclear deterrent. It can easily afford to shut down the Yongbyon facilities, which have no civil energy purpose and which were shut down in 1994, and restarted in 2003. This time too, North Korea publicly claimed that the freeze would only be temporary.

North Korea did not meet the 60-day deadline, however, because of what at first were characterised as technical difficulties over how it would access the $25m in its accounts in Banco Delta Asia (BDA) after the US Treasury, in a 180-degree turnaround, gave Macao authorities the go-ahead to lift their freeze. Hill and Kim Kye Gwan had agreed in Berlin that lifting the freeze would trigger the shuttering of the Yongbyon facility. The $25m was symbolically important to North Korea because of its connection with Kim Jong Il. More important, however, was the chilling impact the action against BDA had on the willingness of banks worldwide to do business with North Korea. Throughout 2006, senior US Treasury officials visited China and other Asian countries to persuade government officials and bankers to shun financial relationships with Pyongyang. In demanding unrestricted access to their BDA accounts, the North Koreans wanted normalisation of their financial transactions worldwide and refused to implement or even talk about any other aspect of the 13 February accord until then. This became complicated when the Bank of China, to whom Macao authorities had tried to transfer the BDA money, refused to accept it because of concerns that the funds had been the focus of a criminal investigation. It took until mid June for parties to work out arrangements to transfer the money first through the US Federal Reserve Bank, then a Russian bank. A 21–22 June visit to Pyongyang by Hill then paved the way for IAEA inspectors to visit to negotiate verification details for North Korea's promise to shut down the facilities.

North Korea's other requirement during the first phase of the February agreement was to 'discuss' with other parties a list of all of its nuclear programmes, and then, in the second phase, to provide a complete declaration. Whether Pyongyang at any stage will admit to a presumed uranium-enrichment programme is questionable. In early 2007, US intelligence claims about the programme became a matter of intense public debate. Hill tried to give North Korea a face-saving way out by setting realistic expectations on what would have to be declared. The evidence is clear that North Korea received some 20 or more gas centrifuges and other elements of an enrichment starter kit from Pakistani nuclear engineer Abdul Qadeer Khan in the late 1990s, and that North Korea from about 2001 sought to procure thousands of aluminium tubes and other equipment that matched the requirements for centrifuge components. The US intelligence community has lowered its level of confidence, however, about whether the uranium-enrichment programme continues to exist, assessing this now with 'moderate confidence' (compared with 'high confidence' that North Korea pursued a uranium-enrichment capability in the past). Some outside analysts believe North Korea never progressed beyond a modest procurement effort. Although it is impossible to fully verify the absence of easily concealed enrichment facilities, North Korea at a minimum was expected to declare the enrichment equipment it obtained, which the United States could then compare with what it learned from intelligence methods and Khan's confession.

Among five working groups established by the February agreement, the working group on normalisation of DPRK–Japan relations ran into the most difficulty, in an impasse over historical differences. While Japan pressed for a full accounting of the Japanese citizens North Korea abducted in the 1970s and 1980s, North Korea demanded settlement of issues stemming from Japan's 1910–45 colonial rule. The working group on DPRK–US relations got off to a better start in early March, discussing, inter alia, replacement of the Korean War armistice with a permanent peace treaty. Hill also laid out what would be involved in removing North Korea from the US list of state sponsors of terrorism and from the Trading with the Enemy Act. Under the terms of the 13 February agreement, the United States must begin the process of removing North Korea's designation in both cases. These steps had been under way in accordance with the 1994 Agreed Framework before they fell victim to the overall unravelling of that accord. Actually removing these sanctions will depend on how the rest of the denuclearisation agreement fares.

The most concrete element of the 13 February agreement called for the provision to North Korea of an initial tranche of energy assistance equivalent to 50,000 tonnes of heavy fuel oil, but this was put on hold until North Korea froze the nuclear facilities. An additional 950,000 tonnes was to be provided in the second phase, for a total value of about $230m, most of it coming from South Korea. Token amounts might come from the other parties, but Japan made clear it would not agree to any form of economic assistance until progress was made on the abductee issue.

In the second phase, the 13 February agreement called for the disabling of all existing nuclear facilities, 'including graphite-moderated reactors and reprocessing plant'. No timetable was given – US officials suggested it should take place by the end of the year or in a matter of months – but this phase can be expected to take up to two years. Staking out a negotiating position on the sequencing, Pyongyang claimed that the 1m tonnes of fuel oil must be provided before it has to dismantle anything. The denuclearisation working group was charged with working out a schedule that would probably set intermediate trade-offs: a certain amount of oil for a certain stage of disabling. In March, however, North Korea reportedly claimed it would implement the next steps (full declaration and disablement) only if it was recognised as a nuclear power.

In large part, the February deal was a reworked version of Clinton's 1994 Agreed Framework with North Korea, which similarly froze the plutonium programme but fell apart during the Bush administration well before reaching the stage of dismantling the facilities or removing the fissile material. Global reactions to the 13 February deal were largely positive, albeit with regret that the agreement had not come six years earlier, before Pyongyang quadrupled its fissile-material stockpile and tested a nuclear weapon. From the right, however, former US ambassador to the UN John Bolton blasted the agreement for rewarding North Korean intransigence and sending the wrong signal to other proliferators.

The change in US policy can be attributed to several factors. While neoconservative policies were in overall retreat over the failure of the Iraq invasion, Democratic Party control of Congress after the November 2006 elections changed the climate in Washington in favour of engagement. The departure of Defense Secretary Donald Rumsfeld, UN Ambassador Bolton and Vice President Dick Cheney's chief of staff Lewis 'Scooter' Libby also changed the dynamics in the administration in favour of Secretary of State Condoleezza Rice's pragmatism. Hill persuaded Rice that the BDA financial issue should be sacrificed for the larger goal of beginning the process of dismantling North Korea's nuclear-weapons programme. To overcome the political obstacles in Washington that had blocked previous State Department attempts at flexibility, Rice went directly to the president for his approval, bypassing the normal inter-agency process. Under Secretary of State for Arms Control and International Security Affairs Robert Joseph, an influential hardliner who had replaced Bolton in the job only two years before, quietly resigned in disagreement.

The February accord left for future discussion any dismantling of North Korea's nuclear weapons. As distinct from closing down the facilities used to produce more fissile material, North Korea will not give up the weapons without a dramatic change in its security calculus. Senior Vice Foreign Minister Kang Sok Ju told reporters in November, 'Why would we abandon nuclear weapons? Are you saying we conducted a nuclear test in order to abandon them?'

The 5MW(e) reactor at Yongbyon produces approximately 6kg of plutonium a year, roughly enough for one weapon. North Korea only has enough fuel on hand for a partial reloading of the reactor, however, and its fuel-fabrication plant deteriorated while it was shut down under the Agreed Framework. A 50MW(e) reactor that would, if completed, increase by tenfold the DPRK's plutonium-production capability, remains in bad repair because of the difficulty of importing materials and equipment.

North Korea is estimated to have enough separated plutonium for 5–10 weapons, assuming each contains 4–5kg of plutonium. Pyongyang's fleet of Russian-made Il-28 bombers represent one possible means of weapon delivery, and North Korea is probably trying to develop small, sophisticated designs for weapons that could be carried by the *No-dong* missile. North Korea has about 200 of the 1,300km-range *No-dongs*, as well as over 600 *Scuds*, according to the United States. Whether North Korea could deliver a nuclear-armed ballistic missile is unknown.

South Korea–US relations

The US and the Republic of Korea both stress the importance of their bilateral alliance, and South Korea has troops in Iraq as well as Afghanistan, where one was killed by a suicide bomber in February 2007 during a visit to Bagram Airbase by Cheney. A number of issues trouble the relationship, however, including a fundamental difference in perceptions about the threat posed by North Korea. Following the latter's missile and nuclear tests, Americans asked why South Korea continued to provide cash to Kim Jong Il through the special economic zone in Kaesong and the Mt Kumgang tours. From a South Korean perspective, both ventures are symbolically important for north–south reconciliation. After an initial reaction of surprise at North Korea's nuclear test, South Korea continued a policy of business as usual, showing little sense of urgency to address the new threat. Indeed, the overall attitude is to live with the nuclear-armed North Korea – most South Koreans believe it would never attack them with nuclear weapons. The generation now in power in South Korea seeks to embrace North Koreans as brethren. Their greatest concerns are being entrapped in another military conflict with North Korea, provoked by a US push for regime change, and unplanned unification if the Northern regime collapses. South Koreans are also concerned that Beijing, with Washington's unintended abetting, will expand its influence in North Korea at Seoul's expense.

Seoul's criticism of the United States sometimes went to extremes. Not long before career diplomat Song Min Soon was selected in October 2006 as the new foreign minister, he said at a conference that the United States fought more wars than any other nation in history. The rift between the two nations widened when Seoul announced in mid November that it would not formally join the

Proliferation Security Initiative (PSI), because of concerns that it could lead to an unintentional naval clash between the two Koreas. Arguments over cost-sharing for US forces in Korea, training opportunities for US Air Force fighter pilots, US base relocations and environmental clean-up of abandoned bases also strained relations. An agreement reached in December 2006 increased South Korea's share of the costs by 6.6%, to approximately $790m, which the commander of US forces in Korea, General Burwood Bell, afterwards criticised as not equitable. According to the United States, it represents less than 15% of the total annual US expenditures required to maintain US forces in South Korea.

One problem that had been troubling the alliance was resolved when the US agreed on Roh's timetable for transferring wartime operational control over South Korea's armed forces by 2012. Roh sought the change as recognition of his country's independent defence capabilities and equal role in the US–ROK alliance, but it was fiercely opposed by conservative Korean forces who argued that pushing for the change compromised national security at a time of crisis with North Korea and could lead to the withdrawal of US forces. Defense Secretary Donald Rumsfeld had complicated matters by agreeing to the transfer *earlier* than Roh had requested. A final roadmap for the transfer was announced at the October Security Consultative Meeting of the US and South Korean defence ministers. As part of the agreement, the US will continue to operate high-tech surveillance and reconnaissance systems to support the Korean forces after the transfer, addressing one of the major concerns raised by former South Korean defence officials. The United States also took every opportunity to reaffirm its commitment to South Korean security.

Agreement on a free-trade pact also helped to mend frayed relations. After months of difficult talks, trade negotiators reached agreement on the pact just in time to meet a US requirement to give Congress 90 days for review before Bush's 'fast-track trade promotion authority' (under which the administration can seek a yes-or-no congressional approval without amendments) expired on 30 June. Disagreements over US application of antidumping regulations, patent rights for US pharmaceutical corporations in Korea, and mutual tariffs on imported vehicles were among the key sticking points. If ratified, the US–ROK Free Trade Agreement would immediately eliminate tariffs on 90% of the categories of goods traded between the two countries. South Korea agreed to phase out trade barriers to US products including cars and beef, while Washington abandoned a longstanding demand that Seoul eliminate subsidies on South Korean rice. One unresolved problem is Washington's refusal to accept products from Kaesong as made in South Korea under the terms of the agreement. Although the deal is expected to cause tens of thousands of South Korean farmers to lose their jobs, it is expected to reverse a decline in South Korea's manufacturing competitiveness vis-à-vis Japan and China. US and South Korean consumers will benefit from more affordable imports and the deal is expected to add $20bn to the current $78bn trade between the two countries. The agreement also helped to clear the way for a similar pact between South Korea and the EU.

Political developments in South Korea

Some of the strains in relations between Seoul and Washington may lighten after the December 2007 elections. As Roh limped toward the February 2008 end of his single five-year presidential term, he was increasingly embattled. Already extremely unpopular because of erratic, divisive and ineffective leadership, Roh came under withering criticism in 2006 when his 'peace and prosperity' policy toward North Korea failed to prevent North Korea's ballistic-missile and nuclear tests. This led in early 2007 to the ruling Uri Party forcing him to resign his party membership. The Uri Party itself was so unpopular that many members left it in early 2007 in the hope of establishing a new centre-left party that could field a viable presidential candidate. As of late spring 2007, presidential hopefuls in the conservative Grand National Party (GNP) were far ahead of potential left-centre candidates in national opinion polls. Victory for a conservative candidate in the presidential election in December 2007 would end a decade of centre-left rule and boost the chances of the conservatives gaining outright control of the National Assembly in parliamentary elections in April 2008. The GNP would not abandon the policy of engagement with North Korea – most Koreans agree with the need to avoid confrontation that could lead either to war or to collapse of North Korea that would lead to a flood of refugees. However, the GNP would demand more conditionality on aid and more reciprocity from the North. The conservatives would also be in greater harmony with the US in paying more regard to human-rights issues in the North and in supporting active participation in the PSI.

South Korean elections are notoriously unpredictable, however. For example, a conservative presidential victory could be stymied if two GNP candidates were both to run, splitting the conservative vote and handing the victory to a 'progressive' politician, as has happened before in South Korea's first-past-the-post electoral system. As of early summer 2007, the front runner was former Seoul mayor Lee Myung Bak, polling well ahead of former GNP leader Park Geun Hye (daughter of former president Park Chung Hee). Park retains strong party support, however, and cannot be counted out. All other potential candidates, whether conservative or progressive, polled only in single digits. Return of the conservatives to power would represent a remarkable reversal of the shift in political alignment that was supposed to have accompanied the generational shift in South Korea over the past several years: the GNP has drawn its support from those over 50, while the Uri Party is the home of the generation of the 30- and 40-somethings who grew up in the turbulent 1970s and 1980s. A GNP victory would probably be attributable to a reaction to the perceived fecklessness of Roh and the Uri Party on economic and quality-of-life issues even more than on North Korea policy.

South Korea's economy is strong, with economic growth of 5% in 2006. However, private-sector investment, which in 1996 was 40% of gross domestic product (GDP), fell to 28% in 2006. Foreign direct investment fell to 7% of GDP, compared to 35% in China. Koreans have increasingly felt sandwiched between low-cost China and high-tech Japan, though a free-trade agreement with the United States should spur reforms and revitalise the economy. The gloomy mood prevailing in the first half of 2007, however, was based on South Korean comparisons with larger neighbours. By global standards, South Korea was doing well in almost every field. Its biotech and information-technology firms were globally prominent. South Korean films, pop stars and soap operas were popular throughout Asia. Indicating South Korea's global reach, Foreign Minister Ban Ki Moon won easy election as UN secretary-general, after an extremely well-run campaign.

North–South relations

The missile and nuclear tests initially appeared to undermine Seoul's engagement strategy toward North Korea. The Sunshine Policy pursued by President Kim Dae Jung (1998–2003) and essentially continued by Roh (who called it the 'Policy of Peace and Prosperity') posited that Pyongyang could be persuaded to yield its nuclear-weapons potential for economic guarantees and security assurances. Roh had invested considerable political capital in opening doors to the North even as Pyongyang expanded its nuclear arsenal, but the missile and nuclear tests demonstrated how little South Korea had gained from that investment. In the wake of the nuclear test several South Korean officials aligned with the engagement strategy resigned, including Minister of Unification Lee Jong Seok. A huge expansion of Kaesong, under which half a million North Korean workers would be employed there by 2012, was put on hold.

As an additional expression of anger in the aftermath of the tests, and as part of the diplomatic strategy to win the UN secretary-general position, Seoul in November for the first time voted for a UN resolution condemning North Korea's human-rights record. The UN resolution criticised Pyongyang both for direct abuses and for mismanagement of a dire humanitarian situation that left severe infant malnutrition. In other ways, however, South Korean officialdom displayed an ingrained posture of overlooking the North's human-rights and humanitarian misdeeds. When South Korean fisherman Choi Wook Il was able to escape to China from 26 years' detention in North Korea after being seized while fishing, his wife received unsympathetic responses from Seoul Foreign Ministry officials until the callous attitude of one bureaucrat was captured on tape and posted on the Internet. According to the Unification Ministry, since the 1953 armistice, North Korea had abducted 3,790 South Koreans, 485 of whom were still being held as of June 2006. The contrast could hardly be greater with Japan, where the demand for North Korea to release information on a small number of abductees takes priority over all other aspects of relations.

Despite the missile and nuclear tests, inter-Korean trade and inter-Korean visits reached record levels in 2006. Trade was up 28% to $1.35bn; visits (not including tourists to Mt Kumgang) up 15% to 102,000, 99% of them from south to north. Even after the nuclear test, an opinion poll in South Korea showed 83% supporting the continuation of economic ties with the North. Following the February agreement, Seoul resumed food and fertiliser aid to North Korea. Amidst other re-invigorated elements of inter-Korea diplomacy, a second North–South summit was reportedly under discussion.

China–North Korea relations

The greatest diplomatic impact of North Korea's nuclear and missile tests was the deep rift it created with China, reflected in Beijing's unprecedented support for the two UN sanctions resolutions. Notwithstanding its 1961 Friendship Treaty with Pyongyang, Chinese officials made clear that the relationship was no longer an alliance. China fears the prospect of Japan seeking nuclear weapons or abandoning its Peace Constitution. It also sees North Korea's provocations as the greatest stimulus to Japan moving rightward. However, in seeking to defuse tensions, Beijing remained cautious about putting too much pressure on North Korea. A key Chinese priority was to prevent the collapse of the North Korean structure, which might result in a flood of refugees and a US military presence right up to China's border. Like South Korea, China still believed that the best way to deal with North Korea was through trade and assistance to gradually reform the economy and engage with the international community.

For its part, North Korea voiced disdain for China's role. In a speech in New York in March 2007, Kim Kye Gwan said Beijing 'is only trying to use' Pyongyang. Calling on the United States to deal directly with North Korea and not rely on China, Kim asked 'What has it achieved? We have test-fired missiles, and conducted a nuclear test, doing what we wanted to do. China has solved nothing.' Pyongyang correctly regarded the energy and economic assistance that China provided as being in Beijing's own interests, since many of Beijing's investments serve to meet China's own need for coal and other raw materials, as well as reinforcing its influence over North Korea.

North Korea's internal dynamics

Several leadership positions in North Korea changed over the past year, mostly through death of the elderly incumbents. Politburo member and party secretary for national security Kye Ung Tae died in November 2006 at age 81. Foreign Minister Paek Nam Sun, who was largely a figurehead, died in January 2007 at 77. (According to North Korean practice, no successors were announced.) Premier Pak Pong Ju was replaced in April 2007 by Land and Transport Minister Kim Yong Il. The latter change may have been due to Pak's failure to reform the destitute economy, but the formal government posts are in any case subordinate to the party and the military, over which Kim Jong Il presides.

The future of the North Korean regime remained intimately tied to the issue of succession of 65-year old Kim, who was reported by the CIA to be in poor health. In what resembles a feudal hereditary monarchy more than a communist state, Kim had yet to publicly name his successor. His second son, Kim Chong Chol, was identified as the Workers Party 'nerve centre' in a 2006 party instruction memo, and appeared to have emerged as the front runner. However, other relatives could not be ruled out, including Kim Jong Il's half-brother Kim Pyong Il, ambassador to Poland. The 'Dear Leader' may have feared that nominating a successor would create a focal point for opposition or set off infighting to curry favour with the chosen successor at Kim Jong Il's expense. His death in office would provoke an intense power struggle with perilous ramifications for the entire region, especially if the nuclear assets became an object of contestation.

It was impossible to determine to what extent, if any, there was internal opposition to Kim Jong Il. A freer economy, more opportunities for travel to China, and greater accessibility to radios and video players may have provided a comparative basis for citizens to question the regime's claims of domestic prosperity. However, there was no evidence yet that North Koreans were making the kind of comparisons that led to the collapse of East Germany. Rioting in Hoiryong in November 2006 was non-political, centring on grievances by vendors over closure of their market, but was nevertheless a significant sign of activity in defiance of local authorities. The regime cautiously continued reforms begun in 2002 allowing a semi-market economy, but reasserted control over food rationing and employment to prevent state workers from moonlighting as traders. Growth was throttled by the contradictions of a command economy, the military-first policy, and a dire capital shortage. North Korea's attractiveness to foreign investors, already seriously undermined by the missile and nuclear tests and the sanctions that followed, was further hurt in December 2006 when accusations surfaced about a fake reinsurance scam discovered by Lloyds and other reinsurers who compared notes on an unusually large and curiously detailed variety of North Korean claims of industrial and personal accidents.

A devastating typhoon that flooded key agricultural areas further weakened North Korea's economy in 2006. According to the South Korean private aid group, North Korea's 2006 grain harvest fell 2.8m tonnes short, equivalent to the famine years of 1996–98. The UN World Food Programme, which was forced by

Pyongyang in 2006 to cut back its operations in North Korea, anticipated a grain shortage of 1m tonnes in 2007. Notwithstanding the dire need, in March 2007 the UN Development Programme (UNDP) suspended activity in the country after the United States alleged that lax accounting meant that UN aid money could be diverted for 'illicit purposes' including developing nuclear weapons. In February the UNDP's board voted to change the way it operated in North Korea, including stopping the payment for local supplies and salaries in euros to the North Korean government. When North Korea refused to accept the new conditions, the UNDP said it had no choice but to suspend the programme. The suspension affected 20 projects with a budget of $4m, including food production and efforts to help Pyongyang improve systems to manage the economy.

Prospects

The 13 February agreement was a promising first step but will not lead anytime soon to the end of North Korea's nuclear programme. There seems little prospect that North Korea will give up the weapons it so recently proved it possesses, and certainly not for one million tonnes of heavy fuel oil. It can be expected to demand, among other things, completion of the construction of the two light-water reactors begun under the Agreed Framework. Although the basic goals of each side are not irreconcilable in principle, differences over which step would have to come first remain a fundamental stumbling block to long-term resolution of the problem and will stretch out negotiations for the rest of the Bush administration, if talks do not break down altogether. North Korea's refusal to continue discussion of any other elements of the 13 February agreement until it had the $25m in its hands foreshadowed its likely behaviour in implementing other steps.

If the Six-Party Talks process breaks down, the United States likely would resume financial and other forms of pressure in order to try to compel or at least to contain North Korea. Preventing North Korea from transferring its nuclear weapons, material or technology is Washington's ultimate red line. Although North Korea announced after the test that it would not 'allow nuclear transfers', the reported presence of Iranian observers at the October nuclear test would, if confirmed, be viewed as equivalent to a technology transfer. The United States still has considerable financial leverage. Strict implementation of UN Resolution 1718 would see an enhanced focus on the PSI to inspect North Korean cargo, although it is difficult to predict how actual interdiction would work in practice without Chinese and South Korean cooperation.

North Korea's propensity for brinkmanship and its willingness to take provocative actions give it the ability to dominate any escalation of the stand-off. It can be argued that the Bush administration's reliance on the tools of coercion had a counterproductive effect, giving North Korea a pretext to accelerate its development and testing of a nuclear weapon. When cornered, North Korea's typical response is to accelerate the crisis. It could well respond to further pressure by a second nuclear test and further missile tests.

Pre-emptive US military strikes are not likely because of the ensuing war and devastation of Seoul that would result, but a naval blockade would be one of the options under careful consideration. On the other hand, if the February agreement is implemented, the Six-Party Talks could evolve into a process with longer-term results, including a formal peace treaty to end the Korean War and a permanent regional body providing security arrangements and dealing with other issues.

Japan: Active Diplomacy

Japan in 2006–2007 continued to pursue more active diplomatic and military policies, especially through continued strengthening of the US–Japan alliance. Security policy was driven by the need to respond to a range of challenges, including the threat from North Korea (highlighted by Pyongyang's missile and nuclear tests in the latter half of 2006); concerns over China's military posture, Sino-Japanese tensions and strategic competition in the region; and enhanced US expectations of closer Japanese support for its regional and global military strategy.

Japan's strategic evolution gathered momentum in spite of a change in political leadership, as Shinzo Abe took over as prime minister when Junichiro Koizumi retired in September 2006. Koizumi is widely regarded as one of the most influential prime ministers in post-war Japanese history. He broke new ground in domestic politics and foreign policy, especially following the 11 September 2001 attacks on the United States, with the dispatch of the Japan Self Defense Forces (JSDF) to provide non-combat logistical support for US-led coalitions in Afghanistan and Iraq. Koizumi was a tough act to follow, and Abe's brand of diplomacy is somewhat different. In some areas he has been willing to take a more moderate and pragmatic stance than Koizumi, whilst in others he has demonstrated a more ideologically motivated and potentially more radical approach. Nevertheless, Abe has maintained much of the Koizumi line, particularly in continuing to challenge post-war taboos and domestic structural constraints, and in strengthening security ties with the United States.

Tokyo's growing assertiveness has, however, been neither entirely smooth – especially over North Korea – nor unhampered by the change of leadership. Japan is developing structures and more explicit values to support a more active, 'normal' diplomatic and security role, but its strategy lacks cohesion; there is insufficient consensus over how it should position itself vis-à-vis the United States and East Asia. Both Koizumi's and Abe's handling of relations with North Korea, China and the United States have also been strongly influenced by their domestic political support base and the need to manipulate foreign policy in support of domestic agendas.

Koizumi's legacy

Koizumi won a landslide victory in the House of Representatives elections in September 2005. Under the governing Liberal Democratic Party (LDP) rules he could not seek a third term as party president, and the political debate from spring 2006 until the 20 September LDP leadership elections focused on his likely successor and how the transition might affect foreign policy. It was a mark of Koizumi's extraordinary impact during his five-year tenure that such a strong association was made between the prime minister and the conduct of Japan's foreign relations.

Although he had taken office with a reputation as a domestic reformer with minimal interest in foreign policy, Koizumi tackled it with the same taboo-breaking approach he applied to domestic issues. He appeared to have been motivated by a strong sense of Japanese national interests, with a willingness at the same time to use foreign policy to bolster his domestic political agenda and popularity. He gave Japanese diplomacy a more active direction along with a distinct streak of expediency and lack of long-term strategic or ideological underpinnings.

Reforms boosted prime-ministerial control over foreign and security policy. Koizumi undertook many foreign-policy initiatives in close consultation with the chief cabinet secretary and other officials in the Cabinet secretariat, with occasional input from key officials in other ministries, bypassing the traditional 'bottom-up' consensus-building approach through the LDP's policy organs and dialogue with the opposition. This led to more rapid but also more erratic and controversial decisions.

In the aftermath of 11 September, Koizumi moved Japan even closer to the United States to demonstrate its indispensability as an ally in the 'war on terror', despatching the Maritime Self Defense Force (MSDF) to the Indian Ocean in support of the US-led coalition from December 2001 onwards, and deploying the Ground Self Defense Force (GSDF) and Air Self Defense Force (ASDF) to Iraq from 2004 onwards. This was intended to retain a degree of strategic leverage over the United States and secure its assistance in dealing with threats from North Korea and China. Koizumi also committed his administration to the introduction of Ballistic Missile Defence (BMD) in cooperation with the United States from 2003 onwards, and pushed through the US–Japan bilateral Defence Policy Review Initiative (DPRI) which concluded in May 2006. The DPRI was designed to enhance the US–Japan alliance whilst reducing the burden of US bases on local communities, particularly in Okinawa, which hosts a disproportionate share of US military facilities in Japan.

The DPRI was significant in stressing that the US and Japan now shared not just common regional but also *global* strategic objectives. The main points of the realignment included:

- Relocation of the command functions of US Army I Corps from Washington State to Camp Zama near Tokyo by 2008. This means Japan will serve as a front-line command post for US global power projection as far away as the Middle East, marking an implicit change in interpretation of the role of US bases under the security treaty as covering only Japan and the Far East. Japan is to complement this by moving its newly established GSDF Central Readiness Force, with rapid-reaction capabilities, to Camp Zama by 2008.
- Relocation by 2014 of the US Marine Corps (USMC) air station from Futenma in the city of Ginowan to Henoko in Nago city, involving construction of runways and redeployment of the Third Marine Expeditionary Force, totalling 8,000 troops and 9,000 dependants. Both locations are in Okinawa, where there is local pressure to reduce the American presence.
- Establishment of a Bilateral Joint Operations Coordination Centre at Yokota air base to co-locate Japan's ASDF Command and US BMD command-and-control information systems. The United States will deploy additional and complementary BMD assets around Japan, including an X-band radar system at Kashiri in Aomori Prefecture, and *Patriot* PAC-3 missiles.
- Relocation of the US aircraft carrier wing at Atsugi air base near Tokyo to the USMC base at Iwakuni, Yamaguchi Prefecture, by 2014.

By the latter stages of Koizumi's administration officials of both governments were fond of stating that bilateral ties were in their 'best condition ever', but many of the changes were highly controversial amongst other policymakers, the general public and local communities affected by the relocation. Koizumi left to his successor the knotty problem of implementing the DPRI domestically.

Koizumi also took on a leading role in diplomacy with North Korea. In consultation with Ministry of Foreign Affairs officials, he concluded that Japan faced major risks in its Korean Peninsula policy. On the one hand, the United States had demonstrated a tendency towards unilateral regime change and military action that might precipitate a new Korean war into which Japan would be dragged. On the other, Japan might risk diplomatic isolation if the United States moved towards rapprochement with North Korea, because of strong public opposition to improving bilateral relations before Pyongyang was forthcoming on the fate of Japanese citizens abducted in the 1970s and 1980s. Koizumi's visits to North Korea in September 2002 and May 2004 were an attempt to break Japan out of this impasse, by demonstrating to Washington the need to exhaust diplomatic means and attempting to clear away the domestic political issues hindering Japan's role in the peninsula's security affairs. He achieved a partial resolution of the abductees issue with Pyongyang's admission of the abductions of 13 Japanese citizens, but when it became clear that eight of the 13 abductees had died in suspicious circumstances whilst in North Korea, domestic opposition to concessions restricted Japan's role in the Six-Party Talks.

Koizumi's stance on Japanese colonial history, and his insistence on annual visits to Tokyo's Yasukuni shrine (where 12 convicted Class-A war criminals are among some 2.5m commemorated war dead), were often seen as motivated by domestic political considerations. He used the issue to undercut right-wing opposition and to ensure that he seized full control of Sino-Japanese relations from other LDP factions. Koizumi's stance seriously damaged political relations with China and South Korea even as economic ties continued to strengthen. A positive direction had been taken in Sino-Japanese relations by Koizumi's visit to China in October 2001 and his reiteration of Japanese apologies at sites commemorating the initiation of Japanese aggression against China. But no direct bilateral summit meetings were held in the following five years. Tensions over history were compounded by friction over exploitation of gas reserves in disputed Exclusive Economic Zones (EEZs) in the East China Sea, the sovereignty of the Senkaku/Diaoyu islands, and Japan's bid for a permanent UN Security Council seat. Relations with South Korea were aggravated by revived tensions over the sovereignty of the Takeshima/Dokdo islands. Koizumi had been unable to hold a summit with President Roh Moo Hyun after June 2005.

On broader regional policy, Koizumi made a positive start with a speech in Singapore in January 2002 offering a vision of an East Asian community that 'advances together and acts together', including at its core the ASEAN+3 forum as well as Australia and New Zealand. An active approach continued with pursuit of bilateral free-trade agreements, termed by Japan Economic Partnership Agreements (EPAs), with individual ASEAN states. However, Japan seemed to lack a strongly articulated vision of how these bilateral agreements would reinforce the wider East Asia vision. Japan sought to block China's competing vision for East Asian regionalism based on the ASEAN+3, successfully proposing, in an attempt to dilute the rising influence of China, that the inaugural East Asia Summit in December 2005 should include Australia and India. Moreover, the impression of an equivocal approach to East Asian regionalism during Koizumi's premiership was reinforced by a general sense that Japan's principal priority was to strengthen security ties with the United States, even to the detriment of its regional leadership ambitions.

Abe's leadership platform

Given the new importance of the prime minister in determining foreign policy and Koizumi's controversial record in this area, the 2006 LDP leadership election became an occasion for a debate on future strategic direction, and in particular on the correct balance among ties to the United States, China and East Asia. In the run-up to the election, then-Finance Minister Sadakazu Tanigaki emerged as the candidate of the Koichi Kato faction, the traditionally pragmatic wing of the LDP, long associated with the post-war 'Yoshida Doctrine' of maintaining a low-profile military stance and close ties with Washington, but also looking to build stronger ties with East Asia. Tanigaki promised to repair ties with China and South Korea and pledged that he would not visit the Yasukuni shrine as prime minister. The far-right wing of the party was represented by Foreign Minister Taro Aso, grandson of Shigeru Yoshida, but noted as a more extreme conservative. Aso promised a tougher stand against North Korea and China, describing the latter as a threat to Japan. He also proposed the nationalisation of the Yasukuni shrine, currently a private organisation under the 1946 separation of state and religion. Nationalisation would open the way for removal of Class-A war criminals to help resolve neighbouring countries' objections. However, the proposal was also fundamentally conservative because it signalled a return to strong links between the state and commemoration of Japan's wartime past.

The two strongest potential candidates for the LDP leadership, Abe and Yasuo Fukuda, emerged from the same Yoshiro Mori faction as Koizumi. Fukuda portrayed himself as an experienced moderate in foreign affairs, having served as chief cabinet secretary until 2004, enjoying close ties to the United States – he was the favoured candidate amongst much of the US policy community early in the race. As the son of Takeo Fukuda (who as prime minister enunciated the 1977 doctrine that shifted Japan towards stronger relations with ASEAN and signed the 1978 Sino-Japanese Treaty of Peace and Friendship), he also maintained good relations with China and the rest of East Asia. Fukuda withdrew in July, citing age reasons (he would have been 70 if elected). It was suspected that the main reason was a wish to avoid a rift within the Mori faction, as he had been vocal in the past in criticising prime ministerial visits to the Yasukuni shrine.

Abe, chief cabinet secretary, then emerged as the front runner. In contrast to Koizumi, he did not attempt to gain the LDP leadership on a platform of domestic economic reform. He was expected largely to continue Koizumi's reforms, although he acknowledged the need to remedy social inequalities brought about by economic liberalisation. In this sense Abe was more of a traditional LDP politician, with less of Koizumi's Machiavellian mastery of domestic politics. Instead, he entered the leadership campaign with stronger nationalist foreign-policy credentials than Koizumi. He was the grandson of Prime Minister Kishi Nobusuke, who was interned for three years as a suspected Class-A war criminal and the prime mover in the 1960 revision of the US–Japan security treaty.

Abe belongs squarely to the 'revisionist' right-wing of the LDP, and, like Koizumi, has been determined to challenge and escape from the post-war course of Japanese foreign policy. In his campaign Abe argued that Japan should break out of the domestic and international structural constraints imposed in the post-war period, and practice 'battling diplomacy' to make Japan a 'beautiful nation'. Abe suggested this should include revising the 'masochistic' view of Japanese colonial history that had forced Japan to keep a low profile in international affairs. He advocated educational reforms to inculcate a stronger sense of 'patriotism' amongst Japanese youth. Though he was known to have visited the Yasukuni shrine in April 2006, during his leadership campaign he stuck to the line that he would not comment on whether he would or would not visit the shrine as prime minister because he believed the issue should not be politicised.

Abe pledged to follow Koizumi in placing US–Japan security relations at the forefront of foreign policy. He argued that Japan could only influence the United States through a more equal partnership and alliance of action and values, involving expanded military cooperation and the lifting of Japan's self-imposed ban on the exercise of collective self-defence. But Abe was hawkish in his views on the impact of China's rise on Japanese security, and had close links to Taiwan's leadership, whereas Koizumi, despite the dispute over Yasukuni, was not predisposed to hostility towards China. Abe was toughest on North Korea, where Koizumi had been disposed to diplomatic engagement. In his previous positions as assistant chief cabinet secretary and secretary-general of the LDP, and as chief cabinet secretary, Abe had been instrumental in preparing economic sanctions to pressure Pyongyang over the abductee issue, and at times had discussed the need for 'regime change'. He stressed strongly in his election campaign that North Korea must be brought to book for 'state terrorism' over the abductees.

Abe put greater emphasis than Koizumi on improving ties with East Asia and sponsoring regionalism, stressing that Japan, with its advanced economic and political status, should be the natural leader of the region. He sought a clearer ideological basis for Japanese foreign policy, abandoning the apparent expediency of the previous five years. Abe argued that Japan's foreign policy should be based on four principles: liberty, democracy, human rights and the rule of law. To achieve this, he argued, Japan had to enact domestic structural change, including revision of Article 9 of the 1946 'peace constitution'; revision of historical interpretations of Japanese imperialism in East Asia as exceptional or wholly destructive; and education reform to promote a greater sense of nationalism. The prime minister's decision-making power was to be boosted through creation of a Japanese National Security Council (JNSC), modelled on that of the United States.

Abe's interest in domestic politics was to drive foreign policy forward, whereas Koizumi had primarily used foreign policy to push ahead on his domestic agenda. Abe's youthful appeal, relatively high public-opinion ratings and tough stance on North Korea, and the belief of LDP politicians that this would gain them electoral success in the upcoming July 2006 elections for the upper house, meant that he won the votes of 70% of the MPs. He was installed as prime minister on 26 September 2006.

The final months of Koizumi's tenure and the early period of Abe's threw up foreign-policy challenges which were to test them both.

Japan and the Korean Peninsula

Japan's principal security concerns in 2006–07 revolved around North Korea. Japan–North Korea relations, already stuck in neutral over the abductee issue, were put into reverse with Pyongyang's test firing of seven ballistic missiles into the Sea of Japan in July 2006. Although the missiles landed far from Japanese territory – and closer to North Korea than Japan – their targeting in the sea bearing Japan's name was viewed in Japan as a highly provocative act almost akin to the North's 1998 *Taepodong-1* test which overflew Japan itself. Tokyo responded with uncharacteristic vigour at the UN. Japan initially introduced a draft UN Security Council Resolution based on Chapter VII of the UN Charter that would have imposed sanctions on North Korea's acquisition of finance and technology for ballistic missiles and WMD. China responded with a proposed chairman's statement that would have condemned the tests while avoiding mention of Chapter VII and sanctions. Intense diplomacy led to eventual agreement on UNSCR 1695, condemning the tests and called for a ban on trade in nuclear or missile technology with North Korea, but without reference to Chapter VII. This was the first time that Japan had introduced a UN resolution on its own initiative, and policymakers were quick to portray it as a diplomatic triumph.

Immediately after the missile tests, Japan imposed a six-month ban on port calls by the *Mangyongbong-92* ferry, the only passenger link between Japan and North Korea and a vital financial resource for Pyongyang. Tokyo also banned the entry of North Korean officials into Japan. On 19 September, relying on UNSCR 1695, Japan imposed a ban on financial transfers to 15 North Korean-linked financial institutions and trading firms. Much of Japan's response was coordinated by Abe as chief cabinet secretary. Hence, by mid 2006, Koizumi's summit meetings and attempted engagement were a fading memory. By the time Abe assumed power, Japan had already shifted towards a harder line.

When North Korea carried out a nuclear test on 9 October 2006, Japan, as rotating chair of the Security Council, played a key role alongside the United

States in helping to pass UNSCR 1718, based on Chapter VII and mandating sanctions on North Korea regarding nuclear and WMD and military equipment. Japan also imposed a ban on all North Korean registered ships entering Japan, as well as on trade in luxury goods with Pyongyang. Abe's government also prepared to ban all financial remittances from North Korean residents in Japan.

Shortly after the passing of Resolution 1718, Abe's administration considered the application of the 1997 revised US–Japan Guidelines for Defence Cooperation to enable Japan to support the United States in interdicting North Korean shipping. Discussions were held over whether Japan had a legal right to strike North Korean missile bases in the face of an imminent attack. In October 2006, Shoichi Nakagawa, chairman of the LDP's Policy Research Council, and Foreign Minister Aso attempted to initiate debate on the utility of nuclear-weapons acquisition, although neither actually proposed that Japan should abandon its non-nuclear principles. Abe suppressed the debate and reaffirmed Japan's non-nuclear stance, but not before the talk had attracted the interest of China, South Korea and the United States. On 16 October President Bush expressed concern that reconsideration of Japan's nuclear stance would cause anxieties for China, and that North Korea's nuclear weapons might produce an arms race in Northeast Asia. Japanese acquisition of nuclear weapons remains unlikely given the US 'nuclear umbrella' and anti-nuclear sentiment in Japan. Nevertheless, the North's nuclear test helped to break down the taboo on the nuclear debate in Japan. Meanwhile, Abe's administration took an even harder line on the abductee issue, ordering the NHK broadcasting service to carry more coverage of the abductions, and even presenting a documentary about them at the World Economic Forum in Davos, Switzerland in January 2007.

Subsequent events undermined Japan's tough stance on North Korea. Abe appeared to have faith in the Bush administration's willingness to face down North Korea over the missile and nuclear provocations, a confidence bolstered by Japanese interactions with John Bolton as the US ambassador to the UN during the passage of UNSCR 1695 and 1718. But Bolton was replaced and the influence of other neo-conservative hardliners, including Vice President Dick Cheney, diminished following the November Congressional elections. Though Tokyo clearly welcomed the restarting of the Six-Party Talks in December 2006, the accord with Pyongyang in February 2007 left it out of step with its partners. Japan was taken aback by the pace at which Washington was prepared to make concessions to Pyongyang.

Talks on normalisation of relations between Japan and North Korea, one of the commitments agreed in the February accord, were held in Hanoi on 7–8 March, but soon broke up in discord over the abductee issue, without a fixed date for resumption. Japan made it clear that it was prepared to refuse US and Chinese requests to provide energy, financial or food aid assistance to Pyongyang until the latter made significant concessions on the nuclear issue, and certainly not until there was substantive progress towards resolution of the abductee issue. Tokyo later indicated some possible flexibility in its position, stating that it might provide assistance indirectly, through the despatch of Japanese government officials to assess North Korea's energy demands. But Foreign Minister Aso reiterated in March that Japan would not provide 'even one yen' until the abductee issue was resolved.

Abe's stance on North Korea negated the diplomatic victories won at the UN in 2006, and instead placed Japan in a bind. On the one hand, Japan risks diplomatic isolation if it fails to fully support the Six-Party Talks, and already faces private accusations from irritated Chinese, South Korean and US officials that fixation on the abductee issue could jeopardise the denuclearisation process. On the other hand, Abe's reliance on the abductee issue to boost his domestic standing means he is unlikely to soften his approach. Japan may only be rescued from this diplomatic bind if North Korea fails to keep its promises, which might provoke a harder US line.

Japan's relations with South Korea in 2006–07 also suffered because of its hardline stance on the North. President Roh Moo Hyun's administration, still looking to maintain engagement with the North, reacted negatively to what it perceived as Japan's seizing on the July missile tests as an opportunity to stoke up a crisis and further isolate the North. Roh and other ministers expressed concerns at Japan's bellicose talk of striking at missile bases, discussion of a nuclear option, and general use of the North Korean threat to push forward its remilitarisation.

Ties between Japan and South Korea were also damaged by ongoing bilateral disputes. They continued to wrangle over sovereignty over the Takeshima/Dokdo islands, and talks held on demarcating their overlapping EEZs held in June and September 2006 and March 2007 produced no agreement. South Korea reacted strongly to Koizumi's visit to the Yasukuni shrine on 15 August 2006, the anniversary of Japan's defeat in the Second World War. Abe's ascension to the premiership brought hopes of an improvement in relations. Although Seoul was clearly suspicious of his right-wing nationalism, it was aware that the new prime minister was predisposed to good relations. Abe planned his first overseas trip as prime minister to China, and South Korea, eager not to be left behind, quickly responded to Japanese requests for a summit. At their summit in Seoul on 9 October Abe and Roh condemned North Korea's nuclear test, and agreed to pursue a 'future oriented' relationship, with Abe stating ambiguously that he would treat the Yasukuni issue 'appropriately'. His visit was followed by a visit of then Foreign Minister Ban Ki Moon to Tokyo in November 2006, the visit of the new South Korean Foreign Minister Song Min Soon in December, a defence ministers' meeting in Tokyo in February 2007, and the visit of Foreign Minister Aso to Seoul in March.

Bilateral relations continue to be troubled by differences of strategy towards North Korea and the problems of colonial history. South Korea has felt increasing frustration with Japan over its foot-dragging on the February 2007 agreement, and over remarks by Abe in March concerning the so-called 'comfort women' (a euphemism for women serving in brothels run by the Japanese imperial armed forces during the Second World War). In January 2007, Mike Honda, a Democrat member of the US House of Representatives, introduced a bipartisan non-binding resolution calling on the Japanese government to acknowledge responsibility for and to offer a full apology to the comfort women. Abe told Japanese reporters on 1 March that there was no evidence suggesting that women were 'narrowly coerced' into prostitution, in the sense that they were physically taken to military brothels. This seemed to suggest that Abe might approve of a review of Japan's 1993 'Kono Statement' under which the government had accepted responsibility for the forcible recruitment of comfort women. It also seemed to contradict his earlier acceptances of Japanese government statements relating to the colonial past shortly after taking office. Abe, in the face of domestic and international criticism, soon afterwards stressed his administration would not change the Kono Statement, and reiterated Japan's sincere apologies for the suffering of the comfort women. However, Abe's retraction was not quick enough to assuage Seoul. The South Korean government expressed its 'strong regrets' over Abe's remarks.

Sino-Japanese relations: back on track?

During the final months of Koizumi's premiership, China began to reach out to Japan in the hope that it could influence the post-Koizumi political landscape. The Fifth Japan–China Comprehensive Policy Dialogue, attended by vice-ministers for foreign affairs, was held in Beijing on 7–9 May 2006; and a foreign ministers' meeting in Qatar on 23 May reached an agreement for the resumption of the Japan–China Security Dialogue, suspended for over two years, in November. Foreign Minister Aso repeated Japan's request for greater transparency in China's military stance, whilst the Chinese side repeated its objections to prime ministerial visits to the Yasukuni shrine as the principal block on efforts to hold a bilateral summit. On 10 June Chinese President Hu Jintao stressed to the new Japanese ambassador that when the conditions were right he was willing to visit Japan, and Koizumi in response repeated that Japan was ready for unconditional dialogue with China at any time.

An immediate upturn in Japan–China relations was halted by Koizumi's provocative visit to Yasukuni on 15 August. Koizumi justified his visit as a matter of individual freedom, designed purely to honour those who gave their lives in the service of Japan, and not to justify war or militarism. But he visited the shrine in his public capacity as prime minister and to fulfil a public promise to visit the shrine on the anniversary of Japan's defeat made during his campaign for the LDP presidency in 2001. China reacted angrily to the visit as an offence to those who had suffered under Japanese wartime aggression, and as damaging to bilateral ties.

However, both sides were already looking beyond Koizumi's administration. Abe, who had put out feelers towards China even before his election, secured a summit with Hu Jintao and Wen Jiabao in Beijing on 8 October. Abe and Hu agreed on the need for enhanced bilateral cooperation to persuade North Korea to return to the Six-Party Talks (North Korea exploded its first nuclear device the following day) and reconfirmed the importance of peaceful consultation on the East China Sea with the aim of eventual joint development. Japan requested support for its bid for a permanent seat on the Security Council, but China simply reiterated the importance of discussions on Security Council reform. On issues of history, Abe acknowledged the damage inflicted on East Asia by Japanese colonialism, and Hu expressed his hopes that Japan would continue to follow its post-war path of peaceful development. Both sides also agreed to establish a joint study group on colonial history. Abe skirted the Yasukuni issue by maintaining his line that he would not comment on whether he would or would not visit the shrine as prime minister. For its part, Beijing appeared satisfied that Abe's agreement to 'remove political obstacles' to political ties could be read as an agreement not to visit Yasukuni during his period of office. Abe invited the Chinese leader to visit Japan at an early date, and continued discussions with Hu on North Korea and history issues on 18 November at the APEC summit in Hanoi. Abe met with Wen Jiabao at the ASEAN+3 and East Asia summits on 13–14 January 2007 in Cebu.

The Japanese government began to refer to Sino-Japanese ties as a 'mutually beneficial strategic relationship'. Similarly, China's silence throughout March on the brewing comfort-women controversy reflected Beijing's eagerness for a more cooperative relationship with post-Koizumi Japan – although Wen made it clear that any future visits to the Yasukuni shrine by Abe would cross a red line for bilateral relations.

Both sides began to put substance into the strategic-partnership concept with Wen's visit to Japan from 11–13 April. Abe and Wen held direct talks on 11 April, and the following day Wen became the first Chinese leader to address the National Diet. Wen also proved adept at popular diplomacy — jogging and practicing t'ai chi in Tokyo's Yoyogi park, and drinking tea and playing baseball in Kyoto. Abe and Wen worked hard during the talks to avoid making history a central issue; and in his Diet address Wen, although he did refer to Japan's 'war of aggression', also noted that China valued highly Japan's apologies for the war and avoided mentioning Yasukuni or the comfort-women issue. Japan and China restated the need for cooperation to deal with North Korea's nuclear progamme, especially through the mechanism of the Six-Party Talks. Abe requested further

Chinese help with resolving the abductee issue. However, Wen simply stated in his talks with Abe that he 'understood the emotions' of Japanese people on the issue, and avoided the abductee issue in his Diet address. Abe and Wen reached a verbal agreement that both sides should continue investigations into the joint exploration of gas resources in the East China Sea; and agreed to promote increased military exchanges and confidence building in security, including visits of defence officials and warships, and a warning mechanism between both countries to avoid unnecessary incidents. Abe stressed Japan's intention to pursue a permanent Security Council seat, but Wen side-stepped the issue, remarking that China had expectations that Japan should have an important role to play in the UN. In addition, Japan and China agreed to cooperate on countering climate change by working for a new post-Kyoto protocol, and agreed that Japan should share technologies for environmental protection and energy saving.

Japanese policymakers largely accepted Wen's appraisal of his visit as 'thawing out' bilateral relations following Abe's 'ice-breaking' visit in October. China appeared to have recognised the importance of improving ties with Japan, stemming from its need for Japanese investment and technology to maintain rapid development, and also for closer political ties to balance the prospects of a Democratic Congress in the US taking a harder line on trade issues. Abe had clearly decided to build better ties with China, in the face of pressure not to upset bilateral relations from his Komeito coalition partner, opposition parties and big business.

Nonetheless, whether Japan–China ties could develop into a real strategic partnership remained questionable. Despite continuing working-level talks on the East China Sea since July 2006, and the statements at bilateral summits, Japan has failed to persuade China to halt exploratory activities, and it appeared in late 2006 that China was moving towards full-scale production in its Chunxiao gas field. Japan also protested in July 2006 and February 2007 about the entry of Chinese maritime survey ships into its EEZ around the disputed Senkaku/Diaoyu islands, breaching a 2001 bilateral agreement for prior notification of research activities. Tokyo continued to stress concerns over the lack of transparency in China's military build-up and viewed with discomfort China's January 2007 anti-satellite test in which a missile shot down a defunct satellite. Moreover, as Abe was mending ties with China, Japan was simultaneously manoeuvring to create new partnerships with India, Australia and Europe to act as counterweights to China's rise. Finally, the issue of history remains, though on the margin, not entirely off the agenda.

US–Japan relations: new growing pains
Abe followed Koizumi in consolidating US–Japan ties, although tricky issues remain. The strength of the alliance was shown by the close diplomatic coor-

dination in pushing through UNSCR 1695 and by accelerating cooperation on Ballistic Missile Defence (BMD) deployment. Japan accepted the deployment to Yokosuka in August 2006 of the USS *Shiloh,* one of the US's first missile defence-capable destroyers, with plans to add BMD capability to four more US destroyers based at the port. Tokyo then speeded up the introduction of *Patriot* PAC-3 missiles from 2006 onwards and the refitting of *Kongo*-class *Aegis* destroyers to carry BMD-capable SM-3 missiles by the end of 2007 instead of March 2008. Japan's other three *Aegis* destroyers will carry SM-3 missiles by 2010 rather than 2011.

US policymakers greeted Abe's accession with the hope that he would continue to move cooperation forward, but also apprehension over his ability to build a personal relationship with Bush, to calm tensions with China over history, and to deal with the unfinished business of implementing the DPRI. Abe's visit to China in October drew praise from Washington as an act of statesmanship, and his administration's active diplomacy in the UN in response to North Korea's nuclear test also drew American plaudits. Japan and the United States subsequently reaffirmed their security guarantees in the face of the North Korean threat, with Secretary of State Condoleezza Rice's statement during her visit to Tokyo on 19 October 2006 that 'Japan's security is the United States' security'. Abe first met with Bush in his capacity as prime minister at the APEC meeting in Hanoi in November, producing standard pledges on continued alliance cooperation and countering North Korea's nuclear programme.

Koizumi had gambled that, although the DPRI meant increased costs for the taxpayer and shifting of the US military presence to local communities potentially opposed to the move, the public as a whole would accept it to attain a stronger US–Japan alliance and a reduced US presence in Okinawa. But there has been resistance to the DPRI from within the LDP, opposition parties and local communities.

The government was relieved when its preferred candidate, Nakaima Hirokazu, was elected as governor of Okinawa in November 2006, defeating candidates who opposed a new facility to replace Futenma and wanted the US to leave the prefecture altogether. However, whilst Nakaima was willing to discuss with the central government plans to create a new facility in Okinawa, he continued to stress the prefecture's opposition to the specifics of the DPRI, and especially proposals to build V-shaped runways at Henoko. The relocation of the US carrier wing aircraft from Atsugi was threatened by wrangling between the mayor of Iwakuni city and the city assembly: the mayor argued against the relocation and received overwhelming support in a referendum, but the assembly censured the mayor for his actions, fearful of losing central government subsidies. Japan's pledge (separate from the DPRI) to the United States to allow, for the first time, a nuclear aircraft carrier to be based in Yokosuka also ran into opposition. The mayor and assembly eventually accepted the deployment, but opposition from citizens' groups forced a debate on the need for a referendum. Abe's administration can only pilot these realignments through by manipulating central-government subsidies. Moreover, there appeared to be no rapid solution to the Futenma issue that has been a political thorn in the side of the alliance for over a decade – the US and Japan first agreed to relocate it in 1996. In the meantime, the government pushed legislation through the lower house in April to facilitate relocation of USMC units to Guam, but is likely to face an inquisition in the upper house from opposition politicians dissatisfied at the government's refusal to fully reveal Japan's share of these costs, thought to be around $6-7 billion.

Abe's government, even if it can work through the base realignment issues, still faces a number of issues that are encumbering smooth management of the alliance. Japan's increasing international confidence and commitment to US-led coalitions means that criticism of US strategy is now more likely to be heard in Tokyo. Although the GSDF withdrew from Iraq in July 2006 after a two-year mission, the Japanese government in April 2007 submitted a bill to the Diet to extend the ASDF mission transporting supplies from Kuwait to Iraq until July 2009 and the MSDF mission in the Indian Ocean supporting the coalition in Iraq until November 2007. Defence Minister Fumio Kyuma in January criticised the US decision to go to war in Iraq and its lack of understanding of the domestic politics of Okinawa. Foreign Minister Aso in February called the American occupation of Iraq 'very naive'. Washington officially complained about Kyuma's remarks and then rejected until April Japanese offers of a defence summit meeting. Similarly, US–Japan ties have been strained by Japan's attitude towards the February agreement in the Six-Party Talks.

The greatest stress to relations was the comfort-women controversy. In February Aso rejected the US congressional draft resolution on the comfort women as 'groundless'. Abe's remarks on the degree of coercion involved in military brothels generated stiff criticism of Japan in the US media. Abe's subsequent moves to adhere to the Kono Statement helped to quell the controversy, but Japanese policymakers feared that this spat over history would dominate the bilateral summit in April. In the end, the 26–27 April summit in Washington helped build personal trust between Bush and the new prime minister, but the event was low-key. Abe avoided media engagements, probably for fear of being quizzed over the comfort-women issue, and Washington and Tokyo announced no new moves in security cooperation; the joint statement focused on energy and environmental cooperation measures.

Japan's East Asian, Pacific, Eurasian and European diplomacy
Abe made important strides in rehabilitating Japan as a regional leader through mending ties with China and South Korea, although his remarks on comfort

women and continued ambiguity over visits to Yasukuni remained potential obstacles for relations with East Asia. Japan pushed on with its strategy of bilateral free-trade agreements, launching negotiations with Vietnam, India and Australia, and finally signing an EPA with Thailand in April 2007, adding to EPAs already concluded with the Philippines, Malaysia and Singapore. Japan's Ministry of Economy, Trade and Industry announced in April 2006 its plan to corral these agreements into a larger EPA across the whole of East Asia, to include the ASEAN+3 states and India, Australia and New Zealand. Japan's plans, though, were hampered by a lack of progress in the Japan–South Korea EPA negotiations, domestic Japanese resistance to a Japan–China EPA, and China's preference for regionalism based on the ASEAN+3 format. The East Asian Summit statement in January 2007, though, acknowledged that there were a number of complementary formats for regionalism in East Asia. Even though Japan was not able to reassert leadership through adoption of a particular format, neither was China.

Abe's strategy to strengthen links with Australia as a counterweight to China's influence was also partly realised by the 13 March 2007 Japan–Australia Joint Declaration on Security Cooperation. The declaration specified a number of areas for cooperation, including counter-terrorism, maritime and aviation security, peace operations and disaster relief. Japan had already built close cooperative relations with Australia since 2004 through JSDF deployments in Iraq and tsunami relief efforts in the Indian Ocean. As liberal democracies and close US allies the countries are natural security partners, but the scope for extension of the security relationship may be limited by Japan's ban on collective self-defence and Australia's close economic relationship with China.

Japan's new emphasis on value-oriented diplomacy and developing a broader set of strategic relationships to reinforce its international position was further evidenced by its diplomacy in Central Asia, the Middle East and Europe. Koizumi paid his last overseas visits to Mongolia, Kazakhstan and Uzbekistan in August 2006, following up on the 'Central Asia Plus Japan' dialogue first launched in 2004 to improve ties, help secure energy supplies and counter Chinese influence in the region. Aso then outlined plans to promote an 'arc of freedom and prosperity' stretching from Australasia, Southeast Asia and South Asia through to Central Asia, the Caucasus, the Balkans, Eastern Europe and the Baltic, based on the common values of freedom, democracy, human rights, the rule of law and the market economy.

Accordingly, Japan sought a higher profile sponsoring the Arab–Israeli peace process, and in March 2006 hosted a meeting of representatives from Israel, Jordan and the Palestine Liberation Organisation with the aim to put in place joint development projects to create a 'Corridor for Peace and Prosperity'. Tokyo also placed renewed emphasis on relations with Europe to implement the arc of freedom and prosperity. Abe visited London, Berlin and Brussels on 9–12

January 2007, and became the first Japanese prime minister to address the North Atlantic Council. At the same time, Aso visited Romania, Bulgaria, Hungary and Slovakia. This initiative was notable for its strong emphasis on strategic reciprocity in security, compared to earlier initiatives focused predominantly on economic and cultural ties or Japanese security assistance for European peace efforts in the Balkans. Abe offered Japanese financial support for NATO peacebuilding operations and even hinted at JSDF participation in Provincial Reconstruction Teams in Afghanistan (a move Japan finally rejected in April), but in return made it clear that Tokyo expected European leaders to fully implement agreed UN sanctions on North Korea, to maintain the embargo on arms exports to China, and to recognise the importance of Japan's Security Council bid.

Developments in security policy

In his election campaign Abe hinted at radical changes in security policy. One was the elevation of the Japan Defense Agency to cabinet-level as the Ministry of Defense (MoD) in January 2007, which will boost its role in security planning alongside the Ministry of Foreign Affairs. The government also planned the JNSC as a small-scale body, comprising the prime minister, chief cabinet secretary, and foreign and defence ministers, to aid more efficient decision-making. Abe also wanted to create the position of standing national security adviser, drawn from the National Diet, who would join the JNSC and draw upon a staff of 10–20 experts. Abe largely succeeded, but bureaucratic opposition to members of the Diet serving as part of the executive weakened the role of the national security adviser in shaping security policy.

Abe also moved forward on constitutional revision. In April 2007 the LDP and Komeito pushed legislation through the lower house enabling a referendum on constitutional reform and Abe established an advisory council on lifting the ban on the exercise of collective self defence. None of the council members were known critics of the move. Abe succeeded in passing a Basic Education Law in December 2006 and prepared a School Education Law in March 2007 which sought to instil greater patriotism in the young. He made no progress toward a permanent law on international peace cooperation activities that would facilitate more routine support for US-led 'coalitions of the willing' and UN operations.

Abe's prospects

As prime minister, Abe has managed to maintain much of Koizumi's forward momentum in security policy, but his weaker grasp of domestic politics than his predecessor may undermine his strategic agenda. He is beholden to domestic pressure on the abductions issue, reinforcing Japan's inflexibility and isolation in the Six-Party Talks. At the same time, he faces criticism from the right in Japan over 'kowtow' diplomacy with China over history issues. Abe also faced elections for the upper house in July 2007, and his popularity had dipped compared to Koizumi's. This was the result of a series of gaffes and domestic scandals, including Abe's allowing LDP anti-reform rebels, ejected by Koizumi following his 2005 landslide, back into the party; Abe's minister of health and welfare referring to women as 'birthing machines' in February; the DPJ's discovery that the government had failed to keep track of 50m pension accounts and Defence Minister Kyuma's resignation in July after saying the atomic bombs that fell on Hiroshima and Nagasaki were inevitable. If Abe experiences a major setback in the July elections his leadership and international strategy might come unstuck, and there could be a challenge for the leadership from more radical right-wingers such as Aso.

South Asia: Indian Growth, Regional Turbulence

India's rapid economic growth and increased business confidence led over the past year to the country's being seen increasingly as a rising great power. This was despite its perennially poor infrastructure and neglect of the agriculture sector – which was the cause of considerable domestic concern. Border talks with China and the proposed civil nuclear agreement with the United States lost momentum, although the United States and India were cautiously optimistic that the latter could be concluded. The peace process with Pakistan entered its third year with little progress in the aftermath of the Mumbai bombings of 11 July 2006, blamed by India on Pakistan, which denied the charge. The intensification of attacks by Maoist Naxalites in central India represented an important additional threat to national security.

In the summer of 2007, Pakistani President Pervez Musharraf was facing his gravest domestic challenge since he took power nearly eight years earlier. His suspension of the Pakistani Chief Justice led to popular street demonstrations which evolved from a campaign to reinstate the judge into a full-fledged movement to end military rule in the country. This greatly weakened Musharraf's power and raised doubts over his ability to secure a second term as president in elections expected in September–October 2007. There was growing international concern over Musharraf's ability to counter Islamic extremism, in view of his reversal of policy in the tribal areas bordering Afghanistan, where controversial peace accords were signed with pro-Taliban tribal leaders.

Nepal made a significant transition from conflict to peace and stability, with the signing of a peace accord with Maoist rebels on 21 November 2006. This formally ended a ten-year insurgency that had killed an estimated 13,000 and displaced some 400,000 people. However, the building of trust between the government and the Maoists required time, with a number of political and security issues remaining of concern.

In marked contrast, the conflict in Sri Lanka deteriorated from low-intensity guerrilla warfare to near full-fledged undeclared conventional warfare. This was marked by artillery exchanges, naval engagements and air strikes by both sides, even though the formal ceasefire remained in force on paper. In a significant development, the Sri Lankan armed forces regained territory from the LTTE for the first time in five years in the east, bolstering their confidence. But this still seemed an unwinnable conflict with little prospect of talks.

With Bangladeshi politics mired in turmoil and bitter confrontation between the two major political leaders in the run-up to general elections that were scheduled for January 2007, a military-backed caretaker government took over. It postponed elections, declared a state of emergency and began to tackle corruption as a pre-condition to restoring democracy. As no firm election schedule was fixed, there was concern about the prospects for democratic government.

India

Politics and economics

Notwithstanding continued unprecedented growth of 9.2% in 2006–07 compared to 9% the previous year, the ruling Congress-led United Progressive Alliance (UPA) faced setbacks in key provincial elections that were an early prelude to the summer 2009 general election. The boom in the service sector, accounting for 55% of the economy, continued, along with 11% growth in the manufacturing sector. Corporate India flourished: a growing number of Indian companies became multinationals, looking for mergers and acquisitions worldwide. Laxmi Mittal of Mittal Steel acquired the European steel producer Arcelor for $35 billion in June 2006, Ratan Tata of Tata Steel acquired Britain's Corus Group for $12bn in April 2007 and Venugopal Dhoot of Videocon acquired Daewoo Electronics (South Korea) for $700 million in October 2006. The stock exchange also remained confident, with the Sensex, India's key stock market index, rising to a new high in June 2007.

However, the agriculture sector, the mainstay of the Indian economy, caused considerable concern. Although two-thirds of the workforce was engaged in farming, the sector's share of the economy dropped to 19%, with cultivable land remaining idle and water available for irrigation declining. With 60% of farmland dependent on a good monsoon for reasonable crop yield, agricultural growth stagnated at 1.8%, raising the prospect of a resumption of the import of grain. The southwest monsoon in June–September 2006 was just below normal in overall precipitation, though a bit erratic. There was a spurt in suicides among farmers in states such as Andhra Pradesh and Gujarat due to poverty.

In February 2007 inflation was at a two-year high of 6.73%. This contributed, along with weak organisational cohesion and an anti-incumbency factor, to losses by the ruling Congress Party in February 2007 in provincial elections in the states of Punjab and Uttarakhand. The Shiromani Akali Dal–Bharatiya Janata Party (SAD–BJP) coalition won the elections in Punjab and the BJP formed the government in Uttarakhand. However, the Congress Party retained power in Manipur as part of a coalition government with the Communist Party of India. In crucial elections in Uttar Pradesh, India's largest state, in April 2007, the Dalit lower-caste leader Mayawati led her Bahujan Samaj Party (BSP) to a surprise electoral victory, defeating the ruling Samajwadi Party-led coalition government and becoming the first party in 15 years to rule Uttar Pradesh on its own. This was achieved by reversing the traditional anti-Brahmin stance of the BSP and engaging with the upper castes. While the BJP was the main loser in the election, the Congress Party, whose electoral campaign was led by Rahul Gandhi, scion of the Gandhi family, was not far behind. On 2 June 2007, the Congress Party retained power in Goa, India's smallest province, as part of a coalition government with the Nationalist Congress Party.

Internal security

Long-standing domestic security problems worsened. The Maoist Naxalites intensified attacks in the central state of Chhattisgarh, focusing on the Dantewada district. On 17 July 2006, approximately 400 Naxalites attacked a controversial civil militia Salwa Judum (peace campaign) camp at Errabore, killing 31 villagers, injuring 20 and abducting another 20. On 1 March 2007, eight people were killed in a landmine blast at Mettagudem; on 15 March some 500 Naxalites killed 55 police personnel and injured 12 others at a police outpost in the village of Rani Bodli. The Naxalites also shot dead Sunil Kumar Mahato, a member of parliament and general secretary of the Jharkhand Mukti Morcha (JMM), at a football match in Jharkhand on 4 March.

The Naxalites' access to small arms was revealed by the seizure of a large haul of rockets, rocket launchers and explosives in Andhra Pradesh on 8 September 2006. Another large arms dump was found on 16 March 2007 in that state's Nallamalla forest. Earlier, on 12 October 2006, large amounts of anti-personnel mines and ammunition were seized in Kolkata. Sourced from a government-run ordnance factory, the arms were reportedly destined for Maoists in West Bengal.

In the northeast, the conflict in Assam with the separatist United Liberation Front of Assam (ULFA) continued, with a surge in violence and little prospect for peace. Talks between the Indian government and the People's Consultative Group, negotiating on ULFA's behalf, failed to make any progress. In an attempt to encourage face-to-face talks with ULFA, without acceding to its demand for the release of five of its leaders in Indian custody, the government on 13 August 2006 suspended all counter-insurgency operations. However, following continued ULFA attacks, the government called off its ceasefire on 27 September 2006. In Guwahati, on 5 November 2006, 15 people were killed and more than 40 injured in two bomb blasts in busy markets; this was followed on 23 November by a bomb outside the railway station which killed three people and injured ten. On 23 June 2007 four people were killed and 20 injured in a bomb explosion carried out by ULFA near a mosque in Guwahati. In Manipur, elections were successfully held in February 2007, despite the spurt in killings. On 9 February, United National Liberation Front militants killed six policemen after the first phase of polling. On 24 February, 15 paramilitary troops were killed after the final polling round.

Social tensions also loomed in Punjab and Rajasthan. In Punjab, the conservative Sikh clergy threatened agitation against the Sikh-based Sachcha Sauda sect in May 2007, accusing it of offending Sikh religious sentiments. In Rajasthan, the Gujjar community, officially categorised as 'Other Backward Castes', violently agitated for 'Scheduled Tribe' status, which brings economic benefits. In late May 2007, thousands of Gujjars blocked the Jaipur–Kota and Jaipur–Agra national highways, and 12 were killed by police gunfire on 29 May 2007. Gujjars in neighbouring states, including Delhi, protested the police action by taking to the streets, where they clashed with the Meena community, which already had Scheduled Tribe status. Following a meeting with the BJP chief minister of Rajasthan on 3 June, the protests were temporarily called off.

Relations with China

On the eve of Chinese President Hu Jintao's visit to India in late November 2006, the first by a Chinese president in a decade, the Chinese ambassador to India raised the issue of Arunachal Pradesh, an Indian state, by publicly stating that it was Chinese territory. The Indian foreign minister rejected this statement, reiterating that Arunachal Pradesh was and would continue to be an integral part of India. This exchange marred the tone of Hu's visit, but with China in the process of overtaking the United States as India's largest trading partner, India and China agreed to double bilateral trade to $40bn by 2010.

Talks in India between the special representatives of the two countries on their border dispute appeared to bog down due to a hardened Chinese stance. The tenth round of talks, on 20–21 April 2007, ended with little to show. India remained concerned over Chinese construction of infrastructure such as roads and rail lines near the Line of Actual Control, the unofficial border between the states. India was also annoyed by China's refusal of a visa to an official from Arunachal Pradesh in June 2007 on the grounds that he was 'Chinese' and did not need one. India cancelled the visit of the large delegation of which he was to be a part, along with two other government delegations scheduled to visit China.

Nonetheless, Prime Minister Manmohan Singh described China at the G8 meeting in Germany in early June 2007 as India's 'greatest neighbour'. On 18 November 2006, a third border point for meetings between border personnel of the Indian and Chinese armies, after Nathula in Sikkim and Bumla in Arunachal, opened at Kibithu in Arunachal Pradesh. India also planned for the first time to carry out joint army exercises with China, on Chinese territory, in October 2007, following an agreement reached during the visit of the Indian army chief to China in late May. In April 2007, China attended as an observer for the first time a meeting of the heads of state or government of the South Asian Association for Regional Cooperation (SAARC) in New Delhi. Afghanistan attended as a new member.

The civilian nuclear deal

Following the 2 March 2006 agreement between Singh and President George W. Bush on India's plan for separating its civilian and military nuclear facilities and putting the majority of its reactors under international safeguards, the focus shifted to the US Congress. Both houses would have to pass an amendment to the US Atomic Energy Act of 1954 for a country-specific waiver to its prohibition of civil nuclear cooperation with any country that did not accept comprehensive safeguards.

In December 2006, the House of Representatives (by a vote of 330 to 59) and the Senate (by 'unanimous consent') passed the requisite legislation, named, after the outgoing chairman of the House International Relations Committee, the Henry J. Hyde US–India Peaceful Atomic Energy Cooperation Act of 2006. The approval was not unconditional, however, and was only the first of a two-stage Congressional approval process. The Hyde Act was the enabling measure that allowed US and Indian officials to negotiate the prospective bilateral '123' civil nuclear cooperation agreement. Named after the clause in the Atomic Energy Act that permits cooperation with outside sovereign entities, the 123 agreement will allow implementation of the deal and requires formal approval by the US Congress. Final Congressional approval depends on agreement by the 45-member Nuclear Suppliers Group (NSG) to grant India an exception to its guidelines requiring comprehensive International Atomic Energy Agency (IAEA) safeguards. India also needs to negotiate a safeguards agreement with the IAEA.

Although the Indian government welcomed the Hyde Act, it said it would 'not accept any conditions that go beyond the parameters of the July 18, 2005 Joint Statement and the March 2, 2006 Separation Plan'. India viewed certain sections of the Hyde Act as contrary to the general provisions of the two prior agreements. The Indian government's differences with the Hyde Act were encouraged by the leftist parties of the ruling coalition government, the opposition BJP and a section of the nuclear scientific community, who saw the Hyde Act as a 'shifting of goalposts'. In an emotive speech, which appeared to lay down India's red lines on this issue, Singh told the upper house of parliament on 17 August 2006 that there were suggestions that 'India's strategic nuclear autonomy is being compromised and India is allowing itself to be pressurized into accepting new and unacceptable conditions that are deviations from the commitments made by me to Parliament in July 2005 and in February and March this year'. He reiterated that 'the proposed U.S. legislation on nuclear cooperation with India will not be allowed to become an instrument to compromise India's sovereignty'.

The two major points of contention at the end of June 2007 were the right to reprocess spent nuclear fuel from civilian power reactors and a formal moratorium on nuclear tests. While India insists on the right to reprocess spent nuclear fuel, the Hyde Act bans it on the basis of a long-standing US policy that goes well beyond India. However, this is a key requirement for India for disposal of spent fuel, which otherwise could be a safety concern. Moreover, Singh had told parliament on 17 August 2006 that India sought 'the removal of restrictions on all aspects of cooperation and technology transfers pertaining to civil nuclear energy – ranging from nuclear fuel, nuclear reactors, to re-processing spent fuel, i.e. all aspects of a complete nuclear fuel cycle', and it would 'not agree to any dilution that would prevent us from securing the benefits of full civil nuclear cooperation'. To seek to break the logjam, India recently offered to set up a dedicated facility for reprocessing spent fuel under IAEA safeguards.

The US Atomic Energy Act stipulates that all 123 agreements must allow the United States the right to require the return of 'any nuclear materials and equipment transferred' if the recipient country 'detonates a nuclear explosive device'. In effect, if India were to detonate a nuclear explosive device, the United States would have the right to cease further cooperation. India argues that this is inconsistent with the separation plan of March 2006, which stated that there would be multi-layered assurances for fuel supplies, including the ability to build a stockpile to meet the lifetime requirements of the reactors. This is a politically sensitive issue for the Indian government in view of the cancellation of the fuel-supply contract for the US-built reactor at Tarapur after India's 1974 nuclear test, which used plutonium produced at the reactor.

Moreover, this may require the text of the 123 agreement to incorporate a reference to nuclear detonation, which would be seen by the Indian government as a restriction on India's future strategic nuclear programme. This would also conflict with Singh's categorical statement in parliament on 17 August 2006 that 'the US has been intimated that reference to nuclear detonation in the India–US Bilateral Nuclear Cooperation Agreement as a condition for future cooperation is not acceptable to us. We are not prepared to go beyond a unilateral voluntary moratorium on nuclear testing as indicated in the July Statement'.

Although not part of the 123 agreement negotiations, India also objected to a section of the Hyde Act that calls on the US president to submit a written determination that India is participating in US efforts to contain Iran's nuclear programme. The Indian government perceives this as an attempt to influence its 'foreign policy and strategic autonomy'. India strongly rejected the linkage of any extraneous issue to the nuclear agreement. India's Foreign Secretary Shiv Shankar Menon reiterated in May 2007 that there was no link between the nuclear deal and the Iran–Pakistan–India gas pipeline project, with both needed to ensure India's energy security.

However, to reassure Washington, India publicly banned the export of all nuclear-related technology to Iran on 9 May 2007. The formal ban had earlier been notified by the director general of foreign trade under the Foreign Trade (Development and Regulation) Act 1992 on 20 February 2007. It prohibits the 'direct or indirect export and import of all items, materials, equipment, goods and technology which could contribute to Iran's enrichment related, reprocessing or heavy water related activities, or to the development of nuclear delivery systems'.

While India and the United States are cautiously optimistic about finalising the 123 agreement, there are still key issues to be agreed, especially reprocessing of spent fuel and lifetime supply of nuclear fuel. It is also unclear whether such an agreement will be reached by the end of 2007, before looming presidential elections in the United States and general elections in India make it harder for either side to compromise. Meanwhile, India and the IAEA have made little progress on an India-specific nuclear-safeguards agreement, which some members of the NSG have said would need to be finalised before they would agree to waive NSG guidelines for India.

The India–Pakistan Peace Process

The peace process with Pakistan entered its third year with little progress to show. Bombings in Mumbai 11 July 2006, blamed by India on Pakistan (which denied the charge), had the effect of suspending the composite dialogue for four months. There was thus little tangible movement on the eight issues under discussion. Nonetheless, both sides moved forward on confidence-building measures (CBMs) in an attempt to normalise relations. Although expectations of an agreement on the Kashmir dispute were publicly generated by Pakistan following the resuscitation of the dialogue in November 2006, they appeared exaggerated. Whereas Pakistani President Musharraf saw the fourth round of the composite dialogue, which began on 14 March 2007, as the time to move forward from conflict management to conflict resolution, India appeared cautious in view of his own growing domestic troubles in mid 2007.

The Mumbai bombings killed 184 people and injured 844. The attack was well coordinated, with seven bombs placed on suburban trains exploding in an

11-minute period during the evening rush hour. Indian intelligence and police officials focused on two active Islamist militant groups, the indigenous Students Islamic Movement of India and the Pakistan-based Lashkar-e-Tayiba (Army of the Pure), as possible perpetrators. Islamabad's offer to cooperate fully with the Indian investigation was dismissed by New Delhi. In turn, New Delhi's request to ban the Jamaat-ud-Dawa (the political wing of the Lashkar-e-Tayiba) and to arrest its leaders, and to hand over the commander of the Hizbul Mujahadeen terror group, was rejected by Islamabad. On 24 October 2007, Singh stated that there was 'credible evidence' of Pakistani involvement in the Mumbai blasts, which Islamabad denied.

Another major terror attack on 19 February 2007 on the Samjhauta Express near Panipat killed 68 people and injured 60 others. The train was travelling between Delhi and Lahore, with 41 of those killed identified as Pakistani nationals. Both governments were quick to condemn the attack, which came a day before the visit of the Pakistani foreign minister to India. Two other terror attacks specifically targeted Muslim places of worship on a Friday. On 8 September 2006, there were three bomb blasts in Malegaon in Maharashtra, killing 31 people and injuring 125 others. Two bombs targeted Muslims gathered for prayers at a mosque and a burial ground; the third went off in a crowded street. Although the Indian government was again initially cautious in directing blame, police focused their investigations on Pakistani and Bangladeshi nationals. On 18 May 2007 another bomb killed 9 people and injured 53 at the historic Mecca mosque in Hyderabad. The subsequent violent protest by Muslims led to shooting by police in which three people died. Earlier, on 20 November 2006, seven people were killed and 50 injured when two bombs exploded on a passenger train in West Bengal, the first major explosion in the state in the past eight years.

Following the Mumbai bombings, India postponed foreign-secretary-level talks with Pakistan scheduled for July 2006 and refused to confirm dates for talks on the disputed border area of Sir Creek, scheduled for August 2006. Tit-for-tat expulsions of diplomats by both countries from 5 August 2006 – the first since the peace process began – were a further setback. Nonetheless, no transportation or communication links were disrupted, and new CBMs continued. On 19 August 2006, the first Thar Express train crossed the border into Pakistan, followed on 27 October by the restoration of cargo-shipping services with Pakistan after 35 years. Expert and technical-level talks also continued. On 1 September 2006, border guards held their joint quarterly meeting, and on 2 November 2006 the countries agreed to boost rail-freight traffic across the border in the Munabao–Khokhrapar and Waga–Attari rail sectors.

Three months after the Mumbai bombings, on 16 September, Singh and Musharraf met on the sidelines of the Non-Aligned Summit in Havana, and agreed to resume the stalled bilateral dialogue. In a significant development,

Singh stated that both countries had suffered from terrorism and suggested the establishment of a 'collective mechanism' to deal with it. They agreed to set up a bilateral 'anti-terrorism institutional mechanism to identify and implement counter-terrorism initiatives and investigations'. At talks between the foreign secretaries in Delhi on 14–15 November, which signified the resumption of the composite dialogue, a three-member anti-terror mechanism was set up to share information. However, its first meeting, held in Islamabad on 6–7 March 2007, made no progress, with the two sides simply agreeing to exchange information to help investigations relating to terrorist acts and to prevent violence in the two countries.

Meanwhile, there appeared to be a hardening of positions by both sides over the Siachen Glacier. While India, whose casualties in the region had fallen to near zero, made it clear that demilitarisation of Siachen could only take place after Pakistan agreed to 'iron-clad' authentication of its troop positions, Pakistan countered that there was no justification for this as Siachen was a disputed area, and 'a part of Kashmir'. This position was contrary to the composite dialogue's structure, under which Kashmir and Siachen were to be discussed separately.

There was little progress on Sir Creek, although for the first time charts were exchanged showing the parties' respective positions on the delineation of the creek and maritime boundaries. A survey was also conducted in February–March 2007 by both India and Pakistan. In accordance with the UN Convention on the Law of the Sea, both sides are required to file claims for their Exclusive Economic Zones and continental shelves by May 2009, requiring a resolution of the dispute. If this does not happen, both sides would have to forgo their claims.

Nonetheless, a significant nuclear CBM was signed on 21 February 2007. An eight-point agreement on 'Reducing the Risk from Accidents relating to Nuclear Weapons' set out guidelines and included information-sharing initiatives. A hotline between the Indian Coast Guard and the Pakistan Maritime Agency was also inaugurated on 14 November 2006. However, an important CBM agreed in principle by both sides, to start a cross-Line of Control (LoC) truck service between Srinagar and Muzaffarabad, was not implemented.

Kashmir
Following the Singh–Musharraf meeting in Havana, there was considerable expectation in Pakistan of a breakthrough in the talks on Kashmir. This was largely for three reasons: Singh's acceptance in Havana of Musharraf's invitation to visit Pakistan, although this came with the caveat that it would take place only if a substantive outcome was likely; the 'back-channel' negotiations taking place between Ambassador Satinder Lambah, the special envoy of the Indian prime minister, and Tariq Aziz, the secretary of the Pakistan National Security Council,

though the content and substance of their talks remained secret; and the ability of both countries to resume talks soon after the Mumbai blasts and the series of accusations and denials.

Building on his proposal of 31 October 2005, Musharraf continued to emphasise four points that in his view should underlie resolution of the Kashmir dispute – identifying linguistic, ethnic and religious regions, demilitarisation, self-governance and joint management. On 4 December 2006, he declared to an Indian TV news channel that Pakistan was prepared to give up its traditional claim to Kashmir if India accepted a solution that included demilitarisation and 'self-governance with a joint supervision mechanism' – though it was later claimed that he had been misquoted and that there was no change in Pakistan's position. In what was interpreted as a hardening of his position, Musharraf stated on 18 February 2007 that Pakistan continued to push for a plebiscite and the right of self-determination in Kashmir, a departure from his earlier stance setting aside UN resolutions on a plebiscite. While India appeared to perceive Pakistan's proposals as ambivalent, Pakistan perceived India's rejections or failure to respond as showing lack of interest in resolving the dispute.

The first practical stage of Musharraf's proposal was demilitarisation of Kashmir. While the Pakistani government was willing to withdraw its troops from the LoC, it would only do so as part of the four-point settlement; there was to be no unilateral demilitarisation of Pakistan-administered Kashmir. The Indian government, on the other hand, stated that withdrawal of its forces from Kashmir could only occur when cross-border infiltration and violence ended. This position diverged for the first time from that of a number of mainstream political parties in Jammu and Kashmir, including the People's Democratic Party, a partner in the ruling state coalition. These groups pushed for a phased withdrawal of troops and repeal of the controversial Armed Forces (Special Powers) Act, applicable in parts of Kashmir in the run-up to state elections in 2008. While ruling out demilitarisation and troop reductions, Defence Minister A.K. Antony conceded on 18 June 2007 that two official committees had been formed to assess the reconfiguration of security forces in Jammu and Kashmir and examine the implementation of the act in parts of the state. At the same time, over 10,000 border troops engaged in counter-terrorist operations were replaced by paramilitary forces. The ceasefire along the LoC and in Siachen continued successfully into its fourth year.

However, there was sporadic violence. On the day of the Mumbai bombings, eight people were killed and 37 injured in serial bomb blasts in Srinagar. On 10 November 2006, five people were killed and 55 injured in a grenade attack outside a mosque. Although cross-border infiltration in Kashmir was considerably reduced for much of the year, it appeared to be on the rise in summer 2007, even though terror attacks did not noticeably increase. Minister of State for External Affairs E. Ahmed said that there were 52 terrorist-training camps in Pakistan and Pakistan-administered Kashmir.

In an attempt to bolster dialogue with provincial leaders, Singh organised a third official roundtable conference on Jammu and Kashmir in New Delhi on 25 April 2007. Boycotted again by the moderate factions of the separatist All Party Hurriyat Conference, its working groups recommended that the Armed Forces (Special Powers) Act and the Disturbed Areas Act be 'reviewed and revoked', a joint consultative group of legislators on both sides of the LoC be formed to exchange views on matters of mutual interest, and a high-powered committee for enforcing human rights be created. To monitor their implementation, Singh proposed the establishment of a Standing Committee along with an Oversight and Monitoring Mechanism. However, the most important group, discussing devolution of powers among different regions, did not reach a consensus.

A fortnightly cross-LoC Poonch–Rawalakot bus service was inaugurated by UPA chairperson Sonia Gandhi on 20 June 2006. For the first time in 60 years, over 4,000 people were permitted to travel across the LoC.

Military developments

India increased its defence budget by nearly 8% to $21.7bn, with significant purchases of new military hardware planned. This included an interim order for an additional 40 upgraded Sukhoi Su-30 aircraft from Russia in view of delays in issuing a $10bn tender for 126 multi-role combat aircraft (expected in August 2007). Defence diplomacy took a major step forward with the first trilateral naval exercise with the US and Japan along the Pacific coast of East Asia in March 2007. This followed the annual *Malabar* series of exercises with the US Navy, held off Japan for the first time. In another bold move, the Indian government permitted the US nuclear-powered aircraft carrier USS *Nimitz* to dock off Chennai for the first time in the first week of July 2007, despite considerable criticism from leftist parties in the ruling coalition. In July 2006, four Indian warships on a routine deployment in the eastern Mediterranean were able to evacuate 2,500 Indians, Sri Lankans and Nepalese from the conflict in Lebanon.

On 27 November 2006, India successfully carried out its first missile interception test, when a *Prithvi* surface-to-surface ballistic missile shot down a similar missile off India's east coast, demonstrating a nascent capability to develop an anti-missile shield. This was followed by the first successful test of the 3,500km-range nuclear-capable *Agni* III missile on 12 April 2007; the first test on 9 July 2006 had failed. While additional tests of the *Agni* III are scheduled, India demonstrated the technical competence for development of a longer-range missile in the near future. On 22 June 2007, the Indian army formally inducted into service the *BrahMos* supersonic cruise missile. The missile, with a range of 290km, was developed as a joint venture between India's Defence Research and Development

Organisation and Russia's Mashinostroyenia research and production centre. The Indian army also planned to hold joint exercises with Russia on Russian territory for the first time in late 2007.

Pakistan
Domestic politics
In summer 2007, President Musharraf faced his gravest domestic challenge since he took power in a military coup on 12 October 1999. His suspension of Chief Justice Iftikhar Mohammed Chaudhry for alleged abuse of office on 9 March 2007 led to popular street demonstrations demanding the judge's reinstatement and Musharraf's resignation. This greatly weakened Musharraf and raised doubts over his ability to secure a second term in presidential elections expected in September–October 2007.

Chaudhry's sudden suspension and referral to a judicial body for disciplinary action appeared to be motivated by his apparent opposition to Musharraf's re-election while a serving military officer. The constitution required him to step down as army chief, the primary source of his power, if he wanted to serve another term.

While the suspension came as a surprise to Chaudhry, the public reaction came as a shock to Musharraf. The judge's public defiance encouraged street protests by thousands of lawyers in Islamabad and Lahore. The televised government crackdown on the demonstrators and opposition parties fuelled greater opposition, with women's groups, journalists and the secular opposition joining street demonstrations. The campaign to reinstate Chaudhry developed into a full-fledged movement to end eight years of military rule.

In the ensuing clashes between demonstrators and police, a number of people were injured and over a thousand opposition-party activists were arrested. But on 12 May, while Chaudhry was at Karachi airport, riots broke out in the city between the pro-government Muttahida Qaumi Movement and local opposition parties and lawyers, leading to 42 deaths. The riots were broadcast live; television stations were attacked and fires started on the streets. In an attempt to subjugate the media, Musharraf promulgated draconian amendments to the Pakistan Electronic Media Regulatory Authority (PEMRA) law on 4 June, which gave him the authority to close down television channels without review. However, under intense media pressure, he agreed to rescind the amendments five days later.

Notwithstanding growing public opposition to Musharraf's rule, the army and its key group of corps commanders publicly supported him. The Bush administration reiterated its confidence in Musharraf and his commitment to the campaign on terror, notwithstanding serious concerns over the tribal areas bordering Afghanistan. There was speculation about political deals between a weakened Musharraf and the resurgent secular opposition, especially former Prime Minister and Pakistan People's Party (PPP) leader Benazir Bhutto – in previous elections the PPP was the largest single party. Such a deal might involve Bhutto returning from exile to stand in elections with all corruption charges against her and her husband dropped; Musharraf could then stand for president but step down as army chief.

Religious extremism

Musharraf attempted to tackle religious extremism in the last year, but without much success. He oversaw changes to inflammatory school textbooks and introduced a new Women's Protection Bill, enabling civil courts to try rape cases. Most of the 13,000 madrassas were finally registered with the government, but there was little progress towards promised reforms. More worrying was a public demonstration of Islamic extremism in the capital, Islamabad, in a stand-off between the radical Lal Masjid (Red Mosque) and its associated women's madrassa, Jamia Hafsa, and the government. Following the occupation of an adjacent library by Jamia Hafsa students in January 2007 to protest against the destruction of mosques illegally built on state land, these students temporarily apprehended on March 27 three women they accused of running a brothel. On 6 April 2007 the top clerics of the Lal Masjid vowed to enforce sharia law in Pakistan and demanded the closure of all brothels and music shops in Islamabad, threatening to unleash a wave of suicide bombers if the government opposed the move. On 23 June Jamia Hafsa students once again kidnapped nine people, including six Chinese nationals, on allegations of immorality. On 29 June Musharraf said that suicide bombers linked to al-Qaeda were believed to be in Lal Masjid. Following several days of clashes, Pakistani troops stormed the mosque on 10 July, leaving more than 70 militants dead.

Tribal areas

In a major policy reversal, the government on 5 September 2006 signed a controversial ceasefire with pro-Taliban leaders in Miran Shah, capital of North Waziristan in the Federally Administered Tribal Areas bordering Afghanistan, where nearly 80,000 troops have clashed with local Taliban and al-Qaeda forces in the past three years. Pakistani security forces were to withdraw from newly installed checkpoints and return to their garrisons. In return, locals were to eject foreign fighters, cease attacks on Pakistani security forces, and desist from launching cross-border raids into Afghanistan.

The Miran Shah accord met considerable criticism. It was viewed as the effective handing over of administrative control of North Waziristan to the Pakistani Taliban and its al-Qaeda associates. The Pakistani government said it was not withdrawing troops from the region and its commitment to the fight against terror had not weakened. It argued that the tribal areas needed to be pacified comprehensively, which required cooperation of pro-Taliban leaders.

While attacks on the Pakistani army decreased, the Taliban and al-Qaeda were able to strengthen their position. In areas under their control in both North and South Waziristan, they killed political opponents, enforced sharia law, banned girls from going to school, forcibly shut video shops, and forbade barbers to shave beards. With a sanctuary in Waziristan, they reportedly increased three-fold their covert crossings into Afghanistan to attack NATO forces and reopened terrorist training camps in the area.

With US concern mounting over the resurgence of the Taliban in Afghanistan, outgoing Director of National Intelligence John Negroponte testified on 11 January 2007 before the US Senate Select Committee on Intelligence that Pakistan 'remains a major source of Islamic extremism and the home for some top terrorist leaders'. He warned that al-Qaeda's core elements 'maintain active connections and relationships that radiate outward from their leaders' secure hideouts in Pakistan'. As a result, on 26 February 2007 US Vice President Dick Cheney, along with CIA Deputy Director Stephen Kappes, made an unannounced visit to Pakistan to reportedly push Musharraf to crack down harder on Taliban and al-Qaeda forces in the tribal areas.

Yet, in March 2007, the government entered into two further peace accords with pro-Taliban elements in the Bajaur agency, north of Waziristan. On 17 March, it reached an official verbal agreement with the Mamoond tribe, followed on 26 March by the Salarzai and Utmankhel tribes. This followed a Pakistani missile attack on an alleged al-Qaeda training base at a madrassa in Bajaur on 30 October 2006, killing 80 people, which had led to the suicide bombing of an army training camp in Dargai in Malakand agency near Bajaur on 8 November 2006, killing 44.

As Islamabad pressed the tribes to implement their side of the accords, there were violent clashes in South Waziristan between tribesmen and foreign (largely Uzbek) al-Qaeda terrorists. The worst took place on 19–22 March and 30 March 2007, when nearly 200 foreign terrorists were reportedly killed. On 4 April, some 50 people were reportedly killed in clashes between pro-government tribesmen and foreign militants in South Waziristan.

Jihadist terror attacks continued to take place throughout the country. On 26 January 2007 a suicide bomber blew himself up at the Marriott Hotel in Islamabad, killing a security guard, followed on 5 February by another suicide bomber injuring three people in the car park of the airport at Rawalpindi. On 17 February, 17 people, including a senior civil judge, were killed and 30 others injured in a suicide bombing in the District Courts compound of Quetta, the capital of Baluchistan. On 20 February, a female minister in Punjab was shot dead by an Islamic extremist for refusing to wear the veil. On 28 April a suiide bomber killed 28 and injured 40, including the target of the attack, Interior Minister Aftab Ahmed Khan Sherpao, in Charsadda in the North West Frontier Province. On 15 May a bomb blast at a hotel in Peshawar killed 24 people and injured 30.

With growing US and UK concern over the rise of cross-border infiltration from the tribal areas of Pakistan into Afghanistan, Pakistani security forces attempted to beef up their border security checkpoints. This had limited impact. With Pakistani and Afghan leaders placing responsibility on each other, the prospect for meaningful bilateral cooperation was limited. At the same time, Pakistan did not permit US-led military forces in Afghanistan to carry out 'hot pursuit' of the Taliban onto Pakistani territory, or joint military operations with the United States against the Taliban on Pakistani territory. In the absence of coercive Pakistani policy in the tribal areas, cross-border infiltration will continue to undermine the security of Afghanistan.

Other security issues and military developments

Long-standing sectarian conflict continued throughout the last year. On 14 July 2006, a suicide bomber killed Allama Hasan al-Turabi, a high-profile Shia scholar and political leader, in Karachi. The former district president of the outlawed Shia group Tehreek-e-Jaferia Pakistan, Syed Bashir Hussain Bukhari, was also shot dead in Punjab on 21 September 2006. On 2–5 October violent clashes between the Sunni Ahl-e-Sunnat and Shia sects over a controversial shrine in the Orakzai tribal area of North West Frontier Province killed nearly 30 people. On 27 January 2007, 15 people, including the city's police chief, were killed and 60 injured in a suicide attack targeting a Muharram procession in Peshawar. This was reportedly followed by sectarian clashes between Sunni and Shia groups in the Kurram agency on 6–11 April 2007, in which there were a number of casualties.

Violence between the military and the Baluchistan Liberation Army (BLA) continued, with a major setback for the nationalists. Baluch militants carried out ambushes, rocket attacks, bombing campaigns and assassinations of security officials, along with attacks on energy infrastructure. On 26 August 2006, a military operation in the Bhambore Hills, between the cities of Kohlu and Dera Bugti, killed Sardar Nawab Akbar Khan Bugti, the popular leader of the local Bugti tribe and a former governor of the North West Frontier Province, and 37 others. Unprecedented violence in the provincial capital Quetta led to the imposition of a curfew.

Following Bugti's death, the level of violence in Baluchistan decreased, but attacks on pipelines and other targets continued. Tensions between Pakistan and Iran increased following bombings in Zahedan in Sistan-Balochistan province in Iran on 14 and 17 February 2007, which killed 11 Revolutionary Guards. The attack was blamed on Pakistani Baluch militants. Earlier, Pakistani security forces carried out operations against militant camps in Baluchistan. Security operations in Kohlu and Sibi districts in mid-January 2007 led to several arrests.

In June 2007, Pakistan increased its defence budget by 10% to $4.5bn. It was in the process of acquiring a number of Chinese-built JF-17 fighter aircraft and other weapons for the army and navy, to reduce India's superiority in conventional arms. Pakistan continued tests of nuclear-capable ballistic and cruise missiles. On 23 February 2007, it carried out the fifth test of its longest-range ballistic missile, the *Hatf-6* (*Shaheen-2*), with a range of 2,000–2,500km, followed a month later by the third test of the new *Hatf-7* (*Babur*) cruise missile with a range of 700km.

Nepal

On 21 November 2006 Prime Minister Girija Prasad Koirala and Prachanda, chairman of the Communist Party of Nepal (Maoist), signed a historic peace accord in Kathmandu formally ending a ten-year insurgency that killed an estimated 13,000 and displaced some 400,000 people. The Comprehensive Peace Agreement (CPA) came about after concessions by both sides; the Maoists agreed to UN supervision of their arms and the Seven Party Alliance (SPA) agreed to include the rebels in an interim assembly in the absence of an electoral mandate. The ceasefire paved the way for inclusion of Maoist rebels in an interim government for the first time on 1 April 2007 and for elections to the Constituent Assembly, expected at the end of the year.

The 'people's movement' that ended King Gyanendra's rule on 24 April 2006 – making him powerless – revolved around a loose political alliance between the mainstream SPA and the Maoists in November 2005. Although the SPA insisted the protests were under their direction, the Maoists played the most important part in organising the mass movement: their dominance in the countryside, and their support and active direction, were crucial in mobilising the rural population. Maoists also played an important role in urban centres, helping to incite the public, boost demonstrations and provide some political direction to the masses.

The previously unthinkable alliance between the mainstream parties and the Maoists was made possible by the rapid polarisation of political forces in Nepal following Gyanendra's declaration of an emergency on 1 February 2005 and his dismissal of Prime Minister Sher Bahadur Deuba's government on the tenuous grounds of the latter's failure to secure a dialogue with the Maoists and his apparent inability to organise elections. Although the king did not ban political parties, political activity was severely restricted and senior political party leaders were placed under house arrest. The king also increasingly relied on heavy-handed repression to restore order and introduced tough emergency measures that obstructed not only political parties, but civil society as a whole.

As a result, the parties weakened their support of the monarchy as an essential pillar of Nepalese politics. The dynamics of conflict, previously three-cornered with the Maoists, the king and the political parties each commanding considerable influence, altered dramatically, with the king increasingly pitted against all others. In a key development, the SPA and the Maoists agreed to a 12-point agreement on 22 November 2005, incorporating the Maoists' 'firm commitment' to accept a competitive multiparty system, fundamental rights, human rights, rule of law and democratic principles. This was reaffirmed in March 2006.

The king lacked the support to contain an insurgency of the magnitude of the Maoists, who organised general strikes, shut-downs and blockades at the local and regional level and carried out armed attacks on the Royal Army. The shut-downs and blockades were extremely effective, as the Maoists controlled the country's three major highways and could lock down the economy virtually at will, isolating Kathmandu by cutting off its supply routes. Confronted by popular mass protests and strikes which shook the country for three weeks in April 2006, aware of his weak military position and under increasing international pressure, on 21 April 2006 Gyanendra asked the SPA to name a new prime minister. Faced with the SPA's refusal, hardening opposition following the deaths of a number of protesters at the hands of the security forces, and mass defiance of curfews following his misjudged offer, the king surrendered power on 24 April and reinstated the House of Representatives, which he had dissolved in 2002. While the Maoists rejected this as inadequate, the SPA welcomed it, and nominated Nepali Congress President Girija Prasad Koirala as the new prime minister.

Although the Maoists and the mainstream parties had worked together to this point, they were plagued by lack of trust and disagreement over how to proceed. On 26 May they signed a 25-point ceasefire code-of-conduct, followed by an eight-point accord on 16 June in which they agreed to ask the UN to monitor weapons and personnel, to dissolve the existing House of Representatives, and to establish an interim government. This set the agenda for subsequent talks, though the details were yet to be negotiated amidst an atmosphere of mistrust. It was not clear how the provisions for UN monitoring called for in the accord were to be implemented. Koirala wrote to the UN Secretary General on 2 July 2006, requesting assistance in the decommissioning, rather than monitoring, of weapons before Constituent Assembly elections. After this letter was made public, Prachanda responded with a separate letter on 24 July 2006 making it clear that any talk of decommissioning of the PLA's arms before elections was 'unthinkable'. With pressure from the UN assessment mission visiting Nepal, both sides sent letters to the UN on 9 August, inviting it to monitor and manage the arms and personnel of the Nepalese army and the PLA. The parties also sought UN assistance to monitor the code of conduct, the human-rights situation and the Constituent Assembly elections.

Difficult and sporadic negotiations continued, and in early October the talks appeared to be on the verge of collapse when the Maoists threatened to launch an urban revolt in the face of what they saw as government foot-dragging. A draft peace agreement was reached on 8 November 2006, but the Maoists failed to sign it eight days later as planned. Additional provisions on land reform, human rights and social and economic transformation were incorporated and the resulting CPA was signed five days later.

The key issue the CPA dealt with was the management of weapons and personnel. For the Maoists, retention of arms was important insurance against being left vulnerable should the talks fail, and provided a useful lever in negotiations through the threat of an urban revolt. The Maoists were also keen to integrate the PLA into the Nepalese army. However, the SPA feared that an armed PLA would not be conducive to peace and could compromise free and fair elections. While the SPA also insisted that the PLA's weapons and personnel be managed before Constituent Assembly elections, the Maoists were adamant that such a process could only be overseen by an interim government in which they were included.

The CPA stated that the PLA would be confined to seven cantonments in Kailali, Surkhet, Rolpa, Palpa, Kavre, Sindhuli and Ilam by 21 November 2006. All PLA arms and ammunition were to be stored in locked containers within these cantonments. While these containers were to be remotely monitored electronically by the UN, the Maoists would retain the keys. At the same time, the Nepalese army was to be confined to barracks and its arms placed in similarly monitored locked storage facilities. The number of Nepalese army weapons and personnel under UN supervision was to be proportional to the number of Maoist cadres and weapons. However, the Nepalese army would be allowed to continue to protect borders, government members and critical infrastructure.

A week later, a separate agreement on arms management was signed by the SPA and the Maoists and handed over to the UN. This allowed the UN to begin its monitoring with the formation on 23 January 2007 of a UN mission in Nepal (UNMIN) with a 12-month mandate to monitor the ceasefire and assist in Constituent Assembly elections. On 9 March 2007 UNMIN completed the first phase of verification of PLA arms and combatants. The PLA voluntarily registered a total of 3,475 weapons and confined 31,152 of its members in the seven cantonments. However, the Nepalese army questioned these figures and stated that some 781 arms, including automatic machine guns, had been hidden. The second phase of verification to ensure that the registered Maoists were over 18 years old when they were recruited was postponed to 14 June 2007 to enable salaries to be paid to the PLA. Following a further postponement due to the killing of Maoist leaders in southeastern and western Nepal, it finally began on 23 June.

The SPA and Maoists disagreed over the form of future democratic political institutions, including an interim legislature and government, and elections to the Constituent Assembly. Whereas the Maoists contested the legitimacy of the House of Representatives reinstated by King Gyanendra on 24 April 2006, the SPA favoured its continuation, with additional seats for the Maoists, as its members were elected representatives of the people. The Maoists' proposal to create an all-party conference comprising a third each of the Maoists, SPA and civil society was opposed by the SPA.

The CPA provided that the reinstated House of Representatives would be dissolved and a 330-member interim parliament set up in its place by 26 December 2006. This would have 209 members from the House of Representatives and Upper House (other than those who opposed the Maoists in April 2006), 73 Maoists to be nominated by the rebels and 48 other seats reserved for professional organisations and underrepresented regions. In addition, the Maoists were to be represented in an interim government to be formed by 1 December 2006. The interim government would hold elections by June 2007 for a 425-member Constituent Assembly. Elections to the Constituent Assembly were to be held through a mixed system of first-past-the-post, proportional representation and appointments by the Council of Ministers under UN supervision. The constitution was to be scrapped and an interim constitution, already drafted by a committee, to be introduced from 21 November 2006, with a final constitution to be adopted by the newly elected Constituent Assembly.

On 16 December 2006, the draft of the 168-point interim constitution was signed by the SPA and the Maoists. Unanimously backed by the House of Representatives on 15 January 2007, it paved the way for the Maoists to enter parliament. On 2 February, the 330-member interim parliament was formed with the Maoists as members. On 1 April, a 22-member interim government was formed with Koirala as prime minister. For the first time, senior Maoists such as Krishna Bahadur Mahara, Hisila Yami (wife of party ideologue Baburam Bhattarai) and Matrika Yadav took part in the formal governance of the country, as ministers for information and communications, physical planning and works, and forest and soil conservation respectively. In late June 2007, the interim government decided to postpone elections to the Constituent Assembly to 22 November.

There was a major disagreement between the SPA and the Maoists over the future of the monarchy. King Gyanendra had been stripped of all powers, including control over the 90,000-strong Nepalese army, on 18 May 2006 and had no further authority in relation to governance. Yet his continuation in office aroused strong suspicion among Maoists that he might yet interfere in domestic politics aided by an external power. They were therefore keen to see an end to the monarchy as soon as possible. On 14 August 2006, Prachanda suggested a suspended status for the king, with his fate to be decided by the Constituent Assembly. However, the SPA was more circumspect, with the Nepali Congress Party seeking to retain the institution of the monarchy by openly suggesting that the king should be given a role, possibly ceremonial, under the new constitution. On 25 August the draft interim constitution proposed that the fate of the monarchy be decided through a referendum to be held along with the Constituent Assembly election.

Although the CPA suspended all the powers of the king until the Constituent Assembly decided on the future of the monarchy, disagreement between the SPA and the Maoists continued. While Koirala on 16 October 2006 reiterated that it should be left to the Constituent Assembly to decide the future of the monarchy, with the king kept to a ceremonial role until then, Prachanda on 27 February 2007 publicly sought to end the monarchy and establish a parliamentary republic. The interim constitution made the king powerless and vested all powers in the prime minister as both head of state and government. On 13 June 2007, the parliament adopted a provision allowing it to abolish the monarchy by two-thirds majority if the king were found to be conspiring against the Constituent Assembly elections.

With Maoist violence, intimidating behaviour and abductions gradually decreasing after the 25 May 2006 ceasefire code of conduct, the security environment across the country improved. Maoist 'donation drives' continued until late 2006, despite repeated allocations of government funds to the PLA for its maintenance. Forcible recruitment to the PLA also continued for much of 2006, as the Maoists attempted to boost troop numbers before the cantonment process began.

Lack of trust is compounded by unrealistic and ambitious timeframes for key political developments which are rarely, if ever, adhered to. This perceived lack of commitment serves to exacerbate suspicions of the other side's motives. The prospective elections to the Constituent Assembly, a key demand of the Maoists, are a case in point. The interim government decided they would be held in mid June on the basis of a wholly unrealistic schedule. When they did not take place on time, the Maoists attributed an ulterior motive to the SPA.

As the Constituent Assembly elections draw nearer, the stakes for representation become greater, with individual parties' electoral interests potentially diverging. With over 50 different ethnic groups, Nepal is prone to such differences. The day after the CPA was signed, organisations representing various indigenous peoples and ethnic minorities claimed they had been ignored. More than 30 people were killed in violence accompanying mass protests over 21 days. The unrest began with agitation by the Madhesi People's Right Forum pushing for the inclusion of ethnic-group rights in the constitution. On 7 February 2007, Koirala was forced to announce that constituencies for elections would be redrawn to increase proportional representation of the Madhesi ethnic groups in the Terai southern region, along with other minority groups. The problem in the Terai, however, is not yet resolved. There has been a proliferation of groups

– armed and unarmed – demanding a fairer electoral system, a federal system with an autonomous and unified Terai and immediate inclusion of Madhesis in state institutions. Sporadic protests continued, and fatal incidents between the armed groups and the state as well as among political rivals increased.

Nepal's peace process was seen internationally as a local and regional problem. International involvement in its peace process has been mostly low-profile, with India, the United States and the United Kingdom as the main players. The US Ambassador to Nepal took a hand by warning that the Maoists would not be taken off the US Terrorist List unless they changed their behaviour. By contrast, India, though concerned with the violence emanating from its own Maoists (Naxalites), assisted in brokering a deal between the SPA and the Maoists in November 2005. As the neighbour most affected by Nepalese developments, India accepted UN involvement in the peace process – thereby formally accepting its own limitations in such a role – but did not appear to be keen on an extended UN mandate in Nepal, in keeping with its traditional opposition to external interference in the region. Although India has been engaging with the Maoists in Nepal and wants them to become a part of the political system, it is at the same time keen that they do not emerge as a powerful and decisive force.

Sri Lanka

In a marked deterioration of political stability, the 24-year conflict between the Sri Lankan military and the separatist Liberation Tigers of Tamil Eelam (LTTE) shifted from low-intensity warfare to near full-fledged undeclared conventional warfare. The Sri Lankan armed forces regained territory from the LTTE for the first time in five years in the east, but there was little prospect of military victory or talks.

Heavy fighting took place between the Sri Lankan military and the LTTE in the east and the north of the country in violation of the five-year-old Norwegian-brokered ceasefire, along with a 'dirty war' carried out by both sides' secretive paramilitary forces. There were human-rights violations on both sides, and allegations of recruitment of child soldiers by the LTTE and attacks on civilians by the military. According to the Sri Lanka Monitoring Mission (SLMM), over 4,000 people were killed in the 15 months to February 2007. Tens of thousands were displaced from their homes.

In the east, Sri Lankan air force strikes in the Sampoor area of Trincomalee in late April 2006, in response to an LTTE suicide attack targeting the army chief, signalled the return to conventional warfare. In a deliberately provocative move, the LTTE on 26 July 2006 blocked an irrigation sluice gate at Mavil Aru, disrupting water supplies to 15,000 families. In an attempt to re-open the gate, the government launched a major air and ground offensive. In response, the LTTE attacked and gained control of the neighbouring town of Muttur, though it was forced out after a few days of fighting. Both sides used heavy artillery, and the government took full advantage of its air force. On 8 August 2006, the LTTE opened the sluice gate. The two-week battle saw some 440 fatalities. On 4 August, 17 locals working for the French charity Action against Hunger were executed in Muttur. The SLMM held government forces responsible for the killing, but the government claimed that the attack had been carried out by the LTTE. After government forces regained control of Muttur, the fighting extended to the strategically important Sampoor area, which provided the LTTE with a base from which to target Trincomalee harbour and attack supply ships travelling north to the troops stationed in the Jaffna peninsula. The military regained control of Sampoor town on 4 September after nine years of occupation by the LTTE, the first real change of territorial control since the 2002 ceasefire.

In the north, heavy military clashes continued, and on 11 August the LTTE broke through government lines on the Jaffna peninsula. The government counterattacked and hundreds were killed on both sides. This led to the closure of the main A9 road between Jaffna and Colombo, completely isolating Jaffna from the rest of the country. The only air/land link was a weekly flight to Colombo; with the LTTE bombardment of the Palaly airbase this was also temporarily suspended. Cut off by land and air, Jaffna became reliant on ships from Trincomalee for food. By refusing to guarantee security for shipping, the LTTE tried to force the government to reopen the A9 road, but failed. On 11 October, the military launched an offensive in the Kilali and Muhamalai sector in an attempt to take Elephant Pass and then Pooneryn. This offensive suffered a major setback, with 129 troops killed and over 300 injured, the highest casualty rate suffered by the military in a single day. Nearly 200 LTTE cadres were reported killed, with over 300 injured.

In view of the heavy fighting, it was not surprising that the Norwegian-brokered Geneva II talks failed on 29 October 2006, over the LTTE's demand that the highway be reopened. The government refused for security reasons, insisting it would only allow sea access to the peninsula. The LTTE also accused the government of escalating hostilities by engaging in provocative offensive preparations along the northern front in Jaffna.

In a defiant statement on 27 November 2006, LTTE chief Velupillai Prabhakaran declared that President Mahinda Rajapakse had rejected his call to find an urgent solution to the conflict, instead intensifying the war. Prabhakaran said the ceasefire agreement had 'become defunct' and the people of Tamil Eelam had only one option: 'political independence and statehood'. Although an LTTE spokesperson subsequently clarified that this did not mean that it had withdrawn from the ceasefire agreement, the statement nonetheless provoked the military to announce plans to intensify operations in the east, to be followed by clearance of the LTTE from the north.

In December 2006 the army mounted an offensive in the east to dislodge the LTTE from its principal stronghold in the Vakarai region close to Batticaloa, which allowed the LTTE a corridor to link north and east. On 19 January 2007 Vakarai and Kathirveli came under the control of the military. Soon after, in *Operation Definite Victory*, a Special Task Force of the Sri Lankan Army overran some 20 LTTE camps in the Ampara district, including a regional intelligence and supply camp. By the end of March, the military had driven the LTTE from its eastern headquarters in Batticaloa. The base appeared abandoned, as security forces entered the compound without resistance. By mid June, the military was deployed outside the Thoppigala jungles, the last stronghold of the LTTE in Batticaloa.

From early 2007 the government became increasingly concerned by suicide attacks by the LTTE's naval arm, the Sea Tigers, on patrol boats and ports, along with harassment of fishermen in the area. Smuggling of weapons and military equipment in support of LTTE operations was also believed to take place across the Palk Strait. On 2 September 2006, the Sri Lankan Navy killed at least 80 Sea Tigers and sank 20 boats during an LTTE attempt to launch a suicide attack on Point Pedro harbour in Jaffna.

Probably in response, on 16 October 2006 the LTTE launched a suicide attack with an explosive-laden truck against a naval bus convoy at Habarana, 80km southwest of Trincomalee. 99 sailors were killed and over 150 injured, making this the worst suicide-bomb attack ever suffered by the military. Two days later, on 18 October 2006, five Sea Tiger boats attacked Galle harbour and the naval camp. Although this was repulsed, it demonstrated the LTTE's intentions to enlarge the conflict to new areas of operation, affecting the country's fragile tourist industry.

These developments led the Sri Lankan government to seek greater Indian naval cooperation to bolster the security of the Palk Strait; the Indian Navy carried out additional deployments and surveillance in the area. At the IISS Shangri-La Dialogue in Singapore in June 2007, the Indian defence minister and the Sri Lankan foreign minister discussed the possibility of coordinated naval patrols in the strait.

Another key concern for the Sri Lankan government is the LTTE's new-found light air power. In a daring move on 26 March 2007, two light aircraft of the Air Tigers for the first time attacked an air force base near Colombo. The two adapted Czech Morovan ZLIN-143 aircraft, capable of carrying four bombs each, attacked the Katunayake air force base adjacent to the country's sole international airport. Although they failed to destroy any aircraft, three Sri Lankan air force personnel were killed and 16 injured. This was followed on 23 April 2007 with an attack by two LTTE aircraft on the main base complex of the military in the Jaffna peninsula and on April 29 against an oil storage facility near Colombo.

Bangladesh

Bangladeshi politics continued to be dominated by bitter confrontation between the two major political parties – the Bangladesh Nationalist Party (BNP), led by Primer Minister Khaleda Zia, and the Awami League (AL), led by Sheikh Hasina – in the run-up to general elections scheduled for January 2007. However this led to new and unforeseen circumstances. Fearing fraudulent voter lists and poll rigging, the AL mounted a series of strikes and blockades against the BNP, resulting in some 80 fatalities by the end of 2006. A military-backed caretaker government took power, postponed elections, declared a state of emergency, and began to tackle corruption as a pre-condition to restoring democracy.

Zia stepped down and dissolved parliament on 28 October 2006, at the end of her government's five-year term, in accordance with the constitution, which required that a neutral caretaker administration be formed to organise free and fair elections within 90 days. The caretaker administration was to be led by the last Supreme Court justice to retire, Justice K.M. Hasan. But the AL opposed him on the grounds that he was a BNP supporter and would not be neutral. It also opposed the other members of the Election Commission, as biased in favour of the outgoing government, and questioned the voter list which, it alleged, contained up to 14 million fake voters. The AL therefore demanded that the commission be entirely reconstituted and the voter lists be purged of false entries before elections were held. In the violent clashes that followed between supporters of the two parties, 13 people were killed and approximately 1,400 injured in less than two days.

Hasan removed himself from consideration as the chief adviser of the caretaker government. In a surprise move on 29 October 2006, the Bangladeshi President Iajuddin Ahmed announced that he would take over as the chief adviser. The AL remained concerned over Ahmed's strong links with the BNP, and civil unrest continued. The 14-party opposition alliance led by the AL presented the caretaker administration with an 11-point charter of demands, including removal of the chief election commissioner, Justice M.A. Aziz, and three of his deputies.

Aziz refused to resign, and the AL attempted to paralyse the country with a transport blockade. Opposition supporters took to the streets, attacking trains and buses, blocking the main thoroughfares and railroad tracks, and forcing the closure of ports, markets and schools. Finally, on 22 November 2006, the caretaker government announced that Aziz would go on leave, and replaced him with Justice Mahfuzur Rahman. But, when the Election Commission abruptly announced on 27 November that general elections would be held on 22 January 2007, the AL rejected this on the grounds that a fresh electoral roll had not yet been published, and announced that it would boycott the polls. AL supporters clashed with BNP supporters, who were keen that elections should take place quickly.

Following the civil unrest, Iajuddin Ahmed ordered the deployment of the army across the country on 8 December 2006. The order was opposed by all ten advisers in the caretaker government, four of whom resigned two days later on the grounds that they had not been informed about the move. The deployment was subsequently cancelled and the armed forces put on standby on 13 December. Clashes between supporters of opposing factions continued into the new year amidst calls by AL supporters for Ahmed to step down as head of the caretaker government.

In a sudden move on 11 January 2007, President Ahmed, backed by the military, postponed the general elections and declared a state of emergency. Fundamental rights under the constitution were suspended, including freedom of movement, assembly and speech. Press censorship was imposed and news broadcasting by privately owned television channels suspended. The government could carry out arbitrary arrests, detain without reason, and hold without trial for an indefinite period. Army troops went on to the streets to enforce this order. Ahmed also dismissed the caretaker administration and appointed Fakhruddin Ahmed, a technocrat and former Central Bank Governor, as the chief adviser on 12 January 2007. Fakhruddin Ahmed appointed ten new advisers. The newly constituted Election Commission formally announced the postponement of the 22 January polls. The major priority for Fakhruddin Ahmed's military-backed caretaker government was the tackling of corruption and crime as a pre-condition to restoring democracy. With the appointment of a new Anti-Corruption Commission headed by Lieutenant General Hasan Mashhud Chowdhury, a retired former army chief, it forcibly began to implement its policies. Several high-profile and visible arrests of senior members of both the BNP and the AL took place. On 8 March 2007, Khaleda Zia's son, senior BNP leader Tarique Rahman, was arrested on corruption charges. Former Aviation and Tourism Minister Mosharraf Hossain of the AL was also arrested. Overall, nearly 100 ministers, businessmen and civil servants were arrested. On 21 June 2007, the first former government minister, the state minister for labour and employment in the Zia government, was convicted and sentenced. To date, however, the military and the police have largely been spared in the fight against corruption.

With the banning of all political activities on 8 March 2007, the caretaker government tried to send Hasina and Zia into exile, on the basis that this was a fundamental condition for holding free and fair elections. On 17 April 2007, it announced that Hasina would be prevented from returning to Bangladesh from a trip abroad, while Zia was said to be negotiating exile in Saudi Arabia. Following domestic and international pressure, the government was forced to back down, and by May 2007 both leaders had returned to Dhaka. On 15 June 2007, Hasina was prevented from leaving for the United States in an attempt to ensure that corruption investigations against her were properly carried out. At the same time, restrictions were placed on Zia's movements in Dhaka.

With the main focus on tackling corruption, government action against Islamist extremist groups and their leaders was limited. This was partly due to an absence of terror attacks in Bangladesh after March 2006, which may have been the result of the arrest of several senior leaders of the banned extremist Islamist group Jama'at-ul-Mujahideen Bangladesh (JMB). Following rejection of an appeal to Iajuddin Ahmed for clemency, on 30 March 2007 six of the group's leaders were executed for killing two judges in Jhalakati in November 2005. Those executed included the chief of the JMB, Shaikh Abdur Rahman; his deputy and operations chief, Siddqul Islam, known as Bangla Bhai; and Ataur Rahman Sunny.

Nonetheless, in the absence of action against Islamist extremist groups such as the Harkat-ul-Jihad-al-Islami Bangladesh, the Jagrata Muslim Janata Bangladesh, or a revitalised JMB, concerns remained over the long-term prospects of the government's security operations and its fight against Islamic extremism.

Although the caretaker government announced plans to revise the electoral lists and provide a level playing field for political parties, there was some concern among political leaders over the military's role in governance. On 27 March 2007, the army chief, General Moeen U. Ahmed, told a gathering of veterans of the 1971 War of Independence that politicians had given Bangladesh nothing but corruption in the past 36 years, and had divided the country by their feuding. General Ahmed then told a conference in Dhaka that the country should not go back to being run by an 'elective democracy' where 'corruption becomes all pervasive, governance suffers in terms of insecurity and violation of rights, and where political criminalisation threatens the very survival and integrity of the state'. Although he did not elaborate on the alternative, he stressed the need for a platform that would incorporate a new sense of direction for the country's governance.

Conclusion

India's rapid economic growth has continued to be the dominant factor in the region, one which has the potential to act as an engine for the entire region if long-standing enmities and security problems could be overcome. As it stands, however, India's economic rise remains at risk from the fragile regional security environment: disputes with Pakistan remain unresolved, and the domestic situations of Pakistan, Sri Lanka and Bangladesh have become more troubled. While domestic security problems in various parts of India are a long-standing feature of the country's politics, they are taken seriously in Delhi and serve as a reminder that all Indian governments must perpetually monitor and control many internal tensions, whether based on ethnicity, religion or caste. To these risks must be added the limitations on India's infrastructural capacity, and the problems of the agriculture sector, which pose a danger of political derailment of reformist economic policy.

Elsewhere in South Asia, much will depend both domestically and for Pakistan's international partners on whether Musharraf can face down political challenges – and if he cannot, on the nature of the government that might replace him. In addition, the long-running sectarian conflicts and especially the developments in FATA and Baluchistan could have spill-over implications for violence in Indian-administered Kashmir, as well as in Afghanistan. The re-emergence of al-Qaeda as an organisation capable of initiating and orchestrating terrorist acts around the world (see essay pages 33–46), with its leaders presumed to be in Pakistan, will ensure that foreign governments continue to view developments in that country – especially those that suggest the rise of Islamic extremism and interference in Afghanistan – with considerable concern. The international community also views with disappointment the deterioration of Sri Lanka's civil war, with long-standing Norwegian-led efforts to end the conflict having clearly suffered a major setback over the past year, and few positive signs for the future. The political turmoil in Bangladesh, where Islamic extremist groups have developed, will also turn out to be a significant setback if it is not resolved by democratic elections that end current de facto military rule.

Afghanistan: Spreading Insurgency

An increase in the military and reconstructive effort of international forces supporting the Kabul government met over the past year with an invigorated insurgency, led by the Taliban and backed by al-Qaeda and jihadist forces. The upsurge in combat activity in the summer made 2006 the most violent year since international forces entered Afghanistan in 2001, with some 4,000 deaths. Following the quieter winter months, an expected Taliban offensive in spring 2007 was blunted by NATO operations in the south, but there were signs of insurgent activity emerging further north. Suicide bombing emerged as a much more commonly used insurgency tactic.

In the face of this change, the strategy of the international community was to give the lead in as many areas as possible to the government in Kabul. Notably, there was an increase in the international effort to train units of the Afghan National Army and Police. A sign in NATO's regional command headquarters in Kandahar quoted British soldier and author T.E. Lawrence: 'It is better to let them do it themselves imperfectly, than to do it yourself perfectly. It is their country, their war, and our time is short.' President Hamid Karzai persisted in his attempt to construct a secular regime and indigenous multi-ethnic security forces, and to rebuild an economy that had been destroyed by years of war. But in a country in which the terrain offers insurgents so many safe havens, and in which they can so easily cast the international forces as 'invaders', the challenge for international and government forces was daunting. Competing sets of law and tribal customs in a feudalistic society often gave the advantage to the Taliban, and clashed with the efforts of the government and international forces to create the stability that would allow the economy to grow. The prospect of achieving Western models of stability, democratisation and economic modernisation remained remote. There were, however, signs of social and economic growth in some areas.

Relations with Afghanistan's neighbours provided a further cause for concern, with rising insecurity in Pakistan to add to historic tensions and disagreement on the nature and location of the Durand Line as an international border.

NATO's challenging task

Over the past year NATO's International Security Assistance Force (ISAF) took almost complete control of the counter-insurgency operation and reconstruction activities. On 30 July 2006 NATO completed Stage 3 of its expansion with the takeover of six southern provinces from US command, and on 5 October the Alliance also took over the eastern provinces, completing Stage 4 and gaining operational control over the whole country.

As of mid 2007, ISAF had 37,000 troops under its command, with 26,000 coming from the 26 member states and 11,000 from other countries. ISAF was headed from July 2006 to February 2007 by General David Richards of the United Kingdom, who handed over to General Dan McNeill of the US Army. Meanwhile the United States retained overall command of Combined Joint Task Force (CJTF)-82, comprising 11,000 troops focused on anti-terrorist operations, mainly in the south and east. NATO commanders in theatre consistently called for more troops and resources, with a particular demand for more helicopters. The UK increased its deployment to over 7,000, Canada and the Netherlands continued to maintain significant contributions to combat operations in the south alongside the United States, along with extra special-force contingents from Norway and Australia. Poland provided an additional 1,000 troops in February. In addition, following pressure at the NATO Riga summit in November, some countries relaxed 'caveats' that limited the activities their forces were allowed to undertake. For example, German troops were made available for deployment outside their northern areas to help allies in an emergency, and German *Tornado* aircraft were assigned a reconnaissance mission in support of NATO ground forces in the south. However, in an example of the debilitating effect of caveats on operational capability, the proposed redeployment of an Afghan battalion from Regional Command-North (RC-N) to support NATO operations in Helmand had to be cancelled because the embedded training team was German, and Berlin refused to allow its troops to deploy outside RC-N. Another battalion with an embedded training and mentoring team from the United States was deployed instead.

The role of ISAF differed between peaceful and less peaceful areas. Efforts at reconstruction involved 25 Provincial Reconstruction Teams (PRTs), mostly deployed in the northern and western regions, while combat operations continued in the southern provinces.

In 2006, the reaction of Taliban forces to NATO's higher operational profile in the south, and in particular in the Taliban heartlands of Kandahar, Uruzgan and Helmand, was to step up their operations. Fierce fighting ensued. In Helmand, British troops moved beyond the towns to set up platoon bases in the villages of Sangin, Gereshk, Now Zad, and Musa Qala. The bases came under persistent attack and took casualties. In Kandahar province Canadian forces confronted insurgents as they gathered in strength in what appeared to be an attempt to take the city of Kandahar, the traditional heart of the Taliban. In September, NATO launched the Canadian-led *Operation Medusa*, a successful two-week effort to clear Taliban fighters from their positions.

However, NATO lacked the troop strength to hold territory once taken, which would permit the reconstruction and development work that would help to build the confidence of local people in the government and NATO. Hence commanders resorted to other solutions. For example, in Musa Qala British commanders struck a deal with local elders and Taliban commanders under which international forces and Taliban alike would withdraw from the village under mutually agreed terms. The agreement held from September 2006 until February 2007, when the Taliban re-occupied the town and detained several elders. The breaking of the agreement came as Richards handed command to McNeill, who was known to be against such deal making. NATO tactics changed to more offensive operations with US air and special-forces support.

Intense combat in Helmand and Kandahar provinces in summer 2006 was followed by a reduction in insurgent activity through the winter months. With the onset of spring, the Taliban offensive increased in intensity and scope, but not to the extent that NATO had expected. The Taliban continued, however, to use psychological weapons, for example 'night letters' warning Afghans not to support the international forces and threatening reprisals against those who ignored the warnings; and with promises of protection for farmers facing the forced eradication of poppy crops. In April and May Taliban operations continued in the southern provinces of Helmand and Kandahar, and increased in the eastern provinces of Khost and Ghazni. On 22 April missile and mortar attacks were launched against the US airbase in Khost province as well as against Bagram airbase. On the same day, perhaps demonstrating coordination of insurgent action, a suicide bomber killed ten people in a market in the city of Khost.

The increasing use of suicide bombing indicated that militant activity was spreading across the country, and that tactical lessons and techniques had migrated from the insurgency in Iraq. An attack on the Bagram airbase on 27 February 2007 when US Vice President Dick Cheney was visiting, demonstrated that insurgents could move with relative freedom beyond the southern provinces and that they possessed a level of intelligence that allowed precision in timing and targeting. The number of suicide attacks increased significantly from 27 in 2005 to 139 in 2006, with the upward trend continuing in the first half of 2007. This suggested an increase in the radicalisation of young men, carried out principally in the Pushtun tribal areas either in Pakistan or Afghanistan, and in defiance of a traditional Afghan aversion to suicide.

In further examples of the geographical spread of the insurgency, fighting took place around Shindand in the western Herat province, between Taliban and coalition forces of the US-led CJTF-82, formerly known as *Operation Enduring Freedom*. Herat had been relatively free from insurgent activity. In the north, a suicide bomber killed three German soldiers on 19 May at Kunduz, and on 23 May at Meymaneh in Faryab province a Finnish soldier was killed in an attack on the Norwegian PRT by an improvised explosive device (IED). These attacks suggested an effort to put pressure on the governments of NATO member states whose electorates were most sensitive to the deployment of their forces in Afghanistan.

In April 2007, NATO forces in the southern region under British command launched *Operation Silicon*, an offensive against Taliban fighters in the Sangin Valley leading to the Kajaki Dam on the Helmand River, which is being refurbished as part of a delayed project to bring electricity and irrigation water to large parts of the southwest. The objective was to retake territory lost since summer 2006. British Royal Marines retook the dam, allowing construction workers to return, but Taliban fighters continued to drive them away with repeated rocket attacks.

The Taliban suffered a significant loss when its military commander in the south, Mullah Dadullah, was killed in a special-forces operation in May. While its promised spring 2007 offensive was muted – suggesting that NATO tactics had achieved a degree of success – it was nevertheless expanding its operations geographically. This was evident from the fighting in Herat province, and in an April attack 75km northeast of Kabul in Kapisa province, where some 300 Taliban fighters attacked government targets in a series of coordinated assaults. This was the closest the Taliban had come to Kabul in strength since they were driven out in 2001.

NATO was put under further pressure by claims of civilian casualties caused by ISAF actions, particularly air strikes. In one week in June over 100 civilian deaths caused by the actions of international forces were reported, including

35–40 deaths from the bombing of villages in Uruzgan province. Karzai reacted angrily to these actions and accused NATO and CJTF-82 of carelessness in carrying out operations. While the Taliban may also suffer losses in such attacks, it gains in the battle for 'hearts and minds', and civil protests weaken the Karzai government. The incidents underlined the difficulty that NATO faced in turning tactical successes into strategic gain.

While it was hard to estimate its precise strength, the insurgency appeared to have little difficulty in gathering sufficient numbers. Recruits could come from amongst disaffected villagers whose livelihoods had been destroyed, or from the refugee camps in Pakistan where young men saw little prospect of returning to a normal life in Afghanistan and so were attracted by the offer of money. For those who had been radicalised and armed for suicide missions, there was the added promised benefit of martyrdom. The Taliban-led insurgency sought to persuade Afghans that it could provide protection against the forces of the 'international invasion', who were 'occupiers'. The constant message was that the Taliban was likely to be a force in Afghanistan for longer than the international forces, and therefore loyalty should be to them rather than the present regime.

Governance and capacity-building

The promise of the presidential and parliamentary elections in 2004 and 2005, which raised the hopes and aspirations of the population, was being met to some degree in the northern part of the country where the majority of new schools have opened and where development initiatives such as the Indian Salma dam project in Herat province could go ahead largely unimpeded by insecurity. However, it remained mostly unfulfilled in the southern ethnic Pushtun provinces, where insecurity and an inability to impose the rule of law continued to hamper reconstruction and undermine the authority of the Kabul government. Nevertheless the creation of development zones laid the framework for development in selected areas which were planned to spread gradually outwards. The principle was that, by creating areas where sustained development could take root, the population would be encouraged to turn away from the insurgency. A more coordinated approach from Kabul helped this process. However, the varying degrees of successful development and reconstruction in different areas of the country created a risk that the country could become divided into an increasingly stable north and a lawless and undeveloped south.

Positive indications of economic and social progress came predominantly from the north and west. Gross domestic product grew 8% in 2006. Between five and six million children were in education, of whom 40% were girls. Amid signs of a re-awakening of cultural activities, 60% of the population had access to radio broadcasts. However, the authority of the president and government came under increasing pressure. Opposition was based around old political adversaries of Karzai. On 3 April 2007 former Afghan President Burhanuddin Rabbani announced the formation of a new opposition coalition party, the United Afghan National Front, composed mainly of former Northern Alliance leaders such as Younus Qanooni, former Defence Minister Mohammed Fahim and former Herat Governor Ismail Khan. Having built up their power bases within the existing political environment, they saw their positions threatened by the Taliban's encroachment northwards, and sensed the possibility of a deal between Karzai and moderate Taliban leaders. The party's formation harked back to former divisions between the Pushtun ethnic majority and the northern ethnic groups such as Tajiks, Uzbeks and Huzzara. In May the Afghan Senate passed a bill urging the government to open negotiations with the Taliban which should include the conditions that during any period of negotiation foreign forces should cease military operations and a timetable for their withdrawal should be drawn up.

The desire of the government to impose secular law across the country was one of the main difficulties. The secular code under the constitution adopted by the Loya Jirga – the grand council of elders – on 4 January 2004 was based mainly on a Western model foreign to many Afghans accustomed historically to other legal and judicial codes. In the past, Afghan governments adopted different approaches. Under most regimes which ruled successfully there was a degree of latitude in applying the law. Pushtun tribes felt that their way of life might be under threat, since they were accustomed to resolving problems according to a traditional code carrying different penalties for crime than the secular law which the central government was attempting to impose. Thus the establishment of the rule of law, fundamental to the future stability of the country, was challenged by old practices.

Karzai's challenge was thus to balance the need to retain Afghan culture and tradition with much-needed new structures. For this he needed capable security forces. The Afghan National Police (ANP) was still far from competent, with local and regional police forces still adhering to feudalistic practices so that they often showed loyalty to local commanders rather than to the Ministry of the Interior. Donors to the Law and Order Trust Fund, set up in 2002 to support police reform, showed signs of reluctance to provide more finance beyond the $200m already gathered. The judiciary was constrained by a lack of trained judges and a paucity of prisons. The United States allocated extra funds to reconstruction, including police reform, but there were doubts about whether reform could take root in the face of an insurgency which targeted poorly paid police.

The Afghan National Army (ANA), though it earned considerable praise for operational achievements, only reached a strength of 35,000, which was 50% of the target of 70,000 to be achieved by 2010. Problems of recruiting and retention were the main causes of the manpower deficit. One US Department of Defense estimate showed that over a period of three years more than half of those recruited will have left the ANA, mainly because of pay. Afghan soldiers received a salary of $100 a month, more than an Afghan policeman but not as much as the wage offered by most private security companies. Meanwhile, an insurgent could receive up to $150 a month. Although the problem was being addressed, the solutions may take time to affect numbers.

To improve capability NATO placed extra emphasis on training the ANA, with NATO Operational Military Liaison and Training Teams and US Embedded Training Teams deployed with most Afghan battalions. The mentoring and training provided by these teams was a crucial part of building the capacity of the ANA and was proving successful. In April, NATO defence ministers decided to allocate an extra 3,400 military personnel to the training mission in addition to the 4,600 already deployed. The emphasis was on building combat capacity. As a result, maintenance and logistic elements received little attention. International forces will need to provide support in these areas for some time before the ANA can be self-sustaining.

Narcotics

For the international community, and particularly European members of NATO with troops serving in Afghanistan, poppy cultivation continued to be a key element in justifying the deployments to domestic audiences. The country produces more than 90% of the global output of opium for conversion to heroin, most of which is consumed in Europe. But despite efforts to reduce the trade, poppy cultivation and production of heroin continued to rise. The UN Office of Drugs and Crime (UNODC) 2006 report showed a record yield, and 2007 is reported to be likely to exceed this volume with the area under cultivation likely to increase in Helmand and also in Nangahar province, previously an area largely considered to be under control. At the same time, there was a new and growing trend in heroin abuse inside Afghanistan.

Under the Bonn Agreement of 2001 the UK took responsibility as the G8 'lead nation' in the fight against illicit drug production. Following the signing of the Afghanistan Compact in London in January 2006, the Afghan government took the lead in all areas of security-sector reform and has been implementing a National Drugs Control Strategy (NDCS) with four priorities: targeting the trafficker; strengthening and diversifying legal rural livelihoods; reducing demand; and developing state institutions. More effort was directed towards interdiction and control of trafficking routes than in the past.

There was general agreement that the illicit trade was inextricably linked to the insurgency, but there was less agreement on a strategy capable of dealing with this complex and long-term problem. The focus tended to be on eradication programmes backed by replacement livelihoods for those farmers who lost their crops. However, replacement programmes may be out of step with eradication efforts, leading to a loss of income for farmers who may then withdraw their support for the government and its allies. As a result, some farmers turned to the insurgency and organised crime for their income. Many NATO commanders believed eradication may hinder efforts to counter the insurgency, because it diverted assets away from combat capability and was counterproductive to their attempts to win over 'hearts and minds'. Other initiatives, such as a programme of crop licencing at village level, remained under consideration. More thought was given internationally to this concept, which aimed to legalise the crop in specific areas based around village communities with a view to selling the product in the form of codeine and morphine. Meanwhile, the UN Office on Drugs and Crime (UNODC) World Drug Report 2007 reports another rise in areas under cultivation and heroin and opium production. Helmand province alone is estimated to have 70,000 hectares under cultivation, accounting for nearly 50% of the world's opium.

Overall, the trend was towards a more flexible approach. All sides of the opium poppy debate agreed on the need to reduce the area under cultivation. Some argued that eradication was the solution with or without replacement livelihoods, whilst others talked of licensing being the key. There was greater consensus that the answer might lie in a mixture of initiatives depending on the conditions in different parts of the country. The crucial element was that deprived farmers must have viable livelihoods. In a country in which nearly 80% of the population live in rural areas, there were few available replacement crops offering the same financial reward as the poppy. The destruction of agro-economic structures over the years of war from 1979 to 2001 meant that for most farmers the only viable crop producing a stable income was the poppy. Reconstruction of the agro-economic sector in all its components, including large portions of the irrigation infrastructure which were destroyed by years of war, was deemed essential if this crop was to be replaced by other crops capable of yielding a decent income for farmers. Agricultural infrastructure was slowly being restored, with an emphasis on irrigation systems, but the actions of insurgents hindered this work.

Neighbourhood tensions

Karzai has claimed that Pakistani President Pervez Musharraf's lack of resolve in dealing with militants in Pakistan has exacerbated the conflict in Afghanistan. Musharraf, for his part, has criticised Karzai's inability to deal with cross-border movement of Taliban fighters. On 29 and 30 April 2007 the Turkish government hosted bilateral talks in Ankara between Karzai and Musharraf aimed at improving the relationship. The talks resulted in the signing of the Ankara Declaration, which contained an undertaking by both sides to respect the territorial integrity of the other, as well as other confidence-building measures to do with border security.

Pakistani troop numbers increased from 80,000 to 90,000 as Islamabad stepped up efforts to control the border and combat militants in the Federally Administered Tribal Areas and North West Frontier Province. The number of manned crossing points also increased and construction of a border fence began along the Durand Line, which has served as the border since 1895 but is not recognised as an international boundary by Afghanistan. The Durand Line is almost impossible to control because of topography and ethnology. Tensions may increase as a result of the fence, seen by many in Kabul as formalising the line as an international border. Pakistan saw it as a sop to Washington's demands for more action in curbing cross-border movement.

On 5 September 2006 the Pakistani government struck an agreement with tribal elders in North Waziristan under which both sides agreed to cease hostilities against the other and militants would stop crossing the border into Afghanistan. The unpopularity of the military deployment in this previously semi-autonomous area, where the Taliban has considerable influence, as well as the considerable cost in logistic support and casualties, was probably a prime reason for Musharraf's move. The United States was opposed to the deal and claimed that violence on the Afghan side of the Durand Line increased after it was signed.

There was also an initiative, proposed by Karzai and other senior figures from Pushtun areas on both sides of the Durand Line, to convene to discuss issues of mutual concern, and security in particular. There are tensions over Afghan refugees in Pakistan, currently numbering some 2–3m. There is increasing Pakistani pressure for them to return. Some 2m refugees have volunteered for biometric registration in an attempt by the UN High Commissioner for Refugees to keep track of the displaced population and to enable more targeted resettlement inside Afghanistan. At the same time, and as an indication of the scale of the cross-border problem, it is estimated that the daily flow of people, which is mostly uncontrolled, across the Durand Line is in excess of 50,000, comprising a mix of local people, refugees and militants. The border fence is unlikely to have a meaningful effect on this traffic as there are many unmanned crossing points and the topography of the area complicates construction.

There has, however, been progress in building cross-border cooperation. In May 2006 1,000 troops from Pakistan, Afghanistan and the United States took part in a training exercise to practice joint procedures. The establishment in January 2007 of a joint command and control centre in Kabul staffed by Pakistani, Afghan and NATO officers also served to improve confidence and coordination.

On Afghanistan's western border, the United States accused Iran of smuggling arms into Afghanistan. General Peter Pace, Chairman of the US Joint Chiefs of Staff, said in April 2007 that Iranian weapons had been found in the country. In June US Defense Secretary Robert Gates said there was evidence of complicity by the Iranian Revolutionary Guard Corps in arms smuggling to Afghanistan. Tehran, however, denied supporting the Taliban and said Iranian investment in Afghanistan had grown this year, as well as pointing to the efforts of Iranian security forces against heroin and opium convoys crossing into Iran from Nimruz and Herat provinces.

Success or failure

Karzai saw a need to reach a political accommodation with moderate Taliban, whom he saw as the only viable political force in the southern and eastern provinces. His attempts were not wholly supported by his international partners, despite encouragement from his own Senate. For Karzai to have the necessary authority to govern the country, a deal with Taliban elements might be required – and the international community would need to support such a deal if the president were not to be undermined. With the insurgency showing no signs of abating and a seeming inability to reduce poppy cultivation, which provides some of the funds for militancy in Afghanistan, the international community was facing the need to acknowledge the realities of the country. For NATO nations which may be wearying of continued troop deployments, a less ambitious mission would entail greater support for Karzai in any effort to deal with Taliban leaders he deemed to be moderate. There may also have to be an acceptance that poppy is too deeply woven into the national psyche and local economy to be eradicated wholesale. A longer-term strategy of reduction of poppy cultivation over many years, with sustainable replacement crops, supported by an extensive international commitment of finance and resources, may prove to be the more realistic option. Overall, NATO may find it more reasonable to construct a mission for the future based on the principle of empowerment and acceptance. While this would still be likely to require commitment of troops and resources for many years to come, it may be more in accordance with political realities both within NATO member countries and Afghanistan. The less palatable alternative would be to seek indefinitely to maintain a high-intensity combat presence at or higher than current levels, which may be neither politically sustainable at home nor likely to produce much more than temporary tactical successes on the ground.

Southeast Asia: Domestic Instability and Sensitive Bilateral Relations

Southeast Asian governments have remained preoccupied with issues of domestic political stability. In Thailand, political tensions between Thaksin Shinawatra's government and the 'establishment' represented by the palace and the military culminated in the armed forces usurping the elected government. In the Philippines, Gloria Macapagal Arroyo's government remained beleaguered. Both Bangkok and Manila still faced significant security challenges from Muslim insurgents. While the Thai conflict escalated, the Philippine authorities registered tactical successes against the relatively small but nevertheless highly aggressive, criminally inclined insurgent-cum-terrorist band known as the Abu Sayyaf ('Sword of God') Group. The Indonesian government faced a continuing separatist challenge in Papua despite a ceasefire there, but provincial elections consolidated the peace process in Aceh. Indonesian security forces continued to take active counter-terrorist measures in the face of indications that the terrorist organisation Jemaah Islamiah was regrouping. Increased patrols by the littoral states, including Indonesia, appeared to have brought the problem of piracy in the Malacca Strait, which earlier in the decade had appeared to be worsening, under control. Timor Leste remained unstable, despite military intervention by an Australian-led force in May 2006 after the local security forces disintegrated. Though relations between certain pairs of members of the Association of Southeast Asian States (ASEAN) improved, progress towards security cooperation amongst Southeast Asian states remained patchy.

Thailand's coup

After months of political instability, on 19 September 2006 the Thai armed forces under army commander-in-chief General Sonthi Boonyaratglin seized power in the country's first coup since 1991, overthrowing a caretaker government led by Thaksin Shinawatra. Shinawatra, a former police colonel and media tycoon, had been prime minister since 2001 at the head of the populist Thai Rak Thai ('Thais Love Thais', TRT) party. The coup promoters justified their actions primarily on the basis of Thaksin's alleged corruption of the democratic process and the stresses and strains this had imposed as he exploited social divisions for political gain. The coup was received ambivalently in Thailand and abroad. Though the military promised a swift return to democracy, political tensions continued over the following months and Thailand's international standing, particularly with foreign investors, suffered.

Despite the military's record of 18 coups between 1932 and 1991, many observers had assumed that Thailand's democratic processes were so entrenched and its armed forces so professionalised that military intervention in politics was a thing of the past. During 2006, however, while senior Thai officers assured foreign visitors that the army would stay in barracks, tensions within the country mounted to the point where military leaders feared that violence might break out between Thaksin's supporters and his opponents. In a political environment where compromise and coalition government had been the norm since democracy apparently became firmly established in the early 1990s, the TRT government was remarkable for its well-defined populist policies. Help for Thailand's 'little people' brought the TRT strong support in the countryside, particularly in the impoverished north and northeast, and the party won the February 2005 elections with a landslide 377 out of 500 parliamentary seats. However, after the elections there was growing discontent among the urban middle class over Thaksin's abuse of his popular mandate by ignoring parliament and compromising state bodies by placing cronies in key positions. There was rising concern over the government's human-rights abuses, trampling of media freedom, and inept handling of the Muslim insurgency in Thailand's southernmost provinces. In January 2006, the Thaksin family's sale of its controlling stake in the telecommunications company Shin Corp to Singapore's state investment arm, Temasek Holdings, was widely seen as improper and boosted support for the People's Alliance for Democracy (PAD) civil-society coalition, which led anti-Thaksin protests.

In April 2006, a snap general election and subsequent by-elections failed to produce a clear result, and pending a fresh general election scheduled for October (later postponed to November), Thaksin – though officially merely caretaker prime minister – resumed control of the government in late May. Celebrations in June of the 60th anniversary of Thailand's revered king temporarily dampened political controversy, but tensions soon rose again. Thaksin's claim that his government was being attacked by 'a charismatic extra-constitutional figure' was widely interpreted as referring to the king's closest adviser and Privy Council president, 86-year-old General Prem Tinsulanonda, a former army commander who had been prime minister from 1980–88. In July, responding to Thaksin's apparent efforts to control the military by promoting his former classmates from the military preparatory school, Prem had reminded the army that it should be loyal to the monarchy rather than to any particular government. Anti-Thaksin elements in the Bangkok establishment apparently saw Thaksin's supposed slur against the palace as a case of *lèse-majesté*, a serious infringement in a country where the monarchy is usually treated with extreme respect.

Fears that growing antagonism between pro- and anti-Thaksin camps might explode into violence reinforced the determination of a small group of senior officers, led by General Sonthi and apparently backed by the palace, to remove Thaksin from power before he could be re-elected. While Thaksin attended the UN General Assembly in New York, on 19 September the army deposed the government and revoked the constitution in a decisive yet bloodless assertion of power. Despite imposing martial law and introducing restrictions on civil liberties, including a ban on public gatherings and the blocking of websites, General Sonthi and his junta, the Council for Democratic Reform – soon renamed the Council for National Security (CNS) – claimed that the army's intervention reflected popular wishes and promised to oversee the drafting of a new constitution and the restoration of democracy within a year. The junta set up an interim parliament, the National Legislative Assembly (NLA), as well as a much larger National People's Assembly to draft the constitution, and on 1 October announced the choice of a former army commander, retired General Surayud Chulanont, as interim premier. Though Surayud was respected as a military reformer, critics claimed that appointing an ex-military man contradicted the commitment to restore democracy. Nevertheless, in early November Surayud spelt out an extensive agenda for his unelected government over the following 12 months: to stimulate a 'national debate' leading to political reform; to restore national unity by reducing social and political tensions, particularly in the Muslim south; to address income inequality through 'pro-poor, anti-poverty policies'; and to strengthen the rule of law through 'drastic' reforms to the police and judicial apparatus, and by strengthening anti-corruption agencies.

Though the coup was executed peacefully, diverse groups opposed the military's takeover. The military intervention severely undermined the cohesion and strength of the TRT, which was formally dissolved by a ruling in May 2007. In early November, within two weeks of the coup, 100 TRT members of parliament (MPs) belonging to three factions had already deserted the party and Chaturon Chaisaeng, the former deputy premier who became acting party leader in mid October, admitted that many of the 200 or so remaining TRT MPs might leave the party even if it survived the eventual tribunal ruling. Nevertheless, the former TRT leader's huge political sway meant that Thaksin's supporters constituted the main source of resistance to the military takeover. Martial law was lifted in 41 provinces in late January 2007, but remained in force in 35 others, including areas in the north and northeast where the CNS evidently still feared what it called 'undercurrents' of well-funded pro-Thaksin activity. Concern over the presence of Thaksin's cronies and clients in the military and the possibility of a counter-coup prompted not only the transfer of some senior officers out of key posts immediately after the coup, but also a reshuffle of 136 battalion commanders throughout Thailand during November. Despite the ex-premier's claims that he would not be a candidate in the next general election, the worst fear of the CNS was from the beginning that Thaksin might return to Thailand, which would pose a serious dilemma: to allow him to mobilise support using his wealth and his extensive network of local officials and politicians; or to arrest him with the attendant probability that he would become a martyr figure akin to neighbouring Myanmar's Aung San Suu Kyi.

While many of Thaksin's urban liberal opponents initially supported the coup, disillusionment set in quickly as it became clear that the main beneficiary of the TRT government's ouster was the conservative Bangkok political establishment rather than the democracy movement. The PAD stressed its continuing mission to secure honest government. Two months after the coup, Sonthi was forced to defend himself and the CNS against public frustration with their apparent lack of urgency in investigating and prosecuting alleged corruption on the part of Thaksin, whose assets had not been seized. At the same time, there was no evidence of significant progress with drawing up a new constitution or any clear indication of when democracy might be restored. The CNS had to deny rumours that it intended to set up its own political party, which would effectively legitimise a long-term political role for the military. On 31 December, a series of bomb attacks in Bangkok killed three people and injured 38, compounding the sense of political instability. Several months later, there was no clear indication of whether these attacks were linked to the southern insurgency or to contention at the political centre.

Interim Prime Minister Surayud became increasingly beleaguered during early 2007 as he faced criticism from not only the democracy movement and activists supporting debt-ridden farmers (formally the beneficiaries of the TRT's rural largesse, which the junta had withdrawn), but also Sonthi and the CNS. In late March, Sonthi made clear his preference for emergency rule in response to swelling anti-junta protests. Though Sonthi refused to contemplate becoming prime minister himself, one CNS plan reportedly involved making him deputy prime minister for security affairs. Responding to criticism, notably from the PAD, of his government's lacklustre performance and continuing fears of Thaksin's return, in early April Surayud revealed that investigations into the former prime minister could be concluded by the month's end. Soon afterwards, an internal leak revealed that the junta was mounting a secret public-relations campaign against Thaksin aimed at discrediting him and his former policies. Later, corruption charges where brought against Thaksin and some of his assets frozen. Amidst questions over Surayud's health, continuing pressure from the democracy movement, and increasingly public disagreement between Surayud and the CNS, there was persistent speculation that military hardliners might stage another coup.

On 19 April, the Constitution Drafting Council, appointed by the military, published the draft of Thailand's proposed new constitution, which included elements drawn from the post-coup interim charter as well as the 1997 constitution and other past national charters, with the intention that after being debated by the 200-member Constitution Drafting Assembly it should be subjected to a referendum in September 2007. Notwithstanding its diverse inspirations, the gist of the draft charter was that popular political participation would be curtailed. The parliamentary lower house would be reduced from 500 to 400 seats and would include 80 'party list' members intended to enhance representation for smaller parties and to obviate the possibility of a single party dominating parliament as Thaksin's TRT had done. The senate, previously comprising 200 elected members, would be scaled down to 160 appointed members. Another provision was for a

National Crisis Council, including the prime minister and senior judges, which would be convened in time of national emergency. Unsurprisingly, the leaders of both main political parties, the TRT and the Democrats, roundly criticised the draft. Demonstrations by monks demanding that Buddhism (the faith of 90–95% of Thais) should be enshrined in the new constitution as the national religion added a further complication for the interim administration, amongst fears that such a measure could exacerbate the alienation felt by Thailand's Muslim minority, particularly in the country's south where a revival of separatist sentiment had erupted in a renewed anti-Bangkok insurgency since early 2004. Critics pointed to the way that in the 1970s a similar impulse towards Buddhist nationalism in Sri Lanka had stimulated the rise of Tamil separatism and terrorism.

Though Surayud initially pledged to continue a free-market emphasis in Bangkok's economic policies and to proceed with Thaksin's infrastructural 'mega-projects', Thailand's protracted crisis, combined with investment restrictions (including proposed new rules on foreign ownership of Thai companies, which would increase penalties for overseas companies using local nominees to circumvent limits on foreign shareholding) and capital controls introduced by the interim government, undermined the confidence of investors and consumers, prompting Finance Minister Chalongphob Sussangkarn to admit in early May that the prevailing political uncertainty had become the biggest threat to the economy, which was also suffering from increased oil prices and a cyclical slowdown. In mid 2007, Thailand's political future remained unclear. Though the interim government insisted that national elections would be held in December, it seemed quite possible that the September referendum would reject the proposed new constitution. While the junta claimed that this was unlikely, it revealed that its response to such a contingency would be to reinstate one of Thailand's many former constitutions – which one, however, remained unclear.

Thailand's southern insurgency

In the weeks immediately following the coup, it seemed that one benefit of the military takeover might lie in Bangkok's handling of Thailand's Muslim separatist insurgency, which had taken almost 2,000 lives since January 2004 in the three southernmost provinces of Narathiwat, Pattani and Yala. Even before Thaksin was overthrown, there were signs of change in Bangkok's policies in the south, the TRT prime minister having ordered the immediate adoption of many of the recommendations of the National Reconciliation Commission that reported in June 2006. Once Thaksin was removed, the new regime indicated that its approach to the south would be significantly different. Even before the coup, General Sonthi – himself a rare Muslim in an overwhelmingly Buddhist government apparatus – had urged negotiations with the insurgents in place of the Thaksin administration's apparently counterproductive hardline approach.

Visiting Jakarta in October, Surayud said that the successful peace process in Indonesia's Aceh province, principally involving the granting of thoroughgoing autonomy in return for a cessation of separatist violence, could provide a model for Thailand's Muslim-majority provinces. In more concrete terms, the regime announced that in order to provide development and justice for the south it would revive the civilian-led Southern Border Provinces Administrative Centre that Thaksin had disbanded. On 1 November, Surayud visited Pattani province and apologised for the October 2004 Tak Bai massacre, in which 92 Muslim protesters died after the army attacked a peaceful demonstration. The new commander of the Fourth Army region asked for forgiveness for Tak Bai and other 'past mistakes' and spoke of the need for compensation. On a second visit to the south, Surayud promised to end the blacklisting of Islamic teachers as well as aggressive searches by the security forces. In mid November, the government appointed a former regional army commander as head of an NLA committee charged with drawing up guidelines for ending the insurgency.

However, early hopes that the interim administration would oversee a significantly new approach in the south were soon dashed, and as bombings, arson and shootings continuing unabated through late 2006 and early 2007 it was clear that there was no easy solution to the insurgency. Indeed, the conflict escalated, with more determined attacks on government security forces and on infrastructure (including railway lines and power supplies). Though the military junta had indicated initially that it might end emergency rule, which allows draconian civil-rights restrictions in the three violence-wracked provinces, in the event it was extended in January and again in April 2007. The 5,000 or so insurgents, mainly affiliated with the Barisan Revolusi National – Coordinate (National Revolutionary Front – Coordinated), according to Bangkok, continued to demonstrate tactical ingenuity, for example by introducing new types of trigger for improvised explosive devices in response to the security forces' blocking of mobile telephone signals, the previously favoured means of triggering roadside bombs aimed at army and police patrols. The Thai police claimed that foreign personnel, suspected to be Indonesian, may have been involved in training the insurgents. Simultaneously, there seemed to be a danger of more open communal conflict as tit-for-tat murders of Buddhists and Muslims became more frequent, and as communities in worst-affected districts lost faith in the ability of Bangkok to protect them and began arming themselves. In mid February, the insurgents attacked ethnic Chinese businesses: 29 bombs in bars, restaurants and hotels killed six people. With 20–30,000 troops already in the three southernmost provinces, in late April it was reported that the government planned to deploy a further 15,000 personnel, particularly to protect lines of communication. At the same time, however, Bangkok was relying increasingly on 'army rangers', poorly-trained, locally recruited militia troops who have earned a reputation in the south for killing innocent civilians and other abuses. In mid May, the cabinet allocated an additional 1 billion baht ($30m) to support security operations in the south.

Yet, despite the intensifying conflict in the south and the failure of their initial efforts at reconciliation there, it was clear that the CNS and Surayud's admin- istration were still interested in finding a peaceful solution. In April, Sonthi reacted quickly and negatively to an offer from Major-General David Fridovich, US Pacific Command's Special Operations Commander, to send US troops to assist Thai forces in the south. Fearing the potentially counterproductive effects of such a deployment, Sonthi turned down the offer and emphasised that the conflict was an 'internal affair'. Shortly afterwards, Surayud revealed that Bangkok was considering an amnesty for rebels who came over to the govern- ment side, following a proposal from Major-General Chamlong Khunsong, army commander in the south. Though Sonthi initially opposed the idea, by early May he had changed his mind and Surayud was able to ask Chamlong to work out the details. In mid May, Surayud claimed that with assistance from Malaysia his government was still pursuing dialogue with the insurgents, after receiving encouraging signals from them.

The Philippines: continuing insecurity in the south

Like Thailand, the Philippines continued to face serious security challenges in its Muslim south. However, from August 2006, Philippine government forces notched significant successes against the Abu Sayyaf Group (ASG), which had been responsible for a series of kidnappings-for-ransom and bombings since 2000, and had killed an estimated 400 civilians over the previous decade and a half. Nevertheless, it seemed unlikely that the ASG could be defeated fully without more determined efforts to resolve the wider political issue of Moro (southern Philippine Muslim) separatism. The victories against the ASG were, however, heartening for the beleaguered administration of President Gloria Macapagal Arroyo, which faced continuing opposition to its attempts to change the constitu- tion fundamentally (in order to allow a unicameral parliamentary government, economic liberalisation, decentralisation of national government and empow- erment of local administrations), legal challenges from political opponents and rumbling discontent within the Armed Forces of the Philippines (AFP) officer corps. At the same time, despite Arroyo's June 2006 declaration of an 'all-out assault' on the New People's Army aimed at achieving victory within two years, it seemed unlikely that the communist insurgents could be defeated so easily or quickly.

On 1 August 2006, the AFP launched *Oplan Ultimatum*, a major offensive in the Sulu archipelago aimed at the ASG and the group's allies from the pan-Southeast Asian terrorist network, Jemaah Islamiah (JI). Although raids which led to the capture of important rebel commanders in April 2006 appeared at the time to have fragmented the ASG's command structure, it nevertheless remained a threat, particularly as surviving members appeared to be making common cause with other Philippine extremist groups and with remnants of JI. The United States, concerned over the continuing threat posed by the ASG (which had in the past kidnapped and killed US citizens) and by its links to JI, deployed a 100-strong military team to provide technical and intelligence support for the 5,000 AFP troops including six army and marine battalions involved in *Oplan Ultimatum*. A specific objective was to capture ASG leader Khaddafy Janjalani, as well as two Indonesian JI bombers, Dulmatin and Umar Patek, who were implicated in the October 2002 Bali bombings that killed more than 200 people, including many Western tourists. The AFP suspended its use of artillery and air strikes during Ramadan (which began on 24 September), but the offensive resumed with full force in late October, soon after President Arroyo authorised deployment of an extra three battalions to Sulu.

The previous major AFP offensive against the ASG was *Operation Endgame* in 2002–03, which reduced the group's strength from 800 to 450 combatants. With substantial indirect support from US forces, AFP search-and-destroy operations extirpated the ASG from its sanctuaries on the island of Basilan, forcing the rebels to move their principal bases to neighbouring Jolo. The ASG had strong local support on this economically deprived island, long a bastion of the Moro National Liberation Front (MNLF), which had spawned the ASG in 1991. Though the United States continued to provide training and advice in support of AFP operations aimed at containing and reducing the ASG, the group not only survived – possibly with support from local MNLF elements disillusioned with the results of their organisation's 1996 settlement with the Philippine government – but also forged links with JI members on the run from the Indonesian authorities' crackdown on extremists following the Bali bombings. In exchange for sanctuary, JI bomb-makers apparently trained members of the ASG (and other Philippine terrorist groups) in their lethal craft.

By early 2007, *Oplan Ultimatum* had substantially weakened the ASG. The AFP claimed that it had been involved in 17 major clashes with the rebels and had captured joint ASG/JI training camps and bomb factories. In January, the Philippine military confirmed that the ASG's commander, Khaddafy Janjalani (brother of its founder, Abdurajak Abubakar Janjalani) had died in a battle the previous September. During January, the AFP also eliminated Abu Sulaiman (alias Jainal Antel Sali Jr), whom the Philippine authorities blamed for several terrorist bombings including a 2004 attack on SuperFerry 14 which killed more than 100 passengers. Overall, the AFP claimed that by late January the continuing offensive had led to the deaths of 72 ASG members, including six senior figures, and the capture of another 28.

The AFP's successes were due partly to the effectiveness of army and marine commanders and a change in tactics involving deployment of small special-forces teams able to fight around-the-clock, denying ASG personnel their previous freedom of movement at night. But US support evidently played a key role. From the beginning of *Oplan Ultimatum*, the Pentagon provided support and advice to the AFP through the 150-strong, forward-deployed Joint Special Operations Task Force – Philippines. US surveillance and intelligence-gathering aircraft helped track the ASG on land and at sea, where US Navy advisers have assisted an AFP blockade of Jolo aimed at preventing insurgents from escaping. Nevertheless, around 350 ASG members remained at large, including five groups totalling around 200 men in Jolo's rugged interior in the vicinity of Tubora Hill. Another 150 were on other islands in the Sulu archipelago such as Tawi-Tawi, or on Mindanao. In early February, the AFP claimed that captured ASG personnel had revealed that 12 JI members comprising Indonesians, Malaysians of Muslim Filipino parentage and a Singaporean were embedded in the ASG contingents in the Sulu islands. One significant JI figure, known as Gufran, was killed in January in a battle at sea with Philippine Navy commandos.

Oplan Ultimatum was scheduled to continue until June 2007. The momentum of the US-supported AFP campaign against the ASG clearly needed to be maintained if the group was to be defeated and, in early February, AFP Chief of Staff General Hermogenes Esperon Jr emphasised that the Sulu operation was his 'chief preoccupation'. Several days earlier an incident in which the AFP attacked and dispersed a nine-strong ASG/JI cell, apparently intent on attacking targets in Metro-Manila, highlighted the danger that the rebels still posed. And in late April, the ASG demonstrated its ability to terrorise civilians on Jolo by capturing and beheading seven civilian road workers there. In early May, security forces blamed the ASG's JI associates for a bombing in Tacurong, Mindanao, which killed eight people.

Meanwhile, the AFP was focusing on neutralising the remaining ASG commanders, notably the elderly Radullan Sahiron (alias Kumander Putol), but also Isnilon Hapilon, Abu Pula and Tandah Sahibul, as well as the two leading JI figures, Dulmatin and Umar Patek. In mid February, additional marines were deployed to Sulu, supported by armoured vehicles and artillery. At the strategic level, the AFP summed up its counter-insurgency approach to the ASG as one of 'clear, hold, develop'. With the ASG pushed into the interior, much of Jolo was at the 'hold' stage, with the AFP establishing local militias, including ASG members who had been 'turned'. However, the development component was clearly also important in order to undercut popular resentment of Manila's rule and support for the insurgents. Indeed, in early February General Esperon warned that new terrorist leaders could emerge from the remnants of the ASG unless development projects were sustained in the south. This point was evidently recognised in Washington as well as in Manila, and there was large-scale US support for such projects. The US Agency for International Development sponsored the GEM ('Growth with Equity in Mindanao') programme, involving port and road upgrading, rural solar power, agricultural training, and school and health projects. In the combat zone on Jolo, US special forces played a key role in implementing development projects. The latest exercise in the bilateral *Balikatan* series, in February–March 2007, involved US and Philippine forces in joint development projects in the south.

Sustained military and development approaches to defeating the ASG, involving continuing support from the United States because of Manila's limited military and developmental resources, were clearly vital elements in resolving the security problem in the south. However, a broad political settlement of the larger-scale issue of Muslim separatism was also badly needed. Recognising this, Manila's new secretary for defence, Hermogenes Ebdane Jr, speaking in early February 2007 soon after his appointment, advocated a 'holistic approach' aimed at addressing socio-economic, political and religious concerns as the most effective way to end the insurgencies that have plagued the country since the 1970s.

However, there was no immediate prospect of a settlement between the Philippine government and the Moro Islamic Liberation Front (MILF), which entered into a fragile ceasefire with Manila in 2001. During 2006, successive rounds of exploratory talks between Manila and the MILF, brokered by Malaysia on behalf of the Organisation of the Islamic Conference (OIC), collapsed over the issue of the extent of the Muslim Moro people's 'ancestral domain' as Manila repeatedly sought extensions of deadlines for its responses to MILF proposals. In late January 2007, the MILF claimed that the peace process was 'at a standstill' because of the government's prevarication. This breakdown in the peace process reinforced tension between the two sides, already running high after conflict between government-sponsored militias and the MILF earlier in the year. At one stage, the Malaysian-led International Monitoring Team (which includes Bruneian, Indonesian and Libyan as well as Malaysian observers) threatened to withdraw, although its mandate was subsequently extended to July 2007.

Although the mainstream MILF command repeatedly distanced itself from more extreme rebel groups in the south, Manila's security forces continued to allege that MILF elements were contravening the 2001 ceasefire. In early February, for example, the AFP claimed that the MILF was responsible for a raid that sprang 48 inmates, including several alleged terrorists, from jail in Kidapawan City in North Cotabato province. In mid February, the Philippine National Police claimed the MILF's Special Operations Group was plotting with the ASG to stage bomb attacks in Manila in a repeat of the 2005 Valentine's Day attacks that killed seven and wounded 150 in the capital. Perhaps the best hope for accelerating a settlement between Manila and the MILF now lies with pressure from interested external parties, which have grown increasingly frustrated over the slow pace of the peace process. In mid February, MILF leaders met the European Union ambassador to Manila and other EU officials, civilian and military representatives of the United States, and Japanese diplomats for detailed discussions. The EU has offered to facilitate peace negotiations, while Japan has indicated willingness to deploy peacekeeping troops.

The MNLF, which the OIC recognises as the only legitimate representative of the Moro people, will need to be included in any peace settlement if it is to be credible and durable. However, a political platform shared by the MILF and the MNLF remains elusive. In the meantime, the MNLF remains dissatisfied with the implementation of its 1996 Final Peace Settlement with Manila, and there seems little prospect of a wider-ranging and more inclusive settlement until outstanding concerns are satisfied. In the meantime, MNLF forces have clashed with AFP troops involved in *Oplan Ultimatum*, against a background of suspicion that the MNLF is sheltering ASG members, including Radullan Sahiron, in its compounds which, under the terms of the 1996 agreement, government forces are not allowed to search. One positive sign, though, has been Manila's agreement to allow jailed former governor of the Autonomous Region of Muslim Mindanao Nur Misuari, who was standing for election as Sulu governor in the May 2007 elections, to lead the MNLF delegation to the preparatory tripartite meeting with the Philippine government and the OIC in Jeddah scheduled for July 2007 and intended to begin ironing out problems connected with the 1996 accord. In April, Manila also emphasised that AFP operations against a rebel MNLF commander, Habier Malik, would not affect its commitment to the talks.

In the absence of a wider political settlement in the south, the frustration of Moro aspirations will continue providing a reservoir of support for the ASG and other extremist groups, which will benefit from the tacit connivance of elements in both the MNLF and MILF. Military victories may grab the headlines, but even when backed by well-funded development projects, they are almost certainly inadequate to resolve a conflict rooted in the frustration of the Moro quest for self-determination.

Indonesia: consolidating stability

The peace process in Aceh, galvanised by the catastrophic impact of the 26 December 2004 tsunami on the province, has represented a major triumph for the Indonesian government led by Susilo Bambang Yudhoyono. Following the disarmament of GAM (Free Aceh Movement) insurgents and the withdrawal of non-organic Indonesian forces, in July 2006 Indonesia's House of Representatives endorsed a governance law which enshrined Aceh's autonomous status. It also allowed for independent candidates to stand in Aceh's provincial elections in December. In these elections Irwandi Yusuf and Mohammad Nazar, both GAM members, won a stunning 38% of the vote and consequently became governor and vice-governor respectively. In January, Irwandi Yusuf underlined his political pragmatism and recognition of the need to collaborate with Jakarta when he promised to oppose Aceh's separation from Indonesia. Given GAM's long-standing and dogged armed resistance to Indonesian rule until 2005, these were remarkable developments. The mandate of the European Union-led Aceh Monitoring Mission ended four days after the December election.

Problems remained in Aceh, however. The crucial issues of sharing resource wealth and power between Jakarta and Aceh were still to be resolved. During April, the Indonesian Home Affairs Ministry produced a draft document giving Jakarta the lead role in 31 policy areas, causing Governor Irwandi Yusuf to protest. At the same time, there was growing popular frustration over the slow pace of post-tsunami reconstruction. At the beginning of 2007, 23,000 Acehnese were still living in temporary accommodation, and activists accused the Aceh–Nias Reconstruction and Rehabilitation Agency of corruption and inefficiency. There was also anger amongst former GAM guerillas and other members of the resistance organisation over delays in the payment of 'reintegration funds'. In late January, more than 500 former GAM members attacked buildings and vehicles in Bireun, 140km from the provincial capital, Banda Aceh. Even when Jakarta provides the promised funding, finding employment for former GAM members will constitute a major challenge for Irwandi Yusuf's administration. In mid February, the new governor went so far as to suggest that ex-insurgents were willing to serve in the Indonesian armed forces (TNI) and police. Civil unrest erupted again in late March over the results of a run-off vote in West Aceh, underlining the province's continuing political volatility.

The settlement in Aceh left Papua, where many amongst the largely Melanesian population resent Jakarta's rule, as the only Indonesian province with an active separatist campaign. In July 2006, the Free Papua Movement (OPM) – which had waged a low-key guerrilla campaign for more than 30 years – unilaterally declared a ceasefire. In response, the TNI claimed that it had not mounted offensive operations in the province for several years. However, subsequent developments suggest that a settlement accommodating the aspirations of Papua's indigenous people is not a near-term prospect. Clashes between OPM and Indonesian forces continued. In early 2007, thousands of people in the central highland region of Puncak Jaya were displaced from their villages and faced serious food shortages because of renewed offensives led by TNI special forces in response to OPM's killing of two Indonesian officers. Jakarta has indicated that it plans to enlarge its already substantial garrison of 12,000 troops and more than 2,000 paramilitary police in Papua, reflecting its concern over not only separatism but also what it sees as the potential for foreign intervention in the resource-rich province.

The Muslim–Christian communal conflicts which plagued Maluku and central Sulawesi in eastern Indonesia at the beginning of the decade had largely been brought under control by the Malino Accords of 2001–02. However, in the district of Poso in central Sulawesi, local members of Jemaah Islamiah and mujahidin from elsewhere in Indonesia subsequently mounted a campaign of violence against Christians, including bombings (one killing 22 people in Tentena market in May 2005), targeted assassinations, and in October 2005 the beheading of three teenage schoolgirls. Though this renewed violence in Poso has been geographically restricted and sporadic, it has represented a major focus for continuing activity by JI, which still comprises at least 900 members across Indonesia despite the success of the Indonesian and other Southeast Asian security agencies, with substantial Australian and other extra-regional support, in apprehending key operatives since the 2002 Bali bombings.

A round-up of terrorist suspects in Poso in January 2007 led the Indonesian police to mount raids in central and east Java, the JI heartland, in late March. One suspect was killed and seven, including members of a cell allegedly responsible for the 2004 attack on the Australian Embassy in Jakarta, were arrested, and a large explosives and weapons cache including more than 70kg of TNT, detonators, M-16 rifles and ammunition was discovered. Captured JI members and documents revealed details of the organisation and strength of the group's military wing on Java, which was organised in four districts: Surakarta, Semarang, Surabaya and Jakarta. The Indonesian authorities claimed that this military wing had held training exercises on the Javanese volcano, Mt Sumbing, and was ready to launch attacks. Prominent amongst the group's plans was allegedly the assassination of key figures who opposed it, including senior police officers, state prosecutors and judges, and possibly foreign diplomats. These revelations tallied with reports in 2006 of a split in JI, broadly between a minority faction, led by the Malaysian Noordin Top, which had been responsible for the large bombings in Jakarta and Bali since 2003 and favoured continued suicide bombings against Western targets and who styled themselves, amongst other titles, the Thoifah Muqatilah (Combat Unit), and a mainstream group that preferred to focus on transforming Indonesia into an Islamic state. The mainstream JI's emphasis was on expanded recruitment, indoctrination and the establishment of geographical bases rather than possibly counterproductive attacks causing indiscriminate casualties. It was the military wing of this mainstream JI organisation which the authorities uncovered – but by no means neutralised – in early 2007. Some reports gave the misleading impression that this Javanese military wing and its offshoot in Poso were all that remained of JI, overlooking the fact that the organisation also continued to maintain cells in other parts of Indonesia, particularly Sumatra.

As well as JI and Noordin Top's splinter group, which mainstream JI may be protecting from the security forces in return for a 'no-bombing' pledge, other terrorist groups still active in Indonesia in early 2007 included Jama'ah Tauhid wal Jihad (in Bandung), Mujahidin KOMPAK, Ring Banten (in West Java), and small independent cells with no organisational affiliations. In May 2007, US officials claimed that the Iranian-backed Hizbullah had a presence in Southeast Asia and might launch attacks on Jewish or other Western targets.

Maritime security had become a major concern for Jakarta in 2004, following an upsurge in attacks by pirates in the Malacca Strait and in other Indonesian waters, and anxiety amongst Western states over the potential for maritime terrorism. Responding to user states' concerns and the Pentagon's Regional Maritime Security Initiative, Indonesia and the other Malacca Strait littoral states, Malaysia and Singapore, significantly enhanced and coordinated their responses to piracy and potential maritime terrorism. While other factors, notably the peace settlement in Aceh, may also have played a part, there have been tangible results, with recorded piracy in the Malacca Strait declining dramatically during 2005 and 2006. During the first quarter of 2007, the number of pirate attacks in Southeast Asian waters overall was the lowest for a decade. Though an April 2007 report by the International Maritime Bureau claimed that Indonesian waters were still the most dangerous in the world despite the significant decline in reported piracy, during the same month US Pacific Commander Admiral Timothy Keating asserted that security in the Malacca Strait had 'vastly improved' over the previous five years.

Timor Leste: saving a failing state

Following the Australian-led military intervention to restore order in the wake of the collapse of Timor Leste's security forces, Prime Minister Mari Alkatiri resigned in late June 2006. In July, President Xanana Gusmão appointed as acting prime minister Foreign Minister Jose Ramos-Horta, the Nobel laureate who had spearheaded Timor Leste's long diplomatic campaign for freedom after the Indonesian invasion of 1975 and who had already been given responsibility for the security forces. After considerable political chaos during the second half of 2006, a presidential election was scheduled for April 2007. Xanana announced that he would not seek re-election. In late February, Ramos-Horta announced he would contest the election as an independent candidate. Among seven other candidates, the leading contender was the Fretilin Party's Francisco Guterres, a former resistance fighter. In the event, Ramos-Horta won a stunning victory with more than 70% of the vote. However, in mid 2007 the format of Timor Leste's government remained in flux, with negotiations between parties taking place following parliamentary elections held on 30 June. The post of president is largely ceremonial, and Xanana was himself seeking the position of prime minister as leader of the newly formed National Congress for Timorese Reconstruction (CNRT) party. The party's initials outraged Fretilin leaders as it clearly represented an attempt to borrow the legitimacy associated with the original CNRT – the National Council for Timorese Resistance – which had led and coordinated opposition to Indonesia's occupation.

The UN Integrated Mission in Timor-Leste (UNMIT), established in August 2006 with the aim of promoting the small country's stability, national reconciliation and democratic governance, included an international police component which, together with the Australian-commanded troops of the International Security Force (ISF), proved vital for maintaining public order in the face of sporadic continuing street violence perpetrated by both criminal gangs and supporters of political factions. On 22 February, the day that the UN Security Council voted unanimously to extend UNMIT's mandate for a further year and provide more than 1,400 additional police officers for the April 2007 elections, 38 UN vehicles were attacked as forces attempted to break up gang fighting; 117 people were arrested. In early March, Australian ISF troops clashed with supporters of fugitive army rebel leader Alfredo Reinado, killing four rebels. Before he was elected president, Ramos-Horta said he hoped that the UN contingent would provide a stabilising presence for at least five more years. There were fears that a parliamentary contest between Xanana and Alkatiri (who in February was cleared of charges linking him to the distribution of arms to civilians during the 2006 crisis) could reignite violence.

Cooperation within ASEAN

A combination of pragmatic cooperation on economic, political and sometimes security matters, and tensions over diverse issues (often deeply rooted in historical suspicions towards neighbours) has always characterised relations among the states which are members of the Association of Southeast Asian Nations (ASEAN). While there has been movement towards multilateral security and political cooperation between ASEAN members – seen in the first ASEAN Defence Ministers' Meetings in May 2006 and the aspiration to establish an ASEAN Security Community (ASC) by 2020 and the anticipated signing of the ASEAN Charter mandating much closer policy coordination at the Association's 40th anniversary summit in November – the success of such efforts will depend in large part on the foundations for trust provided by more robust bilateral relations.

During 2006–07, there were signs that relations between key pairs of Southeast Asian states were improving. After severe strains in bilateral links under Thaksin because of the insurgency in the Thai south (and particularly the presence of Thai Muslim refugees in Malaysia), the restoration of cooperative bilateral relations with Malaysia was an important element in the interim Thai government's initiative to restore peace in the south following the military takeover in September 2006. These improved relations appeared to bear fruit after Thai premier Surayud met Malaysian Prime Minister Abdullah Badawi in February

2007. The two leaders agreed to manage the issue of dual nationality (which is not recognised by Malaysia) amongst residents on the Thai–Malaysian frontier through the sharing of biometric data. The leaders also discussed improving security along the border to control the movement of insurgents and smugglers. Subsequently, Surayud reported that Malaysia was helping Bangkok to establish contact with the insurgents as a precursor to possible dialogue.

There were significant signs of warming in Singapore's perennially complex relations with its two immediate neighbours. When the Singaporean and Malaysian prime ministers met for an informal summit on the Malaysian island of Langkawi in mid May, they agreed to set up a joint ministerial committee to discuss Singapore's involvement in the Iskandar Development Region (IDR) in the nearby Malaysian state of Johor. The two sides recognised the potential mutual benefits of Singaporean investment and other involvement in the IDR, which some observers likened to the Shenzhen Special Economic Zone close to Hong Kong. This discussion highlighted the significant improvement in Malaysia's relations with Singapore since Abdullah Badawi replaced Mahathir Mohamad as prime minister in 2003. However, a range of important unresolved bilateral issues – including the need for a new agreement on Malaysian water supplies for Singapore, the Singaporean air force's use of Malaysian airspace, a dispute over Malaysian railway land in Singapore, and the aborted project to build a bridge to replace the causeway joining the two states – continued to cloud the future of the relationship.

Singapore's relations with Indonesia have also improved since Susilo Bambang Yudhoyono became president in 2004. In June 2006, the two countries agreed jointly to develop the Indonesian islands of Batam, Bintan and Karimun, immediately to the city-state's south, as a Special Economic Zone. Moreover, after two years of negotiations, in April 2007 Singapore and Jakarta agreed an extradition treaty and a new defence-cooperation pact. From Jakarta's viewpoint, the extradition pact was vital in order to fight corruption effectively; the Indonesian government hoped that it could use the agreement to force the return of businessmen who were believed to have hidden large amounts of stolen state funds in Singapore. The Defence Cooperation Agreement (DCA), under which the Singapore armed forces would be allowed to resume use of Indonesian training facilities after a hiatus since 2003, was widely viewed as Singapore's quid pro quo for the extradition agreement. The April 2007 agreements surprised observers who thought that recent bilateral disputes over Singapore's imports of sand from Indonesia, culminating in Jakarta's banning of sand exports in February (which caused a crisis in Singapore's construction industry as the price of concrete more than doubled), would impede closer ties. In fact, the sand-export ban had probably constituted part of Indonesia's negotiating strategy. However, in May delay in agreeing three sets of detailed arrangements for military training areas covered by the DCA provided a reminder that relations between Indonesia and Singapore remained sensitive and unpredictable.

By no means did all bilateral relationships within ASEAN become more productive. Indeed, after the coup in Bangkok, Thailand's relations with Singapore deteriorated substantially. In January, a meeting between ex-Prime Minister Thaksin Shinawatra and Singaporean Deputy Prime Minister S. Jayakumar provoked outrage in Bangkok and the cancellation of a Thai invitation to Singaporean Foreign Minister George Yeo to visit Thailand. Adding to the crisis, General Sonthi claimed that the Thai military's communications were vulnerable to interception by Singapore because of Temasek's acquisition of Shin Corporation, which included Thailand's most important mobile telephone company. In February, Sonthi vowed to take control of 'Thai' satellites operated by Shin Corp., provoking Singapore's Foreign Ministry to protest and request clarification. In the same month, Bangkok's information and communication technology minister, Sittichai Pookaiudom, spoke of the possibility that his government might bring the corporation back under Thai control if it was proven that the Singaporean company had broken Thai foreign-ownership laws, an outcome that seemed likely to damage bilateral relations still further. However, possibly after considering the likely impact on overall foreign investment in Thailand, in April Sittichai spoke merely in terms of Temasek probably needing to reduce its shareholding in the company.

The complex and unreliable nature of relations among ASEAN members, often deriving in part at least from their prevailing domestic political conditions, and their impact on the prospects for intra-ASEAN security cooperation, helps to explain these states' continuing interest in maintaining and in some cases developing security relations with states outside the sub-region. In November 2006, Indonesia and Australia signed an Agreement on the Framework for Security Cooperation, which effectively replaced the earlier bilateral Agreement on Maintaining Security, which had lapsed in 1999 following Australia's role in leading the military intervention in East Timor. In March, Singapore and the United States – which already maintained exceptionally close defence and security ties – signed a Science and Technology Agreement on Homeland Security. At the same time, the web of cooperative endeavours intended to enhance maritime security in Southeast Asia continued to intensify, with the ReCAAP (Regional Cooperation Agreement against Piracy) Information Sharing Centre becoming operational in Singapore in November 2006 and the Western Pacific Naval Symposium holding its Second Mulitilateral Sea Exercise, using Singapore as a base, in May. While one vision for the future – encapsulated in the ASC idea – involved Southeast Asian states collectively taking much fuller responsibility for their own security – the evolving reality suggested that non-Southeast Asian actors were likely to continue playing highly significant roles.

Australia's Global and Regional Role

Elections due to be held in late 2007 will provide a severe challenge for the conservative Liberal Party–National Party coalition of Prime Minister John Howard, who has been in office since 1996 and is in his fourth term – elections are held at least every three years. At mid 2007, opinion polls showed the Australian Labor Party, headed by Kevin Rudd, in the lead and on course for a substantial turnaround. Domestic and economic issues are expected to dominate the election. The leading parties agree on the need for Australia to have a robust foreign and security policy, in close alliance with the United States, in the face of global and regional threats. However, Iraq is a bone of contention: the Labor Party is committed to withdrawing Australian combat troops – about a third of the current deployment in Iraq – though it would first hold consultations with the United States. The government plans to keep Australian forces in Iraq until it believes that their job is done.

Australia was part of the coalition that invaded Iraq in March 2003, and has since been part of the Multi-National Force. On 1 May 2007, the Australian Defence Force (ADF) had about 1,450 personnel deployed, including the 520-strong Overwatch Battle Group–West, based at Tallil Air Base in southern Iraq, overseeing security in al-Muthanna and Dhi Q'ar provinces; a security detachment of 110 personnel protecting Australian Embassy personnel; 30 army instructors at the Iraqi Basic Training Centre near Tallil; a 140-strong RAAF detachment with C-130 *Hercules* transport aircraft; two AP-3C *Orion* maritime-patrol aircraft; a frigate patrolling the Persian Gulf; and headquarters personnel.

Rudd, who replaced Kim Beazley as Labor Party leader in December 2006, is a strong supporter of the Australian–American alliance. However, his party opposed Australia's involvement in the invasion of Iraq, and wants to withdraw the Overwatch Battle Group–West and perhaps the army training team. Labor's preference is to train Iraqi forces outside Iraq. Rudd has indicated that other assets would remain in theatre. Howard has acknowledged the unpopularity of the Iraq deployments, but won a comfortable election victory in 2004 over Labor, then led by Mark Latham, who promised to withdraw all forces from Iraq by the end of that year. Rudd's stance is more measured, reflecting his concern that Labor should not be perceived by the electorate to oppose the Australian–American alliance.

The Labor Party supports Australia's commitment in Afghanistan, where the ADF is part of NATO's International Security Assistance Force. A total of about 950 personnel – an increase from 550 – were due to be deployed by mid 2007, with a 300-strong Special Operations Task Group and an air-surveillance radar capacity being added to existing involvement in the Netherlands-led Provincial Reconstruction Team in Uruzgan province, in training Afghan National Army engineers, and in helicopter transport.

Australian deployments within the Pacific region have also increased. Since mid 2006 Australian troops have been deployed to restore security in Timor Leste, following an upsurge in fighting among security forces there. About 1,100 ADF personnel, as well as 150 members of the New Zealand Defence Force (NZDF), support the government and United Nations police. Around 140 ADF troops, with military personnel from New Zealand, Fiji, Papua New Guinea and Tonga, are deployed along with police as part of the Regional Assistance Mission to the Solomon Islands (RAMSI). Amid growing troubles in Pacific island nations, Australia has difficult relations with leaders in Papua New Guinea, where elections were being held in mid 2007; in Fiji, where a military coup took place in December 2006; and in the Solomon Islands where, in spite of its role in the Regional Assistance Mission, Canberra has been involved in a bitter dispute with the prime minister elected in 2006. Australia and New Zealand have assumed regional leadership in tackling the islands' problems, but this role poses many challenges.

In addition to these commitments, a prime concern for Australia is to tackle international terrorism following the 2001 attack on the United States and attacks in Indonesia in which Australians were among the dead. Following an unsuccessful plan to attack Australia's High Commission in Singapore in 2001, 88 Australians were killed by bombs in Bali in October 2002 and four in another bomb attack in Bali in 2005. There was also a bomb attack on the Australian Embassy in Jakarta in late 2004. Some Australians have been convicted on terrorism-related charges and others are currently awaiting trial in Sydney and Melbourne.

As a result, Australia has sought to build up its defence hardware as well as intelligence sharing and police cooperation in the region. While playing its part internationally as part of a loose Western alliance, Australia wants to increase regional security and to prevent the emergence of failed states in the South Pacific – which might lead to a surge in drug trafficking and people smuggling, as well as providing possible bases for terrorists. In May 2006, the government announced a commitment to increase defence spending by 3% in real terms each year until 2015/16. The plan included a long-term commitment to the construction of three destroyers, two amphibious ships, new combat aircraft and replacement of the army's entire vehicle fleet. It also provided for new helicopters, enhanced satellite capability, refurbishments or replacements for *Hercules* and *Caribou* aircraft, naval weapons and an increase in funding for the army. Under the budget plan, Australia's planned expenditure of A$19.6bn in 2006/07, representing about 1.9% of gross domestic product, is already up significantly from A$12.6bn in 2000/01 and would rise to $26.7bn in 2015/16. Labor has promised not to reduce defence expenditure if elected.

Australia has developed good relations with both China – to which Australia is a key supplier of minerals and liquefied natural gas – and India, and has sought to build its security relationships within the region while maintaining its close alignment with the United States. A Trilateral Security Dialogue, comprising Australia, Japan and the United States, had its inaugural meeting in Sydney in March 2006. In March 2007 Howard and Shinzo Abe, Japan's prime minister, signed a joint declaration on security.

With the government's overall approach to foreign policy and security well supported by voters, Australia's tough-minded stance seems unlikely to change significantly whether or not Howard is replaced following the coming elections.

9 **Prospectives**

Moving towards 2008, there is a sense that the world is approaching key turning points in a number of international crises, but that at the same time, the shifts in the global balance of power do not herald decisive and effective action to deal with these crises.

The Iraq conflict will enter its sixth year during a US presidential election campaign, and decisions on deployments, withdrawals and the redefinition of the mission will be shaped almost uniquely by the US domestic mood. The wilting of American prestige in the deserts of a dysfunctional Iraq will call forth ever more anxious cries for a withdrawal in 2008. Redeployment to some intermediate stance of 'strategic over-watch' is bound to become a persistent demand of the American public. That shift would be strategically consistent with the goal of handing over responsibility to the Iraqi government and redefining the mission to one of training Iraqi security forces. A new Iraqi prime minister might be able to preside over a government in 2008 that for a period may be superficially more capable of being 'benchmarked'. But if lack of confidence in Nuri al-Maliki were to lead to the appointment of a new government leader, this would probably come too late to halt the draining of American willpower to 'stay the course'. In these circumstances, it is probable that 2008 will see the beginning of the difficult game of strategic poker, by which Iraqis are left progressively to their own devices, in the hope that this will inspire more compromise than fratricide.

A withdrawal from the many front-lines of the sectarian conflict in Iraq would also be a condition for any more robust stance against Iran over its nuclear programme, given the proxy war that the United States and Iran appear to be fighting in Iraq. US forces remain hugely vulnerable to an escalation of the asymmetric tactics of America's enemies in Iraq, who can be supplied and trained by Iran.

As the United States continues to put pressure on Iran to renounce any hint of a military element to its nuclear programme, Iran will deploy two principal strategies. Firstly, it will try to ensure that there is enough ambiguity about the pace of its programme and its military aspect to deny the United States and its European allies a wider political coalition providing support for a strong sanctions regime or for military action. Secondly, it will keep up pressure on the United States and its allies through its proxies in the Middle East and to a degree in Southwest Asia to remind Washington of the costs it could be forced to pay in the event the United States and its allies sought to escalate the diplomatic crisis. Iran's ability to build additional centrifuges throughout late 2007 and 2008 theoretically gives it the ability to assemble close to 3,000 in that time. There is therefore a risk that the Iranian nuclear programme could reach a key threshold during the year. Iran could avert a crisis by slowing its programme down or agreeing to participate in negotiations, and the United States could elongate the time frames by re-calibrating its definition of the threshold or its assessment of Iran's genuine capacities. What is certain is that during 2008 policy on Iran will need very refined attention. The principal efforts will be focused on building deeper consensus amongst the permanent members of the UN Security Council.

The problem of how to deal with Iran will also be a focus of the US strategic dialogue with the states of the Gulf Co-operation Council (GCC). All would prefer a diplomatic outcome of the crisis, but most fear in ever-shifting measure both a confirmed Iranian nuclear capacity and the effects on them of any US military strike intended to retard Iran's ability to develop a nuclear military programme. Indeed, a strategic quip making the rounds in the Gulf during 2007 had a senior Gulf official making an apocryphal comment: 'If Iran is close to a nuclear weapon and the US launches a military strike, this region is in extremely deep trouble for at least eighteen months; if Iran is close to a nuclear weapon and the US does not strike, the region is in deep trouble for thirty years.' In fact, many in the Gulf would in current circumstances perceive a US military strike to be more frightening than an Iranian deterrent. That said, the morbid humour of the reported comment and the instinctive concern both about a nuclear Iran and a pre-emptive United States, capture accurately the prisoner's dilemma to which many Gulf leaders are hostage. Iran is their permanent but potentially hegemonic neighbour and the US an unpopular but necessary ally. Caught between the two, it is natural for many of the GCC states to hedge, an attitude that makes the development of a containment policy, the natural strategic response to a potentially nuclear Iran, very hard for the United States to orchestrate. This situation would potentially change if US prestige, or US popularity, were dramatically to increase in the region.

Classically, the prospects for that would only be enhanced substantially if the region were to witness the United States successfully delivering peace between Palestine and Israel. But that seemed to recede even further with the intra-Palestine conflict of 2007. The capture by Hamas of Gaza and the resultant external rush further to empower Fatah in the West Bank certainly complicate the politics of finding a representative and agreeable negotiating partner. Israel's crisis-ridden government and shattered confidence following the operation into Lebanon crucially weakened the chances of dynamic diplomatic activity. In this situation, the focus will shift in 2008 to trying to provide stronger economic underpinnings to peace, with many, especially leaders in the UK, trying to take a leaf out of the Northern Ireland peace process. The most urgent requirement, seen from the outside, would be to create some degree of stability in the West Bank as an example to people in Hamas-dominated Gaza. Limiting Hamas's influence to Gaza will not be easy. Strengthening Fatah carries its risks too. Re-creating a legitimate negotiating partner from the outside is hard. Unfortunately, the international priority will therefore be in the first instance conflict resolution within Palestine, rather than peace between Israel and Palestine. In that sense, the 'peace process' has suffered a real shock and – given the crowded strategic agenda and the international electoral realities of 2008 – will not easily be re-established in a recognisable form. An international peace conference may be called and US engagement more strongly advertised, but the reality will remain that the largely territorial compromise of land for peace will be an insufficient rallying cry when the land in question is being fought over by a fractured Palestinian community.

In Europe, finding a more congenial integration of Muslim minorities will be the most pressing challenge and will hardly be made easier by the ease with which European domestic politics are buffeted by the international politics of the West's relations with the Islamic world.

In the United Kingdom, multiculturalism had for many years been accepted by the political class as both a fact and a goal. The debate in 2007 began to shift towards accepting multiculturalism as a fact, but pointing towards assimilation as the goal. In the same year as one million Turks demonstrated in Izmir in support of secularism, the UK government began internally to debate how British values might be more actively promulgated. When former Foreign Secretary Jack Straw stated that he was reluctant to meet fully veiled women in his constituency, he launched a debate as to how the UK would defend the tenets of its essentially secular society against politically charged assertions of Islamic exceptionalism. That debate will only intensify in 2008, mingled awkwardly with discussion about more measures to meet security challenges from terrorism.

The election of Nicolas Sarkozy in France brought into office a politician who personified the French position that assimilation is the goal and multiculturalism a danger. France's traditional stance in respect of its own Muslim population produces amongst them an objection different to the one normally found in the UK. The Muslims who in previous years demonstrated in Paris were not protesting against France's membership of the West, or seeking special rights for themselves, but instead were demanding more of the fruits of the French politico-economic system. Techniques of affirmative action and more activist assimilation efforts would perhaps answer this call, but some way would have to be found to implement them.

The contrasting, but still unsuccessful, political experiments of the UK and France, combined with the increasingly febrile debate on the incorporation of Muslim minorities in numerous other European countries, point to the fact that there is much work to do to define the terms of the necessary social compact in Europe. Europe can not long delay a more organised debate on the principles by which effective assimilation of Muslim minorities can take place. While there is a consensus among all European elites that the war on terror cannot be fought by military means alone, there is a less overt acceptance that defending the largely liberal and secular nature of the 'public space' in Europe will require a more assertive application of the 'political science' of that liberal-secular tradition. That means looking again at issues as complex as the relative balance between individual and community rights and between secular and religious visions of social organisation. Each European state will have different views on these issues, and this is not an area where unity of approach is essential. The effective assimilation of Europe's Muslim population is, however, an area that would benefit from a greater harmonisation of the attitudes to adopt, and more honest debate about the challenges faced.

Honest debate, bordering on ever franker and crisper discussions, will be the order of the day also between Europe and Russia. The decision by Russia in mid 2007 to suspend its compliance with the Conventional Forces in Europe Treaty in opposition to US plans to station missile interceptors and radar systems in Europe marked the formal rejection by Russia of the terms of the post-Cold War European order. Russia had felt the CFE treaty to be outmoded and unfair from the moment it was agreed. Its annoyance at the West's move eastwards during the late 1990s, especially in the institutional form of NATO, and what it saw as a lack of respect, moved President Vladimir Putin to challenge the terms of the post-Cold War settlement. The more nationalist Russia that he represents, which will probably endure well beyond the scheduled 2008 elections no matter who is in the presidential office, will need a more astute approach from the West.

Putin's efforts to undo what was portrayed as a submissive Yeltsin approach to the West has had as its result a 180-degree about-turn that has been methodical and precise. The result is that Russian political instincts have a distinctly anti-Western quality to them, and occasionally an Orwellian character. It was clear that megaphone diplomacy had become fully entrenched when Russia termed 'immoral' the British expulsion of four diplomats in July 2007 in response to Moscow's refusal to extradite the man accused of the murder of Alexander Litvinenko. Though Russia's political instincts are anti-Western, it retains huge interests in a decent relationship with the West. Unfortunately, Russia's sense of status cannot be satisfied by a more generous standard of admission to Western-invented councils. Russia will be no more happy about being patronised than about being dismissed. The work has instead to begin from scratch, identifying a few clear areas where common approaches can be undertaken, and re-building trust on a step-by-step basis. One can only hope that it is not the work of a generation, and that a new balance can be found in the relationship between Russia and the West that has a twenty-first century feel to it.

In the Asia-Pacific, the nineteenth- and twentieth-century practices of balance of power and alliance politics were boosted during the year and will remain a large feature of regional politics in 2008 and beyond. The strengthening of Japanese and Australian defence ties, the interest shown by India in playing a role in East Asia commensurate with its developing economic might, the enduring concern of China that others seek to contain it, the brinkmanship of North Korea on the nuclear issue all demonstrated how difficult it is to shed the practices of realpolitik. The good news is that discussion of these issues became more public in 2007 in a way that inspired more transparency in the security debate. Previously, it was 'strategically correct' in Asia privately to admit to all sorts of rivalries and disputes, but publicly to diminish them. In 2007 discussion of Japan's ambitions and Chinese concerns about them increased, but lost elements of its shrillness. Australia managed to increase defence cooperation with Japan and the United States while simultaneously seeking closer ties to China, a strategic trick that not many others could turn. Asia remained a place where the deployment of US power remained vital to maintain the balance of power, though the basing and command arrangements were being modernised. Defence and security diplomacy are still a high priority to maintain Asian stability, as distrust remains high and the manoeuvring intense. As China moves into its Olympic year, efforts will be needed to continue to further deepen its evolving self-perception as a responsible stakeholder in global security.

That will be all the more important because it is possible that 2008 will see the dawning of a new nuclear age. Any risk of a confirmed Iranian nuclear programme that is seen as irreversible could well invite many countries, including Egypt, Turkey and Saudi Arabia, to reconsider their position. While there appeared in 2007 to be a negotiated pause to the nuclear programme in North Korea, experience suggests that any pause is succeeded by a new acceleration to eke out another concession. While this ritual continues there are suspicions in the region that some in South Korea would be content for that nuclear programme to be maintained in some sort of state that could permit the South to inherit it when, as surely will one day happen, the North collapses. A united Korean peninsula with a more than latent nuclear programme would pose new questions for the Asian balance of power.

In this potential environment of progressive unilateral proliferation, the permanent members of the UN Security Council will carry heavy responsibilities. Managing the new nuclear age, if it arrives, may require the P5 to think about engaging in some form of multipolar deterrence. Hopefully, the spectre of collaborating on something as daunting as that will unite them to work harder to prevent further proliferation.

In sum, the world in 2008 will be doubly consumed by the politics of parochialism – sectarian rivalries and religious disputes – and by the manoeuvres of balance of power politics – alliance politics and arms races. Intriguingly, these two trends will run side by side and will not much inter-relate with each other. In Europe, the United States and Asia big powers will talk to each other about role, status, alliance, deterrence, containment, balance of power. In the meantime, groups around the world will fight those states and alliances. As *Strategic Survey* has argued this year, the shifts in the global balance of power and the continued growth of anti-state terrorism carry uncertain results.

China is too strong to be seen as just a developing nation, though still too weak definitively to shape its regional environment alone. The United States is too strong to stay on the sidelines of global events, but too weak to implement an agenda that it has set without wide agreement. Russia has accumulated great economic power at the state level but wields it in a way that weakens its reputation and causes distrust. Europe has reputation and economic strength but limited strategic vision and ever-declining military power to support it. In this 'non-polar world', the space for aggressive non-state actors to advance their particularist strategic aims has grown. In 2008, managing nuclear proliferation and terrorism will remain the priorities. But the unsettled relations, rivalries and shifting strengths of the powers that see themselves as custodians of the state system will make the necessary coordination of approaches to these threats immensely hard.

Index